THE PREDICTABLE SURPRISE

THE PREDICTABLE SURPRISE

The Unraveling of the U.S. Retirement System

Sylvester J. Schieber

OXFORD
UNIVERSITY PRESS

OXFORD
UNIVERSITY PRESS

Oxford University Press, Inc., publishes works that further
Oxford University's objective of excellence
in research, scholarship, and education.

Oxford   New York
Auckland   Cape Town   Dar es Salaam   Hong Kong   Karachi
Kuala Lumpur   Madrid   Melbourne   Mexico City   Nairobi
New Delhi   Shanghai   Taipei   Toronto

With offices in
Argentina   Austria   Brazil   Chile   Czech Republic   France   Greece
Guatemala   Hungary   Italy   Japan   Poland   Portugal   Singapore
South Korea   Switzerland   Thailand   Turkey   Ukraine   Vietnam

Published by Oxford University Press, Inc.
198 Madison Avenue, New York, New York 10016

www.oup.com

Oxford is a registered trademark of Oxford University Press

Library of Congress Cataloging-in-Publication Data
Schieber, Sylvester J.
The predictable surprise : the unraveling of the U.S. Retirement System / Sylvester J. Schieber.
   p.   cm.
ISBN 978-0-19-989095-8 (alk. paper)
1. Social security—United States. 2. Old age pensions—United States. 3. Retirement income—United
States. I. Title.
HD7125.S327   2012
331.25'20973—dc23   2011031971

3 5 7 9 8 6 4 2

Printed in the United States of America
on acid-free paper

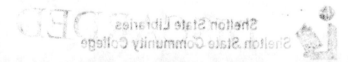

In Memory of
Shannon J. Schieber
August 8, 1974–May 7, 1998
She was willing to fight to her death for her rights,
a reminder to the members of younger
generations to be vigilant and courageous.

CONTENTS

List of figures   *ix*

List of tables   *xiii*

Preface and Acknowledgments   *xvii*

PART I. *Foundations and Fault Lines*

1. Retirement USA   3

2. Early Motivations behind the Pension Movement   24

PART II. *Social Security: The Dream and Reality*

3. Development and Passage of the Social Security Act   33

4. Early Concerns Prove Nagging and Persistent   42

5. Moving to Pay-as-You-Go Financing   52

6. A Deal Too Good to Last   59

7. Operations under Pay-as-You-Go Financing   69

8. Crisis and Reactions: Conflict, Consensus and Surprise   81

9. Sorting Out the Trust Fund Semantics and Realities   92

10. Policy Stalemate at the Demographic Divide   102

11. Understanding Social Security in Modern Times   118

PART III. *Employer-Based Pension Provision*

12. Employer Pensions Taking Root   129

13. Growing Pains for Private Retirement Plans   136

14. ERISA. The Transition to a New Regulatory Regime   146

15. The 1980s: A Decade of Regulatory Schizophrenia   153

16. Good Intentions Gone Awry   164

17. Some Good News . . . or Not   172

18. The Unfolding of a Predictable Defined Benefit Surprise   182

19. And Then, a Predictable Defined Contribution Surprise   200

20. Public Pensions: The Good, the Bad, and the Ugly   215

PART IV. *Delivering Benefits and Providing Retirement Security*

21. Retirement Income Security and Workers' Residuals   239

22. End Game: A Gold Watch, Pat on the Back, and More   253

23. We've Killed the Goose, Let's Gild the Eggs   263

24. Tax Benefits and Benefit Taxes   279

25. Retiree Health Benefits. Misfortune or Malpractice   294

PART V. *Truth and Consequences*

26. The Fellow Behind the Tree   309

27. Securing the Social Security Foundation   328

28. Securing Tax-Favored Benefits and Living Standards   345

29. Remembering the Future   364

Glossary   377

Notes   383

Index   423

LIST OF FIGURES

6.1   Social Security Intercohort Transfers Paid to
Specific Birth Cohorts of Retirees   62

7.1   Historical Beneficiary-to-Worker Dependency
Ratios and Average-Benefit-to-Average-Wage Ratios
in Social Security   70

7.2   Percentage of Final Earnings Replaced by
Social Security Benefits at Various Lifetime
Earnings Levels for Single Workers Retiring at
Age 65 under Various Social Security Amendments   79

9.1   Picture of a Bond Held by the Old-Age and
Survivors Trust Fund in 2007   94

9.2   Social Security Trust Fund Cash Flow Surpluses
and the Unified Federal Budget Balances for
Specified Years in Billions of Dollars   96

15.1   Alternative Pension Cost for a 25-Year-Old Worker
over a 40-Year Career under Alternative Actuarial
Cost Methods   158

16.1   Section 415 Limits on Fundable Pension Benefits,
Defined Contribution Plan Contributions, and
Section 401 Compensation Limits for Providing
Retirement Benefits, in 2010 Dollars   167

16.2   Price-Earnings Ratios on U.S. Stocks for Selected Years   169

17.1   Male and Female Labor Force Participation Rates at
Selected Ages for Selected Years   179

18.1   Price-Earnings Ratios on U.S. Stocks for Selected Years   183

18.2   Value of Accrued Pension Benefit for a New Hire at
Age 30 with a Starting Wage of $40,000 per Year
under a Traditional Pension and a Cash Balance Plan   192

18.3   Value of Accrued Pension Benefit for Worker Converted
        from a Hypothetical Traditional Pension to a Cash
        Balance Plan at Age 45 with 15 Years of
        Completed Service   193
19.1   Percentage of Private Firms Allowing
        Participant-Directed Investing of Employer and
        Employee Contributions to Profit-Sharing or
        401(k) Plans   202
19.2   Share of Private Tax-Favored Plan Assets Held
        in 401(k)s or IRAs and Keoghs, and Share in
        Self-Directed Investment Accounts   204
21.1   Compound Annual Growth Rates of Inflation-Adjusted
        Hourly Pay for Full-Time, Full-Year Workers, by
        Earnings Decile and for Selected Periods   245
21.2   Compound Annual Growth Rates of Inflation-Adjusted
        Hourly Compensation for Full-Time, Full-Year
        Workers, by Earnings Decile and for Selected Periods   246
23.1   Defined Contribution Earnings Replacement Rates
        from Lifecycle Funds with Constant Life Expectancies
        for a Hypothetical Worker Retiring Each Year from 1915
        through 2010   271
25.1   Percentage of Personal Health Care Expenditures
        Paid Out-of-Pocket and Percentage of GDP Spent
        on Personal Health Care from 1960 through 2008   301
28.1   Annuities from Lifecycle Funds with Constant
        Life Expectancies for a Hypothetical Worker
        Retiring Each Year from 1915 through 2010 Based on
        Spot-Market Purchase at Retirement Date and
        Installment Purchases from Ages 55 to 64 with
        Balance Annuitized at Age 65, Constant Interest
        Rates but Variable Asset Values   359
28.2   Annuities from Lifecycle Funds with Constant Life
        Expectancies for a Hypothetical Worker Retiring
        Each Year from 1915 through 2010 Based on Spot-Market
        Purchase at Retirement Date and Installment Purchases
        from Ages 55 to 64 with Balance Annuitized at Age 65,
        Variable Interest Rates but Constant Asset Values   359

28.3   Annuities from Lifecycle Funds with Constant
        Life Expectancies for a Hypothetical Worker Retiring
        Each Year from 1915 through 2010 Based on Spot-Market
        Purchase at Retirement Date and Installment
        Purchases from Ages 55 to 64 with Balance
        Annuitized at Age 65   360

28.4   Installment Group Annuity Bought with 3 Percent
        of Accumulated Retirement Savings Contributed from
        Ages 55 Onward, as a Percentage of an Individual
        Spot-Market Annuity Available to a Hypothetical
        Worker   362

LIST OF TABLES

6.1   Average Net Social Security Windfall Benefits in 2009 Dollars Paid to Single Retirees, by Worker's Gender, Level of Lifetime Earnings, and Year Worker Turned Age 65   68

15.1   Percentage of Workers in Selected Pension Plans Affected by Pension Funding Limits, by Workers' Age and Median Pay Levels in 1998   157

17.1   Estimated Average Age of Claiming Social Security Benefits, Median Age at Retirement and Expected Years in Retirement, by Gender for Selected Periods   180

18.1   Assets Required to Fund an Annual Annuity of $1 Payable at 65, at Alternative Interest Rates   183

18.2   Top 20 Claimants against PBGC Single-Employer Pension Plan Insurance through Fiscal Year 2009   187

18.3   Average Defined Benefit Pension Expense and Average Defined Contribution Expense for Fortune 1000 Companies, 2003–2009   197

19.1   Projected 401(k) and Social Security Wealth, by Lifetime Earnings for Workers Retiring in 2030   213

20.1   Summary Characteristics of Pension Plans for State and Local Workers at the State Level, by Generosity of Benefits Relative to Current Workers' Covered Pay   218

20.2   Funded Status and Contribution Measures for State-Level Public Pension Plans, by Funding Quintiles Based on Plans' Public Disclosure for Fiscal 2009   223

20.3   Illinois' and Louisiana's Annual Required Pension Contributions, Actual Contributions, Unfunded Accrued Liabilities, and Contributions, as a Share of Payroll for Teachers and Public Employee Retirement Plans, 2005–2009   226

20.4   The Distribution of Illinois' 2003 Pension Bond
        Revenues among Its Public Pension Plans, Estimated
        Annual Returns and Accumulations by Year-End 2009   228

20.5   Civil Service Retirement System (CSRS), Federal
        Employee Retirement System (FERS), and Military
        Retirement System (MRS) Populations and Liability
        and Funding Status at October 2008   235

21.1   Cumulative Lifetime Employee plus Employer Payroll
        Taxes as a Percentage of Cumulative Lifetime Earnings,
        Supplemental Retirement Savings Rate, Employer
        Average Contributions for Health Benefits, and
        Totals, as a Percentage of Pay for Workers Retiring
        at Various Dates   241

21.2   Average Annualized Compensation and Pay Levels
        Rounded to the Nearest $100 Levels for Workers, by
        Earnings Deciles in 2009   244

21.3   Share of Total Compensation Increases Absorbed by
        Increases in Payroll Taxes, Employer Contributions to
        Employer-Sponsored Retirement Plans, and Employer
        Contributions to Health Benefit Plans, by Earnings
        Decile and for Selected Periods.   248

21.4   Share of Compensation Gains Provided in the Form
        of More Expensive Benefits Paid by Employers for
        Full-Year Workers, by Earnings Decile and for
        Selected Periods   250

22.1   Percentage of Households and Respondents with
        Any Own, Spouse, or Partner Pension from Current,
        Last, or Previous Jobs, by Health and Retirement
        Sample Members at Ages 51 to 56   255

22.2   Percentages of Respondents in Plan Types among
        the Alternative Cohort Populations in the Health
        and Retirement Study and for Men and Women at
        Ages 51 to 56   256

22.3   Composition of Mean Wealth and Wealth for the
        Median 10 Percent of Wealth-Holding Households
        among 51- to 56-Year-Old Health and Retirement
        Study Participants in 1992, in 1992 Dollars   257

22.4   Average Household Social Security Wealth and
        Pension, 401(k), IRA, and Keogh Wealth, by Lifetime
        Earnings Decile for Health and Retirement Study
        Respondents Aged 63 to 67 in 2000, in 2000 Dollars   258
22.5   Pension Receipt and Monthly Benefits Received by
        the Original Cohort in the Health and Retirement
        Study at Ages 51 to 56 in 1992   260
23.1   Disposition of Employer-Sponsored Retirement
        Benefits by Health and Retirement Study Participants
        at Termination of Employment between 1992 and 2004   264
23.2   Ultimate Accumulated Value of $100,000 in 401(k)
        Plan Savings with 5 or 10 Years to Retirement Invested
        in a Traditional Balanced Fund versus a Guaranteed
        Minimum Withdrawal Benefit Fund   273
23.3   Annuity Values of $100,000 in 401(k) Plan Savings
        Invested 5 or 10 Years before Retirement in a
        Traditional Balanced Fund versus a Guaranteed
        Minimum Withdrawal Benefit Fund   274
24.1   Mean Household Dedicated Retirement Assets, by
        Lifetime Earnings Decile for Health and Retirement
        Study Respondents Ages 63 to 67 in 2000   281
24.2   Expected Value of Social Security Benefits Relative to
        Accumulated Lifetime Contributions with Interest for
        Hypothetical Workers Born in 1949, Retiring at Age 65,
        by Earnings Level   283
24.3   Value of Lifetime Contributions and Present Value of
        Expected Social Security Benefits for Hypothetical
        Workers Born in 1949, Retiring at Age 65, by
        Earnings Level   285
24.4   Value of Lifetime Net Benefits from a Tax-Qualified
        Retirement Savings Account Compared to a Regular
        Savings Account for Hypothetical Workers Born in 1949
        and Retiring at Age 65, by Earnings Level   287
24.5   Combined Value Social Security Net Benefit Gains
        versus Contributions and the Lifetime Net Benefits from
        a Tax-Qualified Retirement Savings for Hypothetical
        Workers Born in 1949 and Retiring at Age 65, by
        Earnings Level   289

24.6 Number and Distribution of Women Aged 62 or Older
Receiving Social Security Benefits by Basis of
Entitlement in December of Selected Years from 1960
to 2008   291

26.1 Projected Federal Spending and Revenues under the
CBO's Long-Term 2010 Alternative Projection, as a
Percentage of GDP   312

26.2 Relative Role of Private and Public Pensions for
Men Retired at Early and Normal Retirement Ages   315

26.3 Quasi-Retirement Income Replacement Rates for
Selected Countries   316

26.4 Projected 401(k) and Social Security Wealth by Lifetime
Earnings Level for Workers Retiring in 2030   317

26.5 Baseline Projections of Growth Rates of Annual
Earnings across Income Deciles for Selected Periods   322

26.6 Percentage of Total Compensation Growth Going to
Finance Increased Costs of Specific Projected Benefits
for Selected Periods   324

26.7 Average Labor Force Participation Rates of Men and
Women at Specified Ages during 2000 through 2004,
and 2005 through 2010   327

27.1 Social Security Benefits Payable at Age 65 under the
Proposals Postulated by the Commission on Fiscal
Responsibility and Reform and the Deficit Reduction
Task Force, as a Percentage of Benefits Payable under
Current Law for Medium, High, and Maximum
Earners in Specified Future Years   343

PREFACE AND ACKNOWLEDGMENTS

I have had the unbelievable good fortune of working in research for most of the last 40 years, so I have been paid over most of my adult life to learn. From 1973 through 1980, I worked in research or policy units at Social Security and I have been in the private sector since 1981. Along the way, by myself or with coauthors, I have written or edited a dozen books and many articles on retirement and the health insurance financing system. During the mid-1990s, I served on an Advisory Council on Social Security organized by the Clinton Administration. From the beginning of 1998 through September 2009, I served on the Social Security Advisory Board and was its chairman during the last three years. In my day work, from 1983 to the fall of 2006, I worked for a consulting firm that advises employers on human resource issues. The firm I retired from was Watson Wyatt, but it has since merged and is now Towers Watson. Over most of my career, I headed up a research unit, but I worked with the company's consulting practices on retirement and health benefit plans. During my last two years with the firm, I headed up North American Benefits Consulting, which helped clients in Canada and the United States establish and manage their retirement and health benefits. In my work in the consulting industry, I have met and worked with people in companies across America and in the trade associations representing them in Washington, and with a wide array of academics interested in health and retirement developments in the business world.

For much of my career, I have studied and dealt with our retirement system—something weighing on many people's minds these days. In this book, I explain the roots of our retirement system, why we seemingly achieved the "golden age of retirement" by the 1970s—and seemingly have lost our way since then. I now believe that the "golden age" was a false dream in some ways, but I do not believe we should abandon the goal of a comfortable retirement supported by the combined efforts of government, employers, and ourselves. Retirement and our various retirement programs arose in response to economic and business necessities, as well as to a personal desire for a well-deserved rest after a lifetime of labor. None of those has gone away. We just have to figure out how to make our programs serve our interests instead of becoming slaves to them. If we can understand how we have gotten where we are, assess our deficits and strengths, and determine where we want to go, we are perfectly capable of plotting a successful and sustainable path forward.

In Lewis Carroll's *Through the Looking Glass and What Alice Saw There,* Alice said that she didn't "much care" where she was going, and the Cat responded, "Then it doesn't matter which way you go."[1] I am convinced that many of the people responsible for steering our retirement system have lost any sense of the context in which the whole thing operates, and that few people who participate have a strong sense of it either. Time after time, we have chosen the easier path, even when doing so led us astray. In the beginning, demographics and other factors made many of these choices work for a while, but they eventually landed us in our entirely predictable predicament.

I tell some parts of this story in the first person, and the tale is peppered with my own opinions and conclusions. I offer this in the way of full disclosure. I have spent most of my working life immersed in the retirement world, and so naturally have drawn a number of conclusions about what has gone right and what has gone wrong. Indeed, one is not appointed to advisory councils and boards without having the capability to assess information and draw conclusions. One of the reviewers of the original manuscript who was evaluating its worthiness for publication observed that I have been "an active participant in most of the controversies" regarding our retirement system over the past three decades. I do not expect everyone to agree fully with all my conclusions and my perspective on the story. Rather, I attempt to provide enough information to enable readers to evaluate my conclusions and, where they do not agree, to draw their own. In the end, if we can reach a broader understanding of our predicament, we have a greater likelihood of resolving our problems and continuing the great tradition of our forebears—handing to the next generation a world that is better than the one we inherited.

I am listed as the author of this volume, but it would be unfair to suggest that this is solely my work. This volume has evolved over 40 years—the period over which I have been doing research and writing—most of which has been about our retirement system. Much of my work has been done in collaboration with others, and without the aid of these good people, the story of *The Predictable Surprise* could not have been told. I have had the tremendous pleasure of working with a number of extraordinary people in doing the research that has formed the basis of books, articles in academic and professional journals, government reports, and policy papers at Watson Wyatt.

The first on the list would be Dr. Dan McGill, who wrote *Fundamentals of Private Pensions*. First published in 1955, the book has been updated periodically to reflect the changing world of private pensions, and Dr. McGill eventually sought help in keeping the volume current. Dr. McGill founded the Pension Research Council early in his career, and I first met this icon of the pension world in the early 1980s, when he was its executive director. In the mid-1990s, I had the privilege of being invited to coauthor the seventh edition of Dr. McGill's classic textbook, which was published in 1996. I have also helped to develop two subsequent volumes, including the ninth edition published in 2010. Another of the book's coauthors has been Kyle Brown, one of the most knowledgeable attorneys on pension law in the United States, with whom I had the opportunity to work for two decades of our professional careers. In drafting the editions of the *Fundamentals*, he was able to explain the complex language of the laws and regulations governing employer-sponsored plans in a way laypersons could understand. Much of the discussion of evolving pension law in this volume has benefitted from my work on updating a classic text that dates back more than half a century.

Another on the list would be Dr. Steven Nyce, an economist at Towers Watson, with whom I have worked on many projects over the past dozen years. He joined my research staff at Watson Wyatt fresh out of graduate school, and we have worked together on a steady stream of projects since then. One that we undertook in 2004 for the World Economic Forum on the effects of aging populations on developed economies led to a book, *The Economic Implications of Aging Societies. The Costs of Living Happily Ever After*, which provides the background for the international references in this volume. We also jointly developed an analysis linking the rising cost of retirement and health systems to many workers' stagnant paychecks, which is a central part of the story told here.

Professor John Shoven, an economist at Stanford University and the head of the Stanford Institute of Economic and Policy Research, has also been an important and highly valued colleague on several projects. Together we edited a book on pension policy, *Public Policy Toward Pensions*, which was published in 1997, and we wrote a book on Social Security, *The Real Deal. The History and Future of Social Security*, which was published in 1999. Both of these projects provided invaluable background for this volume. We have also coauthored several policy papers on both Social Security and employer-sponsored retirement plans over the past couple of decades. Robert Clark, a professor of economics at North Carolina State University, and I have collaborated on a number of papers on workers' participation and investing behavior in 401(k) plans and the reorganization of employer-sponsored defined benefit pensions during the 1990s and early 2000s. This list also includes Professor Olivia Mitchell, an economist at the Wharton School, who now heads the Pension Research Council and who has helped in the editing of several of my books. All of these people have been an ongoing source of information, suggestions, and support that are vitally important for this sort of work. They have also all become fast friends over the years of our associations.

Others with whom I have worked in developing research that is cited throughout the book include Gordon Goodfellow, Dick Joss, Marjorie Kulash, and Lex Miller, all of whom retired from Watson Wyatt. I have also collaborated with Dr. Julia Coronado, now chief economist in North America for BNP Paribas; Dr. Janemarie Mulvey, an economic analyst at the Congressional Research Institute; Dr. Carolyn Weaver, an economist with whom I worked closely on the 1994–1996 Advisory Council on Social Security; and Richard Hinz, now a project manager at the World Bank.

In every substantial endeavor, encouragement and support are vital ingredients. In early 2010, I had dinner with two dear friends and long-time work associates, Walter Bardenwerper, the general counsel at Towers Watson, and Gene Wickes, the global director of benefits consulting at the firm. Both of these men work in their jobs for reasons above and beyond the need to earn an income to support their families. They are both concerned about having a retirement system that provides retirement security across society, and they believe that employers have played a vital role in that system in the past and should continue to do so in the future. They are worried about our current circumstances—in terms of both the income security of those now approaching retirement and the potentially devastating legacy we might be leaving our children and grandchildren. At our dinner, Wally made the case that I needed to write this retirement story and Gene committed to support the project. Both of them followed the progress of the writing as it unfolded and have offered valuable comments and suggestions along the way.

An extremely important source of support from Towers Watson has been the ongoing help I have received from my former colleagues. Brendan McFarland, who is the keeper of retirement plan accounting disclosure information at Towers Watson, has provided much of the statistical data presented here. He also developed the retirement plan annuity calculations presented in chapter 27. Michael Slover ran the tabulations on the U.S. Census Bureau's *Current Population Survey* that are not attributed specifically to other sources. Ann Marie Breheny, who is responsible for keeping abreast of legislative initiatives that affect retiree benefits, helped in tracking down timing, sponsorship, and other important elements of the regulatory story. Michael Orszag's insightful and provocative comments helped me flesh out and sharpen important parts of the story. Susan Farris, who was my executive assistant and primary editor in my last few years with Watson Wyatt, stepped in again to help turn my sometimes Teutonic sentence structuring into readable English.

At the Social Security Administration, Steven Goss, the chief actuary, and Alice Wade, the deputy chief actuary, answered my frequent questions and provided data that is reported in parts of the dialogue. Larry DeWitt, the historian at Social Security, was extremely supportive in the earlier research for *The Real Deal* and once again provided helpful support in understanding and explaining some of the historical aspects of Social Security's evolution. Kate Thornton, the staff director at the Social Security Advisory Board, and staff members Debi Williams, Joel Feinlieb, and David Warner provided background information from reports and testimony by the Advisory Board and helped me find several historical documents important to the research.

David Wray, the president of the Profit Sharing/401(k) Council of America, had special tabulations done on the Council's historical survey member files and provided many useful insights into the evolution of defined contribution plans. Fernando Troncoso of Troncoso Consulting Group helped me sort through some of the insurance industry hurdles that would arise in implementing the proposal for income security included in chapter 28.

In the course of selecting a publisher for the volume, the original manuscript was sent to nine anonymous reviewers. Virtually every one of them endorsed the project, and many gave substantive comments that have helped me clarify and improve the story. I have come to know that three of them are Professors John Shoven and Robert Clark, mentioned earlier, and Brigitte Madrian at Harvard University. Professor Madrian provided some of the more extensive and encouraging comments of all the reviewers. The book has benefitted tremendously from the time and effort invested by all the reviewers of the original manuscript.

Terry Vaughn, the U.S. Economics Editor at Oxford University Press, was extremely enthusiastic and encouraging about the project from our first contact. He provided many valuable comments himself, but he also sent the original draft to his sister, Genevieve Vaughn, a professional editor. Not only did she look it over, she read it cover to cover and provided extensive editorial suggestions for improvement. I am also indebted to Nancy Campbell, who has edited much of my writing over the years and stepped up once again to edit the volume within an abbreviated schedule. Michele Bowman of TNQ Books and Journals did a wonderful job of copyediting the manuscript and catching many inconsistencies in style and format in the presentation plus some remaining grammatical errors that had missed earlier screenings. The myriad of folks at Oxford University Press who helped bring the book through the production process and into readers' hands is too long to list but I am greatly indebted to them for their efforts, contributions and professionalism throughout the process.

Finally, I am deeply indebted to several members of my family. First of all, this book would never have been written if my dear wife Vicki had not persevered with good cheer throughout my preoccupation with putting the story to paper. My brother, George, read every chapter of the first draft of the manuscript as it evolved. He was crucial because he does not work in either the research or retirement fields but is a businessman in the grain industry. It is important to me that this book be understandable and meaningful to people who do not spend most of their time reading about or discussing retirement programs. My brother's comments were invaluable in clarifying the story at many points. I also came to appreciate that he must have paid closer attention in grammar class than I did. My son, Sean, and his wife, Jessica, and their young children, Corinna and Miles, gave me the inspiration to keep focused on the task at hand throughout the long hours involved. Their generations are a reminder that, in providing income security for the current generation in retirement and the next one in line for it, we cannot ignore our responsibilities to those who will follow in our footsteps.

While many people have provided me a great deal of input and support, I am solely responsible for the contents of the volume and for the conclusions and opinions expressed therein.

THE PREDICTABLE SURPRISE

FOUNDATIONS AND FAULT LINES

When no provision is made for an assured retirement income, the majority of elderly wage earners continue to work or to seek employment until they are ultimately forced to dependency either upon their children or upon the community in which they live.

—SUMMARY OF STAFF REPORTS, *Committee on Economic Security,*

1934–1935

Background

The U.S. retirement "system" is a 20th century phenomenon although its roots stretch back to the 19th century. The word "system" is in quotation marks because our amalgam of retirement programs is frequently characterized as a system and described as such through a variety of metaphors. When I first started working in the retirement field some 40 years ago, the system was often described as a three-legged stool. One leg was Social Security; another, employer-sponsored pensions; and the third, personal savings. Later, retiree health insurance became a fourth leg. Finally, some descriptions added a fifth leg, to represent pay earned in "bridge jobs," which serve as a stepping stone between career employment and total retirement. Along the way, analysts pointed out that some legs in this stool were a lot more sturdy than others. With each refinement, the metaphor became less relevant—a stool with five legs, no two of the same size, makes little sense. When the World Bank took up pension issues around the globe in the early 1990s, it characterized the multiple aspects of retirement systems as "tiers." As its work evolved, it revised the characterization to "pillars." No matter how we might characterize our retirement institutions, here in the United States each of the elements of our system evolved largely independently. However, these income sources have evolved into a more rational "system" than one might expect from their separate histories.

Four major forces have played a role in the development of our retirement programs. The first is economics. Since the late 19th century, employers have sponsored retirement plans to help manage the retirement of older workers, and workers rely on them for support in retirement. The second major force has been the political response to workers' desires and economic needs. Social Security has been part of our political dialogue since the mid-1930s, and Medicare since the 1960s. Both programs have been central themes in every recent national election. While employer-sponsored pension and savings plans may not attract as much political commentary, policymakers tinker with them even more than with the government-run programs. The third major force has been the regulatory structure built to govern both public and privately sponsored retirement plans. It is the federal bureaucrats who turn the laws into the rules of the road. And the multitude of rules makes our private retirement system one of the most regulated areas of activity in our economy. Finally, demographics have been a major force in the evolution of retirement. In an economic context, it is workers who produce the goods and services that we consume, and part of that consumption is by retirees—people who are no longer working and producing. As long as there are many workers and few retirees, the retiree claim on workers' production remains small. But when there are many retirees and few workers, the claim on workers' productivity has the potential to become burdensome.

By some measures, our retirement system is an amazing and wonderful achievement. In 2010, the Social Security Administration paid $702 billion in benefits to retired and disabled workers and their survivors and dependents.[1] In 2009, the last year for which there are data, private employers' retirement and profit-sharing plans paid out $502 billion in benefits, the federal government paid out $137 billion in pensions for its civilian and military retirees, and state and local governments paid out $206 billion in pensions.[2] On top of all that, individuals held $4.3 trillion in their individual retirement accounts at year-end 2009,[3] with a substantial amount of those assets held by retirees who were tapping them gradually to support their retirement. Medicare expenditures totaled another half trillion dollars in 2009, and many employer-sponsored retiree health benefit programs were paying out billions more to retirees. Summing up, our retirement programs paid out somewhere between $2 trillion and $2.5 trillion in benefits per year in 2009 and 2010. By comparison, total personal income in the United States was around $12.2 trillion in 2009, and $12.5 trillion in 2010.[4] The benefits paid out by our retirement institutions made up 16 to 20 percent of that total.

But while paying out trillions of dollars may be impressive, it really doesn't tell us much about what has happened to the worker who has gotten up early every workday morning for years, packed a lunch, headed off to a job, and, after all that, finally grasped the brass ring of retirement. At ground level, the evolution of the retirement system has dramatically improved retirees' economic welfare.

In 1967, the Census Bureau estimated that 29.5 percent of people aged 65 and over were living below the poverty line, while the rate for the total population was 16.6 percent.[5] By 2009, the poverty rate had dropped to 8.9 percent among the elderly, compared with 20.7 percent for children under age 18, and 12.9 percent for adults aged 18 to 64.[6] Retirees' relative economic status improved radically as the retirement system matured, but there was more. In the early 1950s, the average claiming age for Social Security benefits was 68 and the typical retiree collected benefits over a remaining life expectancy of about 13 years. By the beginning of the current millennium, the average claiming age was 62.5, and a typical new beneficiary could be expected to remain on the rolls for roughly 21 years.[7]

Not only are today's retirees better off than the rest of the population; on average, they are more insulated from the vagaries of a volatile economy. A 2009

Pew Research Center survey evaluating the effects of the 2007–2008 recession found that fewer people aged 65 and older had to cut back on spending than those aged 18 to 49 or those 50 to 64. When asked whether the recession would make it harder to meet retirement needs or had caused stress in their families, the over-65 group reported fewer adverse effects than either of the younger groups.[8]

Fault Lines Shift under the Retirement Security Foundation

Given the great achievements on the retirement front during the latter decades of the 20th century, many workers came to expect a retirement similar to those enjoyed by their parents or grandparents—maybe even better if early retirement trends continued. But then the retirement train seemed to get sidetracked, and some workers found their retirement plans and aspirations completely derailed.

I will turn 66 in 2012, beyond the age when I could claim my Social Security benefits. Between the time when my parents retired and my thinking about it, our retirement system has gotten more expensive. In 1975, the last year my father worked, the combined employer and employee payroll tax for Social Security was 9.9 percent on $14,100. Today it is 12.4 percent on $106,800, and our contributions will not cover full benefits in the foreseeable future. For many of us, Social Security doesn't seem to be the good deal our parents enjoyed.

On top of that, over the last 10 or 15 years, the pensions that many of my parents' generation enjoyed have either disappeared or been completely re-engineered. Many workers have been left, often mid-career, facing the future with only 401(k) plans, called on to make new decisions about how much to save and where to invest, and then asked to stretch their savings across some unknown years of retirement. As if that were not enough, the first decade of the new millennium was the worst decade for investing since the Depression.

It looks like most of our children can just forget about a monthly employer pension. Many of the private pensions still standing are closed to new entrants, and the phenomenon has even spread to public pensions. Policy mavens in Washington are now suggesting that we need to raise the payroll tax caps and cut Social Security benefits. At the state and local level, public pension costs are edging out funding for educating our children and replacing crumbling infrastructure, in some cases inflicting near paralysis on other normal governmental functions. One young man's view was laid out recently in a front-page editorial of Cornell University's daily newspaper. He said, "My generation is already going to have to pay your social security (a system itself not far from the brink of insolvency) and your Medicare (a system already running huge state deficits). The absolute very least that you can do is craft a stimulus plan void of tax breaks and comprised entirely of transportation, education, energy and technology infrastructure, from which my generation will benefit."[9]

Since the 1980s, the Social Security trustees have been predicting deficits beginning some years after the first baby boomers retired in 2008. In 2009, they reported that the first annual deficit would be in 2016. A year later, the trustees made headlines when their annual report explained that, for the first time since 1983, the system was already running a cash flow deficit expected to be $41 billion in 2010, but that it was expected to bounce back into surplus from 2012 through 2014.[10] Four months later, when the revenues and expenditures were tallied up at the end of 2010, the deficit turned out to be $49 billion. The 2011 Trustees Report projected the surpluses that were anticipated for 2012 to 2014 would not happen. The report explained that the existing trust fund balances plus anticipated tax revenues should cover benefits through 2035 when obligations would still (or only) be funded at a level of 78 percent of payable benefits.[11]

About the same time the Social Security trustees told us that system was running a deficit in 2010, *Chicago Business* reported that Caterpillar was freezing its non-union defined benefit pension plan. The plan freeze affected 28,000 of its 50,000 U.S. employees, and many of those workers would receive smaller pensions.[12] The Pension Benefit Guaranty Corporation reported that in 2007, 18 percent of the total private plan system was no longer providing new service credits (i.e., accruing benefits) to participants.[13] Since then, more plans have been frozen. In 2010, Towers Watson reported that 35 percent of Fortune 1000 defined benefit plan sponsors had at least one frozen plan.[14] Even among plan sponsors still accruing benefits for participants, Towers Watson found that 37 percent of them were no longer admitting new workers into their defined benefit plans.[15] In 1983, there were 175,000 private defined benefit plans covering 29.9 million active workers, according to the Department of Labor. By 2007, the latest year for which there are published data, those numbers had dropped to 49,000 plans covering 19.4 million workers.[16]

So now, many private-sector workers are marching toward retirement with only 401(k) plans—what some people call "do-it-yourself" pensions. At first, this new approach seemed like a wonderful ride, as account balances ballooned in the bull markets of the 1990s. But the first decade of the new millennium was a rude awakening. At the end of 1999, private defined contribution plan balances stood at an aggregate $2.5 trillion. From 2000 through 2002, workers and employers contributed another $612 billion to these plans, but aggregate balances still fell by $399 billion over the same period. And worse was yet to come. In 2007 and 2008, total contributions to these plans were $610 billion but our accumulated balances dropped by $781 billion.[17] Many of us seemed to be on an *Alice in Wonderland* treadmill, contributing more and more and getting further and further behind.

The public sector, for now, is a whole different ball game—for the workers. Government workers have largely clung to their pensions and most of them still get retiree health benefits to boot. But there's a catch. These benefits are expensive, and some state and local governments are buckling under the burden. In California—where a highway patrolman can retire as early as age 50 with a pension up to 90 percent of final-year pay—the state spent more for public pensions in 2010 than on its university system.

By its own accounting, Illinois had unfunded pension obligations of $65 billion at the end of 2009 and should have contributed $5.3 billion, but the state contributed only $3.2 billion to its pension plans. It shorted its "actuarially required contribution" for retiree health benefits another $2.5 billion. Even so, by the end of 2010, the Illinois comptroller was sitting on $5 billion in bills—unrelated to its pensions—from contractors, vendors, and suppliers because there was no money to pay them. In desperation, Illinois has taken to issuing bonds to fund its pensions. It is now borrowing money to fund future pensions, akin to using a credit card to pay the mortgage.

New Jersey should have contributed $4 billion to its pensions and another $5 billion to its retiree health benefit programs in 2010, but it skipped the pension payment and only paid for current retirees' health benefits. The state had not made its required pension contributions in 13 of the last 17 years. The hole kept getting deeper, but the fiscal situation was so dire that in 2010—despite having skipped its pension contribution again—New Jersey had to cut its primary and secondary school budgets by $1 billion and lay off thousands of teachers.[18]

As if this pension story is not bad enough, some now suggest that state and local estimates of their future pension obligations are considerably understated and thus the challenges ahead are even more daunting than the published numbers suggest.[19]

A Growing Public Sense of Confusion, Betrayal and Angst

A friend and colleague of many years' standing recently wrote to me wondering what had gone wrong. Social Security seemed to be in jeopardy, the private pension systems had largely fallen apart, workers were being battered in trying to save for their own retirement, and now we were shutting down schools and jacking up tuitions to provide public-sector workers benefits no one else was getting any more. He wrote:

> How did we take what had become a magnificent achievement in public and private social policy and architecture benefitting both the aged and the generations coming up behind them, and allow it to corrode into a rusted, hollowed-out financial hulk, like an old Studebaker, no longer able to perform the basic functions our parents had thought of as a virtual entitlement? What will be the consequences of this crumbling financial infrastructure? The human costs, the costs to productivity and innovation, the competitive costs to our country in the world economy, the costs in social cohesion?

My friend Walter Bardenwerper happens to be the general counsel at one of the largest benefit consulting firms in the world, Towers Watson. The company consults in a broad range of human resource issues, but the largest share of its U.S. business is consulting with employers on the structure and operation of their retirement programs. If the general counsel in a firm like this has to ask those questions, then it is unlikely that the vast majority of American citizens fully understand what has happened either. While there are some similarities in the story from one segment of the retirement system to the next, there are important differences as well.

Social Security, the Foundation of Retirement Security

Social Security was conceived and became law in the midst of the Depression. It was signed into law on August 14, 1935, and the system paid the first benefit check to Ida Mae Fuller of Rutland, Vermont, in January 1940.

Robert M. Ball, one of the most influential figures in the history of Social Security, was appointed as assistant director of the Bureau of Old-Age Survivors Insurance in 1949. He was named Commissioner of Social Security in 1962 by President John Kennedy and served until 1973. After his retirement from Social Security, he continued to play a predominant role as the chief theologian for the supporters of the system until his death in 2008. His assessment of the program was that:

> [t]he pattern of the program was well set in the [19]39 amendments. One way to consider the whole history of the program from then on is as filling in the structure that had been created in '39. You had to extend

coverage; you had to create programs for the two risks that were not included, disability and health—health insurance for the elderly, at least. But everything was an elaboration of the basic structure and ideas.[20]

While the benefit side of today's Social Security was largely established by 1939, the financing structure was revamped fairly soon after the original Social Security Act was adopted in 1935. The act called for "funding" of the system, meaning that money had to be put aside as workers earned their benefits, so the accumulating savings plus interest would be waiting for the worker when he retired. Franklin Roosevelt insisted on this. But despite frequent protests and a rare veto by President Roosevelt, Congress essentially converted the system to pay-as-you-go financing—using current workers' payroll taxes to pay for current retirees' benefits. Obviously, under this method, there is no large pool of assets to meet future obligations—indeed, there are hardly any accumulated assets at all. Our Social Security system has largely been run this way over the years.

The shift to pay-as-you-go financing delivered a bonanza to early participants in Social Security, who collected benefits as though they had contributed over a full career. When Ida Mae Fuller received her first Social Security retirement benefit check in 1940, she had paid payroll taxes for only three years (since the program started). Over her entire career, she paid a total of $24.75 in payroll taxes. Her first monthly check was $22.54, and she lived to be 100 years old, so her "investment" in the new social insurance system really paid off. But this largess was not available to all the elderly.

My grandfather was born two years later than Ms. Fuller, but he was a farmer and they—along with some other types of workers—were not covered by Social Security until the early 1950s. He lived to be 86 years old but missed out on the windfalls enjoyed by the early participants. Most of my aunts and uncles retired in the 1970s, after having paid into the system for 20 to 25 years at extremely low payroll tax rates compared with current levels. Every birth-year cohort of participants up until those born in 1938 did better, in aggregate, by participating in Social Security than they could have in a conservatively funded pension, according to estimates by Dean Leimer, an analyst at the Social Security Administration.[21] Under the right conditions, this happy outcome could go on indefinitely.

In the late 1950s, Paul Samuelson, who would later receive the Nobel Prize in Economics, developed an analysis showing that, under certain conditions, pay-as-you-go retirement plan financing was not only viable—it could even be superior to FDR's preferred funded approach.[22] The most important factor for success is that the workforce grows over time relative to the retiree population. In a 1967 weekly column for *Newsweek*, Samuelson called Social Security "the greatest Ponzi scheme ever contrived."[23] With the baby boom generation entering the workforce in unprecedented numbers, his rendering seemed to make economic sense and had tremendous political appeal.

If there was ever a pronouncement the Queen got right, it was that "memory works both ways," particularly as it pertains to anticipating future retirement needs. Shortly after the 1970 census, we knew that the high fertility rates that spawned the baby boom had receded. The first baby boomers were born in 1946 and the last of them were born in 1964. It does not require higher mathematics to "remember" when the baby boomers would turn 65 and be eligible for Social Security. We also have a pretty good idea how many workers our economy will have over the next 20 years or so, because the overwhelming majority of them are already here. Twenty years from now it is virtually certain that we will have significantly more retirees than today but only a relatively few more workers. The conditions that made Social Security a successful "Ponzi scheme" in the early 1970s no longer exist.

For a while now, workers have been retiring at younger ages than they did in the 1960s and 1970s and are living longer in retirement, swelling the retirement ranks. As the baby boom generation ages into retirement with the baby bust generation behind them, the growth rate of our retiree population will no longer exceed our workforce growth rate by much, if at all.

Dean Leimer estimates that all birth cohorts from 1938 onward will receive less in Social Security benefits than the value of their lifetime contributions, which he characterizes as "negative intercohort transfers."[24] A more pedestrian description would be that it has become a "bad deal." The baby boom cohorts will not get back nearly the value of their Social Security contributions, and their children will almost certainly do even worse.

Generation waves take a long time to play out, but the leading edge of the baby boom started turning 65 years old in 2011 and the successful "Ponzi scheme" is beginning to feel like a Bernie Madoff investment plan. I recently received an e-mail from a friend who was passing on a message from his brother, a general practice lawyer in Kentucky, expressing common sentiments:

> One question that I keep coming back to is whether Social Security as a pay-as-you-go system was ever sustainable. [We] never appear to confront this question head on. The Social Security promise would have been a good one had the government not been allowed to rob Peter to pay Paul.

We taxpayers sat back and allowed our government to stick it to us because we were never willing to face the music as to the real cost of the government we thought we wanted. And where are we now? If the IOUs that the Social Security Trust Fund holds are of any value, the system still isn't viable if we don't cut benefits or raise taxes.

Despite this fellow's observations to the contrary, there was a great deal of thought and debate about the sustainability of pay-as-you-go retirement systems and the implications for the future.[25] President Roosevelt opposed pay-as-you-go funding for fear it would create a legacy of large obligations for future Congresses. Economists Arthur Altmeyer, the early managing officer presiding over the system and the first Social Security Commissioner, and Edwin Witte, who had been the executive director of the committee that drew up the original Social Security legislation, warned repeatedly that pay-as-you-go financing would push system costs much higher over time and pose major equity issues across generations. They advocated for a "funded" Social Security system in accordance with President Roosevelt's beliefs. But at that time, most people weren't worrying much about developments 30 or 40 years down the road. We are now down the road.

Since the 1970s, we have known how the baby boom generation would affect Social Security's financing. Since the mid-1980s, we have known Social Security would not have sufficient assets to meet current-law claims from the baby boomers over the next quarter century. In 1996, the Social Security trustees told policymakers, "It is important to address this problem soon to allow time for phasing in any necessary changes and for workers to adjust their retirement plans to take account of those changes."[26] Every year since then—over succeeding sets of trustees—this same admonition has been delivered to our national elected officials to no effect. Policymakers have persistently ignored what we can remember forwards.

Employer-Sponsored Retirement Plans, Key to Acceptable Retirement Security

In 1965, Congress enacted the Older Americans Act. Among ten objectives listed, the first was for older people to enjoy "an adequate income in retirement in accordance with the American standard of living."[27] While the Older Americans Act does not suggest an amount, the conventional understanding of that goal is that retirees have roughly comparable standards of living before and after retirement. Social Security was never intended to fill this charter by itself, and President Roosevelt acknowledged as much before the first retirement benefits were paid when he said: "Social Security can furnish only a base upon which each one of our citizens may build his individual security through his own individual efforts."[28] Retirees have been able to supplement the income security base provided by Social Security primarily through employer-sponsored retirement programs.

The employer-sponsored elements of our retirement system are distinctly different than Social Security's. These plans were instigated by employers, sometimes at their workers' urging, without any government mandate. Employers started their retirement plans under a largely *laissez faire* regulatory environment. The earliest private plans predated Social Security by more than a half century and were developed as a human resource management tool. They originated in the railroads but spread to other industries with substantial numbers of older, long-tenured employees. In their early decades, these plans tended to be operated on a pay-as-you-go basis. As some of the early plans matured, benefit obligations escalated more rapidly than anticipated, leading to plan curtailments or defaults as companies were driven into bankruptcy. By the 1920s, technical expertise was sufficient to help these plans remain viable, but many of them still failed to do so.[29] The Depression took its toll on many plan sponsors.

During World War II, wage controls capped workers' salaries but allowed employers to essentially pay them in the form of retirement and health benefits. After the war, labor unions won the legal right to negotiate for pensions, setting off a stampede to set up plans in the late 1940s and early 1950s. The union plans, in particular, were plagued by underfunding, and several collapsed as their sponsors went bankrupt. This phenomenon came to a head in 1964 when Studebaker went bankrupt, and the media focused on the plight of the workers and retirees who were victimized by the pension collapse.

In 1974, policymakers passed the Employee Retirement Income Security Act, commonly known as ERISA. This far-reaching legislation established a regulatory structure that reflected its stated intentions to make benefits available to more workers and require employers to fund benefits as employees earned them. As a backstop, it created the Pension Benefit Guaranty Corporation to protect plan participants if their employer went bankrupt and could not pay workers their rightful pension benefits.

Many early private pensions failed when the sponsoring companies that had not sufficiently funded their plans ran out of money during economic downturns. This was also the case in the late 1950s and early 1960s when several second-tier auto producers failed, leaving unfunded pensions behind.

Many of the workers and retirees who had participated in these plans received little or nothing for their efforts. The Studebaker collapse was the culmination of that story, and ERISA seemed to be the public "remembering" of what caused the disasters and how to ensure they didn't happen again.

But our remembering was suppressed by our appetite for forgetting. The bankruptcies of companies like Delphi, the auto parts producer, United and Delta Airlines, and Bethlehem Steel at the beginning of the new millennium echoed the Studebaker collapse some 40 years earlier. Each of these companies was swamped by unfunded retirement promises. Despite ERISA's protections, many workers lost pension benefits, some along with their jobs. Dozens of other large, well-known companies had gone down the same path during the 1980s and 1990s and scores of smaller ones as well.

ERISA clearly required pension sponsors to lay aside funds for pension benefits as they were being earned, although lawmakers effectively gave sponsors of union pensions a pass on the funding requirements. In the law's first several years, plan funding improved markedly and coverage of workers under the system grew.

Then, in the early 1980s, policymakers became interested in increasing tax revenues without increasing tax rates. One avenue was to restrict the funding of private pensions to reduce contributions, which were not taxed until the benefits were paid. Several new laws adopted during the 1980s and early 1990s significantly curtailed the amounts sponsors could contribute to their pension plans, which had the effect of slowing funding for young workers' retirement benefits. When these laws were passed, few took notice, but shifting the funding of the baby boomers' pensions from early in their careers to much nearer retirement had ominous ramifications. It meant that funding requirements would accelerate as workers aged for two reasons: first, to make up for the earlier reductions and second, to make up for the interest that was not earned because the contributions were delayed.

During the 1980s, pension plans were cheap because most companies were not contributing much. In fact, under federal funding restrictions, many were making no contributions at all. The phenomenon continued through the 1990s because the booming financial markets were outperforming expectations and "growing" pension funds without requiring much from sponsors. Any realistic assessment of historical asset returns and understanding of the pension obligations around the corner would have warned of serious funding challenges ahead. Some employers spotted trouble on the horizon and began to change their plans in the 1990s. For many, the wake-up call arrived with the beginning of the new millennium.

By the beginning of the new millennium, pension liabilities exploded because of falling interest rates and the aging of the work force. When the financial markets collapsed in 2001–2002, asset values in the pension trust funds tanked. Pension funds went from being reasonably well funded to dramatically underfunded in the wink of an eye. Unsurprisingly, many companies reacted by closing their plans—some shutting them to new hires but many shutting them down entirely. Many sponsors that chose to stay in the defined benefit game reengineered their plans, curtailing their plans' generosity in the process. Finally, in 2004 Congress reversed some of the funding limitations it had imposed during the 1980s and 1990s, but by then the damage was done. The baby boomers were closing in on retirement, the financial markets had dipped significantly and company managers who had not made substantial pension contributions for years, if ever, were dumbfounded by exploding pension funding demands. They rediscovered that if you sponsor a program to "save" for workers' retirement security, along the way some saving has to be done. If you don't start early and stay at it over time, the bill is going to be mighty costly at the end.

While the events that prompted so many employers to give up on their defined benefit plans were playing out, defined contributions plans were undergoing their own revolution. In 1978 tax legislation, Congress laid the foundation for the 401(k) system. The regulations for these new plans were not published until the early 1980s, but proliferation of 401(k)s was rapid and widespread. Initially, these plans were intended to supplement traditional employer pensions.

For younger workers, the shift to 401(k) plans was welcome, because defined benefit plans pay small benefits early in workers' tenure but progressively more as service in a plan increases. Benefits are earned more consistently in defined contribution plans. Early-career and short-term workers can amass benefits much faster in a defined contribution environment. For many older workers, however, the shift was traumatic. Having watched their older colleagues age into a pensioned retirement, they looked forward to their turn. But just when the value of their benefits was about to take off, their plans were frozen or yanked out from under them, in the midst of a turbulent financial environment no less.

Learning Lessons and Applying Them

When Alice told the Queen that she could "only remember backwards," she was expressing a sentiment with which many of us might agree. But we often fail to apply even the lessons we have learned from what we remember of the past. The collapse of the Morris Meatpacking Company in the 1920s was well documented in pension history, but Studebaker's managers failed to take to heart its lessons about the perils of running up large unfunded pension obligations. Studebaker's collapse in the 1960s was also well documented, but it did not prevent Wheeling Pittsburgh Steel from following in its path in the 1980s or Eastern Airlines in the 1990s or Delphi in 2009. Often, instead of using our recollections to help divine the way forward, we lament our current predicament with scant attention to how we got here or how we can correct our risky ways. Our past is our past and we cannot get it back for a redo. But we should at least begin to remember backwards, as Alice declared she could, and discern what enlightenment we can from our history. The evolution of our retirement system offers up many lessons that could guide us as we deal with the system's problems and promises.

Retirement programs are extremely long lived, necessitating long-term perspectives. Gertrude Grubb Janeway, the last surviving widow of a Union soldier, died on January 19, 2003. She received a Civil War pension check from the federal government until her death. She had married her husband, John, in 1927, 62 years after the Civil War ended when he was 93 and she was 18.[30] Ms. Janeway's was clearly a unique case, but Social Security's time tail often crosses many decades. For example, young workers might start paying payroll taxes in their mid-teens and make their last payments in their 60s, 70s or even later. Contributions, the entry fee to the system, can easily span six decades and the retirement period another 30 or 40 years.

All elements of the U.S. retirement system have been stressed in recent years. Both Social Security and the private employer pension system have been affected by demographic developments over the last 50 years. The aging of the baby boom is about to present the biggest claim on the system to date. One common theme with retirement programs that pay out monthly annuities—Social Security and employers' traditional defined benefit plans—is "remembering" to fund benefits as they are being earned. Because pension participation spans so many decades, pension obligations can be hidden as they accrue—and then overwhelm the plan when they come due. The real threat to the Titanic was not the part of the iceberg that sailors saw; it was the part hidden from the naked eye that did them in.

A careful look at the factors that drive Social Security costs boils the determinants down to two important ratios. One of them is the ratio of average benefits paid to recipients to the average covered earnings of workers paying payroll taxes—basically the ratio of grandpa's monthly benefit to his son's monthly paycheck. The other is the ratio of the number of beneficiaries to the number of workers supporting the system with their payroll taxes—the ratio of grandpas and grandmas to their working sons, daughters and grandchildren.

The factors that drive Social Security's costs are a good example of why it is important that we remember forwards as the Queen suggested to Alice. If a social insurance program is properly designed, the relationship between workers' average earnings subject to the payroll tax and the average benefits paid to retirees can be anticipated. The ratio between the number of workers paying such taxes and the number of retirees receiving benefits can also be anticipated by studying a population's demographic structure and its work and retirement behavior. In 1939, Dorrance Bronson, a senior actuary at Social Security, estimated 1980 program costs at around 10.6 percent of covered payroll on a "current cost" or "pay-as-you-go basis."[31] As it turned out, in 1980, the cost of the program was 10.77 percent of covered pay. The Queen would likely cite this example as proof that remembering forward is possible and necessary.

But remembering forward is never absolutely perfect and we can still get off track. In the early 1970s, when Social Security benefits were first automatically indexed to inflation, the actuarial estimates suggested the new benefit adjustments would not significantly affect future program costs. Those estimates were wildly wrong, leaving the program rushing headlong toward insolvency throughout the 1970s, until legislators finally enacted a resolution. A technical mistake in the 1972 indexing changes triggered much faster benefit growth than the actuaries had anticipated—average benefits were exploding but the wages on which payroll taxes were being collected were not. The legislative correction resulted in a close approximation of the way the program had worked previously, with the average-benefits-to-average-covered-wages ratio being fairly constant over time. The 1983 response to the 1970s funding crisis increased the normal retirement age—the age at which unreduced Social Security benefits could be claimed. Congress was remembering the future when it made those changes, anticipating evolving demographic developments and encouraging more workers and fewer retirees to manipulate the ratio of the number of retirees to workers in the system.

In regard to the current concerns that our Social Security system is again underfunded and must be reformed, some people contend that ideologues are stoking fears about Social Security because they're out to kill the program. Certainly some people would like to see us shut it down. I believe these suggestions reflect a lack of appreciation for the facts. At the end of 2010, contributing workers had earned some $21.6 trillion in benefits in today's dollars—for which no contributions have been set aside, according to Social Security actuaries' estimates.[32] Walking away from Social Security would mean walking away from a $22 trillion debt to these workers. Some of them, including some already retired, are mightily dependent on these benefits. Walking away is not a viable option. But neither is ignoring the projected deficits that threaten the benefits of retirees—current and future. Most people understand this, although they might not see a path to solvency.

Many proposals suggest that solutions are at hand if only policymakers would sit down and thrash out the details. You can review various proposals at the Office of the Actuary's web page on the Social Security Administration's website.[33] The site also provides analyses explaining the various proposals' implications. Certainly we must approach changes with caution, but the ramifications of not changing the system, and soon, constitute a comparable risk. The analyses are not advocacy documents but dispassionate, technical estimates of how things might work under alternative policies. The analyses show that under every one of the 45 proposals reviewed there, the reformed system would be paying substantial benefits 75 years from now, and the results suggest that it could continue to do so even longer. The ultimate size of the remaining Social Security defined benefit pension system varies considerably under the different proposals, and that is an issue worthy of careful consideration because some proposals would put substantially more responsibility on workers, and others would retain all responsibility withinin the central program. These are elements of potential reform that have implications for retirees' security and welfare.

Failing to respond to anticipated developments in Social Security would not be the first instance of our remembering the future but refusing to act. By the late 1980s, there were clear signals that recently adopted pension policies were going to cause problems down the road. In 1990, I testified before the Subcommittee on Retirement Income and Employment of the House Select Committee on Aging and explained the implications of the path we had taken:

> Every year since 1981, the Congress and Administration have toiled with the need to raise additional federal revenues to meet their combined appetite for spending. We have become engrossed with the political charade of raising additional federal revenues without overtly raising taxes. The result has not always been good. The provisions in the Deficit Reduction Act of 1984 limiting the ability of plan sponsors to fund retiree health benefits is at least partially accountable for the elimination and curtailment of plans now occurring.
>
> Another result, in particular, that should raise concern is the change of maximum funding of DB [defined benefit] pensions put in law by the Omnibus Budget Reconciliation Act of 1987 . . .

The potential effect of the new funding limits is that many plans have lower funding limits under the new method. . . . Under the new provisions, contributions will tend to be pushed back toward the end of the worker's career. This is especially ominous when one considers the size of the baby boom and the fact that employers are going to be hit with funding a larger share of this particularly big group of workers late in their careers. Congress is merely delaying employer contributions to the plans, and thus the deductions they take in calculating their tax obligations.

As we move through the 1990s and into the next century, the delays in pension funding are going to have to be made up if the benefit promises now implied in the benefit formulas are to be met. The important question that will remain unanswered is whether or not employers will be able to play catch-up to the extent the current law implies. The alternative will be that employers will have to reduce their future benefit promises, which they can do in a number of ways, many of them subtle.[34]

Some have blamed the demise of private pension plans on greedy corporate managers pumping up their bottom lines or, even more cynically, scalping the benefits of folks on the shop floor to feather the nests of those in the executive suites.[35] It would be foolish to argue that corporate managers are not trying to earn profits—that is what they are paid to do. But why did they set up plans after World War II if such plans reduce corporate profits? Or is there something different about our modern times that makes these plans a greater threat to profitability than they used to be? Certainly the Sarbanes-Oxley Act passed in 2002 has given corporate boards greater authority and responsibility to look out for stockholders' rights. But the charge that a sharper focus on profitability is responsible ignores a long history of corporate profitability while sponsoring these plans.

If we do not address Social Security's financing problem until the trust funds are nearly depleted, 20 to 25 years from now, Social Security actuaries estimate that using payroll taxes to pay for benefits will leave a deficit of about 3.5 to 4.0 percent of covered pay—meaning payroll taxes would have to rise by that percentage to cover the shortfall.[36] Or if we tinker with benefits to achieve a fix, Dean Baker, the co-director of the Center for Economic and Policy Research, says that a delay of that duration would necessitate an immediate reduction of around 25 percent of current benefits. Baker argues that if policymakers simply sit on their hands until then, they will not dare impose such painful cuts. The only remaining realistic alternative, according to Baker, would be to raise taxes.[37]

What if policymakers wait until 2030 to act but Baker is wrong, and they reduce benefits by 25 percent to eliminate the financing shortfall? Why would we delay a solution for 20 to 25 years when we could implement much less draconian changes now? Alternatively, what if Baker is right that policymakers would simply raise taxes to fill the financing void as they did in 1983? If they raise the payroll tax by 3.5 percent of pay in 2030, which is roughly what the actuaries' projections suggest would be necessary, my grandson Miles, born in 2009, would pay far higher payroll taxes at age 21 than I ever paid. If he starts working at age 21 and works steadily until he could claim full Social Security benefits at 67, 1.5 to 2.0 years more of his lifetime earnings would be taxed away to pay Social Security benefits than a 45-year-old will have paid. Is this the legacy we wish to leave our grandchildren?

President Bill Clinton gave a succinct summation of the generational considerations in Social Security policy in a speech to Georgetown University students in 1998:

> This fiscal crisis in Social Security affects every generation. . . . But if it gets in trouble and we don't deal with it, then it not only affects the generation of the baby boomers and whether they will have enough to live on when they retire; it raises the question of whether they will have enough to live on by unfairly burdening their children and, therefore, unfairly burdening their children's ability to raise their grandchildren. That would be unconscionable, especially since, if you move now, we can do less and have a bigger impact . . .
>
> It's very important you understand this . . . [:] {If} we wait too long to fix it, the burden on society of taking care of our [the baby boom] generation's Social Security obligations will lower your income and lower your ability to take care of your children to a degree most of us who are your parents think would be horribly wrong and unfair to you and unfair to the future prospects of the United States.[38]

A more immediate example of the consequences of failing to act despite the fact "that memory works both ways" is illustrated by some of those caught up in the transition from the employer-based defined benefit system to the do-it-yourself world of defined contribution plans. I recently viewed a video clip of a focus group of people in their 50s talking about how they acquired information on investing retirement savings and retirement planning in their new environment. There was a palpable aura of angst in the group. One woman said that her young adult children already had financial advisers helping them prepare to meet their future financial needs, but it had never occurred to her to do such a thing when she was young. She said she had watched her parents retire with a pension and Social Security and she expected to follow suit. But well along in her career, her pension was shut down, leaving her to fend for herself in the world of 401(k) saving and investing decisions. She found much of the available guidance confusing, especially given the stock market's crazy gyrations. She was afraid her retirement security would end up like a child's yo-yo, hanging at the bottom of its string.

What This Book Is About

We keep forgetting to remember backwards and often ignore our ability to remember forwards. This behavior has tremendously negative human consequences. This book attempts to explain, in somewhat more detail than in this opening discussion, how we got ourselves into this retirement predicament and where we can go from here.

The rest of Part I describes the foundations of our modern-day retirement system, the roots and motivations that led to its creation. Some people contend that pensions are no longer relevant in today's "knowledge economy." That runs counter to the reaction of several major universities when they could no longer require faculty to retire after 1994. Several of them implemented plans that offered faculty members with 20 years or more service who were at least 60 years old two years of pay to retire. After the first offer, the value of the retirement incentive declined by 20 percent per year. That is essentially a pension plan with strong retirement incentives. These universities and their faculty are at the pinnacle of the knowledge economy, proving the point that retirement plans remain important for the same reasons they were created in the first place.

Part II of the volume describes the development and evolution of our Social Security system. Some elements of this discussion are closely related to a book I coauthored in the late 1990s about Social Security.[39] The discussion here is more succinct than in the earlier volume but includes new information on developments before 1999 and describes developments since then.

Part III focuses on employer-sponsored retirement plans. It describes the early development of these plans and the problems that spurred the passage of ERISA. Many of the results of that regulation have been positive, but policymakers' failure to understand the need to "remember forward" has led to disastrous funding patterns. State and local plans are not subject to ERISA, and many forgot the need to set aside funds to cover obligations and are now in a fiscal mess. The jury is still out on the shift to defined contribution plans, but after two substantial financial market downturns in the last decade, broad concern remains that these plans are not as effective as they should be at providing retirement security. Policymakers are adding default options and other tweaks to 401(k)s, but getting defined contribution plans to fill the role once played by traditional defined benefit pension plans will not be easy.

Part IV presents evidence on the results—costs and benefits—of operating the retirement system at year-end 2010. There is a natural tendency to think about the retirement benefits we receive without appreciating the costs. This section starts with an analysis of who has borne these costs in recent decades and the implications for workers' living standards. It then describes the benefits being provided and looks at the integration of Social Security and employer-sponsored plans on a financing and benefit delivery basis. The last chapter in this section looks at retiree health benefits, which pose many of the same societal challenges and avoidances as our retirement income programs. The retiree health and income programs—both essential elements of the retirement system—are integrated in retirees' lives and draw on the same national economy. A full treatment of retiree health care would require a volume of its own, but it is impossible to consider retirement security without understanding how retirees acquire their health insurance and meet their health care needs.

The last part of the book takes up the policy issues that we face and explores some of our available options. Our situation is not hopeless if we act. If we fail to act, we threaten the prosperity of younger generations, a prospect President Clinton declared would be "horribly wrong and unfair." We have now squandered 14 years since his declaration, and the deterioration has continued apace. Social Security is fixable if politicians on both sides of the aisle can rise to the occasion and get on with the business at hand.

Employer-sponsored defined benefit pension plans have already undergone significant adjustments and are now much more sustainable. Funding challenges remain for defined benefit obligations, and we should find a mechanism to help workers, who are increasingly dependent on individual retirement savings, convert their 401(k) and other savings into retirement security. State and local governments are in a particularly difficult fix. Many of them guarantee workers the pension coverage in effect on the day the worker was hired, regardless of changing conditions and later pension reforms. While some believe that the government's power to tax exempts them from the prospect of bankruptcy, the case of Prichard, Alabama, a small city outside of Mobile with a population of around 27,000, suggests otherwise. It failed to properly fund its pension benefits for years and, despite repeated warnings, finally depleted its fund. The city stopped sending pension checks to 150 retirees on September 1, 2009. The retirees sued, and the city filed for bankruptcy. Despite a state law mandate to pay the benefits and a judge's ruling that the bankruptcy filing did not cancel the city's debt to the retirees, the checks are not in the mail. R. Scott Williams, a lawyer representing the city, responded, "The reality for Prichard is that if you took money to build the pension up, who's going to pay the garbage man? Who's going to pay to run the police department? Who's going to pay the bill for the street lights? There's only so much money to go around."[39] If we refuse to remember forward, the laws of arithmetic will ultimately catch up with us.

Since 1996, the Social Security trustees have been warning policymakers that the system is out of balance. The conditions that brought down private pensions were known years before that system started to collapse. The unsustainable nature of state and local pensions has also been clear for some time. Yet when the ramifications of closing our eyes comes crashing down on us, we are absolutely startled at the denouement. We may be able to ignore the people who are remembering forward for a while, but that path will only lead to one predictable surprise after another. If we do not resolve some of these issues soon, our grandchildren's remembering backward about the legacy we have left them will not be fond remembrances.

2 EARLY MOTIVATIONS BEHIND THE PENSION MOVEMENT

Entire books have been written about the evolution of retirement and income support mechanisms. The overview presented in this chapter is much briefer but will at least give a high-level sense of the roots of our retirement system. Some pension historians point to the diminishing demand for older workers in industrializing economies as the motivation for the creation of pensions.[1] Others attribute the retirement phenomenon to a growing taste for leisure as workers' productivity and earnings rose.[2]

Military pensions in the United States can be traced back to the Revolutionary War.[3] Pensions spread to public-sector workforces shortly after the Civil War, and the American Express freight company offered the first private plan in 1875. By the early 20th century, public pensions were becoming more common but were still generally limited to police officers, firefighters, and teachers and were concentrated in larger cities. Eighty-five percent of cities with populations of 100,000 or more had retirement plans, versus 66 percent in cities of 50,000 to 100,000 and 50 percent in cities of 30,000 to 50,000.[4] As industrialization took off during the 19th century, private employers began operating on a larger scale than ever before. Division of labor became increasingly important as tasks became more specialized. Large firms in the rail industry were the first to implement bureaucratic structures and offer private pensions.

By the second decade of the 20th century, retirement benefits were on offer by public utilities, employers in the banking and insurance industries, and in higher education. By the end of the 1920s, the academic community viewed pensions as one of the most important new economic developments since the Civil War and began to analyze the phenomenon.

In a 1936 study of the U.S. private pension movement, Birchard Wyatt developed a theoretical explanation of what motivated employers to sponsor a pension program. Wyatt argued that without a pension plan, large companies were vulnerable to "hidden pensioners" on the payroll.[5] He surmised that during a typical worker's prime working years, productivity exceeded pay for some period of time, but eventually pay caught up to and surpassed the worker's productivity. Wyatt's rationale was that the surplus created during the worker's peak productivity period could be used to fund a pension benefit. So when his or her productivity level waned, the employer could hold out the accumulated benefit to entice the worker to retire. In the 1970s, Edward Lazear, considered the founder of modern-day human resource economics, agreed, and his analysis of this phenomenon added empirical support to Wyatt's theoretical intuitions.[6]

Meanwhile, older workers were increasingly attracted by the concept of retirement. Industrialization had increased worker productivity and boosted their earnings. Dora Costa points out that "when retirement incomes were low, men remained in the labor force even if they could do so only by switching to a less physically demanding but lower-paying job."[7] Higher incomes gave rise to the possibility of a financially comfortable retirement.

If the post-Civil War economic environment enabled pensions to take root, demographic trends increased the social need for such plans. In the decades after the Civil War, both the absolute and relative size of the aged population grew significantly. By 1930, the U.S. population was four times its size in 1900, but the number of people aged 65 and older had grown six times.[8] Actuarial projections in 1935 estimated that the portion of the population over 65 would roughly double—thereby making up 11.3 percent of the total—by 1980.[9] Forty-five years later, this projection proved to be almost precisely correct—a prime example of "remembering forward" discussed in chapter 1.

By the 1920s, the U.S. pension movement had spread and matured to the point of coming under public scrutiny. At that time, many plans financed current benefits out of current contributions of participating workers or the company's current revenues. Plan sponsors were often unprepared for how quickly benefit obligations would accumulate or how long the retirees would be alive to cash their annuity checks. By the mid-1910s, the retirement system that Andrew Carnegie had set up for university faculty members around the turn of the century was facing financing shortfalls and had to be scaled back.[10] In 1923, the Morris Packing Company closed operations, sold off its assets, and distributed the proceeds to stockholders. The cost of its pension plan was a central contributing factor to the company's financial demise. After the shutdown, the company quit contributing to the plan and the assets were valued at less than one-quarter the obligations to workers. Workers not yet retired had the right to

withdraw from the plan and to get back their contributions. Younger participants quickly brought the plan to collapse with a run on the bank.[11]

Pension shortfalls were not confined to failing companies or unique circumstances like those in higher education. U.S. Steel started paying out pensions in 1911. By 1915, the financial burden forced the company to raise the
retirement age from 60 to 65. The Pennsylvania Railroad, which adopted its
plan in 1900, saw its costs swell from 0.5 percent of payroll in its early years to
2 percent of payroll by the end of the 1920s. Early plan administrators lacked
the expertise to accurately project future cost (although they knew they would
be higher). Making matters worse, pension costs did not behave like other
labor-related costs—going up with expanding production and falling during
contractions. When product markets went soft, retirement rates tended to
rise, bringing up pension costs with them.[12]

Public-sector plans were similarly vulnerable to the financing dilemma,
and even at the federal level, pension financing was often a struggle. The
Navy's early pension system was funded by selling prizes captured from ves-
sels of countries at war with the United States. During periods of hostilities,
the Navy would watch the horizon for ships sailing under enemy flags, and
then brave sailors would claim their bounty. But during peace time, plun-
dering cargo from ships sailing under foreign flags was piracy, and the Navy
plan went bankrupt more than once during the 19th century.[13]

State- and local-level administrators succumbed to the same behaviors that
weakened pensions in the private sector. For example, New York City, like the
Morris Meatpacking Company, set up an employee contributory program with
a benefit schedule that was steeper than its supporting revenue stream. By
1910, pension payouts had outgrown revenues and, in short order, accumulated assets dwindled to nothing. New York City turned to an outside "consultant," George B. Buck, to help reorganize the plan and make its financing
viable. The modern pension consulting industry can trace its roots back to this
engagement as Buck went on to set up a consulting firm aimed at providing
actuarial services to pension sponsors. He started with public sector clients
and then branched out to work with private firms.[14]

Pension historian Steven Sass maintains that guiding principles for establishing ongoing affordable pensions were understood by the end of the 1920s.[15]
First and most importantly, pension expense was not the cost of benefits paid
out to current retirees. Rather, true pension expense was the value of benefits
as they were being earned by current workers. This tied pension expense to
the value of associated labor inputs. Second, pension expense had to be covered by a cash contribution to a secure, independent fiduciary. This enabled

the benefits to be "funded" as they were earned, so retirees' benefits did not depend on the future success of the sponsoring firm. Third, plan participants had to be vested with legal rights to their pensions or cash withdrawal after some reasonable period of service. This last principle would insure that workers whose productivity has been tapped to finance the benefits in question actually received them.[16] While the principles for establishing sound pensions might have been understood by the 1920s, they would prove to be forgotten time and again over the coming decades.

By the latter part of the 19th century, it was becoming clear in many countries that the "older worker problem" would not be solved by the offer of a firm pension by a rail company here and a banking firm there. Older people were losing jobs in all sectors of the economy. Workers were becoming restive, resenting the demands of the grindstone of productivity and their meager rewards in this new industrial era. In part to calm the populace, Otto von Bismarck created the first national retirement program in Germany in 1889. The system originally covered about 40 percent of the German workforce and expanded coverage to roughly 55 percent of German workers by 1895. At first it was a disability program for workers only, but benefits were soon extended to dependents, survivors, and the aged. The system paid out the first disability benefits in 1891 and the first old-age pensions in 1899. The benefits were modest—less than those provided through the poor relief system at the time.[17]

Germany's system and those that followed came to be known as social insurance—income protection for workers and their dependents that was required in the new industrialized and urbanized society. When a worker became too old to be a viable economic cog in the ever modernizing industrial machine, or when he became disabled or died and left dependents too young to fend for themselves, the state's collective insurance plan stepped in with income support. The Germans were at the vanguard of the social insurance movement for various reasons. First, industrialization proceeded more rapidly in Germany than in other European countries. Second, German philosophers and economists advanced the perception that it was the proper role of the state to provide for the general welfare. Finally, organized labor developed early in Germany under the auspices of the "socialist" movement.[18] Across Europe, rising cries for socialism were seen as a threat to the established political and economic order. One of Bismarck's goals in instituting social insurance programs was to stem the rising tide of socialism.

The social insurance movement became quite popular around the world, but the United States resisted the modern-day institutions that now figure so prominently in all our lives. There are many reasons why we were so much slower to set up our Social Security program than many other countries. Part of it was Americans' view of their own "rugged individualism." The "free land" opportunities in the massive area settled under the Homestead Act undoubtedly played a role, and our melting-pot citizenry with its resulting lack of homogeneous kindred relationships probably was a factor as well.[19]

From the early part of the 20th century, movements cropped up that were motivated by the sentiments that we suffered many of the same conditions that had prompted other countries to establish their social insurance programs. Two schools of thought emerged on how to provide income security for the elderly, the unemployed, and the disabled. One emanated under the leadership of John Commons at the University of Wisconsin, and his colleague John Andrews. They advocated basing retirement programs on insurance principles that used experience rating, funding, and reserving. Contributions would be accumulated over workers' careers and invested at interest to finance the benefits paid in retirement. The other, more loosely organized school of thought was led, in spirit at least, by the writings and advocacy of Isaac Rubinow and Abraham Epstein, two Russian émigrés, who argued that such "prefunded" programs would not give older participants enough time to accumulate substantial benefits. They believed in contributory programs in which the government subsidized workers' contributions as necessary to pay sufficient benefits from the start. By the time Congress considered Social Security legislation, 44 states had some form of workers' compensation programs, 46 provided "pensions" for widowed mothers, and 24 had "old-age pension" systems.[20] These were public assistance benefits provided only to those who could demonstrate financial hardship.

In 1928, Franklin D. Roosevelt was elected governor of New York. During his gubernatorial campaign, FDR promised to call for a study to guide the development of legislation creating an "adequate old age pension" system. In 1930, FDR signed a state pension bill into law. His later comments about its structure reflected his opinions on the issues being debated by the social insurance theorists of the day. As the Social Security Act was being debated while he was President, he said: "As Governor of New York, it was my pleasure to recommend passage of the Old-Age Pension. . . . In approving the bill, I expressed my opinion that full solution of this problem is possible only on insurance principles. It takes so very much money to provide even a moderate pension for everybody, that when the funds are raised from taxation only a 'means test' must necessarily be made a condition of the grant of pensions."[21]

The Great Depression ultimately forced federal policymakers to take up the "aging dependency" issues that the states had been addressing in their piecemeal and varied ways. Unemployment peaked in 1932 at 25.2 percent of the total workforce, reaching a high of nearly 38 percent among the nonfarm workforce. While all segments of the workforce were hit hard by unemployment, the elderly suffered most. By 1930, 54 percent of men over age 65 were out of work and looking for a job, with another quarter temporarily laid off without pay.[22] Making matters worse, the stock market crash and rash of failures among financial institutions wiped out the limited resources that many older workers had accumulated. Furthermore, many of those who had pensions lost them when businesses collapsed. Andrew Achenbaum reports that "forty-five plans, covering one hundred thousand employees, were discontinued between 1929 and 1932; other plans lacking an adequate fiscal base, curtailed benefits."[23]

The collapse of economic markets during the Great Depression in the United States and around the world sparked fundamental concerns about the capitalist system. British historian Arnold Toynbee commented that 1931 was different than prior years in "one outstanding feature. In 1931, men and women all over the world were seriously contemplating and frankly discussing the possibility that the Western system of Society might break down and cease to work."[24] Developments in places like Russia showed what could happen when the economic and social orders broke down. There was palpable fear of radical outcomes even in countries like the United States unless the economic devastation of the Great Depression could be stanched.

At one extreme, the perceived failure of capitalism led some observers to turn to communism or socialism. A more moderate set of proposals to deal with excess industrial capacity was for the government to tax "surplus funds" and spend the money on social insurance programs. The so-called surplus funds included the incomes and inheritances of the well off.

The Great Depression proved to be the catalyst that motivated U.S. policymakers to respond to the stewing cauldron of economic and social forces that had already led other countries to establish large national retirement systems. In 1935, Congress established Social Security. It was up and running by 1936, registering private-sector workers who were paid hourly wages or salaries. It began to collect payroll taxes in 1937 and paid the first retirement benefits in 1940. The story in the chapters that follow chronicles Social Security's development and evolution into what, for a while, seemed to be one of the greatest achievements of modern economic development. Today, Social Security faces a financing shortfall, and there is considerable skepticism about how that came about and no coalescing around specific solutions.

Shortly after World War II, there was a "stampede" by large employers to expand employer-sponsored retirement benefit programs. But along the way, our unwillingness or inability to remember the lessons we learned as these programs evolved has led to where we sit today. The employer-based element of our retirement system has undergone tremendous change in the past 20 years, and we do not know yet whether the evolving structure can support the income security needs of future retirees. Beyond explaining how we landed here, this story explains the options for reestablishing the retirement income security system to meet the needs of workers and retirees in the future.

SOCIAL SECURITY: THE DREAM AND REALITY

We can never insure one hundred percent of the population against one hundred percent of the hazards and vicissitudes of life, but we have tried to frame a law which will give some measure of protection to the average citizen and to his family against the loss of a job and against poverty-ridden old age.
This law, too, represents a cornerstone in a structure intended to lessen the force of possible future depressions. It will act as a protection to future Administrations against the necessity of going deeply into debt to furnish relief to the needy.

—PRESIDENT FRANKLIN D. ROOSEVELT, *Signing Statement,*
Social Security Act, August 14, 1935

DEVELOPMENT AND PASSAGE OF THE SOCIAL SECURITY ACT

Franklin Roosevelt coined the term "New Deal" during the 1932 presidential campaign. The New Deal was not a specific set of programs, but rather a "concept" meant to offer hope to all the victims of the Great Depression. It "was an idea that all the political and practical forces of the community should and could be directed to making life better for ordinary people."[1] It was out of this "idea" that a range of programs, including Social Security, evolved. The New Deal was Roosevelt's answer to the public perception that America's traditional economic structures had crumbled.

Growing Clamor for Income Relief for the Elderly

Within months of taking office, Roosevelt was facing challenges from both the left and the right on how to help the elderly. A retired physician in California, Francis E. Townsend, proposed giving $200 a month to all citizens over 60 who were not employed or a felon, on the condition that he or she spend the benefit within 30 days. To put the generosity of this proposal into context, $200 per month in 1934 is roughly equivalent to $3,200 per month in 2009 dollars. The average monthly Social Security benefit for a retired worker at the end of 2008 was slightly less than $1,500 per month. Despite its impracticality, Townsend organized a movement and collected around 25 million signatures in support of his plan.[2] Its popularity made it impossible to dismiss on the political front.

Even more disconcerting than the Townsend plan was a flanking move executed by Senator Huey Long (D) of Louisiana. Long had supported Roosevelt during the 1932 Democratic convention, delivering the Louisiana and Mississippi delegates for Roosevelt's nomination. But by the middle of 1933, the end of FDR's "First Hundred Days," Long and Roosevelt had parted company and by 1934, it was clear that Long was positioning to run against Roosevelt in 1936. Long published a book, *Every Man a King*, and delivered a series of speeches advocating massive redistribution of wealth. Among other things, he proposed old-age pensions for everyone over age 60 with less than $10,000 in cash. FDR considered Huey Long to be one of the most dangerous men in the country.[3]

These proposals created two concerns for FDR. One was political—the Depression had stimulated the public appetite for social change. The Townsend and Long plans were too popular to ignore. The Townsend plan was the pivotal political issue in some congressional districts, and more than one candidate had ridden its coattails to victory.[4] Long was gaining popularity with his "chicken in every pot" and "share the wealth" campaign, and FDR feared he could siphon off 10 percent of the Democratic vote in the 1936 presidential election, which might give the White House back to the Republicans.[5] Roosevelt may have taken up the Social Security issue on his own at some point, but these populist developments forced his hand.

FDR's other set of concerns focused on the practical policy issues involved in providing an old-age retirement program. The plans being proposed by Townsend and Long went against the grain of his own fiscal conservatism. FDR worried that these plans would eventually create significant liabilities for the federal government. He believed that it was "dishonest"[6] or "immoral"[7] to set up a program that would create burdens for future congresses and presidential administrations and constrain their ability to manage the government's fiscal and other operations. Roosevelt concluded that while economic, social and political dynamics called for an old-age retirement proposal, it had to be affordable, fiscally sustainable and acceptable to the vast majority of Americans.

Formulating a National Retirement Program

On June 8, 1934, President Roosevelt submitted a message to Congress addressing broad security issues. In FDR's words, "People want . . . . some safeguard against misfortunes which cannot be wholly eliminated in this man-made world of ours."[8] He said that these related "to security against the hazards and vicissitudes of life," especially those associated with "unemployment and old age."[9] He thought a "social insurance" program was the way to address these problems and said he was launching a study to formulate a comprehensive proposal to be submitted to Congress in the next year.

On June 29, 1934, President Roosevelt created a cabinet-level Committee on Economic Security and a citizen Advisory Council on Economic Security.

Both groups were to make recommendations to the president by December 1, 1934, regarding proposals to "promote greater economic security."[10] The Committee designated Secretary of Labor Frances Perkins, the committee chair, to lead the effort and create a technical advisory board. In doing so, she relied heavily on her assistant secretary, Dr. Arthur Altmeyer. By Perkins' account, they "brought in other people who were familiar with social insurance problems [but] at the President's request we steered clear of people who were too theoretical and who would take months of research before they could make a brief report."[11] Assistant Secretary Altmeyer had a Ph.D. in economics from the University of Wisconsin, where he had been a student of John Commons.

When Altmeyer was at the University of Wisconsin, one of his associates was Dr. Edwin Witte. Altmeyer selected Witte to be the executive director of the Committee on Economic Security.[12] Witte brought Wilbur Cohen, one of his students at the University of Wisconsin, to serve as his assistant. On August 13, the Committee on Economic Security named Altmeyer chairman of the technical board. Thus the leadership of both the Committee's staff and the technical board were from the Wisconsin school of social insurance.

After a decade-long battle between the two factions on the social insurance battlefield—Isaac Rubinow and Abraham Epstein versus Commons and Andrews—disciples of the Wisconsin school were put in charge of developing Roosevelt's initiative. Rubinow and Epstein had done far more research and writing on the needs of the elderly and how to address them in the modern economy. Witte and Altmeyer, however, were more closely aligned with FDR on how best to finance a national retirement system.

Altmeyer acted as the liaison between the Committee on Economic Security and the working staff. He considered himself an administrator, keeping programs on course and on schedule. For him, the organization took precedence over the individual. He believed that "if you have any desire to be a public character, you're not likely to be interested in administration as such. I think anonymity is desirable so that you don't get the public involved in making decisions based on personality rather than accomplishments. . . . So I have said many times that a successful administrator ought to be about as interesting as spinach—cold spinach at that."[13]

Edwin Witte was an academic with practical skills in framing legislative solutions to social problems. He was more builder than architect. Witte's biographer would write of him that "he could treat limited, immediate problems and subjects incisively and lucidly, but he did not conceptualize in a grand manner." Witte directed his energies "towards working out the technical details of new legal and institutional structures . . . . rather than in conceiving radical new designs for social order. As he designed institutions, he used blueprints that were compatible with what he understood to be prevailing American political and economic concepts."[14]

Witte brought in three other outside associates who were largely responsible for the development of the proposals that would cover the elderly. These were Barbara Armstrong, a professor of economics and law from the University of California at Berkeley; J. Douglas Brown, a professor of economics from Princeton University; and Murray Latimer, the head of the Railroad Retirement Board and a pension expert who had written extensively about the employer-based pension movement in the United States. They were supported by a small group of analysts and actuaries, including a young actuary named Robert J. Myers. It would turn out that Armstrong and Brown were much more attuned to the ideas of Rubinow and Epstein than the Wisconsin crowd on the desirable structure of social insurance for the elderly.

Witte and Altmeyer were practical men who were willing to accommodate differences of opinion in the interest of making progress. Armstrong and Brown were headstrong academics. An air of intellectual superiority or haughtiness seeps through Armstrong and Brown's recollections of their work. Armstrong found the accommodation to practicality to be particularly disagreeable and clearly disdained those who engaged in it. She referred to Witte as being "half Witte" and Altmeyer as being "quarter Witte."[15] Brown was less harsh but made it clear that the academics on the committee staff were not bound by the practical considerations that worried Witte and Altmeyer. Both Armstrong and Brown went back to their academic posts after their work for the Committee on Economic Security was finished. Brown continued to play an active role in the development of Social Security policy for many years to come.

Despite differences among the staff members' perspectives, there was consensus that the program should include employer and employee contributions. The state plans then in existence generally were not financed this way and most included means tests—requirements for applicants to demonstrate the inability to support themselves. Everyone was convinced that a national program that did not include contributions from workers and their employers would almost certainly have to include means testing. Virtually all students of social insurance found means tests demeaning and beneficiaries of traditional welfare programs that included such testing were commonly considered to be personal failures by the broad cross-section of society.

Proponents of old-age social insurance saw inadequate income security in old age as largely a fault of industrialization and economic organization rather than personal failure. They felt strongly that solutions to a systemic economic problem should not stigmatize participants. If benefits were financed by workers' contributions, the elderly would have earned the right to their benefits without stigma. FDR, who understood public sentiments on many matters as well as anyone, felt strongly that the system should be "contributory" because it would give participants a sense of ownership and create a sense of "rights" or "entitlement" that would not be dismissed lightly. One reason it is so hard to reduce benefit levels in Social Security today is because of the strong "I have paid for my benefits" conviction among so many workers.

There was disagreement about what to do for people who were already retired at the inception of the new program. These retirees' careers were over, and they had no earnings on which to contribute. The issue was even more complicated than the black and white of people who worked under the system versus those who did not. How would benefits be linked to contributions? If benefits were linked to a worker's total contributions, someone who worked five years under the new system would get a very small benefit. Someone with 20 years under the system would receive a proportionately larger benefit, but only workers who had contributed over a relatively full career—35 or 40 years—would receive a full lifetime benefit. A program that would not pay full lifetime benefits for another four decades or so would not help those already in need. The proposal had to make some provision for them. Under traditional insurance principles, such financing would not be available. The alternative model, however, could finance subsidized benefits for early beneficiaries out of the government's general revenue.

The debate over the structure of the national program for the elderly was conducted among a group of feisty theoreticians, but the differences in what they were proposing had practical implications. In addressing an outside panel of experts in mid-November 1934, the president said the program for the elderly should encourage employment based on sound insurance principles and should avoid the comingling of insurance and relief elements.[16] FDR's position was that anyone receiving a pure "gratuity" should be paid under some sort of relief program. Those who were to qualify for benefits based on contributions would be covered under the "insurance" program.

Ultimately, the Committee on Economic Security crafted legislation to provide benefits to the elderly under two titles of the bill. Title I would establish a means-tested, old-age assistance program operated at the state level but partially financed by federal funds. This would extend federal support for the sorts of welfare programs that many states had already adopted for the low-income elderly. Title II called for old-age insurance benefits that would be based on wages on which contributions were made. The proposal on old-age insurance developed by Armstrong, Brown, and Latimer called for contributions to begin in 1937 and benefit payouts to begin in 1942.

Armstrong and Brown were clearly in the Epstein/Rubinow camp on how to design the benefit structure under Title II, but Witte and Altmeyer were in charge and much more aligned with the approach desired by President Roosevelt. As the proposal evolved, it is clear that the authors tried to split the baby—benefits would be linked to the worker's covered earnings, out of which contributions would be made, but there would be some subsidization. Over time, workers who had made larger contributions by virtue of higher earnings or longer contribution periods would receive higher benefits.

Financing a program purely on the basis of contributions based on workers' earnings, however, meant that benefits would be extremely small during the program's early years. The architects of the proposal resolved the conflict through several plan features. Although the proposal was based on the "insurance principles" of paying retirees based on their contributions, the initial proposal called for two forms of benefit subsidization. First, lower-earning workers would receive a higher percentage of their preretirement earnings than higher-earning workers. Second, in the early years of the program, retirees would receive higher benefits than would be economically warranted, purely on the basis of contributions on their behalf.

To make the program self-sustaining, subsidies to one group of workers had to come at the expense of benefits to another group. But the architects of the proposal developed for the Committee on Economic Security did not want the subsidization of early retirees' benefits to come at the expense of those retiring later. Thus, they proposed that, starting in the 1960s, the government would contribute the amount of the worker contributions used to subsidize benefits for early beneficiaries.

The retirement plan put together by the Committee's staff envisioned that initially private-sector hourly wage and salaried workers earning less than $3,000 per year would be covered under the system. This would include about 60 percent of the total workforce at the time. Initial benefits were to be paid only to those who were at least 65 in 1942 and who had contributed to the system in each of the five years from 1937 through 1941. In 1942, the beneficiary pool was expected to be a relatively miniscule portion of the total population over the age of 65. Under the Committee's proposal, early retirees' benefits would be subsidized by tapping the contributions of current workers. Excess contributions were to be accumulated in the form of government bonds.

A Funding Question Arises at the Outset

By Christmas Eve in 1934, there was general agreement among the members of the Committee on Economic Security on the package to be sent to Congress. They completed their final sign-off and accompanying legislative recommendations in mid-January 1935. The package would be submitted to Congress on January 17, and press materials announcing the proposal had already gone out. But as President Roosevelt was reviewing the final package on the afternoon of January 16, he discovered a table showing that the old-age insurance program would run significant deficits after 1965,[17] requiring a government subsidy sometime later, around 1980.[18] He assumed this was an error and summoned Secretary Perkins and then Edwin Witte to help sort out the matter. Upon being informed that this was an element of the plan design, FDR insisted that it be changed. Perkins quoted FDR as saying, "This is the same old dole under another name. It is almost dishonest to build up an accumulated deficit for the Congress of the United States to meet in 1980. We can't do that. We can't sell the United States short in 1980 any more than in 1935."[19]

FDR clearly intended Social Security to be contributory and self-supporting. He wanted the plan to operate like a commercial retirement plan that might be offered by an insurance company rather than what Barbara Armstrong and J. Douglas Brown had put together. He did not tell Perkins and Witte to take out the subsidization elements of the package but indicated that a portion of early contributions had to be accumulated to help pay future benefits. After the meeting at the White House on January 16, at the president's insistence, the offending table was taken out of the report and the package was modified to indicate that the schedules of tax rates and benefits included were merely one approach to providing old-age benefits that Congress might consider. The report was not filed with the president in final form until the morning of January 17, although it still bore the date of January 15.[20]

The staff who had worked on the old-age insurance provisions came up with a new set of provisions and cost estimates. J. Douglas Brown identified the projections around the new plan as the "M 9 tabulation," which he translated as Robert Myers' "ninth shot at it."[21] The modified plan and the projected financing suggested that the old-age insurance element of the program would be self-supporting indefinitely. Roosevelt's demand for modifications so late in the game shows how strongly he felt about the matter. The modified plan was not introduced in Congress until Committee hearings on the package were underway. The modifications were introduced by Secretary of Treasury Henry Morgenthau and came to be known as the Morgenthau amendment.

Moving from Design to Legislative Action

On January 17, 1935, President Roosevelt transmitted a message to Congress recommending legislation on economic security. Ultimately, the Ways and Means Committee redrafted the legislation, making several substantive changes to the provisions and changed the name of the bill from the "Economic Security Act" to the "Social Security Act." Ways and Means reported out the bill on April 5 and the House began its consideration on April 11. Roughly 50 amendments to the committee bill were offered but none were adopted. On April 19, 1935, the House of Representatives adopted the Social Security Act by a vote of 371 to 33.[22]

In the Senate Finance Committee, Senator Bennett Clark from Missouri introduced an amendment to exempt employers with pension programs from participation in the old-age insurance program. Given the redistributional nature of benefits, this would have left the program holding the most expensive beneficiaries minus the redistributional contributions from better-off workers. The amendment was defeated on a tie vote, but the full Senate adopted the Clark amendment on a vote of 51 to 32. Then the Senate passed the full bill by a vote of 77 to 6 on June 19.

Inconsistencies in the initial bills adopted by the House and Senate had to be reconciled in a conference committee. All differences but the Clark amendment, which was in the House version of the legislation, were worked out by July 16. Both the Senate and House accepted the changes in this conference report on July 17, but each chamber instructed its conferees to hold firm to their respective positions on the Clark amendment. The conference committee then attempted to redraft the Clark amendment to be acceptable to both chambers. Ultimately, the conferees recommended that the Social Security Act be adopted without the Clark amendment with the understanding that a joint committee would be formed to push such legislation through the next session of Congress. The conference report was adopted by the House on August 8 and by the Senate on August 9. The Clark amendment was never heard from again.

The final provisions in the 1935 Social Security Act called for a schedule of payroll taxes to begin at a rate of 1 percent each on workers and their employers on the first $3,000 of annual earnings. The initial payroll tax rate paid by workers and their employers was to increase in half-percentage-point increments every three years until it reached 3 percent of covered wages in 1949. Hourly-wage and salaried workers in private businesses were covered under the original Social Security Act, except for railroad workers, who were to be covered in their own separate federally mandated retirement system. People over the age of 65 who quit working would be eligible for benefits. To receive a retirement annuity, scheduled to commence in 1942, a worker had to have had covered earnings for the prior five years. Workers who turned age 65 before 1942 would have their contributions returned with interest. Estates of workers who died before receiving an annuity would also receive a return of the employee's contributions with interest.

The original act anticipated that workers with low earnings would receive subsidized benefits relative to those with higher earnings. It also provided that initial beneficiaries receiving retirement annuities would receive subsidized benefits. These subsidized early benefits were to be financed through the payroll tax schedule adopted in the law. The tax rates were projected to be somewhat higher in the long-term than the cost of benefits that would be paid to workers once the system had fully matured. In other words, future beneficiaries would receive benefits worth slightly less than the contributions on their behalf would warrant, in order to give initial retirees adequate benefits.

EARLY CONCERNS PROVE NAGGING AND PERSISTENT

Some critics contend that Social Security has become a welfare program. But in fact, the 1935 Social Security Act essentially called for "subsidizing" benefits for some workers, and that redistributional component has persisted, at least in theory, into the present.

Another common complaint about Social Security is that the government has squandered workers' contributions. Those voicing this complaint believe the original intention was to save contributions, invest them and then pay them out as benefits over time. Our political leaders often reinforce this line of thought.

These two issues—paying welfare benefits through Social Security and misusing the trust fund—are interlinked. FDR clearly intended for the system to accumulate a much larger share of Social Security payroll taxes than it has. Because that did not happen, there was greater subsidization of benefits during the program's start-up years than was authorized in the original legislation. But the original legislation clearly intended the income redistribution to persist even as the system matured. Spending payroll taxes as they were collected had profound implications for the program in which our grandparents participated, and it has equally profound implications for the baby boom and subsequent generations of workers.

Operation of Social Security Trust Funds

Social Security's trust funds have always been invested in government bonds. The U.S. Treasury collects Social Security revenues (payroll taxes), and, as revenues flow in, uses some of the money to pay immediate benefits. For the money left over, Treasury issues a special bond to the Social Security trust funds. Initially, it issues short-term bonds. But on June 30 each year, it cashes the short-term bonds and issues a longer-term bond—today it issues a 15-year bond. Each of the bonds earns the same interest as other Treasury bonds of similar duration at the time. These are par value bonds, and their immediate redemption value always equals the face value on their issue date. Social Security can cash them anytime as needed to meet its benefit or administrative obligations. There is no evidence suggesting that any of these bonds have ever been misappropriated or cashed for any other purpose than paying benefits and operating the program under law.

Social Security Funding Concerns and Controversy

When the U.S. Treasury collects more payroll taxes than it needs at the time, it issues bonds to the Social Security trust funds and spends the excess cash from tax collections on other governmental functions. This is when the funding of Social Security becomes confusing, and it does so in a couple of different ways. First, when Social Security needs the money, it tenders a bond to the Treasury in trade for cash. At that juncture, the federal government has to either raise general revenues to cash out the bond or borrow from lenders to pay it off. Surely if the trust funds were real assets, say critics, we would not have to go back to the taxpayers or credit markets to collect more money to pay off the money we already collected as payroll taxes. Second, Social Security delivers cash to the Treasury outside Treasury's normal channels of revenue, such as personal and corporate income taxes, excise taxes, and user fees. Here the concern is that Social Security serves as a cash cow for policymakers.

These modern-day concerns about the trust funds date back to the beginning of the program. The initial legislation had no sooner passed than conservative critics focused their ire on the trust fund. Under the 1935 law, the trust fund was expected to hold $47 billion by 1980.[1] Many found such an enormous accumulation of government bonds too fantastic to comprehend. The government itself had accumulated only $27 billion in debt in its first 159 years, and people could not fathom accumulating another $20 billion over the next 45 years. Moreover, policymakers hoped to pay down the debt after the Depression, not increase it.

Accumulating the trust fund was supposed to hold program cost at a reasonable level across generations. The system designers knew that workers would willingly pay only so much in payroll taxes. The original legislation scheduled the payroll tax rate to go up to 6 percent of covered wages, again split between the employer and employee. The problem was that, by 1980, benefits were expected to equal as much as 10 percent of covered pay, which virtually everyone agreed was too high for a regressive payroll tax—a tax that imposes the heaviest burden on low earners. As FDR saw it, if early contributions were saved and invested, then much of the cost of benefits in 1980 and later would be covered by interest income on the accumulated trust funds.

It was the discrepancy between the projected cost of benefits and what was widely considered a reasonable contribution from workers that prompted the Committee on Economic Security to originally propose that the government make regular contributions to the mature system. When FDR balked at that approach, the revised package called for phasing in higher payroll taxes more rapidly, which also sped up projected trust fund growth. The larger trust fund would generate higher levels of interest than the smaller one. Under the 1935 Social Security Act, 1980 total tax collections were projected to be $2.2 billion compared to benefit payments of $3.5 billion, with the difference made up by interest on the trust fund.[2]

Conservative critics asked whether the government could "save" the accumulating trust fund. One pundit put this into a personal context: Suppose a worker saved $10 per week and put it in a box marked "Reserve." Over a one-year period, the worker would save $520, but from time to time he would need money. Instead of borrowing from a bank, he would borrow from his reserve fund and put in an IOU promising to return the "loan" plus 6 percent interest. The worker continued contributing to the fund and borrowing for 10 years, at which point he had a box full of IOUs with an accumulated value of $8,000. The analyst argued that it is clear the worker has accumulated no savings and that the reserve was "pure fiction."[3]

Those who argued that the trust funds represented real savings said the excess cash would be used to buy back existing federal debt held by the public, and reducing outstanding debt would be "saving." That, critics responded, would essentially be paying off government debt on the "shoulders of the lowest income group of the country."[4] The average-wage worker earning roughly $2,000 would pay 1 percent of his wages, rising to 3 percent in time, and a worker earning $3,000 per year would pay the same tax rate. But a worker earning $4,000 would only pay taxes on the first $3,000 of earnings, thereby lowering his overall tax rate to just 0.75 percent, and someone earning $10,000 would enjoy an even lower overall tax rate of 0.3 percent. The regressive payroll tax would be the source of the accumulating trust fund—or pool of federal debt, depending on how you looked at it.

Critics also worried that, rather than paying down the federal debt, the government would use the accumulating trust fund as an excuse to spend more. Policymakers in 1935 expected that, by 1960, the projected trust fund would exceed total federal debt. They could not fathom the amounts of federal debt that would be piled on during World War II and later decades. There was no serious discussion at the time about investing the trust fund in the private capital base of the economy. So it appeared the government would have to create added debt just to accommodate payroll tax accumulations. If the government simply held the collected money, it would act as a tremendous drag on the economy. The only other option was to spend the excess payroll taxes as they were collected. So the funding mechanism could potentially generate federal spending totally unrelated to the purpose of Social Security.

Some six decades after this debate began in Congress, there was a replay during a Senate Finance Committee hearing on Social Security financing. In August 1998, Social Security Commissioner Kenneth Apfel defended the policy put in place in 1983 that led to our roughly $2.5 trillion accumulation in the trust funds today. In that session, Apfel insisted that we must save the surplus payroll tax revenues now to keep the system solvent until 2032 rather than 2020. Senator Robert Kerrey, a Democrat from Nebraska, responded in highly emotional tones:

> We are not prefunding. . . . Are we holding the money in reserve some-place? We are not prefunding! The idea in 1983 was that we would pre-fund the baby boomers. We began to use it immediately for the expenditures of general government. We didn't prefund anything. What we are doing is asking people who get paid by the hour to shoulder a disproportionate share of deficit reduction. That's what we're doing! And the beneficiaries on the other hand, they suffer under the illusion inflicted by us very often, that they have a little savings account back here. They are just getting back what they paid in. They don't understand that it's just a transfer from people that are being taxed at 12.4 percent.[5]

The 12.4 percent that Senator Kerrey referred to is the combined percentage of workers' covered paychecks split by employers and employees in the form of the payroll tax.

When the first payroll taxes were collected in 1937, conservatives in Congress were poised to fight the financing provisions of the Social Security Act. Senator Arthur Vandenberg, a Republican from Michigan, and several of his congressional colleagues set the stage. They argued that the

> reserve is unnecessary in a compulsory tax-supported system; that its ultimate accumulation of a $47,000,000,000 reserve is a positive menace

to free institutions and to sound finance and that it is a perpetual invitation to the maintenance of an extravagant public debt; that it will, in effect, transfer the burden of debt retirement from the shoulders of general taxpayers to the shoulders of the lowest income group of the country in the form of a gross income tax on labor; and that it involves . . . a needless postponement of earlier and more adequate benefit payments.[6]

Social Security Financing Revisited

Linking the trust fund accumulation to benefit adequacy opened an opportunity for conservatives to form an alliance with interested parties at the other end of the political spectrum. From the left, the critics of the Social Security Act focused on the meager pension benefits that would be paid in the program's early years. In many states, the benefits paid under Social Security's Title I—means-tested welfare benefits financed out of general revenues for indigent people 65 and over—were larger than those being paid under Social Security's Title II pension program financed out of the payroll tax. Some of the architects of the Social Security package sent to Congress in 1935 became ardent spokesmen for shifting to pay-as-you-go financing—called "pay-as-you-go" because it draws from current revenues and involves virtually no buildup in a trust fund.

J. Douglas Brown, who had helped formulate the Old-Age Benefits proposal in the Social Security Act, was committed to pay-as-you-go financing and had testified in 1935 against the trust fund accumulations that FDR had insisted upon. After the passage of the Social Security Act in 1935, which included FDR's funding approach, Brown concluded that improving benefits at the outset was likely to be the best way to "win" pay-as-you-go financing.[7] Barbara Armstrong originally had favored an expanded package of benefits to be paid for by pay-as-you-go financing from the start and, although she opposed the trust fund provisions in the original package, she had gone along with them to get the bill approved.[8]

In January 1937, Senator Vandenberg introduced a resolution calling for the abandonment of "full reserve" funding of Social Security, which was to be accomplished by either raising benefits or cutting taxes. At a Senate Finance hearing on the proposal, Arthur Altmeyer made the case for staying the course. As the hearing was ending, Senator Vandenberg and Altmeyer agreed that the Social Security Board and the chairman of the Senate Finance

Committee would create an advisory group to look into funding mechanisms for Social Security and report back to both of them.[9] The Advisory Council was appointed in May and included representatives from the employer community and labor organizations, actuaries and economists. The council's charter went beyond the pure funding and reserves questions to consider accelerating the date that benefits would be paid, increasing benefits, and extending coverage to additional groups.[10] J. Douglas Brown chaired the council.

While Altmeyer, as chairman of the Social Security Board, had been pushed into forming the Advisory Council, the Board and the Roosevelt Administration took it as an opportunity to enhance the system. Altmeyer had Roosevelt write him a letter in April 1938, asking that the Board develop a plan for enhancing Social Security's provisions. In addition to extending coverage, accelerating payments and increasing benefits for early beneficiaries, FDR also asked the council to consider "providing benefits for aged wives and widows, and providing benefits for young children of insured persons dying before reaching retirement age. It is my hope that the Board will be prepared to submit its recommendations before Congress reconvenes in January."[11]

Members of the Advisory Council represented the full range of opinions on funding. Among the most liberal members was Alvin Hansen, the noted Keynesian economist, who was worried about the payroll tax being a potential fiscal drag on the economy. He wanted to use benefit expenditures to fuel consumer demand and act as an economic stimulus. On the conservative side was M. Albert Linton, president of Provident Mutual Life Insurance Company. An adviser to Senator Vandenberg, he had served as an actuarial consultant to the Committee on Economic Security and had consistently advocated the pay-as-you-go approach.[12] Another council member was Edwin Witte, who remained committed to the "reserve funding" approach in the original Act.

Under the program he sent to Congress in 1935, President Roosevelt envisaged that the trust funds would accumulate assets over time in rough accordance with the accumulating benefit obligations. In pension parlance, this is known as a "funded" plan. A funded plan does not have to rely on future generations of workers to pay benefits to retirees. The alternative funding mechanism favored by Albert Linton, Senator Vandenberg, and others would use the taxes paid by current workers to finance immediate benefits.

The debate within the Advisory Council on the appropriate funding approach boiled down to choosing whether to base the system on "banking or savings" principles or "social insurance" principles.[13] Linton argued that relying on the former meant that adequate pensions would not be available for many years, thereby penalizing middle-aged and older workers. He also argued that the benefits promised by the 1935 Act would be overly burdensome for future taxpayers. He cited the projected benefit levels equivalent to 10 percent of pay in 1980 as the true costs that would fall to taxpayers.[14]

Alvin Hansen viewed the accumulating trust fund differently than Linton. Linton was concerned about the trust fund leading to federal budget deficits. Hansen saw them in the context of their macroeconomic effects and worried that the government having raised $400 million more in 1937 than it spent would act as a contractionary force on the economy. That year's payroll tax had raised $500 million, so Social Security was to blame for the aggregated federal budget being contractionary precisely when an expansionary influence was needed. He felt that higher benefits in the short term would ameliorate the fiscal problem the payroll tax was creating in the larger economic context.[15]

On the matter of the "banking" versus "social insurance" principles, Witte clearly embraced the former, arguing that "banking" payroll taxes was the only way to secure workers' benefits. He had an individualistic view of the program and believed that, at a minimum, every worker should get back his own contributions plus interest. He acknowledged that "insurance might be a better institution, if it did not include the savings element, but it does include the savings element."[16]

Linton and his allies viewed the income security challenges associated with old age as risks that should be socialized and spread broadly across society. Witte viewed these risks as individual responsibilities that needed to be funded across time. Because workers were shortsighted about saving for old age, a mandated savings program was the way to overcome their myopia. The Social Security program with its individualistic contribution rates and benefits was the best mechanism for achieving this goal.

Those opposed to funding Social Security argued that instead of "banking" contributions, current payroll taxes should be used to pay full lifetime benefits for all eligible elderly recipients. When the younger generations of contributors reached retirement age, the next generation of workers would finance their benefits. FDR and Witte countered that losing the interest accumulation on the "savings" would push program costs much higher as the system matured. The groups understood and appreciated each other's arguments— they simply had different perspectives on what was most important. Possibly the clearest articulation of the difference in the two perspectives occurred when Witte confronted Brown with the prospect that moving away from reserve funding to pay-as-you-go financing would impose tremendous costs on future generations. Brown blew off Witte's concern, responding: "We will all be dead"[17] when the higher costs materialize. High costs down the road were not his concern.

Early Change in Directions on Program Financing and Benefit Structure

The Advisory Council recommended a significant overhaul of the program that was largely incorporated into the Social Security Act through amendments adopted in 1939. These amendments maintained the principle of linking benefits to the number of years of coverage and contributions, but the link was much weaker than it had been in the original act. First, benefits became payable in 1940 after only three years of contributions. Second, the amendments increased the earnings replacement rates for short-term beneficiaries and reduced the long-term replacement rates for single workers.[18] These changes were accomplished by moving from a formula that based benefits on lifetime, cumulative, covered earnings to one based on average monthly covered earnings.

The 1939 redesign further redistributed benefits to spouses. For example, a 65-year-old wife would be entitled to 50 percent of her husband's basic benefit, which significantly increased replacement rates for early retirees with spouses. The amendments also increased the potential long-term benefits for those workers. There would now be a new category of beneficiaries—survivors. The net effect of these provisions, as with dependent benefits, was to redistribute benefits toward nonworkers.

On the financing side, the start date for the payroll tax increase was rolled back from January 1, 1940, to 1942—against the recommendations of the Social Security Board. The Advisory Council called for future government contributions to the trust fund but did not get into the specifics of when or how much. Under the amended schedule of benefits and tax provisions, the projected 1955 trust fund balance declined from $22.1 billion under the original act to $6.9 billion.[19]

Secretary of Treasury Morgenthau testified on behalf of the modified financing proposals and stated two reasons for doing so. In developing the original Social Security Act, it was assumed that coverage under the Old-Age Benefits program would be relatively limited, so general revenue financing would be unfair to the taxpayers outside the program. As program coverage turned out to be far broader than originally anticipated, that became less of an issue. The second reason for his support related to concerns about the payroll tax being a fiscal drag on the overall economy. During the second half of 1937, the U.S. economy appeared to be heading back toward full-blown Depression, and neither Morgenthau nor Roosevelt wanted to do anything that would exacerbate the economy's precarious condition.[20]

The 1939 Amendments were significant. Instead of being heavily weighted toward individual equity—that is, basing benefits on wages, albeit with a redistributive aspect—the program provided much broader protection against hardship across a broader range of contingencies. Over the years, debate has continued over the proper weight of the "equity" and "adequacy" goals, and we will cover some of that discussion later.

But while the amendments modified the program substantially, the operational changes did not represent a radical departure from the original benefit goals. The rationale that society needed to provide "insurance" protection for workers who had aged out of jobs could be easily extended to protection for the workers' dependents as well. Benefits for dependent spouses made sense in a society where most people were married and husbands were typically the breadwinners. The more consequential change in direction was on the financing side of the ledger.

Social Security's current benefit structure was, for all practical purposes, put in place by the 1939 Amendments. Disability insurance benefits were added in the 1950s, early retirement was introduced in 1956 for women and in 1961 for men, and automatic inflation protection was added in the early 1970s. Adjustments have been made to the relative generosity of benefits for workers at various income levels, and average benefits have modulated somewhat relative to average wages of workers. The benefit formula no longer pays out an additional 1 percent for each extra year a worker contributes, but workers who contribute for more years still receive something for their efforts, at least until 35 relatively full years of work are recorded. For the most part, these changes do not represent fundamental structural changes.

In presenting and defending the recommendations of the Advisory Council to Congress, J. Douglas Brown argued that there were only two practical ways to deal with old-age dependency: old-age assistance or old-age insurance. He maintained that a hybrid program with a mix of the two would not work. Brown articulated the philosophy that contributory insurance was vital to maintain workers' self-reliance in that it "permitted" them to finance their own old-age protection. Self-reliance permeated our contributory Social Security program as well as our economic and political system—it was the American way. People who worked harder and contributed more should receive more. If we deviated from this route, "mounting dependencies [would become] both an economic and political hazard."[21] Brown's philosophical statement did not address the contradiction between the significant expansion of the welfare embedded in the Social Security program and his and the Social Security Board's articulation of the superiority of "incentives" and "self-reliance" in a contributory social insurance program. Apparently giving money to people outright created a moral taint whereas heavily subsidizing their retirement benefit did not.

If the 1935 Social Security Act represented a victory for the Andrews/Commons model of social insurance, the 1939 Amendments represented some degree of defeat. As Abraham Epstein said in his assessment of the revisions: "The victory which transcends every other is, of course, the complete revision of the national old age insurance program. . . . The results achieved, frankly, exceed our fondest hopes."[22]

Edwin Witte took a very different view of the 1939 Amendments. He believed the really important change was that the "principle that everyone who has paid taxes gets at least some benefits has been discarded."[23] He was critical of delays in the payroll tax increase originally scheduled for 1940. He believed the system's financing was faulty. Witte was aware that the program's true costs in the early years were not the benefit payments, but rather the accruing liabilities for the workers contributing during their working lives. He knew the new model would not come close to covering those costs and was convinced that the 1939 amendments portended long-term financing trouble ahead.

MOVING TO PAY-AS-YOU-GO FINANCING

The 1939 Amendments to Social Security did not fully resolve the disagreements between the advocates of the original design and its critics. Indeed, both groups could and did claim their vision of the system was embodied in the restructured program. Virtually everyone embraced expanding benefits to protect U.S. citizens from a wider array of "vicissitudes of life," accelerating payment of the first benefits, and making benefits for early beneficiaries bigger.

The three-year delay in the increase of the payroll tax only temporarily pacified the pay-as-you-go proponents. Meanwhile, the funding advocates were worried about the revised law's silence on how future funding shortfalls would be covered. These issues would preoccupy policymakers throughout most of the 1940s, although the public took little notice—people seemed not to share FDR's concerns about leaving long-term obligations for future generations.

Concerns Raised with Shift toward Pay-As-You-Go Financing

After the Social Security Act passed in 1935, Edwin Witte returned to Wisconsin, but he remained engaged in discussions about the program's evolution. His strong belief that the system should be funded never wavered. He was convinced that the shift in funding policy would create a "Santa Claus state."[1] He worried in 1938 that Senator Arthur Vandenberg and his allies would succeed in "convincing the American public that it is not necessary to pay any attention to accruing liabilities."

Witte knew that the tax rate required to finance a pay-as-you-go retirement plan was the product of 1) the ratio of the number of people receiving benefits to the number of workers paying payroll taxes, times 2) the ratio of average benefits paid to recipients to the average wage of those working and contributing to the system.[2] People who study retirement programs refer to the ratio of the number of beneficiaries receiving benefits to the number of workers paying into the system as the "dependency ratio." The ratio of average benefits paid to the average wage of workers contributing to the system is called the "earnings replacement rate."

The denominator in the dependency ratio for Social Security was the number of workers paying payroll taxes. In the first year of payroll tax collection, slightly less than 60 percent of all U.S. workers were employed in a covered job. In 1950, farm workers and domestics were brought under Social Security. Subsequent amendments in 1954 brought in farmers and the self-employed, and gave state and local governments the option of covering their employees even when they had their own pension plan. By the mid-1950s, close to 90 percent of the U.S. workforce was participating in Social Security.[3] Those still outside the system included federal civilian employees, employees of a number of state and local governments that chose not to enter the system, and some employees of nonprofit organizations. The 1983 Social Security Amendments brought employees at nonprofits and federal civilians hired after 1983 into the system. The approximately 30 percent of state and local government employees still outside the system at that time and covered by their own retirement plans were not required to participate.

The numerator in the dependency ratio was the number of people receiving Social Security benefits. In the early years, Social Security recipients had to be at least age 65 and to have made payroll tax contributions over the prior three years. In 1940, Social Security paid benefits to 112,000 retired workers—roughly 1 percent of the population over age 65. By 1950, 17 percent of those over age 65 were receiving benefits. The percentages of those over 65 receiving benefits kept growing: to 62 percent in 1960, 86 percent in 1970, and finally 90 percent in 1975.[4] Since the percentage of the elderly receiving benefits was much lower than the percentage of the working-age population paying taxes, the system's dependency ratio was artificially suppressed. This turned out to be important because the dependency ratio is a direct cost driver under pay-as-you-go financing.

Edwin Witte worried that the artificially low dependency ratio would encourage policymakers to be overly generous with benefits. To understand Witte's concerns, consider this scenario: A retiree is paid $10,000 per year, and 20 workers, all earning equal salaries, contribute $500 a year to the retiree's pension. If the number of workers drops to five, they must contribute $2,000 a year. During the implementation of pay-as-you-go financing in 1940, there were roughly 400 workers paying into Social Security for each retiree. But the ratio was expected to drop rapidly: to 14 workers per retiree in 1950, 5 workers per retiree in 1960, and 3.5 workers per retiree in 1970,[5] where it would remain relatively stable for the next 40 years.

Witte understood all this and was afraid that when there were 100 workers, or even 50, supporting each retiree, Congress would be tempted to boost benefits because they were so cheap. Then, after the rich benefits were firmly in place, the number of workers supporting each retiree would dwindle to three or four. Simple arithmetic told Witte that any boost of benefits early on would be subject to a large multiplier on the cost side as the program matured.

When he served on the Advisory Council that formulated the 1939 Amendments, Witte warned his fellow council members that "the real question is whether the younger workers will get their benefits in full" under a pay-as-you-go system. "There was grave danger that rather than appropriating general funds" to secure benefits when the costs of the pay-as-you-go system ramped up, "future Congresses would increase payroll taxes or lower benefits."[6] By the time the Advisory Council's recommendations were being finalized, Edwin Witte was publicly lamenting the creation of the "Santa Claus" welfare state to whomever would listen, warning of the accruing unfunded liabilities that would eventually become more federal debt. He feared that large payroll tax increases would be required to cover costs that should have been paid, in part, by the dividends on real savings.

During the debate over the proper way to finance Social Security, President Roosevelt, Arthur Altmeyer and Edwin Witte all articulated their concerns about future costs, which were based on estimates developed in Social Security's Office of the Actuary. In a memo prepared as background material for the development of the Fourth Annual Report on the system's operations, Dorrance Bronson, an assistant actuary at Social Security, presented estimates of benefits as a percentage of payroll for various years from 1940 through 1980. This memo was prepared after the adoption of the 1939 Amendments, so the estimates reflect its provisions. Under "estimate[s] based on probable maximum cost assumptions" the benefits that would be paid in 1980 under the Old-Age Insurance program were estimated at 10.6 percent of covered payroll, up from 0.37 percent of covered payroll in 1940.[7]

The Social Security Board's records include a paper, kept in Chairman Altmeyer's files, that details "principles concerning the financing" of the Old-Age Insurance program. The paper raised a concern about the "future load" that the system would pose. It cited three reasons that costs would rise over time. First, the over-65 population was expected to increase by 2.1 times between 1940 and 1980. Second, the number of people drawing Social Security benefits was expected to increase by six times between the 1942-to-1946 period and

1980 because an ever-larger share of the elderly population would qualify for benefits. Third, benefits were expected to be considerably more in 1980 than they were in 1940. On a level premium basis, which would have funded obligations as they accrued, the system was estimated to cost 5 percent of covered payroll. The report cited revised estimates developed after the passage of the 1939 Amendments suggesting that, under a pay-as-you-go system with no accumulation of reserves, "an eventual load of 10 percent" would result.[8] This was undoubtedly a reference to the Social Security actuaries' cost estimates.

The repeated focus of the president, Altmeyer and Witte in their statements about the potential costs of Social Security in 1980 indicated their understanding of the timing of the maturing of the system. They clearly understood that the increasing dependency ratio would drive up costs in a system that was not funded. They understood that once we reached the mid-1970s, the percentage of the population over age 65 receiving benefits would catch up to or surpass the percentage of workers paying payroll taxes. In Bronson's memo conveying the cost projections developed by the Social Security actuaries, he noted that:

> . . . some of the tables and charts estimates are included beyond the year 1955, which year was the stopping point for testimony furnished the recent session of Congress. I should also mention that another display which has not heretofore been publicly given is the component of costs according to beneficiary category.
>
> While we believe that it is desirable that the two above-mentioned extensions of estimates be not withheld as if they had not been made, it may be a question whether they should be included in the Annual Report. If it is decided that 1955 should be the limiting years this will drastically curtail the extent and value of some of the tables and charts contained in this material.[9]

In 1955, only 40 percent of the over-65 population was receiving a Social Security benefit, while 85 percent of the U.S. workforce was paying payroll taxes. The dependency ratio was less than 50 percent of what it would be when the system matured. That means that the pay-as-you-go costs of the system would have been less than half of what they would become once the percentage of the elderly receiving benefits equaled the percentage of workers paying into the system. Bronson's point was that a comparison of funded versus pay-as-you-go financing that stopped with 1955 would be totally misleading.

While Altmeyer and Witte fretted about the cost of the Old-Age Insurance program rising to 10 percent or more, they also were mindful of the expansionary goals they shared with President Roosevelt. They all envisioned a program that would ultimately feature disability coverage, maternity benefits, and health insurance, and they knew that these would come with their own set of costs.[10]

The 1943 Annual Report acknowledged that the expenditures for old-age and survivors benefits would continue to increase for "some decades" and anticipated a similar pattern of growth in "long-term benefits for disability." It concluded that the current cost of benefits could ultimately reach 12 percent or more over time.[11] Altmeyer knew that the long-term cost of the program he envisioned would be much higher than workers were bearing in the 1940s and that keeping future costs within reasonable limits was crucial.

Momentum toward Pay-As-You-Go Overwhelms Resistance

The 1939 Amendments delayed the first increase in the payroll tax by three years—to January 1, 1943. The Revenue Act of 1942 slid the increase to January 1, 1944. President Roosevelt went along with the first delay but opposed all subsequent delays. When Congress was considering the delay under the Revenue Act of 1942, FDR protested to the chairmen of the Senate Finance and House Ways and Means Committees: "A failure to allow the scheduled increase in rates to take place under present favorable circumstances would cause a real and justifiable fear that adequate funds will not be accumulated to meet the heavy obligations of the future and that the claims for benefits accruing under the present law may be jeopardized."[12] When Congress ignored his objection, FDR vetoed the Revenue Act of 1942—his second veto in ten years as president. Nevertheless, Congress overrode him, and the payroll tax increase was delayed until January 1, 1945. Toward the end of 1944, new legislation again postponed the scheduled payroll tax increase, this time to January 1, 1946. The Revenue Act of 1945 moved the first increase in the payroll tax to January 1, 1948. In 1947, Public Law 379 deferred the increase to January 1, 1950.[13]

The repeated delays in the payroll tax increases moved the program inexorably toward pay-as-you-go financing. FDR continued to protest. At the end of 1944, in signing legislation that delayed the payroll tax increase to January 1, 1946, the president's accompanying statement noted, "I have felt in the past and I still feel that the scheduled rate increase, which has been repeatedly postponed by Congress, should be permitted to go into effect. The long-run financial requirements of the Social Security System justified adherence to the scheduled increases."[14] On April 12, 1945, President Roosevelt died. Social Security had become the central foundation of the welfare state in America and was well on its way to pay-as-you-go funding.

The repeated confrontations between congressional leaders and Arthur Altmeyer led to the creation of a second Advisory Council in 1947, with Robert Ball as executive director. The focus of the 1947 Council's study was on ways to enhance Social Security benefits, and the council recommended expanding coverage to the agricultural sector, the self-employed and domestic workers. To provide sufficient benefits for newly covered groups, they advocated a "new start" in determining benefits.[15] The Council's recommendations evolved into the 1950 Amendments to the Social Security Act.

The payroll tax rate would not increase during the 1940s. In 1948, after pay-as-you-go financing was largely in place, Edwin Witte observed that it was "a very bad practice not only to fail to meet current liabilities but to keep from the public the fact of an ever-growing debt additional to the acknowledged debt of the United States."[16] The 1950 Amendments marked the end of the financing wars. After the law passed, J. Douglas Brown observed that "the early issue between 'pay-as-you-go' and 'large reserves' seems to have faded into the background. In old-age and survivors insurance, we have let the actuaries worry about the problem of balancing income and outgo over time."[17]

Growing dependency rates and higher benefits under the 1950 Amendments finally demanded an end to the low contribution rates of the 1940s. If policymakers waited until the reserves accumulated during the 1940s were spent, the payroll tax would have to triple, which would pose the risk of political turmoil. The leaders at Social Security knew it was much better to phase these increases in gradually and many members of Congress agreed. The 1950 Amendments called for the payroll tax to rise to 1.5 percent each on employers and employees in 1951, and scheduled further step increases up to 1970.[18] By 1960, the statutory payroll tax rate was 3.0 percent of covered pay each for workers and their employers. By 1970, it was up to 4.2 percent each.[19]

Edwin Witte's concern about low dependency ratios enticing Congress to offer "Santa Claus" benefit increases did not materialize in the early years of the program's operations. The level of Social Security benefits established in the 1939 law remained constant through the 1940s. One possible explanation was the country's preoccupation with the war. Another is that the management at Social Security was more interested in expanding the program in other ways. By the end of the 1940s, benefits were not keeping up with the cost of living, which was threatening to trivialize the Social Security program. In 1949, more than twice as many people were receiving old-age assistance as were getting

Social Security retirement benefits. The average monthly benefit paid under old-age assistance was $42 per month, compared to the average Social Security benefit of $25. With wages growing during the 1940s while benefits were held constant, the average Social Security benefit declined by 40 percent relative to the average pay rates subject to the payroll tax.[20]

The 1950 Amendments expanded Social Security coverage to roughly 10 million additional workers, including the non-farm self-employed (other than those in selected professional groups, such as doctors, lawyers, and engineers). Coverage was also extended to regularly employed domestic and farm workers, employees who worked for state and local governments not covered by alternative retirement systems, and employees of nonprofit organizations who wished to join.

The 1950 Amendments increased benefits for existing beneficiaries by nearly 80 percent. In June 1950, the average benefit paid to a retired worker was around $26 per month. Under the new schedule, the estimated average benefit rose to $46 per month. For those who retired after the new law took full effect, the average benefit was expected to be $50 to $55 per month. Benefits for widows and orphans rose by similar percentages. Spousal benefits were provided for men whose wives had earned benefits.[21] After the 1950 benefit increases, Congress adjusted average benefits periodically, but the increases over most of the next two decades closely paralleled the growth rate of average wages subject to the payroll tax[22] and held the relationship between average benefits and average wages subject to the payroll tax nearly constant.

The 1950 Amendments marked an accord on Social Security policymaking. For the next couple of decades, the program would continue to evolve and expand but without the earlier controversy and contentiousness. The debates over how to finance the system had been put to rest for at least a couple of reasons. First, Social Security was widely perceived as an extremely good deal. And second, the senior players at the administrative and legislative levels were in substantial agreement on the direction that policy should take and had a plan for getting there.

Franklin Roosevelt never wavered from his opposition to pay-as-you-go financing. He had condemned the immorality of running up large unfunded liabilities in 1935. With the exception of 1939—when other overriding fiscal considerations warranted—he consistently maintained that his Social Security program should be funded to cover future liabilities. Despite losing the funding battle, much of FDR's vision for Social Security was achieved in the 50 years after his death.

6 A DEAL TOO GOOD TO LAST

When President Roosevelt insisted that Social Security be based on "insurance principles," he had more in mind than just the funding issues that have been discussed so far. Roosevelt visualized Social Security as a retirement savings program—one reason for his insistence on its being funded—but he also expected it to provide an annuity to retirees.

Providing retirement annuities under insurance principles requires that participants save during their working years and that their savings—or, in a program like Social Security, their contributions—be collected and invested. The combination of the savings and the investment income is used to finance the annuity for the rest of their lives. In a large participant pool, some participants die before reaching their full life expectancy and their unused benefits are used to support those who outlive actuarial predictions.

Actuaries develop their estimates on the basis of the anticipated evolution of a number of factors that affect pension benefits over time and the required contributions to fund them as they are earned. These factors include life expectancies or mortality rates, employment and earnings patterns, expected rates of return on assets in the pension trusts, and so forth. All these different factors affect contribution rates and are rechecked periodically and adjusted as new experience warrants. As the factors change, plan sponsors must adjust contribution rates to ensure that when workers retire, there are sufficient assets to pay their benefits.

When FDR took his stand on "insurance principles" for Social Security, he was implicitly saying that participants should receive fair market rates of returns on their contributions over their working lives. The collective rate of return on participants' contributions is the rate of return earned by the total pool of assets. The annualized rate of return results from investing in the financial markets over the annuity's operational period—both the accumulation and the payout stages. As Social Security diverged from funded to pay-as-you-go financing, President Roosevelt, Arthur Altmeyer and Edwin Witte became concerned about economic fairness. Altmeyer articulated it this way:

> It is a mathematical certainty that the longer the present pay-roll tax remains in effect, the higher the future pay-roll tax must be if the insurance system continues to be financed wholly by pay-roll taxes. Therefore, the indefinite continuation of the present contribution rate will eventually necessitate raising the employees' contribution rate later to a point where future beneficiaries will be obliged to pay more for their benefits than if they obtained this insurance from a private insurance company.
>
> I say it is inequitable to compel them to pay more under this system than they would have to pay to a private insurance company, and I think that Congress would be confronted with that embarrassing situation.[1]

Start-up Benefits and Initial Equity Concerns

Roosevelt, Altmeyer, and Witte were well aware that Social Security would be particularly generous to early participants. They accepted that as the price of getting the program up and running quickly and providing meaningful benefits from the start. But they hoped to transition quickly to workers "paying for" their benefits and so were concerned about the repeated delays in scheduled payroll tax increases.

Unexpected benefits are what economists often call "windfalls." The term windfall literally comes from the concept of fruit being blown from a tree, sparing the person the effort of picking it. The Social Security windfall benefits were unexpected income that required no saving or investing from beneficiaries. The term "windfall" is not used pejoratively—the recipients of these benefits did nothing untoward to get them. The windfall benefits had—and are still having—significant economic ramifications for both the trust funds and the program participants.

In Chapter 1, I introduced Ida Mae Fuller, who received the first Social Security benefit check of $22.54 in January 1940. Fuller and her employer each contributed $24.75 in payroll taxes over the prior three years. Accumulated with interest, the total value of their contributions would have been around $60 when she retired, which Fuller received back in the first three months of her retirement. At the time she turned 65, an average retiree lived another 12 to 13 years, receiving a monthly check all along the way. Ms. Fuller and the other early recipients received substantial windfalls from the new retirement program.

Robert Myers, in the Office of the Actuary, estimated that under the start-up benefit formula, typical workers who earned $50 per month in covered employment for five years and then retired at age 65 received roughly 100 times their own contributions. Adding in the employer's contributions reduced the return by half, but it was still a real bonanza.[2] At the end of the 1940s, however, only about one-seventh of the elderly population was receiving old-age insurance benefits, and many of the recipients were among the most affluent of the elderly. Giving a relatively small and well-off minority big retirement subsidies prompted criticism and questions about Social Security's fairness.

Early congressional criticism of the inequities in Social Security's startup led some to advocate adopting a universal non-contributory pension program. Senator Sheridan Downey on the Senate Finance Committee fell into this camp.[3] He argued that Social Security was not a "contributory plan but almost wholly a fake scheme of social dividends in which payments of public money will be disbursed in the inverse order of need; that is substantial payments to the prosperous and meager pittances to the miserable."[4] Arthur Altmeyer countered that if benefits were to be "adequate" in a social insurance system, early beneficiaries would have to receive far more than the actuarial value of their own contributions.[5] Altmeyer strongly believed that benefits had to bear a relationship to preretirement wages and that this was "the fundamental purpose of contributory social insurance."

The architects of the Social Security program expected the inflated benefits paid to early beneficiaries to be a relatively short-lived phenomenon, which would be mitigated by the ramp up of the payroll tax rate. The delays in payroll tax increases extended the period of actuarially unbalanced payouts, which would mean higher tax rates and intergenerational inequities for later generations of workers.

Benefit Equity across Generations

Generally, analysis of how various people fare under a program like Social Security focuses on groups of people or a hypothetical individual within some group. A common grouping is by birth year or "birth cohort." Demographers consider all those born in 1875 as belonging to the 1875 birth cohort. The Social Security program has treated—and continues to treat—different birth cohorts quite differently. Many analyses over the years have focused on equity issues from both intra-and inter-cohort perspectives.

Dean Leimer, a research analyst at the Social Security Administration, estimated how various birth cohorts fare under Social Security. He characterized the difference between outcomes under Social Security and a pension based on FDR's insurance principles as something called "net intercohort transfers" for each birth cohort. In this context, a "transfer" is shifting income from one birth cohort to another. The mechanism for acquiring the workers' income is the payroll tax and the mechanism for distributing it to retirees is the Social Security benefit. Since the retirement benefits were financed by workers' payroll tax contributions, the start-up transfers in the system were from younger cohorts to older ones.

Dean Leimer's analysis segregated birth cohorts from 1875 through 2005, estimating payroll tax contributions from each cohort and their employers, along with interest. He then estimated expected lifetime benefits for each age cohort. For the older cohorts, Leimer used administrative data for his estimates. For the younger cohorts, he projected contributions and benefits using the same assumptions used by the Social Security actuaries to project future operations—the remembering forward process that was discussed in chapter 1. Leimer essentially compared the estimated Social Security benefits paid to each generation of workers with the amount they would have received from a funded pension invested in government bonds. If a birth cohort received more from Social Security than it could have expected from a funded pension, he characterized the cohort as receiving a "positive intercohort transfer." If the cohort received less, it was a negative cohort transfer.

Leimer's estimates were stated in 1989 dollars, which are updated in this presentation to 2009 dollars (see figure 6.1). The birth cohorts where the line

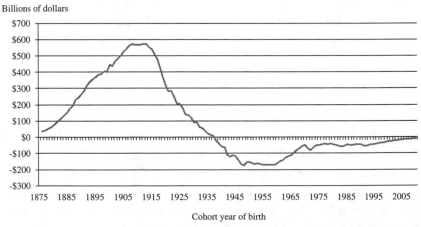

FIGURE 6.1 Social Security Intercohort Transfers Paid to Specific Birth Cohorts of Retirees (Annual amount in billions of 2009 dollars)

Source: Dean R. Leimer, "Cohort-Specific Measures of Lifetime Net Social Security Transfers," ORS Working Paper Series, Number 59 (Washington, D.C.: Social Security Administration, February 1994), pp. 76-77 and calculations by the authors. Leimer used the interest rate on trust fund assets to convert current dollars into 1989 dollars. We convert the series into 2009 dollars using corresponding interest rates between 1989 and 1997. All figures are present values as of 1997.

is above the $0 level—those born from 1875 through 1937—received more from Social Security than they would have received from the funded pension invested in government bonds. A more colloquial term might be that they received a good deal, some a spectacular deal. At first, the transfers were relatively small, because few people in the initial Social Security cohorts qualified for benefits, and benefits were relatively smaller to start. As benefit levels and elderly recipiency rates climbed, the value of the transfers increased. The positive inter-cohort transfers peaked for those reaching retirement age around the mid-1970s, the point when recipiency rates among the elderly finally equaled participation rates among the working population. Since then, the windfall benefits provided to succeeding cohorts have declined.

The members of the 1937 birth cohort—the last cohort to receive positive net transfers—turned age 62 in 1999, the early retirement age under Social Security. Leimer's results suggest that Social Security was a "good deal" in economic or actuarial terms if you were old enough to claim benefits in the 20th century. Leimer's total estimated "intercohort transfers" for the participants born before 1938 accumulated to the present day would be $18 trillion. Even if the comparison were between Social Security windfalls and returns from a funded plan invested in stocks and bonds, the start-up of Social Security was an incredibly good deal for early participants.

If Social Security had been operated under insurance principles, as FDR had originally intended, the trust funds would hold the value of the intercohort transfers that have been given away thus far, plus the roughly $2.5 trillion reserves in the fund today—a total of around $22 trillion.[6] This estimate of what the trust funds would now hold if the start-up windfalls were still in the system was calculated independently of the method used by the Social Security actuaries to estimate the system's current accrued liabilities. The estimated $18 trillion extra balance the trust funds would have held at the end of 2009 had the windfalls not been paid corresponds closely to the actuaries' estimate of the program's unfunded accrued obligations of $20 trillion at the end of 2009. If the extra funds were in the system today, it would be funded today at nearly the levels FDR, Altmeyer, and Witte hoped it would be.

Since the windfalls were given away, the interest they would have earned in the trust funds has been lost. Without that interest to help support benefit payments, higher payroll taxes have been required to cover the benefits of subsequent generations. But their higher contributions will not generate commensurately higher benefits. For participants reaching retirement age in the current millennium, the retirement story will not have the same happy outcome it had for those eligible to retire before 2000. The birth cohorts born from 1938 through 1950 will contribute, in aggregate, $1.4 trillion more in today's dollars accrued with interest than they will receive in benefits. The cohorts born from 1951 through 2010 will contribute an extra $4.3 trillion. For cohorts not born yet, a $12 trillion bill is waiting for them to help cover the start-up costs of our Social Security pension system.

Early Windfalls at the Ground Level

The problem with considering Social Security in an aggregate context is that the numbers quickly explode into trillions of dollars, making it impossible to comprehend what it means to real people. In the late 1990s, I wrote a book on Social Security with John Shoven, an economics professor at Stanford University.[7] We estimated how the "intercohort transfers" were distributed to workers and their spouses based on age, gender, marital status, and earnings. Our hypothetical workers were consistent with a set of such workers developed by the Office of the Actuary at the Social Security Administration based on lifetime earnings patterns. The workers have steady earnings patterns, which are characterized as low, average, high or at the maximum taxable earnings rate. The low earner's steady wage equals 40 percent of the average earnings of all covered workers in any given year. The high earner consistently earns 1.6 times the average earnings level, and the maximum earner earns the taxable wage maximum under Social Security.[8]

We estimated workers' and their employers' annual contributions based on earnings and contribution rates, and accumulated these over workers' careers with interest.[9] We also estimated monthly benefits for each retiree at retirement. Monthly benefits were summed to arrive at annual benefits and adjusted, as necessary to reflect any cost-of-living adjustments. They were then calculated as lifetime benefits stated in present value terms over each birth cohort's life expectancy at retirement. We used government bond rates of return paid on the Social Security trust funds to calculate the present values of lifetime benefits at retirement.[10]

According to our calculations, updated to 2009 dollars, a single male characterized as a "low earner," whose wages were about 40 percent of the average wage, who retired in 1940 would have received about $38,000 more in benefits from Social Security than from a funded annuity. For the average wage earner, the extra benefit was nearly $50,000 and for the maximum wage earner, it was slightly more than $77,000. Between 1940 and 1970, the additional benefits Social Security participants received compared to what they would have received under an insurance annuity grew because of enhancements to Social

Security benefits in the interval. For workers retiring in 1970, the windfall in 2009 dollars was $115,000 for the low earner, $146,000 for the average worker and nearly $159,000 for the maximum earner. Additional results are shown in the table in the appendix at the end of this chapter.

The estimates of single workers' windfalls helps to explain the early start-up benefits of Social Security but still fails to capture the real magnitude of windfall benefits provided to many retiring workers. For workers coming to retirement in the 1940s, 1950s or even as late as the 1970s, the two-earner household that we are familiar with today was a much rarer phenomenon. In 1950, labor force participation rates for 25- to 60-year-old women were consistently below 40 percent but, by 2000, had risen to nearly 80 percent at the prime working ages.[11] When men retired in 1970, most of their wives had been homemakers which meant that most women were receiving a Social Security benefit based on their husbands' earnings rather than their own. This outcome is significantly different today.

When the value of spousal benefits is factored into the computations on the early windfall benefits, the results are even more dramatic than they are for a single earner. Many workers retiring at the peak of the windfall phenomenon—during the 1960s and 1970s—received unearned benefits in 2009 values ranging from nearly one-quarter of a million dollars for a worker at 40 percent of the average wage to more than one-third of a million dollars for workers at the maximum income levels.

The distribution of windfall benefits helps to clarify some of the early criticisms of the benefit structure. One such criticism was that the distributions of the gratuitous benefits were extremely uneven. In 1940, less than 1 percent of those older than 65 were receiving benefits. By 1950, only 17 percent of those over age 65 were receiving benefits, and by 1960, the percentage was only 62 percent. The significant subsidies to some retirees and not others naturally raised equity questions. Another criticism was that Social Security was billed from the outset as being redistributional—with lower earners supposed to get the better deal. So why were the high earners receiving the lion's share of the unwarranted benefits?

From a practical perspective, these numbers explain why Social Security was so popular over the years. For the vast majority of workers who have passed through both the contributing and benefiting sides of the program until recently, it has been a fantastic deal from an actuarial or economic perspective. The way our Social Security system was structured, we could give away literally trillions of dollars in unearned benefits and yet almost all the windfall recipients had the sense that they had paid for what they received.

This is partly attributable to the contributory financing of the program. Shortly after the system was getting under way, a reporter challenged President Roosevelt on the potentially adverse economic incentives embedded in the payroll tax. Roosevelt responded:

> I guess you are right on the economics, but those taxes were never a problem of economics. They are politics all the way through. We put those payroll contributions there so as to give the contributors a legal, moral, and political right to collect their pensions. . . . With those taxes in there, no damn politician can ever scrap my Social Security program.[12]

The Backside of the Shift to Pay-As-You-Go Financing

There is a direct correlation between the winners of Leimer's intercohort transfers shown in figure 6.1 and the windfall benefits paid to individuals within specific birth cohorts—shown in table 6.1. They both peaked in the 1970s and then began to decline. As the program matured, the number of beneficiaries increased relative to workers paying into the system, and the system depended entirely on payroll taxes—there was virtually no trust fund to accumulate investment income. For those who retired at the end of the century, the windfall benefits had largely dried up, and for those who retire during this century, the "net intercohort transfers" will be negative. From 2000 onward, on average, the "return" for workers in each retiring cohort will be less than it would be from a funded pension program invested solely in government bonds. Having spent young workers' contributions on inflated "start-up" benefits for earlier retirees meant the program had to forego the interest income on those contributions. So as an investment vehicle, Social Security could not match a funded system no matter how conservative the funded system's investments.

We have now reached the point that Roosevelt, Altmeyer, and Witte had warned would come under pay-as-you-go financing. As FDR predicted, Congress is confronting large unfunded liabilities. As Arthur Altmeyer rued the delays in the payroll tax increases time and again, he argued that the "financial deal" offered by Social Security would deteriorate, finally reaching a point where workers could get a better deal from commercial markets than through the government program. Witte worried that the costs of benefits in a pay-as-you-go system would rise to the point that policymakers could not raise the payroll tax high enough to cover them. The combined employer-employee payroll tax for Social Security now stands at 12.4 percent of covered pay and is insufficient to cover current benefits costs. Policymakers are reluctant to raise the tax rate because it is already the largest tax many households bear. To meet benefit obligations in 2030, payroll taxes would have to climb another 4 percent, making an already bad deal even worse. Altmeyer suggested that, when Social Security became a bad deal, policymakers should divert general revenues to sweeten the deal and make later retirees "whole." But there are other pressing contingencies at the moment, again as Franklin Roosevelt had feared.

APPENDIX TO CHAPTER 6

Estimating Social Security Windfall Benefits

Workers from each birth cohort considered had steady earnings patterns developed by the Social Security actuaries at one of four levels characterized as being low, average, high, or at the maximum taxable earnings rate under the program. The low earner was assumed to have a steady wage equal to 40 percent of the average earnings level of all covered workers in any given year. The high earner had consistent earnings that were 1.6 times the average earnings level and the maximum earner had earnings each year at the maximum of taxable wages.[13]

Workers' and their employers' contributions were estimated each year based on their earnings level and the statutory provisions in the law that set contribution rates and accumulated these over their working lives with interest.[14] Monthly benefits for each retiree were estimated at the point of retirement. Monthly benefits were summed to give annual benefits and adjusted, as appropriate, to include any cost-of-living adjustments and were then summed to lifetime benefits stated in present value terms over each birth cohorts' life expectancy at the point of retirement. Government bond rates of return paid on the Social Security trust funds were used in calculating the present values of lifetime benefits at retirement.[15]

To explain how the windfalls during the start-up of Social Security were distributed, windfall gains were calculated by subtracting the lifetime value of payroll taxes paid for a particular worker from the lifetime value of benefits he or she could expect to receive over an average life expectancy at age 65 for each birth cohort and gender. We calculated the estimated windfalls in 1998 dollars and those results have been further adjusted to bring them up to 2009 levels by using the CPI for all urban consumers. The results of the calculations for single males are shown in the top section of table 6.1.

Table 6.1 Average Net Social Security Windfall Benefits in 2009 Dollars Paid to Single Retirees, by Worker's Gender, Level of Lifetime Earnings, and Year Worker Turned Age 65

Year worker turned age 65	Lifetime earnings level			
	Low	Average	High	Maximum
single males				
1940	38,114	49,878	58,874	77,365
1945	39,985	44,745	52,134	63,948
1950	37,712	39,724	44,091	47,515
1955	77,701	111,147	118,191	116,700
1960	92,234	134,348	146,908	145,381
1965	101,567	147,442	158,739	157,016
1970	115,043	146,298	160,480	158,674
1975	97,108	134,378	151,566	149,640
1980	73,093	106,075	126,320	126,350
Married male worker with non-covered spouse				
1940	66,416	85,523	100,411	131,605
1945	71,366	79,695	92,569	113,056
1950	70,331	74,773	82,986	89,476
1955	146,546	212,157	227,651	226,159
1960	182,308	270,032	297,835	296,307
1965	203,855	304,004	330,812	329,089
1970	228,378	303,433	337,583	335,777
1975	194,644	284,627	326,994	325,070
1980	150,115	234,463	286,453	289,231

Source: Sylvester J. Schieber and John B. Shoven, *The Real Deal: The History and Future of Social Security* (New Haven: Yale University Press, 1999), 106 (updated to 2009 prices by the author).

The benefits for single female earners, not shown here, were somewhat higher at each earnings level because women have longer life expectancies than men and so receive more lifetime benefits on average, other things being equal.

For single-earner couples, we assumed that the husband was the individual who earned the Social Security benefit and further assumed that both spouses were the same age. That meant that when the husband retired at age 65 under our assumptions his wife also began to receive a spousal benefit that was 50 percent of his.

7 OPERATIONS UNDER PAY-AS-YOU-GO FINANCING

A pay-as-you-go pension system generally runs on payroll taxes. The tax rate required to finance benefits is the product of the dependency ratio and the ratio of average benefits to average wages. The values for these factors are determined, to an extent, by the system's operating rules. The Social Security Act specifically defines who must pay payroll taxes and the amount of their earnings that is subject to the tax. The Act also specifies in some detail how benefits will be determined, which has some effect on who works and who retires.

Social Security Cost Drivers Trend Upward as Program Matures

Demographics have an enormous effect on Social Security's costs, with the fertility rate a central element. Once you know the number of births in a given year, you can map out a relatively predictable timeline from birth to working career to retirement. Fertility rates fell to their lowest levels during the Great Depression. After World War II, from 1946 through 1964, the fertility rate surged, resulting in the "baby boom" generation. After 1964, the fertility rate again fell below Depression levels.

Not only is the baby boom generation far larger than earlier birth cohorts, but more baby boom women also entered the workforce—and stayed there through their childbearing years—than did earlier generations of women. By the mid-1980s, the mass of the baby boomers were in the workforce, while the smaller Depression cohorts were nearing retirement age. Many workers and few retirees kept the dependency ratio low.

The cost drivers for Social Security from 1940 until recently are shown in figure 7.1. The two lines in the graph are the two ratios discussed earlier—the dependency ratio and the ratio of average

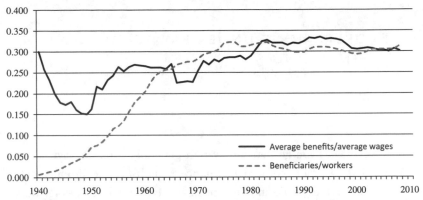

FIGURE 7.1 Historical Beneficiary-to-Worker Dependency Ratios and Average-Benefit-to-Average-Wage Ratios in Social Security

Source: Social Security Administration, *Annual Statistical Supplement to the Social Security Bulletin*, 1970, 1981, 1991 and 2009.

benefits to average wages. The evolution of the dependency ratio, the dashed line in figure 7.1, can be divided into two stages. During the phase-in stage, the dependency ratio grew steadily as ever more elderly people became eligible for benefits. After peaking around 1976 or 1977, the dependency ratio fell back a bit during the 1980s and has remained level over the past two decades.

The progression of average benefits to average wages, the solid line in figure 7.1, has been somewhat more erratic than the dependency ratio. During Social Security's first decade, the ratio declined steadily as wages grew but benefits did not. In 1950 and again in the mid-1950s, Congress increased benefits compared to covered wages. Because wages continued a steady climb, Congress had to increase benefits periodically to keep the solid line in the figure from dropping. It did so again in the late 1950s and early 1960s. But in the mid-1960s—with the Vietnam War consuming resources and policymakers preoccupied with creating Medicare—benefits declined relative to covered wages.

The 1965 Amendments to the Social Security Act created the Medicare program, which began providing health benefits to retirees in 1966. With the adoption of Medicare, Social Security had reached the full breadth of FDR's intended protections against the "vicissitudes of life." It was the last significant expansion of coverage through the remainder of the century, although the government extended Medicare to the disabled in 1972 and added drug benefits in 2003. The scope of protections the total Social Security system would provide had been put in place before the full phase-in of the system had been completed.

Drive to Expand Benefits Prior to Reaching Program Maturity

Each expansion of Social Security cost less at implementation than it would later on, because the dependency ratio was growing. It may seem farfetched to suggest that program managers orchestrated the expansions to bring added costs on slowly. But the initial phase-in of the payroll tax, starting at 2 percent of covered earnings split evenly between workers and employers, was certainly an acknowledgement that the full throttle of 6 percent of covered payroll might spark a revolt.

Amazingly, two men, Robert Ball and Wilber Cohen, played a primary role in developing and implementing the expansionary agenda between adoption of the 1939 Amendments and the mid-1970s. Bob Ball joined the Social Security staff in 1939. Wilber Cohen, who had come to Washington as Edwin Witte's assistant in 1934, stayed on after the passage of the Social Security Act and was the first employee of the Social Security Board.

Robert Ball served as Social Security Commissioner from 1962 to 1973 but effectively started running Old-Age and Survivors Insurance operations in 1953.[1] Even after his departure in 1973, Ball continued to play an advisory role in virtually all major Social Security legislative and policy developments until he died in January 2008. Wilbur Cohen stayed with Social Security into the early 1950s but remained a powerful influence on policy even after his departure. He served in senior-level political positions during the Kennedy and Johnson Administrations and as Secretary of the Department of Health, Education and Welfare (DHEW) in the latter. At that time, the Social Security Administration was part of DHEW. It was during Cohen's tenure as secretary of DHEW that Medicare was passed as part of the Social Security Act.

In June 1942, the Social Security Board outlined a "cradle to grave" social insurance program in its annual report to the President. It called for expanding Social Security coverage to all workers, providing benefits to the temporarily or permanently disabled, and offering hospital benefits.[2] This agenda was too large to be consumed in one single bite, and President Roosevelt never pushed for comprehensive legislation along these lines, but FDR later claimed ownership of the concept of "cradle to grave" social insurance protection, which was usurped by Sir William Beveridge in pushing comprehensive legislation in the United Kingdom during the 1940s.[3]

Robert Ball and Wilber Cohen ultimately found another way to achieve their ends. Instead of taking their whole agenda to Congress at once, they advanced it in small bites, increasing a benefit here, adding disability coverage there, and so forth, until they completed their grand design. Cohen summarized the recipe:

> The men and women I worked with, while they were populists, while they were progressives, while they were strong believers in social legislation, they were also strongly of the belief of the inevitableness of gradualism. In other words, they felt it was more important to take one step at a time. Or perhaps I ought to put it this way—to digest one meal at a time rather than eating breakfast, lunch, and dinner all at once and getting indigestion. This was their philosophy. I think it's the right social philosophy.[4]

After Medicare was in the bag, Commissioner Ball's next goal was to increase the benefits already in force.[5] He and Cohen crafted a legislative package on Social Security that the Johnson Administration submitted to Congress in 1967. It would be 17 years before Dean Leimer would develop his analysis of "intercohort transfers" among Social Security participants, but Ball and Cohen understood how the program worked and its implications. They were concerned that "future generations of covered workers will get protection that is worth less than the combined employer-employee contributions with respect to their earnings."[6] The seeds of concern that Altmeyer and Witte had planted throughout the 1940s were beginning to ripen.

Ball and Cohen's package called for increasing benefits 15 percent across the board for existing retirees. For those not yet retired, they had more ambitious plans. For workers through the middle part of the earnings distribution, they proposed raising initial benefits by the same 15 percent they advocated for current retirees, but they wanted to increase benefits at the upper end of the covered earnings range by 50 percent.[7] Ball and Cohen were proposing to significantly dampen the redistributive characteristics of the benefit structure by increasing benefits at higher earnings levels relatively more than at lower levels.

Now that Social Security was reaching maturity, raising benefits had become more complicated. To bring benefits to the level in the 1967 legislative package, Congress would have to increase the contribution base and the payroll tax rate. Ultimately, Congress increased benefits by 13 percent, but additional increases for high earners failed to gain support. The legislation increased the payroll tax on employers and employees from 4.4 percent in 1967 to 4.8 percent in 1969, and covered earnings rose from $4,800 in 1965 to $6,600 in 1967, and then to $7,800 in 1968. The new covered earnings provisions would capture roughly 82 percent of total U.S. earnings.[8]

Even after Richard Nixon became president in 1968, Robert Ball remained commissioner and continued to push an expansionary agenda. In 1971, another Advisory Council was empanelled, and its members spent much of their time considering new valuation methods that would anticipate wage growth in projecting Social Security's future costs. They also analyzed the implications of automatically increasing benefits over time to account for inflation.[9] This council's conclusion was that Social Security benefits could be raised further without having to push up the payroll tax. Ultimately, the Nixon administration proposed Social Security benefit increases to keep up with the estimated increases in the cost of living. Before that, it proposed increasing benefits by 10 percent in 1969, 6 percent in 1971, and 5 percent in 1972. The Democrats in Congress "outbid" each proposal, granting 15 percent in 1969, 10 percent in 1971, and 20 percent in 1972.[10] A retiree receiving a benefit of $500 per month at the beginning of 1969 would receive $759 per month at the end of 1972—a 52 percent increase. From 1968 to 1972, the span of the first Nixon administration, the cost of living as measured by the consumer price index (CPI) had risen by only 20 percent. The sweet deal, Social Security, was made even sweeter for the beneficiaries at the time.

The most important set of changes adopted in 1972 involved the automatic indexation of benefits. The intent was for initial benefits paid to new retirees to go up at the rate of wage growth. The maximum amount of earnings subject to the payroll tax was also set to increase at the rate of wage growth. Benefits for retirees were to be automatically indexed for increases in the cost of living using the CPI developed by the Department of Labor.

The 1972 Social Security Amendments were a high-water mark for the program. They culminated a 35-year campaign to build the program that President Roosevelt had envisioned. Social Security was approaching maturity and further benefit enhancements would bring along fully loaded cost increases.

Richard Nixon was re-elected as president in November 1972. After the election, he asked for the resignations of all the government managers holding positions that were reserved for appointment by the sitting president. Bob Ball, who had been kept on as commissioner during the first Nixon term, was caught in this house cleaning. He left behind a remarkable legacy of achievement.

As the program reached maturity, the cost of current Social Security benefits as a percentage of covered payroll was nearly 11 percent, reaching levels that Edwin Witte and Arthur Altmeyer had worried would spark antagonism. By the time Bob Ball was cleaning out his desk at Social Security, the concerns about pay-as-you-go financing seemed baseless. Paul Samuelson, the prominent American economist, was writing the articles for *Newsweek* described in chapter

1 in which he called Social Security "the greatest Ponzi scheme ever contrived."[11] Samuelson was telling the American public that:

> The beauty of social insurance is that it is actuarially unsound. Everyone who reaches retirement age is given benefit privileges that far exceed anything he has paid in. And exceed his payments by more than ten times as much (or five times, counting in employer payments)!
>
> How is it possible? It stems from the fact that the national product is growing at compound interest and can be expected to do so for as far ahead as the eye cannot see. Always there are more youths than old folks in a growing population. More important, with real incomes going up at some 3 percent per year, the taxable base on which benefits rest in any period are much greater than the taxes paid historically by the generation now retired.
>
> Social security is squarely based on what has been called the eighth wonder of the world—compound interest. A growing nation is the greatest Ponzi game ever contrived.[12]

It was hard for skeptics to argue with the beauty of Paul Samuelson's formulas that proved his theory. Policymakers and program supporters pointed to his profound work to justify the system as it had been operating for at least a quarter of a century by the time he wrote his *Newsweek* article.

The Great Social Security Financing Faux Pas

The agreement to automatically adjust Social Security benefits in 1972 was one of the happy intersections of public policy interests. Conservatives suspected that Congress was inclined to increase benefits every other year coinciding with elections and wanted to limit benefit growth to no more than inflation. Liberals were worried that when Congress was distracted by other pressing matters it often failed to keep or protect benefits from inflation so they saw automatic indexation as an expansion of system protections. In the 1973 Social Security Trustees Report, the actuaries estimated that the Social Security programs were underfunded over the next 75 years by about 0.5 percent of covered payroll. This was worthy of note but nothing to become alarmed about—it simply meant that payroll taxes needed to rise by 0.25 percent on covered workers and their employers to cover benefits.

In 1974, a more pessimistic economic outlook raised the estimate of underfunding by another 0.19 percent. The deteriorating economic picture in 1974 and its implications for the long-term Social Security financing outlook were lost in the demographic headlines that came out of that year's Trustees Report. By then, the results of the 1970 Census had been published and demographers realized that the post-World War II baby boom had come to an end. For Social Security, that meant far fewer workers in the future making payroll contributions and a much less favorable dependency ratio.

The first automatic cost-of-living adjustment of Social Security benefits took effect in June 1975, a few weeks after the release of the annual Trustees Report. That report projected lower income for the Social Security trust funds than anticipated every year from 1975 onward. Actuaries estimated long-term underfunding at 5.32 percent of taxable payroll. The short-term outlook was bad and was expected to steadily worsen over time. After roughly 25 years of experience operating on a pay-as-you-go basis, program administrators tried to maintain a trust fund balance equivalent to one year of benefits in case of unforeseen economic turmoil. The 1975 Trustees Report projected that the trust funds would be fully depleted by 1980.[13] The program had suddenly gotten badly off track.

The financing failure that had caught policymakers unaware related to the automatic indexation of retirement benefits. Social Security's benefit formula has always been complicated because of the goal of replacing a larger share of preretirement earnings for low earners than for high earners. Actuaries, who are applied mathematicians, design formulas like Social Security's to transform policymakers' goals into financial realities. For the policymakers, the actual details of the formulas get lost in the "sausage making" as they put together legislation.

The automatic inflation adjustments of Social Security benefits were supposed to mechanically replicate the previous ad hoc adjustment process. What policymakers wanted was for initial benefits paid to new retirees to grow at the same rate as average wages of covered workers. The benefit formula bases initial benefits on a worker's average earnings over his or her 35 highest years of covered earnings. Partly because of inflation and partly because of productivity gains, average wages tend to rise gradually over time. To arrive at the retiree's benefit amount, the formula used three different rates or multipliers for successively higher levels of average covered earnings in a worker's earnings record. At the end of 1972, the formula called for the basic benefit to be 108.01 percent of the first $110 of average monthly wages, plus 39.29 percent of the next $290 of average monthly wages, plus 36.71 percent of the next $150 of average monthly wages. A worker retiring at age 65 would receive this monthly benefit.

Under the 1972 legislation, any time the CPI rose by 3.0 percent or more from the last adjustment in the formula, the multiplication factors used in determining the basic benefit were indexed by the growth rate in the CPI. This indexing formula was also used for automatically increasing benefits already in payment status. Because the wages were already automatically indexed by inflation and productivity growth, the indexing of the factors in the benefit formula compounded the indexing of initial benefits; the problem came to be known as "double indexing." Ultimately, the proposed solution was called "decoupling"—separating the processes for indexing original benefits and those already in current pay status.

The assumptions used to develop the 1972 legislation projected that benefits would grow at about the same rate as wages, which was the policymakers' goal. Nevertheless, between January 1975 and January 1977, benefits for new retirees had grown nearly 10 percent relative to their preretirement average wages[14]—Congress had intended the relationship to be constant. Under the benefit adjustment method adopted in 1972, benefits soared relative to covered wages under then-current economic conditions.

The indexing procedure adopted in 1972 made benefits sensitive to the interrelationship of wage and price growth. Under the assumptions supporting the indexing legislation, between 1972 and 1976, wages were expected to grow 1.8 times faster than prices as measured by the CPI. In compounded terms, prices were expected to grow 14.5 percent over the five-year period but actually grew by 81.0 percent. Wages were expected to grow by 11.8 percent more than prices, but they fell by 0.7 percent relative to prices.[15] The adjustments had made the system hypersensitive to inflation during the worst inflationary period in the century.

It is puzzling that this turn of events could come to pass some 35 years into the program's operation. In 1971, Social Security actuary Bob Myers wrote an article for a trade periodical aimed at the financial services sector. Myers was a self-professed Republican who thought Bob Ball and his cronies were pushing an expansionist agenda for Social Security. Their agenda was incompatible with Republican philosophy and his own vision of what the program should be. He saw the legislative package that was being prepared for 1972 as part of that whole initiative. In comments about cost estimates for the system, he observed:

The relationship of the assumption as to increases in prices and increases in wages is extremely sensitive. For example, if it is assumed that wages rise twice as rapidly as prices (which was the case for the considerable period some years ago), the program will be shown to be quite adequately financed.

On the other hand, if the ratio of wage increases to price increases is in the order of only 1½ to 1, then the system will be in financial difficulties and higher tax rates will be required. . . . And in this respect it should be noted that, in recent years, this critical and sensitive ratio has only been 1¼ to 1.[16]

Myers was writing about the new "dynamic assumptions" for valuing Social Security that the actuaries were being pushed to use, but these assumptions and the valuation technique corresponded with the indexation proposal that was then under consideration. The point was that as long as wages were growing twice as fast as prices, Social Security costs as a percentage of covered payroll would be relatively stable in the future. If something significantly less than that were to occur, there would be a problem. Myers' final comment is ominous. He noted that recent history would be problematic if it persisted into the future.

Myers was not the only one to appreciate the interactions of wage and price growth as an important determinant of the system's cost projections. A 1970 staff paper developed by the Bureau of the Budget suggested that some indexing provisions could lead to increases in benefits relative to covered wages.[17] The Bureau of Budget, today known as the Office of Management and Budget, had government-wide oversight of proposals that would affect federal revenue or expenditures. The memo in question suggests that staff members were paying attention to this matter.

The staff paper observes: "There are two changes in the computation of Social Security currently being talked about—the implications of which are not widely appreciated. Especially if these provisions overlap, they might . . . affect the system far beyond the intentions of the decision-makers."[18] Later on in the discussion of the cost implications the paper states: "There will be no additional cost to this proposal provided that it is tied to the decoupling of benefit formula from automatic benefit increases."[19]

Nothing in the public record disclosed so far indicates that Bob Ball understood the implications of the indexing provisions before their adoption. He may not have sorted out the nuances the way that Bob Myers would have. Myers had been the prominent numerologist developing cost estimates for most of the program's history. He knew the system mechanics better than anyone and how pressure at one point would affect operations elsewhere. Ball was the consummate policy maven—he knew what he wanted to achieve and how to achieve it. There is no doubt, however, that by early 1973, Ball knew there was a potential problem. In his final written report as Social Security commissioner, which he left behind as a roadmap for the agency's managers, Ball indicated that a new Social Security Advisory Council was being formed. Among other things, he said the council would be looking at "decoupling," which he described as follows:

> The issue has to do with the mechanisms that should be used to keep the social security system up-to-date: specifically the question arises as to whether in the long run the coupling of increases for those on the rolls and those coming on in the future that is inherent in the present statutory formula is the best, or whether a change should be made so that only benefits after people retire would be tied to the cost-of-living index and benefits at the time of retirement would be more closely related to the worker's retirement earnings.[20]

A New, Difficult Experience in Making Social Security Policy

As it turned out, the benefit indexation in the 1972 legislation was a catastrophe. In 1976, President Ford's administration drafted legislation to address the rapidly unfolding financing fiasco, but it garnered little support in Congress. Until then, Social Security policymaking had always been about expanding the pie, and Ford's proposed curtailment was a new and unwelcome recipe. President Carter sent similar legislation to Congress in July 1977 and signed the 1977 Amendments into law on December 20. The amendments fixed the long-term indexing problem, thereby resolving half of the projected long-run actuarial deficit. But it also reduced benefits for future retirees. The new formula reduced 2010 benefits by 33 percent for low earners, 25 percent for average earners, and 31 percent for maximum earners.[21]

After the dust had settled, the benefit structure under the 1977 amendments was remarkably similar to that legislated in the 1939 Amendments. Figure 7.2 shows earning replacement rates provided under various amendments to the original Social Security Act, at three different earnings levels. All three lines show benefit growth across the board between the mid-1960s and mid-1970s and the fairly dramatic reductions brought about by the 1977 Amendments. Clearly Congress was willing to cut Social Security benefits when costs threatened to spiral out of control. If you draw a horizontal line across from the 1939 observation for each of the three earnings levels to the far

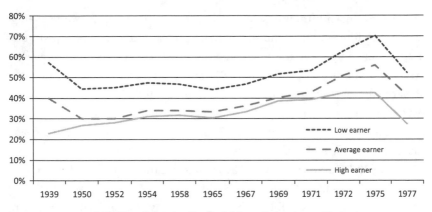

Initial benefit level set by Social Security law in specified year

FIGURE 7.2 Percentage of Final Earnings Replaced by Social Security Benefits at Various Lifetime Earnings Levels for Single Workers Retiring at Age 65 under Various Social Security Amendments

Source: Robert J. Myers, "History of Replacement Rates for Various Amendments to the Social Security Act," Memorandum no. 2 (Washington, D.C.: National Commission on Social Security Reform, 1982), p. 3 and 1994-1996 Advisory Council on Social Security background materials.

right of the figure, benefits under the 1977 Amendments were slightly lower than those under the 1939 Amendments for a low earner, almost identical for an average earner, and slightly higher for a high earner.

To make the transition to the lower benefits more palatable, the law guaranteed all those reaching age 62 before 1984 a benefit no lower than what they would have received under the old law as of December 1978 based on earnings through age 61. The workers first eligible for benefits immediately after the 1977 Amendments finally took effect received smaller benefits than the recipients of the substantial windfalls bestowed by double-indexing. These reductions came to be known as the benefit "notch" and those affected by it were called "notch babies."

Various groups representing the notch babies have campaigned for years to win back the benefits they would have received before the 1977 Amendments, but they never succeeded. The notch babies were not cheated—they received the benefits Congress had intended to pay them rather than unintended windfalls introduced by the 1972 indexing snafu. In any event, it was not the first time the program had treated one group of workers much differently than another, otherwise similar, group.

The 1977 Amendments also accelerated a scheduled set of increases in the payroll tax rate and raised the maximum covered earnings levels. After 1981, the earnings maximum was scheduled to go up automatically when average wage rates climbed. The combination of tax increases and benefit adjustments dramatically improved the financing outlook. The projections suggested system surpluses at least through 2011 and reduced the projected long-run actuarial deficit from more than 8 percent to less than 1.5 percent of covered payroll.[22] The 1977 Amendments had begun to plan for the baby boomers' retirement but left it to some future Congress to fully accommodate the seismic demographic shifts in progress.

By July 1979, some 18 months after President Carter signed the 1977 Amendments, Social Security Commissioner Stanford G. Ross observed that: "The optimistic expansionist philosophy that underlay Social Security planning since World War II has now changed to one of guarded hope that the best of the past can be preserved while the considerable needs of the future are addressed." He predicted that the coming decade would witness "painful adjustments in which finances and benefits will have to be closely scrutinized and balanced."[23]

The 1977 Amendments had corrected the indexing fiasco in the 1972 Amendments, but Social Security was still being financed on a pay-as-you-go basis, and system costs remained sensitive to the economic factors that affect benefits and wages. Furthermore, the transition guarantees meant that remnants of the earlier indexing would persist into the early 1980s for new beneficiaries. By the time the 1977 Amendments passed, the reduced trust funds could offer very little buffer against further economic turmoil.

When the 1977 Amendments were being considered, the actuaries assumed inflation would drive up benefits by 28.2 percent from 1977 to 1981. In fact, the CPI skyrocketed 60 percent over that period. They expected inflation-adjusted wages to grow by 12.9 percent over the period, but they fell by 19 percent relative to inflation.[24] By the time of the 1980 presidential campaign, Social Security financing clearly remained a significant policy problem that would land in the lap of the next administration.

8 CRISIS AND REACTIONS: CONFLICT, CONSENSUS AND SURPRISE

Shortly after President Ronald Reagan was inaugurated in January 1981, Secretary of Health and Human Services Richard Schweiker announced the administration's plan to keep the Social Security "system from going broke, protect the basic benefit structure and reduce the tax burden of American workers."[1] The package called for significantly lower benefits for those who retired before age 65. At that time, you could retire at age 62 and still receive 80 percent of the full age-65 benefit, with the benefit between those ages adjusted on a pro rata basis. Under the proposal, early retirement benefits would decline to 55 percent of full benefits, and the average earnings replacement rate would drop from 42 percent to 38 percent at age 65. The package proposed delaying the annual cost-of-living increases by three months for those receiving benefits and tightening the eligibility and administration of the disability program.

The public was stunned, and those close to retirement age were outraged. The reaction triggered a political consensus probably not matched again until the terrorist attacks of September 11, 2001. Congressional leaders in both parties attacked the plan. Senator Moynihan (D-NY) thought the proposal would make it "financially impossible to retire at 62."[2] Senator William Armstrong (R-CO) called the proposal a "masterpiece of bad timing."[3] House Speaker Tip O'Neill described it as "despicable . . . a rotten thing to do . . . that robs the system of its most important feature: the confidence of the American public."[4] The Democrats were convinced that the proposals were motivated by Reagan's desire to reduce the deficit and declare victory for Reaganomics. Speaker O'Neill said the Republicans were "willing to balance the budget on the backs of the elderly,"[5] a new and potent mantra for the Democrats.

A May 20 resolution adopted by the Democratic Caucus of the House stated that President Reagan's proposals to reduce early retirement benefits "represent an unconscionable breach of faith with the first generation of workers that has contributed to Social Security for their whole lives."[6] On the same day, the Senate unanimously (96–0) adopted a resolution expressing the sense of the Senate that "Congress shall not precipitously and unfairly penalize early retirees." The author of the latter resolution was Bob Dole, the Republican chair of the Senate Finance Committee.[7] In the floor discussion of Dole's proposal, not a single Republican rose to defend the president.[8]

Creating Political Dialogue to Address the Financing Crisis

With his proposals soundly rebuffed, President Reagan moved to create a National Commission on Social Security reform. It was to be a bipartisan group with one-third of its members appointed by Speaker Tip O'Neill, one-third by Senate Leader Howard Baker, and one-third by the president. The composition of the committee was announced in December 1981.[9] It came to be known as the Greenspan Commission after its chair, Alan Greenspan, chair of the Council of Economic Advisors during the Ford Administration. House Speaker Tip O'Neill appointed Bob Ball, who was clearly O'Neill's special representative on the group. Greenspan appointed Robert Myers as executive director of the commission, so the two Bobs, Ball and Myers, held positions of power over Social Security once again as they had for most of the program's history.[10] The Commission was to report its findings and recommendations by the end of 1982.

The 1982 Trustees Report said that full benefits likely could not be paid in July 1983. The Social Security Act made no provisions for borrowing money if current revenues and trust fund assets would not cover current payments. So the Social Security Administration was facing the prospect that in July, it could choose between sending partial checks or not sending checks until later.

As the commission neared its December 1982 deadline, the members were at political odds over an acceptable solution. The nation's political leaders were facing exactly the dilemma President Franklin Roosevelt had hoped to avoid: dealing with unfunded Social Security obligations. President Reagan gave the Greenspan Commission 15 extra days to resolve its members' disagreements, but the stalemate continued. Then, Senator Robert Dole wrote a *New York Times* editorial arguing that "Social Security overwhelms every other domestic priority." He suggested that "through a combination of relatively modest steps, including some acceleration of already scheduled taxes and some reduction in the rate of future benefit increases, the system can be saved."[11] Up until then, the Republicans on the commission had resisted any consideration of tax increases.

Senator Daniel Patrick Moynihan grabbed the opening. He and Dole drafted Ball, Greenspan, and Barber Conable, a respected Republican and long-serving member of the House of Representatives from New York, into a small working group carved out of the larger commission. The White House joined the discussions with David Stockman, James Baker, Kenneth Duberstein, and Richard Darman participating. Stockman was the head of the Office of Management and Budget at the time, Baker was the secretary of Treasury, and Duberstein and Darman were White House advisors to the president. This group negotiated a package aimed at striking a balance between raising taxes and curtailing benefits and submitted it to the full Commission for approval. Three members refused to endorse it because of the tax increases,[12] but President Reagan and House Speaker O'Neill compromised because the alternatives seemed even worse. Older Americans had become so dependent on Social Security that the chaos a breakdown would bring was unacceptable to either political party.

The recommendations were projected to sustain the system through the short term and to gradually build up the reserve fund sufficiently to avoid further financing crises. But even the small working group of Commission members and Administration representatives could not agree on how to deal with the long-term financing challenges the baby boomers' retirement would bring, although the options were the same for the short and long term—increasing taxes or reducing benefits.

Congress Accepts Commission Recommendations and More

It is said that "facing the gallows at dawn focuses one's mind." The prospect of being unable to send full Social Security checks in July as February was approaching focused policymakers on compromising as necessary to keep things going over the short term. Both the House Ways and Means Committee and the Senate Finance Committee convened hearings on the Greenspan Commission's recommendations. While there was far from universal agreement, the negotiated agreement stood.

Some important Congressional leaders also insisted on long-term financing reforms. After heated debate, the Ways and Means Committee approved a 5 percent cut in benefits for 2000—17 years in the future—and a tax hike to commence in 2015.[13] J. J. Pickle, a colorful Democrat from Texas who chaired the Ways and Means Subcommittee on Social Security, had an alternative proposal, namely to raise the "normal retirement age" to 67, but on a delayed basis. People who wanted to retire sooner could collect reduced early retirement benefits.

Jake Pickle was cut from similar cloth as Franklin Roosevelt—a progressive who fully supported the underlying philosophy behind Social Security, but a conservative when it came to paying the bills. Pickle wanted to raise the retirement age to balance the books for the long term, and increasing the retirement age made sense because life expectancy was expected to continue its steady improvement.

Congressman Pickle understood that shortly after the turn of the century, the system's dependency ratio—the number of retirees compared to contributing workers and a major driver of costs—would start rising. From 2000 to 2030, the dependency ratio would increase from around 0.30 to 0.50, driving up the payroll tax cost proportionately, according to the 1982 Trustees Report. That is why Pickle proposed to start phasing in the higher normal retirement age in 2000. Mindful of how important the age 62 early retirement option was to many people—given the outraged response to President Reagan's 1982 proposal to reduce the age-62 benefits—Pickle was willing to leave the option there but wanted to reduce benefits for those who took it although not nearly as dramatically as President Reagan had proposed.

Opponents to Pickle's proposal argued that increasing the normal retirement age amounted to an across-the-board benefit cut. The leader of the opposition was Claude Pepper, a fellow Democrat who had represented Florida in the Senate from 1936 to 1951 and the Miami area in the House from 1963 until he died in 1989. The House passed Pickle's proposal to increase the normal retirement age to 67, with the age to begin rising in 2000 and reach 67 in 2022. The Senate's proposal increased the normal retirement age to 66, but ultimately Pickle's plan won out in the conference committee.[14] Under the final legislation, the first increases in the retirement age were 17 years away, and most people didn't even seem to notice at the time.

The 1983 Amendments would keep the system fully financed for the next 75 years, according to the actuaries' projections. The short-term financing appeared to be sufficient for the economy to right itself. President Reagan signed the 1983 Social Security Amendments on April 20, 1983, on the South Lawn of the White House. Tip O'Neill, Claude Pepper, Bob Dole, Daniel Patrick Moynihan, and Howard Baker shared center stage with the president, who remarked that the legislation "demonstrates for all time our nation's iron-clad commitment to Social Security." He reaffirmed "Franklin Roosevelt's commitment that Social Security must always provide a secure and stable base so that older Americans may live in dignity." He concluded by saying that in reaching agreement on the 1983 Amendments, "Each of us had to compromise one way or the other . . . but the essence of bipartisanship is to give up a little in order to get a lot. And, my fellow Americans, I think we've gotten a very great deal."[15]

New Surprises in the Crisis Aftermath

When the Social Security system was young, the actuaries made their cost projections in perpetuity, assuming that the system would go on forever. Of course, they didn't actually project out to infinity but approximated it in their calculation processes. As time went on, they started limiting projection periods to 75 years and considered long-term financing adequate when it was in "close actuarial balance"—meaning that revenue and costs come within 0.5 percent of each other—over 75 years. The actuaries were using a 75-year projection period for their calculations when the 1983 Amendments were under deliberation.

After the 1983 legislation passed, policymakers focused on the current trust fund balances. The surplus climbed to $42 billion in 1985 and crossed the $100 billion mark during 1988. The trust fund balance reached $225 billion by the end of 1990 and continued climbing through the end of the century. Social Security's short-term financing problem had been solved in 1983.

Harry Ballantyne, then the chief actuary at the Social Security Administration, presented new long-term projected costs and revenues after the 1983 Amendments. According to these estimates, the Social Security trust funds would grow from around $27.5 billion in 1983 to about $20.7 trillion in 2045.[16] The trust funds could pay promised benefits until the youngest of the baby boomers turned 100. The system was projected to be in balance until at least 2063, some five years beyond the 75-year projection window. In 2063, the youngest of the baby boomers will celebrate their 99th birthdays, so there was a general sense that the 1983 Amendments had fixed Social Security financing for the baby boom generation.

The projected trust fund accumulations under the new legislation reflected a marked departure from earlier funding practices. It was not a shift to full funding by any stretch of the imagination, but it tilted sufficiently in that direction to reignite the earlier debate about holding trust fund assets in government bonds. There had been virtually no discussion about accumulating a significant trust fund during the debates over the 1983 Amendments, and the news of accumulations surprised some policymakers and analysts. Everyone had been so intent on bringing the system back into close actuarial balance that they were oblivious to the implications of the 1983 changes within the context of historical policies or practices.

In the 1985 Trustees Report, the actuaries revised their estimate of the ultimate trust fund accumulation downward to a maximum of around $12 trillion and estimated that the system would need more money by 2049. By 1995, the Trustees Report suggested the trust fund would only accumulate roughly $3.5 trillion and funding would run short by 2029. Between 1983 and 1995, the actuaries revised their estimate of the trust fund accumulation downward by around $18 trillion. Once again, these trillion-dollar figures are hard to imagine, but other markers were more easily grasped.

In 1983, the government told the public the system was secure until 2063. In 1995, the public was told the system would remain solvent until 2029. The youngest baby boomers will turn 66 in 2029, but they will not yet be eligible for an unreduced retirement benefit. In a little more than a decade, we traveled from system solvency for all baby boomers to the prospect of coming up short about halfway through their retirement. The shortfall was projected to be about 25 percent to 30 percent of expected benefits when the trust fund was depleted.

Four factors accounted for most of the bad news: (1) changes to the calculation methods used for the estimates, (2) the realization that the economic assumptions underlying the 1983 projections were overly optimistic, (3) the determination that the assumptions about disability rates in 1983 were too low, and, finally (4) the 75-year projection period turned out to be deceptive. Some good news actually emerged over the period, which was lost in the sea of adverse developments. By the mid-1990s, the demographic outlook had improved considerably, suggesting a somewhat lower dependency ratio in the future than previously anticipated.[17]

An important lesson learned from the 1983 Amendments is that basing Social Security policy on any given 75-year period can create or leave in place structural problems that lead to financing imbalances. Formulating an appropriate period for evaluating policy has become controversial. But the 1983 Amendments and the developments that followed proved that the 75-year perspective can mislead policymakers into thinking they have resolved funding issues that are merely looming beyond the projection horizon.

Accumulating Trust Funds and Déjà Vu All over Again

While the trust fund accumulation would be considerably lower than first anticipated, it was projected to be much larger than ever before. At the end of 2010, the trust funds held around $2.6 trillion. The 2011 Trustees Report assumes that the trust funds will accumulate roughly $3.7 trillion by 2022. Under the 1983 Amendments, at least in theory, the baby boom's benefits would be partly prefunded by contributions during their working lives and accumulated for redemption during their retirement. The policy result has been nearly as contentious as the original policy that Franklin Roosevelt had insisted upon when the Social Security Act was under consideration.

As to whether accumulating the trust fund is prefunding future benefits, that depends on whether the growing balances are being "saved." The question has proven, time and again, to be controversial. The term "saved" can mean different things in different contexts. In a macroeconomic context, savings is the portion of income earned in a specific period that, rather than being spent on consumption, is invested in a way that boosts the value of our national balance sheet, making us collectively richer. Savings are used to accumulate equipment, software, and other tools that workers use to produce goods and services that will generate additional income in the future. Much of the added income flows to workers in the form of wages, and a portion flows back to the owners of the capital to repay their investment and pay them interest for having given up or deferred earlier consumption. One form of saving is paying down outstanding loans, thereby reducing the amount of future income required to pay interest. In some ways, our national economics work the same as our household economics. Paying off our debts means we spend less on interest payments, freeing up income for other things.

Are Social Security trust funds making us collectively richer? Or are they simply being used to finance current consumption? In practical terms, what happens when Social Security collects $10 billion more in tax revenue in a year than it spends? If the $10 billion is used to reduce outstanding federal debt, it is saved. If it is used to pay for farm subsidies, emergency relief programs, military operations and much of what else the government does, it is being consumed. Some government expenditures on education, highways, and the like that will increase productivity in the future are forms of national investment. These make up a small share of government expenditures.

During the 1930s and 1940s, Senator Arthur Vandenberg (R-OH) had railed against Edwin Witte and Arthur Altmeyer's arguments that Social Security should be funded. In 1937, Senator Vandenberg argued that the proceeds of workers' payroll taxes "are currently diverted to foot the general bills of the Government."[18] By the end of the 1980s, the trust fund accumulations drew policymakers' attention. In the fall of 1989, Senator Ernest Hollings (D-SC), a member of the Senate Budget Committee, summoned ghostly memories of Senator Vandenberg in addressing his colleagues: "The public fully supported enactment of hefty new Social Security taxes in 1983 to ensure the retirement program's long-term solvency and credibility. . . . Well, look again.

The Treasury is siphoning off every dollar of the Social Security surplus to meet current operating expenses of the Government."[19]

A year later, Senator Patrick Moynihan (D-NY), chairman of the Social Security Subcommittee of the Finance Committee, introduced legislation to reinstate pay-as-you-go financing. In explaining his motivations, Moynihan recalled his service on the Greenspan Commission and the development of the 1983 Amendments and earlier work on the Finance Committee in developing the 1977 Amendments, and he noted how the taxing provisions were leading to the trust fund buildup. He said almost no one noticed at the time and admitted that the implications of their actions probably did not fully dawn on him "that we had changed the whole basis of Social Security, but we had."[20]

About the same time Senator Hollings was ripping into Social Security's funding policies on the Senate floor, Senator Moynihan was reading an article in the *Rochester Democrat Chronicle* that described what was happening to the trust funds as "thievery." Early in 1989, Moynihan appeared on the *NBC Today Show* with Senator John Heinz (R-PA), and the host asked Heinz whether he agreed with the characterization that what was going on was "thievery." Moynihan said that Heinz responded with great candor: "Certainly not. It is not thievery. It is embezzlement."[21] But despite the railings in Congress about the trust fund accumulations, legislation to switch back to pure pay-as-you go financing never got off the ground.

By the mid-1990s, another Advisory Council had been appointed with Ned Gramlich, an economics professor from the University of Michigan, as chairman. Bob Ball was a member again. I was also a member of the council. Among other things, this group focused on the funding issue in some depth and addressed whether the current trust fund practices were an effective way to save accumulating payroll contributions and lower the system's long-term cost.

Barry Bosworth, an economist from the Brookings Institution addressed the matter with the Advisory Council. He claimed that policymakers had been "playing games" with the Social Security trust funds. "It just takes the Social Security surplus and makes it available for other funds and uses it to finance our consumption."[22] He admitted that retirees would try to reclaim the trust fund accumulations when incoming payroll taxes were not enough. But he argued that with the federal budget in deficit, the Social Security surplus contributions were being spent on current consumption for current generations of taxpayers and were not being saved.

Bob Ball did not buy Bosworth's assessment or that of several others presenting to the Advisory Council. He claimed that "it's a political judgment as to whether Social Security isn't already contributing to savings by reason of the fact that it has reduced the government's dissaving if you think that the Congress would not have come any closer to balancing the budget anyway."[23] Within the Advisory Council, we agreed that the issue could not be resolved. But that did not end the 60-year long debate about the role of the trust funds in securing future Social Security obligations and in the larger economy.

In March 1998, Senators Bob Kerrey (D-NV) and Patrick Moynihan introduced a revised version of legislation that Moynihan had introduced earlier calling for an immediate reduction in payroll tax rates. Compared to Moynihan's earlier legislation proposing a return to pay-as-you-go financing, the Kerrey-Moynihan bill of 1998 did not depend nearly as much on increasing future payroll tax rates. It called for a technical adjustment to the way benefits were indexed, increasing the number of working years considered for determining benefits from 35 to 38 years, and gradually increasing the age at which full benefits are paid. Kerrey-Moynihan also proposed to allow workers to contribute their portion of the immediate payroll tax cut to an individual retirement account. If workers contributed a 1 percent reduction in the tax rate to such accounts, their employers would be required to match it with the other half of the payroll tax reduction. Some people saw this as a significant step toward individual accounts by Senator Moynihan, a long-time supporter of the current Social Security system. Henry Aaron, a prominent Washington economist, Social Security advocate, and ally of Bob Ball, characterized Moynihan's proposal as "the My Lai approach to Social Security reform—burn the system down in our attempt to save it."[24]

Bob Ball had been a close advisor to Moynihan on Social Security through the 1970s and into the 1980s, and he felt betrayed by the Senator's advocacy for pay-as-you-go financing. In his later years in the Senate, Moynihan turned to a Finance Committee staff member, economist David Podoff, for advice. Podoff had joined the Social Security Administration and worked in its policy research unit from the early 1970s until he went to work for the Senate Finance Committee toward the end of his federal career. He knew a great deal about Social Security but did not always agree with Bob Ball, who concluded that Moynihan was no longer getting the quality of advice that he himself had provided in the past. He seemed to overlook the possibility that Moynihan simply disagreed with him.

When Senator Moynihan informed Ball that he planned to introduce legislation to shift the system back to pay-as-you-go financing, Ball advised: "Well, don't do that! At least retain the overall rate, because Medicare is way under-funded, and we're going to need it for that."

But Moynihan was convinced that the accumulating trust funds were being misused and he was determined to stop it. Ball concluded that Moynihan was "on a collision course with people who had traditionally been supporters of the program. . . . Note that the unraveling of his support depends entirely on the belief that you can't advance-fund for Social Security; that the government can't save. This is the key point I disagree with him on. If you accept his view on this point, the rest of his positions become quite reasonable."[25]

With the short-term payroll tax cuts that Moynihan was proposing, Ball could see that there would be no trust fund to buffer the higher rates ahead in the pay-as-you-go environment. Trailing out the logic, Ball saw that "under a pay-as-you-go system, the rates would be so high for sustaining the benefits levels set in current law that you really couldn't expect support for such high rates." What Arthur Altmeyer and Edwin Witte had predicted in the 1930s was now a looming possibility, which Ball clearly recognized but did not want to acknowledge because of the consequences.

Bob Ball understood that if the Social Security trust funds were not a mechanism for saving and accumulating wealth in a macroeconomic context, "the only consistent solution with pay-as-you-go financing was to lower the cost of the system to make sure that you could handle it with pay-as-you-go rates in the long run. This led [Senator Moynihan] into proposing benefit cuts."[26] Bob Ball, who had gone along with pay-as-you-go funding for decades and thrived on it during the expansionary days of the 1950s, 1960s, and early 1970s, was now praising the benefits of funding.

When Senator Moynihan added voluntary individual accounts to his proposed reforms, it was just salt in the wounds for Ball. He saw individual accounts as being antithetical to the "social" elements of the existing system. He worried that if these accounts did well, workers would want to make them larger, which would become a potential and ever-growing threat to the joint commitment to the existing system.

In early 1999, President Clinton proposed using the federal government surpluses to increase Social Security funding (which I discuss in more detail in chapter 10). The Republicans wanted to create a "lock box" by using the Social Security surplus to pay down publicly held debt and directing any general budget surplus to tax reductions and defense. But legislation would have had to go through the Senate Finance Committee, which has jurisdiction over Social Security financing. With Senator Moynihan as the ranking Democrat at Senate Finance supported by allies like Senator Kerrey, President Clinton's ideas about greater funding of Social Security were not warmly embraced even by the Democrats.

As it turned out, neither Senator Moynihan nor Senator Kerrey ran for reelection in 2000. When they left office, the system was still operating under the structure put in place by the 1983 Amendments. The Social Security trust funds continued to grow along with the general budget surplus. Both of these retiring senators were convinced the accumulating surpluses were not being saved, just as their predecessor, Senator Arthur Vandenberg, had been convinced the originally projected surpluses would not be saved. Ken Apfel, who served out the remaining period of President Clinton's presidency as Social Security commissioner and had sounded a lot like Arthur Altmeyer in front of the Senate Finance Committee, could not convince any of the doubters that the Social Security surpluses were real savings.

SORTING OUT THE TRUST FUND SEMANTICS AND REALITIES

The assets in the Social Security trust funds are special-issue federal bonds prescribed by the law that defines the rest of the program. Most working Americans pay more payroll taxes than income or other taxes, but Social Security does not collect its own revenues. The U.S. Treasury Department collects the money for Social Security and writes the monthly benefit checks (or, these days, makes auto-deposits). Massive in scope, Social Security is a colossal administrative task, involving some 130 to 135 million workers contributing payroll taxes, and some 50 to 55 million beneficiaries receiving payments. Despite widespread and long-standing involvement with Social Security, many people do not understand how their taxes are collected, invested, and paid out as benefits.

Trust Fund Operations

Payroll tax deposits flow into the Treasury continuously, and expenses come due on a continuous basis as well. At the end of each day, trust fund revenues and expenses are tallied. Separate trust funds are maintained for the Old-Age and Survivors program and the Disability program, so each has its own accounting and cash management. When the Treasury collects more Social Security payroll taxes than it needs to pay out in benefits, it issues the trust funds an electronic bond at the current short-term interest rate. Thus, rather than receiving cash, the trust funds receive interest-bearing bonds from the Treasury—essentially a promise to pay back the cash upon redemption—that the trust fund can redeem any time. As interest credits accrue, Treasury issues additional bonds to the trust funds. If the trust funds need extra cash, bonds are cashed in interest-rate order, with the bonds accruing the lowest interest rates cashed first. At the end of each month, the trust fund cashes all electronic bonds accumulated during the past month and Treasury issues a paper bond with a term through the next June 30 at an interest rate equivalent to the rates on government bonds with similar terms. On June 30 each year, the trust fund cashes all the paper bonds issued over the past year and the electronic bonds issued over the past month, and Treasury issues a 15-year paper bond at current rates for government bonds of such duration. The trust fund bonds can be redeemed any time at their full face value at purchase. The paper bonds are printed on a regular laser printer of the sort you might have on your desk, on three-hole-punched white paper. All the paper bonds for each trust fund are kept in a three-ring binder and put in a filing cabinet located in Parkersburg, WV at the Federal Bureau of Public Debt, which is a unit of the U.S. Treasury Department.

In recent years, the trust fund has held a minimum of 15 bonds and a maximum of 55 bonds. It never holds more than 15 of the longer-term bonds because after 15 years, the oldest bonds are redeemed and reinvested. It never holds more than 11 of the monthly bonds because only one is issued for each month from July through the following May. So it never holds more than 26 paper bonds, as the remaining monthly bonds are electronic. At the end of June each year, the monthly bonds from the last 11 months and the electronic bonds from the current month are cashed and rolled into the newest 15-year bond. The trust fund never holds more than 30 of the daily electronic bonds, and on June 30 holds no more than 29 of them because, at most, one bond is issued daily and none needs to be issued for June 30, because the net cash proceeds for that day are rolled into the next 15-year bond being purchased.

In 2006, the Social Security Advisory Board traveled to Parkersburg to see the trust fund and its operations. I was a member of the board at the time, and the picture in figure 9.1 shows what we saw and held in our own hands: one of the monthly paper bonds, held by the Old-Age and Survivors Trust fund, in the notebook that held the complete set of paper bonds in this trust fund. This particular bond was earning a 5.25 percent annual rate of return with a maturity date of June 30, 2007. The binder in the picture held 19 of these pieces of paper when I took this picture. Their face value was approximately $1.6 trillion. The binders in which the bonds are kept, one for the retirement and survivors program and the other for the disability program, are held in a metal filing cabinet drawer with a keypad lock—a proverbial lock box.

FIGURE 9.1 Picture of a Bond Held by the Old-Age and Survivors Trust Fund in 2007
Source: Picture taken by the author.

Controversy over Trust Funds as Savings

One area of confusion—and sometimes contention—is whether the Social Security trust funds represent savings in an economic sense. The answer is "not usually." Suppose the government runs a balanced budget in the general accounts and a $50 billion surplus in the Social Security trust fund. This gives the unified budget[1] a surplus of $50 billion, exactly the trust fund surplus. Since general account expenses are paid by general revenues, the Treasury would use the $50 billion Social Security surplus to buy back federal debt. The Treasury would issue new bonds to the trust fund in trade for the surplus cash, but the American public would end up with $50 billion less in public debt. Reducing the federal debt increases the wealth position of the government and future taxpayers—it is savings in a macroeconomic context, as discussed in the previous chapter. If the government were running a surplus in its general accounts, it is straightforward that any surplus in trust fund cash income contributes to national savings.

Things get more complicated when the government is running a deficit in its general accounts. The logic can get so contorted that it is like the scene in an old W. C. Fields movie where he performs the carnival trick of hiding a pea under one of three walnut shells and shuffles the shells around with observers trying to keep track of where the pea is hidden. Suppose the government were running a $50 billion deficit in its general accounts and a $50 billion surplus in the Social Security cash flow. Then the Treasury would use the $50 billion Social Security surplus to cover the $50 billion of general account deficit and issue new government bonds to the trust fund. In this case, there would be no cash to buy back any public debt. Here is where the issue of trust fund savings gets confusing, if not contentious.

At issue is whether a Social Security cash surplus prompts policymakers to spend the surplus amount on other government programs—which they would not spend if the surplus did not exist. In chapters 4 and 5, we saw that during the 1930s, Senator Arthur Vandenberg argued that cash surpluses in Social Security would be spent on other government expenditures rather than saved. In chapter 8, we saw that during the 1990s, Senators Earnest Hollings and Daniel Patrick Moynihan argued the same thing. The contention that Social Security surpluses are not saved suggests that our federal deficits are larger than they would otherwise be simply because Social Security ran surpluses between 1983 and 2009.

The top two lines in figure 9.2 show the Social Security trust fund gains over the full terms of Presidents Bill Clinton and George W. Bush, and the first year of Barack Obama's term. The top line shows the trust fund gains from an internal Social Security accounting perspective, which includes payroll tax revenues and interest credits net of expenses. Both tax revenues and interest income add to the resources available in accounting for trust fund activities. However, interest credits to Social Security have no effect on the unified budget because they appear as income in the Social Security budget but as an expense to the government in its general operating budget. Since Social Security is a subcomponent of the unified budget, the income is offset by the expense. In figure 9.2, the solid line shows the incremental cash surpluses that the Social Security trust funds generated over the period, which is the amount included in deriving the unified budget balances that are shown by the lower broken line. The solid line is what worried Senators Vandenberg, Hollings, and Moynihan when they discussed the effects of Social Security's surpluses on the larger federal budget.

The argument over whether the trust funds contribute to savings is about the amounts shown by the solid line in figure 9.2. Over most of the period from 1993 to 2009, the cash surpluses in the trust funds have been relatively trivial compared with the unified budget deficits. The only unified budget surplus was from 1998 to 2001, when the trust fund cash surpluses accounted for 56.5 percent of the unified budget surpluses. During those four years, the Social Security surpluses plainly helped the government pay

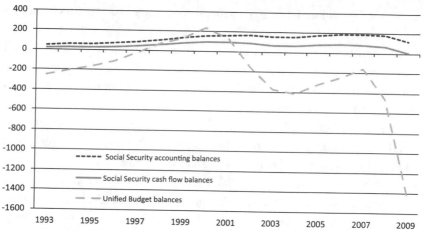

FIGURE 9.2 Social Security Trust Fund Cash Flow Surpluses and the Unified Federal Budget Balances for Specified Years in Billions of Dollars

Sources: 2010 Annual Report of the Board of Trustees of the Federal Old-Age and Survivors Insurance and Disability Insurance Trust Funds, unpublished data provided by the Office of the Actuary, Social Security Administration, and *Budget of the United States Government, Fiscal Year 2011, Historical Tables.*

off government bonds held by investors, so the trust fund accumulations contributed to national savings. In every other year in the table, indeed in every other year since 1969, the unified budget ran a deficit, and the net savings effect of the Social Security surpluses is debatable.

The Social Security Commission appointed by President George W. Bush acknowledged the theoretical possibility of trust fund accumulations adding to national savings, but concluded that the developments after the 1983 funding legislation had taught the "nation a clear lesson about how unlikely this is as a practice. The Social Security surpluses have enabled the government to finance other government spending, rather than raising current-year taxes and effectively saving Social Security funds for the future."[2]

Not everyone agrees with this assessment of our fiscal operations. Some observers believe policymakers segregate the accounts and act independently on each. Peter Diamond and Peter Orszag, two economists and noted participants in the debate over Social Security reform, fall into this camp. They looked at congressional attempts to reduce federal budget deficits throughout the 1980s and early 1990s. On the basis of the efforts to reduce the unified budget deficits, Diamond and Orszag concluded that it is "plausible" that policymakers were not raiding the Social Security surpluses to finance other government operations.[3]

Evidence That Social Security Surpluses Are Not Saved

To introduce some evidence to the issue, Sita Nataraj and John Shoven studied the relationship between governmental trust fund accumulations and government spending. They estimated that a dollar increase in the Social Security trust funds increased federal deficits in other operations by $1.73. Carrying the analysis further, Nataraj and Shoven broke their analytical period into two segments, 1949 to 1969, and 1970 to 2003. This split was important because in 1970, the U.S. government combined the trust fund with all other government operations on a unified budget basis. Back when the budgets were segregated, Nataraj and Shoven found that the accumulating trust funds were not statistically associated with deficits in other government operations. After 1970, the accumulating trust funds led to added deficits in other government operations, once again statistically on a dollar-for-dollar basis.[4]

Barry Bosworth and Gary Burtless, two economists at the Brookings Institution in Washington, D.C., studied the pension funding in national pension systems around the world and the government deficits associated with other government operations. They had data on thirteen member countries of the Organization for Economic and Cooperative Development (OECD) from 1970 through 2000. Bosworth and Burtless found that a 1 billion currency unit increase in social insurance trust funds increased the government deficit in other operations by 0.57 billion currency units. When they limited the analysis to the five countries whose policies require them to fund a portion of their national pensions—Canada, Denmark, Finland, Japan, and Sweden—they estimated the offset at 0.64 billion currency units. An increase of $1 worth of pension funding increased other government expenditures by 57 to 64 cents worth of spending, according to their estimates. In any event, the authors concluded that a unit increase in national pension funding significantly increased net deficits in other government operations.[5]

The evidence suggests that in pooled budgeting, Social Security surpluses are generally not saved. This does not mean the trust funds are worthless. The bonds are an obligation of the federal government that can be cashed as needed to pay benefits. In fact, in 2010 and 2011, Social Security ran a cash deficit, so trust fund bonds were cashed to pay benefits. Since the government was also running a deficit during those two years, cashing the trust fund bonds necessitated greater federal borrowing because of Social Security operations than would have otherwise occurred.

Social Security and Saving in a Larger Context

In one regard, the discussion about whether the Social Security trust funds contribute to national savings has been drawn too narrowly. Suppose Norman begins with a bank account balance of zero, earns $50,000 from his job, net of taxes, and, after paying his expenses, deposits $5,000 in his savings account. He also runs up another $20,000 in credit card debt. Given his $20,000 credit card debt, no one would say that Norman saved $5,000. Yet that is essentially the logic behind the claim that the U.S. Social Security program's trust fund accumulation is adding to national savings.

Following Norman's example, we can track the reported financial activities of Social Security during 2010. That year, the trust funds realized income, including all tax revenues collected and credits for interest, of $781.2 billion. It had total expenditures, including benefits and administrative expenses, of $712.5 billion. In net then, it looked to the naked eye as though the system added wealth to the tune of $68.7 billion. But the Social Security actuaries also estimate total accrued benefit obligations—that is benefits earned to date by people currently alive who have earned a future benefit stake—and those total obligations increased from $22,770.7 billion at the end of 2009 to $24,174.8 billion at the end of 2010. From this perspective, it is foolish to argue that adding $68.7 billion to Social Security's trust fund is a contribution to our national saving. We might have had added $68.7 billion to our Social Security banking account in 2010 but we also added $1.3 trillion in unfunded obligations to our credit account—essentially a credit card charge against our children's future earnings.[6]

The Power of Compound Interest and Unfunded Obligations

The gulf between the assets in our Social Security trust funds and the unfunded obligations for benefits already earned gets much wider as time passes. There is a very distinct trend here and we should expect it to continue. One reason for the trend goes back to the actuarial methods used for calculating liabilities and how these change over time. Other reasons include variations in assumptions underlying the estimates and recent economic developments. But the power of compound interest is a primary factor widening the chasm between assets and benefit obligations. If you invest $1,000 today at 5 percent simple interest, you'll have $4,321.94 in 30 years. Only $628.89 of the $3,321.94 in interest is earned in the first ten years, $1,024.40 is earned in the second ten years, and $1,668.64 is earned in the last decade.

The longer the money remains in the investment account, the more potent the interest compounding becomes, and the timing effects increase exponentially as the interest rate rises. In calculating the value of an investment 30 years from now, the initial balance is multiplied by one plus the interest rate raised to the power of 30—that is 1.05 multiplied by itself 30 times in the example here.

When the actuaries estimate Social Security's current obligations for future benefits, they use the reverse of the process I just used to calculate compound interest. To calculate the present value of a benefit that will be paid in 30 years, the future amount is divided by one plus the interest rate raised to the power of 30. For example, assume you must pay someone $10,000 in 30 years. At 5 percent interest, the present value of the $10,000 is $2,313.77. In other words, if you invested $2,313.77 today at 5 percent interest, it would compound to $10,000 in 30 years. This is basically how the Social Security actuaries estimate the present value of earned benefits payable in 30 years. But there's a catch: There is no compound interest because of the program's pay-as-you-go financing. If you dealt with your future obligation like Social Security does, 10 years down the road, you would still owe $10,000 but in 20 years instead of 30. At this point, the present value of the obligation would have grown to $3,768.89 because the future obligation would be "discounted" by the compounding factor raised to the 20th power instead of the 30th power. In another 10 years, the obligation's present value would have climbed to $6,139.13, because it would be only discounted for 10 years. Finally, on the due date, you would need to come up with $10,000.

When the term of the $10,000 future obligation declined from 30 to 20 years, the present value of the obligation rose from $2,313.77 to $3768.89—an increase of $1,455.12 over the 10 years. When the obligation was 10 years away, the present value rose to $6,139.13—a $2,370.24 increase in the second 10 years. Finally, when it was time to actually pay the $10,000, the present value grew another $3,860.87 in the last 10 years leading up to when the obligation was due. As time passed and the payoff date drew nearer, the net increase in the value of the obligation grew more in each decade than it had in the decade before. This phenomenon is accelerating the growth in Social Security obligations.

When the 1983 Social Security Amendments passed, the baby boomers ranged in age from 19 to 37—an average of some 38 to 39 years from normal retirement age. Their obligations were nearly 35 to 40 years in the future, on average, and they were being discounted accordingly. In 2010, the baby boomers ranged in age from 46 to 64—an average of 11 to 12 years from retirement. In nominal terms, the present value of a dollar's worth of Social Security benefits for the baby boomers was 3.7 times greater in 2010 than it was in 1983, simply because of the shorter discounting period used to calculate the obligations. As the baby boomers get closer to retirement, the unfunded Social Security obligations will continue to balloon.

In 2010, Social Security registered its first annual deficit since the passage of the 1983 Amendments—eight years ahead of schedule. The financing deficits were early because of high unemployment during the 2007–2008 recession and even during the recovery. Unemployment delivers a double whammy, reducing the number of workers paying payroll taxes and pushing more workers into early retirement when they can't find jobs.

The second era of "funding" our Social Security system has come to an end. Arriving at this state had nothing to do with Senator Moynihan or anyone else putting a legislative stop to funding. It was the natural aging of the baby boom in conjunction with an unanticipated and powerful economic downturn. The irony of having arrived here so far ahead of schedule is that we will realize a whole new set of experiences in the next few years that have been anticipated for decades.

The only quasi-precedent to our current situation is the financing crisis of the 1970s and early 1980s. But there are also tremendous differences between the two crises. The 1970s funding calamity was sudden and unexpected, whereas our current predicament has been forecast for at least 20 years. The need for adjustment in the 1970s could be blamed on a technical flaw introduced by the 1972 legislation and by particularly adverse economic conditions. Now we're talking about changing a program that has been operating under current rules for a couple of decades and potentially reducing benefits even as we are still phasing in the higher retirement age adopted in 1983. In 1977 and 1983, there was relatively universal agreement that we could not continue paying benefits unless modifications were made. Now, there is not even universal acceptance that we have a real financing problem, despite the fact that virtually all mainstream analysts from both political parties believe the demographic forces ahead demand changes.

Every group formed to examine Social Security policy since the early 1990s has concluded its financing must be addressed. The Social Security Trustees have broadcast the need for change in annual report after annual report. A former comptroller general of the United States, David Walker, has raised alarms about the extent of underfunding in Social Security, as well as other entitlement programs, suggesting we are digging ourselves a deeper and deeper hole. Alan Greenspan, as chairman of the Federal Reserve Board, and his successor, Ben Bernanke, have called repeatedly for balancing the program because of the long-term fiscal implications of its current configuration. Commissions both with and without congressional participation have recommended that we take up this matter with dispatch. Presidents Bill Clinton and George W. Bush both found the issue pressing enough to put their National Economic Council staffs to work developing major Social Security reform proposals and spent considerable amounts of time trying to win over the public to the idea of reform. Since the mid-1990s, the Social Security Advisory Board has issued four reports calling for policymakers to take up this matter "sooner rather than later," so the fixes can be less draconian and more incremental. But despite all the talk, not one legislative solution proposed since the 1980s has come under serious consideration by Congress.

POLICY STALEMATE AT THE DEMOGRAPHIC DIVIDE

The 1994–1996 Advisory Council on Social Security shocked many in the Washington policy community because its results and recommendations were remarkably different from those of earlier councils. President Clinton had been concerned about Social Security policy and so had appointed this group to make recommendations on setting the system right for the future. Instead of coming up with a single set of marginal recommendations to keep the existing structure standing, the thirteen council members fractured into three groups, two of which recommended individual accounts.[1] Among the issues this council was to consider were the *adequacy* of benefits and *equity* for people at different ages and income levels, as well as in various family patterns.[2] Bob Ball was on this Council, and so was I.

The two individual account proposals called for increasing contributions to Social Security. Bob Ball and his colleagues did not support individual accounts and could not bring themselves to propose higher payroll taxes. Both the individual account proposals called for restricting the available investment options to protect participants' retirement savings and streamline the investment process.

The traditional proponents of Social Security lashed out at the recommendations for individual accounts. In July 1996, Dean Baker at the Economic Policy Institute wrote that under one plan, "the individual accounts will add significant administrative expenses with no obvious benefit." Of the other plan he wrote: "The only clear winner from this plan is the finance industry. . . . The plan would not guarantee anyone a secure retirement, but it would guarantee large profits for Wall Street brokerages and banks."[3] After the report came out, Gerald Shea, an assistant to the president of the AFL-CIO at the time and a member of the Advisory Council, said the labor unions were organizing to "prevent these ideas of radical reform from getting beyond the fantasy stage."[4]

On the other side, long-time supporters of basic reforms built around individual accounts were ecstatic that an Advisory Council, traditionally an institutional mechanism for expanding the program, had legitimized the concepts they had been advocating. Until the Council's report, calls for personal savings accounts within Social Security were perceived as coming from libertarian groups ideologically opposed to the system. But the Advisory Council endorsers of individual accounts had been largely motivated by the fairness issues just over the horizon, as future cohorts of retirees faced the prospect of extremely low returns on their lifetime contributions. Even Bob Ball conceded that this was an important matter. Ball commented later:

> So the money's worth issue really became a significant part of an argument about whether to retain the system [in its current structure]. I don't see that you can duck it and I think it's a real point that needs to be dealt with.
>
> Some people try to make the case that it's irrelevant . . . which inevitably means that down the road you will have pretty high dedicated taxes for Social Security, that are quite clearly vulnerable from the standpoint of whether people who pay those rates over their lifetime are going to do as well as if they put their money in a private savings plan. So, I don't think it can be ducked.[5]

Political Stirring on Social Security Reform

After President Clinton's re-election in November 1996, he brought Erskine Bowles to the White House as his chief of staff. A Democrat and an investment banker from North Carolina, Bowles was also a practical, results-oriented manager with close ties to several prominent Southern Republicans. His first political task was negotiating a balanced budget deal with Republican leaders in the House of Representatives. The Republicans liked Bowles and felt they could trust him. At the same time, Dick Gephardt, then the House minority leader, was worried that Bowles was insufficiently committed to the Democrats' agenda. In August 1997, Clinton and House Speaker Newt Gingrich managed to wrest enough votes from moderate Republicans and conservative Democrats to pass a budget bill.[6]

About the time the president was signing the budget agreement with Newt Gingrich by his side, Clinton's pollster, Mark Penn, was reporting that 73 percent of Democratic voters favored Social Security reform that included some element of individual accounts, with younger respondents especially disposed to this approach.[7] A policy wonk by nature and a baby boomer by birth, President Clinton wanted to take on the long-term Social Security financing problem. He knew he had to build support for any policy changes and moved toward doing that on multiple fronts.

Before becoming president, Clinton had helped organize and lead the Democratic Leadership Council (DLC) to develop centrist analyses of various social problems and solutions to resolve them. The DLC was an extension of Clinton's staff but could operate outside the bright lights of scrutiny and accountability. The DLC was clearly interested in Social Security. In the fall of 1997, it invited me to spend a weekend at a private retreat in Florida, with several of its leaders and financial contributors, for a series of roundtable discussions on Social Security. They also invited Alicia Munnell, an economist closely aligned with Bob Ball; Al Fromm, president and founder of the DLC; Will Marshall, president of the Progressive Policy Institute, the DLC's research arm; and Mark Penn, the president's pollster. Dr. Munnell and I were invited to conduct a debate, of sorts, on reforming Social Security with individual accounts as part of the package.

At the end of the first day's roundtable discussions, we broke for cocktails and dinner. My wife and I were seated with Al Fromm and Will Marshall for dinner and we continued the discussion from earlier in the day. Fromm and Marshall had many questions but clearly supported reform to increase funding and seemed to embrace the idea of individual accounts. After dinner, Mark Penn described public attitudes about Social Security and various approaches to securing it for the future.

After we returned to Washington, D.C., Will Marshall and I kept in touch. He was interested in continuing developments in the Social Security reform debate. During 1998, John Shoven and I were working on *The Real Deal*, our book on the history of Social Security, and Marshall took great interest in it. In our book, Shoven and I outlined a Social Security reform proposal that included individual accounts. Our proposal was a modified and updated version of the proposal I had worked to develop with Carolyn Weaver and several other council members during my time on the Advisory Council. As we were finalizing our manuscript, we solicited a number of people familiar with Social Security policy to provide brief endorsements on the dust jacket. Will Marshall provided such an endorsement. His comment was:

> For historical perspective and analytical depth, *The Real Deal* stands
> head and shoulders above other recent books on Social Security's

future. Cutting through partisan polemics, authors Schieber and Shoven give readers a balanced and lucid account of Social Security's dilemmas, along with a well-crafted plan for modernizing the system for the demands of the twenty-first century.[8]

The Democratic Leadership Council had helped President Clinton reform the welfare system when many prominent Democrats in Congress were strongly opposed. The DLC would be vital in any Clinton effort to move forward on Social Security reform.

Clinton Seeks a Bipartisan Accord on Social Security Reform

In the fall of 1997, President Clinton seemed ready to take on Social Security. He realized he would need Republican support because a strong Democratic faction would vehemently oppose reform. Dick Gephardt, the minority leader in the House, was closely affiliated with organized labor. Making matters even more complicated for the president, Gephardt and Vice President Al Gore were both positioning themselves for presidential runs in 2000.

By the end of 1997, Clinton was laying the groundwork for both Republican political leaders and the public to start the journey toward Social Security reform. In reaching out to Republican leadership, Clinton started with House Speaker Newt Gingrich and Bill Archer from Texas, the chairman of the House Ways and Means Committee, who would play a pivotal role in Social Security policy. Historian Steven Gillon provides a fascinating glimpse into the Clinton inner sanctum and how the president and Newt Gingrich built on the relationship they developed in the budget battle to lay the groundwork for Social Security reform. Erskine Bowles proved to be the mediator who enabled the president and the Speaker to work together—neither of the political leaders trusted each other, but they both trusted Bowles.[9]

In late 1997, Clinton told Chairman Archer he wanted to solve Social Security's and Medicare's financing problems and was willing to take the political heat of working with the Republicans. Archer was convinced that Clinton was sincere and was impressed with his overture. At the same time that Clinton was reaching out to Archer, Erskine Bowles was reaching out to New Gingrich with the same proposition.[10] In subsequent negotiations between President Clinton, Speaker Gingrich, and Chairman Archer, the broad parameters of reform took shape. Gillon later interviewed Gingrich and Bruce Reed, who served as Clinton's domestic policy advisor and director of the Domestic Policy Council. Gillon's take is that both Clinton and Gingrich "believed that any effort to update Social Security would require government to incorporate some measure of choice, and that meant some form of privately managed account." Gillon quotes Reed as saying, "There was really only one plausible policy compromise. That was to have private accounts on top of security. That would give the Republicans what they wanted but leave Social Security intact." Gingrich was willing to go along with a tax increase if the reforms included personal accounts.[11]

At the same time that President Clinton was negotiating with Republican leaders from the House of Representatives, other developments bode well for their efforts. As the Social Security Advisory Council was winding down at the end of 1996, the National Commission on Retirement Policy—a group convened by the Center for Strategic and International Studies, a Washington think tank—was getting under way. This group issued a report in early 1998 calling for several adjustments to bring Social Security financing back into balance, including diverting two percentage points of the payroll tax into individual accounts. The most notable aspect of this development was that the Commission's members included Senators John Breaux, a Democrat from Louisiana; Judd Gregg, a Republican from New Hampshire; Representatives Jim Kolbe, a Republican from Arizona; and Charlie Stenholm, a Democrat from Texas. Bipartisan congressional support would be critical in bringing Social Security reform to closure.

In early 1998, Clinton launched a yearlong, bipartisan national conversation about our aging population and Social Security financing. At a forum in Kansas City, the president laid down several principles that should guide reform:

1. Strengthen and protect Social Security for the 21st century
2. Maintain universality and fairness
3. Provide a benefit people can count on
4. Preserve financial security for low-income and disabled beneficiaries
5. Maintain fiscal discipline

The president also made clear that all reform options—other than higher payroll tax rates—should be on the table.[12] He indicated that he would entertain "letting workers invest part of their Social Security taxes in the stock market, instead of having the Social Security Administration invest those taxes in Treasury bills."[13]

President Clinton's ideas did not meet with universal approval. *The Progressive*, a publication describing itself as a "monthly leftwing magazine of investigative reporting, political commentary, cultural coverage, activism, interviews, poetry, and humor,"[14] editorialized that Bill Clinton would go down as the "gravedigger of the New Deal." As for his "privatization" proposal, the editorial continued, "for people who depend on Social Security for survival, it could be a nightmare. . . . Privatization would also undermine the commitment to universality, the idea that our government has an obligation to all of us to ensure that we have certain basic necessities, like the ability to retire without going broke."[15]

Forming a Concrete Social Security Reform Proposal

As the public discussion of Social Security that President Clinton was orchestrating was getting under way, a series of high-level meetings were convened within his Administration. A working group, jointly chaired by Gene Sperling, the director of the President's National Economic Council, and Larry Summers, the deputy secretary of Treasury, met once or twice a week. Sperling and Summers were busy with broad portfolios of responsibilities but attended meetings at least once every two or three weeks. The president joined periodically as well. The last Advisory Council had been widely criticized because of its split, but the Clinton Administration's working group used the Council's results as their launching pad for further work on the options. Insiders later observed that "despite the divisions on the [advisory council], the majority of members supported some sort of individual accounts as part of Social Security. Thus, the idea of individual accounts had, in a few short years, made a remarkable transition from the white papers of libertarian think tanks to the mainstream policy debate."[16]

The working group within the Clinton Administration never specifically proposed individual accounts, but it was clearly heading in that direction. The plans scoped out the resources that would be required for the administration of private accounts and even considered forming a group to set up an administrative system, so the program could be up and running before President Clinton left office. Three of the individuals involved later described the level of detail as follows:

> The information technology staffs at the Treasury Department and the Social Security Administration were given the task of determining exactly how information and dollars would flow from workers' earnings statements to private investment managers. Extremely detailed estimates were produced of how much additional manpower would be necessary for such a system to function. For example, one option was for workers to indicate their choices of private sector fund managers on

their 1040 tax forms. The working group went so far as to determine how many digits would be needed for each fund's ID number and therefore how many key strokes would be required to enter all of the ID numbers each year. Separate estimates of cost and necessary manpower were produced depending on whether the processing would occur by May of each year (sharply increasing IRS workload during its peak period) or by early August (which was much cheaper).[17]

When the 1994–1996 Advisory Council published its multiple recommendations, Bob Ball characterized individual accounts as "radical" reengineering of Social Security. Only a year later, here was a Democrat, President Bill Clinton, developing such a proposal down to the detail of how many keystrokes it would take to record workers' annual account contributions. By early 1998, Clinton was ready to lay out his plans in the State of the Union scheduled for January 27.

Reform Derailed by Unrelated Events

On January 21, 1998, the lead story in the *Washington Post* was about Bill Clinton's affair with Monica Lewinsky. This is not the place to retell the Clinton-Lewinsky story. What is important is Erskine Bowles's summary that "Monica changed everything"[18] in the discussions between the president and Gingrich. Clinton had been strong-arming the liberal House Democrats and Gingrich was doing the same with the fire-brand conservatives among the House Republicans. But Clinton could not push House Democrats to vote for Social Security reform, including individual accounts, if he wanted Dick Gephardt's support in the impeachment battle ahead. On the other side, partisan Republicans smelled Clinton's blood and were not about to let Gingrich's aspirations to be a historical figure on Social Security stop their feeding frenzy. The journalist Joe Klein, interviewing Clinton toward the end of his term, asked him about the damage done by the Lewinsky affair. Clinton said he regretted that "we didn't get to do Social Security. I think maybe we could have gotten it if we hadn't had that whole impeachment thing."[19]

The next year, in his 1999 State of the Union address, President Clinton unveiled a reform proposal calling for contributing budget surpluses to the Social Security trust funds instead of creating individual accounts. He also proposed that the trust funds be partially invested in the stock market. Under the Clinton proposal, the government would use the budget surplus to pay off government bonds held by private investors and credit Social Security's trust funds each year for the subsequent reduction in interest charges. So the credits would not be for revenues collected but rather for expenses not incurred.

One criticism of the proposal was that most of the surpluses in the unified budget were due to the Social Security surpluses for which the trust funds had already been credited. Some critics saw this as double counting. In 1998, the federal unified budget ran a surplus of $82.1 billion. The Social Security trust funds collected $97.2 billion more in tax revenues that year than the program spent on benefits and administrative expenses. But the Social Security surplus was already embedded in the unified budget surplus. This meant that, not counting Social Security transactions, the rest of the budget was in deficit by $15 billion. Social Security had already been credited with the $97.2 billion but would have been credited for another $50 billion or so under the Clinton proposal. For every dollar of Social Security surplus in the unified surplus, Social Security was going to be credited with $1.62. The president's own staff understood this proposal was open to criticism, as a group of them would later write:

> One important disadvantage of these plans was their vulnerability to the charge of "double counting" the Social Security surplus. Much of the projected unified budget surpluses originated in Social Security and therefore were already credited to the Social Security trust fund under current law. Thus, according to the critics, transferring unified surpluses to Social Security caused the same dollars of revenue in effect to be counted twice to the benefit of Social Security.[20]

The people who worked on Clinton's Social Security reform proposals were smart, and President Clinton was widely recognized as having a better grasp of the substance of such proposals than many who have occupied the Oval Office. They knew that any proposal for Social Security reform or financing would come under tremendous scrutiny. So you may wonder how they could rationalize bringing this sort of proposal to the table. Here it is:

> . . . the status quo involved precisely the same approach to budgeting: as long as the budget process was focused on balancing the unified budget, dollars that were credited to the Social Security trust fund were still perceived to be available for new spending or tax cuts. The administration's economic team believed that a dollar of the unified budget surplus could therefore legitimately be transferred to Social Security and credited to the trust fund, provided that the [transfer] would take the dollar off the table and prevent it from being used for other

purposes. In that case, the transfer would result in an extra dollar's worth of public debt being paid down relative to the status quo, and therefore an extra dollar of government saving.[21]

Arguing that double counting Social Security revenues was okay because those revenues have historically been counted as both trust fund and unified budget surpluses in the past did not pass the smell test for most involved observers. Developers of the package admitted that "the administration was well aware that the approach had 'bad optics' and internally a number of economists argued vigorously against adopting a plan that would be subject to this criticism."[22]

An added wrinkle in Clinton's plan was the proposed creation of Universal Savings Accounts called USA Accounts. These accounts would receive an automatic contribution by the government, a refund of a portion of the budget surplus, for all workers earning less than a specified amount and a matching contribution for workers earning more than that amount but with incomes below a certain threshold. The underlying motivation for these accounts was to serve as a bridge between the proponents and opponents of individual accounts for Social Security.

After Clinton was out of office, Bob Ball claimed that he had played an important role in developing the structure of the plan that the Clinton Administration ultimately released.

> I had a lot to do with what the Clinton Administration came out with. Gene Sperling chaired the continuing group in the White House that was looking at Social Security for a couple of years. It was a group made up of top people—it wasn't some technical group. . . . I must say they started with some willingness to consider individual accounts—Summers and Sperling both. At Sperling's request, I wrote a series of memos that were circulated to the group and I met with them a couple of times. That's really the measure of my involvement with the Administration.[23]

The Clinton package received no support from Republicans and little from Democrats in Congress.

Shifting from Policy Development to Political Rhetoric

In the 2000 presidential election campaign, Social Security was a hot issue and candidates had to discuss their plans with voters. As the race narrowed to George W. Bush and Al Gore, the focus became sharper. The two candidates were clearly committed to different visions regarding Social Security policy.

Bush made Social Security reform a central element of his agenda. He advocated sparing retirees and those near retirement any changes, and preserving disability and survivor protections. His reform would allow young workers to voluntarily invest part of their Social Security taxes in personal retirement accounts, and the government would not invest Social Security funds in the stock market. He believed people should be able to invest—not politicians. Finally, he would not increase Social Security payroll taxes. Protecting survivors, the disabled, and those retired or close to it would garner virtually universal approval by Washington policymakers on both sides of the aisle. But proposing to finance individual accounts out of existing payroll tax rates became the basis for the Democrats to accuse Bush of being out to destroy Social Security.

Al Gore talked about setting up a "lock box" so the trust funds could not be spent elsewhere. He also advocated paying down the federal debt with the surplus and crediting the trust funds with the saved interest, retreading Clinton's proposal that had never gained traction. He kept the USA account element of the Clinton package and regularly referred to his plan for reform as "Social Security Plus," echoing Bob Ball's description of the plans he was supporting. But the campaign literature that Gore and the Democratic National Committee ran during fall 2000 did not mention Al Gore's Social Security proposals—the ads focused on George Bush's proposal.

Bush's refusal to increase the payroll tax rate but to allow younger workers to divert a share of their payroll taxes to their individual accounts implied that some of Social Security's projected revenue stream would be unavailable to pay benefits. The Democrats quickly put a $1 trillion price tag on this part of the plan. With the system already scheduled to run short in the 2030s, diverting a trillion dollars of revenues while paying current benefits to near-term retirees would bring the system to insolvency that much sooner.

Al Gore stated the argument clearly in one of the nationally televised campaign debates—the Bush proposal was promising young workers they could take a trillion dollars out of the system for their own accounts while also promising beneficiaries that the trillion dollars would be available to pay their benefits.[24] If the Republicans could make hay by attacking Bill Clinton's Social Security reforms for double counting, turnaround was fair play. During the campaign that fall, Gore ran three commercials on Social Security, one of them featuring Bob Ball. All three focused entirely on the $1 trillion that George Bush intended to take out of the trust funds for individual accounts while also promising the money to retirees. The Democratic National Committee ran two ads making the same point.[25] None of their commercials mentioned how they intended to resolve the Social Security financing problem.

Another Commission and Sharp Reactions Hold Stage

Shortly after George Bush assumed office, he pressed forward with his plans to reform Social Security. On May 2, 2001, his Administration announced the formation of a 16-member Commission to Strengthen Social Security. The commission was charged to make recommendations to modernize and restore fiscal soundness to Social Security.[26] As soon as the commission and its membership were announced, the attacks began. Critics claimed the president had a litmus test for membership—support for individual accounts. While the membership included eight Democrats and eight Republicans, the appointed Democrats had not been vetted and approved by congressional or other party leaders. Democrats in Congress complained that there were no "real" Democrats on the commission. One vice chair of the commission was former Democratic Senator Daniel Patrick Moynihan, whom many considered a traitorous "privatizer" for proposing to cut payroll taxes and let workers put the difference into individual accounts. Richard Parsons, CEO of AOL/Time Warner at the time, was the Republican vice chair. Many Democrats viewed the entire commission as a "Cato-dominated Trojan Horse,"[27] referring to the conservative Cato Institute think tank in Washington.

The commission published two reports, one in August 2001, which set out the problems facing the current system, and the final report in December 2001, which recommended solutions. Once again, there were three proposals instead of one, but each featured some form of voluntary personal account. Commission members, along with the Bush Administration, favored option two, which proposed allowing workers to redirect up to 4 percentage points of the payroll taxes—up to $1,000 annually—to a personal account. The $1,000 maximum would be indexed to wage growth. Workers with individual accounts would receive a lower traditional Social Security benefit when they retired to reflect their reduced contributions plus interest. Under the plan, anyone with at least 30 years of covered wages would receive a benefit of at least 120 percent of the official poverty line. In the future, the initial benefit calculation would be based on the growth rate of the consumer price index (CPI) rather than the growth of wages. While the actuarial projections indicated that the combined system would need to borrow from general revenues starting in 2025, it would pay off all loans by 2054. After that, the long-term financing outlook would be positive, according to the projections.[28]

The Commission's reports came under blistering attacks. In addition to rhetorical condemnation of the concept of individual accounts, the critics focused on two primary issues: the transition cost of creating the individual accounts and the reductions in traditional benefits. There were also concerns about the future of disability benefits, the effects on women's benefits, and others, but most of the objections focused on transition costs and benefit reductions.

The transition costs arise from the shift toward greater funding of Social Security obligations than had occurred in the pay-as-you-go past. Building up savings while paying current benefits requires extra money. Peter Diamond and Peter Orszag estimated the transition costs of implementing option two at $2.2 to $2.8 trillion in 2001 dollars.[29] However, Diamond and Orszag purposefully omitted two crucial elements from their analysis. First, they only assessed the implications of the proposed reform on the 75-year projection period. While shifting to individual accounts, whatever the size, has up-front costs, funding a greater share of benefits becomes much more economically efficient over the long term, given our demographic outlook. Second, they ignored the significant underfunding in the current system over the next 75 years. In 2002, the Social Security actuaries estimated the underfunding at $3.3 trillion in present value terms, and in early 2011, the estimated underfunding rose to $6.5 trillion.

In 2011, we faced at least $6.5 trillion in transition costs no matter what policy path we followed—even under the current structure. To comply with the law, benefits over the projection period must be fully financed by revenues and assets. In fact, because we could not invest an extra $6.5 trillion in our pay-as-you-go system, the cost will be $6.5 trillion plus foregone interest on that amount. To top that, we know that, barring corrective legislation, the $6.5 trillion shortfall estimated for the 75-year period starting in 2011 will be much larger in future 75-year periods. A fair comparison of the Bush Commission package with Diamond's and Orszag's favored proposal, which they published later,[30] would have made the transition cost in the commission plan look like a bargain.

Diamond and Orszag also compared the modified benefits under the commission's proposal to the benefits under current law, specifically projected benefits for future retirees. They concluded that indexing initial benefits to the CPI rather than to wages would reduce benefits.[31] Wages generally grow more rapidly than prices. Basing initial benefits on wage growth keeps the replacement rate—the share of preretirement earnings paid out—relatively constant over time.

Many Social Security participants do not understand the implications of wage-indexing initial benefits. The Social Security actuaries estimate that a worker they classify as a "low earner" (based on her average lifetime earnings used to determine benefits) qualified for a benefit of $10,232 at age 65 in 2011. They project that a low earner retiring at age 65 in 2061 will qualify for a benefit worth $17,080 in 2011 dollars, an increase of $6,848. For the medium worker, the 2011 benefit was estimated to be $16,860, and the 2061 benefit $28,143 in 2011 dollars, an increase of $11,283. For the maximum earner, the corresponding numbers are $26,573 and $45,466, or an increase of $18,893.[32] The system is structured to provide much greater inflation adjusted increases in initial benefits to higher earners over time than to those at lower earnings levels. In a system that is underfunded, this feature of the system suggests that slowing benefit growth for higher earners might be one way to provide financing relief.

Given the state of Social Security's funding and its dire need for rebalancing, it is hard to look at those numbers without considering that future benefits could be adjusted without inflicting undue hardship, especially for higher earners. In table 10–1, the purchasing power of benefits at all earnings levels grows by 75 percent to 80 percent for a 65-year-old retiring in 2066 versus 2011, and purchasing power increases nearly three times as much for maximum earners as for low earners.

The Bush Commission's option two sought to increase traditional Social Security benefits for lower-earning workers and trim them a little for higher earners—but to give higher-earning workers the opportunity to make up the reduction in the individual accounts. In their analysis of option two, Diamond and Orszag characterized the net effect of the proposal as a benefit cut—a 10-percentage-point reduction for low earners, a 21 percent reduction for medium earners, and a 25 percent reduction for high earners in 2075.[33] But these "reductions" were calibrated against benefits under current law, which the system was projected to be unable to pay. Diamond and Orszag did not mention that in 2075, incoming revenue will equal 13.28 percent of covered payroll while projected benefits will be 17.03 percent of payroll, according to the actuaries' projections. In other words, promised benefits are underfunded by nearly 30 percent, and under current law, unfunded benefits cannot be paid.

Charles Blahous, executive director of the Commission to Strengthen Social Security and a staff member working for President Bush on Social Security policy, wrote a book about their proposals, describing in some detail the motivations for what they recommended and the reactions to them.[34]

In retrospect, George W. Bush's no-new-taxes rule proved to be a serious problem for Social Security reform. Current payroll taxes—at 12.4 percent of covered payroll—should be enough to finance a reasonable benefit in a funded retirement program. It clearly falls at the outside range of what Franklin Roosevelt, Arthur Altmeyer and Edwin Witte thought would be tolerable to workers.

Bill Clinton had also insisted that Social Security reform could not include raising taxes.[35] When President Bush called for individual accounts but without higher payroll tax rates, however, the Democrats accused him of creating an unacceptable precondition. They told the American people that Bush was creating an added "trillion-dollar" hole in Social Security financing and that his proposals would make the situation worse, not better.

Critics of Bush's proposal admitted that staying the current course was not an option, and that the choices were to increase benefits or reduce taxes, but going the Bush route would require us to do it sooner. Andrew Biggs, a strong advocate of individual accounts who left the Cato Institute to become a principle staffer for Bush's Commission to Strengthen Social Security, has recently written:

> With personal accounts, we face the same choices, only sooner. If workers invest part of their Social Security taxes in personal accounts, they could indeed earn higher returns and generate higher benefits without taking more risk. But diverting taxes to accounts leaves the program short of what is needed to pay benefits to today's retirees. To cover these "transition costs," we would need to generate new revenues for the program, either by raising taxes, cutting other programs, or borrowing.[36]

After President Bush was reelected in 2004, he intended to spend some of his political capital on pushing Social Security reform. In a series of public meetings around the country in 2005, the president explained the problems we faced and the general approach he wanted to take. I participated in two of those public meetings. They were staged for the president to open the meeting and outline the problem, after which a technical expert would explain the issues in somewhat more detail. Then the president would conduct a round-table discussion of Social Security with three or four people from the local community. After each session, the participants were escorted offstage and the president spoke briefly with each of them. He also posed for pictures with local participating citizens and their families.

I participated in the sessions he held in Omaha, Nebraska, and Galveston, Texas. I had a brief private chat with the president about Social Security after each of the public sessions. In Omaha, the president commented in his opening remarks that because we are:

> . . . living longer, you've got people who have been made promises by the government, receiving checks for a longer period of time than was initially envisioned under Social Security. Secondly, the benefits that had been promised are increasing, so you've got more—and thirdly, baby boomers like me and (Senator) Hagel and a bunch of others are getting ready to retire. So you've got *more people retiring, living longer, with the promise of greater benefits.* The problem is that the number of people putting money into the system (per beneficiary) is declining. So you can see the mathematical problem, right? Greater promises to more people who are living longer, with fewer payers. That's a problem—particularly when you start doing the math.[37]

After the session in Galveston, which would have been toward the end of his tour, he said to me: "You know Syl, I think these individual accounts are getting in the way of us having a meaningful discussion about the Social Security financing issue we are facing." The president clearly understood the problem, and I think he came to appreciate that the individual-account tack was getting in the way of the ultimate goal. Policymakers ultimately will have no choice but to consider benefit reductions or else new revenues when they take up Social Security reform—with or without individual accounts.

Roadblock to Reform

The fact that Bill Clinton and George W. Bush reached similar conclusions about Social Security suggests the possibility of common ground for Republicans and Democrats. President Barack Obama's repeated references to addressing Social Security and other entitlement claims is an encouraging sign. But the roadblocks that threw Bill Clinton and George Bush off the track suggest tremendous hurdles to conducting a rational conversation on reform.

For several years, I believed that some of those who headed off Social Security reform feared a groundswell supporting individual accounts, which are an anathema to them. But now I think their opposition is more fundamental. In my last three years on the Social Security Advisory Board, while I was chairman, one of the members was Barbara Kennelly. In a conversation with her shortly after Obama became president, she helped me understand why it is so difficult to hold an open dialogue about reform.

Kennelly is a Democrat who represented the first congressional district of Connecticut from 1982 to 1999. As a member of the House Ways and Means Committee, she was exposed to Social Security policy debates from the program's crisis early on to the seemingly golden period toward the end of Bill Clinton's White House term. She served as the House Democratic Whip. From 2002 until 2011, she was president of the National Committee to Save Social Security and Medicare, which has millions of members and raises millions of dollars annually to lobby Congress on Social Security and Medicare issues.

In our conversation, Kennelly expressed her consternation at the President's intention to tackle Social Security after enacting health care reform. I suggested that it was quite natural—he had campaigned for the youth vote, was by nature a bit of a policy wonk drawn to big issues, and that Social Security reform posed a natural challenge from both a political and practical perspective. Barbara conceded all of that but said that no serious politician would consider raising payroll taxes now, which leaves reducing benefits as the only option. The unsaid but implicit conclusion in her statement was that we can't increase our contributions now and save them in a way that gives us meaningful financing relief later—added revenues put into the trust funds cannot be saved. All that is left is benefit cuts if we do anything now. She could not understand why any elected Democrats would ever want to put themselves in that no-win position. The implication of Kennelly's observation, as I see it, is that some policymakers will avoid taking up Social Security reform until the trust funds are nearly depleted and we again face the prospect of coming up short on the monthly payroll.

UNDERSTANDING SOCIAL SECURITY IN MODERN TIMES

After all the discussion about Social Security's evolution and operations, it is probably worthwhile to step back and review what the program does for us. In its early years, there was some dispute over whether Social Security was "insurance," and arguments over its nature have continued. The program serves several purposes and can be characterized in different ways. Some roles have been purposefully blended, which can complicate sorting out the different functions. A clear understanding of Social Security's provisions and their operations clarifies the program's place in our retirement system.

The Role of Insurance in Our Lives

Insurance is a mechanism that allows a group of people to join together to spread individual risk, usually from a financially devastating contingency. For example, imagine that you live in a small society of 100 households, and each householder owns a home that, with its insurable contents, would cost $100,000 to replace. For simplicity, further assume that when a house catches on fire, it burns to the ground. Finally, assume a consistent probability that 1 percent of the houses—that is, one house—will burn down each year, but no one knows which one. Lacking insurance, the homeowner whose house burned down would face a catastrophic financial burden. A way out of the risk is to buy fire insurance and insure the house for $100,000. In this simplified example—ignoring administration and other costs—the insurance company collects $1,000 in premiums from each homeowner to cover the known probability of its annual fire claims. The insured homeowners receive value equivalent to the probability of their house burning down (1 percent) times the replacement value of the structure and its contents ($100,000) or $1,000 (i.e., .01 x $100,000 = $1,000). In other words, all insurance-holders receive the actuarial equivalent of their insurance premium in value each year, whether or not their house burns down.

Social Security's Insurance Protections

Theoretically, Social Security could operate very much like the above fire insurance example. The program replaces the earnings of those who can no longer work. These "hazards," in insurance language, or "vicissitudes," as Franklin Roosevelt called them, include dying and leaving dependent children, becoming disabled, and getting too old to earn a living anymore. In an insurance context, however, the nature of the risks insured under Social Security varies considerably from one program element to the next.

Preretirement Survivor Insurance

Social Security provides insurance protection against the risk of workers dying and leaving children younger than 18 without enough money. The probability of a U.S. worker between the ages of 20 and 65 dying and leaving behind a child under age 18 is less than 0.25 percent. This is similar to the house fire example in that it doesn't happen often and insurance can spread the risk across the broad working population.

Private insurance companies can provide much the same insurance protection as Social Security, but some public-good features would be difficult for private insurance to replicate. For example, Social Security's benefits are redistributional—they replace a larger share of earnings for surviving children of low earners than of high earners, who are more likely to have supplemental life insurance policies. Running the program through the national government with mandatory participation for virtually all workers is economically efficient. As it now stands, we can guarantee universal coverage, no marketing costs, and efficient administration.

Disability Insurance

Disability Insurance provided through Social Security extends earnings protection to people unable to support themselves by working. The probability of becoming disabled under the program is less than 2 percent in any given year, even for workers in their late 50s, according to the 2005 incidence rates. Given the stringent definition of disability and qualification process, once someone becomes eligible, he or she generally remains on the rolls. As a result, as workers age, the cumulative probability of being disabled rises steadily. By the time covered workers reach their early 60s, the probability of being disabled under the program climbs to 15 percent. While that may seem high, people entering the disability program at those ages would qualify for early retirement benefits anyway at age 62. Across the disability-insured population, the disability prevalence was 4.3 percent at the end of 2004.

The disability program realizes the same relative efficiencies as the preretirement survivor insurance, namely a government-run, nationalized, mandatory participation program. After more than a half century, however, it is time to revisit the definition of disability. While Social Security is making progress on cleaning out processing backlogs, the program desperately needs modernizing.

Insurance against Bad Labor Market Outcomes

As has been discussed in earlier chapters, Social Security benefits are intended to replace a higher share of earnings for low-wage workers than for high earners. This was built into the system from the time benefits were first paid in 1940. The program literature describes this redistributional feature as an attempt to meet an "income adequacy" goal. While it has not been widely characterized this way, the redistributive benefit formula is actually an insurance feature that protects workers from having bad labor market outcomes carried fully into retirement.

At the outset of our careers, none of us can be certain we will succeed. Many people born into the most modest circumstances become smashing successes. Similarly, others seem destined for glory when they're starting out but then fail miserably along the way. We cannot expect private insurance to match the redistributional element in Social Security. As long as we do not want to force those who were unsuccessful in their working careers to live out their retirement in poverty, this mechanism should be part of our retirement structure. The stated goals of Social Security's redistributional mechanism, however, are not met by the outcomes, and so this area deserves review, and benefit enhancement is likely in order.

Some believe the discrepancy arises from Social Security's spousal benefits, which are paid to a worker's spouse based on the worker's earnings. This is different from a survivor retirement benefit, which will be discussed later. Spouses who have no earnings subject to payroll taxes can receive 50 percent of the benefit their covered spouse is collecting in retirement. If a husband's or wife's benefit is less than half the spouse's benefit, the system tops up the benefit to 50 percent of the benefit of the more highly paid spouse. Empirical evidence suggests that the spousal benefit provided by Social Security overrides much of the redistributive aspect of the benefit formula.[1]

Insurance against Myopia Regarding the Need to Save for Retirement

Without Social Security or other retirement savings programs, people would be left on their own to figure out when to start saving for retirement, how much to save, what to do with the accumulating balances, and so forth. Many people are simply not very good at this. Some wait too long to start saving or don't save enough or both. In chapter 9, I talked about the power of compound interest and the time value of money. When left to their own druthers, however, even those who know they should start early are often inclined to put it off as long as possible, sometimes too long to ever catch up. Savings programs like Social Security protect us by not giving us the choice of when we begin the game or how much we save.

Some workers do not like being "forced" into Social Security because it intrudes on their own free choice and abilities to manage their own lives. Society has a larger interest, however, in ensuring acceptable standards of living for the elderly. To the extent the public agrees on this, it is reasonable to force people to save for their retirement. One of Franklin Roosevelt's fundamental motivations for signing the Social Security Act was to avoid having the elderly become wards of the state. He clearly viewed his Social Security program as vastly superior to the "dole."

Insurance against Longevity Risk

Social Security pays its benefits monthly until a beneficiary dies. Providing retirement security entails delivery of income to meet an individual's economic needs from the date he or she retires until death. Without an annuity, people must cope with the uncertainties of life expectancy as they prepare for retirement, which poses multiple problems. First, not knowing the duration of retirement makes it hard to know how much to save. Saving too little leads to an impoverished old age. But saving too much could impose deprivation on young and middle-aged workers. In retirement, people face a different dilemma, namely how much they can spend without running out of assets. Spending too much in the early retirement period could mean poverty later. But skimping too much early on could subject the retiree to unnecessary hardship and leave a pot of money for somebody else to enjoy after the retiree dies.

Participating in a group can ameliorate many of these retirement saving and spending risks. President Roosevelt insisted on providing benefits in the form of annuities, so Social Security recipients could not outlive their monthly retirement checks.

Spousal Survivor Insurance during Retirement

The original Social Security Act provided benefits only for retirees. The 1939 Amendments added survivor protection for retirees' spouses, which has proven to be a crucial benefit. When a primary breadwinner dies, the surviving spouse is often left in dire straits. Yet research has shown that, unless survivor protection is required in retirement plans, it is often not provided. Virtually all the research analyzing the low rates of joint-and-survivor annuity selection before the adoption of the Retirement Equity Act in 1983—which requires written consent from a spouse if a joint-and-survivor annuity is not chosen—found that a surviving spouse, generally the wife, lost pension income when the annuitant died, and suffered a subsequent deterioration in economic status. This phenomenon largely accounted for the high rates of poverty among aged widows. The ongoing prevalence of poverty among older widows suggests the need to enhance survivor benefits, which could be financed by an adjustment to retiree benefits when both spouses are still living.

Insurance against Inflation

When the Social Security Act was adopted in the midst of the economic challenges of the 1930s, no one was overly concerned about the potential effects of either wage or price inflation on benefits. But it soon became apparent that both forms of inflation required policymakers' attention. Through the end of the 1960s, policymakers reacted to inflation largely on an ad hoc basis, which prompted concerns that they were adjusting benefits for political purposes. In 1972, Congress adopted automatic benefit adjustment features to protect workers and retirees against the corrosive effects of inflation.

Most people receiving Social Security benefits have little recourse against inflation. The automatic indexation of Social Security benefits almost fully protects retirees with little or no other income against inflation. As few other forms of retirement income have this protection, Social Security benefits have become an increasingly important part of retirees' income portfolio the longer they live after retiring. While major financial institutions could provide inflation-protected annuities, Social Security is the only broadly available retirement system providing such protection to date.

The high rates of poverty among the older elderly, especially older women, suggest a need for added benefit protections. In 2008, the poverty rate was 4.9 percent for married men ages 65 and older and 5.0 percent for married women. For those 65 and older who were widowed, the poverty rates were 10.2 percent for men and 15.4 percent for women. Rates were higher for the divorced—11.0 percent and 19.5, respectively—and for the never married—16.8 percent and 18.1 percent, respectively.[2] The higher poverty rates among the divorced and widowed may arise from a flaw in the benefit design but more likely reflects the low benefits paid to workers with a history of low earnings. In any event, the poverty rates deserve review.

Social Security Is Only Part of U.S. Retirement Security

When Franklin Roosevelt introduced the proposals that ultimately became the 1935 Social Security Act, he wanted to provide immediate relief for the elderly who had been badly battered by the Depression, but he also wanted an ongoing retirement saving program that would enable workers to contribute enough to cover their own retirement claims. In a message to Congress on January 17, 1935, the president outlined his goals:

> In the important field of security for our old people, it seems necessary to adopt three principles: First, non-contributory old-age pensions for those who are now too old to build up their own insurance. It is, of course, clear that for perhaps thirty years to come funds will have to be provided by the States and the Federal Government to meet these pensions. Second, compulsory contributory annuities which in time will establish a self-supporting system for those now young and for future generations. Third, voluntary contributory annuities by which individual initiative can increase the annual amounts received in old age. It is proposed that the Federal Government assume one-half of the cost of the old-age pension plan, which ought ultimately to be supplanted by self-supporting annuity plans.[3]

What President Roosevelt referred to as "old-age pensions" developed into the Old-Age Assistance provisions in the Social Security Act. These were means-tested benefits provided to people older than 65 who could not support themselves. This program was jointly financed with the states on a 50-50 basis. The compulsory contributory annuity program evolved into what most people today consider Social Security. The voluntary annuity program was dropped during the legislative consideration of Roosevelt's proposals.

Roosevelt strongly believed that workers needed help in saving for retirement but he also recognized the limitations of government. After the Social Security Act passed, he reflected on the motivation and purpose of the new law:

> Because it has become increasingly difficult for individuals to build their own security single-handed, Government must now step in and help them lay the foundation stones . . .
>
> The Act does not offer anyone, either individually or collectively, an easy life—nor was it ever intended so to do. None of the sums of money paid out to individuals in assistance or in insurance will spell anything approaching abundance. But they will furnish that minimum necessity to keep a foothold; and that is the kind of protection Americans want.[4]

Roosevelt firmly believed that workers needed to save on their own to build on the base that Social Security would provide. In a message to Congress on January 16, 1939, Roosevelt said: "We shall make the most lasting progress if we recognize that Social Security can furnish only a base upon which each one of our citizens may build his individual security through his own individual efforts."[5]

From time to time, one hears it said that Social Security is not a retirement program. In part, this comes from its supporters' descriptions of the program. For example, the Social Security historian's website has a series of posters published by the Social Security Administration after the passage of the 1939 Amendments, which added survivor and spousal benefits to the program. Under each poster, the historian has added the statement: "This poster announces the passage of the 1939 Social Security Amendments. These important amendments transformed Social Security from a retirement program for individual workers into a family income security program—providing retirement, survivors, and dependents benefits."[6] The contention also emanates from critics arguing that Social Security is an old-age welfare program that takes money from people who work and gives it to people who, for the most part, do not.[7]

From the worker's perspective, accumulating pension rights through a pay-as-you-go system is no different from accumulating wealth through personal savings or a funded pension, although they each pose very different legal and political risks. Indeed, many analyses of the economic status of individuals approaching retirement treat Social Security wealth, pension and retirement plan savings, and other personal wealth as equivalent.[8]

James Poterba, Steven Venti, and David Wise developed estimates of household asset holdings among a representative sample population aged 63 to 67 in 2000. They based their estimates on the Health and Retirement Study financed by the National Institute of Aging, which is part of the National Institute of Health. They divided the study population by lifetime earnings based on Social Security records, and then estimated the lifetime values of Social Security, employer pension and savings plans, home equity and other assets for the sample members, all of whom were retired or approaching retirement. Ignoring the bottom 10 percent and top 10 percent of the income distribution, both of which are unique, Social Security and employer-sponsored pensions and retirement savings plans averaged roughly the same values consistently across the earnings spectrum. Social Security also averaged about one-third the value of total assets across all earnings levels.[9] Social Security is an extremely important part of the "retirement" security portfolios of almost all workers. Anyone who contends that it is not a retirement program, albeit one with a number of unique features, is ignoring the facts.

EMPLOYER-BASED PENSION PROVISION

The greatest griefs are those we cause ourselves.

—SOPHOCLES

EMPLOYER PENSIONS TAKING ROOT

We briefly explored the early development of employer-sponsored pensions in chapter 2 and now take a closer look. Today, U.S. employer-sponsored retirement plans pay out more in annual benefits than Social Security. Yet, this vital cog in our retirement system has been buffeted by political missteps and economic setbacks in recent years and is in the midst of a tremendous transition. Many workers are as dismayed about the state of our employer-sponsored retirement programs as they are about Social Security, and some blame their employers. They believe they had a deal—a pension in exchange for their loyalty and hard work—and now the employer is reneging. The real story is more complicated than what appears in the periodic news story about employer pensions.

Through the end of the 19th century, private-sector pensions in the United States were largely concentrated in the rail industry. But by the turn of the century, Yale, Harvard, Cornell, and the University of California had established pension plans to retire elderly faculty members. Around the turn of the century, Andrew Carnegie became concerned that the low wages paid to faculty members in higher education doomed them to an impoverished old age. In 1905, with an endowment of $10 million, Carnegie established a free pension system for college professors. By 1906, 52 institutions had been accepted under the umbrella of the system. Ultimately, 96 institutions retired eligible faculty under this system. While Carnegie's system ran out of funding and had to be closed to new entrants, it served as the predecessor of the Teachers Insurance and Annuity Association of America created in 1918.[1] Around the turn of the century, public utilities also began setting up retirement plans. By 1911, street rail employers sponsored 7 of the 11 public utility plans, which tended to be structured like those in the larger railroad firms.[2]

During the second decade of the 20th century, retirement benefits spread to other industries, including banking and insurance.

Employers that required organization-specific "human capital" began to structure their plans to encourage longevity, according to Leslie Hannah. He also points out that the second decade of the 20th century witnessed a growing appreciation that retirement plans could be structured to encourage desirable behavior on the job. The pension—paid only to workers upon successfully completing a career—provided a capital lever that employers could use to encourage desirable behavior in lieu of a fidelity bond.[3] For example, Steven Sass claims that pensions in the banking sector took their shape because of the "great discretion over cash and credit that banks by necessity delegated to their staffs."[4]

The evolution of employer-sponsored pensions from the 1910s until the passage of the Employee Retirement Income Security Act (ERISA) in 1974 was strongly influenced by two key factors: governmental regulations, primarily for the tax treatment of pension plans and benefits, and the implementation of Social Security.

Early Federal Regulations of Employers' Retirement Plans

Since the start of the federal income tax in 1913, even before the tax code specifically addressed pensions, reasonable employer pension payments to retirees or contributions to trust funds have been tax-deductible expenses for plan sponsors. The Internal Revenue Code grants tax-deferred status to a range of deferred income arrangements. Sponsors can deduct contributions to their plans as a business expense in the year the contributions are made. The contributions are deposited to a tax-exempt plan trust, meaning neither contributions nor interest accruals are taxable. These benefits are taxed only when they are dispersed. In recent decades, these tax preferences have been controversial, and government tinkering to raise short-term revenue has set off waves of change throughout the pension system.

At first, the government did not impose funding requirements on employer-sponsored pensions. Many plans were funded on a pay-as-you-go basis or another basis that did not require liabilities to be funded as they accrued. Over time, many plan sponsors found that their pension costs grew larger than they were willing or able to meet. In a seminal study of the industrial pension system in the early 1930s, Murray Webb Latimer wrote:

> The rate of growth of pension payments, rapid as it is, requires some time to become burdensome. In those companies where the expense factor has been determinant in forcing abandonment of the system, whether so stated or not, its operation probably requires a long time

before its significance appears. The relatively short experience of most pension schemes, the rapid growth in the number of employees of most companies until recent years, and possibly the relatively low age distribution of the employees as compared with what it may be after another generation, explain why the expenditures for pensions have not yet mounted sufficiently to compel the abandonment of many plans.[5]

Latimer went on to report that, between July 1, 1929, and April 30, 1932, plans were being discontinued at unprecedented levels, and the company's financial condition was usually to blame.[6]

Until 1938, plan sponsors could set up retirement trusts when business was good and then revoke them when things got tight. The 1938 Revenue Act modified the revocability provisions for retirement trusts and required that such trusts be for the exclusive benefit of plan participants until all obligations were met. During this time, plan sponsors could offer pension benefits to some workers but not others. The 1942 Revenue Act, along with certain amendments to it in the 1954 Internal Revenue Code, changed the tax code to stop plan sponsors from reserving benefits for owners and officers.[7]

Before the passage of ERISA, federal pension regulations focused primarily on preventing discrimination in favor of officers, managers, or highly compensated employees and on limiting the loss of federal revenues through excessive deductions. Until 1974, the law did not address the actuarial soundness of plans. There were no requirements for vesting or preservation of benefits for workers who terminated employment before becoming eligible for retirement. There were no requirements to report benefit accruals or enforce benefit rights for participants. Beyond general trust law and the criminal code, the law offered little protection against mismanagement of plan assets.

Social Security's Start-Up Encouraged Employer Plan Sponsorship

From their outset, employer-sponsored retirement plans relied on earnings replacement targets in setting benefit levels. To encourage workers to retire, employers had to give them sufficient retirement income. If workers could not or would not save enough on their own to retire, the pension plan would have to do so.

Early pension literature was often quite specific about income-replacement goals. The Committee on Economic Security that developed the Social Security Act in 1934 stated that "payment of benefits at a rate . . . approximating

50 percent of previous average earnings is socially desirable."[8] Although the committee spelled out no justification for that threshold, it is consistent with the pension goals that Dan McGill laid out 20 years later in the first edition of his classic pension textbook, *The Fundamentals of Private Pensions*. There he wrote that "pension technicians have generally regarded as adequate a plan which will replace, inclusive of OASI benefits, one-third to one-half of the employee's average earnings during the five or ten years preceding retirement."[9]

Two elements of Social Security played important roles in the spread of employer-sponsored pensions in the late 1940s and over the next 30 years. First, Social Security initially covered workers in the private, for-profit sector who were not self-employed and not farm or domestic workers. Covering the entire industrial base of the economy and the financial sector captured the more prosperous elements of the workforce and a significant share of those working in larger firms—the segment of the private sector where pensions had been taking root anyway. Second, the windfall benefits paid out by Social Security over its initial decades of operation, as discussed in chapter 6, provided a tremendous subsidy for employers that wanted to give workers a lifetime pension when they retired.

Suppose you were an employer who had set up a pension plan in the 1920s that would pay your retired workers a lifetime annuity of 50 percent of their final salary. For simplicity, assume you needed $250,000 in the pension fund for each retiree to fully cover his or her annuity. So along comes Social Security. Instead of having to fund the whole pension on your own, Social Security will now cover a generous share. Some of the early windfalls were worth $100,000 and more for workers earning industrial-level wages and retiring in the 1950s, 1960s, and 1970s. With the advent of Social Security, it suddenly became considerably cheaper to provide a relatively rich pension benefit. By the mid-1950s and for the next 20 years, as much as half the annuity benefit deemed appropriate by pension experts was being covered by Social Security windfalls.[10]

The new pension opportunity was not a secret. In October 1951, the U.S. Chamber of Commerce ran an article expounding the tremendous benefits to be had. The article began: "If you got a letter in this morning's mail telling you that you had suddenly inherited $41,000 free of income and estate taxes, how would you feel?"[11] The article explained that under the recent amendments, a worker could "be entitled to $20,000 worth of pensions by paying as little as $81 in social security tax."[12]

Marion Folsom, a Kodak executive who served on several Social Security Advisory Councils and who ultimately was appointed secretary of the Department of Health, Education, and Welfare, explained the situation from Kodak's perspective. After about 40 years in business, he said, "Some of the older people had passed their peak productiveness. The management was becoming quite concerned about what they were going to do with them. They looked into it and found that some of them couldn't get along very well if retired. The company didn't have a pension plan." After a while, George Eastman, the inventor of roll film and founder of Eastman Kodak, was convinced to set up one of the first funded plans in industrial America. Folsom said that many business "people were worried about what effect the government plan would have on existing pension plans" when the original Social Security Act was under consideration. Folsom told his business counterparts that "as far as Kodak was concerned, we simply would make a reduction in our plan. Part of it would come from Social Security, part from the company plan."[13] These Social Security subsidies dramatically facilitated employers' sponsorship of their own pension plans.

Other Factors Stimulate Plan Creation

During the first half of the 1940s, as the country fought World War II, the high demand for workers combined with the impact of tax legislation, the regulated economy and the beginnings of Social Security gave private pensions a considerable boost. Some employers began offering retirement plans because there were wartime restrictions on pay increases, which did not apply to benefits. High marginal tax rates made the tax treatment of pensions much more valuable than it had been in the early days of the federal income tax. By 1945, the employer-based pension system would cover 6.5 million workers.[14] Only a small fraction of workers covered in collectively bargained plans had pensions at the end of World War II.[15]

During 1943 and 1944, 49 percent of men ages 65 and older in the United States were still in the workforce.[16] By the end of the war, many large American businesses had become holding pens for older workers. One pension actuary suggested that most companies had a larger share of their workers over the age of 65 than ever before.[17] Many of the older workers were in unions, and the high demand for workers during the war had strengthened the unions' bargaining position. The purchasing power of Social Security benefits had eroded during the war, and these workers were not eager to exchange their working salaries for meager retirement benefits. The unions wanted these older workers to move on so they could give their jobs to younger returning veterans.

The Republicans won the majority in Congress in the 1946 elections. Labor leaders were pessimistic about pushing through higher Social Security benefits and so decided to push for pensions more directly under their own control. In 1946, the United Steelworkers filed a grievance with the National Labor Relations Board (NLRB) alleging that the Inland Steel Company's unilateral enforcement of compulsory age-65 retirement constituted a breach of the general labor contract. The company refused to negotiate with the union on the grounds that compulsory retirement was an essential part of the company's pension plan, which did not fall within the scope of collective bargaining. In January 1947, an NLRB examiner ruled that the Inland Steel Company had engaged in unfair labor practices when it refused to negotiate. In 1948 the NLRB ruled, in effect, that the Labor-Management Relations Act of 1947 imposed a duty on employers to bargain with representatives of their employees over pensions.[18] Upon appeal by the company, the U.S. Court of Appeals for the 7th Circuit approved the NLRB's view that the terms of a pension plan are subject to mandatory collective bargaining on the grounds they were "conditions of employment."

Pensions became a priority for the Congress of Industrial Organizations (CIO), and the United Auto Workers (UAW) and United Steel Workers (USW) led the way. In the negotiations with Ford Motor Company in 1948, Walter Reuther and his UAW colleagues demanded a retirement plan for union workers. Similar demands in the steel industry led to the threat of a nationwide strike, which prompted President Truman to appoint a fact-finding board to evaluate the issues. This board supported the union demand for a pension and within three weeks of issuing a report to that effect, Ford reached an agreement with the UAW. The steel firms resisted but gave way on the matter in short order.[19] The CIO used their successes at Ford and in the steel industry as a springboard to negotiate pension coverage across member companies. It took the American Federation of Labor (AFL) a while to join in, but it came on board in the 1950s and made employer-sponsored pensions a priority across most of organized labor.[20] The unions generally preferred pensions that paid benefits in the form of lifetime annuities.

Defined benefit plans have come to be known as pensions. These plans virtually always provided an annuity benefit payable for the remaining lives of retiring workers. The benefits were typically based on years of service and average salary, either over a worker's career or averaged over the last few years of service. Many of the union plans were negotiated on the basis of a flat dollar amount per year of service. For example, under the original benefit that the CIO negotiated with General Motors, retiring workers would be paid $1.50 per month for each year of service with the company—a retiree with 30 years of service would receive $45 per month.

In addition to defined benefit plans, two types of defined contribution plans came into being: profit sharing and money purchase. Today these plans are often characterized as savings or capital accumulation plans. They are plans in which workers accumulate a pool of funds that is made available to them when they terminate their employment with the plan sponsor. Under a profit-sharing plan, employer contributions can vary depending on the firm's profitability. Under a money purchase plan, fixed contributions are made each year on a worker's behalf. These can be stated as flat-dollar amounts but typically are a percentage of pay. At retirement, the individual's benefit, in most cases, is the accumulated amount allocated to his or her account.

By 1950, roughly one quarter of the private-sector workforce was participating in a pension plan.[21] After the war, labor demand slackened, and many employers used pensions as a tool for encouraging targeted retirement. From 1950 to 1970, the share of the private workforce participating in plans grew from 25 percent to nearly 45 percent.[22] But there were troubling signs that all was not well with pension developments in the private business world.

Early pension regulations focused almost exclusively on tax matters, leaving most of the structural issues to sponsoring employers and their consultants to work out. When the unions took an interest in pensions, their motivations also played an important role. In the early years, employer-sponsored pensions proliferated, and the promise of secure retirement income seemed within grasp. But by the end of the 1950s and early 1960s, a number of troubling developments had captured the attention of the public and policymakers.

13 GROWING PAINS FOR PRIVATE RETIREMENT PLANS

Three risks associated with employer-sponsored pensions emerged during the 1950s and 1960s, according to James Wooten. The first was agency risk, which is the risk of plan managers improperly handling or disposing of plan assets for a purpose other than providing benefits to participants under the stated plan rules. The second was forfeiture risk, the chance of a worker's employment being terminated before he or she has earned a vested right to a retirement benefit. The third was default risk, the probability of a plan sponsor not being able to sustain a plan and pay retirement benefits.[1]

Principal Agent Problems in Pension Management

In January 1955, Jimmy Hoffa negotiated a pension plan for 100,000 teamsters working across the Midwest and South. Initially, the employers were to pay $2 per worker per week into the pension fund—nearly $1 million per month. By 1965, the contributions would rise to $6 million per month. For Hoffa, the real treasure in the pension plan was the money. The mishandling of pension assets in the Teamsters Unions' Central States Pension Fund while under his direction is one of the more notorious examples of agency risk. Hoffa promoted loans for friends, associates and influential people outside his immediate circle. By 1962, nearly 70 percent of the plan assets were invested in mortgages and collateral loans made at special interest rates. Hoffa and his friends got a piece of the action from commissions for acting as loan intermediaries or brokers. By the mid-1960s, loans representing 18 percent of the Central State Pension Fund assets were in trouble. There were other cases of pension mismanagement, but the antics of Jimmy Hoffa and his union pension fund attracted special attention. When Robert Kennedy was Attorney General in the early 1960s, he investigated Hoffa's activities and scrutinized the union pension operations under his influence. Hoffa and seven colleagues were indicted for fraud,[2] and Hoffa was convicted in 1964. He served four years in prison for the pension charges and a separate jury-tampering conviction that was handed down that same year. President Nixon commuted his sentence in 1971.[3]

Forfeitures and Defaults in Employer Pensions

In 1964, two other pension developments focused public attention on private pension risks: the bankruptcy of Studebaker, and a book by Merton Bernstein, who was a professor at Yale Law School. His book, *The Future of Private Pensions*, featured case studies of private pension plans.[4] His overarching criticism of private employers' pensions was that they only covered between 22 and 25 million workers out of the roughly 61 million workers in private, non-farm wage and salary jobs. He found the operations of pensions for those covered problematic as well.

Beyond pensions providing limited coverage, Bernstein's basic contention was that the eligibility requirements in many private plans precluded the vast majority of workers—covered at some point during their career—from ever collecting benefits. In other words, these workers thought they were earning a pension but at some juncture would fail to meet a requirement, thus forfeiting their benefits. Many plans back then had extremely long service requirements to qualify for a benefit—15, 20, and even 30 years. If a worker terminated employment before then, the plan would often provide no benefit whatsoever. There were myriad reasons—many beyond workers' control—for leaving employment before becoming vested. Bernstein investigated turnover rates, facility closure rates, layoffs over economic cycles, business failures and other factors that might account for workers losing or changing jobs, and estimated that a minority of workers—possibly one-third—covered under plans would likely ever collect the benefits.[5] Bernstein's book is not an easy read but his story garnered attention from both the press and policymakers.

Bernstein's indictment of the private pension system documented pension defaults arising out of bankruptcy cases, but the announcement of Studebaker's insolvency arrived too late for the book. The Studebaker Company came to be the poster child for problems with employer-sponsored pensions. The company had agreed with the United Auto Workers (UAW) to establish a plan for its blue-collar workers in 1950. The Studebaker contract committed the company to contribute to the pension trust in accordance with its bargaining agreement and to pay pensions to retirees.

Employers and unions shared a desire to retire older workers who had prolonged their careers during World War II. Doing so meant paying substantial benefits from the outset of plan operations. So employers adopted a pension formula that gave older workers retroactive credit for service under the plan. The benefits for the first retirees were supposed to be for a lifetime of work, but no one had funded or otherwise secured the benefits. The Ford Motor Company started its plan with an immediate liability of $200 million[6] and not a dollar in the trust fund to cover it, according to George Buck. This was pay-as-you-go financing.

Most companies were neither able to make nor interested in making a large upfront gratuitous payment for departing workers. So unions and employers usually agreed to amortize the "unfunded liabilities" over 30 years. Thus, the benefits would become much more secure after two or three decades than during the pension's early years of operations. In the heavy manufacturing industries, however, union contracts were usually renegotiated on a three-year cycle and pension benefits were generally part of the negotiations. Employers could not prefund expected benefit enhancements, even if they wanted to, because the federal tax code only allowed them to deduct the funding of current benefits. Thus, every contract negotiation created a new set of pension liabilities, and it was common practice to treat them like start-up liabilities, namely to amortize them over 30 years or even longer in some cases. As a result, many of these plans were perpetually behind in their funding.

Studebaker was a second-tier auto producer at the end of World War II. It had done well during the war and its immediate aftermath as consumer demand surged, but by the end of 1953, demand for new autos was declining. With the lifting of war-time economic restrictions, the big auto producers, General Motors, Ford, and Chrysler, were positioned to cut prices to maintain demand, thereby squeezing the second-tier companies out of the market. In January 1954, Nash and Hudson merged to establish American Motors.

In October 1954, Studebaker and Packard announced they were merging. Studebaker's production operations were in South Bend, IN, and Packard's in Detroit.[7] Packard had started its own pension plan for its union workers in 1950, as negotiated with the UAW. Both Packard's and Studebaker's pensions were defined benefit plans that would pay $1.50 per month for each year of service up to 30 years. Both of them intended to amortize their substantial start-up obligations over several decades. Their pension problems arose because the combined Studebaker-Packard company was in financial difficulty from the outset and collapsed in 1956.

Packard's intent to amortize its pension obligations over many years assumed the revenues would be there, but bankruptcy cut off the company's revenue stream. The ramifications piled up quickly. In 1956, Studebaker contributed $1.8 million to the Packard pension plan, $1.2 million to amortize past-service credits and $616,000 for active workers' benefits earned that year. In 1957, after operations had ceased, Studebaker contributed another $1 million, of which $36,900 was for current service. The remaining Studebaker production facilities in South Bend—with their own challenges to face—had to pay all these costs out of their own productivity. In 1958, facing recession and a large debt payment it could not pay, Packard terminated its pension plan, and the Studebaker union had a hand in the decision.

In October 1959, the union and company agreed to reduce benefits for Packard retirees to 85 percent of their prior level, paid $43 per year of service as a lump sum to anyone eligible to retire when the plan was terminated who had not filed for retirement benefits then, and paid nothing to the remaining participants. The UAW local in South Bend went along with the benefit cuts for their brothers in Detroit because they could not afford to do otherwise.[8] Packard's collapse, along with that of other small car producers, prompted Walter Reuther, the head of the UAW, to press federal policymakers to establish something like the Federal Deposit Insurance Corporation, which protected depositors' bank accounts against default, to protect pensions.

Concerns about private pensions were sufficiently widespread that President John Kennedy appointed a President's Committee on Corporate Pension Funds in 1962, a committee that sowed the seeds for regulatory reform. This cabinet-level committee was chaired by Willard Wirtz, the Secretary of Labor, and included the secretaries of Treasury, Health, Education and Welfare, the director of the Bureau of the Budget, and the chairs of the Council of Economic Advisors, the Securities and Exchange Commission and the Federal Reserve Board. The rank of the members indicated the president's sensitivity to the issues and implied the findings would receive high-level attention.

In December 1963, Studebaker announced that it was closing its production operations. When it closed its plant in South Bend on November 1, 1964, it could not pay accrued pensions. In the plan liquidation, Studebaker paid full benefits to the 3,600 people already retired and those at least age 60 with 10 years of service who were eligible to retire under the plan. These benefits were covered by annuities purchased through Aetna, which cost the pension fund $21.5 million of its $24 million in assets. The next group to receive benefits included 4,080 participants over age 40 with at least 10 years of service. Their average age was 52 and average service with the firm was 23 years.

They received lump sums equal to about 15 percent of the benefits they had earned to date. The amounts ranged from $200 to $1,600, with an average of $600. The remaining 2,900 participants received nothing.[9]

The Wheels of Reform Begin to Turn Slowly

President Kennedy was assassinated in November 1963. The Committee on Corporate Pension Funds that he had appointed submitted its report to President Lyndon Johnson in June 1964. The report recommended the following:

- Private plans should continue to play a major role in the retirement security system.
- Public policy should provide tax incentives to encourage the growth and improve the reliability of private plans.
- The combination of Social Security and employer-sponsored pensions should be reasonably related to wage levels and living standards.
- The Internal Revenue Code should require that tax-qualified plans have reasonable vesting schedules.
- Plans should fully fund current service accruals and amortize existing unfunded liabilities over no more than 30 years.
- For negotiated plans, contributions should realistically reflect benefits.
- Plan funding should be certified by a qualified actuary on a regular basis.
- The IRS should review the assumptions used in actuarial valuations against reasonable standards.
- A qualified public accountant should certify the value of the assets in the pension fund.
- A serious study should examine the possibility of creating "a system of insurance which, in the event of certain types of termination, would assure plan participants credit for accrued benefits."[10]

Before he died, President Kennedy had been informed of the general direction that the Committee on Corporate Pension Funds was headed in its recommendations. Kennedy had appointed the Committee in March 1962 and it had submitted a "provisional" report in November, knowing that its recommended regulatory policies would be controversial. President Kennedy's Advisory Committee on Labor-Management Policy, which included representatives from both business and unions, reviewed the preliminary report. The Advisory Committee's response did not reach the White House until after Kennedy's death, but both business and organized labor members strongly opposed the vesting and funding proposals. They warned that these provisions would raise pension costs and likely reduce benefits.[11]

In early 1964, Walter Reuther visited President Johnson in response to Studebaker's bankruptcy announcement. Reuther told the president about the UAW's pension termination insurance proposal and gave him a copy. For political reasons, the president was not willing to advance the issue at that time, and Reuther turned to Congress for support.[12] President Johnson also sat on the report of the Committee on Corporate Pension funds for the rest of the year. With the public already riled up about the Bernstein book and the Studebaker bankruptcy, he apparently did not want to add anything else to the caldron of public opinion in an election year—especially a proposal opposed by both the unions and business.

Federal policy had always viewed private pensions from the employers' perspective. Now the public policy discussion was turning toward the treatment of workers and their retirement security.[13]

Both business and union members on President Kennedy's Advisory Committee on Labor-Management Policy felt that government had no business interfering in labor contracts, but officials at the Treasury Department were coming to believe that government had a prominent and legitimate interest in regulating employer-sponsored retirement plans. In the mid-1950s, Walter Blum began to develop a concept that ultimately became known as "tax expenditures." Writing in the Joint Economic Committee's 1955 study *Federal Tax Policy for Economic Growth and Stability*, Blum argued that if the government "decided to subsidize a certain activity, we should be hesitant about administering the subsidy by way of a tax preference. Subsidies in this form vary directly in amount with the tax brackets of the recipients; they are invariably hidden in the technicalities of the tax law; they do not show up in the budget; their cost frequently is difficult to calculate; and their accomplishments are even more difficult to assess."[14]

Stanley Surrey, who was lead tax-policy advisor to President Kennedy in the Treasury Department, embraced this concept. In 1967, while he was serving as the Assistant Secretary for Tax Policy at the Treasury Department, Surrey gave a speech in New York in which he said: ". . . through deliberate departures from accepted concepts of net income and through various special exemptions, deductions and credits, our tax system does operate to affect the private economy in ways that are usually accomplished by expenditures—in effect to produce an expenditure system described in tax language."[15] Surrey went on to say, "When Congressional talk and public opinion turn to reduction and control of Federal expenditures, *tax expenditures* are never mentioned. Yet it is clear that if these tax amounts were treated as line items on the expenditure side of the Budget, they would automatically come under closer scrutiny of the Congress and the Budget Bureau."[16]

If the tax preferences that favored employer-sponsored retirement plans were government expenditures, then the government could clearly claim a role in determining how those expenditures were made. Treasury officials had a number of concerns about the existing structure. They felt that tax-preferred plans were giving high earners excessive benefits, and leaving lower earners out altogether or giving them the short end of the stick. The Treasury staff began to formulate remedies.

President Johnson released the report of the Committee on Corporate Pension Funds in January 1965 against the urging of Ford Motor Company, which had been a strong Johnson supporter. Organized labor found the prospect of pension insurance appealing but was cool to the mandates for funding and vesting requirements. But this was not one of those government reports that faded into the sunset as its ink dried.

Moving the Discussion from the Committee Rooms to Family Rooms

James Wooten describes pension reform and identifies the key players and how they contributed to moving legislation forward or having it scuttled. By 1970, he reports, Republican Senator Jacob Javits and Senator Harrison Williams, a Democrat from New Jersey, decided to bypass employers and organized labor, taking their case directly to the public. The senators sensationalized inequities in the pension system and paraded case study victims in front of the public. Public indignation mounted, and it made little difference whether the victims numbered only 1 or 2 percent of plan participants. The employers and unions who resisted proposed solutions were perceived as looking out for their own narrowly defined interests, not the welfare of hard-working Americans.

In August 1970, the Senate Labor Subcommittee chaired by Senator Williams sent out a questionnaire developed by Senator Javits' staff to pension plan sponsors to document presumed problems. Senior members of the actuarial consulting community were livid, believing the survey was intended to make plans look bad. Ewan Clague, former director of the Bureau of Labor Statistics, was asked to tabulate the results. Wooten quotes Clague as saying the survey results were not trustworthy. Actuaries in the Government Accountability Office said the data were unusable and the study should be redesigned, starting with the questionnaire. Still, Williams and Javits presented statistics on two groups of plans at a March 1971 press conference. In the first group of 51 plans, the senators said that only 5 percent of participants who had left their employers between 1950 and 1970 ever qualified for benefits. In the second group of 36 plans, only 16 percent of the workers who had left the firm between 1950 and 1970 qualified for benefits.[17]

The senators' data were flawed according to virtually all expert assessments. In addition, the results ignored the vesting of benefits for employees who stayed with the employer. There might have been 15 to 20 times the number of employers remaining with the firms and vesting in their benefits as the number who had left with nothing. One study presented to the Treasury Department found that about half of active covered plan participants had already vested and another 50 percent of those not yet vested would likely do so before terminating employment based on worker turnover patterns.[18] Finally, the samples were extremely small and there was no indication they represented the universe of plans.

Senators Javits and Williams were less concerned with statistical validity and more interested in headlines that would stir the public. There was no need to statistically demonstrate beyond reasonable doubt that the pension system was failing most workers when the *Philadelphia Inquirer* would print a front-page article under the headline, "The Pension Game: Many Sign Up but Few Collect."[19] When *60 Minutes* took up the issue, they turned to Mert Bernstein as their principal outside advisor. Karen Ferguson, who now heads up the Pension Rights Center in Washington, D.C., a Ralph Nader spinoff, says of the program, "The magic of *60 Minutes* worked—it transmuted a dauntingly complex subject into simplicities that incited outrage. When the show aired in 1971, pension reform got onto the national agenda."[20]

Having helped CBS transmute a dauntingly complex subject into outrage-inciting simplicities, Bernstein moved on to help NBC prepare an hour-long show, characterized as a "White Paper," that aired on September 12, 1972, under the title *Pensions: The Broken Promise*. Edwin Newman, the long-time NBC reporter and news anchor, narrated the story, which presented several case studies of people losing their pensions due to bankruptcy, long vesting requirements, inadequate pension funding and so forth. Newman summarized the situation as "deplorable." The program's one caveat was a passing statement by Newman that there are many good pension plans. Predictably, the public was outraged. The show won a George Foster Peabody Award for being a "shining example of constructive and superlative investigative reporting." Not everyone was as enthused.

Accuracy in the Media, a nonprofit, nonpartisan watchdog group, complained to the Federal Communications Commission (FCC) that the program presented an inaccurate and one-sided view of private pensions, and NBC's refusal to present the other side violated the commission's fairness doctrine. An FCC staff finding agreed with Accuracy in the Media's complaint. NBC appealed and requested a full FCC review, and in December 1973, the FCC unanimously voted in agreement with the staff finding and ordered NBC to present a counterpoint to its show.[21] NBC appealed this ruling to the D.C. Circuit Court. The three-judge panel ruled in NBC's favor, overturning the FCC ruling, but the full court immediately voted to hear the case *en banc*. The full court mulled the issues—or sat on the case—for the next three years and then kicked it back to the original panel.[22] By that time, the charges against NBC had put a damper on one-sided documentary exposés, but Javits and Williams got the public reaction they had hoped for when they shifted from a constructive engagement with the major players in the pension world to stirring up public sentiment by presenting horror stories.

In addition to winning over public support for pension reform, legislators had to formulate the legislation. There were many players at the table. Senior bureaucrats in the interested agencies worried about their jurisdictions. The Senate Finance and House Ways and Means Committees traditionally had jurisdiction over tax issues, and tax considerations were a major element of pension reform. The Labor Committees in both chambers traditionally had jurisdiction over the treatment of workers and the employment contract. On top of everything else, the potential impeachment of President Nixon complicated the legislative environment, in which lawmakers from both parties had to forge legislation drastically expanding the regulatory powers of government. It would take too long to describe all the political maneuvering behind the developing legislation for this story. James Wooten's book provides an excellent summary of the legislative "sausage making" and political gamesmanship during the development of the Employee Retirement Income Security Act (ERISA), an extremely important piece of legislation that has touched millions of lives.

Legislative Twins, One Sired by Controversy, the Other in Spite of It

Despite the Watergate investigation, in early 1974 President Richard Nixon tried to thwart excessive government spending by "impounding" funds appropriated by Congress for activities he perceived as unwarranted. While his attempt had nothing to do with the pension legislation winding its way through Congress, it led to the passage of the Congressional Budget and Impoundment

Control Act of 1974. This legislation limited the president's power to unilaterally impede the intent of the Congress. The president vetoed the act, but Congress overrode his veto on July 12, 1974, establishing the Congressional Budget Act as law. It had a wide range of ramifications, but it had particular implications for retirement policy that were largely unnoticed in the heat of other ongoing controversies.

The summer of 1974 was a hot and contentious period in Washington. After the Watergate hearings, the House was considering Nixon's impeachment. President Nixon announced his resignation on August 8 and left office the next day. Through it all, Congress had been able to forge sweeping pension reform. On August 20, the House of Representatives passed the conference report on pension reform by a vote of 407 to 2. The Senate passed the measure two days later by a vote of 85 to 0. On September 2, 1974, Labor Day, President Gerald Ford signed ERISA into law, the first piece of legislation presented to him by Congress in his presidency.

14 ERISA: THE TRANSITION TO A NEW REGULATORY REGIME

The Employee Retirement Income Security Act (ERISA) dramatically refocused federal oversight of employee-sponsored retirement plans. The overall intent was to insure that pension coverage was made available to workers on a fair and equitable basis and that participants received their benefits.

ERISA and its implementing regulations make up one of the most massive and complex sets of federal rules controlling business activities.[1] The law includes four titles and its structure alone created some complexity. The mass is attributable to the scope of issues covered and the detail with which Congress articulated its intent. The complexity derives partly from the technical nature of the subject matter, as well as the multiplicity of legislative committees involved in developing the legislation and holding jurisdictional authority.

Title I of ERISA protects employee benefit rights. It addresses reporting and disclosure by plan sponsors, participation and vesting standards for participating workers, plan funding, and fiduciary responsibilities. Title II of ERISA is primarily concerned with tax matters. It contains essentially the same standards for participation, vesting, and funding that appear in Title I but specifies the conditions for tax-qualification status. Title III directed the Secretaries of Labor and Treasury to establish a Joint Board for the Enrollment of Actuaries who would be qualified to certify the periodic valuations of pension obligations and assets. Title IV created the Pension Benefit Guaranty Corporation to provide pension benefit insurance.

The new law established a couple of alternative vesting schedules but essentially required that all participating workers vest in their benefits after 10 years of service. Workers generally became eligible for participation after one year. Plan participants who terminated employment before retirement and received a cash distribution of their accumulated benefits could roll their benefits into an individual retirement account (IRA). Under ERISA's funding requirements, the plan sponsor's annual contributions must equal the plan's normal cost—a measure of the benefits earned in a given year—plus amortization of any unfunded liabilities associated with past service credits. Unfunded liabilities acquired before ERISA took effect could be amortized over 40 years, but all others had to be amortized over 30 years. Plan sponsors must file periodic disclosure forms with the government indicating worker coverage, participation and vesting levels, funding levels, and so forth. The Pension Benefit Guaranty Corporation would protect accrued benefits of workers up to a limit. Premiums would be $0.50 per participant per year for multi-employer plans and $1.00 per participant per year for single-employer plans. It was generally understood that, while these premiums would not fully finance the insurance, they would give Pension Benefit Guaranty Corporation administrators time to figure out appropriate premium rates. There were provisions to allow the Pension Benefit Guaranty Corporation to increase premiums in the future with Congressional approval.

Early Operations under ERISA

While there were concerns about government over-regulation as ERISA was implemented, retirement plans seemed to flourish during the early years under the new regulatory regimen. Between 1975 and 1987, the number of tax-qualified defined benefit and defined contribution plans escalated. Growth was steady over the period—the number of defined benefit plans grew by 70 percent between 1976 and 1982 while the number of defined contribution plans doubled.[2]

The names of these plan types are literal descriptions of the two major classes of employer-sponsored plans. Defined contribution plans are accounts holding contributions from the employer, employee or both, and the contributions accumulate investment returns over time. The total benefit is the account balance. The most common of these plans today we know as 401(k) plans, which include employee contributions and, frequently, employer contributions based on the company's profitability or "matched" to workers' contributions. Defined benefit plans are generally what people mean when they refer to "pensions." These plans have a formula for calculating the benefit at retirement, which is typically based on years of service and average salary. In 1985, hybrid plans arrived on the scene, which share certain characteristics with both defined contribution and defined benefit plans. These plans include cash balance, stable value, and pension equity plans.

As ERISA was implemented, the universe of plans offered by private employers gradually expanded. From 1975 through 1979, the annual growth rate was 1.8 percent for private defined benefit plans and 4.7 percent for defined contribution plans.[3] Most large employers already had defined benefit plans by the time ERISA was adopted, so there was not much room for growth in that group. Many mid-size and smaller firms were holding off on setting up defined benefit plans to see what the new regulatory environment would ultimately entail. Defined contribution plans were spreading more rapidly for two reasons. First, they were cheaper to operate. Second, ERISA encouraged defined benefit plan sponsors to also adopt supplemental defined contribution plans. Before ERISA, there was no upper limit on the benefits paid to an individual from a defined benefit plan. Likewise there was no limit on the dollar amount of contributions made to a defined contribution plan on a worker's behalf. The limits prior to ERISA permitted a maximum annual deduction of 15 percent of covered pay to a profit sharing plan and 25 percent of pay to all plans.

ERISA added section 415 to the Internal Revenue Code, which limited the amount of benefits tax-qualified plans could pay. Under section 415, defined benefit plans could pay the lesser of $75,000 per year or the average salary paid in a worker's highest three years of earnings. Contributions to defined contribution plans were restricted to the lesser of $25,000 per year or 25 percent of a worker's earnings. The $75,000 and $25,000 limits were indexed to the annual rate of increase in the consumer price index. This new section of the tax code was intended to limit the tax subsidy for highly paid individuals, and it meant that many executives would receive smaller pensions.

Under Section 415, sponsors of both defined benefit and defined contribution plans could contribute fully to the primary plan up to the limit for that plan type and still contribute another 25 percent of the full limit to the other plan type. For any plan sponsor with significant numbers of workers affected by the limits, the treatment of multiple plans offered the opportunity for greater benefits under the tax preference for qualified plans. The U.S. Department of Labor estimates that the percentage of workers covered by such supplemental defined contribution plans doubled from 9 percent to 18 percent between 1975 and 1984.[4]

Once ERISA was fully phased in, growth rates for both plan types accelerated. Between 1979 and 1982, the annual growth rate was 10.9 percent for defined benefit plans and 17.3 percent for defined contribution plans.[5] ERISA's ultimate goal, however, was expanding the worker population covered by pensions, not merely creating more plans.

Between 1975 and 1982, the number of active participants in defined contribution plans roughly doubled, about the same as the expansion in the number of plans; the number of defined benefit plans increased by roughly 70 percent over the same period, but the participant count increased by only about 9 percent.[6] The corresponding growth in both the plan and participant counts in defined contribution plans suggested the new plan sponsors were similar in size to the earlier ones. The difference in the growth of plans and participant counts in the defined benefit case suggests that the new plans were much smaller, on average, than existing plans. A substantial part of the growth in defined contribution plan coverage reflected the supplemental coverage extended to defined benefit plan participants that was triggered by the section 415 limits mentioned above.

A major goal of the stepped-up regulatory oversight of employer-sponsored retirement plans was to increase benefits. During ERISA's first five years, benefit payouts grew by 0.7 percent a year in private defined benefit plans and by 1.9 percent a year in defined contribution plans, in inflation-adjusted terms. From 1979 through 1982, benefits began to grow more rapidly—at an annual rate of 10.9 percent for defined benefit plans and 17.3 percent for defined contribution distributions.[7] This was a time when Social Security benefits seemed to be in jeopardy because of the 1970s funding crisis. While the private employer-sponsored system had been maligned during much of the decade leading up to the passage of ERISA, it was becoming an increasingly meaningful contributor to the retirement security of American workers at a critical time.

In addition to the other good news, ERISA had made workers' private retirement benefits more secure at exactly the time many people were beginning to worry about the long-term outlook for Social Security. ERISA decreed that plan sponsors must fund workers' benefits as they were earned, with provision to pay off over time the "mortgage" arising from any previously earned, unfunded benefits. The thinking was that if a worker earned $1,000 worth of benefit rights in a year, in present value terms, the plan sponsor ought to put in trust $1,000 to secure that benefit. Excepting malfeasance by plan administrators—which ERISA was now regulating more aggressively than had been done in the past—and barring an economic catastrophe, workers could count on receiving their benefits at retirement.

One measure of a pension plan's security is the extent to which accrued benefits—those earned to date by participants—are secured with matching funds. If assets fully cover aggregate accrued benefits, the plan is fully funded. The percentage of large plans that were fully funded rose from 25 percent in 1977 to roughly 85 percent by 1986.[8]

Not all the news was good. In 1977, 40 percent of defined benefit plan participants were fully vested and another 6 percent were partially vested in plans with sliding vesting schedules permitted under the law. By 1982, these percentages were 41 percent and 5 percent. The vesting story for defined contribution plans was somewhat better, with 59 percent of active workers reported as fully vested and another 24 percent partially vested in 1977, but by 1982, those numbers had hardly budged: 60 percent and 24 percent. ERISA did not seem to be improving the vesting situation.[9] Workers do not lock in their rights to these benefits until they vest.

The stagnant vesting rates were a concern in the early 1980s, but the ERISA requirement was a 10-year standard, so many thought it might be too soon for results. But there were other troubling and more immediate concerns. In 1975, 39 percent of private-sector workers were participating in defined benefit plans and another 6 percent were in defined contribution plans. By 1984, participation rates in defined benefit plans had declined to 34 percent, and rates in defined contribution plans had risen to 11 percent.[10] Moreover, the total percentage of private workers covered by employer pensions was stagnant between 1975 and 1984. In developing ERISA, policymakers had assumed the new one-year participation requirements would boost rates of plan participation.

In 1978, President Jimmy Carter formed a President's Commission on Pension Policy to examine existing retirement and disability systems and address remaining inadequacies. In assessing employer-sponsored retirement plans, the commission concluded that "the most serious problem facing our retirement system today is the lack of pension coverage among private sector workers."[11] The Commission's ultimate recommendation was for a Mandatory Universal Pension system that would mandate savings of 3 percent of payroll for all workers. The system would consist of funded individual accounts to be administered by Social Security but kept separate from its taxing and benefit structures. By the time the President's Commission on Pension Policy released its report, President Carter had been replaced by President Ronald Reagan, who was not inclined to propose a new mandatory pension program.

Tax Treatment of Pensions Becomes a Growing Focus

In the late 1960s, the Treasury Department began to estimate the cost to the federal government of the tax preferences accorded private pensions. They calculated the cost by estimating (1) the foregone federal income taxes due to contributions being made to a pension trust instead of being paid directly to workers as wages, plus (2) the amount of taxes foregone because pension trust fund earnings were not taxable, minus (3) the amount of taxes collected on pension benefits actually paid. The estimated tax expenditures associated with private employer-sponsored retirement plans had been increasing steadily but accelerated after ERISA passed.

In 1968, the tax preferences were estimated at $2.8 billion. The estimated cost grew at a compound annual rate of 11.2 percent, reaching $5.3 billion in 1974. From 1974 to 1982, the estimated tax expenditure grew by 15.5 percent per year and reached $16.8 billion in 1982.[12] From 1975 to 1982, annual contributions climbed from $37 billion to $79 billion per year, and the trust fund assets grew from $260 billion to $789 billion. Benefits had risen, but only from $19 billion to $55 billion per year, so they were not offsetting the effects of larger contributions and trust fund accumulations.[13]

The magnitude and growth path of the tax expenditures associated with private retirement plans were considered problematic primarily because upper-income workers were disproportionately reaping the rewards. In 1977, the Treasury Department estimated that the bottom 50 percent of wage-earners were receiving 5 percent of the value of the tax benefits being provided to employer-sponsored retirement plans and only 2 percent of that value for individual retirement accounts (IRAs). Treasury estimated that the top 5 percent of earners were receiving 36 percent of the tax benefits for employer-sponsored retirement plans and 65 percent of the IRA preferences.[14]

While many considered the greater sums of money flowing into and residing in pension funds a virtuous result of ERISA, not everyone agreed. Treasury staff was concerned about the public subsidization of private retirement plans and in 1977 developed a proposal to change their tax treatment. Under the proposal, plan contributions would remain deductible, but earnings on the funds would be taxable income to vested workers. Earnings that could not be attributed to vested workers would be taxable income to the plan sponsor. Benefits would still be taxed at distribution.[15] The proposal did not progress but it clearly laid out the Treasury's sentiments about these plans.

One reason Treasury became more aggressive about the tax preferences was the 1974 Congressional Budget Act, which formalized the concept of "tax expenditures" as a required budget item that the president submits to Congress each year. Before then, tax expenditures had been a theoretical concept. The Congressional Budget Act defined tax expenditures as "revenue losses attributable to provisions of the federal tax laws which allow special exclusion, exemption, or deduction from gross income or which provide a special credit, a preferential tax rate, or a deferral of tax liability."[16] The notion that tax breaks cost the government revenue just as a spending program does had been formally legitimized, so "tax expenditures" from tax breaks were now calculated along with actual spending.

The relative implications of moving from the current tax treatment of pensions toward a more comprehensive income tax treatment can be demonstrated algebraically.[17] An example may be more straightforward. Suppose I contribute $5,000 today to a 401(k) plan, and my marginal income tax rate is 34 percent. I intend to invest this money for 15 years until I retire and buy a bond that yields 8 percent per year. Suppose also the 34 percent tax rate will continue to apply in the future, and that my income in 15 years will require me to pay 34 percent on the benefit distribution. My tax reduction in the year I make the initial contribution is $1,700 because I put the money in my 401(k) rather than taking it as regular income. In 15 years, my investment will be worth $15,860.85.[18] When I take that as a benefit, I will pay federal income taxes of $5,392.69—34 percent of the accumulated benefit. The present value of those future taxes at the time I make my contribution is $5,392.69 discounted by 8 percent over 15 years or $1,700.[19] In this example, I ultimately pay the $1,700 in income taxes that I earn on my original investment one way or the other. If I take it as regular income and invest it in a savings account with 8 percent interest per year, I would have to pay income taxes on that interest income each year. By investing it through a tax-deferred account, such as a 401(k) plan, I do not pay taxes on the interest accruals. The Treasury considers that a tax expenditure.

Understanding how the tax treatment of retirement-plan contributions favors their utilization also helps to explain the justification for former Senator William Roth's sponsorship and Congress's adoption of Roth IRAs and 401(k) plans. If you follow the same steps as in the last paragraph, except you tax the income when it is earned, let interest accumulate tax-free and impose no taxes on the distribution, the net distribution will be the same from both the Roth 401(k) and the traditional 401(k). Senator Roth, who was chairman of the Senate Finance Committee when he introduced the new Roth approach to 401(k) contributions, was trying to move forward the timing of tax collection.[20]

There have been many criticisms of the concepts behind these measures and the methods used to estimate them. There are demographic issues, timing issues, and even fundamental questions about what tax treatment would be on funds invested with post-tax dollars.[21] The idea that the government was spending something when employers made contributions to their employees' retirement plans, often extra contributions under the new government-mandated funding requirement, did not sit well with plan sponsors and their professional advisors. The matter was controversial as a conceptual idea and its real-world effects on public policy would be even more so.

15 THE 1980S: A DECADE OF REGULATORY SCHIZOPHRENIA

The Employee Retirement Income Security Act (ERISA) was fundamentally about securing pension benefits as workers earned them. That's why ERISA required defined benefit plan sponsors to fund benefits on an orderly basis as they accrued. Under the "tax expenditure" concept introduced in chapter 14, the funding was viewed as a cost to the government because neither the worker's income on which contributions were based nor the income on pension assets were taxed. Pension funding was taxed only when the benefits were paid, which could be decades after the contributions were made. So the bureaucrats at the Treasury Department took a keen interest in minimizing the tax losses to the Treasury and keeping high earners from getting the lion's share of benefits from the "tax expenditures." The interests of Treasury dovetailed with those of policymakers in the 1980s, pushing the funding goals of ERISA into the background.

Drive to Lower Tax Rates but Maintain Tax Collections

In his 1980 campaign for president, Ronald Reagan promised to reduce federal income tax rates. He assumed office during a severe recession, and Congress was anxious to stimulate economic growth. When President Reagan submitted his tax proposals, Congressional leaders from both parties embraced his recommendations and expanded on them. By the time they had finished, the Economic Recovery Tax Act of 1981 called for a 23 percent reduction in federal income tax rates over three years, with the top rate dropping from 70 percent to 50 percent.

When the Reagan Administration submitted its 1982 fiscal budget, the attempt to cut expenditures by reducing Social Security benefits set off a political firestorm, as discussed in chapter 8. Representative Charles Rangel, a Democrat from New York, introduced legislation to reduce maximum pensions that could be provided on a tax-preferred basis, which ended up in the Tax Equity and Fiscal Responsibility Act of 1982. The rationale for cutting retirement benefits was that it would add federal tax revenues without raising tax rates.

Despite lower tax rates under the Economic Recovery Tax Act of 1981, federal expenditures held steady relative to the size of the economy. In 1980, federal outlays for the fiscal year were 21.7 percent of gross domestic product (GDP). During 1988, Reagan's last full year in office, federal outlays were 21.3 percent of GDP.[1] To keep federal tax rates low but raise the same amount of revenue, much of the 1980s legislative agenda was built around reducing "tax expenditures"—the cost of tax preferences to various activities. This put employer-sponsored retirement plans front and center on the legislative agenda. Every tax discussion included further deliberation over how to limit the tax preferences for employer-sponsored retirement plans while also broadening their distribution.

After the 1982 passage of the Tax Equity and Fiscal Responsibility Act, the tax expenditures associated with retirement plans steadied, rising from $30.2 billion in the fiscal 1982 budget to $31.3 billion in fiscal 1983. Then pension tax expenditures started rising, to $60.8 billion in fiscal 1984, $67.7 billion in fiscal 1985, and $70.2 billion in fiscal 1986. For comparison, in 1981, the estimated tax expenditure for retirement plans had been 1.2 times that of the home mortgage interest deduction. By the mid-1980s, the retirement tax preference was more than 2.5 times that for the mortgage deduction.[2] The largest increase in the tax expenditures for retirement plans was between 1983 and 1984, with no explanation in the budget to account for it. In fact, what drove the increase in the 1984 budget was the first-time inclusion of federal civilian, state, and local government employee pensions in the estimates. Including public workers' pensions put the pension tax preference at the head of the class. The combined magnitude of this set of tax expenditure estimates captured policymakers' attention, but the resulting legislation focused primarily on private retirement plans.

The 1984 Deficit Reduction Act extended the freezes on the funding and contribution limits for pensions that had been adopted in 1982. That same year, the Retirement Equity Act expanded pension benefits by requiring ERISA plans to cover workers over age 21 with more than one year of service (it had been age 25). The Retirement Equity Act also established survivor benefits as the default for pensions, so a worker could not waive survivor benefits without written consent from his or her spouse.

During this era, policymakers across the political spectrum continued to pursue lower tax rates. President Reagan and many conservatives felt that low tax rates encouraged workers to be more productive because they could keep a greater share of the rewards. Many liberal policymakers believed the federal income tax system was riddled with tax incentives skewed toward upper-income individuals, which encouraged actions most of them would take anyway, like buying houses. Eliminating these preferences would allow lower taxes for everyone. A harmonious chorus singing the virtues of lower taxes ultimately resulted in the adoption of the Tax Reform Act of 1986.

The Tax Reform Act of 1986 imposed more limits on tax-preferred pension benefits and rebalanced the limits for defined benefit and defined contribution plans.[3] It reduced the vesting requirements allowed under tax-qualified plans and vastly limited the ability to discriminate in favor of highly paid workers, including, among other things, fundamentally changing the rules for integrating employer plan benefits with Social Security.

After the passage of tax reform, pension tax expenditures rose to an estimated $77.4 billion for 1987. Congress adopted the Omnibus Budget Reconciliation Act of 1987, which reduced the full funding limits for private defined benefit plans—a contribution that increased the pension trust beyond the limit would not be tax deductible.[4] In effect, this new law prevented plan sponsors from putting aside sufficient money to fund eventual retirement benefits for younger workers. Reducing current contributions meant they would have to be increased later.

When the Omnibus Budget Reconciliation Act funding limits took effect in 1988, the leading edge of the baby boomers averaged 33 years old. This law significantly pushed back the funding of the baby boom generation's defined benefit pension promises. While the legislation was being considered, an analysis based on a 1986 survey of 664 plans, each with more than 1,000 participants, estimated that 40 percent of them would bump up against the new contribution limits, compared with only 7 percent under prior limits.[5]

By the time the fiscal 1988 budget was released, the lower marginal tax rates under the Tax Reform Act of 1986 and reduced plan contributions under the Omnibus Budget Reconciliation Act of 1987 were achieving the desired results. Pension tax expenditures for fiscal 1988 were estimated at $53.9 billion. Despite the repeated legislative measures to curtail the pension tax preferences, this was the first reduction in their estimated cost during the decade. Nevertheless, the estimated cost of the tax preference for fiscal 1988 was more than three times the estimated cost for fiscal 1981, the year before the Tax Equity and Fiscal Responsibility Act had been adopted.

The legislative onslaught during the 1980s also aimed to distribute retirement benefits more broadly among workers. The 1982 Tax Equity and Fiscal

Responsibility Act classified certain tax-qualified plans as "top heavy." In a top-heavy plan, key employees and their beneficiaries receive more than 60 percent of the value of all accrued benefits. The law required top-heavy plans to provide minimum benefits or contributions to all participants. It also capped the compensation on which benefits are based at $200,000 for both defined benefit plans and defined contribution plans. Although the top-heavy provisions were primarily targeting pension abuses among small employers, all plans had to be tested for top-heavy status each year.

The Tax Reform Act of 1986 extended the top-heavy annual compensation limit of $200,000 to all plans, with the limit indexed to the consumer price index. Changes enacted in the 1993 Omnibus Budget Reconciliation Act had the effect of forcing employer pension plans to put aside an even smaller share of pension cost early in a worker's career. The new law reduced the limit on compensation that could be considered in funding employer pension plans from $235,840 to $150,000. In 1993, the Social Security average wage index was around $23,130 and the maximum taxable cap was $57,600, so you might wonder why the $150,000 limit caused problems. The earnings cap for benefit funding for many workers was actually much less than the $150,000 cap. The issue arises from the duration of the funding horizon.

For example, a 35-year-old worker earning $35,000 who received 5.5 percent annual raises would have a final annual salary of $165,344 at retirement. The funding rules looked at expected salary at retirement and worked backwards. For this worker, 9.3 percent of final salary—that is, $15,344/$165,344—could not be considered in funding the pension benefit. In practical terms, this means that 9.3 percent of the worker's $35,000 current salary—roughly $3,255—could not be considered in funding the benefit the worker earned this year.

An analysis in the late 1990s estimated the effects of the funding limits on workers at various ages, based on 15 companies with 165,000 plan participants. By 1999, the cap had grown to $160,000 because of indexing. The data analyzed included age, service, and pay information necessary to project workers' salaries forward to see how many were affected by the $160,000 cap. The average rate of expected annual wage growth used to value large pension plans was 5.2 percent. As in the earlier example, projected wages for a 35-year-old worker earning $35,000 with annual raises of 5.2 percent would exceed $160,000, thus preventing the employer from funding all of his or her accruing benefit.[6] The results of the analysis are shown in table 15.1.

The limits were affecting workers at every age. While the limit affected few workers in their 60s, the majority of workers in their 20s and 30s bumped up against it. With median earnings of those affected by the cap under $30,000

Table 15.1 **Percentage of Workers in Selected Pension Plans Affected by Pension Funding Limits, by Workers' Age and Median Pay Levels in 1998**

Age of workers	Percentage of workers with projected pay above $160,000 limit	Median pay of workers affected by the $160,000 limit
Less than 20	17.5	20,280.00
20 to 24.9	47.2	27,831.50
25 to 29.9	59.7	36,614.09
30 to 34.9	57.4	44,875.01
35 to 39.9	45.5	53,982.00
40 to 44.9	30.5	66,573.07
45 to 49.9	17.9	90,100.00
50 to 59.9	12.0	128,893.29
60 to 64.9	6.5	179,301.06

Source: Sylvester J. Schieber, "The Employee Retirement Income Security Act: Motivations, Provisions, and Implications for Retirement Security," paper presented at ERISA After 25 Years: A Framework for Evaluating Pension Reform, conference sponsored by The Brookings Institution, TIAA/CREF and the Stanford Institute for Economic Policy Research, Washington, D.C., August 1999. The paper was published under the title "The Evolution and Implications of Federal Pension Regulation," in *The Evolving Pension System,* ed. William G. Gale, John B. Shoven, and Mark J Warshawsky (Washington, D.C.: The Brookings Institution, 2005), 11–50.

for those in their 20s and under $55,000 for those in their 30s, the regulatory net was snaring far more than the "fat cats" who were its purported targets.[7] The results were hard to make sense of given ERISA's intention to make retirement plans more secure by encouraging companies to fund benefits as workers earned them. Every significant pension law adopted between 1982 and 1993 slowed pension funding by limiting plan sponsor contributions.

In 1994, Professor John Shoven from Stanford and I presented a paper in which we projected the private pension system forward over 75 years, the same period the Social Security actuaries use to project that program's future funded status. Our estimates suggested that for the private defined benefit system to deliver aggregated benefits belonging to the baby boom generation, contribution rates would have to increase by 60 percent, effective immediately.[8] During the general discussion that followed our presentation, an analyst from the Office of Pension and Welfare Plan Administration from the Department of Labor, John Turner, observed that our results simply indicated that employers would have to contribute more in the future to give workers pensions. We suggested that an alternative possibility was that plan sponsors would curtail their plans.

Accounting Rules Change and Employer Practices Follow

Another element of the regulation story relates to the financial accounting of pension benefits and obligations. In the early 1980s, the Financial Accounting Standards Board reviewed the actuarial methods plan sponsors used to calculate and report pension obligations and expenses on their financial statements. The board was interested in aligning assets with liabilities on corporate balance sheets. In 1980, nearly two-thirds of private defined benefit plans that based benefits on workers' salaries used the "entry age normal" cost method to fund benefits.[9] Using this method, and assuming actuarial assumptions came true, an employer would contribute a steady percentage of a worker's pay over his or her career.

The Financial Accounting Standards Board ultimately promulgated accounting rules that required plan sponsors to use the projected-unit-credit cost method for accruing pension benefits. As shown in figure 15.1, the projected-unit-credit method reduces costs early in a worker's career and increases them later. After employers changed the way they valued their pension plans

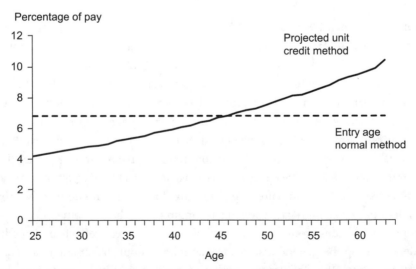

FIGURE 15.1 **Alternative Pension Cost for a 25-Year-Old Worker over a 40-Year Career under Alternative Actuarial Cost Methods**

Source: Developed by the author.

for accounting purposes, many changed the method for calculating their annual funding obligations as well, moving from the entry age normal method to the projected-unit-credit alternative. In 1983, 10 percent of final-pay defined benefit plans were funded on a projected-unit-credit basis. By the mid-1990s, nearly two-thirds of them were being funded that way.[10] The baby boomers were in their 20s and 30s as the accounting rules were being changed. The shift further delayed the funding of this large cohort's retirement benefits, pushing costs from the first half of the baby boomers' careers to the last half.

Some Sponsors Tap Pension Assets for Other Uses

Given that policymakers had come to the conclusion that private pensions could operate successfully with less funding, it was not surprising that some business managers came to the same conclusion. During much of the 1980s, the stock market performed well and interest rates were relatively high. Asset values rose and the high interest rates made it look relatively cheap to fund future benefits, so many pensions were considered overfunded. Some companies terminated their pensions to tap the excess assets in the pension trusts, despite having to pay income taxes on the reversions. From 1980 to 1988, 1,827 private plans, with nearly 2 million participants, were terminated, and plan sponsors took nearly $20 billion out of the plans.[11] In 1988, there were still 146,000 private defined benefit pensions in operation with $912 billion in assets,[12] so the plan closings represented a relatively small percentage of plans, but the optics were bad and the spirit of the transactions rubbed pension regulators the wrong way.

ERISA required pension funds to be used for the exclusive benefit of plan participants but allowed plan sponsors to recapture assets in terminated plans as long as all liabilities to participants and their beneficiaries were settled—and the plan provided for excess assets to revert to the sponsor. To settle liabilities, plans had to provide annuities for participants. The reversion provision was important because some plans provided for excess assets to revert to participants.

There was widespread antipathy to the idea of plan sponsors terminating pension plans at the expense of workers' benefits or retirement security. The perceptions about what was going on were worse in many cases than the effects of the plan terminations themselves, and many workers' full benefits were protected in the transactions. But there were a number of highly publicized cases where the pension assets were used in leveraged buyouts of the sponsoring firms. "Overfunded" pension plans were becoming targets for corporate raiders who would make an offer to buy the company and then "raid" the assets from the terminated pension plan to finance the deal.

An empirical analysis by David Cather, Elizabeth Cooperman, and Glen Wolfe found that firms terminating their plans were more likely to be involved in mergers and acquisitions than other firms. The terminating firms also tended to have larger pension surpluses and to be less profitable in their general business operations than other firms.[13] In another study, Mitchell Petersen found that firms that were financially weak or failing, as well as those with the lowest tax rates, were more likely to terminate their plans.[14] Petersen's study was somewhat unique in that he focused on the termination of specific plans, including cases where a firm with more than one plan would terminate one or more—but not all—of its plans with surplus assets. He concluded that "the size of the transfer from workers to shareholders significantly affects which plans are chosen for reversion."[15] Financiers clearly more interested in a company's excess pension assets than its long-term success created a robber baron environment that many policymakers found unseemly.

The IRS established guidelines regulating termination/reversions in 1983. The guidelines required the purchase of annuities for all plan benefits to protect employees against market fluctuations and confirmed that employers could reestablish plans after a reversion. The Tax Reform Act of 1986 applied a 10 percent excise tax to reversions, which later rose to 15 percent. The Omnibus Budget Reconciliation Act of 1990 pushed the reversion tax as high as 50 percent, in addition to corporate income taxes. The tax penalty—on top of the regular federal and state corporate income taxes on cash reversions—would generally consume any recaptured assets from terminated plans. The excise tax virtually ended the practice of terminating plans for the surplus funds, although the lower interest rates in the 1990s would have made such terminations less attractive anyway. While the flow of funds from tax-qualified plans for irregular purposes had been largely stanched, the new rules locked up plan contributions tighter than ever before.

Birth of 401(k): Nothing Would Ever Be the Same

The Revenue Act of 1978 included a provision that would become section 401(k) of the Internal Revenue Code. Congress provided that workers' voluntary deferrals of some portion of their pay into an employer-sponsored saving or profit-sharing plan would not be taxable until the benefits were distributed. As long as the worker could make the choice to contribute and how much, the contribution would receive tax-favored treatment. Before then, employer contributions to retirement plans received tax preferences but employee contributions did not. Adding section 401(k) to the tax code put employer and employee contributions on similar tax-deferred footing.

The tax code and its incentives affect behavior in very important ways. The tax preferences for qualified retirement plans provide real economic benefits and shaped the way retirement saving was done. Before section 401(k), employers' contributions, which were made with pre-tax dollars, were more effective in building up retirement plan wealth than employee contributions, which were made with post-tax earnings. Because of this, the overwhelming majority of private, employer-sponsored defined benefit plans did not require employee contributions. Even today, employee contributions to defined benefit plans are not tax deductible and virtually all private plans are funded entirely with employer contributions. With the deductibility of workers' contributions to 401(k) plans, employee contributions became predominant in the defined contribution world.

The Treasury Department and the IRS were not enthused about section 401(k) at first, but it was the law and employers took notice. The IRS released proposed regulations for the operations of plans with 401(k) features in November 1981, indicating that employee contributions from their regular pay could be saved on a pre-tax basis. Technically, there is no such thing as a 401(k) plan because this section of the tax code merely allows employers to add a 401(k) feature to existing profit-sharing or thrift-savings defined contribution plans that allowed pre-tax employee contributions. But today, almost all of these plans are called 401(k) plans. When section 401(k) came into effect, most large employers merely modified their savings or profit-sharing plans to add a salary deferral option for workers, thus creating a 401(k) plan.

The 401(k)s proved to be more popular than anyone expected. By the end of 1984, there were 17,300 401(k) plans with 7.5 million participants and nearly $92 billion in assets. During that year, Congress adopted the Tax Reform Act of 1984, which required 401(k) plan sponsors to perform discrimination tests to ensure that plan contributions did not favor the highly compensated.[16] The 1984 legislation was a precursor to the tax reform legislation then under development, and 401(k) plans drew special attention in discussions of tax policy.

In 1984, the Treasury Department released its initial blueprint for tax reform and recommended eliminating section 401(k). The initial markup of tax reform legislation from the House Ways and Means Committee released by Chairman Dan Rostenkowski called for repeal of 401(k). Trade associations and consulting firms organized a massive letter-writing campaign in support of workers' 401(k) benefits. The deluge convinced Congressional representatives and the Ways and Means Committee to back away from repeal.

When President Reagan released his proposals for reforming the federal income tax system in 1985, section 401(k) survived, but he called for tougher discrimination standards and more stringent contribution limits. The existing rules followed those that applied to noncontributory defined contribution plans, which allowed contributions up to 25 percent of pay subject to the overall limits. For defined contribution plans, the contribution limit was $30,000 as set in the Tax Equity and Fiscal Responsibility Act for 1983 and frozen for three years. The president's proposal would have allowed employees to defer up to $8,000 per year into their 401(k), and Congress reduced it to $7,000.

The second restriction on 401(k) contributions in President Reagan's tax reform package was to further tighten the anti-discrimination provisions. These were part of the Treasury Department's initiative to force more equitable distribution of benefits to lower-wage earners. These rules split the workforce into two groups: "highly compensated" and the rest. The rules put limits on the average contribution rates of highly compensated workers based on the average contribution rates of lower earners. Tax reform further reduced the contribution rates allowed for highly compensated workers.

The third limit in the President's tax reform package was the cap on compensation that could be considered for funding or contributing to retirement plans. The Tax Equity and Fiscal Responsibility Act had introduced the $200,000 compensation cap on top-heavy plans, and the Tax Reform Act of 1986 extended it to all plans, including 401(k) plans. Its ramifications did not seem so apparent when it was paired with the $7,000 contribution cap, but they were significant in practice.

The changes to the 401(k) rules were intended to encourage plan sponsors to cover as many rank-and-file workers as they could and to give them meaningful benefits. The changes were also meant to keep highly compensated workers from enjoying excessive tax benefits based on their own savings decisions. Linking savings rates for the highly compensated to the average savings rates of the lower-paid improved the lot of rank-and-file workers. Plan sponsors took care to pass the discrimination tests to avert having to limit the savings potential for their middle and upper managers. To encourage lower-paid workers to join the plan and contribute, employers offered matching contributions and used sales-oriented communications programs. The match rates varied but typically ranged from a 25 percent match on each dollar of contribution up to a full dollar-for-dollar match on contributions up to 6 percent of pay. The most common match rate was 50 percent of employee contributions up to 6 percent of pay.

Seeds for Pension Change Were Now Germinating

By the end of the 1980s, employer-sponsored retirement plans were operating under a very different regulatory infrastructure than they were under a decade earlier. When the decade began, ERISA was already firmly in place and many employers' funding patterns suggested they had accepted its basic tenets. The 401(k) plan was an easy means of expanding retirement benefit offerings on a relatively efficient basis, and many sponsors were optimistic about workers' enthusiasm for their new savings option. The evolution of the accounting regulations was raising awareness of the costs of retirement plans and creating an understanding that a traditional pension was a long-term commitment that could get out of hand if not managed prudently. The discrimination standards that were seemingly aimed at doctors, lawyers, and other small employers thought to be abusing their employees were being applied universally, imposing considerable costs and aggravation on plan sponsors despite having little to do with their fundamental business or how they treated their workers.

The messages from regulators about funding pension obligations were the most confusing of all. Initially ERISA set out to ensure that accruing pension obligations were secured by meaningful assets and backstopped by an insurance program that would have few claims. The idea was that if a worker earned a benefit this year that was going to be paid in 30 years, the employer needed to deposit the necessary funds this year to make sure the benefit was secured. This view linked the retirement benefit to the worker's long career of steadily increasing productivity and pay. By the end of the decade, the perspective had changed from a future to a present orientation—from the benefit to be paid down the road to how much was owed if the plan was shut down today. The difference in these two perspectives was dramatic and would have tremendous ramifications for the young workforce of the 1980s.

16

GOOD INTENTIONS GONE AWRY

The retirement plan regulations adopted during the 1980s were intended to bring more lower-earning workers into retirement plans and ensure they received an equitable share of the tax-preferred benefits. Nevertheless, during the five years following the passage of the Employee Retirement Income Security Act (ERISA), coverage under private tax-qualified plans remained essentially flat. In 1980 and again in 1985, private employer-sponsored retirement plans covered 46 percent of the workforce. Coverage dropped to 45 percent in 1990 and inched back up to 46 percent in 1995. Possibly offering a glimmer of hope, coverage climbed to 50 percent in 1999.[1]

Push for Expansion Leads to Contractions

One reason for the lack of pension progress was that the regulations changed the fundamental economics of the tax preferences for defined benefit plans. All the new pension rules and restrictions dramatically increased administration costs for defined benefit plans, with a disproportionate effect on the per capita costs of running smaller plans.[2] Employer-sponsored retirement plans offered more economic value to workers than simply the face amount of annual contributions and asset income—the preferential tax treatment is valuable, too. But that value was limited by the contribution amounts and workers' marginal income tax rates. The heavier regulatory burdens imposed on defined benefit plans during the 1980s added administrative costs that simply outweighed the economic value of the tax preferences to workers. This was especially true for lower-earning younger workers in smaller firms.[3] When the benefits stopped being a good deal, many employers closed their defined benefit plans and shifted to less costly defined contribution plans.

The regulatory message to defined benefit plan sponsors was clear, and their reactions were straightforward. There were 83,311 operating private defined benefit plans with fewer than

100 participants in 1975. By 1982, the number of these plans in operation had climbed to 149,600. With the passage of the various burdensome regulations after that, these plans started to fold—there were 93,821 in operation in 1990, only 35,214 in 2000.[4] More than 75 percent of the small plans had disappeared less than 20 years after the passage of the Tax Equity and Fiscal Responsibility Act. Among plans with more than 100 participants, there were 20,035 in operation in 1975, climbing to 55,979 in 1983 and then declining to 19,241 in 1990 and dropping to 13,557 in 2000. Nearly half of the larger plans had been closed between 1983 and the beginning of the new millennium.

As noted, the pension regulations adopted during the 1980s were designed to encourage greater distribution of benefits to workers on the lower rungs of the economic ladder. But for workers to have a chance of receiving a benefit from an employer-sponsored retirement plan, they had to be covered by one. From 1979 to 1990, private retirement plan coverage dropped by 8.2 percent for workers earning between $25,000 and $50,000, by 17.2 percent for workers earning between $15,000 and $25,000, and by 20.3 percent among workers earning less than $15,000 per year. Private plan coverage rates were declining across the board, but the decline was considerably steeper at lower earnings levels as the legislative onslaught played out.[5] Some believed that although smaller plan closures were reducing formal coverage rates, the closures would have little effect on the ultimate delivery of benefits because many of the small plans had been paying most of their benefits to business owners. The "top heavy" rules discussed in chapter 15 targeted these abuses of the tax preferences.

The lower plan coverage rates did not rule out the possibility that the new rules were helping many lower earners. Peter Orszag suggested that the 401(k) rules likely prompted many plan sponsors to offer generous matching contributions, and that these almost certainly both encouraged lower earners to participate and made their contributions go further.[6] It is undeniable that reducing service requirements for participation and imposing more worker-friendly vesting standards expanded the percentage of workers who would ultimately receive benefits. It is also clear that requiring a spouse's written permission to reject joint and survivor pension coverage expanded the number of workers who chose it, likely reducing poverty rates among surviving spouses. The discrimination testing of 401(k) plans had a tremendously beneficial effect on both participation and contribution rates for lower earners. At the same time, however, the changing regulatory environment was largely responsible for the loss of 114,000 small defined benefit plans and another 12,000 larger ones between 1982 and 2000. Not all of these plans were tax dodges.

Moves to Curtail Pension Funding and Benefits Take Hold

These regulations also affected pension funding behavior. The initiatives to reduce contributions to the employer-sponsored retirement system came from two directions. First, the caps on contributions, benefits and compensation were intended, at least ostensibly, to keep high earners from enjoying too many spoils from the tax preferences for retirement plans. Second, the Omnibus Budget Reconciliation Act of 1987 was a legislative maneuver intended to push funding from earlier in workers' careers to later. The shift in the timeline of pension funding was exacerbated by the new regulations that effectively locked up every dollar in the pension fund, even after all pension obligations were met. The regulations had consequential implications for plan funding. Whereas the Employee Retirement Income Security Act (ERISA) was all about securing pension promises, the new funding limits and restrictions were about delaying funding, and plan sponsors took the message to heart. In 1980, private defined benefit plan sponsors contributed $3,747—stated in 2010 dollars—per active participant in their plans. By 1990, the contribution per active worker declined to $1,466 (also in 2010 dollars). In 1999, per capita contributions were $1,732. From the time the Omnibus Budget Reconciliation Act of 1987 was implemented through 2004, the per capita contributions to private defined benefit plans, in inflation-adjusted dollars, averaged 54 percent of what they had been in 1980.[7]

ERISA established the first dollar limits on benefits that could be funded in a defined benefit plan and limited annual contributions to a defined contribution plan.[8] Lawmakers indexed the limits to inflation in parallel to Social Security benefits indexation. The Tax Equity and Fiscal Responsibility Act of 1982 reduced the limits and froze them for a time. The freezes were extended in tax legislation subsequently adopted in 1984 and 1986.

Figure 16.1 shows the evolution of the section 415 limits adjusted to restate the historical series in 2010 dollars. In the late 1970s and early 1980s, a defined benefit plan could pay a retiring 65-year-old worker benefits worth 50 percent more than those the plan could provide in 2010. For anyone retiring at younger ages, the reductions were even steeper. The maximum contribution to a defined contribution plan before 1982 was more than twice the maximum in 2010.

Figure 16.1 also shows the compensation limits that factor into calculations of benefits and contributions. The compensation limits were first introduced for top-heavy plans in 1982 and then extended to all plans under tax reform in 1986. The effects of the 1993 adjustment are particularly striking. When these limits were introduced, the message was that policymakers were cutting back

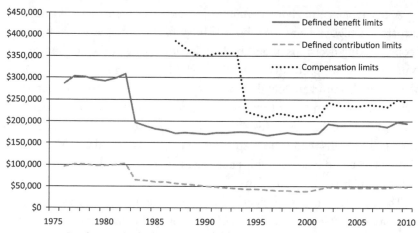

**FIGURE 16.1 Section 415 Limits on Fundable Pension Benefits, Defined Contri-
bution Plan Contributions, and Section 401 Compensation Limits for Providing
Retirement Benefits, in 2010 Dollars**

Source: Internal Revenue Code, section 401 and section 415 limits adjusted using the
Bureau of Labor Statistics' Urban Wage Earner consumer price index series.

on excessive tax incentives for fat cats making hundreds of thousands of
dollars a year. But these limits hurt many rank-and-file workers. The defined
benefit paid to a full-career worker was generally a percentage of his or her
final earnings, with high and low earners receiving roughly the same percentage. Employer contributions to defined contribution plans were generally
a percentage of pay for all workers. When the regulations essentially reduced
percentages for higher earners, the reductions often rippled down the line.

Pension Curtailments in a Larger Retirement Policy Perspective

It is interesting to juxtapose the policy environment for pensions in the early
1980s with that for Social Security. As documented in chapter 6, higher-income
Social Security beneficiaries were receiving tremendous windfall benefits in
the late 1970s and early 1980s, even as the program was facing a financing
crisis. Yet no one proposed putting a stop to that largesse. But the possibility
of essentially the same people receiving excessive benefits through their private pensions prompted a Congressional hue and cry. Reducing Social Security benefits for the big winners would not have sent comparable cutbacks
rippling down the income distribution, but the opposite was true for employer-
sponsored retirement plans.

A major concern about curtailing private retirement benefits for high earners has always been that those subject to the reductions are the same people making decisions about the benefits offered to rank-and-file workers. While there is no proof that executives who lost benefits from tax-qualified plans turned around and cut them for regular workers, the subsequent prolif-eration of non-tax-qualified retirement plans for the higher paid is undeni-able. Many retiring executives today will receive far more from their nonqualified plans than from their tax-qualified plans. Regular workers might be much better off today if highly paid executives had more retirement income riding on their tax-qualified plans.

There is much harder evidence that the funding limits imposed under the Omnibus Budget Reconciliation Act of 1987 slowed the funding of pension ben-efits during the early part of the baby boomers' careers. After the 1987 law, many employers that had been contributing regularly to their plans suddenly found that their plans were "overfunded." Contribution holidays—during which the plan sponsor contributed nothing—became common, some lasting for years. But as the plans matured, their funding "excess" often gave way to deficits.

Under the Omnibus Budget Reconciliation Act of 1990, taking assets out of a closed or frozen pension plan essentially subjected the plan sponsor to a tax lia-bility comparable to the withdrawn excess assets. So sponsors of overfunded pen-sion plans could not easily recover the surplus funds. The various regulatory messages about pension funding policy changed the way plan sponsors operated their plans. One can make a case that funding beyond the minimum require-ments was not acting in the plan sponsor's economic interests. Indeed, for corpo-rate sponsors, one could argue that irrevocably tying up surplus assets in a pension would not be in the stockholders' best interests. In other words, corporate management could be accused of violating its fiduciary responsibility to stock-holders by funding the pension plan as though it were an ongoing commitment.

Irrational Exuberance Hits Pension Financing Perspectives

It was not uncommon for the averages of age and service of workers partici-pating in private pension plans to be increasing by one-half to a full year per year during the 1990s.[9] With workforce aging and increasing tenures, pension liabilities should have been catching up with whatever overfunding still existed at the beginning of the 1990s. That dynamic should have restarted pension funding with vigor as the 1990s evolved because the baby boom was aging. But at exactly the point when the full ramifications of the funding pol-icies of the 1980s would otherwise have become starkly visible, another "angel

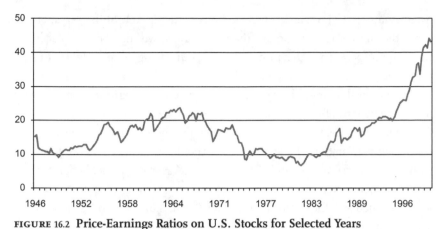

FIGURE 16.2 Price-Earnings Ratios on U.S. Stocks for Selected Years

Source: Robert J. Shiller, updated data used in developing *Irrational Exuberance* (Princeton, NJ: Princeton University Press, 2000), found at: http://www.irrationalexuberance.com/index.htm.

of good fortune" showed up on the doorstep of pension sponsors. In retrospect, the good fortune may have been the devil in disguise.

Figure 16.2 shows the price-to-earnings ratios for U.S. stocks after World War II, when private pensions became widespread in the United States, through the end of 2005. Robert Shiller, a finance professor from Yale University, developed data on the price-earnings ratios on U.S. stocks back to the early 1880s. Over the whole period of Shiller's data, the average price-to-earnings ratio has been 16.2, and since 1946, the average has been only slightly higher at 17.9. At the end of 1999, it stood at 44. The value of a company at any given time reflects investors' assessment of its future earnings stream. Investors convey their assessment to the market by buying or selling the company's stock at prevailing prices. With stock prices at all-time highs relative to current earnings by the end of the 1990s, investors were signaling their belief that corporations would significantly outperform their own history in the future.

As stock prices and price-to-earnings ratios climbed during the 1990s, there was widespread talk of a "new economy" in which the old economic rules no longer applied. But there was a nagging concern among some that the new economy was too good to be true. Alan Greenspan, the chairman of the U.S. Federal Reserve Board, asked: "But how do we know when irrational exuberance has unduly escalated asset values, which then become subject to unexpected and prolonged contractions as they have in Japan over the past decade?"[10] The phrase "irrational exuberance" stuck in the public mindset, and Shiller made it the title of his best-selling book, published in 2000, on the over-valuation of U.S. stocks. On the book's dust jacket, Shiller says, "If we think the market is worth more than it really is, we may be complacent in funding our pension plans, in maintaining our savings rate, in legislating an improved Social Security system. . . ."[11]

Despite the booming financial markets, which took pension assets up with them, the pattern of pension funding started to take on a new shape. In 1987, the median plan held assets valued at 45 percent more than the value of its currently accrued liabilities. Plans whose asset holdings exceeded their obligations earned to date were overfunded. Those whose assets were less than already earned benefits were underfunded. The story is straightforward—funding levels declined over the decade after the 1987 restrictions on funding took effect. The median funding ratio dropped from 1.45 in 1987 to 1.15 by 1995, grew modestly during the latter 1990s, but then fell to 1.11 in 2000. Among overfunded plans, the median funding ratio fell from 1.57 in 1987 to 1.25 in 1995, rose a bit in the late 1990s stock market boom and then fell to 1.22 by 2000. In 1987, 83 percent of all plans reported holding more assets than accumulated liabilities. The percentage of these "overfunded" plans dropped to 69 percent in 2000. While underfunded plans made modest funding gains during the 1990s, they remained significantly unfunded when financial markets peaked in 2000.[12] The next decade would be the roughest financial market investors had faced since the Great Depression, and the private pension system had reduced its margin for coping with the bumpy ride that was about to unfold.

Transition to a New Era

In many respects, the 1970s were the pinnacle of the golden era of the private defined benefit pension movement. ERISA was going to make workers' benefits more secure than they had ever been. The subsequent increases in funding levels were exactly what policymakers had in mind, and the Pension Benefit Guaranty Corporation was a backstop for workers' benefits in case the sponsor was hit with an economic catastrophe. As ERISA was implemented, new plans were created, making system expansion seem possible despite the new regulatory burdens. During the 1980s, however, perspectives changed. Legislators imposed new laws to limit federal tax losses and to spread the remaining ones down the economic ladder. The new regulatory regimen levied costs that overwhelmed the economics of plan sponsorship in many cases—instead of expanding, the system started to contract.

The golden era was over. Early declines in the numbers of private defined benefit plans and reductions in worker coverage during the late 1980s were early warnings signs of a transition under way. The shifting attitudes toward pension funding were more subtle but would ultimately prove more consequential.

Richard Ippolito, the former chief economist at the Pension Benefit Guaranty Corporation, was concerned about the pension funding trends evolving during the 1990s. He was well aware that falling funding levels could lead to more plan defaults and thus more participant claims. Ippolito developed an empirical analysis of funding patterns across nearly 20,000 plans.[13] He was interested in sorting out the effects of the reversion taxes, which were established in 1986 and raised in 1990, and the funding limitations imposed by the Omnibus Budget Reconciliation Act of 1987. The reversion taxes had been imposed to discourage plan sponsors from raiding their pension funds for other financial purposes and effectively cut off sponsors' access to surplus pension assets. Ippolito was convinced that it was discouraging sponsors from making more than minimum required contributions for fear of tying up corporate assets. The funding limits were quite explicitly intended to shift pension funding to later in workers' careers. Ippolito's empirical results led him to conclude that the reversion tax had about three times the effect of the funding limit changes in reducing private pension funding,[14] but that the latter were not trivial.

According to Ippolito's estimates, without the reversion taxes, employers' pension contributions would have averaged 6.6 percent of covered pay per year beyond 1987. He estimated that the 10 percent reversion tax passed in 1986 reduced contributions by 1.5 percent of covered pay and that the steeper rates in the 1990 legislation reduced contributions by another 1.3 percent. He estimated that the excise tax on reversions reduced pension contributions by 42 percent overall. When he split the sample into groups by funded levels at the beginning of the period, he found that the most overfunded plans reduced their contributions by 60 percent while the most underfunded plans reduced theirs by 16 percent. Ippolito concluded: "Even in the face of historically high investment returns, plan sponsors succeeded in reducing their excess pension assets by 60 percent. . . . The law is directly responsible for the growth industry in cash balance conversions, which are de facto terminations that often confer the kinds of capital losses on workers that the legislation sought to prevent. The occupation of creating new defined benefit plans effectively no longer exists."[15]

SOME GOOD NEWS . . . OR NOT

The employer-sponsored retirement system might have been fraying at the margins by the late 20th century, dramatically so in some instances, but it was also becoming an increasingly larger slice of the retirement pie. When Congress adopted the Employee Retirement Income Security Act (ERISA) in 1974, Social Security delivered $57.6 billion in benefits, while private-sector defined benefit and defined contribution plans delivered only 22.5 percent of that amount—slightly less than $13 billion. But private retirement programs gained steadily and, by 2000, these programs were paying out benefits worth two-thirds of those provided by Social Security.[1]

Private Retirement Benefits Measurement Controversy

While aggregate data suggested that private retirement plans were steadily increasing their contribution to the retirement security of American workers, other evidence told a different story. The Office of Research, Evaluation and Statistics at the Social Security Administration publishes a report every few years measuring income amounts, sources and distribution for the population aged 55 and older. In 1976, Social Security analysts estimated that households with at least one member 65 or older received 16 percent of their income from employer-sponsored pensions. By 1990, they estimated that these households were receiving 18 percent of their income from employer-sponsored plans. Over the same period, the income that elderly households derived from personal assets climbed from 18 percent to 24 percent of their total income.[2]

The recurring Social Security analyses are based on the *Current Population Survey* (CPS), a monthly national survey by the Census Bureau of a representative sample of the U.S. population. Each March, the monthly survey includes a special supplement on the sources and amounts of income that people received over the prior year.

While the Social Security analyses were widely accepted, they were puzzling to anyone closely following reported coverage and benefit levels in private pensions. The *Current Population Survey* estimated that Social Security provided twice the income provided by employer-sponsored retirement plans. However, using administrative and disclosure data, the *National Income and Product Accounts* developed by the Department of Commerce's Bureau of Economic Analysis suggested that private and public employer-sponsored retirement programs paid out $243.3 billion during 1990, while OASDI paid out $244.1 billion.[3] Billions of dollars were disappearing somewhere between the survey and administrative data.

The IRS creates Annual Tax Files, which are part of its Statistics of Income program allowing analysis of tax-filing unit income data for research purposes. The data are based on annual income tax filings (personal information is deleted) and allow exploration of the discrepancies between the survey and administrative data on Social Security and employer pension income. The files enable users to simulate the revenue and administrative impact of tax law changes and to access statistical information on filers' income sources and tax payments. Unfortunately, the files contain little information about tax filers other than income tax filing data. And very low-income individuals are not required to file income tax forms, so the IRS Tax Files do not represent the lowest-income segments of the population.

The IRS Tax Files revealed that employer-sponsored retirement plans were providing considerably more income than the *Current Population Survey* reported.[4] Nearly two-thirds of the elderly tax filing units reported having received pension or annuity income during 1990, and the average pension or annuity income was a significant share of the filers' total income. Among filers in the lower half of the income spectrum, benefits accounted for one-third or more of reported income. At higher income levels, pensions take on less relative importance but provide progressively higher benefits.[5] As one leg of a retirement system composed of private savings, Social Security and employer-sponsored plans, the employer-sponsored benefits were providing a substantial base of retiree income security for many people.

The Tax Files for 1990 represented 13.5 million filing units that included a person over age 65. The *Current Population Survey* estimated that there were 21.3 million individuals over 65 or couples where at least one partner was over age 65.[6] The difference suggests that roughly 63.4 percent of potential tax filing units with someone over aged 65 filed a tax return in 1990. Despite the fact that the tax filers were only a subset of the CPS population, the IRS reported income of $112 billion from employer-sponsored pensions compared to $88 billion from the *Current Population Survey*.[7] The estimate of the total pension and annuity income paid to elderly units based on the tax files was 27 percent greater than the CPS estimate, even though there were 37 percent fewer elderly units represented in the tax files. The *Current Population Survey* seems to have significantly underreported the benefits provided by the employer-based retirement system. But it was analyses like those coming out of Social Security that seemed to be defining the general understanding of pension operations in public policy discussions.

Retirement Plan Accumulations and Economic Savings

The benefits paid by the private retirement system were large and growing, but these plans furnish other benefits to society as well. The plans were a tremendous accumulator of capital that helped to underpin the U.S. economy. Between 1985 and 2000, private defined benefit assets grew from $589 billion to $2.2 trillion.[8] Private defined contribution balances grew from $432 billion to $2.5 trillion, and Individual Retirement Account (IRA) balances grew from $241 billion to $2.6 trillion.[9] In total, private retirement plan assets had grown from $1.3 trillion in 1985 to $7.3 trillion by 2000.

It is difficult to pin down the effect of the tax preferences on savings rates. Over the years, several economists have attempted to sort out whether the tax incentives for retirement savings are adding to our savings pool, with a particular focus on 401(k) and IRA savings.

James Poterba from MIT, Steven Venti from Dartmouth, and David Wise from Harvard have consistently concluded that the saving in tax-favored plans is not simply offsetting saving that would take place without the tax preferences, although clearly the participation rules affected the extent to which workers used these vehicles.[10] Venti and Wise documented that when IRAs were open to everyone, higher earners were more likely than lower earners to contribute. For example, 32.5 percent of individuals with incomes between $50,000 and $100,000 contributed to an IRA in 1984, while only 19 percent of those earning $30,000 to $40,000 did so. In aggregate, however, 90 percent of contributions were from workers earning less than $50,000 per year. Venti and Wise concluded that conventional wisdom claiming that contributions were concentrated among high earners was wrong. Their results indicated that the savings in IRAs were largely independent of any other saving by workers.[11]

As to 401(k) plans, Poterba, Venti, and Wise reasoned that if workers saved in them as a substitute for saving in other vehicles, then 401(k) participation should have little effect on workers' total asset accumulations. In that case, workers' growing 401(k) balances should have been offset by declines in assets held in other forms. They found that the non-401(k) savings of the two groups of workers, one in a 401(k) plan and the other not, were the same and their debt status was comparable. The authors concluded that the 401(k) contributions represented new savings.[12]

In a second test, Poterba, Venti, and Wise concluded that at the outset of the 401(k) system, those offered coverage versus those who were not had previously had similar savings patterns. But in 1991, when they compared total savings behavior in the two types of households, they found that households eligible to participate in a 401(k) plan had two to eight times the financial assets of families not offered a 401(k). Still, there was little difference in the non-401(k) assets held by the two types of households. Here again, they concluded that the 401(k) savings were new savings.[13]

As with most things in economics, not everyone agreed. In a series of articles, Eric Engen at the Federal Reserve, William Gale at Brookings, and John Karl Scholz at the University of Wisconsin published a range of studies reaching the opposite conclusion. Engen, Gale, and Scholz's empirical work consistently concluded that the savings in IRAs and 401(k) plans are merely a reallocation of saving that plan participants would do with or without the tax incentives.

Gale and Scholz argued that IRA savers and non-savers are not comparable. They estimated that in 1983, the median IRA contributor held $77,000 in net worth and $16,000 in non-IRA financial assets, whereas non-contributing households held an average of $20,448 in net worth and $2,050 in financial assets. Gale and Scholz attribute some of the differences in financial status of IRA contributors versus non-contributors to differences in age and earnings, but they concluded that even after controlling for those factors, significant variations attributable to differing inclinations to save persisted between the two groups. They concluded that an increase in the IRA saving limit between 1983 and 1986 would have increased saving by 2 percent compared to Venti and Wise's estimate of 45 percent to 66 percent.[14]

Engen, Gale, and Scholz reviewed Poterba, Venti, and Wise's analysis of the effects of 401(k) plans and again reached the opposite conclusion. They found that the incentives have a strong effect on where savings are held but almost no effect on the level of saving and wealth.[15] Poterba, Venti, and Wise conceded that alternative analytic approaches can lead to opposite conclusions about the impact of tax incentives on workers' savings patterns. Their conclusion, however, after assessing the full body of evidence, was that the vast bulk of IRA and 401(k) savings were new savings.[16]

Retirement Plans and Workers' Retirement

While opinions might vary about the private retirement system's delivery of retirement benefits and contribution to household savings, there is wider agreement about how the system affects retirement patterns. When the baby boom generation entered the workforce, the system responded by encouraging older workers to retire at earlier ages.

When the Social Security Act was adopted in 1935, the retirement eligibility age was 65. In 1940, 81.3 percent of men between ages 60 and 64 were still working, as were 61.7 percent of men between ages 65 and 69. By 1950, these percentages hadn't changed much, with 81.3 percent of the younger group and 60.9 percent of the older group still in the labor force. But by 1960, labor force participation rates fell to 45.2 percent for men ages 65 to 69. It declined very slightly for the younger group, from 81.3 percent to 79.2 percent.[17]

In 1956, the government established an early retirement age of 62 for women. As wives, on average, were three years younger than their husbands, policymakers thought it would be nice to let couples retire together. In 1961, the government also established an early retirement age of 62 for men to reduce unemployment. This latter reduction set the stage for reducing the retirement ages under employer-sponsored pensions.

In 1964, the United Auto Workers won $400 monthly retirement benefits for 60-year-old workers with 30 years of service. Under this arrangement, the normal retirement benefit was reduced to account for the early retirement, but a supplemental benefit brought the combined benefit up to $400 per month. These "supplements" were payable until age 65 as long as the retiree did not take another job. Retirees who took another job lost $2.00 worth of pension supplement for each dollar they earned.[18]

Most of the baby boom generation entered the labor force between 1965 and 1985. During that period, the number of workers covered by Social Security increased by 42.9 million, and the number of Social Security beneficiaries grew by 17.2 million.[19] For every new beneficiary, there were an additional 2.5 workers. Employers enjoyed an unprecedented pool of available labor. An analysis by Diane Macunovich showed that when the baby boomers entered the labor market *en masse*, young workers' earnings rates fell relative to older workers' earnings.[20] So not only were employers able to choose from an outsized pool of workers as the baby boomers came on board, but the new workers were cheap to boot.

The early "30-and-out" union contracts that allowed workers beyond a specified age to retire once they had attained 30 years of service under a plan whetted workers' appetites for pure 30-and-out provisions where there were no age requirements. This trend, coupled with the influx of the baby boom workers, made strictly service-related 30-and-out provisions a negotiating priority by the early 1970s. During the auto negotiations in 1973, the young workers were as committed to 30-and-out as older workers. Younger workers were more interested in clearing rungs up the ladder than in the minimal additional value of their retirement benefits. During the first half of the 1970s, the 30-and-out plan became common in the steel and auto industries and then spread to other industries as well.[21]

Early-out provisions spread to white-collar plans partly because unionized companies feared that their white-collar workers would unionize if their compensation packages suffered in comparison. In addition, the baby boom's entry into the workforce increased competition for jobs. Under the age discrimination laws, employers increasingly had to rely on financial incentives to entice older workers to retire, which they willingly did to clear the way for the new workers streaming into the workplace.[22]

A number of studies in the 1980s investigated the relationship between increased Social Security benefits and the trend toward earlier retirement.[23] Generally these studies found a statistically significant relationship between the level of Social Security benefits and retirement levels at various ages. But they also estimated that changing Social Security benefit levels would result in relatively small changes in retirement probability at various ages. Social Security does not seem to have been a predominant force in the trend toward earlier retirement.

During the 1980s, economic research also began looking at the implications of retirement incentives in employer-sponsored pensions.[24] When an employer offers a retirement subsidy for retiring by a specific date, the worker will suffer a penalty—that is, lose the subsidy—if he or she continues working beyond that time. In general, these studies found that traditional defined benefit pension plans introduced or strengthened these early retirement incentives during the late 1960s and throughout the 1970s. Richard Ippolito estimated that the number of defined benefit plans offering age-55 retirement benefits increased from 30 percent to 57 percent between 1960 and 1980. At the end of this period, 69 percent of these plans offered full benefits to some workers before age 65 compared to none in 1960. Finally, over these years, the percentage of plans providing some actuarial subsidies for early retirement benefits increased from 10 percent to 95 percent.[25] Empirical studies of the behavioral responses to retirement incentives consistently found that these incentives changed behavior—workers retired earlier when they received pension subsidies for doing so.[26]

From the early 1960s through the mid- to late-1980s, male labor force participation rates dropped steadily for men age 55 or older. The rates fell somewhat more rapidly for men 62 and older than for younger men in the group, but even at the younger ages, they declined significantly. In 1962, shortly after Social Security adopted the early retirement age of 62, 56 percent of men aged 65 were still working, along with 77 percent of men between the ages of 62 and 64. By 1971, only 46 percent of 65-year-old men were still working. Seventy-six percent of 62-year-old men were still working, but labor force participation rates for those aged 63 and 64 had dropped from 77 percent to 65 percent in a decade. By 1981, fewer than half of 63- and 64-year-old men were still in the workforce, and by 1991, more than half of 62-year-old men had retired. Labor force participation rates for men ages 55 to 59 dropped from 92 percent in 1962 to around 80 percent 20 years later.[27] Retirees were happy with earlier retirements, which seemed like a good idea at the time.

In the late 1980s and early 1990s, labor force participation trends for Social Security-eligible men began to change. After the long decline, participation rates started to flatten and then to rise again, although there was variation from year to year. The effects of the recessions in the early 1990s and since 2000 seemed to result in more significant drops in participation at ages 62 and 65 than among those ages 63 and 64 or 65 to 69. But workforce participation trends were up for those 62 or older from the mid-1990s onward. Participation rates for 62-year-old men climbed from 52 percent to 63 percent in 2009 before dropping back to 60 percent in 2010. Among those 63 to 64 years old, participation rates rose by 27 percent between 1990 and 2010. For those ages 66 to 69, participation rates were 10.5 percentage points higher in 2010 than they had been in 1990—an increase of nearly 40 percent. Labor force participation rates for men ages 55 to 59 and 60 and 61 flattened out after the mid- to late-1980s and have remained flat since then.[28] The dichotomy in the patterns between men before and after Social Security eligibility has been too pronounced to be random and undoubtedly relates to developments in the structure of retirement plans.

The labor force participation story for older women since the 1960s has been remarkably different from that of men. Among women ages 55 through 61, labor force participation rates rose slightly from the early 1960s through the early 1980s. Rates were relatively flat for women ages 62 and older. For example, 45 percent of women ages 55 to 59 were in the labor force in 1962, rising to 50 percent in 1982 and 63 percent in 2002. Among 60- and 61-year-old women, participation rates were 37 percent in 1962, 40 percent in 1982 and 52 percent in 2002. In 1982, 32 percent of 62-year-old women were in the labor force—exactly the same level as 20 years earlier—but by 2002, participation rates had climbed to 42 percent. At older ages, workforce patterns were consistent with those for 62-year-old women.[29]

The baby boom women entered the workforce at somewhat higher rates than the generations of women that had come before them. A more dramatic change in their behavior, however, was that once they entered the workforce, they stayed in it at much higher rates than prior generations. This progression in increasing labor force participation rates played out over the 20 to 25 years that the baby boomers completed their educations and joined the work world. Each successive birth cohort tended to have slightly higher labor force participation rates than the one before it. By the time the youngest post-baby boom women reached their 30s, their labor force participation rates were roughly equivalent to those achieved by the oldest baby boomers when they had been in their 30s. Labor force participation rates for women seem to have peaked.

The increases in women's labor force participation rates since the late 1960s have more than offset the reduced labor force participation rates of older men. As a result, since 1970, the percentage of time in the workforce has increased for the prime-age adult population. This has been a major contributing factor in our economic growth and higher standards of living over the latter part of the century. The trends raise the question of whether higher female workforce participation rates will change long-term retirement patterns. The answer is, probably not.

Figure 17.1 shows the workforce participation rates of men and women by age in 1960 and 2005. Despite the decades of increasing participation rates for women of all ages, older women have retirement patterns similar to older men. There is no reason to believe that women will find work inherently more rewarding than men do late in their careers. The rapid labor supply expansion

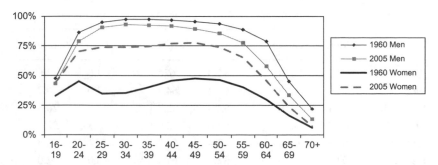

FIGURE 17.1 Male and Female Labor Force Participation Rates at Selected Ages for Selected Years

Source: Tabulations of the U.S. Census Bureau's *Current Population Survey*, various years.

during the 1970s and 1980s had pretty much dried up by the 1990s, when growth rates were more akin to the 1950s than to the intervening decades.

Implications of Retirement Patterns on Retirement Plans

The changes to the retirement system dramatically changed employment patterns and the duration of retirement. As shown in table 17.1, between the early 1950s and 2000, the average age for claiming a Social Security benefit dropped by six years, and the median retirement age declined by five years for men and by seven years for women. The duration of retirement has increased by seven years for men and by 9.5 years for women—a 58 percent increase for men and a 70 percent increase for women.

As the new millennium was about to dawn, all eyes were focused on the potential Y2K meltdown of our information systems. Few noticed the implications of the unfolding developments in the retirement system. We knew there would be problems with Social Security down the road. Some parts of the employer-based traditional pension system were fraying, but workers' defined contribution plans were amassing double-digit annual returns. Many workers were convinced they could do much better with their own retirement savings accounts than with a traditional pension anyway.

Table 17.1 Estimated Average Age of Claiming Social Security
Benefits, Median Age at Retirement and Expected Years in Retirement,
by Gender for Selected Periods

Period	Average Social Security claiming age		Median retirement age		Expected years in retirement	
	Men	Women	Men	Women	Men	Women
1950–1955	68.5	67.9	66.9	67.6	12.0	13.6
1965–1970	63.4	64.3	64.2	64.2	13.9	16.7
1980–1985	62.9	62.8	62.8	62.7	16.0	20.5
1985–1990	62.8	62.8	62.6	62.8	16.3	20.3
1990–1995	62.7	62.6	62.4	62.3	17.2	21.3
1995–2000	62.6	62.6	62.0	61.4	18.0	22.0
2000–2005	62.6	62.5	61.6	60.5	19.0	23.1

Source: Murray Gendell, "Older Workers: Increasing Their Labor Force Participation and Hours of Work," *Monthly Labor Review* (January 2008): 42.

By the end of the 1990s, some defined benefit plan sponsors had been on contribution holidays for 10 or 15 years. Even back in 1967, when Paul Samuelson was writing about Social Security being "the greatest Ponzi scheme ever contrived,"[30] the Social Security system at least required contributions. Pension operations in the 1990s seemed to be one-upping Samuelson's assessment of Social Security. But along the way, we had forgotten that saving for retirement requires some actual saving. Samuelson's assessment of Social Security would prove wrong when economic and demographic fundamentals changed. And the employer pension system would also run into problems when economic fundamentals changed at the beginning of the new millennium.

18

THE UNFOLDING OF A PREDICTABLE DEFINED BENEFIT SURPRISE

Chapter 16 described the evolution of price-to-earnings ratios for corporate stocks in the United States from 1946 through 2000. Figure 18.1 begins with the data from figure 16.3, starting in 1981, and extends it through the third quarter of 2010. From the time policymakers started cutting back on private plan funding in the early 1980s until the end of the century, stock values climbed ever upward. The new millennium was a rude awakening to old realities.

Pension Funding Collapses amid Financial Market Chaos

If the 1980s had been a mostly pleasant ride in the equity markets and the 1990s an exhilarating one, the first decade of the new millennium would prove too rough for comfort. Stock market declines early in the decade drove aggregate asset values substantially lower for the first time in more than 15 years. Between 1999 and 2002, the value of private defined benefit plan assets dropped by 21 percent. But worse was yet to come, and it came shortly. Between 2006 and 2008, the value of equities in the private pension system dropped by 48 percent. Over those two years, the private pension system lost almost $700 billion, nearly 30 percent of its value.[1]

The equity market declines driving down pension assets were only part of the problem. Liabilities are the other half of the funding equation, and they escalated after 2000—at exactly the same time that asset values were plummeting. One of the crucial variables in determining a pension obligation is the interest rate, and lower interest rates were also hurting pension plans. Table 18.1 shows the assets required to fund a $1 annuity payable at age 65 at various interest rates. Low interest rates increase the amount of capital required to deliver pension benefits. Following table 18.1, a plan that is required to pay a 65-year-old retiree $1,000 a year would require

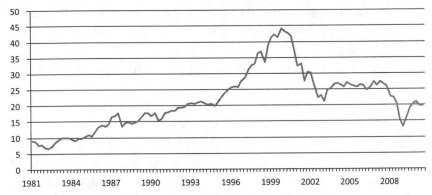

FIGURE 18.1 Price-Earnings Ratios on U.S. Stocks for Selected Years

Source: Robert J. Shiller, updated data used in developing *Irrational Exuberance* (Princeton, NJ: Princeton University Press, 2000), found at: http://www.irrationalexuberance.com/index. htm.

Table 18.1 Assets Required to Fund an Annual Annuity of $1 Payable at 65, at Alternative Interest Rates

Interest rate	Annuity cost
4.0%	$12.58
4.5	12.05
5.0	11.55
5.5	11.09
6.0	10.67
6.5	10.27
7.0	9.89
7.5	9.54
8.0	9.21
8.5	8.90

Source: Annuity rates were calculated using the Pension Protection Act Unisex Mortality Table for annuitants.

$8,900 in assets when interest rates were 8.5 percent, but $10,670 if interest rates were 6 percent. The average interest rates used to calculate pension liabilities in corporate pensions fell from 8.49 percent in 1991 to 5.97 percent in 2009.[2] This suggests that plans needed about 20 percent more funds in 2009 than in 1991 if everything but interest rates remained the same. But everything else was not the same. The largest single segment of the U.S. workforce, the baby boomers, had aged nearly 20 years closer to making their pension claims. The power of compound discounting which, as I showed in chapter 9, has been accelerating the growth in Social Security liabilities over the past couple of decades was doing exactly the same thing to employer-sponsored defined benefit plans.

In addition to their effect on liabilities, interest rate variations often affect a plan's cash flows. Many pension sponsors now allow retiring workers to choose between monthly annuity payments for life or a lump sum. The lump sums are equivalent to self-annuitizing, so the annuity must be converted back into a capital amount when the worker terminates employment. The lower the interest rate, the more capital the plan must pay a retiree to buy out a promised annuity. When interest rates are very low, retirement rates sometimes increase in plans with lump sum options because the higher lump-sum payouts make retirement seem attractive.

In 1999, assets exceeded liabilities by 14 percent in the median private defined benefit plan. Ten years later, the median plan's assets had fallen to only 75 percent of liabilities. From 1999 to 2009, for plans at the 90th percentile of the funding distribution, plan funding had plunged from 153 percent of liabilities to only 92 percent.[3] In 1987, an estimated 85 percent of larger private pension plans were fully funded. By the end of 2009, less than 10 percent of sponsors had sufficient assets to pay their estimated liabilities. The baby boomers were no longer young, the stock market was no longer exuberant, and the pension bill had come due with a vengeance.

Exploding Claims Reveal Pension Insurance Flaws

Chapter 13 explained the risk of pension default, where the plan sponsor cannot sustain a plan, usually because of bankruptcy. Lawmakers intended for the Employee Retirement Income Security Act (ERISA) to address default risk by requiring sponsors to fund their plans more fully and establishing the Pension Benefit Guaranty Corporation to pay some share of workers' benefits if the plan sponsor could not. For single-employer plans, the guaranteed annual benefit in 2011 is $54,000.[4]

One would think that the backstop of pension insurance would become less important over time as ERISA improved plan funding, but such was not the case. The history of the agency's claims since the passage of ERISA goes as follows: $252 million in claims between 1975 and 1979, $2.4 billion during the 1980s, $3.6 billion during the 1990s, and $36.6 billion from 2000 through 2009.[5]

The pattern of terminations in the 1980s waved a red flag about the insurance program. Economic conditions were horrible in the early 1980s. Things started to improve later in the decade, but the last five years of the 1980s witnessed a new phenomenon. By the end of 1989, total claims on the Pension Benefit Guaranty Corporation were $2.7 billion, and $1.1 billion—or 41.75 percent of all claims—involved four companies: Allis-Chalmers, an agricultural equipment manufacturer; LTV-Republic Steel; Wheeling Pittsburg Steel; and Kaiser Steel.

All four of these pension insurance claimants had CIO unions that negotiated pensions. When ERISA was adopted, companies were allowed to amortize existing unfunded obligations over 40 years. Under the federal tax code, sponsors of the flat-dollar plans that covered union workers could not fund anticipated benefit increases until they were part of a contract. Under the typical three-year negotiation cycle, these companies acquired new unfunded pension obligations every three years, to be amortized over 30 years. Often neither the unions nor the firms' management teams wanted to accelerate funding, which would have reduced the rewards available for firms and workers; accumulating unfunded obligations was easier. Workers at these companies did not risk losing everything the way their Studebaker predecessors did, but if financial calamity hit underfunded firms, the Pension Benefit Guaranty Corporation had to pick up the tab, which it passed on to remaining plan sponsors.

Under any sort of insurance program, more claims lead to higher premiums. When ERISA originally established the Pension Benefit Guaranty Corporation, it set the "premiums" for single-employer pension plans at $1 per plan participant. It became clear fairly quickly that premiums would not cover claims, so it was raised to $2.60 per plan participant in 1978, and to $8.50 in 1986. The Omnibus Budget Reconciliation Act of 1987 increased the minimum premium to $16 per participant and created a variable-rate premium linked to funded status, so higher-risk plans would pay more. Plan sponsors had to pay an additional $6 for every $1,000 of unfunded vested benefits with a cap of $34 per participant. In 1990, the base premium was raised to $19 and the capped variable premium jumped to $53 per participant. In 1994, the cap on the variable premium was lifted. In 2010, the flat-rate premium was $35 per participant and the variable premium was $9 per $1,000 of unfunded vested benefits.[6] The variable premium has been in effect for more than 20 years now, but it has not solved the large employer termination problem.

Table 18.2 tracks the history of terminations for the largest 20 companies making a claim against the Pension Benefit Guaranty Corporation's single-employer insurance program, which counts LTV-Republic Steel and the LTV

Steel Company as a single company (yes, one company managed to go bankrupt twice and leave unfunded pension obligations behind both times). The three summary lines at the bottom of the table compare the top 20 claims with all other claims made through the end of 2009. While the top 20 claims represent only 2.2 percent of the plans terminating with a claim, they represent 39 percent of affected participants—and 71 percent of total claim amounts.

The bankruptcies listed came in waves, brought on by economic conditions outside the companies' control, but they were exacerbated by the need for ongoing cash flows to support unfunded pension obligations accrued decades earlier. In the first wave, the steel firms collapsed because a worldwide glut of capacity intersected with a falloff in demand from recessions during the early 1980s and again in the early 1990s. In the second wave, several airlines collapsed under the crushing effects of recession and public reaction to the terrorist attacks on September 11, 2001. The third wave caught the U.S. auto industry in the crosshairs of declining demand and competition with international producers not burdened by unfunded retiree obligations. Delphi is the only auto supplier in the top 20 in table 18.2, but several other smaller suppliers were caught in the same economic squeeze that led them to dump their pension obligations as they went into bankruptcy.

Structural Defects Plague Private Pension Insurance System

The private pension insurance system was badly flawed from the outset, and its evolution over the years reflects its unsound foundation. In a well-designed insurance program, higher risks mean higher premiums. Drivers with perfect driving records pay lower premiums than those with multiple accidents and claims. Those who drive less pay lower premiums than those who drive more, and it is cheaper to insure a $20,000 car than a $75,000 car. The likelihood and potential cost of insurance claims affect the premium price, so drivers with more risks try to reduce them. In that way, the structure of the insurance distributes costs to those that create them and the incentives work to encourage those buying insurance to reduce their risks.

Most of the Pension Benefit Guaranty Corporation's income is from the flat premium, which bears no relationship to participants' risk of default. A solid company with a fully funded pension and a miniscule chance of bankruptcy poses virtually zero risk, while one with a few billion in unfunded pension obligations teetering on the edge of bankruptcy represents a major risk. Introducing the variable premium ameliorated the problem but only minimally. In 2003, the flat premiums generated $647 million in revenues and the variable

Table 18.2 Top 20 Claimants against PBGC Single-Employer Pension Plan Insurance through Fiscal Year 2009

Company	Plans terminated	Termination year(s)	Claims ($ millions)	Vested participants	Average claim per participant
Allis Chalmers	11	1985, 1986	185.7	9,055	20,512
LTV Republic Steel	1	1986	221.9	8,208	27,037
Wheeling Pittsburg Steel	7	1986	495.2	22,144	22,364
Kaiser Steel	4	1987, 1988	221.6	8,403	26,373
Eastern Airlines	7	1991	552.7	51,182	10,799
Pan American Airlines	3	1991, 1992	841.1	37,472	22,446
CF&I Steel	1	1992	184.0	4,239	43,412
Uniroyal Plastics	1	1992	149.9	5,212	28,766
Blaw-Knox	6	1992, 1994	118.9	5,659	21,016
Sharon Steel	5	1994	290.8	6,886	42,229
Trans World Airlines	2	2001	710.5	34,189	20,782
Polaroid	1	2002	357.0	11,353	31,447
Bethlehem Steel	1	2003	3,650.2	97,015	37,625
National Steel	7	2003	1,216.1	35,404	34,349
LTV Steel	6	2002, 2003, 2004	2,135.0	83,094	25,694
US Airways	4	2003, 2005	2,699.9	55,770	48,412
Weirton Steel	1	2004	640.5	9,410	68,064
United Airlines	4	2005	7,256.5	122,541	59,217
Delta Airlines	1	2006	1,739.7	13,028	133,533
Kaiser Aluminum	7	2004, 2007	597.3	17,727	33,694

(continued)

Table 18.2 (*Continued*)

Company	Plans terminated	Termination year(s)	Claims ($ millions)	Vested participants	Average claim per participant
Delphi	6	2009	6,108.5	69,042	88,475
Top 20 total	86		30,373.1	707,033	42,959
Total all others	3,907		12,544.9	1,103,554	11,368
Total all terminations	3,993		42,918.1	1,810,587	23,704

Source: Pension Benefit Guaranty Corporation, *Pension Insurance Data Book*, various years, http://www.pbgc.gov/practitioners/plan-trends-and-statistics/content/page13270.html.

premiums $301 million. That year, there were $6.4 billion in new insurance claims—none of them by well-funded plans.[7]

In 2005, the Bush Administration proposed to raise the flat pension insurance premium to $30 per participant and index it to future wage growth. At the time, the flat premium was $19 per participant and the variable premium was $9 per $1,000 of unfunded vested benefits. The administration's proposal would have allowed the Pension Benefit Guaranty Corporation's board to set variable premiums based on the program's economic status and risks. In a significant departure from past policy, the Bush proposals called for limits on benefit enhancements in severely underfunded plans. Under the proposal, companies "at risk" of financial default could not pay lump sums from pension plans unless asset levels exceeded 80 percent of liabilities. Lump sums are particularly problematic for underfunded plans because terminating workers take the full value of their benefits out of the trust, leaving the plan in even worse shape for remaining participants.

An analysis released at the time of the Bush Administration recommendations explained the problems with the pension insurance program and why the new proposals would not fully resolve them. In 2004, firms rated as "below grade" investment paid premiums that represented only 8 percent of the value of the expected claims they posed for the Pension Benefit Guaranty Corporation that year. Among firms that were "above grade" investment, their estimated premiums covered only 66 percent of the value of the expected claims they posed. The fact that premiums for both groups were less than their risk exposures was an indicator of the system's underfunding—higher premiums were necessary to keep the system solvent. But the extremely low premiums for high-risk plan sponsors were the insurance program's biggest problem. Yet under the Bush proposal, premiums for below-investment-grade firms would equal only 16 percent of their expected losses, while premiums for above-investment-grade firms would be 340 percent of their expected losses. This was like charging the most dangerous drivers the lowest auto insurance premiums.

The Pension Protection Act, adopted in 2006, followed the general outline of the Bush Administration proposals. In fiscal 2009, total pension insurance premium revenues were $1.8 billion dollars, with $1.1 billion paid in flat-rate premiums. Only 38 percent of the total revenues came from the risk-based premiums. The $6.1 billion Delphi claim showed there were still large employers posing significant risks. The low levels of funding among some of the worst-funded plans in 2011—five years after the adoption of the Pension Protection Act—suggest the problem is not going away anytime soon.

The Pension Benefit Guaranty Corporation's insurance structure for single-employer pensions may be protecting some workers' benefits, but it does not support the long-term viability of the private defined benefit system. Every time an underfunded plan sponsor goes bankrupt and turns over its pension obligations to the insurance program, plan sponsors that have complied with the spirit of ERISA's funding requirements must patch the gap with their own higher premiums.

Flaws in Multi-Employer Pension Plan Insurance

ERISA established a separate insurance program for multi-employer plans under the Pension Benefit Guaranty Corporation. In multi-employer plans, two or more employers agree to contribute to a common retirement plan for their workers. The plans are maintained under collective bargaining agreements. These plans are common where there are multiple firms in similar businesses and workers tend to move from one firm to another within the industry. In 2008, 54 percent of multi-employer insured plans were in the construction industry alone.[8] Trucking was another large component. Workers earn credits under their multi-employer plan as long as they are employed by any firm in the group. The plans are subject to ERISA funding requirements. Even after withdrawing from the group, employers are required to pay off the obligations accrued by their workers while they were part of the system.[9]

In 2011, the insurance program guaranteed participants in multi-employer plans up to $12,870 in benefits per year—considerably less than the $54,000 maximum for participants in single-employer plans. Multi-employer premiums are a flat $9 per participant per year versus the $35 flat premium and variable premium for single-employer plans. Pension insurance is activated when a multi-employer plan becomes insolvent, in which case the insurance agency helps the plan pay benefits and meet administrative expenses up to the guarantee amount. The Pension Benefit Guaranty Corporation does not assume administration of multi-employer plans in the way it does in the single plan system. If the plan recovers, it is required to repay the assistance with interest. Since the program began, only 62 plans had received financial assistance through 2009—43 of them during 2009. As of year-end 2009, only one plan had repaid the insurance program for its assistance.[10]

In 2009, the insurance program covered approximately 1,500 multi-employer plans with 10.4 million participants. The financial market turmoil hit these plans hard, and funding eroded accordingly. In 1990, the combined total of multi-employer plans' assets were $166 billion compared to liabilities of $156 billion. By 2000, the system held $357 billion in assets covering liabilities of $340 billion. By 2007, the plans reported $435 billion in assets and $628 billion in liabilities. On average, plan assets would cover only 70 percent of liabilities.[11] In 2007, the underfunded plans were short $195 billion. Of this, $59.8 billion—30.7 percent—was concentrated in 10 plans, and another $48.9 billion in the next 40 plans.[12] The Pension Protection Act considered plans less than 80 percent funded "endangered" and those less than 65 percent funded to be in "critical" status. Between the end of their plan years 2007 and 2008, private multi-employer trust balances declined by $100 billion.[13] By the end of 2008, the average multi-employer plan was in critical status on the funding meter.

In 2002, the Pension Benefit Guaranty Corporation estimated that the assets in its reserve funds would more than cover the liabilities of prospective claims. By 2007, the agency estimated that its multi-employer insurance program was underfunded by $1 billion. The funding picture improved slightly with the next year, but by 2009, the multi-employer insurance program was estimated to be underfunded by $869 million.[14] Once again, firm bankruptcies were playing a role in the deteriorating insurance program. In theory, an employer who pulled out of a multi-employer group retained liability for pension credits earned by its workers while they were in the plan. In reality, many companies simply went out of business or into bankruptcy. There are no plans in the works to distribute the costs associated with the risk of pension underfunding to those responsible for making pension promises but not funding them.

Default Risks Persist Despite Funding and Insurance Requirements

The Pension Benefit Guaranty Corporation has eliminated the worst of the pension default risks for covered workers, but there are caps on the benefits workers can recover. In 2008, the Pension Benefit Guaranty Corporation released a study evaluating the benefit limitations on 125 plans with 525,000 participants that it had taken over between 1990 and 2005. Sixteen percent of the participants had benefits reduced and the average reduction was 28 percent, according to the report. This was particularly problematic for high-income plan participants with very generous pension benefits, such as airline pilots. The limits also tended to affect groups like the steelworkers, who have early retirement supplements in their plans.[15]

Other remaining default risks became prominent as plan sponsors responded to evolving regulations, economic pressures, and changing demographics. By the mid-1990s, smaller employers had closed down most of their defined benefit pensions. Among larger employers, the mid-1980s introduced a new approach to pension provision: cash balance pensions. Cash balance plans and a subsequent variant, pension equity plans, came to be known as hybrid pensions. Hybrid pensions combine features of both defined benefit and defined contribution plans. In terms of contributions and participation, hybrid plans act like traditional defined benefit plans in that both are automatic rather than self-instigated. The plan sponsor retains the investment of assets and the risks associated with financial market volatility. Benefit accumulation and lump-sum benefits in hybrid plans facilitate communication and portability, as is the case for defined contribution plans.

Hybrid plans are regulated as defined benefit plans, and the employer is responsible for ensuring that the pension account has sufficient funds to pay vested benefits. Benefits are specified as an account balance similar to defined contribution plans. In cash balance plans, the account grows each year from new contributions and from the crediting of a specified return on the account assets. In pension equity plans, benefits are still accumulated as a multiple of pay, but the benefit is stated as an account balance. Both types of plans generally pay departing workers the full account value as a lump sum, similar to distributions under defined contribution plans.

During the latter part of the 1990s, many sponsors still offering defined benefit plans began converting them to hybrid plans. The shift to cash balance and other account balance plans by large employers was significant. Virtually all the conversions to these new hybrid plans eliminated early retirement incentives, and some further scaled back plan generosity.[16] In many cases, when plan sponsors restructured their defined benefit plans they also enhanced their defined contribution plans—often increasing the rates at which employee contributions were matched—but employees had to contribute to the plans to benefit. The trend of providing ever more generous pension benefits that had prevailed since World War II was not only over—it was being reversed.

Many affected workers were unhappy with the conversions. They were being shifted from plans where accruals sped up as the worker neared retirement to plans where accruals were steadier from start to finish. But these employees had worked 10, 20, or more years under a plan that had slow accruals in the early years and the promise of higher accruals at the end. The accrual pattern was being changed just as they were about to hit the jackpot.

Figure 18.2 shows how benefits accrue in traditional versus hybrid pension plans. The solid line shows the benefit accrual pattern under a traditional defined benefit plan for a worker who joined the plan at age 30. The line traces the value of the earned benefit stated as a multiple of the worker's pay at each age. The steep increase in the benefit value at age 55 relates to the early retirement subsidy that most plans provided during the 1980s and into the 1990s.

The broken line in figure 18.2 shows the accumulated benefit for the same worker under a typical cash balance plan. For a worker who terminated

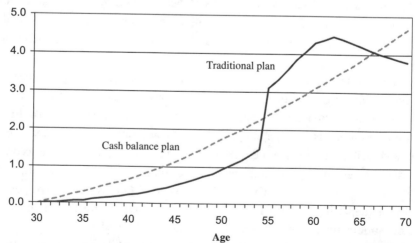

Accrued benefit as a multiple of annual pay

FIGURE 18.2 **Value of Accrued Pension Benefit for a New Hire at Age 30 with a Starting Wage of $40,000 per Year under a Traditional Pension and a Cash Balance Plan**
Source: Developed by the author.

employment before age 55, the cash balance plan would provide a higher benefit. But for a worker who stayed with the company until age 55 or later, the traditional plan would provide a richer benefit. The cash balance line has no "cliff" similar to that in the traditional pension line.

Figure 18.2 compares benefits for the same worker with a full career under both traditional and hybrid plans. The cash balance controversy arose where workers were shifted from one type of plan to another mid-career. Figure 18.3 illustrates this situation, with the worker converted to a cash balance plan at age 45 with 15 years of service under the old plan. In this case, when the worker is 45, the accumulated pension under the traditional plan is converted to its equivalent cash value, after which the worker earns additional credits under the cash balance plan. The pension path in the old plan is plotted by the solid line, with the dashed line showing the actual path after the conversion. It is easy to see why many workers caught in these conversions were unhappy, although most employers provided transition benefits that protected workers with substantial service under their traditional plans.[17]

The shift to hybrid pensions stirred heated policy discussions during much of the 1990s, with the controversy spilling over into the courts. Plan sponsors were reasonably certain the conversions were legal, but many workers were convinced that their employers were in the wrong. In several prominent lawsuits,

Accrued benefit as a multiple of annual pay

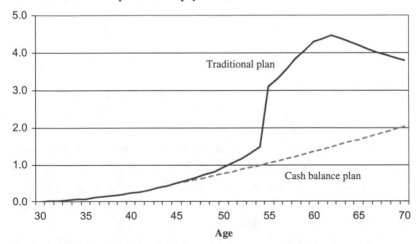

FIGURE 18.3 **Value of Accrued Pension Benefit for Worker Converted from a Hypothetical Traditional Pension to a Cash Balance Plan at Age 45 with 15 Years of Completed Service**

Source: Developed by the author.

employees sought to reverse the conversions. In probably the most well-known of these, plan participants brought a class action suit against IBM in the U.S. District Court for the Southern District of Illinois for changes to its plan adopted in 1995 and 1999. On July 31, 2003, Judge G. Patrick Murphy found that IBM's pension plan conversions were age discriminatory.[18]

To understand the age discrimination claim against IBM, consider two workers covered under a cash balance plan. The employer credits employee accounts with 6 percent of pay and a 5 percent interest credit on the accumulated balance annually, with the balance payable at termination. The normal retirement age is 65. Assume that both workers earn $40,000 per year, but one is 45 and the other 55. The court considered IBM's plan age discriminatory because the younger worker's account balance would accumulate to $6,367.91 by age 65, while the older worker would have only $3,909.35 at that age. Never mind that compound interest accounts for the difference here, and if the employer put $2,400 in a defined contribution account rather than a cash balance plan, the different account payouts would not be considered age discriminatory.

By the end of 2003, the Pension Benefit Guaranty Corporation estimated that 25 percent of participants in insured plans were in hybrid plans.[19] Many people, including many critics of some conversions to hybrid plans, called for a regulatory remedy to the glaring inconsistency in the treatment of benefit accruals under defined benefit and defined contribution plans after the IBM ruling. Shortly after the ruling, the Treasury Department decided to develop modified regulations to clarify whether hybrid pensions were age discriminatory. In December 2003, however, Congress stopped the Treasury Department from finalizing its regulations. Early in 2004, the Treasury proposed new transition rules for hybrid plan conversions, under which future hybrid plans would generally meet age discrimination requirements so long as the pay credits were level or increased with age in the same manner as those in defined contribution plans.

Despite widespread concerns about the legality of hybrid plans and the clear desire of Congress to have a public hand in resolving the perceived unfairness to workers, it took until August 3, 2006, for the Pension Protection Act to formulate rules to govern these plans going forward. Still, that legislation did not resolve the legal status of plans already in existence when the new rules took effect. Ironically, on August 8, 2006, the United States Court of Appeals for the Seventh Circuit overturned *Cooper vs. IBM*. In its ruling, the author of the opinion, Judge Easterbrook, wrote "Treating the time value of money as a form of discrimination is not sensible."[20]

In 2001, when the first IBM ruling had come down, the Pension Benefit Guaranty Corporation reported 1,541 hybrid plans in its single-employer insurance program, which was only 5 percent of the universe of plans but covered a quarter of plan participants. The shift to hybrid plans tended to be a large plan phenomenon. At the end of 2008, the insurance agency reported 2,984 hybrid plans—10.3 percent of the total—covering 31.3 percent of defined benefit participants.[21] The shift to hybrid plans and consequent elimination of generous early retirement subsidies dramatically reduced the pension accruals of the affected baby boom workers late in their careers. Many employers grandfathered workers with long tenures under the old formulas, but some did not. For many workers, though, worse was ahead.

Shifting from Pension Conversions to Pension Closures

When the Pension Benefit Guaranty Corporation analyzed its universe of single-employer plans in 2005, using 2003 enrollment data, it reported that 9.3 percent of its plans had implemented a hard freeze. In a hard freeze, the sponsor closes the plan to new entrants and existing participants no longer accrue benefits. By 2007, 18 percent of covered plans were under a hard freeze. Participants in frozen plans represented only 7.6 percent of all participants, implying that plan freezing was predominantly a smaller plan phenomenon.[22] But many larger employers were also curtailing their plans.

A pension industry analysis of pension freezes among Fortune 1000 firms by Brendan McFarland and Erika Kummernuss used financial disclosure data and a broader definition of a "plan freeze" than the "hard freeze" measure used by the Pension Benefit Guaranty Corporation. The broader definition included both freezes that stopped all accruals and freezes where the plan provides accruals for some participants. For example, it is fairly common to close an existing plan to new hires but continue operating it for current plan participants. Or an employer might freeze future service accruals based on service but not on pay, or the reverse.

In 2004, among the 633 companies on the annual *Fortune* list of the largest corporations in the United States, 633 reported sponsoring a defined benefit plans. Of these, 7.1 percent reported one or more frozen defined benefit plan. The number of firms on this list reporting that they sponsored a defined benefit plan has declined since 2004, dropping to 607 companies in 2009 and 586 in 2010. By 2010, 35.5 percent of the companies with such plans reported that they had frozen at least one of them.[23]

The composition of the *Fortune 1000* list changes every year, and new additions to the list are less likely to have ever sponsored a defined benefit plan, which likely accounts for part of the decline in plan sponsorship. To control for the potential effects of list turnover from one year to the next on defined benefit plan sponsorship and freezing patterns, Brendan McFarland at Towers Watson ran a separate set of tabulations estimating freeze rates among the 481 companies that both sponsored a defined benefit plan and remained on the *Fortune 1000* list over the entire analysis period. While 723 companies made the *Fortune* list every year from 2004 through 2010, 242 of them did not sponsor a defined benefit plan during the period. Among the 481 companies that sponsored a defined benefit plan at some point in the analysis, one terminated its plan in 2009 and eight more followed in 2010. These nine companies may signify a new pattern for large plan sponsors, although it is too early to say with certainty. The percentage of defined benefit plan sponsors that froze one or more of their pension plans shows the growing trend of large employers freezing their defined benefit plans. The percentage of plan sponsors that reported having at least one frozen plan in this group followed the trends reported for the larger list where the companies on the list were simply tabulated from year to year. Among the plan sponsors on the list in every year, the percentage with at least one frozen plan increased from 6.9 percent in 2004 to 34.1 percent in 2010.[24] It is clear the system continues to be constricted.

In the early 2000s, falling interest rates drove up pension liabilities and stock market declines depressed trust fund asset values. After two decades of cutting back on pension funding for the various reasons that have been explored, these financial market developments in the 2000–10 period drove up pension costs dramatically, and the exploding costs were a major motivation for the pension freezes. Table 18.3 helps to clarify why so many plan sponsors are giving up on their defined benefit plans. The table summarizes average retirement plan costs for 335 companies that were on the *Fortune 1000* list from 2004 through 2009 in the Towers Watson analysis.

Focusing first on the defined benefit plans, the average plan expense for sponsors that had no frozen plans in 2010 rose from $57 million in 2003 to $102 million in 2009—an 80 percent increase. Meanwhile, the average defined benefit plan expense for sponsors that froze one or more plans between 2004 and 2010 dropped from $75 million to $68 million—a 10 percent decline. The frozen plans had higher average pension costs in 2004 but dramatically lower average costs in 2010. Pension costs for companies that froze their plans before 2004 were so low that comparing pension costs in 2003 and 2009 hardly seems relevant.

Table 18.3 Average Defined Benefit Pension Expense and Average Defined Contribution Expense for Fortune 1000 Companies, 2003–2009

	Number of companies	Average defined benefit plan expense		Average defined contribution plan expense	
		2003	2009	2003	2009
(dollar amounts reported in thousands)					
All companies	335	$56,888	$86,070	$35,723	$56,888
No frozen DB plans	227	56,078	101,633	34,799	49,337
First froze 2004–2009	82	75,012	67,772	41,856	84,356
Froze prior to 2004	26	6,801	7,902	24,441	27,947

Source: Brendan McFarland and Erika Kummernuss, "Pension Freezes Continue among Fortune 1000 Companies in 2010," *Insider* (September 2010), http://www.towerswatson.com/united-states/newsletters/insider/2761, and unpublished tabulations from the authors on the firms in all seven Fortune 1000 lists.

The costs for defined contribution plans add considerable context to the fate of defined benefit plans, at least among larger private plan sponsors. Among plan sponsors whose defined benefit plans were still fully active in 2010, the average defined contribution plan cost rose from $35 billion to $49 billion, an increase of 42 percent. Most of these companies have 401(k) plans with substantial matches of employee contributions. Much of the higher expense was probably from employers matching workers' bigger contributions, which reflected rising incomes and workers' attempts to offset their investment losses. Among the companies that froze plans between 2003 and 2009, the average defined contribution expense doubled. While large employers were spending less on defined benefit plans, they were spending substantially more on defined contribution plans. Still, overall retirement spending was much higher in companies that stayed the course with their defined benefit plans.

Late in 2007, the Government Accountability Office (GAO) surveyed a sample of private defined benefit pension plans with more than 100 participants in order to evaluate the implications of plan freezes. The GAO concluded that 21 percent of active participants in single-employer defined benefit plans were affected by a plan freeze at that time. It estimated that nearly half the sponsors in its study population had one or more frozen plans. Nearly 51 percent of the plans were closed to new entrants and 23 percent of all plans were under a hard freeze. Among the sponsors with one or more frozen plans, 83 percent reported offering participants a replacement savings plan, and some allowed affected participants to join an existing plan or increase their plan contributions. But 11 percent of these sponsors offered no replacement plan after freezing their defined benefit plan. When the GAO survey asked plan sponsors why they froze their plans, 72 percent cited the required annual contributions and subsequent reduced cash flow as the primary motivation, but 69 percent identified the unpredictability and volatility of plan funding requirements as important factors.[25]

In a separate survey, the GAO focused on 94 companies that appeared on the *Fortune* 500 or Global 500 list of sponsors of the largest defined benefit plans in the Pension Benefit Guaranty Corporation's 2004 Form 5500 Research Database.[26] These defined benefit plans represented 50 percent of total pension liabilities and 39 percent of all plan participants covered by the insurance program. Out of the 94 companies, the 44 ultimate respondents represented 25 percent of all defined benefit plan liabilities and 19 percent of all participants in the system. The data were collected between late December 2007 and the end of October 2008. This was before the ramifications of the financial market turmoil were fully understood by plan sponsors. Focusing on the plans that were not collectively bargained, 48 percent of the respondents said they had scaled back the generosity of the pension plans over the last decade and cited unpredictability or volatility of funding requirements as the primary reason for the cutbacks.[27]

New Pension Funding Rules: A Day Late and Dollar Short

The Pension Protection Act changed the rules—pension funding was back in vogue. The new rules, which took effect in 2008, require that single-employer plan sponsors fund 100 percent of unfunded accrued liabilities over seven years. They also restrict actuarial flexibility in determining funded status.[28] Plans whose asset balances are less than 80 percent of accrued liabilities are subject to benefit restrictions, and those whose funded status is between 60 percent and 80 percent cannot increase benefits and can only pay partial lump-sum distributions. Plans that are less than 60 percent funded cannot increase benefits, pay lump sums, or accrue additional benefits, and special shutdown benefits are frozen until funding improves.[29] The requirements are less stringent for multiemployer plans, which must amortize unfunded accrued liabilities over 15 years.

The legislation set out to put the private pension system on a more secure footing and reduce the Pension Benefit Guaranty Corporation's exposure to underfunded plans, primarily by putting the monkey on the back of private pension sponsors—particularly those who were not creating the problem. The timing was terrible, as the new requirements came online as plan funding was plummeting from the financial market upheaval. Plan sponsors that had been discouraged or stopped from contributing during the prosperous 1980s and 1990s now had to make enormous extra contributions in one of the worst economic environments since the Great Depression.

Many workers have been blindsided by the changing pension system, and some of the changes, while legal, were unfair to some workers. Many of the "unjust cutbacks" in pensions, however, were motivated less by greedy corporate managers than by the economic realities of global competition. While many of the companies that modified their plans have remained profitable, other firms that refused to modify their plans were driven into bankruptcy by their underfunded retirement obligations. Those workers and retirees also lost benefits, and many of the workers also lost their jobs. The choices employers would have to make and their outcomes were predictable more than 20 years ago. As I noted in chapter 1, I testified before the House Select Committee on Aging in 1990 and told the committee members that the delays in pension funding that had been imposed in the prior decade were going to lead to much larger contributions in the future. I warned them that if employers could not meet the obligations embedded in federal funding policies when the bills came due, then they would cut back the generosity of their plans.[30] If we had awakened a long time ago to the reality we now face, the outlook would be more favorable.

19

AND THEN, A PREDICTABLE DEFINED CONTRIBUTION SURPRISE

In 1975, almost 68 percent of the benefits that were paid out of private employer-sponsored retirement plans came from defined benefit plans.[1] The next 35 years would bring a reversal in the roles of defined benefit and defined contribution plans. But there was more than just a simple shift from defined benefit to defined contribution plans going on over the period.

Retirement Plan Participants Become Investment Managers

When the Employee Retirement Income Security Act (ERISA) was implemented in the mid-1970s, the operations of defined contribution plans were remarkably different from those today. Partly for historical reasons and partly for technological reasons, most defined contribution plans held their assets in pooled trust funds, and the plan sponsors managed the investments. Employers contributed on a periodic basis as specified in the plans, and assets were valued periodically, generally quarterly, but sometimes only once or twice a year. If a worker quit or retired between valuations, the benefits paid out were based on the most recent valuation.

The Conference Report on ERISA included section 404(c), which provided a "special rule . . . for individual account plans where the participant is permitted to, and in fact does, exercise independent control over the assets in his account. In this case . . . other persons who are fiduciaries with respect to the plan are not to be liable for any loss that results from the exercise and control by the participant." The report stated that whether or not participants "exercise independent control is to be determined pursuant to regulations prescribed by the Secretary of Labor."[2] This provision was included in ERISA because in professional service firms, like law firms, it was common for the partners to "manage" their retirement assets through individual brokerage accounts. It did not make sense to hold plan sponsors accountable for the investment results of individuals who were managing their own accounts. It is unlikely that anyone back then anticipated the changes to come over the next couple of decades. While the IRS took its time in proposing 401(k) regulations, the Department of Labor took even longer to develop regulations on participant-directed accounts, publishing its recommended rules on September 3, 1987. A child born the day ERISA was passed was already in high school by the time the regulating agencies released these preliminary rules.

On Black Monday, October 19, 1987, the Dow Jones Industrial Average dropped 22.6 percent—the largest one-day percentage decline in the market's history.[3] The historic drop set off another revolution in the defined contribution world that led to a restructuring of the way plan assets were managed. These events and reactions to them had remarkable implications for the evolution of the employer-based component of our retirement system.

Plan sponsors recognized that workers who quit their jobs before the year-end plan valuation would qualify for a distribution based on the September 30 valuation of plan assets—well before Black Monday. So terminating workers could walk away with assets worth considerably more than their share of the fund on the day they left—leaving that much less in the trust for the workers who stayed behind.

ERISA required that fiduciaries discharge their duties with "prudence and diligence," and events after Black Monday called into question whether fiduciary standards had been met. Sponsors faced the prospect of having to make special contributions to protect remaining participants, but any contributions in excess of legal maximums could trigger a 10 percent excise tax. Added contributions could not discriminate in favor of officers or highly compensated employees. Sponsors worried about the implications of setting a new precedent: Would making an extra contribution now mean they would have to do so whenever the stock market fell?

Some defined contribution plan sponsors had been allowing workers to direct the investment of their retirement assets since ERISA took effect. Now there was widespread interest in turning asset direction over to plan participants. The only source of information available on the evolution of self-directed investment in private defined contribution plans after the passage of ERISA to the present is the Profit Sharing/401(k) Council of America, a trade association the members of which tend to be large employers.

The Profit Sharing Council surveys its members annually, and its 2009 survey had 931 respondents with an average of almost 10,000 participants per firm. Since 1980, the survey has asked whether the plan sponsors allowed participants to invest the funds arising from either employer or employee contributions.

Figure 19.1 shows the survey results. Starting in 1982, with the advent of the 401(k) system, the percentage of assets being managed by participants began to trend up steadily to the early 1990s. By 2009, 97 percent of plans had self-directed investment of employee contributions and 85 percent of plans had self-directed investment of employer contributions. Ninety-one percent of the plans were allowing participants to direct the investment of some of the employer-financed assets in their plans.

Until the 401(k) rules were clarified, employee contributions to these plans were small, although many larger employers had thrift-savings plans that accepted after-tax contributions from workers, with the returns not taxed until distribution. The regulatory wheels were slowly grinding out the rules for self-directed accounts, but employers were under mounting pressure to give workers more control over their own assets. The Department of Labor issued modified proposed regulations for participant-directed investment of defined contribution assets in March 1991 and final regulations in October 1992. The child born the day ERISA became law was out of high school by the time the

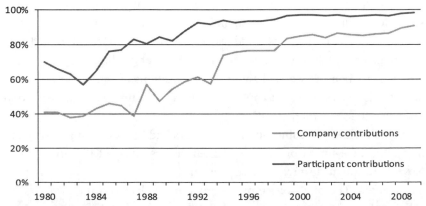

FIGURE 19.1 Percentage of Private Firms Allowing Participant-Directed Investing of Employer and Employee Contributions to Profit-Sharing or 401(k) Plans

Source: Annual surveys of the members of the Profit Sharing/401(k) Council of America.

rules finally codified the principle that protected sponsors from fiduciary responsibility for asset management when participants do the investing.

Growing Role of 401(k) Plans

After the 1987 financial market downturn, defined contribution plan sponsors pushed their record-keeping vendors for more frequent plan valuations. The regulations on participant-directed investment management required more frequent opportunities for participants to move their assets among investment choices. The rules required that plan participants be offered at least three types of funds in which to invest—equities, bonds or fixed income, and money market—in order to be able to diversify their investments to manage the risks they faced. Large mutual fund companies quickly became the gold standard for operating defined contribution plans, partly because their families of funds met the alternative investment class requirements of the rules. Once the sponsor chose a set of plan options that met the risk and return requirements, participants could move their assets among them as frequently as they wished. Participants' account balances could be determined daily based on their holdings in the alternative funds and the end-of-day closing price for fund shares.

By the mid-1980s, retirement plan sponsors were offering matching contributions to encourage workers to take advantage of their 401(k) opportunities. As 401(k)s matured, there was a dramatic shift toward a private retirement system dependent on worker contributions. In 1984, about 16 percent of private retirement plan contributions and slightly more than one-third of defined contribution plan contributions were to 401(k) plans. By 2007, 75 percent of all private retirement plan contributions and more than 90 percent of defined contribution plan contributions were to 401(k) plans. When employee contributions started flowing into 401(k) plans in the early 1980s, private retirement plans held slightly more than a half trillion dollars. The share of 401(k) assets grew steadily from the early 1980s through 2007. By then, nearly 50 percent of assets in all private, employer-sponsored retirement plans were in 401(k) plans, and nearly 85 percent of the assets in all private defined contribution plans were in plans dependent on participant contributions.[4]

Before IRAs were created in 1974, workers generally had to leave tax-qualified plan accumulations in their plans of origin. After 1974, workers could roll their qualified plan assets into an IRA and continue to enjoy tax-deferred accumulation until retirement. Today, most of the growth in funds being added to IRAs, beyond investment returns, comes from rollovers of distributions from tax-qualified employer plans.

From the outset, IRA holders had to manage their own investments, and by the early 1990s, employers were shifting responsibility for managing the investment of 401(k) plan assets to participants as well. Technological developments allowing daily valuations, and the Internet, which allowed participants to manage their accounts online, made self-directed investment feasible for large and small 401(k) plans alike. The predominant role played by mutual fund companies in managing investments for the vast majority of savers facilitated the process.

Figure 19.2 shows the share of private, tax-favored retirement plan assets in 401(k) plans and IRA or Keogh accounts between 1981 and 2007. Keogh accounts are retirement plans for the self-employed, and the Federal Reserve combines Keogh and IRA assets in their data. Figure 19.2 also shows the estimated percentage of total private plan assets in self-directed investment accounts. The estimates assume that two-thirds of 401(k) contributions were from employees, consistent with employee contributions being matched at a 50 percent rate, the most common matching rate in private plans. I used the rates for self-direction derived from figure 19.1, adjusted to account for the Department of Labor's focus on large plans after 1999, and followed the trends from the Profit Sharing Council data. In the early 1980s, slightly less

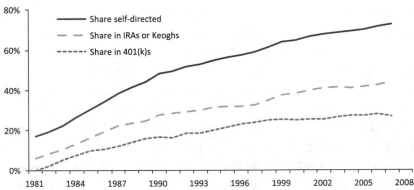

FIGURE 19.2 **Share of Private Tax-Favored Plan Assets Held in 401(k)s or IRAs and Keoghs, and Share in Self-Directed Investment Accounts**

Source: Derived from U.S. Department of Labor, Pension and Welfare Benefits Administration, *Private Pension Plan Bulletin Historical Tables and Graphs: 1975-2007*, various tables, found at: http://www.dol.gov/ebsa/pdf/1975-2007historicaltables.pdf and the Federal Reserve Board's *Flow of Funds*.

than 20 percent of private retirement assets were self-directed, while by 2008, it was nearly 75 percent.

Shift to Do-It-Yourself Pensions Raises Retirement Security Concerns

The rise of 401(k)s corresponds almost precisely with the fall of defined benefit pensions. From 1984 through 2008, there was only one year when per capita contributions to private defined benefit plans exceeded per capita contributions to 401(k) plans.[5] In 1984, private defined benefit plans had four times as many active workers as 401(k) plans and took in about three times the annual contributions of 401(k) plans—$47.2 billion versus $16.3 billion. By 2007, 401(k) plans had 2.6 times as many active participants as private defined benefit plans and received roughly four times the contributions made to defined benefit plans—$273.2 billion versus $68.3 billion.[6]

Around two-thirds of the contributions to 401(k) plans come directly out of workers' paychecks. And workers then must figure out how to manage account investment and, eventually, their distribution. Retirement security has become a "do-it-yourself" proposition, and some critics are concerned about the job workers are not doing in the new world order. An analysis by Richard Hinz and John Turner, from the Department of Labor, used 1993 Census data and national survey data to look at plan participation. Hinz and Turner showed that among all those offered a 401(k) plan, participants tended to be older, have longer tenures, earn higher pay and work for larger companies than nonparticipants. Women were less likely to participate than men. Workers tended to contribute more to their plans as their pay levels climbed.[7] The results suggested that those who needed help the most in acquiring retirement security were being left out.

By the early to mid-1990s, some concerned employers explored ways to motivate reluctant workers to join their 401(k) plans. Sponsors' concerns were motivated, in part, by the discrimination tests that 401(k) plans must pass each year. While evidence suggested that higher match rates and more intensive communication increased plan participation,[8] some employers could not afford a higher match and, even if they could, some workers stayed away despite a higher match and more and better communication.

In 2001, Bridgette Madrian and Dennis Shea published an analysis of participation, contribution rates, and investment behavior in a Fortune 500 company in the health care industry. Before April 1, 1998, the plan had offered a 401(k) plan to workers with at least one year with the company. Workers could contribute up to 15 percent of their pay, subject to the contribution limits, and the company provided a 50 percent match on contributions up to 6 percent of pay. To enroll, the worker had to fill out an enrollment form or call the plan record keeper to authorize deductions from pay, and choose a contribution rate and investment options.[9]

On April 1, 1998, the company eliminated the one-year service requirement for participation but maintained it for matching contributions. Newly hired workers were automatically enrolled in the plan—unless they made an affirmative election to opt out—at a default contribution rate of 3 percent of pay. New enrollees were free to change their contribution rate. The plan managers were convinced that automatic enrollment would boost participation and ensure compliance with the discrimination rules.[10]

The results were impressive. The participation rate was 72 percent among all those eligible to participate, and 86 percent among those automatically enrolled. Among workers hired in the one-year period before April 1, 1998, the participation rate was only 49 percent. None of these workers would have been eligible for participation before the introduction of automatic enrollment because of the prior one-year service requirement. They all became eligible to join the plan on April 1 but were not automatically enrolled. Among those who had been with the firm between one and two years on April 1, 1998, the participation rate on June 30, 1999, was 57 percent. They had a full year of eligibility before the employer changed the plan. Automatic enrollment made the biggest differences for blacks and Hispanics, younger workers and lower-earners. The changes were a resounding success and eliminated the discrimination testing failures.[11]

Unfortunately, the effects on contributions were less positive. The average contribution rate among all participants was 6.4 percent of compensation, with 6 percent being the most frequently selected rate. Among automatically enrolled participants, the contribution rate averaged 4.4 percent, with 76 percent of participants contributing the default rate of 3 percent. When the automatically enrolled group was compared to the group hired in the year before the new plan features were adopted, 80 percent of the participants who self-enrolled were contributing more than 3 percent of compensation. The authors concluded that automatic enrollment reduced the contribution rate by 2.9 percentage points among the newly eligible, and that the results were generally applicable across all demographic subgroups.[12]

In a series of subsequent papers, Madrian and several coauthors continued to study worker behavior in companies that offered 401(k) plans with default features.[13] They consistently found that default enrollments dramatically altered behavior. Workers tended to be passive when they were auto-enrolled in 401(k) plans, but automatic enrollment was typically linked to default contribution rates of only 2 or 3 percent of pay, while workers who voluntarily joined 401(k) plans tended to contribute 6 percent or more of pay. The solution of one problem was potentially causing another.

Richard Thaler and Schlomo Bernatzi, two behavioral economists, suggested that once workers got used to plan participation, employers could successfully use other default features to nudge them into saving more. Thaler is a pioneer in the behavioral economics field with an orientation toward experimentation. The hypothesis was that workers would save more over time if their deferral percentage rose whenever they got a raise, so part of the pay increase would go into the plan instead of the paycheck. In a live test, workers who signed up for their plan tended to increase their contributions to their savings plans over time.[14]

Madrian and her coauthors' research suggested that default increments in savings rates could get workers to save more. Instead of asking workers beforehand to give up part of their pay increases, as Bernatzi and Thaler did, plan sponsors simply told workers that part of their annual pay increase would be added to their savings rate unless they elected otherwise. Increasing participation rates while bringing default enrollees' contribution rates up to the level of motivated savers would be a winning combination.

Researchers have also been concerned about participants' asset management skills. Policymakers and employers had concerns about workers' understanding of important financial concepts and the investment advice they received. Douglas Bernheim summarized his research by saying that for retirement savers to be turning to family or friends for advice on investing their nest eggs was often the "blind leading the blind."[15]

Much of the same economic research that studied the implications of automatic enrollment in 401(k) plans also evaluated investment behavior. The researchers found that 401(k) participants tend to be passive investors. Once they allocate their contributions, they seldom reallocate either their contributions or their account balances, which increases their investment risk. For example, suppose a worker allocated 40 percent of contributions to bonds and 60 percent to stocks in 1985 and never rebalanced the account. By 2000, the participant would have had far too high a concentration in stocks, leaving the account vulnerable to heavy losses when the stock market took a nosedive.

Institutionalizing Automatic Features
of Defined Contribution Plans

The Pension Protection Act of 2006 recognized the virtues of automatic enroll-ment and contribution increases and created "safe harbors" for 401(k) plan sponsors that introduced these auto features, meaning the sponsors could act without fear of reprisal as long as they followed the rules. Many employers had been cautious about auto-enrollment because of potential conflicts between default elections and other laws, especially state laws requiring employees' permission for payroll deductions. The Pension Protection Act preempts state laws that conflict with auto enrollment.

Since 2006, there has been a substantial shift to auto enrollment. Fidelity Investments has tracked auto enrollment among its customer base for some time. Between December 2004 and March 2009 Fidelity tracked 16,600 plans with 11.1 million participants. One-third of its clients with between 500 and 1,000 participants had auto enrollment by the end of the period, compared to 1 percent at the beginning. For sponsors with 2,500 to 5,000 participants, auto-enrollment increased from 6 percent to 43 percent. For those with 10,000 to 25,000 participants, the jump was from 17 percent to 40 percent. The trends were consistent across the size spectrum of plans.[16] In September 2010, Charles Schwab reported that 38 percent of its defined contribution clients were of-fering automatic enrollment, up seven times from just five years earlier.[17] Van-guard Investments reported that at year-end 2008, 19 percent of its defined contribution clients had automatic enrollment, broken down to 19 percent of its plans with fewer than 1,000 participants, 42 percent with 1,000 to 4,999 par-ticipants, and 43 percent with 5,000 or more participants. Among the partici-pants in plans it administered, 43 percent were in automatic enrollment plans.[18]

Fidelity, Schwab, and Vanguard all found that the higher prevalence of automatic enrollment after the Pension Protection Act was boosting plan par-ticipation rates. Participation rates across most ages rose from the middle-to-low 80 percent range to the low 90 percent range, according to Fidelity's results.[19] The almost 10-percentage-point increase in participation rates was good news, but 62 percent of Fidelity's clients were enrolling workers at a 3 percent default contribution rate. Only 22 percent brought workers in above that rate and only 7 percent brought them in at a 6 percent contribution rate. The analysis suggested that higher automatic contribution rates do not dis-courage participation, which seems to be a fear of plan sponsors.

Considerable evidence now exists that automatically increasing contribu-tions in tandem with pay boosts savings rates. The Pension Protection Act allowed plan sponsors to automatically increase their 401(k) participants' deferral percentage by at least 1 percentage point annually up to 10 percent of compensation or until the employee says stop. As to whether workers increase their contribution rates once they're participating in a plan, Fidelity reports that more than a third had increased their deferral rate but 60 percent did not in plans including the feature. Three-quarters of Fidelity's plans offer annual auto-increase programs, but the vast majority of plan sponsors do not automatically enroll participants in this feature. Among workers who default into an automatic increase in contribution rates, 71 percent stay there.[20] This important feature could significantly rev up the economic horsepower of these plans, but it is not yet fully utilized. Plan sponsors can help workers achieve more financially secure retirements simply by adopting auto features with proven track records.

Pioneers of automatic enrollment were concerned about fiduciary liability and so tended to direct contributions to conservative investments, and most participants simply left the assets in those funds. Madrian and Shea found that workers perceive default investment options as recommendations by the plan sponsor.[21] Even automatically enrolled workers who proactively increased their contribution rates still disproportionately left their assets in the default fund.[22] In many cases, the defaults were money market funds with little risk of capital losses but also slim prospects for the lucrative returns so important to successful retirement saving.

A large industrial company I worked with from 2005 to 2006 developed a detailed analysis of the relative rates of return realized by its defined benefit and defined contribution plans going back a couple of decades. These defined contribution plan participants had to make affirmative choices on allocating contributions and funds. According to the company's estimates, the pension assets chosen by its investment managers outperformed participant-directed investments in the defined contribution plan by an average of 200 basis points per year, net of expenses. Over a full career, earning 6 percent a year versus 4 percent could amount to a 50 percent gain—or loss—in savings. In a larger context, Alicia Munnell and colleagues estimated that between 1988 and 2004—most of the period over which workers have directed the investment of substantial accumulations in 401(k) or similar plans—private defined benefit plans collectively outperformed 401(k) plans by 1 percentage point per year, net of expenses.[23]

The Pension Protection Act directed the Department of Labor to develop regulations to encourage employers to offer higher-yield default investment options. The Department issued regulatory guidelines in October 2007, which attempted to balance the competing interests of capital preservation and growth. The rules allowed three different types of default investments. The first included life-cycle funds, also called target-date funds, which reflect a plan participant's age, target retirement date, or life expectancy. The second included balanced funds, which take into account the characteristics of the plan participants as a whole. Balanced funds periodically rebalance holdings in equities and bonds to maintain a fund-specified ratio of stocks to bonds. The third is for an investment service that allocates contributions among plan options to provide an investment portfolio that considers the individual's age, target retirement date, or life expectancy. This latter option would essentially put plan participants' funds under professional management.

Fidelity Investments published data showing the shift in the use of default investment options among its clients during the months leading up to the Pension Protection Act and for 18 months after the regulations spelled out the rules for using default investment funds. Their data tracked 17,500 plans with 11.3 million participants on a quarterly basis from September 2005 through March 2009. In December 2005, only 4 percent of the plans used a life-cycle fund as the default investment option, but by March 2009, 62 percent of Fidelity's entire client base and 96 percent of its plans with auto-enrollment were doing so.[24]

Among all private defined contribution plans, 38.2 percent of assets were invested in stocks in 1990, with the share climbing to 68.2 percent by 2007.[25] Given the concerns that plan sponsors, researchers, and policymakers have had about defined contribution investors being too conservative, it is somewhat ironic that, in the aggregate, the workers left to direct their own investment became so exposed to the equity markets. The risky allocation partly reflects participants' disinclination to reallocate their assets even as economic conditions change. To the extent participants select life-cycle funds, balances will be automatically reallocated periodically. Vanguard reported that among its 401(k) client plans, only 11 percent of the assets were invested in balanced funds at the end of 2008 and another 7 percent in life style or target-date funds. As of 2008, most of the equities in the defined contribution system were still in accounts that were not automatically rebalanced on any regular basis.

Remaining Concerns Plague Defined Contribution Plans

Enticing more workers into savings plans, increasing their contributions over time, and moving them into reasonable investment patterns still leave a major problem unsolved: preretirement leakages. These occur when workers change jobs and cash out their savings. James Moore and Leslie Muller cite Department of Labor surveys showing that by 1997, defined contribution participants were four times more likely than defined benefit plan participants to have the option of lump-sum payouts at employment termination.[26] Since then, lump-sum payouts have become much more common in defined benefit plans, so the potential problems created by early distributions affect both types of plans.

Many studies published by a range of authors during the 1990s looked at lump-sum distributions from retirement plans. The studies consistently found that participants who cashed out tended to be younger workers with relatively small balances. While the majority of people who changed jobs cashed out their plans, more than half of the associated lump-sum distributions were rolled into another tax-qualified retirement plan like an IRA. That most of the money was being rolled over was some solace, but the fact that young workers were "losing" their early-career retirement savings was still troubling. To discourage workers from taking premature distributions, the Tax Reform Act of 1986 imposed a 10 percent excise tax on preretirement distributions on top of regular income taxes. In 1992, Congress required plan sponsors to withhold and remit to the IRS 20 percent of any distribution not rolled into another tax-favored account for all those younger than age 59½. In 2005, the Department of Labor issued regulations requiring plan sponsors to roll accumulations of $1,000 to $5,000 into an IRA unless the participant specifically directed them otherwise.

Alicia Munnell and her colleagues recently developed an analysis of the cashing out phenomenon that describes recent trends and retirement dollar losses. They considered only funds that workers actually withdrew when they terminated employment. In 2001, 55 percent of workers cashed out their 401(k) benefits when they changed jobs, but their accumulated assets were only 21 percent of the 401(k) assets held by participants who could have cashed out. By 2007, the percentage of job changers taking cash-outs had dropped to 40 percent and their accumulated assets equaled only 16 percent of the total assets that could have been cashed out.[27]

Andrew Samwick and Jonathan Skinner developed an analysis suggesting the cash-out phenomenon in defined contribution plans might not be much different from what happens to traditional defined benefit plan participants who change jobs before retiring. Samwick and Skinner developed a range of simulated wage histories and job turnover patterns and tested them against defined benefit plan formulas from 1983—before the defined benefit world was turned on its head. They also tested them against a sample of defined contribution plans from 1995. Based on contribution and investment allocations from a nationally representative sample of defined contribution plans, mean and median defined contribution pension benefits were substantially higher than the corresponding defined benefit pensions. Although some of the defined contribution plans did not provide adequate retirement incomes, neither did many of the defined benefit plans.[28]

Their results held up when they changed the simulated equity rates of return, productivity growth and variations in earnings patterns. When employees changed jobs, pension benefits tended to be lower under the defined benefit plans. Samwick and Skinner's simulation suggested that employees with defined contribution plans needed to roll over approximately 25 percent of distributions received early in their careers and 50 percent of distributions received late in their careers to maintain parity with benefits provided under traditional pensions. Their analysis showed that defined contribution plans were riskier, meaning that retirement income varied more widely, but overall expected returns were also higher. In their results, the defined contribution plans provided higher benefits in all but the bottom 20 percent of the retirement income distribution.[29]

The 401(k) Story May Not Be as Bad as the Telling

Before the recent innovations to increase 401(k) participation rates, contribution levels, and investment allocations had evolved, James Poterba, Steven Venti, and David Wise projected the system forward to 2040. They used evolving participation and contribution patterns from the 1980s and 1990s and accounted for leakages of preretirement distributions. They projected contributions based on wage growth consistent with assumptions used by the Social Security actuaries for their annual valuations. Poterba, Venti, and Wise estimated accumulating account balances based on existing asset allocation patterns and past returns on various asset classes. Ultimately, they estimated the 401(k) wealth of individuals retiring in 2010, 2020, 2030, and 2040 by income classes, where each class represented one-tenth or decile of the retiring group in each year. The authors also developed a Social Security wealth estimate in 2000 for the classes of people retiring in 2010, based on Social Security historical earnings records matched to the individual-level data in the Health and Retirement Study, a nationally representative sample of older Americans.[30] The Social Security wealth measure they developed is the present value of expected lifetime benefits for each individual given his or her historical earnings pattern and normal life expectancy based on age and gender.

Table 19.1 Projected 401(k) and Social Security Wealth, by Lifetime Earnings for Workers Retiring in 2030

Earnings decile	401(k) wealth	Social Security wealth	Ratio of 401(k) to SS wealth
1	$1,372	$98,843	0.014
2	21,917	135,926	0.161
3	47,770	153,377	0.311
4	120,706	193,294	0.624
5	272,135	248,299	1.096
6	390,004	270,238	1.443
7	508,402	314,541	1.616
8	647,329	338,877	1.910
9	622,449	360,685	1.726
10	895,179	387,250	2.312
Total	3,527,263	2,501,331	1.410

Source: The 401(k) projections came from James M. Poterba, Steven F. Venti, and David A. Wise, "Rise of 401(k) Plans, Lifetime Earnings, and Wealth at Retirement," NBER Working Paper 13091 (Cambridge, MA: National Bureau of Economic Research, 2007), http://www.nber.org/papers/w13091. The Social Security wealth projections were derived by the author based on Poterba, Venti, and Wise's estimates of Social Security wealth for people reaching retirement age in 2010.

Poterba, Venti, and Wise's Social Security wealth estimates for 2010 can be projected forward to 2030 by indexing them by the rate of real wage growth used in developing their projected 401(k) accumulations. A projection of the 2010 Social Security wealth estimates in this fashion is consistent with the method Social Security actuaries use to estimate future benefits.

Table 19.1 compares Poterba, Venti, and Wise's projected accumulation of 401(k) wealth in 2030 to the projection of Social Security wealth that year. The estimated values of projected average 401(k) wealth at the lowest earnings levels are modest, and the auto-enrollment and auto-contribution features discussed earlier should give those values a boost. Still, accumulations for low earners will remain modest for three reasons. First, many low earners do not have the opportunity to enroll in a 401(k) plan. Second, low earnings mean low contributions. Third, these workers are more likely than higher earners to have irregular employment patterns, thus having shorter periods of 401(k) plan

participation and being more likely to take cash distributions when they terminate or lose jobs. Social Security is important to almost everyone, but particularly to lower earners, an observation that should be kept in mind when
considering potential policy changes.

Moving up the earnings distribution, projected 401(k) wealth accumulations increase much more rapidly than Social Security wealth estimates. By
the middle of the earnings distribution, projected 401(k) wealth exceeds Social
Security wealth. At the top of the distribution, 401(k) wealth is projected to be
more than double Social Security wealth. Across the whole distribution, 401(k)
accumulations are projected to be as much as 40 percent greater than Social
Security wealth.

If these projections come to pass, it will be an amazing outcome. In 2030,
the Social Security system will celebrate its 95th anniversary, and the 401(k)
system will have been operating for 50 years—about half the life of Social Security. The projections in table 19.1 assume the Social Security benefits in
current law will be delivered. For that to happen, the Social Security actuaries
project program costs of around 16.5 percent of covered payroll in 2030. By
comparison, average contributions to 401(k) plans have been somewhere
around 9 percent of participants' compensation, and all contributions are
voluntary. Once again, these differences illustrate the profound implications
of funding retirement benefits.

Scanning back over the 30-year evolution of the private retirement system
leading up to 2010, the defined contribution system has absolutely exploded,
while the defined benefit system seems to be dying. When policymakers
choked off the flow of funding into the defined benefit system, they limited its
ability to expand or even build in a buffer to soften severe financial blows.
Policymakers also tried to choke off the 401(k) system, but this time they were
taking on the public instead of "corporate interests," and the fierce backlash
stopped them cold. The 401(k) system has been far more vibrant in the new
millennium than the defined benefit system and has adapted more readily to
financial shocks. Still, it was not impervious to them.

20 PUBLIC PENSIONS: THE GOOD, THE BAD AND THE UGLY

Retirement plans for public-sector workers are coming under increasing scrutiny, and the focus is likely to get even sharper in the future. These workers make up a significant share of the labor force, and their retirement benefits comprise a disproportionately large share of the retirement system's total outflow. The locked-in generosity of these public-sector plans—particularly compared with the current state of private-sector retirement plans—is fast becoming a political issue as well as a fiscal one.

The Scope of State and Local Public Employee Retirement Plans

Public employers' retirement benefit programs are predominantly defined benefit plans. Some public employers have recently adopted defined contribution plans, but these are for employees hired after the new plan is adopted or for defined benefit plan participants who want to switch. In recent years, public employers have offered their workforces 401(k)-style plans, but these tend to be supplemental plans rather than the primary retirement accumulation vehicles they have become for private-sector workers.

By conventional measures, some public employers have done a respectable job of plan funding while many others have done poorly. In the aggregate, state and local pensions are estimated to be underfunded to the tune of about $500 billion against total liabilities of around $3 trillion.[1] Recently, however, a number of academic economists have questioned the way public plans measure their liabilities, casting doubt on their estimates of the obligations lying in wait for governments—and, by implication, taxpayers—to pay. From the revised perspective of these economists, unfunded state and local pension obligations may be five or six times larger than current estimates.[2]

The U.S. Census Bureau annually surveys state and local government retirement systems about their plan membership, revenues and sources, expenditures, and asset levels. At the end of fiscal 2008, the latest year for which data are available, 2,550 of these systems were operating across the country, with 218 at the state level and the remaining 2,332 at the local level. Of the 26.8 million participants, 14.7 million were workers accruing benefits, 4.4 million were inactive, and 7.7 million were receiving benefit payments. Eighty-nine percent of active participants and 85 percent of retirees were in state-level plans.[3]

During fiscal 2008, total contributions to state and local plans were $79.6 billion, of which 31.1 percent came from employees, 30.5 from states, and 38.4 percent from local governments. Employee contributions make up a much larger share of defined benefit financing in the public sector than in the private sector. Although the vast majority of participants and beneficiaries are in state plans, local governments account for the largest share of government contributions because the vast majority of local government employees, usually including teachers, participate in state-level plans. Public plans paid out $175.4 billion in benefits or an average of $22,650 per beneficiary in fiscal 2008.[4] The public-sector retirement plans were hit by the same financial market forces that rocked the private plan world in recent years. Assets in state and local government retirement plans dropped from $3.2 trillion at the end of 2007 to $2.3 trillion a year later—a decline of 27.6 percent.[5]

Public plans are exempt from most of the Employee Retirement Income Security Act's (ERISA's) requirements. Some IRS rules apply to public plans, but nothing nearly as complex and restrictive as the regimen for private plan sponsors. The more lenient regulatory environment means that the public retirement system operates differently than the private-sector system. As a white paper published by the National Association of State Retirement Administrators puts it, "In lieu of ERISA, public pension plan sponsors (state and local governments) establish their own governing standards and rules. One beneficial outcome of this arrangement has been a wide range of policies and benefit structures, each suited to the unique needs of their plan sponsors."[6]

At the beginning of 2011, only Nebraska, Michigan, and Alaska did not offer a traditional defined benefit plan to new employees. In 1964, Nebraska established a money purchase defined contribution plan for its employees. In 2003, it closed that plan and started a cash balance plan for new hires and anyone who wanted to switch from the old plan. In 1997, Michigan shifted from a traditional defined benefit plan to a mandatory defined contribution plan for all new hires and allowed existing employees to switch into the new system. Since July 1, 2006, all newly hired state and local workers in Alaska have been covered under a defined contribution plan.

As of July 1, 2011, Utah offers newly hired workers the option of participating in a defined contribution plan or a new defined benefit plan that is fully funded by participant contributions. The employee contribution rate is set at 10 percent of pay. If that amount exceeds the defined benefit plan costs, the excess goes into a 401(k) account. A number of other states—including Colorado, Florida, Montana, North Dakota, Ohio, and South Carolina—already have optional defined contribution plans available for employees who do not want traditional defined benefit plans. A number of states now sponsor combination defined benefit/defined contribution plans.[7]

While the benefit formulas are generous in many public defined benefit plans—especially viewed from the perspective of a private worker who must contribute to the defined contribution plan to get anything—there are certainly private defined benefit plans with comparable formulas. However, many public plans provide unreduced benefits at much earlier ages than typical private plans—it is not uncommon for public-sector workers with 30 years of service to qualify for unreduced pensions, regardless of age.

Table 20.1 summarizes the average salaries of workers covered under state defined benefit pension plans and the plans' average levels of benefits. It includes data from virtually all such plans in operation at the end of fiscal 2009. The table classifies states into five groups of 10 states each on the basis of average benefit generosity relative to the average earnings of participants. Plan generosity does not necessarily vary in lockstep with workers' earnings. The average benefits vary from a low of just under $13,800 per year to nearly $29,300. The average benefits-to-earnings ratio naturally increases going down the rows because that is how the states were ranked, but it is important to consider the benefits-to-earnings ratio in the context of the "Percentage of workers covered under Social Security" column. Not all state and local workers are covered under Social Security, so their benefits must cover both Social Security and employer-plan benefits. Where Social Security coverage rates are lower, state and local pension benefits tend to be more generous. But more than 90 percent of the state and local workers in three of the 10 states in the top (most generous) quintile—Wisconsin, New Jersey, and New York—are covered by Social Security. Average benefits ranged from $7,850 in Montana to $37,700 in New York.

Table 20.1 Summary Characteristics of Pension Plans for State and Local
Workers at the State Level, by Generosity of Benefits Relative to Current
Workers' Covered Pay

Replacement rate quintile	Average covered earnings	Average benefits	Average benefits to earnings ratio	Percentage of workers covered under Social Security
1	$42,202	$13,771	32.4%	90.9%
2	44,982	18,128	40.5%	83.4%
3	40,893	19,481	47.6%	84.8%
4	46,176	24,320	52.9%	74.0%
5	44,927	29,288	65.7%	57.8%

Source: Developed by the author based on disclosure information in state government Consolidated Annual Financial Reports or from actuarial reports based on individual pension plans. Much of the information is as of December 31, 2009, or June 30, 2009, depending on ending fiscal year dates for the various entities.

Public Pension Controversies over Public Plan Generosity

Anyone who followed the news in the early months of 2011 could not have missed the public pension stories coming out of Wisconsin or New Jersey. The governors of both states waged highly visible campaigns against the largess of their public pension plans. Many other states not in the national spotlight were struggling to deal with public pension costs as well.

In chapter 15 I discussed "agency risk," which is the risk of private pension managers improperly handling or disposing of plan assets for some purpose other than providing benefits to participants as called for under the plan. Agency risk is different in public plans, where the worry is that public policymakers will utilize, some would say manipulate, retirement plans for their own benefit. This occurs in two ways. First, lawmakers typically include themselves in public pensions, so their decisions are about the disposition of public money for their own personal benefit—certainly a potential if not actual conflict of interest. Second, they are setting the benefits for a sizable group of potential supporters in the next election. In this case, the agency problem is compounded by the constitutional or contract law provisions in many states that prohibit future benefit reductions for current participants.[8]

Press reports and public concerns about some public retirees receiving out-landish pensions, often more than $100,000 per year, are not discernable in table 20.1. Someone receiving a public pension benefit of $100,000 or more would generally have to earn a much higher salary than the averages in table 20.1, along with having a relatively long tenure. In a larger context, focusing on jumbo pensions paid to a few public retirees can be misleading.

Consider a hypothetical state worker who retires after 40 years of public service, having risen through the ranks of several state agencies to become the state comptroller, whose final three-year average salary is $200,000 per year. If this worker's pension paid a benefit of 1.25 percent of final average salary per year of service, this retiree would receive a $100,000 pension. The 1.25 percent accrual rate is not out of line with the accrual rates in traditional private retirement plans.

In a country where the average full-time worker earns $35,000 to $40,000 per year, many people may not understand why a state comptroller should be paid $200,000 per year. If that is the market rate for a competent comptroller, the alternative to paying a competitive wage is to hire an incompetent one. State governments today are multibillion-dollar enterprises, and their man-agers face complex issues that are extremely important for all stakeholders. A competent comptroller at $200,000 a year—even including the generous pension—might well be a far better value than someone much less compe-tent who would accept a lower salary. While there may be some egregious cases of outlandish pensions, we should be careful with the brush strokes when we paint these issues.

Public Pensions in a Compensation Context

Many people are convinced that public workers are better paid than their pri-vate-sector counterparts. According to the March 2010 *Current Population Sur-vey*, annual salaries in 2009 were around $39,000 for full-time private-sector workers, $45,000 for state and local workers, and $53,000 for federal workers. But apples-to-apples comparisons require more data than pay levels. Neither the nature of the work nor the characteristics of the workers required to do it are directly comparable in the private and public sectors.

Comparing pay for public employees and comparable private-sector workers is complicated, and many economists have weighed in on the issue. Some conclude that public workers are more highly paid than comparable private-sector workers,[9] others find the pay comparable,[10] while still others determine that public-sector workers earn less.[11] The results partly depend on the time frame. And most of these analyses tend to focus only on wages rather than on wages plus benefits, which turns out to make a big difference.

In a recent analysis of public and private pay, Keith Bender and John Heywood control for workers' characteristics and concluded that state employees earn 11 percent less than comparable private-sector workers, and local workers earn 12 percent less.[12] Bender and Heywood used the Bureau of Labor Statistics' latest National Compensation Survey to develop their comparison of benefits provided to workers in the public and private sectors during 2008. State and local employers paid an estimated 7.9 percent of compensation in retirement benefits and 11.4 percent in the form of health benefits, while private employers paid 3.5 percent and 7.5 percent on retirement and health benefits, respectively, according to the survey results. Private-sector employers with more than 500 employees spent 5 percent of compensation on retiree benefits and 8.5 percent on health care.[13] If public plan costs were estimated similarly to private plan costs, both the public pension and retiree health costs would be higher.

Andrew Biggs replicated the Bender and Heywood results and concluded that their estimates of cash pay are reasonable. When he introduced benefit comparisons on the basis of a more equitable valuation of their respective costs, he found that public-sector workers were "almost one-third better paid overall."[14] Even based on a more conservative valuation of public workers' benefits, once benefits are factored in, state and local employees are better paid, on average, than workers in the private sector after controlling for differences in the nature of their work.[15]

Abuses Demonstrate Agency Risk Issues with Public Pensions

The presumption that public retirement plans are more generous than private plans is supported by the relative cost of benefits as a percentage of payroll as measured by the Department of Labor's National Compensation Survey, but the outliers have become the lightning rods grounding the widespread antipathy toward public pensions. The stories abound and the reporting follows a pattern. A front-page article in the *New York Times* in May 2010 opened: "In Yonkers, more than 100 retired police officers and firefighters are collecting pensions greater than their pay when they were working."[16] In June 2010, the *Times* ran another story with a headline about a Metropolitan Transit Authority (MTA) conductor whose salary topped $200,000 in 2009. The headlining conductor retired on a pension after his bonanza year.[17] The *Miami Herald* opened its version of the story this way: "Mind-numbing numbers hung over the commission chamber. Miami city commissioners voted to cut salaries and pensions without mentioning the $300,000 a year firefighters and 100 percent pension packages after 30 years." The commission didn't provide body counts, but the *Herald* could not resist. It counted 19 city of Miami firefighters making more than $300,000 per year in salary and benefits, another 161 making more than $200,000 and 47 making more than the mayor.[18]

Some of the more egregious stories draw national attention. For example, the *Wall Street Journal* turned the spotlight on a retiring chief of a fire department shared by two towns in Northern California. The fire chief in Orinda and Moraga had been making $186,000 per year when he retired in January 2009. Three days before announcing his retirement, the department's trustees allowed him to "sell" unused vacation days and holidays and treat it as salary for his final year of service, thus boosting his annual pension to $241,000. Adding insult to injury, the 50-year-old retiree was hired back as a consultant at a rate of $175,400 per year to help find his replacement.[19]

These stories are not all about retiring firefighters and police officers. The *Chicago Sun Times* reported that the former president of the state senate was collecting a pension 30 percent larger than his salary while in office.[20] It is one thing for policymakers to feather the nests of public servants but even worse when they pad their own retirement featherbeds.

Pension administrators have known for decades that final-year-pay plans that factor in overtime pay or other supplemental income in calculating the pension are prone to abusive practices. It is hard to fathom that the trustees of the fire system in Orinda and Moraga did not comprehend that adding the value of many years of accumulated sick leave in the retiring chief's final pay would grossly inflate his pension benefit. Frank Sperling, the vice president of the fire board that approved the earnings recalculation maneuver, has been quoted as saying that the former fire chief "abided by existing rules and guidelines for optimizing his retirement pay. . . . I don't fault him. The system itself is broken. We need to change the system."[21]

Adding in the extra earnings for this one pension created an extra $1 million obligation for the citizens. The cost of income-spiking in public pensions in California alone is estimated to cost taxpayers $100 million per year. No one has applauded Frank Sperling's candid admission that "the system is broken" after being publicly exposed for awarding a pension more generous than the private sector could legally allow. This case embodies "agency risk" in its most flagrant form, when those in charge knowingly and publicly continue to cash in on a broken system or at least take no initiative to fix it. It is little wonder that this became a public scandal, and even less remarkable that it spawns what is now widely referred to as "pension envy" from private-sector taxpayers whose own retirement security has taken a nosedive.

Challenges in Measuring Public Pension Costs and Paying for Them

As bad as these exorbitant benefits are, the bigger public pension problem is the cost and funding of public-sector plans and the fiscal threats to other government activities that many of these plans pose. Table 20.2 was compiled from public disclosure documents from states or their pension plans. The states are classified in groups of 10 by the percentage of their stated pension obligations that are funded. The first group has the smallest share of their obligations covered by accumulated assets. Their reported underfunding when measured against their active covered workforces is the equivalent of roughly 2.5 years of pay on average. When the Pew Center on States developed an analysis of public pension funding recently, plans that were less than 80 percent funded were considered to pose security risks for plan participants.[22] At the end of 2009, more than half the state plans fell into that risk category.

Accounting for public pensions has become controversial. At issue is the appropriate interest rate to use for discounting future liabilities. As we saw in the private pension discussion, as the discount rate falls, pension liabilities increase. Some economists are convinced that state and local governments are using inappropriately low interest rate assumptions in calculating their pension obligations—which would make the taxpayers' future tab much bigger. The Governmental Accounting Standards Board propagates accounting rules for state and local governments. The board does not have enforcement authority, but because of the widespread compliance with its rules, information like that in table 20.2 can be compiled.

One measure of public pension burdens is the "actuarially required contribution," which is the amount required to fund the plan's "normal cost"—that is, the cost of benefits accruing this year—plus amortize any unfunded obligations over 30 years. The "Actuarially required" column shows the average required contribution while the "Average" column shows the average contributions states made that year, each stated as a percentage of pay. In all groups, average actual contributions were lower than the actuarially required percentages, suggesting that most states were losing ground in their pension funding in the 2008–2009 period.

According to the Accounting Standards Board, the interest rate used to derive the present value of future public pension obligations "should be based

Table 20.2 Funded Status and Contribution Measures for State-Level
Public Pension Plans, by Funding Quintiles Based on Plans' Public
Disclosures for Fiscal 2009

Funding quintile	Average funding shortfall per active worker	Percentage of pension obligations reported as funded	Contributions as percentage of payroll	
			Actuarially required	Actual
1	$106,293	59.0%	18.0%	15.8%
2	75,124	69.9%	12.4%	8.2%
3	53,006	77.3%	8.1%	7.7%
4	31,147	84.8%	18.7%	16.6%
5	20,234	94.8%	25.9%	22.6%

Source: Author's tabulations of state reports on their public pension plans.

on an estimated long-term investment yield for the plan, with consideration given to the nature and mix of current and expected plan investments."[23] In recent years, most states have used an 8 percent discount rate, with the rates ranging from 7 percent to 8.5 percent.[24] In recent years, a group of financial economists has argued that these interest rates are much too high and are understating pension obligations.

The argument boils down to a theorem that is the cornerstone of modern-day finance theory, which states that the value of an enterprise or activity is independent of how it is financed.[25] Applying this theorem to valuing public pension obligations means estimating the obligations on a basis that is independent of the assets used to cover them. Jeffrey Brown and David Wilcox summarize an article by Cynthia Moore, Nancy Aronson, and Annette Norsman[26] and a legal memorandum by the law firms Morrison and Foerster, and Greenebaum Doll & McDonald[27] to indicate that most public-sector workers have strong contractual rights to their pension benefits. Brown and Wilcox argue that if the obligation to pay the benefits is a virtual certainty, then the liabilities should be valued using expected rates of return for assets with risk-free return characteristics—that is, government bonds.[28] This would mean that state plans should have been using an interest rate of 4 percent or less to discount future public pension obligations at the end of 2009 instead of 7 to 8.5 percent. The implications are significant.

In an analysis of 116 state-level pension plans, Robert Novy-Marx and Joshua Rauh estimated plan assets at $1.94 trillion and liabilities at $2.98 trillion as of December 2008. Using conventional measures, these plans were underfunded by $1 trillion at the bottom of the most recent investment cycle. Using a Treasury rate would increase liabilities to $5.17 trillion and unfunded obligations to $3.2 trillion. Using municipal bond rates would increase liabilities to $3.25 trillion and unfunded obligations to $1.3 trillion.[29]

Novy-Marx and Rauh extended their analysis to several local government pension systems as of June 2009. They gathered data on 78 plans scattered across 50 county or municipal jurisdictions—an estimated two-thirds of the universe of local government employees. Under Governmental Accounting Standards Board rules, the plans had a collective unfunded liability of $190 billion—more than $7,000 per household in the jurisdictions covered. Using federal Treasury rates to value the obligations pushed unfunded liabilities up to $383 billion. By their lights, unless the missing one-third of plans are much better funded than the two-thirds Novy-Marx and Rauh included, the total unfunded obligations would be around $500 billion. Adding in state-level unfunded obligations would bring the combined underfunding for state and local plans up to around $3.5 trillion.[30]

Many actuaries involved in valuing public pensions do not agree with Novy-Marx and Rauh or other economists who advocate using the market valuation of current liabilities.[31] The Governmental Accounting Standards Board issued a comment draft in June 2010 of "Preliminary Views . . . on major issues related to Pension Accounting and Financial Reporting by Employers," sticking to its view that future benefit payments should be "discounted at the long-term expected rate of return on plan investments."[32]

Growing Unfunded Public Pension Obligations Pose Fiscal Threats

The argument over appropriate measurement of public pension obligations may be distracting attention from the more serious problem at hand. For many of these plans, the hole is getting much deeper year in, year out, and the cash requirements to pay obligations—no matter how they are measured—are not sustainable. The actuarially required contributions calculated under the accounting standards call for pension sponsors to pay off unfunded liabilities in addition to contributing the cost of current benefit accruals.

Joshua Rauh has drawn attention to the implications of public plan sponsors' failures to make amortization payments for unfunded obligations. He assumed that plans would realize annual returns of 8 percent on their assets and contributions would cover normal cost contributions going forward—but make no amortization payments. He predicted that under this scenario, Illinois' public plans will deplete their assets in 2018; Connecticut, Indiana, and New Jersey will follow suit by 2019; and Hawaii, Louisiana, and Oklahoma in 2020. Of all the states, only Alaska, Florida, Nevada, New York, and North Carolina would still have funds beyond 2047.[33] Indiana and New Jersey both adopted legislation to slow growth in pension obligations during 2011 but such changes usually have no effect on prior pension obligations that have been accrued but have not been funded.

Many states have been amortizing unfunded obligations, contrary to Rauh's assumptions in developing his projections. But there are a number of states that have simply been watching their pension funding hole grow deeper. Table 20.3 tracks funding patterns of teacher and public employee retirement plans in Illinois and Louisiana from 2005 through 2009. Both states sponsor additional public pensions, but the two plans included in each case comprise the largest share of each state's pension obligations: 65 percent of total state obligations in Illinois, and 93 percent in Louisiana. These two states are good illustrations because they are both in the top 10 of poorly funded pension systems and they have chosen different funding paths. Illinois has consistently contributed significantly less than its annual required pension contributions—just under half the amount of its actuarially "required" contributions between 2005 and 2009. Louisiana contributed more than its required contribution in four of the five years and cumulatively over the period. Nevertheless, unfunded obligations increased by 67 percent in Illinois and by 37 percent in Louisiana.

The story in Illinois is actually worse than the numbers in table 20.3 suggest, because the table does not include the costs of the "pension obligation bonds" the state has been issuing to come up with contributions to its pension plans. On June 12, 2003, Illinois issued $10 billion in pension funding general obligation bonds with maturities of up to 30 years. The state contributed $7.3 billion of the funds raised directly to the state pension systems in the year the bonds were issued. The government used most of the rest to cover the state's contribution obligations in the fourth quarter of fiscal year 2003 and for fiscal year 2004. Some of the proceeds paid the interest for the first year of the bonds' debt service. If this seems like using one credit card to pay off the bill on another one, that's because it is.

In explaining why they issued the bonds to fund the pensions, Illinois State Comptroller Daniel W. Hynes opined that the actuaries expected an 8.5

Table 20.3 Illinois' and Louisiana's Annual Required Pension Contributions, Actual Contributions, Unfunded Accrued Liabilities, and Contributions, as a Share of Payroll for Teachers and Public Employee Retirement Plans, 2005–2009

	Annual required contribution (ARC) ($millions)	Actual contribution ($millions)	Unfunded obligation ($millions)	ARC as a percentage of payroll	Actual contributions as a percentage of payroll
Illinois teachers and public employee retirement plans					
2005	1,335.2	711.1	15,810.1	24.0%	12.8%
2006	1,334.6	387.8	17,488.5	23.1%	6.7%
2007	1,529.7	618.6	17,578.4	25.1%	10.2%
2008	1,693.9	933.1	23,177.3	26.6%	14.6%
2009	1,877.4	1,229.2	26,332.4	28.2%	18.4%
Total	7,770.8	3,879.7		25.5%	12.7%
Louisiana teachers and public employee retirement plans					
2005	966.9	994.7	10,790.6	18.5%	19.0%
2006	978.8	966.8	10,420.3	20.1%	19.8%
2007	1,013.7	1,038.3	10,036.4	18.8%	19.2%
2008	1,093.8	1,267.4	10,977.7	17.9%	20.7%
2009	1,189.6	1,293.3	14,825.8	18.4%	20.0%
Total	5,242.9	5,560.5		18.7%	19.8%

Source: Compiled by the author from the respective states' *Consolidated Annual Financial Reports*.

percent annual return for most of the state's pension plans. Since the state was borrowing money at 5.05 percent interest, it could come out a net winner in the transaction. But there was another benefit as well. The government had to honor the payment schedule for the pension bonds, while it could adjust direct payments to the pension system by changing the law stipulating that contributions be made in accordance with the annual actuarial valuation results.

If Hynes's calculation proves correct—that Illinois can use money borrowed at 5.5 percent to fund its pension plans and realize 8.5 percent per year on the pension assets—it will be the ultimate free ride. It has an eerie resemblance to the ruse of Joseph Heller's *Catch 22* mess officer, Milo Minderbinder, who could acquire eggs for his mess hall by buying them in Sicily for a penny, selling them in Malta for four and a half cents, buying them back for seven cents, and finally selling them to the mess hall for five cents, with everyone making a profit.[34] Somewhere in the chain, most people conclude that the results of the transactions don't quite live up to the billing.

In 2007, Hynes acknowledged the real-world risk that investment returns might be lower than the interest cost on the bonds. Indeed, he cited New Jersey, which issued $2.7 billion in pension obligation bonds in 1997. Unfortunately, the equity markets the money was invested in flopped between 2000 and 2002, so New Jersey had to continue making the scheduled debt service payment on the bonds, while also making higher retirement contributions not forecasted in the original optimistic funding plan.[35] One wonders whether Hynes decided that the financial markets would never again hit a rough patch. If that was his assessment, 2007 to 2009 must have been a rude awakening, with the potential to turn the free-ride approach to financing public pensions into a case study on "Wizard of Oz" funding.

The money Illinois raised by selling pension obligation bonds in 2003 was distributed across five state pensions based on their underfunding. Table 20.4 shows estimates of contributions to all five plans based on their publicly disclosed unfunded obligations at fiscal year end 2002. Public disclosures were also used to estimate the annual rates of return on pension plan investments from 2004 through 2009. The plans report their income by major source each year as well as their annual expenses. The rate-of-return calculation is not precise because it simply divides the annual investment income in each plan by the beginning-of-the-year asset balance. The disclosure documents do not give month-to-month flows of income and expense, so the estimates in table 20.4 are slightly off actual returns, but they are more than adequate for our purpose.

The annual returns on the various funds were used to calculate the accumulating assets in each pension plan that could be attributed to the cash infusion financed by the pension obligation bonds. The result is shown in the bottom line of table 20.4. The accumulated total in all five plans at the end of 2009 was $12.25 billion. At first blush, this might seem like the "free ride"—a 25 percent increase in the $10 billion investment over six years. But we have to net out the interest payments on the bonds to uncover the true economics of the transaction. In the July 2010 issue of *Pensions and Investments*, Barry Burr reported that few of the Illinois pension obligation bonds had been redeemed.[36] Had none of them been redeemed, the annual interest payments would have summed to a little over $3 billion. If they were being paid off at a

Table 20.4 The Distribution of Illinois' 2003 Pension Bond Revenues among Its Public Pension Plans, Estimated Annual Returns and Accumulations by Year-End 2009

	Assembly	Judges	University	State employees	Teachers
	(All dollar amounts are stated in thousands)				
2002 under-funding	$130,532	$677,187	$4,162,000	$6,617,151	$20,681,389
Share of under-funding	0.4%	2.1%	12.9%	20.5%	64.1%
Bond infusion	$47,582	$244,052	$1,225,322	$1,948,135	$6,088,745
2004 return rate	23.8%	22.4%	18.9%	18.9%	19.4%
2005 return rate	9.2%	9.5%	10.2%	9.5%	10.6%
2006 return rate	9.4%	10.9%	11.5%	10.6%	11.7%
2007 return rate	15.8%	16.4%	17.8%	16.3%	18.7%
2008 return rate	-5.4%	-5.7%	-4.2%	-5.6%	-4.8%
2009 return rate	-19.3%	-20.0%	-19.6%	-20.1%	-22.6%
2009 balance	$50,302	$260,108	$1,621,816	$2,462,759	$7,850,148

Source: Derived by author, using disclosure data from various actuarial reports and *Consolidated Annual Financial Reports* issued by the respective pension plans.

rate of one-thirtieth of the issue each year, the interest would have been nearly $2.8 billion. If the interest payments are subtracted from the fund totals, the value of the extra assets in the pension fund at the end of fiscal 2009 would have ranged between $9.25 and $9.45 billion. The magic money machine had turned $10 billion into something substantially less in just six years; as in The Wizard of Oz, there was less behind the curtain than first appeared.

Hope springs eternal and many people remain convinced that investing in risky assets will pay a larger reward than investing in relatively secure bonds.

In January 2010, Illinois issued an additional $3.5 billion in pension obligation bonds to help cover its pension contribution requirements in 2010. In early 2011, Governor Pat Quinn was pushing legislation to raise another $3.7 billion to meet the next scheduled pension contributions.[37] In December 2010, Dan Hynes said on CBS's *60 Minutes* that he had $5 billion in bills unrelated to its pensions but no money to pay them. Dan Croft, the interviewer, concluded that Illinois had become a "deadbeat."[38] Indeed, some might wonder who would loan the state another $3.7 billion to fill in a debt hole that is likely to be even deeper next year.

Other states have also issued pension obligation bonds, but Illinois and California are by far the largest issuers of these instruments.[39] California has been in the press lately because of its own public pension deficits and abuses, but it is generally considered to have done a much better job of funding its pensions than Illinois. Any state issuing bonds to raise funds for pensions is deluding the public about the immediate costs of the plans and is making a bad bargain worse.

When state budgets are stressed, some lawmakers respond by skipping pension contributions. But if these plans run out of assets, they must revert to pay-as-you-go financing, which is economically inefficient in the contemporary setting. For example, if the Illinois and Louisiana systems described in table 20.3 were running in pay-as-you-go mode, their annual cost of delivering benefits would be around 33 percent of payroll. If state and local governments find themselves too strapped to keep up with growing pension liabilities, ignoring the problem will simply dig a deeper hole. The major problem in making public pensions solvent is that, in many states, the plans are legally locked in for existing workers, so the current cost structures will persist for many workers for decades to come.

Public Pension Legal Protections Stir Political Controversy

In a recent summary of state pension laws, Amy Monahan describes the legal protections public workers enjoy.[40] Most public pensions are covered under contract or property rights laws, and some states provide explicit protection in their constitutions. For example, Monahan writes, "The constitutions of New York and Illinois specifically provide that rights are fixed as of the date the employee enters the retirement system and cannot thereafter be diminished or impaired (N.Y. Const. art. V, sec. 7; Ill. Const. art. XIII, sec. 5). Unlike federal retirement plan protections for private employer plans, which protect only the benefits accrued to date, this type of state protection is significantly more generous."[41]

In most states that treat public pensions as contracts, protections not specified in the state constitution are either embedded in public statutes or are based on the facts and circumstances of claims. The fact that legal protections are not in a state's constitution does not make them any less secure. Monahan quotes the U.S. Supreme Court as saying that merely because the government "believes that money can be better spent or should now be conserved does not provide a sufficient interest to impair the obligation" of a contract.[42]

In the private sector under ERISA, a benefit earned cannot be reduced, but a benefit offered can be modified. For example, consider a worker covered under a plan that pays out 1.5 percent of final average salary for each year of service under the plan for 10 years. The plan sponsor can change the plan going forward but must pay the benefit earned for the 10 years. If the employee works for another 10 years, the employer can change the future accrual rate under a similar plan, switch to a completely different plan or offer no plan at all. In a public plan with a stringent anti-cutback provision, the employer cannot make any change that would reduce workers' future accruals from their first to their last day of coverage.

In many states, it is now easier to furlough or fire workers than to change their pension plans, even where benefits will not be paid for another 20 to 30 years. The anti-cutback provisions severely limit a public jurisdiction's authority to modify its pension costs structure for its existing workforce. While a number of states have modified their public pensions in recent years, the modifications will apply only to new hires or employees who volunteer to switch plans in most cases.

In some states, pension obligations are so onerous that political leaders are trying to roll back benefits even for current workers. Shortly after Chris Christie was inaugurated as governor of New Jersey in January 2010, he declared public budgets a financial disaster and laid much of the blame on public retirement costs. He summed up the situation saying, "Make no mistake about it, pensions and benefits are the major driver of our spending increases at all levels of government—state, county, municipal and school board. We cannot in good conscience fund a system that is out of control, bankrupting our state and its people, and making promises it cannot meet in the long term."[43]

The article that reported Governor Christie's plans for New Jersey said that 16 other states were considering pension changes that could mean lower benefits, later retirement ages or reduced cost-of-living adjustments, but that most were considering the changes only for new hires. Some states reportedly were considering raising employee contribution rates for all workers immediately.[44]

When Governor Christie assumed office, his domain included six state-sponsored pension plans for public workers. The combined annual required contribution for the five plans in fiscal 2011 was $3.5 billion, up from $1.6 billion in 2006. Between 2006 and 2010, the aggregate actuarially required contributions for the five plans were $10.1 billion. The state had contributed only $2.6 billion over the five-year period—25.7 percent of required contributions—partially accounting for the dramatic jump over the period. When Governor Christie assumed office, New Jersey was facing a $10.7 billion budgetary short-fall. The governor managed to maneuver a deficit-reduction package through the legislature, which called for skipping another $3 billion pension contribution, but he pledged to confront pensions through future legislation.[45]

Governor Christie proposed to increase employee contributions for their pensions, increase the ages at which they could claim them, adjust pension formulas and roll back a 9 percent across-the-board benefit increase awarded in 2001. On the funding front, the proposal called for reducing the anticipated annual rate of return on pension assets from 8.25 percent to 7.5 percent and speeding up the amortization of unfunded liabilities.[46] When the dust settled in late June 2011, pension reform passed the New Jersey legislature. Fire-fighters and police contributions were raised from 8.5 to 10 percent of pay; other workers' contributions were raised from 5.5 percent of pay, on average, to 7.5 percent. Cost-of-living adjustments to benefits for current and future retirees were eliminated until the pension funds become stable, which is not expected before 2040. Retirement ages for new school employees were increased from 60 to 65 and the service requirement for early retirement was raised from 25 to 30 years. For new police officers and firefighters, the benefit formula was scaled back to pay 60 percent of preretirement earnings after 25 years of service rather than the 65 percent payable to current uniformed workers. The state's annual contribution was to be "mandatory" and the unions were given the right to sue if the state failed to comply.[47]

When Governor Christie was first pushing pension reform, union leaders said they would sue if the legislature delivered on the governor's recommenda-tions. The attorney general during former Governor John Corzine's tenure had warned that these types of pension cuts could be found unconstitutional, but Governor Christie said, "If they want to sue me, tell them to get in line[;] I've got plenty of lawyers to defend our positions."[48] The legislation ultimately adopted in New Jersey clearly did not go as far as the governor had wanted, but the unions still were outspoken in their reactions. On August 31, 2011, more than 20 unions and public employee organizations in New Jersey filed a federal lawsuit challenging the public pension reforms adopted in June. The lawsuit claims that the new law "violates the federal and state constitutions by suspending cost of living increases for pensions, increasing pension contributions for public workers, allowing the government to make only a portion of its pension contribution until 2019 and increasing how much employees with less than 20 years of service will have to pay for health benefits as a retiree."[49] The outcome of this suit and the implications of New Jersey's attempt to control public pension costs may not be known for some time. Even if the provisions hold, the idea that the funds will remain too unstable to support cost-of-living increases until 2040 calls into question whether New Jersey has solved its pension funding problems.

It would appear that constitutional amendments can go both directions, as the history of prohibition in the United States demonstrates. In Illinois, the escalating costs associated with mounting unfunded pension obligations may ultimately pit voters wanting state pension rollbacks—like those pushed by Governor Christie in New Jersey—against constitutional protection of public workers' pensions. On the other side, the legal framework of contract law is an important element of our social and economic infrastructure, and abrogating legal contracts is not going to be undertaken lightly, no matter how much public angst is expressed. But pension envy is not likely to go away as the pension rollbacks in the private sector continue to play themselves out in the future.

Federal Pensions, Maybe the Grandest of Them All

The vast majority of federal civilian workers are covered under either the Civil Service Retirement System or the Federal Employee Retirement System. Members of Congress are covered by one or the other of these but accrue benefits somewhat faster than regular participants. Certain federal employees, such as those in the Federal Reserve System, the Coast Guard, the Public Health Service, and officers of the National Oceanic and Atmospheric Administration, participate in separate pension programs.

Military personnel are covered under the Military Retirement System, although military disability benefits are coordinated with benefits provided by the Veterans Administration (VA) for soldiers who receive disabling injuries in service. The VA benefits generally have certain tax advantages over regular military retirement benefits, so the disability payments by the retirement system are relatively small. The following discussion about military retirees focuses solely on the Military Retirement System in the context of the federal provision of regular pension benefits.

These major pension systems covering federal civilian workers and military are partially funded, but all funding consists of special-issue federal securities. The funding works essentially the same way as Social Security—it makes little difference to the taxpayers whether these systems are funded or not. The bonds in federal pension trust funds are pension obligation bonds that will either be sold into the financial markets or cashed out with tax revenues when the system needs money. The Office of Management and Budget acknowledges that these trust funds are available to pay future benefits

> . . . only in a bookkeeping sense. The holdings of the trust funds are not assets of the Government as a whole that can be drawn down in the future to fund benefits. Instead, they are claims on the Treasury. From a cash perspective, when trust fund holdings are redeemed to authorize the payment of benefits, the Department of Treasury finances the expenditure in the same way as any other Federal expenditure—by using current receipts or by borrowing from the public.[50]

The Civil Service Retirement System covers federal civilian workers hired before January 1, 1984. Until then, most federal civilian employees were not covered under Social Security, so the system is more generous than the one that replaced it in 1984. Workers covered under the Civil Service system can retire with unreduced benefits as early as age 55 with 30 years of service. Participants contribute 7 percent of their salary to their pension but do not pay Social Security payroll taxes.

The Federal Employee Retirement System covers federal civilian workers hired after December 31, 1983, and contributions and benefits are coordinated with Social Security. In this system, the early retirement age is gradually being raised from 55 to 57. Participants contribute 7 percent of pay minus their Social Security payroll taxes. Participants who earn more than the Social Security wage base contribute the full 7 percent of the extra pay to the federal retirement plan. Participants also receive defined contribution benefits through the Federal Thrift Savings Plan. The employing agencies automatically make a 1 percent contribution to workers' accounts and match employee contributions up to 3 percent of pay on a dollar-for-dollar basis. Contributions of more than 3 percent of pay up to 5 percent are matched by the employing agency at a rate of 50-cents-on-the-dollar. For regular employees, government contributions vest after three years in the plan. For members of Congress and certain other participants, primarily those in public safety positions, they vest after two years.

The Military Retirement System covers members of the Army, Navy, Marine Corps, and Air Force. It is a noncontributory system that covers both active and reserve members of the military. Retirements can be approved at any age for members with 20 years of service, but reservists must generally be at least 60 years old and have 20 years of qualified service to receive benefits. Benefits do not vest before retirement.

Three separate formulas are used to determine benefits, depending on when the participant joined the military. All three provide a benefit that is 2.5 times each year of service times a pay factor. For soldiers who joined the military before September 8, 1980, the pay factor is their basic pay rate at retirement. The second group includes those hired on or after September 8, 1980, and their pay factor is the average of the three highest years of basic pay. The third formula applies to members who joined the service on or after August 1, 1986, and involves a choice on their part. They can stay under the 2.5 percent per year of service times the high-three average pay formula or take what is called a "Career Status Bonus/Redux" benefit. Soldiers who opt for the latter are offered a $30,000 Career Status Bonus in their 15th year of service. If they take it and then retire with less than 30 years of service, their retirement benefit is reduced until they turn age 62, when it is recomputed to a full benefit. If they remain in service for the full 30 years, their immediate benefit is still the 2.5 percent of high-three pay per year of service. In addition to their military pensions, retired soldiers also receive Social Security benefits based on their military service. Most soldiers are eligible to retire by their mid-40s.

Civil service retirement and military retirement benefits are indexed to the consumer price index (CPI) for Urban Wage and Clerical Workers, which is also used for Social Security benefit indexation. This is a more generous indexation of retirement benefits than virtually any private, state, or local pension plan provides. Benefit indexation in the Federal Employee Retirement System is more limited than that in the civil service and military systems. If the CPI increase is 2 percent or less, benefits in the Federal Employee Retirement System are fully incremented by the CPI. If the CPI increase is 2 percent to 3 percent, the benefit increase is still 2 percent. If the CPI increase exceeds 3 percent, the federal system's cost-of-living increment is the CPI increase minus 1 percent.

Table 20.5 presents the participation and actuarial summary of the three major federal retirement systems. To put the participation data in perspective, the state-level plans had about 2.7 times the number of active workers accruing benefits as the three federal plans—approximately 1.4 times the number of beneficiaries. The estimated liabilities in the state systems were around $3

Table 20.5 Civil Service Retirement System (CSRS), Federal Employee
Retirement System (FERS), and Military Retirement System (MRS)
Populations and Liability and Funding Status at October 2008

	CSRS	FERS	MRS	Total
Active personnel	477,000	2,195,000	2,226,630	4,898,630
Retirees & disabled	1,566,000	320,000	1,880,871	3,766,871
Deferred vested	16,000	25,000	85,502	126,502
Survivors	591,000	32,000	289,943	912,943
Total annuitants	2,173,000	377,000	2,256,316	4,806,316
(dollar amounts in billions of dollars)				
Actuarial accrued liability	$1,096.5	$311.4	$1,157.3	$2,565.2
Actuarial value of assets	$423.2	$310.5	$253.1	$986.8
Unfunded liability	$673.3	$0.9	$904.2	$1,578.4
Employer cost as % of payroll	18.8%	11.5%		
Full time			40.3%	
Part time			27.3%	

Source: Compiled from the 2008 Actuarial Reports developed by the Offices of the Actuary at the Office of Personnel Management and Department of Defense.

trillion by their estimates versus $2.6 trillion in the federal plans. Disregarding the lack of "real" funding in the three federal plans, both the Civil Service Retirement System and the Military Retirement System are dangerously underfunded under the standards used to evaluate state and local pensions.

The "employer cost as a percent of payroll" in table 20.5 is the result of an actuarial computation. In the 2009 annual valuation report prepared on the Military Retirement system, a table reflecting actual contributions indicates that there are more costs here than meet the eye. In 2010, the Department of Defense contributed $19 billion to the retirement system to cover currently accruing obligations for service that year. In addition, the Treasury made a contribution of $4.5 billion to cover current plan accruals but it also made an additional contribution for $58.6 billion as an amortization payment to partially cover unfunded obligations based on prior service and past actuarial losses against expected income. In each instance, these contributions were book-keeping entries and there was no actual transfer of cash between the various accounts and the trust funds. While there was no cash changing hands, the trust funds ended up with Treasury bonds reflecting the contributions. In total, contributions equaled $82.1 billion against reported payroll of $60.3 billion.[51] In other words, the Military Retirement System contributions in 2010 were 136.2 percent of pay for currently active soldiers.

In table 20.5, the costs associated with the Federal Employee Retirement System may look like a bargain compared to the older system, but in addition to covering pension costs, the government must contribute 6.2 percent of covered pay to Social Security on behalf of participants, plus pay matching contributions to the Thrift Savings Plan. The implications of early retirement costs under the Military Retirement System are clearly reflected in the employer costs as a percentage of payroll.

The shift to the Federal Employee Retirement System is instructive in thinking about the implications of pension reforms that affect only workers hired after the fact. That is what happened in early 1984 when the Civil Service Retirement System was closed to new entrants. More than a quarter century later, the Civil Service program is still accruing massive benefits for current employees, including those now retiring at relatively young ages, and it will be facing ongoing benefit claims for another 20 years. The 1984 system was not developed to cut pension costs. After Social Security coverage was extended to federal workers in 1984, policymakers needed to adjust the pension plan accordingly. If the motivation had been to reduce costs, leaving all employees hired before the transition in the old plan would have drastically limited any cost savings for a couple of decades or more.

IV DELIVERING BENEFITS AND PROVIDING RETIREMENT SECURITY

It was the best of times, it was the worst of times, it was the age of wisdom, it was the age of foolishness, it was the epoch of belief, it was the epoch of incredulity, it was the season of Light, it was the season of Darkness, it was the spring of hope, it was the winter of despair, we had everything before us, we had nothing before us, we were all going direct to Heaven, we were all going direct the other way—in short, the period was so far like the present period . . .

—CHARLES DICKENS, *Tale of Two Cities*

21 RETIREMENT INCOME SECURITY AND WORKERS' RESIDUALS

Money flows into various components of the retirement system from different sources. Social Security payroll taxes are generally evenly split between employees and employers. Most private defined benefit plans are financed purely by employer contributions. Public-sector defined benefit plans typically require employees to contribute something, but the employer finances most of the benefits. Most defined contribution plans now rely on workers' contributions for the largest share of their financing, although roughly one-third of the annual deposits into these plans are from employers.

Most of us might prefer that our employers pay for our retirement benefits rather than our having to do it ourselves, but there is no free ride. Companies consider retirement plan contributions as a cost of hiring and keeping employees on the payroll, similarly to how they view wages. To employers, wages and benefits are both labor costs.

Accountants, economists, human resource managers, and corporate executives tend to lump the costs of all workers' rewards under the more comprehensive label of compensation. For 25 years of my career, I developed annual budgets for units that I managed, and compensation was invariably the largest expense. In accounting for labor costs, I had to itemize wages, benefit costs, and the employer's share of payroll taxes. Compensation was the total of these individual labor costs, and when it came to hiring or dismissing a worker, overall compensation mattered more than cash wages. Over time, workers who do not contribute value to an employer at least equal to the cost of their total compensation become an economic burden to the organization. In for-profit organizations, positions are generally eliminated if workers' productivity does not cover the cost of their employment. If health or retirement benefit costs rise faster than workers' productivity growth, it will likely slow wage growth or even lead to the elimination of jobs.[1]

Cost Implications of Retirement System Developments

To understand what has happened to retirement costs and the implications for workers' take-home pay, consider a worker, Jane, who begins her career at age 21 and earns average wages every year until she retires and starts collecting Social Security benefits at age 65. If Jane had reached age 65 in 1955, she and her employer(s) would have paid 2.2 percent of her lifetime wages to finance her Social Security benefits. For the Jane who turned 65 in 1965, the lifetime contributions would have climbed to 3.6 percent of her lifetime earnings, showing the effects of the payroll tax rates that had started to climb in the early 1950s. In the mid-1960s, Medicare was added to the retirement package under the Social Security Act and it was partially financed by payroll taxes. Each subsequent Jane reaching age 65 in later years would have paid successively higher payroll taxes throughout her working life. The one who turned age 65 in 2011 would have incurred payroll taxes equal to 13.1 percent of her lifetime pay. The average cost rates at various 65th birthday years appear in the second column in table 21.1. At almost every point in time, Jane's Social Security benefit would have been around 40 percent to 45 percent of final pay when she retired, but the cost over her career would have depended on when she retired. The Jane who retired in 2011 would have paid over six times more than the one who retired in 1955.

As mentioned in chapter 17 and shown by table 17.1, retirement patterns changed markedly between 1950 and 2005. In 2005, Jane's retirement lasted longer because of both her earlier retirement age and her longer life expectancy. These developments have also affected the cost of providing Jane with a supplemental pension. The third column in table 21.1 shows the savings rates required to finance a benefit to replace an additional 40 percent of Jane's final earnings.

In developing the calculations, I employed certain assumptions. Jane received pay increases of 4 percent per year throughout her career, and her retirement savings earned a constant 7 percent return. Her retirement benefit from this portion of her retirement portfolio increased 2 percent per year during her retirement to cover part of the cost of inflation. To simplify the calculations while reflecting changing retirement and longevity trends, I assumed Jane would retire at age 65 in 1955, 64 in 1965, 63 in 1975 and 1985, 62 in 1995, and 61 in 2005 and 2011. I assumed she would die 14 years after retiring in 1955, 16 years after retiring in 1975, and then incrementing by one year for the other four retirement years in table 21.1. These retirement ages and durations do not exactly match the results in chapter 17, but they are close enough for our purposes.

Table 21.1 Cumulative Lifetime Employee plus Employer Payroll Taxes as a Percentage of Cumulative Lifetime Earnings, Supplemental Retirement Savings Rate, Employer Average Contributions for Health Benefits, and Totals, as a Percentage of Pay for Workers Retiring at Various Dates

Year reaching age 65	Lifetime payroll tax as percentage of lifetime earnings	Required supplemental savings rate	Total retirement cost per year	Annual health benefits cost	Retirement plus health costs
		(All amounts stated as a percentage of salary or wages)			
1955	2.1	4.6	6.7	1.0	7.7
1965	3.6	5.4	9.0	2.1	11.1
1975	5.9	5.9	11.8	3.5	15.3
1985	9.0	6.1	15.1	5.6	20.7
1995	9.9	6.7	16.6	8.0	24.6
2005	12.0	7.1	19.1	9.9	29.0
2011	13.1	7.5	20.6	10.6	31.2

Source: Retirement plan costs derived by the author as described in the text; the health benefits costs were derived from the U.S. Department of Commerce, Bureau of Economic Analysis, *National Income and Product Accounts*.

The third column in table 21.1 shows the percentage of Jane's income required to finance her supplemental benefit. The Jane retiring in 1955—or her employer—would have to have saved 4.6 percent of her pay each year. For the one retiring in 2011, 7.5 percent of pay would have been required, because this Jane has fewer years over which to accumulate her savings and the savings must last over a longer retirement. Changes in the supplemental savings rates were much smaller than they were for Social Security because of the greater efficiency of funded versus pay-as-you-go systems.

The fourth column, "Total retirement cost per year" helps to explain why many people today find the sort of retirement their parents and grandparents enjoyed beyond their grasp. That column sums the percentages of salary required to finance Social Security benefits and supplemental pensions for workers of various vintages. For a worker retiring in 1955, the combination of Social Security and a roughly matching supplemental benefit would cost slightly less than 7 percent of lifetime earnings. For the same worker retiring in 2011, the cost would have been 20.6 percent of earnings. My father turned age 65 in 1974—in what might be considered the golden era of retirement. Social Security windfalls were at their zenith and employers were offering early retirement subsidies to entice older workers to make way for the incoming baby boomers. I turned 65 in 2011, and my generation needed to save around 21 percent of pay year in, year out, to draw a similar level of retirement benefits as my father's generation. To put this in a slightly different context, the generation retiring in 2011 would have had to surrender roughly 3.5 to 4 more years of their lifetime earnings to finance their retirement benefits than the generation retiring in the mid-1950s. A relatively small share of this generational penalty is the self-induced cost of retiring younger.

Workers' health benefits are also financed out of compensation budgets, and the fifth column in table 21.1, "Health benefit costs," are the average total employer costs for health benefits stated as a percentage of cash wages. These averages are based on total wages paid to all workers—including those not covered under an employer-sponsored health plan. Omitting non-participants' pay from the calculations would have made the average costs for plan participants considerably higher. These data do not reflect the workers' own premium payments and out-of-pocket expenses.

As shown in the "Retirement plus health costs" column in table 21.1, providing workers retiring in 2011 with retirement and health benefits comparable to those enjoyed by earlier generations costs, on average, roughly 31 percent of their pay—a full 23.5 percent of pay more than the cost for workers who retired in 1955. The difference over a 40-year career is more than nine years' worth of pay. While employers pay much of this cost, compensation dollars siphoned off to retirement programs and health plans cannot make their way into paychecks. Mounting evidence traces stalling wages—a source of increasing public frustration—to the higher costs of retirement and health benefits.[2]

Factoring Benefit Costs into the Measurement of Rewards

While the results in table 21.1 provide a stylized explanation of why retirement costs have been rising over the past half century, they are not consistently grounded in real-world developments affecting Social Security and employer pension programs. Both the Social Security costs and the supplemental savings rates are reasonable estimates, but the world is a great deal messier than the assumptions underlying those estimates. Many of us do not start saving or accruing pension benefits at age 21 and stay on course until we retire. Our investment results are not as well behaved as those in the assumptions. And we have seen that policymakers and employers—acting on their own incentives—may intervene from time to time in ways that affect our retirement savings patterns.

A few years ago, a colleague, Steven Nyce, and I developed an analysis to sort out how the various costs discussed in table 21.1 were distributed across the earnings spectrum over time.[3] We started with the fundamental premise that employers reward workers for their labor with compensation, but we wanted to track the relationships among the components of compensation and tie back our findings to various public policy, demographic, and business developments. Our original analysis was based on data that ran through 2007, and we recently updated the analysis to reflect data from 1980 through 2009.[4] The analysis tracks earning levels and other components of compensation paid to full-year, full-time workers from 1980 through 2009.

Our analysis relied on two national data series that monitor the evolution of our economy and society. The annual March Supplements to the *Current Population Survey* are conducted by the Census Bureau on a sample of U.S. households representative of the civilian, non-institutionalized population. The survey asks participants how much they worked over the past year, how much they earned and whether they were covered by an employer-sponsored pension or health plan. We augmented the survey data with information from the *National Income and Product Accounts,* which report employers' annual contributions to Social Security, Medicare, and employer-sponsored pension, savings, and health benefit plans.

While we noted criticism of pension data from the *Current Population Survey* in earlier chapters, we believe the data we used are more reliable. There is evidence that elderly respondents with asset holdings frequently report having no asset income on the *Current Population Survey* and similar surveys.[5] Where workers are asked whether they have a job, how much they earn, and whether they have an employer-sponsored health benefit plan, a pension plan, or a savings plan, the questions and answers are more straightforward and likely more reliable. To minimize complications, we focused on full-time workers.

We used the Census survey data to divide workers into 10 groups (deciles) ranked by annual earnings level. We had to exclude the top 1 percent of the earnings distribution because the Census Bureau does not disclose extraordinarily high earnings as it might identify the few people who earn that much. They promise survey respondents anonymity and this is one of the ways they assure it. The Census Bureau simply codes all earnings responses above a certain break-off point, a practice referred to as "top coding." We eliminated all instances of "top-coded" earnings by excluding the top 1 percent of reported earnings in each year.

The top 1 percent of earners clearly receive more than 1 percent of cash salaries, but their payroll taxes, health benefits, and contributions to tax-qualified retirement plans are much less skewed. Social Security payroll taxes and the limits on income considered for tax-qualified retirement plans are capped well below the earnings level of the top 1 percent. In most cases, highly compensated individuals are enrolled in the same health plan as their lower-paid colleagues. Excluding the top 1 percent of the income distribution should not distort the results.

In order to give a frame of reference, table 21.2 shows the estimated annual compensation and pay levels in each of the earnings deciles for 2009. The averages shown in the table are derived by multiplying the average hourly rates developed in our analysis by a potential work year of 2,080 hours—40 hours per week for 52 weeks in a year—including paid leave time. The averages shown have been rounded to the nearest $100. Over most of the earnings distribution, pay was close to 80 percent of total compensation. The share of compensation paid as cash has declined somewhat since the end of World War II.

We first look at wage growth patterns across the earnings spectrum on a decade-by-decade basis. Figure 21.1 shows the compound annual growth rates in inflation-adjusted average hourly pay across the 10 pay groups from 1980 to 1990, 1990 to 2000, and 2000 to 2009. The patterns vary considerably

Table 21.2 Average Annualized Compensation and Pay Levels Rounded to the Nearest $100 Levels for Workers, by Earnings Deciles in 2009

Earnings decile	Average compensation	Average pay
1	$15,800	$12,700
2	26,000	20,700
3	33,200	26,000
4	39,400	30,600
5	46,000	35,900
6	53,400	41,600
7	61,000	48,000
8	73,000	57,800
9	91,400	73,200
10	145,900	121,900

Source: Derived from tabulations of the Current Population Survey and augmented by data from the National Income and Product Accounts for various years.

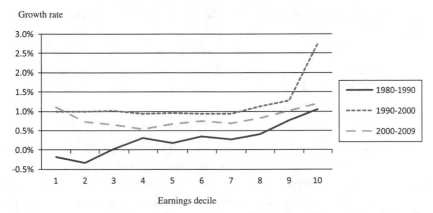

FIGURE 21.1 Compound Annual Growth Rates of Inflation-Adjusted Hourly Pay for Full-Time, Full-Year Workers by Earnings Decile and for Selected Periods

Source: Derived from tabulations of the *Current Population Survey*, various years.

over time. During the 1980s, wage growth was negative at the bottom of the earnings spectrum, modest but flat across the middle-income segments, and progressively higher across the top 30 percent of the distribution. In the 1990s, wages grew significantly across all earnings categories—but considerably more for higher earners than for lower earners. In terms of take-home pay growth, the 1990s enjoyed the most uniform advancement of the three decades. While take-home pay rose more rapidly for lower-and middle-earning workers than it did in the prior decade or would in the next, it was the high earners who realized the greatest bonanza in the era of "irrational exuberance." The rate of wage growth fell off during the 2000s.

In recent years, there has been considerable concern about whether our rewards structure disproportionately benefits highly compensated workers. The root of this concern is embedded in the figure by the tilt upward at higher earnings levels in all three of the wage growth lines. The results focus purely on wages paid to workers; factoring in the higher unemployment in the new millennium would make the tilt even steeper because unemployment has been higher among lower earners.

Table 21.1 shows the increasing cost of benefits and payroll taxes in recent decades. Employers pay half the growing Social Security contributions, which do not show up on workers' W-2 tax forms. Most employer contributions for retirement plans and health benefits fall into the same category. By 2009, employer contributions for social insurance and benefit programs amounted to 20 percent of workers' compensation, according to the Bureau of Economic

Analysis, so figure 21.1 does not reflect all the rewards accruing to workers in recent decades.

No single database links the value of the benefits workers receive to what they are paid in cash. To develop our analysis, we had to estimate how much employer contributions for payroll taxes and benefit plans added to workers' compensation. We did this by relying on Census survey respondents' indications that they were covered by an employer-sponsored health plan and/or a retirement plan and distributing the aggregate costs of employer contributions for these benefits from the *National Income and Product Accounts*. We based estimates of employers' payroll tax contributions on prevailing law governing annual contributions. Employer contributions to retirement plans were calculated from coverage rates at each earnings level and the progressive structure of benefits across the earnings distributions. Employer health benefit costs were allocated according to coverage rates at each earnings level and based on differential rates of single and family coverage within those earnings levels.

In figure 21.2, we added to cash pay employer costs for retirement plans—including both employer-sponsored plans and social insurance benefits—and for employer-sponsored health plans. While wage growth in the 2000s falls short of that achieved during the 1990s, there was more compensation growth across much of the earnings spectrum in the 2000s than in either of the prior two decades. Compensation grew at virtually all earnings levels in the first decade of the new millennium as it had during the 1990s, and those in the fourth through the eighth or ninth deciles did better in the later decade. Looking

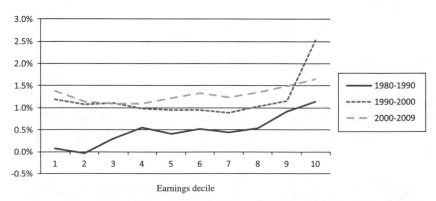

FIGURE 21.2 Compound Annual Growth Rates of Inflation-Adjusted Hourly Compensation for Full-Time, Full-Year Workers by Earnings Decile and for Selected Periods

Source: Derived from tabulations of the *Current Population Survey* and augmented by data from the *National Income and Product Accounts* for various years.

at compensation, the 2000s have not been worse for middle America than the prior decade. The rate of growth in compensation from the third through the ninth deciles during the 2000–2009 period equaled or exceeded that of the 1990s. If people feel dissatisfied with their paychecks in a decade when compensation growth actually became more robust for most American workers, we need to look at other elements of compensation and their effect on workers' take-home pay in order to understand the nature of the disappointment.

Putting the Benefits Story into the Compensation Picture

Table 21.3 shows the extent to which employer contributions to the three major categories of non-cash compensation have absorbed workers' compensation increases over the three decades from 1980 through 2009. The 1980s were a particularly turbulent period in the labor markets—the baby boomers were still flooding in, there was a harsh recession at the beginning of the decade, and total compensation growth at the bottom of the earnings distribution was virtually nonexistent. It was barely above zero in the first decile and negative in the second. On average, it was negative over the first two deciles combined. Above those earnings levels, the effects of the payroll tax increases to resolve Social Security's financing crisis at the beginning of the 1980s are apparent in table 21.3. The share of compensation growth absorbed by the payroll tax increases was much greater during the 1980s than in later years when it was simply the tax rate applied against the growth in wages. The share taken by the payroll tax in the 1990s was greater than in the first decade of the 2000s because a much larger share of compensation was paid out in the form of benefits in the latter decade with most of it not subject to the payroll tax.

The negative rate of compensation growth absorption reported in table 21.3 for employer contributions to their retirement plans reflects the cutbacks in pension funding that occurred in the 1980s and 1990s. As a result of public policies to reduce tax expenditures, employers' plan contributions shrank across the board during those two decades, even as the workforce was gradually aging. Few retirement planners would recommend progressively cutting back on retirement savings as you age during your prime working years, but that is exactly what we did as a matter of national policy during the 1980s and 1990s.

The old saying that "the sons have to pay for the sins of the fathers" explains, to a substantial degree, why the growth rates in retirement contributions represented by the 2000–2009 period in the figure are so high. The long spell of low contributions changed dramatically around 2000, as maturing pension obligations and the financial market downturn necessitated

Table 21.3 Share of Total Compensation Increases Absorbed by Increases in Payroll Taxes, Employer Contributions to Employer-Sponsored Retirement Plans, and Employer Contributions to Health Benefit Plans, by Earnings Decile and for Selected Periods

Earnings decile	1980–1990	1990–2000	2000–2009
	Payroll tax increases		
1	NA	5.3%	5.0%
2	NA	5.9%	4.0%
3	44.3%	5.7%	3.6%
4	26.3%	6.0%	3.0%
5	33.9%	6.3%	3.4%
6	28.6%	6.2%	3.4%
7	32.6%	6.7%	3.5%
8	28.0%	6.9%	3.8%
9	20.6%	7.1%	4.2%
10	17.8%	4.2%	4.3%
	Employers' retirement plan cost increases		
1	-130.0%	-1.7%	6.6%
2	NA	-3.6%	13.3%
3	-60.4%	-4.3%	18.6%
4	-29.4%	-5.8%	21.3%
5	-44.3%	-8.3%	23.5%
6	-30.8%	-9.9%	25.2%
7	-39.5%	-9.8%	25.6%
8	-30.0%	-9.5%	26.4%
9	-12.3%	-8.4%	25.8%
10	-8.5%	-0.4%	24.3%
	Employers' health benefit costs increases		
1	> 100%	26.8%	23.6%
2	NA	20.8%	30.4%
3	> 100%	23.6%	30.1%
4	57.2%	21.0%	36.5%
5	74.4%	19.8%	28.9%
6	45.2%	22.5%	26.7%
7	55.5%	15.5%	25.8%
8	38.7%	12.1%	20.1%
9	21.4%	9.1%	15.0%
10	12.1%	2.9%	9.1%

Source: Derived from tabulations of the *Current Population Survey* and augmented by data from the *National Income and Product Accounts* for various years.

much larger employer contributions. The even steeper financial market declines in 2008 and 2009 resulted in more cash demands on retirement plan sponsors. This erratic pattern of retirement contribution claims on workers' compensation is rooted in the regulatory schizophrenia over pension funding early in the baby boomers' work lives and the timing of financial market swings.

The last major benefit cost—employer-provided health insurance for workers and dependents—has grown faster than all the others. As table 21.3 shows, these costs have been a substantial drain on workers disposable income over virtually the entire study period, absorbing a greater share of compensation in each one of the three decades than either Social Security or employer-sponsored retirement plans. In fact, health benefits costs have grown more rapidly than wages or inflation ever since World War II. There was a brief respite during the mid-1990s, when managed care practices and health providers' reaction to the Clinton Administration's attempt at health care reform slowed the growth of health benefit costs. They still grew by an average of 2.5 percent more per year than inflation for the bottom two-thirds of the earnings distribution, while wages grew by only about 1 percent per year. By the end of the 1990s, pent-up anger at managed care programs among the provider community, consumers, the media, and public policymakers forced insurers to eliminate several cost-effective but unpopular managed care features in their health benefit plans.

In the new millennium, health costs escalated again, although not at the furious pace of the 1980s. Looking back at table 21.1, you can see that between 1985 and 2010, employers' contributions to health benefit plans diverted an added 5 percent of total compensation of all workers in the American economy to pay for health insurance. This is roughly four times the rate at which added resources would be claimed under reasonable savings patterns to finance extended retirement years given our growing levels of life expectancy.

One aspect of this story which is not depicted in these figures is that many employers reacted to escalating costs by curtailing—sometimes eliminating— their health plans. Reductions in employer-provided health coverage shift more costs to workers. Our analysis simply distributes employer costs for their benefit plans, as reported in the *National Income and Product Accounts*, across the covered workforce for each earnings decile. For workers who lost employer-sponsored health insurance coverage, the loss appears as a cost reduction in the analysis. For example, the growth rate of hourly health benefit costs for the lowest earners declined after 2000 when averaged across all low earners because fewer of these workers had employer-sponsored coverage. What appears as a cost reduction is actually a cost transfer. Workers who lost employer coverage had to acquire and pay for health insurance and retirement protection on their own or do without.

When benefit costs grow more rapidly than the compensation budget, they consume a larger share of cash wages. When we add total compensation growth across the earnings spectrum, decade-by-decade as well as across benefits categories, and calculate the share diverted to benefits, as we show in table 21.4, it explains some of the public consternation about what has been happening to disposable earnings. The sluggish growth in disposable income has been attributed to a variety of factors, including changing reward structures in the corporate world and tax policy. Those factors may have played some role, but growing benefit costs were likely a much larger reason for the stagnant pay.

Stepping Back and Looking Forward

In many ways, the 1980s was a decade of discontent. Women's workforce participation rates were higher than ever before and the number of families with two earners jumped significantly. Yet many of these families felt like they were running in place. And one reason for that perception was that most of

Table 21.4 Share of Compensation Gains Provided in the Form of More Expensive Benefits Paid by Employers for Full-Year Workers, by Earnings Decile and for Selected Periods*

Earnings decile	1980–1990*	1990–2000	2000–2009
1	100.0%	30.4%	35.2%
2	100.0%	23.1%	47.7%
3	90.8%	25.0%	52.3%
4	54.1%	21.3%	60.8%
5	63.9%	17.8%	55.7%
6	43.0%	18.8%	55.3%
7	48.6%	12.4%	54.8%
8	36.8%	9.6%	50.3%
9	29.7%	7.8%	45.0%
10	21.4%	6.8%	37.7%

Source: Updated results of projections presented in Steven A. Nyce and Sylvester J. Schieber, "Health Care Inflation, Must Workers Bear the Brunt," *Milken Institute Review* (Second Quarter 2010): 46–57.
* Total benefit cost increases in the 1980s for the first and second earnings decile exceeded 100 percent of compensation growth. In both cases, benefit costs increased significantly, but total compensation growth was negative in the first decile and negligible in the second.

the rewards for all that extra work were diverted to benefit costs, especially among the bottom half of earners. During the 1990s, on the other hand, workers across the income spectrum seemed to be getting ahead—most compensation rewards were paid out as higher wages. In the early 2000s, however, employers were again diverting a substantial portion of compensation to benefit costs, although the effects on paychecks were somewhat more equitable than they had been during the 1980s. Still, the perception remained that rank-and-file workers were losing ground. Two recessions in the decade did not help matters.

For the past quarter century, Social Security's long-term financing outlook has consistently called attention to the underfunding for the baby boom's retirement. Despite the long lead time, policymakers have not reacted to the warnings. The 2010 Trustees Report indicated that the combined Social Security retirement and disability programs would run a cash-flow deficit that year—some seven years sooner than previously predicted. With the program now in deficit and adding to rather than subtracting from the federal deficit, pressure will mount to find a solution. While it is impossible to predict how policymakers might respond, the solution is likely to involve some combination of benefit reductions and tax increases. Higher payroll taxes would stake a further claim on workers' compensation packages.

In chapter 20, we saw that—under the most optimistic projections—the public employer system was funded to the tune of around 75 percent to 80 percent of accrued obligations at the end of fiscal 2008, on average. Private employer plans were funded at 77 percent of projected benefit obligations at the end of fiscal 2009, up from 71 percent a year earlier, according to annual reports from Fortune 500 companies.[6] The baby boomers' aging toward retirement will put additional pressure on pension funding. Some of the pension underfunding could be ameliorated by a few good years of financial market performance, but counting on that is fraught with risks. It is likely, in any event, that employers will continue making hefty contributions to these plans for the next few years, and these contributions will continue reducing the amount left in the compensation package for wages and salaries.

As plan sponsors catch up on their funding and defined benefit plan curtailments continue rolling out, pension plan costs should decline over time, but most employers will still contribute to the replacement or enhanced 401(k) and other defined contribution plans. In 401(k) plans, the typical plan provides a 50 percent employer match on employee contributions of up to 6 percent of pay, meaning employers contribute about one-third of such contributions and many also make additional profit-sharing contributions. Between 2000 and

2008, total contributions to private defined contribution plans grew at a compound rate of 5.8 percent per year and contributions per active participant in these plans have been growing at a compound rate of 4.3 percent per year, much more rapidly than either compensation or wage growth.[7] Although some companies hit hard by the recession reduced contributions to their profit-sharing plans and workers' 401(k)s, in most cases the cuts were temporary.

Health care costs have long been a culprit in the missing productivity rewards for workers. But given the implications of health cost inflation, we are now in a much more sensitive spot than ever before. In 1980, a median-wage, full-time worker's health benefit costs represented roughly 4.3 percent of compensation. By 2010, health benefits claimed 10.6 percent of worker's compensation. To the extent that health costs continue spiraling upward, we will be indexing the share of compensation diverted to health care against a base that is 2.3 times higher than it was in 1980. The risks associated with health cost inflation under health care reform are substantial and troubling.

The prosperity of workers and their retirement security are closely linked, and that linkage is complicated by an extremely expensive and out-of-control health financing system. Workers expect to "trade" their sustained commitment and hard work for gradual improvements in their economic stability and prosperity. But many workers today feel trapped on the Alice in Wonderland treadmill, working harder and harder and going nowhere. When our efforts do not seem to pay off, there is a natural inclination to suspect that somebody else must be reaping our rightful rewards. These perceptions are easily fueled by political aspirants and pundits who are more interested in stirring public reaction against scapegoats than in the hard work needed to understand the problems and address them.

In assessing economic status, it is easy to count the dollars in the paycheck and to understand what they will provide. It is more difficult to value the compensation we receive in the form of health and retirement benefits and discern that they are making us better off. It may be even harder to appreciate what refusing to address our current problems might mean to our children and grandchildren. If we simply sit on our hands until 2030, those workers would have to divert roughly 16 percent of their pay to make up Social Security's financing shortfalls. Under recent health cost growth rates, the tab for health benefits could be as much as 17 percent of workers' pay. Given the need to save for their own retirement, these costs could consume more than 40 percent of workers' earnings. What are we leaving the next generation?

END GAME: A GOLD WATCH, PAT ON THE BACK, AND MORE

When I was in college in the 1960s, Walter Cronkite would run periodic stories on his national CBS news program about poverty among the elderly. I recall one segment about elderly people being forced to buy dog or cat food because they could not afford a proper diet. This was the era of President Lyndon Johnson's War on Poverty. In 1967, the Census Bureau estimated that 29.5 percent of those aged 65 and over had incomes below the poverty line, while the rate among the total population was 16.6 percent.[1] The disproportionate destitution of the nation's grandparents played a major role in motivating policymakers to boost Social Security benefits in the 1969-to-1972 period. Concerns about the economic security of retirees were clearly in the background as policymakers crafted the Employee Retirement Income Security Act (ERISA).

In October 2010, the Social Security Administration announced there would be no cost-of living-increase for Social Security in 2011, the second year in a row there was no inflation adjustment. House of Representatives Speaker Nancy Pelosi worried that the lack of a benefit increase would "fall hard" on many retirees.[2] But a month earlier, the Census Bureau had released a report on poverty rates for 2009 and changes from the prior year. In the accompanying press release, the Census announced that, from 2008 to 2009, the poverty rate increased from 19 percent to 20.7 percent for children under age 18, and from 11.7 percent to 12.9 percent for those aged 18 to 64, but it had declined from 9.7 percent to 8.9 percent for people 65 and older.[3] Between the War on Poverty and 2010, the elderly made great economic strides, both in absolute terms and compared with the rest of the country. Poverty rates among the elderly were dropping even before the big Social Security benefit increases—they fell from 35 percent in 1959 to 25 percent in 1969. After the benefit increases, the elderly poverty rate dropped to 15 percent by 1979, then to 11 percent in 1989, 10 percent in 1999 and, finally, 8.9 percent in 2009.

Documenting the Extent of Retirement Income Security

During the 1990s, the National Institute on Aging began a remarkable research program to track the retirement experience of successive generations. We have talked about the Health and Retirement Study elsewhere, but a brief recounting is worthwhile. Beginning in 1992, a group of researchers at the Survey Research Center in the Institute for Social Research at the University of Michigan surveyed a representative sample of people ages 51 to 61. Those remaining from that original group have been resurveyed every other year since 1992. In 1998, the survey added a "war baby" cohort, which included a representative sample of individuals ages 51 to 56. In 2004, an "early baby boomer" cohort—a representative sample of individuals ages 51 to 56—was added. In the discussion that follows, I refer to these three groups as the "original" cohort, the "war baby" cohort and the "early boomer" cohort. All these groups continue to be surveyed every other year.

In 2010, Alan Gustman, Thomas Steinmeier, and Nahid Tabatabai published a 367-page volume summarizing much of the pension and savings plan data from the 1992 through the 2006 waves of the Health and Retirement Study databases.[4] We summarize some of their results here to provide an understanding of what employer-based retirement programs currently provide, how they are changing for retirees or those nearing retirement, and a sense of the context in which they deliver benefits.

Table 22.1 shows the percentage of households and participants who reported having earned an employer-sponsored retirement benefit at some point in their career. Members of each of the three sample groups were interviewed between the ages of 51 and 56. The interviews were in 1992 for the original sample, in 1998 for the war baby sample and in 2004 for the early boomer sample. In much of the discussion thus far, we have differentiated between pensions—shorthand for defined benefit plans—and defined contribution or savings plans. Gustman and his colleagues refer to all of these as pensions, and since we are borrowing their results we follow their convention here.

Retirement benefits are much more common among workers approaching retirement age than the 50 percent often cited in criticism of the employer-based system. Almost 90 percent of couples had earned a benefit. Single women fared worse, but well over half in each sample had a retirement benefit from an employer plan by their early 50s. Single women were more likely than married women, considered on their own, to have a pension. Since the passage of the Pension Equity Act in 1981, the vast majority of married defined benefit recipients taking an annuity cover their spouse in a joint-and-survivor

Table 22.1 Percentage of Households and Respondents with Any Own, Spouse, or Partner Pension from Current, Last, or Previous Jobs, by Health and Retirement Sample Members at Ages 51 to 56

	Original sample	War baby sample	Early boomers sample
Household members	in 1992	in 1998	in 2004
All respondents	78.8	81.2	80.4
All households	76.9	79.3	78.4
Couples	83.9	87.1	87.5
Males	74.8	76.6	75.4
Females	49.2	57.9	62.4
Singles	58.8	62.1	59.2
Males	64.8	62.8	61.1
Females	55.1	61.6	58.0

Source: Alan Gustman, Thomas Steinmeier, and Nahid Tabatabai, *Pensions in the Health and Retirement Study* (Cambridge, MA: Harvard University Press, 2010), 95.

benefit. Gustman and his colleagues consider that one person in a couple having a pension benefit provides value to both, as suggested in table 22.1.

But having earned a retirement benefit at some point does not mean these workers still have it "in the bank" the day they retire. When workers terminate employment before retiring and take distributions from their employer-sponsored plans, some of that money leaks out of the retirement system. That leakage, though, is not the fault of the plan or the sponsor. If the leakages need to be plugged, we need to focus on doing so rather than faulting plans for not delivering benefits more broadly.

The plan types in which the Health and Retirement Study participants earned benefits are shown in table 22.2. In earlier chapters, the shift away from defined benefit plans and toward defined contribution plans was documented and discussed, and the table clearly reflects the shift. Of the original cohort turning 51 to 56 in 1992, 68 percent were covered by a defined benefit plan and 58 percent by a defined contribution plan. For the war baby cohort—ages 51 to 56 in 1998—the split shifted to 60 percent in defined benefit plans and 70 percent in defined contribution plans. For the early boomers first interviewed in 2004, the divide was 49 percent in defined benefit plans and 72 percent in defined contribution plans.

The type of plan workers have affects their retirement behavior for a couple of reasons. Traditional defined benefit plans have generally paid benefits as annuities, which makes it easier for workers to evaluate when the monthly amount will pay their monthly bills. For workers starting retirement with a lump sum of cash from a defined contribution plan, it is much more difficult to know when they have "enough" money to last some unknown remaining lifetime.

Moreover, traditional defined benefit plans have often provided financial incentives to encourage workers to retire early. Such provisions became popular in the 1960s and 1970s to encourage older workers to retire to make room for the baby boomers. As a result of these early retirement incentives, retirement ages for men declined from the 1960s through the mid-1980s and then leveled out. In recent years, men's retirement ages have been rising, partly because of shifting plan structures. Meanwhile, older women's labor force participation rates have

Table 22.2 Percentages of Respondents in Plan Types among the Alternative Cohort Populations in the Health and Retirement Study and for Men and Women at Ages 51 to 56

	Total in a defined benefit plan	Total in a defined contribution plan	Total in both types of plans
Original sample			
Males	70	60	31
Females	64	54	21
All	68	58	27
War baby sample			
Males	63	71	35
Females	57	68	26
All	60	70	31
Early baby boomer sample			
Males	51	75	29
Females	48	69	21
All	49	72	25

Source: Alan Gustman, Thomas Steinmeier, and Nahid Tabatabai, *Pensions in the Health and Retirement Study* (Cambridge, MA: Harvard University Press, 2010), 98.

steadily increased since the early 1960s, but the climb largely reflects higher workforce participation for all women. Among all three of the Health and Retirement Study samples, workers with a defined benefit plan expected to retire one to two years earlier than those with only a defined contribution plan.[5]

Gustman and his colleagues developed estimates of wealth in Health and Retirement Study households in order to compare the values of components in workers' financial portfolios as they were approaching retirement age. Table 22.3 shows their results for the 1992 cohort as two sets of averages. Some survey participants have very substantial wealth holdings, which tend to push the overall average values higher than what many would expect for a "typical" individual. The average values on the right side of table 22.3 are more typical because they are for the 10 percent of survey participants in the middle of the wealth holdings distribution. Comparing the two sets of averages shows that the more representative survey participants—aged 51 to 56 in 1992—were more dependent on Social Security than the overall cohort was. More affluent participants held larger shares of their retirement wealth in financial assets such as individual retirement accounts and employer-sponsored retirement plans.

Table 22.3 Composition of Mean Wealth and Wealth for the Median 10 Percent of Wealth-Holding Households among 51- to 56-Year-Old Health and Retirement Study Participants in 1992, in 1992 Dollars

	Average for whole cohort		Average for the median 10 percent of wealth-holding households	
	Value in $s	% of total	Value in $s	% of total
Total	409,765	100.0%	312,253	100.0%
House value	72,171	17.6%	57,499	18.4%
Real estate	26,048	6.4%	9,297	3.0%
Business assets	21,919	5.3%	6,155	2.0%
Financial assets	38,536	9.4%	19,238	6.2%
IRA assets	15,569	3.8%	10,218	3.3%
Social Security	123,953	30.2%	135,859	43.5%
Pension value	98,186	24.0%	60,493	19.4%
Net value of vehicles	13,383	3.3%	13,494	4.3%

Source: Alan Gustman, Thomas Steinmeier, and Nahid Tabatabai, *Pensions in the Health and Retirement Study* (Cambridge, MA: Harvard University Press, 2010), 287.

The results in table 22.3 might exaggerate the ultimate value of Social Security by the time these people actually retired. James Poterba, Steven Venti, and David Wise analyzed members of the Health and Retirement Study sample population who were ages 63 to 67 in 2000—eight years after the data in table 22.3 were collected on the same group. The analysis by Poterba and his colleagues reflected the older half of that group in 2000, while Gustman and his colleagues were looking at the younger half of it in developing table 22.3 in 1992.

Some of the Poterba, Venti, and Wise results appear in table 22.4. The table shows Social Security wealth compared to private retirement plan wealth across the Social Security lifetime-covered earnings deciles. The lowest covered earnings decile is misleading because it includes a significant number of public-sector workers who were not covered under Social Security. The results in table 22.4 suggest greater parity between Social Security and private plan values across much of the earnings distribution than the two-thirds to one-third split in the right-hand column of table 22.3. One explanation for the different results is accrual patterns under the respective systems.

Table 22.4 Average Household Social Security Wealth and Pension, 401(k), IRA, and Keogh Wealth, by Lifetime Earnings Decile for Health and Retirement Study Respondents Aged 63 to 67 in 2000, in 2000 Dollars

Lifetime covered earnings decile	Social Security wealth	DB + 401(k) +IRA/ Keogh wealth	Social Security share of total
	(dollar amounts in 2000 dollars)		
1	$74,074	$88,697	45.5%
2	97,345	55,028	63.9%
3	109,638	99,956	52.3%
4	131,219	120,897	52.0%
5	176,401	133,386	56.9%
6	196,484	161,593	54.9%
7	225,868	185,314	54.9%
8	244,630	226,140	52.0%
9	260,767	283,005	48.0%
10	279,080	571,331	32.8%
All	$178,373	196,102	47.6%

Source: Derived from James Poterba, Steven Venti, and David A. Wise, "Rise of 401(k) Plans, Lifetime Earnings, and Wealth at Retirement," NBER Working Paper 13091 (Cambridge, MA: National Bureau of Economic Research, 2007), 6.

Social Security bases benefits on the highest 35 years of earnings and indexes past earnings to align them with current average earnings. For most full-career employees, working beyond 35 years nets little benefit advantage because each extra year merely removes an earlier year from the computation and, with indexing, the marginal value of the later year is negligible in the 35-year averaging process. Many workers reach 35 years of covered earnings in their early to mid-50s—the age of the Health and Retirement Study cohort in table 22.3. While Social Security benefits often grow slowly late in one's career, private plan benefits usually grow faster as retirement nears, for several reasons. First, many workers can contribute more to their retirement savings plans late in their careers—their children have grown up and the home is paid off. Second, compounding works more powerfully on larger accumulations than on smaller ones, and total lifetime savings should be larger later in life. Third, the power of compound discounting means the pension values grow more rapidly as benefit payouts get closer.

Large Pension Wealth Accumulation Seemingly Nets Little Benefit

After 275 pages of analyzing the Health and Retirement Study samples and their pension wealth, Gustman, Steinmeier, and Tabatabai spend only three pages discussing actual retirement payouts. Table 22.5 is from the segment of their analysis that traces the pension income reported by the cohort aged 51 to 56 in 1992. The table shows reported pension income for each survey year for which data were available. The number of households declines from year to year as members of the group die off. The essence of the table is the "Percentage receiving pension income" column, which never even reaches 40 percent. The benefit levels drop off over time, in part, because they are stated in 1992 dollars, and benefits are not indexed in most private plans and not fully inflation-indexed in state and local plans. And those with smaller benefit levels might be claiming their benefits later in life. Benefits also decline as primary beneficiaries die, leaving the surviving spouse with a smaller monthly pension.

The low percentages of the cohort receiving pension income shown in table 22.5 can be used to demonstrate the ineffectiveness of the employer-based retirement system. When I wrote, "Why Do Pension Benefits Seem So Small?" in 1995, which explained why the impression was misleading, John Woods at the Social Security Administration published a lengthy critical article

Table 22.5 Pension Receipt and Monthly Benefits Received by the Original Cohort in the Health and Retirement Study at Ages 51 to 56 in 1992

Year surveyed	Total households	Households with pension income	Percentage receiving pension income	Average monthly benefit in 1992 $s
1992	4,494	520	11.6%	1,073
1994	4,128	696	16.9%	1,511
1996	3,994	851	21.3%	1,265
1998	3,976	914	23.0%	1,032
2000	3,785	1,189	31.4%	1,041
2002	3,724	1,285	34.5%	945
2004	3,612	1,418	39.3%	925
2006	3,172	1,183	37.3%	817

Source: Alan Gustman, Thomas Steinmeier, and Nahid Tabatabai, *Pensions in the Health and Retirement Study* (Cambridge, MA: Harvard University Press, 2010), 277.

in the *Social Security Bulletin* defending the estimates of pension receipt and benefits based on the Census Bureau's *Current Population Survey*.[6] In the conclusion to his critique, however, Woods wrote:

> Schieber is justifiably concerned that some of the IRA income reported by the aged undoubtedly originated as rollovers from employer-sponsored pension plans and thus should be considered when evaluating the contributions of the pension system. He is further justified in pointing out that some of the money classified as asset income among the aged probably has its origins in lump-sum distributions from employer-sponsored plans. In addition, data on the uses of preretirement lump-sum distributions suggests that the pension system may also be contributing to other aspects of economic well-being among the aged, such as home ownership and the lack of indebtedness. Unfortunately, there are no data available to help us untangle these complex issues, and it is certainly an area where further research is needed . . .
>
> Although it is not the purpose of this article to take positions on pension policy, we should take a position on the quality of data analyses underlying policy debates. And here, the evidence seems clear: The system of employer sponsored pensions in the United States—indirectly subsidized by one of the largest tax expenditures in the Federal budget—has been

doing a poor job of providing widespread retirement income security to lower wage workers and their families: instead, it is serving its intended role in the 3-legged stool only among majorities of the aged at middle and upper income levels.[7]

The data in table 22.4 clearly demonstrate substantial retirement wealth accumulations across the earnings distribution from employer-based retirement plans. The surveys of retirees' pension income, however, suggest that the system delivers virtually nothing to most of them. One of those conclusions must be wrong. We cannot assess how our public policies are working if we do not measure the outcomes on some reasonable basis. We cannot see past misleading data if we know nothing about the substance of the matter to which the data pertain. Employer plans play an extremely vital role in the retirement wealth of many workers nearing retirement—as attested to by Poterba, Venti, and Wise's body of work and that of Gustman, Steinmeier, and Tabatabai—but their contributions disappear on surveys when workers retire.

The argument that public policy supporting employer-sponsored retirement plans has failed because the plans have done a "poor job of providing widespread retirement income security to lower wage workers and their families" ignores two practical considerations. The first is that many low earners pay no federal income tax. If their tax rate is zero, the immediate net tax benefit of putting money into a tax-preferred saving plan is zero times the amount they put into the plan. No matter how much we multiply by zero, the product will always be zero. Second, we need to understand the constraints of nature. When people are barely scraping by, their appetite for retirement savings is greatly diminished.

In recent years, some analysts have concluded that simply asking retirees about their pension income does not accurately measure the effectiveness of employer-sponsored retirement plans. Barry Bosworth and Gary Burtless from the Brookings Institution observe:

One way to assess the effectiveness of a nation's pension system is to measure its success in bringing the incomes of the aged close to those enjoyed by nonaged adults. The comparability of income estimates for the aged and nonaged depends, however, on the relative accuracy of the income reports for the two populations. Unfortunately, some income items that are particularly important to the elderly, including occupational pensions and interest and dividend income, may be significantly underreported in the Census Bureau's Current Population Survey.[8]

In addition, Gustman, Steinmeier, and Tabatabai conclude at the end of their analysis:

> Not all pensions continue in a form that is easily connected back to its origin as a pension. Although defined benefit plans are much more likely to be preserved in a form that is directly recognizable as originating from a pension plan, defined contribution plans are not.
>
> The role of pensions will be understated in surveys of retiree incomes by source. This may explain why the frequency of pension incomes among retirees and the value of income from pensions received by retirees are typically so much smaller than are comparable figures reporting the coverage and value of plans held by those who are still employed.
>
> When we consider both the smaller share of DC plans that continue in the form of a pension, together with the trend to defined contribution plans, this suggests a factor that will continue to reduce the fraction of retired respondents who will report that they are receiving income from a pension plan and the share of retiree incomes measured as originating from pensions.[9]

The shift toward defined contribution plans does not mean that employer-sponsored plans are no longer contributing to workers' retirement security. But the shift has created a new set of concerns about whether defined contribution plans can provide true retirement income security. The increasing prevalence of lump-sum retirement benefits does not stop retirees from converting their retirement savings into steady income streams. But the evidence is indisputable that many of them do not. Reliable estimates are that up to 80 percent—or $360 billion—of private retirement plan distributions in 2007 were available as lump sums. The evidence suggests that a very small share of those lump sums are being annuitized, and many policy analysts are concerned that workers' decision-making is far from optimal, thereby threatening their financial security in retirement. I explore that concern in the next chapter.

23 WE'VE KILLED THE GOOSE, LET'S GILD THE EGGS

Policy analysts and policymakers are concerned about the decisions workers make in their participant-directed retirement savings plans. While recent restructuring has made defined contribution plans considerably more effective savings vehicles, concern remains about what people do with these portable accounts when they switch jobs or retire. If many workers have trouble making sound financial decisions, does it make sense to hand them a bag of money as they walk out the door and expect them to handle it wisely?

Growing Concerns over Move from Retirement Annuities

Table 23.1 is based on the Health and Retirement Study participants who terminated a job between the 1992 and 2004 waves of the survey and had a vested retirement plan benefit. Nearly 60 percent of defined benefit plan participants—accounting for two-thirds of plan assets—started receiving an annuity upon leaving their jobs. Another 22 percent left their money in the plan, presumably planning to take an annuity later. It appears that roughly 90 percent of these plan assets would be paid out in regular monthly annuities to around 80 percent of plan participants. But this was the early 1990s, when most defined benefit plans were paying out benefits as annuities, and lump sums have become increasingly common since then. In defined contribution plans, only 5 percent of the money was converted into annuities when workers—all of whom were relatively far along in their careers—left their jobs. Over the last couple of decades and going forward, far more people are managing their retirement accumulations on their own.

Table 23.1 Disposition of Employer-Sponsored Retirement Benefits by Health and Retirement Study Participants at Termination of Employment between 1992 and 2004

	Average value of benefit at distribution in 2004 $s	Percentage of individuals	Percentage of total dollars
Defined benefit plan participants			
Cash out	64,114	6.65	2.13
Roll into an IRA	164,034	7.99	7.56
Leave in plan for later	166,892	22.28	22.12
Start immediate annuity	206,144	59.23	67.29
Other	102,673	1.54	0.80
Defined contribution plan participants			
Cash out	27,184	17.55	7.61
Roll into an IRA	86,794	32.23	41.45
Leave in plan for later	72,679	38.62	39.46
Convert to an annuity	75,940	3.55	4.98
Other	64,799	7.10	6.32

Source: Dan M. McGill et al., Fundamentals of Private Pensions, 9th ed. (Oxford: Oxford University Press, 2010), 275.

In the 2008 wave of the Health and Retirement Study, respondents were asked a series of questions aimed at evaluating their financial literacy, sophistication, and inclinations to make appropriate investment decisions. The questionnaire framed many of its questions from two alternative perspectives. For example, one group of participants was asked whether they agreed with the statement, "Even older retired people should hold some stocks." The remaining participants were asked whether they agreed with the statement, "Older retired people should not hold any stocks." One group was asked whether "[i]t is best to avoid owning stocks of foreign companies," and the other whether "[i]t is a good idea to own stocks of foreign companies." One group was asked whether the following was true or false: "If the interest rate falls, bond prices will fall." For the other, the statement was, "If the interest rate falls, bond prices will rise." Annamaria Lusardi, Olivia Mitchell, and Vilsa Curto published an analysis of the resulting data from the Health and Retirement Study participants who were over age 55 when the survey was conducted.[1] They found that responses varied substantively depending on how questions were phrased.

A large majority of respondents did not understand that bond prices fall when interest rates rise. There were three questions about risk diversification, and many respondents answered one or two correctly, but only one-third knew the answers to all three. Older women were less likely than men to say they understood the stock market reasonably well. Compared to men, women were more likely to avoid investing in foreign stocks, were less knowledgeable about the interest rate and bond pricing relationship, and knew less about risk diversification. The women were also less likely to be able to do complex calculations of asset returns and potential outcomes of investment options. Educational attainment was important in determining knowledge of the financial markets and an understanding of concepts like asset pricing and risk diversification. Racial differences were also pronounced but undoubtedly were partly related to the differences in educational attainment. The authors concluded that many of the deficits they identified could be addressed with educational materials and seminars, but they cautioned that the needs vary from one segment of the population to the next.[2]

Lusardi, Mitchell, and Curto's research did not link age to the Health and Retirement Study respondents' knowledge and abilities to deal with investment matters, but the relationship between aging and dementia suggests that retirees' ability to handle financial affairs may diminish over time for some. There is evidence that even without a diagnosis of dementia, some of the elderly find the prospects of managing their finances more difficult as they age.

Tara Queen and Thomas Hess reported the results of comparative testing of a group of 17- to 28-year-olds and a group of 60- to 86-year-olds who were still living independently. When tasked with decisions based on intuitive evaluation, study participants in both groups were equally adept. Older people can choose from a restaurant menu as well as younger ones. But when study participants read printed descriptions of criteria to use in choosing an apartment and were then expected to rely on memory in making a choice, some of the older adults had more difficulty than their younger counterparts. Those with a higher education did a better job remembering the selection criteria and using them in the decision-making process.[3] In describing the implications of their research, Hess said that age differences are likely to "crop up when it comes to complex decision-making, such as choosing a health-care plan based on a complex array of information."[4] Queen added, "Presenting older adults with overwhelming amounts of information is less beneficial to them."[5] This is only one study, but it suggests that some older people might find it difficult to manage their retirement security. The default features that make workers more effective savers will not necessarily make them effective shepherds of retirement wealth when left to their own druthers.

Even for retirees who know how to manage money effectively and who remain capable of doing so throughout retirement, the challenge remains of covering both anticipated and unanticipated expenses over an indeterminate period. At retirement, people might have some expectations about the duration ahead, but not knowing where they might be on the mortality curve complicates budgeted spending from a likely nonrenewable source for the rest of their lives.

Understanding Annuity Avoidance by Retirees with Choice

Economists who have studied retirement behavior have been perplexed by the fact that so few people buy annuities.[6] Consider a simplified case where two workers each save $40,000 during their working period to finance their consumption needs in retirement, and interest adds another $10,000 to the nest egg. The presumption is that the workers actually save to achieve some reasonable standard of living in the retirement period. Ignore, for now, the possibility of passing on some of their savings to their children. Acting independently, the two workers amass $50,000 each during their working period to spend during the retirement period. Now assume that each worker faces a random 50 percent probability of dying at the end of the working period—one of them is going to die but neither knows which one. For the one who dies, the accumulated $50,000 has no value in terms of financing retirement consumption. Both of them can improve their potential consumption in retirement by pooling their resources, so the survivor enjoys the benefit of the combined savings. The potential value that both workers realize is the individual savings amount divided by the probability of being alive in second period of $50,000 /0.50 = $100,000. In trying to understand why so many people refuse to buy annuities—even though they would be better off by doing so—some have called into question a couple of assumptions in the above example.

The first questionable assumption is that death is totally random. Life insurance companies have determined that people who buy annuities live longer than those who do not.[7] Presumably, people in ill health are basing their annuity decisions on a rational assessment of their life expectancies and economic interests. The second assumption subject to challenge is that a dollar of unspent retirement savings has no value to the person who saved it. Some people want to leave money to their surviving heirs, and converting accumulated assets into an annuity with no residual for a survivor would defeat that goal. A third good reason not to purchase annuities is because marketing costs and profit margins are high for these products. Jeffrey Brown and colleagues estimated that commercial insurers charge individual annuity buyers an additional 6 percent to 10 percent fee over and above the charges associated with the expectation of longer than typical lives for annuity buyers.[8] In modeling the economics of annuity offers, however, Brown and colleagues concluded that even given the substantial extra costs, retirees should be buying annuities more than they do.[9]

Jeffrey Brown and another group of colleagues turned to behavioral economics to help sort out the annuity puzzle. They hypothesized that resistance to annuities was a framing issue—that potential buyers' choices depended on whether they considered the annuity as an investment or as income security. Would-be buyers who viewed the annuity as an investment would compare its risk and return characteristics to those of other investment options. If they considered the annuities riskier—including the risk of dying shortly after purchase—and less profitable, they shied away. Those who considered annuities from a consumption perspective—in other words, in terms of income security—found the lifetime guarantee very attractive.[10]

To test their hypothesis, Brown and his colleagues conducted an Internet survey during December 2007 of 1,342 individuals, all age 50 or older, split into four groups. Two groups were asked questions about buying annuities from a "consumption frame," using terms such as "spend" and "payment" to describe a series of decisions made by two fictitious retired men. The other two groups were asked questions from an "investment frame," using terms like "invest" and "earnings." The two groups were each split into two more groups, with one told that any assets remaining after their death would be donated to charity, and the other that the assets would be passed on to their children. In each instance, the respondents were asked which was the better choice: a life annuity or the alternative option.[11]

In virtually every case, posing the annuity options in the consumption frame elicited significantly greater choosing of an annuity than when the questions were posed from an investment perspective. The survey participants showed some bequest motivation in their choices—they were more likely to choose the annuity option in each case if any excess assets at their death under the non-annuity option were to go to charity rather than their children. Among the consumption-frame group, the majority chose the full-life annuity in all cases but one, the exception being the consol bond option paying a monthly benefit of $400 in perpetuity. Then 49 percent chose the annuity versus 51 percent the consol option. Among the investment-frame group, the majority of the respondents chose the alternative to an annuity in every instance.[12]

Proposals to Automatically Annuitize Retirement Savings

In 2008, William Gale and colleagues proposed that when retirees take a distribution from their 401(k)s or similar plans, a substantial portion of the distribution be automatically deposited into a two-year trial income plan that did not entail buying an annuity but scheduling payouts in a way to provide income support over the individual's remaining life expectancy. During the two years, plan participants would receive a monthly check. After two years, unless they elected an alternative form of payout, they would default into a permanent income distribution plan. The authors hoped "to lay out the issues and begin a dialogue that ultimately would lead to a strategy that provides improved retirement outcomes for workers."[13]

Shortly after Barack Obama became president, he created the White House Task Force on Middle-Class Working Families and designated Vice President Joe Biden as chair of this cabinet-level group. Mark Iwry, a senior advisor to Secretary of Treasury Timothy Geithner, influenced the Task Force's deliberations. In early 2010, the task force issued a "Fact Sheet" previewing their forthcoming recommendations for supporting middle-class families. In "Updating 401(k) Regulations to Improve Transparency and Reliability," the fact sheet suggested "promoting the availability of annuities and other forms of guaranteed lifetime income, which transform savings into guaranteed future income, reducing the risks that retirees will outlive their savings. . . ."[14]

Also in early 2010, Jeffrey Brown laid out the rationale and a proposal for defined contribution plan sponsors to make annuities the default form of benefit distribution from their plans, which could be overridden by the account holder who preferred a lump sum benefit over the annuity. Brown observed that defined benefit plans have traditionally paid benefits as annuities because federal regulations require that they offer annuities, and that most participants in these plans receive annuities. He also noted that when Congress passed the 1978 tax provisions that led to the 401(k) revolution, its focus was on the capital accumulation phase—not the distribution phase. Moreover, Congress failed to predict how popular these plans would become or that they might be the only employer plan. Given these developments and the financial security offered by annuities, he suggested that annuities become the "default" option for benefit payouts in all employer-sponsored retirement plans.[15]

On February 2, 2010, the Department of Labor and the Treasury Department issued a joint request for information on the use of lifetime income products in retirement plans. These included questions about general practices for such products and problems associated with offering them. One of the questions noted the use of "behavioral strategies" adopted by sponsors of 401(k) and similar plans and asked, "To what extent are these or other behavioral strategies being used or viewed as promising means of encouraging more lifetime income? Can or should the 401(k) rules, other plan qualification rules, or ERISA rules be modified, or their application clarified, to facilitate the use of behavioral strategies in this context?"[16]

There were 789 written responses, which the Department of Labor published on its website. The vast majority of these were personal statements, some quite colorful and many of them clearly hostile to the idea. Frequently, those commenting viewed the proposal as a government attempt to seize control of their retirement savings and spend them. A few even drew a linkage to the government's handling of Social Security's trust funds. For example, one commenter wrote:

> It is obvious that the government's plan is a device to obtain large amounts of money to cover current expenses and that it is likely (actually absolutely certain!) that the funds will be spent rather than being invested. Any legal restriction on the use of the funds could be circumvented by legislation. The plan is very reminiscent of how the government has used social security funds to disguise deficits in the budget. One result of that policy is that that there claims that [sic] there is no money to pay benefits and that the funds in the "trust fund" are not really available.[17]

The comments from benefit consultants, trade associations, and other public interest groups tended to be more measured, with some in favor and others opposed to requiring defined contribution plan sponsors to offer annuities. There was also a public hearing where 40 witnesses representing various groups testified on the matter, and once again, they were fairly split between supporters and opponents.

The supporters of default annuity options in defined contribution plans cited longevity risks, the need for lifelong retirement income, the potential for higher income levels than those most people can achieve by self-managing their assets, and other reasons. Some of the concerns about such options were practical administrative concerns, while others focused on the effects on retirees' income security.

One of the problems with automatic annuitization of balances in defined contribution plans is that many workers terminate employment before retirement and roll their assets into their individual retirement accounts (IRAs). Craig Copeland presented tabulations of Investment Company Institute pooled data from several mutual fund companies on the distribution of funds in the IRAs of 11.1 million individuals with 14.1 million accounts holding $732.9 billion at the end of 2008. His results suggest that much of the money saved in employer-sponsored plans is out the 401(k) plan door long before people would be committing to a retirement annuity.[18] While workers leaving a job to retire might accept an automatic annuity, younger workers are less likely to do so.

Residual Risks even if Annuitization at Retirement is Automatic

Even if we could automatically shift workers' defined contribution assets into an annuity at retirement, the timing of the annuity purchase is a problem. Brendan McFarland and Mark Warshawsky considered a worker—call her Louise—who saved 6 percent of her pay for 40 years and retired at age 65.[19] Louise invested in a lifecycle fund—one of those funds workers default into in some 401(k) plans. In this fund, 88 percent of Louise's assets were invested in equities when she was 25, and this allocation gradually declined to 34 percent in her final year before retiring. The fund was rebalanced each year to keep the allocation in alignment with the investment strategy. The accumulating fund incurred an annual fee of 100 basis points—that is, 1 percent of total assets—for administrative and investment fees.

The exercise showed how Louise's annuity would vary depending on when she turned 65. Historical annual returns on stocks and bonds from 1875 through 2010 from Robert Shiller's updated data from *Irrational Exuberance* were used to calculate Louise's accumulated savings based on alternative career and retirement dates.[20] In the first simulation, Louise was assumed to have worked, saved, and had her retirement funds invested from 1875 through 1914, and then retired in 1915. In the second simulation, she was assumed to have worked, saved, and had her retirement funds invested from 1876 through 1915, retiring in 1916, and so on through 2010. At various retirement dates, Louise's accumulated lifetime retirement savings were converted into an annuity based on prevailing interest rates on her retirement date and on current life expectancies.[21] McFarland and Warshawsky assumed that a worker buying an annuity in the retail marketplace would face charges of 15 percent of the purchase price to cover the loading costs associated with the longer life expectancy of annuity purchasers, marketing costs, and profit margins.

The benefits Louise would receive appear in figure 23.1. On average, Louise's benefit was 28.4 percent of her final earnings, which, when combined with a Social Security benefit of roughly 40 percent of final earnings, would allow typical workers to approximate their preretirement standard of living. Most of the benefit outcomes since 1960 have been above the 28.4 percent average, suggesting long stretches of time when Louise would have outperformed the long-term average and lived a retirement of relative luxury. However, remember the underlying assumptions: Louise saved religiously from age 25 until she retired at 65; there were no breaks in employment or in plan coverage; and there were no premature distributions. This is an optimistic picture for many workers.

The results in figure 23.1 are based on a single-life annuity. Buying a joint-and-survivor benefit would reduce the benefit by 10 percent or so. Many people worry about outliving their retirement resources, particularly given the financial turmoil of recent years, and are looking for more protections against these and other retirement risks. Annuity providers have created new retirement income vehicles in recent years to address many of these concerns. Some people want inflation protection during retirement. An indexed annuity to keep purchasing power constant over retirement could easily reduce the initial nominal benefit by another 20 to 30 percent or more. Those who want to preserve capital for heirs would also receive lower benefits during their lifetimes.

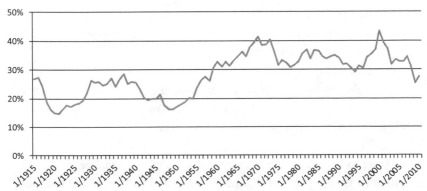

FIGURE 23.1 **Defined Contribution Earnings Replacement Rates from Lifecycle Funds with Constant Life Expectancies for a Hypothetical Worker Retiring Each Year from 1915 through 2010**

Source: Brendan McFarland and Mark J. Warshawsky, "Balances and Retirement Income from Individual Accounts: U.S. Historical Simulations," *Benefits Quarterly* (Second Quarter 2010), p. 39.

There are ways to reduce or eliminate timing risks in purchasing annuities, but they carry other risks. For example, one alternative is to "ladder" annuities by purchasing small annuities on a periodic basis building toward an accumulated total annuity for retirement. By buying some portion in down markets and some in up markets, the purchaser receives the benefit of annuitization without being at the mercy of market ups and downs. But implementing such a strategy would be difficult in a default context under an employer plan.

No Magic Solutions to Retirement Security Dilemmas

Variable annuities allow purchasers to enjoy the upside benefit of financial returns, but annual fees may be as high as 200 basis points or 2 percent of asset value each year.[22] A recent twist on variable annuities is adding guarantees that the benefit will not fall below some specified level in declining markets. This is an investment account—a balanced or lifecycle fund—with an annuity wrapped around it. At retirement, $1,000 in the account might generate a retirement benefit of $50 per year for the owner. With better-than-expected investment returns during retirement, the guaranteed income could climb accordingly. The investor owns the underlying account and can withdraw money, which, of course, reduces the number of annuity units that are available at retirement and may also trigger withdrawal penalties.

In its submitted testimony, the American Council of Life Insurance (ACLI) wrote:

> ACLI believes that efforts to educate employers and employees about the value of guaranteed lifetime income and to reframe defined contribution plan savings as a source of guaranteed lifetime income will help solve the annuity puzzle. From a recent survey [sponsored by the Council], employees are interested in guaranteed lifetime income options and find it valuable to see how much guaranteed income they could obtain by using their retirement plan savings.[23]

A plan in which retirement savings accumulate toward a guaranteed benefit with downside insurance and upside potential has considerable appeal at first glance. Further scrutiny suggests caution.

Several responses to the Treasury-Labor Department's Request for Information mentioned that guaranteed annuities have high fees. The Principal Financial Group, itself an insurer, quantified the implications. First, they evaluated being in a Guaranteed Minimum Withdrawal Benefit fund versus saving in a traditional 60/40 equities/bonds account during the working period. They used S&P 500 returns and Barclay's Aggregate Bond Index from 1927 through 2008 to identify the historically "best," "average," and "worst" five-and 10-year investment periods to simulate total returns, net of investment costs, for a worker investing $100,000 either 5 or 10 years before retirement. They calculated compound annual returns for historical periods and the accumulated balances at retirement.

The simulation results presented in table 23.2 suggest that the guaranteed account plan would have cost participants who joined it 5 years before retirement 4 to 5 percent of their accumulated balances across the investment cycles. For those making the commitment 10 years before retirement, the cost would have been 7 to 9 percent, with higher costs for those caught in a bad investment cycle. Longer participation clearly increases the costs.

Table 23.2 shows the investment implications of buying one of the guaranteed variable annuities for accumulating assets, but the ultimate goal is securing a lifetime income stream. The Principal extended its

Table 23.2 Ultimate Accumulated Value of $100,000 in 401(k) Plan Savings with 5 or 10 Years to Retirement Invested in a Traditional Balanced Fund versus a Guaranteed Minimum Withdrawal Benefit Fund

Market performance			Impact on retirement savings		
Type of return	Years to retirement	Annual return average	Traditional 60% stock 40% bonds	Guaranteed minimum withdrawal benefit	Reduction in account value due to fees
Best	5	20.08%	$249,663	$240,446	4%
	10	16.50%	$460,531	$426,166	7%
Average	5	9.32%	$156,134	$149,812	4%
	10	9.71%	$252,617	$232,642	8%
Worst	5	-4.20%	$80,691	$76,972	5%
	10	16.80%	$118,129	$108,080	9%

Source: Principal Financial Group, *Comparing Guaranteed Income Options*, attachment to comment letter by Greg Burrows on the Departments of Treasury and Labor Request for Information on Certain Issues Relating to Lifetime Income Options for Participants and Beneficiaries in Retirement Plans, October 13, 2010, http://www.dol.gov/ebsa/pdf/Principal101410.pdf, 2.

analysis to estimate the retirement benefits that could be purchased under the two approaches. The worker in the traditional balanced fund account with 60 percent stocks and 40 percent bonds was assumed to annuitize the accumulated balance at age 65 as of October 1, 2009. The annuity was assumed to include an installment refund—that is, the annuitant's heirs would receive a rebate if the annuitant died before the original investment was paid out. The guaranteed benefit was assumed to be the larger of 5 percent of the account value or 5 percent of the original $100,000 investment.

The annuities that a retiree could purchase under the two plans are shown in table 23.3 under the "Income guaranteed annually" heading. In every case, the traditional income annuity is larger than the guaranteed benefit. In the best and average periods where the money would have been invested for 5 years before retirement, the traditional income annuity is 45 percent larger than the guaranteed minimum benefit, and in the worst case it is 13 percent

Table 23.3 Annuity Values of $100,000 in 401(k) Plan Savings Invested 5 or 10 Years before Retirement in a Traditional Balanced Fund versus a Guaranteed Minimum Withdrawal Benefit Fund

Type of return	Years to retirement	Income guaranteed annually		
		Traditional income annuity	Guaranteed minimum withdrawal fund	Traditional annuity as a percentage of guaranteed minimum benefit
Best	5	$17,476	$12,022	145.4
	10	$32,237	$21,308	151.3
Average	5	$10,929	$7,491	145.9
	10	$17,683	$11,632	152.0
Worst	5	$5,648	$5,000	113.0
	10	$8,269	$5,404	153.0

Source: Principal Financial Group, *Comparing Guaranteed Income Options*, attachment to comment letter by Greg Burrows on the Departments of Treasury and Labor Request for Information on Certain Issues Relating to Lifetime Income Options for Participants and Beneficiaries in Retirement Plans, October 13, 2010, http://www.dol.gov/ebsa/pdf/Principal101410.pdf, 3.

larger. In the 10-year investment simulations, the traditional annuity was at least 50 percent larger in every part of the return cycle.

On top of everything else, Greg Burrows, an executive from Principal, pointed out that

> [i]f an employee leaves an employer for any reason, there is currently no viable solution that allows the employee to continue making contributions [to a Guaranteed Minimum plan], even if they become eligible to contribute to another defined contribution retirement plan because the new plan may not offer this kind of option or it may be with a different company. This can result in small balances that are insufficient in providing lifetime retirement income. Alternatively, the employee may cash out the account. That means the employee will have paid fees, potentially for many years, for an income guarantee that will not be used.[24]

So here we have the American Council of Life Insurance, the trade association and lobbying group for the insurance industry, claiming that these guaranteed products are the solution to defined contribution plan participants not appropriately insuring themselves against longevity risk. Alternatively, we have a senior vice president of the Principal Group—among the largest vendors to employer-sponsored retirement plans—commenting on Principal Life Insurance Company letterhead that the guaranteed annuity products are less efficient than traditional annuities from almost any perspective. A number of the other comments to the Treasury and Labor Departments' Request for Information suggested that employers need to know what choices make sense before they offer their defined contribution participants an annuity option, much less default them into an annuity payout program.

The employer responses to the solicitation for information on automatic annuitization of defined contribution balances were made mostly through trade associations such as the American Benefits Council, the ERISA Industry Committee, and the Profit-Sharing/401(k) Council of America (PSCA). A common vein running through the comments was about fiduciary liability. If automatic annuitization comes to pass, plan sponsors must choose the annuity providers, which is fraught with risks. Participants might discover other providers offering better rates, or a provider that appeared financially sound could become insolvent, thereby putting retirees' income at risk. Former workers who conclude that the employer chose poorly could sue. The

Department of Labor has published regulations establishing a "safe harbor" from claims as long as employers follow certain steps in setting up an annuitization option.

Allison Klausner, Assistant General Counsel for Honeywell, testifying on behalf of the ERISA Industry Committee noted that the harbor was not so safe:

> The Department has characterized its regulation as a safe harbor. In fact, it is not. Merely characterizing a regulation as a safe harbor doesn't make it a safe harbor.
>
> Under the regulation, a fiduciary's selection of an annuity provider satisfies the duty of prudence only:
>
> - if the fiduciary engages in an *objective, thorough and analytical* search;
> - *appropriately considers* information that is sufficient to assess the annuity provider's ability to make all future payments;
> - *appropriately considers* the cost of the contract in relation to the benefits and services to be provided;
> - *appropriately concludes*, at the time of the selection, that the annuity provider is financially able to make all future payment; and
> - *if necessary*, consults with an *appropriate* expert or experts.
>
> The Department's regulation is not a safe harbor. It does not provide that the law will be considered satisfied if specific objective steps are taken. Rather, the Department's regulation is laced with critical but vague terms that require subjective judgments.[25]

In a similar vein, Janet Boyd, director of government relations for the Dow Chemical Company, on behalf of the American Benefits Council, testified:

> . . . due diligence includes an assessment of the annuity provider's continued ability to fulfill its contractual obligations and plan sponsors, including Dow, are understandably concerned that courts will make this assessment with the advantage of hindsight, resulting in potential litigation liability years later. A clear, simple safe harbor is a necessary first step to increase the interest of plan sponsors in adding lifetime income options to their plans.[26]

Finally, David Wray, the president of the PSCA observed:

The current safe harbor guidance while helpful, is not a safe harbor in the conventional sense. It merely lays out a subjective process that constitutes a prudent selection process for selecting an annuity provider. To effect a behavior change by plan sponsors, the government will have to take responsibility for the safe harbor status of certain decisions, particularly the long term viability of the product provider.[27]

This suggests the government might have to set up a Pension Benefit Guaranty Corporation-like backstop for insurance companies offering annuities that become employer plan defaults. Given the experience with the pension insurance program, this is a step that should be taken carefully.

Across the spectrum of respondents, a number of the commenters noted the dynamic and immature nature of many of the annuity products now in the marketplace, and pointed out that adopting a norm now could potentially inhibit further experimentation that could lead to more effective retirement distribution vehicles. Some of the commenters noted that the earlier movement to default options in 401(k) and similar plans was driven by employers exploring ways to make their plans more effective, which then drove the development of regulations to provide needed guidance and protections for the new processes. They urged regulators to give the laboratory of ideas time to percolate before dictating a solution.

In a discussion with David Wray as I was developing background material for this volume, he recounted a bit of the Profit Sharing/401(k) Council of America's history. Originally organized as an educational and information sharing association, the organization encouraged company benefit managers to share ideas and information on how to structure their plans and operate them most effectively. In the early 1950s, an initiative by public policy regulators in Washington would have required profit-sharing plans to annuitize their benefits. At that juncture, the Profit Sharing Council was converted from an educational association to a lobbying association to fight the proposal. It orchestrated a massive letter-writing campaign, through which its members urged their own plan participants to express their views about the initiative to policymakers. The initiative died quickly. Based on that outcome, the Association of Associations honored the Profit Sharing Council of America with an annual award as the most effective association in America in supporting its members' interests.

It is instructive to read some of the personal comments at the Department of Labor's website that published the responses and testimony to the Departments of Treasury and Labor Request for Information on annuities in employer plans. In the 1980s, the tax reform initiative to eliminate section 401(k) was met with an intensive letter campaign much like that organized by the PSCA in the 1950s, and it was equally effective. Any initiative to require employers to make annuitization the default option in their defined contribution plans is likely to face a similar groundswell of opposition.

We are chasing around this bush because policy analysts, advocacy groups, and policymakers are dismayed that defined contribution plans do not provide the same retirement security that traditional defined benefit pensions provide. But the goose that was laying those golden eggs has been largely dispatched the way of the dodo bird. Now it seems as though we are trying to gild eggs to see if we can't match what we had in an earlier era. It is a mighty challenge.

Since the passage of the Employee Retirement Income Security Act (ERISA), much of the policy dialogue about employer-sponsored pensions has focused on the "who" and the "how much" of the tax preferences. Policymakers' concerns about high earners reaping too great a subsidy from the tax deferral have led to repeated restrictions and reductions in pension contribution and benefit limits. Essentially the same concerns prompted policymakers to legislate widespread discrimination provisions and testing to ensure that retirement benefits were spread widely and fairly.

The discussion of Social Security also addressed the distribution and costs of benefits, but it had a distinctly different tenor than the employer-plan story. Higher earners received much larger windfall benefits over the first four decades of the program's operation than their lower-earning counterparts, but that was perceived as necessary to accommodate early participants who had not had much time to contribute. But the price of their windfalls was for later generations to receive less than their accumulated contributions. We have now reached the point that the early system architects and managers—people like Edwin Witte and Arthur Altmeyer—had warned us about. Put plainly, for many workers Social Security has become a bad deal. Now, policymakers must rebalance an under-financed system in the relatively near future or it will not be able to pay out already promised benefits. One reason that policymakers have avoided the inevitable for so long is that whatever reforms they enact will make an already bad deal even worse.

Considering Social Security and Private Retirement Plans Together

The remarkable thing about the policy discussions of employer-sponsored retirement plans and Social Security is that they are virtually never linked. It could be because of historical timing or the programs' separate regulatory and administrative structures. When Social Security began, private employer pensions were few and far between. After World War II, many employers rushed to fill out the retirement portfolio with supplemental benefits, but their goal was to "retire" workers whose productivity levels were declining due to age.

Social Security was centralized and had smart, motivated managers who understood how to use data and research to show how expanding the program could deliver added benefits and then document the success of their efforts. To ensure continuing support, they continually reinforced the need for the program. To this day, public defenses of the program often start with a recitation of how many retirees have no other income and would fall into poverty without it. The pitch is made even more effective by the fact that much of the employer-sponsored pension income never shows up on surveys, as discussed in chapter 22, so Social Security seems even more dominant in providing retirement income than it actually is. The employer-sponsored world, on the other hand, was loose and fragmented, and even when a regulatory structure was put in place to gather information, regulators couldn't be bothered to actually use the data to analyze the benefits the system was delivering.

Between the time Social Security got off the ground and the end of the 20th century, the retirement world had become a different place. Table 24.1 shows an estimate of the accumulated wealth in various components of the retirement system held by a retirement-age population sample in 2000 as measured by the Health and Retirement Study. For Social Security and defined benefit pensions, the "wealth" holdings in each earnings bracket are the estimated "present value" of lifetime benefits assuming a normal life expectancy. The 401(k), individual retirement account, and Keogh (plans for the self-employed) wealth is the accumulated balances in defined contribution plans.

The relative mean values of Social Security wealth and private retirement plan wealth are remarkably comparable across the earnings spectrum. In 1935 and for quite a while, it made sense to make Social Security policy without considering employer-sponsored retirement plans—there were few of them around in the 1930s and 1940s. They became more popular in the 1950s and 1960s, but they were considered—and often proved to be—unreliable. Likewise, in formulating ERISA in the 1970s, the structure of Social Security had little relevance to securing benefits for participants in employer-sponsored plans. But today, these two elements are of comparable proportions, although

Table 24.1 Mean Household Dedicated Retirement Assets, by Lifetime Earnings Decile for Health and Retirement Study Respondents Ages 63 to 67 in 2000

Covered earnings decile	Social Security wealth	Defined benefit pension wealth	401(k) + IRA + Keogh wealth	Total dedicated retirement wealth	Social Security wealth as percentage of total
1	$74,074	$65,372	$23,325	$162,771	45.5%
2	97,345	42,877	12,151	152,373	63.9%
3	109,638	76,101	23,855	209,593	52.3%
4	131,219	72,846	48,051	252,117	52.0%
5	176,401	89,382	44,004	309,787	56.9%
6	196,484	73,890	87,703	358,077	54.9%
7	225,868	94,841	90,473	411,182	54.9%
8	244,630	118,559	107,581	470,770	52.0%
9	260,767	129,356	153,649	543,772	48.0%
10	279,080	151,608	419,723	850,412	32.8%
All	$181,373	$92,288	$103,814	$377,475	48.0%

Source: James Poterba, Steven Venti, and David A. Wise, "Rise of 401(k) Plans, Lifetime Earnings, and Wealth at Retirement," NBER Working Paper 13091 (Cambridge, MA: National Bureau of Economic Research, 2007), 6.

they do not coordinate their respective benefits. As policymakers grapple with the retirement issues posed by developments in both Social Security and the private system, completely ignoring the other sector no longer makes sense. They cannot consider them together, however, unless they understand the features of each and how they interact.

Payroll Tax Costs and Benefits of Social Security Participation

For years, the Social Security actuaries have developed analyses of "money's worth" for program participants. These analyses focus on specific birth cohorts and their lifetime contributions to the system, including those made by their employers on their behalf, accumulated with interest. They compare the lifetime contributions in each birth cohort to their lifetime benefits in present value terms. Payroll taxes are accumulated based on the statutory payroll tax rate and workers' hypothetical earnings levels over the analysis period. The contributions and accumulating balances are credited with interest at the rates that the bonds in the trust fund earned interest. In developing their estimates, the actuaries account for the comprehensive package of benefits provided by the system, including retirement, disability and survivor benefits. The most recent such analysis included results for 11 different birth cohorts, with the first born in 1920 and the last born in 2004. Historical contributions were based on statutory provisions, and future contributions were based on current law. Historical benefits were based on administrative records, and future benefits were based on projected earnings, contributions, and assumptions used in developing the annual Trustees Report.[1]

Money's worth calculations are done for five hypothetical workers with different earnings levels. Four of the workers have salary patterns scaled off of a large sample of participants' actual Social Security earnings records.[2] These four are characterized as "very low, low, medium, and high" earners. Their career average earnings closely approximate 25 percent, 45 percent, 100 percent, and 160 percent, respectively, of the average wage index for all workers in the economy. The fifth worker is assumed to always have earnings at or above the taxable wage base for Social Security.[3]

The money's worth results for the 1949 birth cohort are shown in table 24.2. These hypothetical employees got jobs at age 21 in 1970 and worked continuously through 2013, retiring on their 65th birthday at the beginning of 2014. According to the results, a very-low earning single male can expect to receive a Social Security benefit that is 1.25 times the value of his lifetime contributions—and his employer's on his behalf—accumulated at trust fund interest rates. As earnings levels rise, the value of the benefit relative to contributions falls. Workers at the maximum earnings level throughout their career can expect to receive only 46 percent of the value of their lifetime contributions. This pattern clearly reflects the redistribution to lower-earning workers that was built into the system by the original plan architects and President Franklin Roosevelt. Variations over the years have been minimal.

The expected value of lifetime benefits being less than the value of lifetime contributions for many workers is what worried Edwin Witte and Arthur Altmeyer when they warned that financing Social Security on a pay-as-you-go basis would eventually mean people could buy a better deal from insurance companies.

Table 24.2 Expected Value of Social Security Benefits Relative to Accumulated Lifetime Contributions with Interest for Hypothetical Workers Born in 1949, Retiring at Age 65, by Earnings Level

	Single male	Single female	One-earner couple	Two-earner couple
Very low	1.25	1.41	2.47	1.41
Low	0.91	1.02	1.81	1.03
Medium	0.67	0.76	1.36	0.77
High	0.56	0.63	1.12	0.64
Maximum	0.46	0.52	0.92	0.52

Source: Michael Clingman et al., "Money's Worth Ratios under the OASDI Program for Hypothetical Workers," Social Security Administration, Office of the Actuary, *Actuarial Note* no. 7 (July 2010): 9–10, http://www.socialsecurity.gov/OACT/NOTES/ran7/index.html.

Benefits for single women relative to their contributions are somewhat higher at every earnings level than they are for men. Men and women are subject to the same payroll tax rates and their earnings rates are assumed to be identical for each of the income levels represented by the hypothetical workers. Thus, at a given earnings level, single women's accumulated contributions would be equal to those of single men under the assumptions and methods used to calculate the ratios in the table. Single women appear to do somewhat better than men because of their longer life expectancy—on average, women can expect an extra three years of benefits.

One-earner couples' benefits are by far the most generous. At normal retirement age, the couple receives 150 percent of the benefit payable to the worker, which is usually the man. Benefits continue at that level until one spouse dies, after which the surviving spouse receives 100 percent of the worker's benefit. The money's worth for one-earner couples is double that for single men. If both spouses work, the money's worth is the same as that for single women. When one spouse dies, the other spouse starts receiving the higher of the two benefits paid when both spouses were alive. In most cases, that would mean a higher benefit for the surviving widow when her husband dies. The specific results depend on the couple's respective earnings—if one significantly out-earned the other, the results would more closely approximate those for a single-earner couple.

Measuring Interactions of Social Security and Private Retirement Saving

The hypothetical workers used to explain Social Security benefits can also be used to explain how private retirement savings benefit from tax preferences and how the two retirement systems interact. This does not exactly replicate the Social Security estimates because the focus here is solely on retirement benefits.

Members of the 1949 birth cohort are assumed to start their careers at age 22, work until age 65 and then retire in 2014. Starting their careers one year later than the workers represented in table 24.2 has virtually no effect on their Social Security benefit levels. We use the Social Security scaling factors to project annual earnings at the low, medium, high, and maximum earnings levels. The benefits and contributions in both systems are maximized by assuming that all workers survive until retirement age. Retirement benefits were calculated using a calculator developed by the Social Security actuaries and available at http://www.socialsecurity.gov/OACT/anypia/anypia.html.

The accumulated contributions and present value of benefits for the hypothetical workers are shown in table 24.3. For the "Medium earner," estimated payroll taxes accumulated at trust fund interest rates would be worth $353,800 just before retirement. At this earnings level, a single male could expect to receive a lifetime payout of $273,049, assuming he lives a normal life expectancy. He would be a net loser to the tune of $80,751 for having participated in the program. For a single woman, on the other hand, the lifetime expected benefit would be $304,767 because of her extra three years of benefits. Since her payroll taxes would be the same as those paid by her male counterpart, her net loss would be $49,033.

Following on through the calculations, one-earner couples could expect to receive lifetime benefits of $554,229—they would be net winners of $200,429. Working couples with medium earnings would have accumulated lifetime payroll taxes of $707,600 and benefits of $609,534—thus losing $98,066. The results in table 24.3 are shown in dollar terms instead of relative terms as they were for table 24.2. Calculating the ratios of benefits to payroll taxes would show a similar pattern to that in table 24.2, although there would be some differences because these lifetime payroll tax values include only the Old-Age and Survivors Insurance component of Social Security. Paying disproportionately high benefits to one-earner couples completely changes the nature of the program for this select group of participants.

Table 24.3 Value of Lifetime Contributions and Present Value of Expected Social Security Benefits for Hypothetical Workers Born in 1949, Retiring at Age 65, by Earnings Level

Value at retirement date	Low earner	Medium earner	High earner	Maximum earner
Lifetime payroll taxes	159,225	353,800	566,077	898,346
Present value of single male benefit	166,175	273,049	365,057	402,884
Net lifetime gain for single male	6,950	-80,751	-201,020	-495,462
Present value of single female benefit	185,478	304,767	407,462	449,682
Net lifetime gain for single female	26,253	-49,033	-158,615	-448,664
Present value of one-earner couple benefit	330,524	554,229	730,113	789,968
Net lifetime gain for one-earner couple	171,299	200,429	164,036	-108,378
Lifetime payroll taxes by two-earner couple	318,450	707,600	1,132,154	1,796,692
Present value of two-earner couple benefit	370,956	609,534	814,924	899,364
Net lifetime gain for two-earner couple	52,506	-98,066	-317,230	-897,328

Source: Developed by the author.

I next calculate the tax benefits of employer-sponsored retirement plans for these same workers in order to consider how the Social Security system and the private systems interact. To simplify the analysis and presentation, all calculations assume participation in a defined contribution plan. The low earner is assumed to contribute 6 percent of pay each year of the career; the medium earner 10 percent of pay; the high earner, 10 percent at the beginning of the career, increasing 1 percent per year from age 40 to 44, and by another 1 percent per year from age 55 to age 59; and the maximum earner is assumed to contribute 15 percent of pay at the outset until age 32 and then rising at 1 percent of pay per year until reaching 25 percent of pay and remaining at that level until retirement. All workers were assumed to participate in the plans throughout their careers. In keeping with known savings patterns, higher earners are assumed to contribute at higher rates than lower earners.

In developing estimates of the tax benefits that workers receive from participating in a tax-preferred defined contribution plan, I compared lifetime accumulations in such a plan to what would be accumulated in a regular savings account. In the former, contributions are made on a pre-tax basis with no taxes collected on the annual income from the assets earned but with benefits being fully taxable. In the latter, contributions were assumed to be made with post-tax earnings each year and the annual returns on the assets were taxable each year during the worker's career as well. In a normal savings account, the money taken from it during retirement would not be subject to any additional tax. The difference in the value of the two ultimate accumulations, net of taxes due on the tax-preferred account, is the calculated value of the tax preference.

The same historical rates of return on Social Security's trust fund assets were used in calculating the returns to the accumulating assets in the defined contribution accounts for these workers. In calculating the value of the tax preferences, benefits were accumulated over the worker's lifetime and distributed at retirement at an annual rate of $1 \div n$, where n is the remaining life expectancy of the individual each year. Income tax rates were assumed to be the same before and after retirement. Taxes on annual benefits were accumulated on a discounted basis to determine the lifetime value of taxes at retirement age. The gross distribution, tax obligation and net distribution after taxes from this account are compared to the accumulated value of a normal savings account at retirement.

The results of this exercise are reflected in table 24.4. Once again, look at the results for the "Medium earner." The top row of data suggests that at retirement, this worker will have accumulated retirement savings of $359,015,

Table 24.4 Value of Lifetime Net Benefits from a Tax-Qualified Retirement Savings Account Compared to a Regular Savings Account for Hypothetical Workers Born in 1949 and Retiring at Age 65, by Earnings Level

	Low earner	Medium earner	High earner	Maximum earner
Gross retirement plan accumulation	$96,944	$359,015	$722,417	$1,904,088
Assumed marginal tax rate	15%	15%	25%	28%
Value of income tax liability at retirement	14,542	53,852	180,604	533,145
Net pension distribution	82,402	305,163	541,813	1,370,943
Accumulated value of savings if taxed as a taxable savings account	65,217	241,521	389,799	937,339
Value of the tax preference versus a regular savings account	17,185	63,642	152,014	433,604

Source: Developed by the author.

which will be subject to a 15 percent federal income tax when benefits are distributed. The value of the worker's tax liability at retirement is $53,852 or 15 percent times $359,015, leaving a net of $305,163 in after-tax benefits. If instead of saving through a 401(k) or similar plan the worker had saved through a regular savings account, the accumulation at retirement would be $241,521. Because the savings was done through a tax-preferred retirement account, the worker received a net additional benefit of $63,642 ($305,015 minus $241,521).

The progressively higher value of the tax preference at higher earnings levels, as reflected in the bottom line of table 24.4, is what has worried many policy analysts for years. They ask why our public policies should favor higher-paid workers over those who earn less. Their concerns generally ignore the workings of Social Security. To be fair, most of those complaining about the poor money's worth results under Social Security do not consider the way the tax preferences for private retirement plans work either.

These examples suggest that many of those with a poor outlook under Social Security can expect a better deal under the tax treatment of their retirement savings plans. The combined effects of the two systems are reflected in table 24.5. The Social Security gains are from table 24.3 and the value of the tax preferences for employer-sponsored plans, from table 24.4. The single-earner male "Medium earner"—a net loser to the tune of $80,751 under Social Security—is a net gainer by $63,642 under the private pension system, for a net loss of $17,109. The values of the tax preferences shown here for two-earner couples are simply double the single-earner values based on the assumption that both spouses fall into the same earnings category.

The intent of this exercise was to develop the series of combined values shown in the bottom four rows, which represent the net effects of Social Security and the employer-based retirement systems operating in tandem. Most single male workers covered by both Social Security and an employer-sponsored retirement plan are net losers in the combined retirement system despite the tax benefits in the private savings component. Single female workers fare a bit better, as only the high and maximum earners are net investors in the system. According to the estimates from the Social Security actuaries reflected in table 24.2, a high earner retiring in 2008 had a lifetime average indexed annual earnings level of around $65,000, a level that many might consider to be solidly middle class. The two-earner couples' results are simply double the single female results. The ratio of the two-earner couples' lifetime Social Security benefits to lifetime contributions is almost the same as that for single females, and lifetime tax benefits from the employer-sponsored component of the retirement system are identical for spouses under the assumptions used to develop the earnings and contribution histories.

The overall winner of the retirement lottery is the couple with only one earner. This result is driven solely by the larger net benefits paid to one-earner couples under Social Security—it has nothing to do with the employer-sponsored retirement system. Some portion of the spousal benefits also accrues in situations where one of the spouses earns a benefit on his or her own account that is less than one-half that earned by the other spouse.

Table 24.5 Combined Value Social Security Net Benefit Gains versus Contributions and the Lifetime Net Benefits from a Tax-Qualified Retirement Savings for Hypothetical Workers Born in 1949 and Retiring at Age 65, by Earnings Level

Value at retirement date	Low earner	Medium earner	High earner	Maximum earner
Net lifetime Social Security gains				
Single male	$6,950	-$80,751	-$201,020	-$495,462
Single female	26,253	-49,033	-158,615	-448,664
One-earner couple	171,299	200,429	164,036	-108,378
Two-earner couple	52,506	-98,066	-317,230	-897,328
Value of the tax preference in tax-favored retirement plan				
For one earner	17,185	63,642	152,014	433,604
For two earners	34,371	127,284	304,028	867,209
Combined value of Social Security gains plus pension surplus from tax preference				
Single males	$24,135	-$17,109	-$49,006	-$61,858
Single females	43,438	14,609	-6,601	-15,060
One-earner couple	188,484	264,071	316,050	325,226
Two-earner couple	86,877	29,218	-13,203	-30,119

Source: Developed by the author.

Implications of Social Security Spousal Benefits in the Larger Context

Social Security benefits are sharply skewed in favor of single-earner couples. In 1944, 11.6 percent of Social Security retirees were women. Labor force patterns changed after World War II, and by 1960, 35 percent of Social Security retirees were women.[4] But the majority of women receiving Social Security benefits continue to claim spousal benefits, as shown in table 24.6. By 2008, 44 percent of the women drew benefits based solely on their own earnings, but 28 percent received benefits purely on the basis of their husbands' earnings. The other 28 percent were drawing a benefit based on their own earnings, but it was small enough that they also received a supplement based on their husbands' benefit entitlements.

No one would claim that four or five wage profiles can capture the diversity of career outcomes in our dynamic, evolving economy. Still, the analytical results developed by Social Security's actuaries and those presented here suggest that the program's spousal benefits create benefit disparities. Other factors, such as differential mortality rates across the income spectrum, play a role as well.

In recent years, a growing body of research has focused on distributional outcomes under Social Security. These studies reflect the development of new microsimulation models that provide more detailed looks at public policy issues, and the availability of databases like that associated with the Health and Retirement Study. As the need to revisit Social Security financing has become increasingly apparent, it makes sense to assess whether the program is accomplishing what policymakers had intended in the first place.

Once again, the Health and Retirement Study career summary data provide empirical evidence of how the system is working. For married couples, the study collects information on both parties. Alan Gustman and Tom Steinmeir analyzed Social Security benefits relative to contributions for the Health and Retirement Study population. They conclude:

> When families are arrayed according to the total lifetime earnings, and spouse and survivor benefits are taken into account, the extent of redistribution from families with high lifetime earnings to families with low lifetime earnings is roughly halved. Much of the remaining redistribution is from families where both spouses spend much of their potential work lives in the labor market, to families where a spouse, often with high earnings potential, chooses to spend a significant number of years outside of the labor force. When families are arrayed by their earnings potential, that is, earnings during years when both spouses are engaged in substantial work, there is very little redistribution from families with high to low earnings capacity.[5]

Jeffrey Brown, Julia Coronado, and Don Fullerton look at the same issue using a completely different data set, the Panel Study of Income Dynamics, to

Table 24.6 Number and Distribution of Women Aged 62 or Older Receiving Social Security Benefits, by Basis of Entitlement in December of Selected Years from 1960 to 2008

	Number receiving benefit (000s)	Worker only benefit	Own worker + spouse benefit		Receiving only spouse benefit	
			Husband still alive	Widow's benefit	Husband still alive	Widow's benefit only
1960	6,619	38.7%	2.4%	2.1%	32.8%	23.4%
1970	11,374	42.1	3.4	5.0	22.4	26.8
1980	16,350	41.0	6.2	9.6	17.6	25.4
1990	19,954	36.9	10.4	13.0	15.3	24.3
2000	21,381	38.0	12.0	15.6	12.9	21.5
2008	22,868	44.2	12.0	15.7	10.3	17.7

Source: Social Security Administration, *Social Security Bulletin, Annual Statistical Supplement* (2008), table 5.A14.

follow a sample group over time. Their analysis considers people of all ages, and is less specifically focused than the Health and Retirement Study on aging and retirement. The Panel Study collected information on participants' earnings, family status, and other variables salient to sorting out how Social Security treats different income groups. Brown, Coronado, and Fullerton use data for 1968 through 1993, and they include all households that remained in the sample for at least 10 of the 26 years and were under age 55 in 1968. They studied the results from more than 6,000 respondents with some over-representation of lower-income individuals. They conclude that

> . . . when evaluated using potential labor earnings at the household level (rather than actual individual earnings), the Social Security retirement program exhibits virtually no overall impact on inequality . . . We find that the lack of impact on overall inequality is largely driven by the lack of impact across the middle and upper part of the income distribution, whereas most of those in the bottom income quintile may, in fact, still get net benefits from the program. Third, even when redistribution does occur, we find that it is not efficiently targeted, with

many high income households receiving net transfers, while many low income households pay net taxes.[6]

The empirical results from these two studies support the conclusion that policymakers' stated intent for Social Security to redistribute income from higher earners to lower earners is largely undone by the spousal benefits for married couples where one spouse earns significantly less than the other. This outcome is amplified when tax-favored retirement plan participation comes into play.

Fitting the Results into Stated U.S. Retirement Policy

In 1965, Congress enacted the Older Americans Act, which listed first among its 10 objectives for older people that they enjoy "[a]n adequate income in retirement in accordance with the American standard of living."[7] Social Security by itself does not do that and was never intended to do it. As I noted in chapter 11, during one of his famous "fireside chats" President Franklin Roosevelt stated very clearly that the role of Social Security was limited in terms of providing an adequate retirement income. He stated unequivocally that Social Security was not intended to nor would it ever provide retirees "an easy life" or anything "approaching abundance." It was to "furnish that minimum necessity to keep a foothold"[8] for retirees. For there to be true retirement security, workers have been expected to save since the outset of Social Security, and the federal income tax was structured to encourage them to do so. Spanning the generations, President Bill Clinton in his 1999 "State of the Union" said, "we must help all Americans, from their first day on the job—to save, to invest, to create wealth. From its beginning, Americans have supplemented Social Security with private pensions and savings." If the intent of public policy is for workers to acquire an adequate income in retirement and the structure of Social Security means that workers will need other savings to accomplish that goal, does it make sense to have policies that impose "penalty taxes" on workers who save?

No one is disputing that the tax treatment accorded qualified retirement savings favors workers who use these plans. But the extent of the benefits that accrue to those workers is considerably less straightforward than often portrayed. When tax-qualified plan utilization is aligned with the underlying economics of Social Security, the net picture changes considerably. Given the net investment of tax expenditures in the qualified plan component of the retirement system, continuing to ignore the breadth and depth of this system in our considerations of Social Security policy could lead us down the wrong path. At the same time, continuing to regulate the qualified plan component of the system without bringing Social Security into the picture could lead to equally distorted results. We need to view the system from a more holistic perspective.

25 RETIREE HEALTH BENEFITS: MISFORTUNE OR MALPRACTICE?

Almost all retirees are covered under Medicare—the health services component of the retirement system—but many also are covered under supplemental insurance. Employers also have played a role in retiree health care, although they have backed off from that role dramatically over the last quarter century. The financing of retiree health consumption is an extremely important consideration in the retirement income security picture.

Before 1935, health insurance plans were rare in the United States. In response to the Depression, hospitals—in cooperation with doctors—formed non-profit Blue Cross organizations in several states. Subscribers paid nominal "dues" for hospital insurance. The insurance programs paid participating hospitals a substantial portion of charges for member services, and members paid the rest.[1] In 1934, only 26,000 people were covered by Blue Cross plans.[2] Once these plans took root, however, health insurance spread rapidly, and before long, many employers were financing some or all the cost of health insurance for workers and their dependents.

The same factors that encouraged employers to become a primary provider of retirement income security enticed them to provide health benefits as well. The National Labor Relations Act, adopted in 1932, requiring that employers negotiate with workers over wages and conditions of employment, was a significant catalyst for employer health benefits. The labor unions sought health insurance and other benefits as concessions for their members, and employers generally extended them to the non-union population as well. The government encouraged these benefits by making employer contributions to health plans tax deductible to the employer and offering tax concessions to the workers. By the early 1950s, health benefit plans were widespread but still cheap— between one-fifth and one-third of 1 percent of payroll.[3]

Movement to Establish Medicare

As with pensions, employers were pioneers in offering health insurance to workers, but there was a long history of social support for the government to take on a central role in health care financing. In his State of the Union message in 1944, President Franklin D. Roosevelt urged the adoption of an "economic bill of rights" that would include the "right to adequate medical care and the opportunity to achieve and enjoy good health."[4] The next week, the Social Security Board, in its annual report to Congress, proposed a national health insurance program. Presumably, President Roosevelt intended to make the program a high priority after the war ended, but he died before he could do so. President Truman took up where Roosevelt left off, but national health insurance proved impossible to achieve during his presidency. Accordingly, in the early 1950s, the Social Security Administration began to scale back its health care agenda to include only the aged.[5]

Throughout the 1950s, various bills were introduced in Congress to establish a health insurance program for the elderly. In 1960, legislation was passed expanding medical vendor payments under the state/federal public assistance programs for the elderly. Believing the legislation inadequate, Senator John F. Kennedy made Medicare a major element of his campaign for president that year. Kennedy pushed the Medicare proposals after his election as president, but public hearings were only getting under way before the Ways and Means Committee in November 1963 when he was assassinated. The legislative case for Medicare was built upon the lack of health insurance coverage for half of the population over the age of 65.[6] Medicare was approved by Congress in the summer of 1965. In 1972, the Social Security Act was amended to extend Medicare benefits to Social Security disability beneficiaries; Congress concluded that the disabled shared many of the same characteristics that justified Medicare for the elderly.

As with Social Security, Medicare was broadly based, but it was not so extensive that it completely crowded out private insurance. Medicare was structured to provide a broad base of health care protection for the elderly and disabled, but it required substantial cost sharing from members and did not limit out-of-pocket spending. This explains why, to this day, as many as three-fourths of Medicare participants carry some form of private health insurance. When lawmakers established Medicare but left employer-sponsored pension and health plans in place, they created the opportunity for overlapping coverage by social and private insurance programs.

Employers' Retiree Health Insurance and More Regulatory Conflicts

The historical record of the origins of employer-provided health care coverage for retirees is not nearly as rich as that of pensions. Lawrence Atkins, a health policy analyst, suggests that employer-provided health benefits for retirees evolved mostly without "design or intent" as a result of collective bargaining over benefits during the 1950s and 1960s. At the time, relatively few retirees were covered by them, and the low cost of providing the benefits on a pay-as-you-go basis made them virtually a "throwaway" in union negotiations. With the passage of Medicare, offering retiree health benefits became even cheaper. Atkins argues that employers adopted these benefits "because they needed them to make their retirement packages work, because they helped in collective bargaining, because they were attractive to labor in competitive labor markets, and because the costs were rarely significant."[7] There were so few retirees at the time that employers simply kept workers on the active employee health plan after they retired.

As with pensions, these programs got under way without employers fully appreciating how covered populations mature over time. Steven Sass's observation about the "science of reform" that swept the U.S. pension movement in the 1920s, as discussed in chapter 2, is equally applicable to retiree health benefit plans. The retirement plan's expense, whether a pension or retiree health plan, was not the cost of benefits paid out to current retirees but the value of benefits as they were being earned. Second, the benefits had to be "funded" as they were earned, so retirees' benefits did not depend on the future success of the sponsoring firm. Third, plan participants had to be vested with legal rights to their pensions or cash withdrawal after some reasonable period of service.[8]

A retiree health benefit plan might seem different from a pension, but both are promises to pay retirees a benefit in the future—the pension is a cash promise, the retiree health benefit is a promise in-kind to finance health benefits. Pension plan experts of the time understood the importance of eliminating risk for both employees and plan sponsors.[9] But as we saw with pensions, knowing the right way to accrue and finance retirement obligations was one thing, and doing it was quite another.

In the early 1980s, the Financial Accounting Standards Board undertook a project to rationalize the accounting for post-employment benefits. The Accounting Standards Board's initial focus was on pensions, but in 1984, it issued standard no. 81, which required that employers sponsoring "welfare benefit plans" report either the current cost of retiree welfare benefits or the unfunded liability if the amounts were lumped in with benefit costs for active employees. Welfare benefits primarily included health and life insurance benefits. This new standard raised general awareness about the implications of unfunded liabilities. A 1988 study by the Government Accounting Office estimated that the unfunded liabilities represented 8 percent of the value of company stock.[10] Another study estimated that the annual costs of amortizing these liabilities could run as high 12 percent of payroll or 10 times the current rate of pay-as-you-go spending.[11]

The earlier discussion indicated that despite the cutbacks to the pension system, most workers covered under defined benefit plans since the passage of the Employee Retirement Income Security Act (ERISA) have not lost accrued benefits. That has not been true for retiree health benefits. Congress significantly restricted funding of retiree health benefits in the Deficit Reduction Act of 1984. Lawmakers were concerned that the plans were sheltering corporate income and that smaller employers were using trusts set up in the guise of benefit plans to acquire ski chalets, yachts, and the like. The 1984 tax law prohibited employers from taking medical cost inflation and utilization trends into account when funding retiree medical benefits and limited funding to current retirees. Further adjustments were made by the Omnibus Budget and Reconciliation Act of 1989 and the Omnibus Budget and Reconciliation Act of 1990. These legal restrictions substantially eliminated any tax-preferred means of funding the health care liabilities of future retirees. Existing funding vehicles, which are largely for current retirees, limit contributions and do not reflect growing utilization and medical inflation.

In late 1990, the Financial Accounting Standards Board issued Statement No. 106 dealing with Employers' Accounting for Postretirement Benefits Other than Pensions, which focused primarily on retiree health benefits. Its stated purpose was to change the common "pay-as-you-go" practices to an accrual accounting of the obligation during the working period. The board surmised that these benefits were a form of deferred compensation earned over a worker's service, and that the employer's obligations should be recognized as that service is provided. Similar to the pension accounting requirements, Standard No. 106 required that sponsors annually report the compensation cost of retiree health benefits earned in a given year, interest cost resulting from deferred payment of those benefits, and the investment results for the assets in the plan from which the accrued benefits will be paid.[12]

Pay-As-You-Go Funding on Retiree Health Benefits Prevails

Retiree health benefits spotlight regulatory schizophrenia in even more sublime glory than pensions. The tax rules required that employers run their retiree health benefit plans almost entirely on a pay-as-you-go basis, while the accounting rules forced accrual recognition of obligations and costs, which mounted rapidly without funding. While regulations might be causing private pensions to become underfunded, at least there was still substantial funding. At the end of fiscal 2009, Towers Watson reported that, among Fortune 1000 firms reporting pension liabilities, plan assets averaged 77 percent of projected benefit obligations (the actuarial present value of all benefit participants have earned up to the measurement date).[13] Among the Fortune 1000 firms still sponsoring retiree health benefit plans at the end of 2009, 37 percent of companies with postretirement medical benefits reported some funding of those benefits. In fiscal 2009, for those companies with any funding, the median level of assets as a percentage of the projected benefit obligation was 33 percent.[14] The combination of 37 percent of plans holding assets equal to 33 percent of obligations translates into an average funding level across all plans of around 12 percent. The different rules for retiree health plans versus defined benefit plans have led to remarkably different funding outcomes.

In terms of funding retiree health obligations, the rules have been dramatically different for public-sector employers. Policymakers had limited private-sector funding of retiree health plans to stem income tax leakages. As public-sector employers pay no federal income taxes, the concept did not apply. Yet public-sector employers did not start funding their retiree health obligations even after the private-sector experience. Private-sector employers had to disclose accrued obligations and annual expense associated with sponsoring retiree health benefit plans from the early 1990s, but there was no similar requirement for public-sector plans from the Governmental Accounting Standards Board until 2004. The board's Statement No. 45 requires states to report the value of future health care promises to current workers as these benefits are earned, plus the present value of obligations to current retirees. The rules took effect for financial disclosure periods starting after December 15, 2005.[15] Public employers generally did not report their long-term retiree health obligations until then. The Pew Center on States summarized the fiscal 2008 reporting of costs associated with non-pension retiree benefits—predominantly retiree health benefits—as $587 billion of liabilities versus $32 billion of funding. Of the total liabilities, 95 percent were concentrated in half the states.

Only two states—Alaska and Arizona—had assets that covered more than half the accrued liabilities in their plans.[16]

With funded levels for retiree health obligations at 12 percent in the private sector, about 5 percent at state and local levels, and zero at the federal level, this is yet another component of our retirement system being operated on a pay-as-you-go basis. Once again, costs are driven by the product of the dependency ratio—the ratio of total beneficiaries to the number of active workers in the system—times the ratio of the average benefit costs paid to current retirees to the average wages earned by workers in the system.

In 1950, 22 workers were participating in private pension plans for every retiree receiving a benefit, so the dependency ratio was $1 \div 22 = 0.045$. By 1965, when Studebaker was at bankruptcy's door, the number of workers participating in pension plans had dropped to 7.9 per retiree drawing benefits, bringing the dependency ratio up to $1 \div 7.9 = 0.127$. By 1975, when ERISA was being implemented, there were only 4.3 active workers in pension plans for each retiree drawing benefits, so the dependency ratio climbed to $1 \div 4.3 = 0.233$.[17] Twenty years after the adoption of ERISA, among plans with more than 100 active lives, there were 2.9 active workers for each retiree, bringing the dependency ratio up to $1 \div 2.9 = 0.344$, according to tabulations of the Form 5500 filings that pension sponsors are required to file annually. A decade later, at the end of 2005, the number of active workers per retiree had dropped to 2.0 and the dependency ratio was up to $1 \div 2.0 = 0.500$.[18] By 2005, dependency ratios had increased by 10 times their base in 1950. When the dependency ratio rises by 10 times, the cost of providing a benefit financed on a pay-as-you-go basis rises by 10 times.

When ERISA was adopted, most large pension plan sponsors also sponsored a retiree health benefit plan. The dependency ratio for the two types of plans would have been virtually identical in terms of retired workers being covered. In retiree health benefit plans, however, most retirees would have a spouse or other dependents who also qualified for benefits, thereby making retiree health dependency ratios 40 to 60 percent higher than the rates for pension plans. So a pension plan with a 0.5 ratio of retirees to active workers would translate into a retiree health benefit dependency ratio of 0.7 to 0.8. For many mature plans, which were common among large unionized workforces, the dependency ratios would have been much higher than these averages suggest. The low dependency ratios that made pay-as-you-go retirement benefits cheap in the 1950s and 1960s were long gone by the beginning of the new millennium. The cash flow costs of retiree health benefit programs were driven up accordingly—and subject to an accelerator.

Not only has the dependency ratio exploded in recent years, but average benefit costs have also risen much faster than average wages, driving up the average-benefits-to-average-wages ratio as well. One reason is that the character of benefits provided under employer-sponsored health benefit plans has changed dramatically in the past 40 years. Another reason is that wage growth has lagged behind health care cost inflation. Two factors account for this cost inflation. First, the price of services and products provided under health plans has risen faster over the years than other economic factors, such as wages. Second, plans cover more services and products today than they did in the past.

From 1980 through 2009, medical prices, as measured by the medical component of the urban consumer price index (CPI), have grown 38 percent per year faster than average wages.[19] Although retiree health costs are not associated with current work, they are a component of labor costs for plan sponsors, a form of deferred compensation. In addition to price inflation, the changing nature of health insurance over the past half century also drove up health benefit costs. The solid line in figure 25.1 shows the share of total health expenses that consumers paid directly out-of-pocket. In 1960, the typical consumer paid 55 cents for services that cost a dollar and insurance paid the rest, whereas by 2008, the typical consumer paid only 14.2 cents of the $1 charges. The dashed line in the figure shows the total expenditure for personal health consumption across the United States stated as a percentage of gross domestic product (GDP). It was 4.4 percent of GDP in 1960 but climbed to 13.5 percent by 2008. The spending levels shown here do not include capital investments in the health sector, certain research programs, or other spending that is not for the delivery of personal health services. As insurance paid a larger share of health consumption costs, consumers spent increasingly large amounts on medical consumption. Employer-sponsored plans bore much of the brunt of increasing expenditures.

Economic Irrationality Leads Employers to Retrench on Benefits

Financial Accounting Standard No. 81 was a wake-up call to the private sector about incurring the expense of pension benefits as they were earned, rather than as they were paid many years later. Standard No. 106 was the final indication that the way forward would be very different for retiree health benefits. State and local government sponsors of retiree health benefit plans might be able to ignore the financing implications a while longer, but private employers

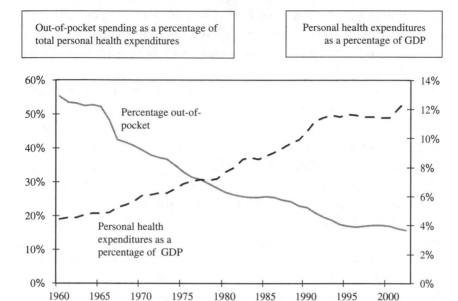

| Out-of-pocket spending as a percentage of total personal health expenditures | Personal health expenditures as a percentage of GDP |

FIGURE 25.1 **Percentage of Personal Health Care Expenditures Paid Out-of-Pocket and Percentage of GDP Spent on Personal Health Care from 1960 through 2008**

Source: Center for Medicare and Medicaid Services, Office of the Actuary, found at: http://www.cms.gov/NationalHealthExpendData/02_NationalHealthAccountsHistorical. asp#TopOfPage.

were forced to face the hard realities of current expenses and future obligations hitting their financial statements. Many companies that had appeared financially sound looked much less robust with their unfunded retiree benefits in full view.

Employers were required to report retiree medical liabilities but were unable to fund them, so many responded by curtailing the benefits. Retiree health coverage dropped steadily after 1980, when 86 percent of firms with more than 250 employees offered such plans.[20] By 1990, only 62 percent of firms this size were still sponsoring retiree health benefits. By 2000, only 35 percent of the larger firms were still offering the benefits and by 2009, it was down to 31 percent.[21] Many employers that still offered benefits capped their liabilities in a variety of ways. Some passed all cost increases beyond a certain amount directly to plan participants through higher premiums, while others closed their plans to new workers. Other responses included limiting benefits to those who left the firm into immediate retirement and even eliminating benefits for current retirees. Those workers who kept their retiree health benefits usually had to shoulder a rapidly growing share of the premiums, sometimes the total premium. Few retiree medical plans today provide the sort of protections offered before 1980. Still, these benefits have proven problematic for those plan sponsors who have been forced to keep them.[22]

In some firms with large unionized workforces, union bargainers have refused to accept reductions in health benefits, often including retiree health benefits. Consequently, these firms still offer extremely rich retiree health benefits. Over time, the rich benefits in conjunction with maturing workforces and retiree populations have driven retiree obligations up accordingly. The combination of unfunded retiree health benefit obligations and unfunded pensions has driven some plan sponsors into bankruptcy.

The industries hardest hit by the failure to manage their retiree health liabilities effectively were steel, the airlines, and then the auto industry. Virtually all the largest pension collapses that shifted pension obligations to the Pension Benefit Guaranty Corporation shown in table 18.2 in chapter 18 also were burdened by underfunded or unfunded retiree health obligations. For retiree health benefits, however, there was no Pension Benefit Guaranty Corporation waiting in the wings when workers lost their benefits after the company collapsed under the deadweight of these programs.

When the managers of steel firms promised workers retiree health benefits but did not fund them with some part of the product they actually controlled—namely the output produced under their management—they were making promises for future stakeholders to keep. In the 1990s, when the airlines promised workers benefits to be paid in the 2000s but did not fund them, they were signing IOUs for someone else to pay, having no idea of what political developments or recessions might be lying in wait to devastate their industry. When their product or service markets came under severe economic pressures, the firms could not keep their promises. These benefits are economically irrational for all parties involved with them.

The patterns of restricting and eliminating retiree health insurance in the private sector have not occurred in the public sector. The fiscal pressures on state and local governments from their pension programs spill over to their retiree health plans. As they do, the fiscal impossibilities may become more pronounced for health benefits than for pensions. Almost all public health benefits for retirees are run on a purely pay-as-you-go basis, and many of these plans are likely to buckle under future demographic conditions. The Governmental Accounting Standards Board's financial disclosure rules are much newer than the equivalent in the private sector, so public officials have had much less time to respond to a problem just coming into public view.

Ninety-five percent of unfunded retiree health obligations in state plans are concentrated among half the states, suggesting that the scope of the problem varies significantly across the country. The differing perceptions of the "contractual" obligation on public retirement benefits are interesting, given the parallel tracks that pension and retiree health benefits seemingly occupy. In response to a query about why so few public sponsors of retiree health benefits have funded these plans, one executive director of a state pension plan who wished to remain anonymous told me:

> Very few states have stepped in with OPEB [Other Post Employment Benefits-namely retiree health] financing because in most states the retiree health benefit is not a contractual right and is subject to revision unlike pension benefits. States are actively looking at a combination of benefit reductions, more significant cost sharing and changes to health care generally as a means to close the funding gap. In [my state] the legislature has many different approaches under review including elimination of the retiree subsidy for those still actively employed.

This observation suggests that public employers' commitments to their employees' retiree health benefits is little different than those many private-sector employers were accused of violating when they closed, froze, or converted their defined benefit plans in recent years. This potential notwithstanding, Robert Clark and Melinda Morrill suggest that retiree health benefits in some states may be subject to constitutional and legal contractual protections comparable to those for state and local pension programs.[23]

Shifting the Burden to the Government . . . or Taxpayers

Retirees have generally relied on employer-provided health insurance or purchased their own policies for two reasons. First, Medicare traditionally does not provide the same level of comprehensive insurance protection as employer plans. Second, most retirees do not qualify for Medicare until they turn age 65.

When Medicare was enacted, it provided benefits through two insurance components that mimicked the traditional structure of Blue Cross-Blue Shield insurance programs. Part A of Medicare covered hospitalization costs through its Hospital Insurance program, and Part B covered the cost of physicians through its Supplementary Medical Insurance programs. Medicare benefits came with substantial deductibles and coinsurance. Moreover, Medicare did not limit enrollee out-of-pocket costs and provided no coverage for outpatient prescription drugs. To fill these gaps, many retirees bought private supplemental plans or received them from employers. The Medicare Prescription Drug, Improvement, and Modernization Act of 2003, generally referred to as the Medicare Modernization Act, created a new Part D benefit package covering prescription drugs. Although less comprehensive than the prescription drug benefits offered by many employers, the standard Part D benefit pays approximately half the cost of prescription drugs.

The Patient Protection and Affordable Care Act of 2010 will change the operating environment for employer-sponsored retiree medical plans in several ways. First, it provides more comprehensive coverage of drug benefits under Medicare and so reduces the need for supplemental insurance. It also reduces some of the subsidies for employers continuing to sponsor insurance for retirees that covers drug benefits. Employers have been backing off from these plans anyway, but health care reform will likely exacerbate that trend.

Pre-Medicare retirees may be among the biggest winners from the individual market reforms in the new law. Health care reform prohibits insurers from denying coverage due to pre-existing conditions and limits age rating to a factor of three-to-one—much higher factors have been common in the past. Those whose family incomes are less than four times the federal poverty level will qualify for premium subsidies if they cannot buy a plan for less than 9.5 percent of their income, and the lower the income, the more generous the subsidies. The health insurance exchanges are supposed to ensure that pre-Medicare retirees have readily available options in the individual insurance market. Few employers are likely to continue sponsoring early retiree plans when a cost-effective alternative is available.

It is too soon to know how employers will react to health reform until its rollout in 2014, but the reforms appear to significantly reduce employers' incentives for providing health insurance. A recent Wall Street Journal editorial by the Democratic governor of Tennessee, Philip Bredesen, outlines why employers might stop offering any health benefits to active employees, and by inference, to retirees. He begins by describing the subsidies, slated to come online in 2014, for those shopping for insurance in the public "exchanges." The subsidy for a family of four with an annual income of $90,000 and a 45-year-old policyholder will be 40 percent of the premium price. At an income level of $50,000, the subsidy will be 76 percent of the cost. Tennessee has around 40,000 state employees in its health plan who pay 20 percent of total plan cost. Employees' contributions are roughly $86 million, and it would take another $38 million to cover workers' premiums if they bought insurance through the exchange. For the state to cover that amount and make sure none of the employees were worse off in the bargain, the governor estimated tripling this amount to $114 million. The new law would impose a penalty of $2,000 per employee on the state for not offering health insurance as a large employer, adding another $86 million to shift to the new financing approach. The state's total cost would come to around $200 million, but it could jettison its health benefit plan that costs around $346 million dollars. Adding in the state's 30,000 retirees under age 65, the 128,000 local school system employees, and the 110,000 employees in local government jobs, the economics begin to look very interesting from an employer's perspective.[24] The economics for any corporation on the Fortune 1000 list are essentially the same.

I noted at the outset of this discussion that President Franklin Roosevelt had advocated a national health insurance program in 1944, and the issue has reemerged repeatedly. The gradual collapse of employer-sponsored health benefits and general dissatisfaction with the bifurcated health care financing of retiree health benefits have increased support for restructuring our health care system. Whether it will work and whether it will provide greater retirement security remain to be seen. In the last several chapters, I have focused on the benefits being delivered by various components of the retirement system. Clearly there is considerable dissatisfaction and restiveness about how much of the system is working, or not.

V TRUTH AND CONSEQUENCES

"Would you tell me, please, which way I ought to go from here?"
"That depends a good deal on where you want to get to," said the Cat.
— LEWIS CARROLL, *Alice's Adventures in Wonderland,*
Chapter 6, "Pig and Pepper"

26 THE FELLOW BEHIND THE TREE

There are at least three distinct views of the current condition of the U.S. retirement system—a Goldilocks' porridge of perspectives. Some believe the system is too hot, costing more of our public and private resources than is reasonable or that we can bear. Others believe it is too cold, not providing the level of retirement security that other developed nations manage to provide to their seniors. Finally, some conclude that while the system might not be "just right," things are not as grim as the news media and surveys on retirement preparedness would have us believe.

The Too Hot Perspective

In chapter 21, the discussion of table 21.1 focused on the dramatically rising cost of financing our retirement benefits. The cost of financing a livable replacement income has risen from around 7 percent of workers' earnings in the mid-1950s to nearly 21 percent of earnings by 2011, according to the data. With the current payroll tax structure having been in place since the early 1980s, this will rise to around 23 percent of earnings by 2020. At current health cost growth rates, adding health care expenses will push up the benefits bite to at least one-third of workers' compensation by 2020. This percentage, while oppressively high already, fails to recognize the underfunding among the public and private components of the retirement system, so trying to maintain the status quo would likely cost considerably more.

The implications of retirement costs for the federal budget are a major concern. Much of the worried public discussion focuses on the long-term budget projections by the Congressional Budget Office. In August 2010, the CBO published projections that presented two scenarios. The baseline scenario assumed current law conditions.[1] According to the CBO, several aspects of current law are unlikely to prevail, and their repeal or amendment will significantly affect the federal government's financing. The Economic Growth and Tax Relief Reconciliation Act of 2001 and the Jobs and Growth Tax Relief Reconciliation Act of 2003 reduced tax rates. Known as the Bush tax cuts, these reduced individual income tax rates, and taxes on corporate dividends, capital gains, and estates. The tax reductions were scheduled to sunset on January 1, 2011, but under an accord reached by President Obama and Congressional Republicans after the 2010 elections, they were extended for another two years. Beyond that, it is difficult to predict. During his presidential campaign, Barack Obama promised not to let the tax provisions expire for those with annual incomes under $200,000—$250,000 for couples—but he advocated restoring the higher tax rates for those with higher incomes. Republican policymakers generally want to leave the lower tax rates in place for everyone. The fight over whether to raise taxes on higher-income individuals led to the U.S. government nearly defaulting on its debt obligations in August 2011 as government borrowing bumped up against the legal limit on total federal debt. While an accord was reached to avoid the default, the legislation did not resolve the differences between Democrats and Republicans on appropriate federal tax or spending policies, and they will be a major element of contention throughout the national election campaigns in 2012.

The alternative scenario "incorporates several changes to current law that are widely expected to occur or that would modify some provisions of the law that might be difficult to sustain for a long period."[2] In this scenario, the CBO assumed the tax cuts would remain in place only for those whose incomes fall below the thresholds that Barack Obama campaigned on. The CBO also assumed the extension of relief from the Automatic Minimum Tax, and the 2009 estate tax parameters would persist and be indexed in the future. In 2009, the estate tax exemption was $3.5 million, and the tax rate was 45 percent of the value of estates worth more than that amount. For married couples, this means a potential exemption of $7 million indexed for inflation in the future.

In chapter 21, I discussed the fact that health care costs were siphoning off a significant share of workers' compensation rewards. Health care costs also represent a major threat to future federal budgets. When Congress passed health care reform in 2010, one of its goals was to rein in growing health costs, and budget projections since then assume that goal will be met. On the expenditure side of the ledger, there is a widespread concern that the cost assumptions under health care reform will not be realized. Possibly the most damaging critique of these assumptions has come from Richard Foster, the chief actuary for the Centers for Medicare & Medicaid Services, and his staff. As the chief actuary responsible for the development of cost estimates for Medicare included in the annual Trustees Report, he provides a "Statement of Actuarial Opinion" that is part of the formal report. His 2010 statement raised a number of concerns:

> . . . the financial projections shown in this report for Medicare do not represent a reasonable expectation for actual program operations in either the short range (as a result of the unsustainable reductions in physician payment rates) or the long range (because of the strong likelihood that the statutory reductions in price updates for most categories of Medicare provider services will not be viable).[3]

Similar concerns motivated the CBO to project an alternative scenario from current law for Medicare and other federal spending on health care programs under the Patient Protection and Affordable Care Act. The CBO's alternative scenario also used different assumptions about noninterest spending and entitlements from the base scenario. Both scenarios assumed that short-run expenditures responding to the economic crisis would be phased down. Beyond that, the baseline scenario assumed spending on other programs would gradually be reduced as a percentage of gross domestic product (GDP) by restricting program growth to less than GDP growth. The alternative scenario assumed that spending growth in these programs will remain at the rate of GDP growth beyond 2012. The results of the alternative projection are shown in table 26.1. The expenditure data in the table includes Medicaid, the Children's Health Insurance Program, and anticipated federal subsidies to the new health insurance exchanges under health reform.

Under this scenario, total federal spending as a percentage of GDP declines over the next few years, but after 2015, it climbs steadily to levels not seen since World War II. Because these revenue projections track more closely to the historical pattern of federal revenues, burgeoning interest rates are part of the dilemma. Richard Foster's observation that the Medicare projections in the 2010 Trustees Report are not credible is extremely credible. The projections that are likely closer to reality and their implications, however, raise fundamental credibility questions about our fiscal outlook under current policies.

Under the CBO projections, health care is clearly at the heart of the adverse outlook. Some people view these projections as an indicator that Social Security is not causing our fiscal dilemma and that we can address its financing

Table 26.1 Projected Federal Spending and Revenues under the CBO's Long-Term 2010 Alternative Projection, as a Percentage of GDP

	2010	2015	2020	2025	2030	2035
Major entitlement programs	(All amounts are stated as a percentage of GDP)					
Social Security	4.8	4.8	5.2	5.6	6.0	6.2
Medicare, Medicaid CHIP and exchanges	5.5	6.0	7.2	8.4	9.7	10.9
Major entitlement spending	10.3	10.8	12.4	14.0	15.7	17.1
Other non-interest spending	12.5	9.9	9.7	9.6	9.5	9.3
Interest spending	1.4	2.7	3.8	5.4	7.0	8.7
Total spending	24.2	23.4	25.9	29.0	32.2	35.1
Revenues	14.9	18.7	19.3	19.3	19.3	19.3
Deficit (-) or surplus	-9.3	-4.7	-6.6	-9.7	-12.9	-15.8
Debt held by the public	62	72	87	112	146	185

Source: Congressional Budget Office, *Long-Term Budget Outlook* (August 2010 revision), http://www.cbo.gov/doc.cfm?index=11579.

imbalance in the narrow context of its own operations. But this is akin to the homeowner behind on his mortgage payments who asks his banker to finance a new car. While the banker sees a creditor already in over his head wanting to take on more debt, the applicant insists that his mortgage is the problem, and the new car a separate issue.

The Too Cold Perspective

During the summer of 2010, I testified at a hearing held by the Social Security Subcommittee of the House Ways and Means Committee, at which several of the witnesses detailed the inadequacies of various elements of our retirement system and how to deal with them.

Virginia Reno from the National Academy of Social Insurance, which Robert Ball helped to establish and in which he played a prominent role until his death, argued that our Social Security system is much less generous than retirement systems in most other developed countries. She said:

The adequacy of retirement income is often measured by replacement rates—the percent of prior earnings that benefits replace. By international standards, U.S. Social Security replacement rates are modest. The Organization for Economic Cooperation and Development (OECD) found that U.S. replacement rates rank near the bottom among its 30 member countries. U.S. replacement rates were 4th from the bottom for low-earning workers (at 50 percent), 5th from the bottom for average earners (at 39 percent), and 9th lowest for high earners (at 28 percent).[4]

Given the meager nature of the U.S. Social Security system by developed country standards, Reno argued that we needed to find resources to shore it up and enhance its protections. She cited a recent National Academy of Social Insurance survey done with the Rockefeller Foundation as evidence that American workers would rather pay more taxes than see benefit reductions in Social Security. Roughly three-quarters of the survey respondents said they were willing to pay more for Social Security because they value it for themselves and their families. The survey also found out that:

- 78 percent of respondents wanted to extend the age from 19 to 22 years for benefits to children in college or vocational school whose working parents died or became disabled.
- 76 percent supported increasing benefits by $50 per month for recipients at age 85.
- 76 percent wanted to improve benefits for low-income widowed spouses.
- 69 percent supported guaranteeing that Social Security benefits for steady workers—even those who retire early—exceed the poverty line.
- 64 percent supported giving service credits for time working parents take off to care for children.

Nancy Altman, another protégé and collaborator of Robert Ball, also testified at the same hearing. Altman is the co-director of Social Security Works, a lobbying group sponsored by a coalition of unions and interest groups like AARP and the National Committee to Preserve Social Security and Medicare. A significant component of Altman's testimony amplified a series of quotations from an editorial that Robert Ball had written and published in the *Washington Post* shortly before his death in 2008. She quoted Ball as writing, "Social Security has never been more important to more Americans than it is now. Private pension plans continue to dwindle—currently covering only about 20 percent of private sector employees—and the national rate of savings hovers around zero. We just can't afford to cut Social Security benefits further. There's no way to make up for the loss."[5]

The Just Right Perspective

If you look at the summary of Virginia Reno's and Nancy Altman's comments to the House Ways and Means Committee's Social Security Subcommittee in the prior paragraphs, or consider their entire testimonies, which are available at the websites listed in the footnote references, you can see they either implicitly or explicitly dismiss employer-sponsored programs. Reno does so implicitly by including only Social Security benefits in her comparison of American retirees with those in other developed countries. Altman does so explicitly when she says that private pension plans cover only 20 percent of private-sector workers.

Alan Gustman, Thomas Steinmeir, and Nahid Tabatabai portray a different perspective in summarizing their volume-length analysis of the pensions of participants in the Health and Retirement Study.[6] They conclude that participation in employer-sponsored plans "is much more extensive than commonly portrayed."[7] They note that many surveys fail to capture the origin of retirement income—once the benefits leave the employer plan and are deposited into individual retirement accounts, they are no longer linked to employer plans. Moreover, "because household assets are treated collectively, it seems fair to argue that members of the same household are covered by a pension when either spouse is covered. Yet most pension surveys collect information at the level of the individual or individual employee but do not collect the data needed to analyze coverage at the household level."[8]

Virginia Reno's point that the U.S. Social Security system replaces a smaller share of workers' preretirement income than systems in many other developed countries is correct but extremely misleading. It is a classic case of missing the forest for the trees. The United States has a more balanced reliance on public and private retirement systems than several of the countries with which she compared us. This is an extremely important distinction.

Table 26.2 shows the prevalence of men ages 65 and older receiving public and private pensions during the mid-1990s in several developed countries. It also shows average benefits as a percentage of the average disposable income of the working-age population. In every developed country, almost all men receive public pensions by their mid-60s. Private pension sponsorship is common in some countries and rare in others. In countries like Canada, the Netherlands, the United Kingdom, and the United States, which have high levels of dependency on private pensions, benefits from the public pensions tend to be smaller than those in countries like Finland, Germany, Italy, and Sweden, which rely almost exclusively on public pensions. Ignoring the benefits delivered by the U.S. private pension system misses a substantial share of retirees' income.

Ultimately, retirees' economic well being depends on their level of income. Table 26.3 compares the incomes of people aged 65 to 74, 51 to 64, and 41 to 50 in various countries in the mid-1990s. The overwhelming majority of people in all countries in the table are retired by age 65. In many developed countries, most workers retire before age 65,[9] so those in the 51-to-64 age range include varying shares of retirees. It makes sense, then, to focus on the right-hand column in table 26.3 when comparing incomes

Table 26.2 Relative Role of Private and Public Pensions for Men Retired at Early and Normal Retirement Ages

	Percentage of men receiving:		Benefits as percentage of average disposable income of the working-age population for:	
	Public pensions	Private pensions	Beneficiaries of public pensions	Beneficiaries of private pensions
Men ages 65 +				
Canada	99.8	60.7	41.0	30.6
Finland	100.0	3.3	95.2	0.0
Germany	100.0	16.4	79.3	4.6
Italy	97.5	5.2	75.0	4.2
Netherlands	95.0	82.7	50.2	52.5
Sweden	100.0	88.2	87.8	25.8
United Kingdom	99.0	80.7	27.2	36.6
United States	96.8	54.4	39.6	27.8

Source: OECD, *Ageing and Income* (Paris: OECD Publication Service, 2001), 172.

for the retiree and working-age populations. By that comparison, our retiree population does relatively well. Only Canada has a higher ratio of income for those 65 to 74 compared to those in their 40s. Canada, coincidentally, was extremely low on Virginia Reno's ranking of countries on the basis of Social Security income. Canada also has a robust private retirement system. The economic position of retirees in the United States, as measured by comparison to the working population, stacks up quite well in this comparison.

The claim that private pensions cover only 20 percent of private-sector workers ignores defined contribution plans—now the predominant form of retirement savings programs sponsored by private employers. In Ball and Altman's one-dimensional world, most retirees depend entirely on Social Security, thus making any proposal to adjust benefits untenable. As I noted in chapter 19, Poterba, Venti, and Wise project that 401(k) wealth for the top 60 percent of the lifetime earnings distribution of workers retiring in 2030 will exceed their Social Security wealth under current law. It makes little sense to ignore significant retiree resources as we consider broad retirement security policy.

Still, analyses suggest that lower earners have fared less well in employer-sponsored plans than higher earners, and that this deficit is likely to persist. This implies there is a peril in ignoring the benefits of the larger system

Table 26.3 Quasi-Retirement Income Replacement Rates for Selected Countries

	Percentage of mean disposable income of people aged 65 to 74 compared to:	
	People aged 51 to 64	People aged 41 to 50
Canada	86.9	86.6
Finland	75.5	71.6
Germany	84.4	78.2
Italy	78.7	78.1
Netherlands	80.7	78.9
Sweden	76.1	80.3
U.K.	74.1	65.0
U.S.	79.9	83.6

Source: OECD, Ageing and Income (Paris: OECD Publication Service, 2001), 22.

when we take up consideration of Social Security policies. Table 26.4, a modified version of table 19.1, shows 2030 projections of Social Security and 401(k) wealth balances at various lifetime earnings levels. For the sake of discussion, suppose the 401(k) system is the only employer-sponsored retirement saving in 2030, and it—in combination with Social Security—make up the total retirement income system at that time. The Poterba, Venti, and Wise projections suggest that, in 2030, the lowest-earning workers would be 98 percent dependent on Social Security for retirement plan income in 2030, but the highest earners would receive only 30 percent of their retirement system income from Social Security. Thus, cutting Social Security benefits across the board by 20 percent would reduce combined retirement system payments to the lowest-earning retirees by 19.7, but the reduction would be only 6.0 percent for the highest earners. If we consider Social Security policy from the myopic view of that program alone, such a policy might make sense but it would not be an equitable way to rebalance the U.S. retirement system.

Table 26.4 Projected 401(k) and Social Security Wealth by Lifetime Earnings Level for Workers Retiring in 2030

Earnings decile	401(k) wealth	Social Security wealth	Combined wealth	Social Security share
1	$1,372	$98,843	$100,215	98.6%
2	21,917	135,926	157,843	86.1%
3	47,770	153,377	201,147	76.3%
4	120,706	193,294	314,000	61.6%
5	272,135	248,299	520,434	47.7%
6	390,004	270,238	660,242	40.9%
7	508,402	314,541	822,943	38.2%
8	647,329	338,877	986,206	34.4%
9	622,449	360,685	983,134	36.7%
10	895,179	387,250	1,282,429	30.2%
Total	3,527,263	2,501,331	6,028,594	41.5%

Source: The 401(k) projections came from James M. Poterba, Steven F. Venti, and David A. Wise, "Rise of 401(k) Plans, Lifetime Earnings, and Wealth at Retirement," NBER Working Paper 13091 (Cambridge: National Bureau of Economic Research, 2007), http://www.nber.org/papers/w13091; the Social Security wealth projections were derived by the author based on Poterba, Venti, and Wise's estimates of Social Security wealth for people reaching retirement age in 2010.

Paying for Retirement Security

To continue enjoying the benefits of Social Security and employer-sponsored retirement plans, we must continue putting money into them. When Virginia Reno testified before the House Ways and Means Subcommittee on Social Security, she described the National Academy of Social Insurance's survey results that showed three-quarters of the respondents would rather pay higher taxes than reduce Social Security benefits. Because the system is currently underfunded and she was proposing to expand benefits, Reno also proposed ways to close the financing gap, including increasing the cap on Social Security taxable earnings, applying the same tax treatment to all earnings reduction plans that we apply to 401(k) plans, and scheduling future payroll tax increases for workers. While she did not summarize the implications of her proposals for the Social Security Subcommittee, a review of its components indicates that 19.8 percent of her financing solution would come from taxing higher earners and 71.5 percent from taxing future generations of workers. Only 8.7 percent of her proposed added revenue would come from the broad cross-section of workers who she claimed now want to expand Social Security benefits.[10]

Nancy Altman's proposed response to Social Security's financing shortfall was one she had crafted with Robert Ball. The "Ball-Altman" plan would raise revenues "without raising anyone's contribution rates." The plan has three elements, which Altman finds are "good policy in and of themselves." First, raise the payroll tax cap to cover 90 percent of all earnings; second, invest some of the trust fund in the stock market; and third, reinstate the estate tax and dedicate the proceeds to Social Security financing. The particular benevolence of the latter element was that most of the money would come from the top wealth-holding 1 or 2 percent of the population.[11]

Apparently, even though a broad cross-section of Americans would be willing to pay higher taxes to avoid Social Security benefit reductions, the program's strongest proponents do not want to directly raise revenues from the broad masses of program participants. Social Security is now running a growing deficit. There is likely to be a strong political inclination to consider necessary Social Security reforms soon because its cash flow deficit is now part of the unified budget deficit. Social Security reform almost certainly means that someone will have to pay more—the question is who that will be.

In the discussion about Franklin Roosevelt's organization of an initiative to develop the Social Security legislation, one of the figures credited with motivating him was Senator Huey Long, a Democrat from Louisiana. Senator Long was assassinated in 1935 while preparing to run for the presidency against Roosevelt in the 1936 election. In 1948, his son, Russell Long was elected to the U.S. Senate from Louisiana. A Democrat as well, Russell Long served in the Senate from 1948 until retiring in 1987. He was appointed to the Senate Finance Committee in 1953, became chairman in 1966, and held that position until Republicans assumed the leadership in 1981. According to one biographer, he "possessed the rare gift of simplicity. He spoke in plain English. Always, he reduced issues to their most basic, fundamental terms."[12] Long believed that tax preferences or loopholes, if we want to be pejorative, are "something that benefits the other guy. If it benefits you, it is tax reform."[13] In the fall of 1975, the Senate was considering a bill to cap federal spending, but the measure was hung up over an amendment proposed by Senator Ted Kennedy of Massachusetts to include $1.5 billion in tax reform changes. Senator Long explained that "tax reform" was a misnomer and made the point with doggerel: "Don't tax you, don't tax me, tax the fellow behind the tree." The Kennedy amendment was defeated 76 to 21.[14]

After the initial remarks are made by all witnesses at hearings like the one at the Social Security Subcommittee of Ways and Means described earlier, the members of the subcommittee ask the witnesses questions. The first question I was asked was from a Republican member who had received a letter from a constituent just before the hearing. In it, she complained about the taxation of her Social Security benefits and the Congressman asked me how he should respond to his constituent. I suggested my response would likely disappoint but that Social Security benefits actually receive more generous tax treatment than other defined benefit pensions partially financed with employee contributions. In those cases, only the benefits financed by employee contributions are not taxed when the pension is paid. Social Security benefits already receive more beneficial federal income tax treatment than other pensions.

I explained that his constituent's letter along with the proposals from Virginia Reno and Nancy Altman should remind us of Russell Long's conclusion that we all want to "tax the fellow behind the tree." The problem is that none of us believe we should be the fellow behind the tree. We don't know what Congress will do with the estate tax, but why should any resulting revenues be dedicated to Social Security? Do we really want to spend accumulated capital on virtually pure consumption—especially when most of it goes to people in the middle and upper ends of the income distribution, much of it to people who could afford to cover some of the Social Security funding gap themselves without threatening their living standards? If we are going to capture significant amounts of estate wealth in the public purse, shouldn't we consider "investing" it for the future, such as by improving infrastructure and educational opportunities for needy youth, or paying down our public debts?

The Fellow behind the Tree

In chapter 21, I explored the relationship between compensation and earnings. We saw that higher Social Security payroll taxes in the 1980s siphoned off a substantial portion of workers' added compensation rewards. We also saw that higher health benefits and employer-sponsored pension costs had a similar effect on cash rewards. The same mechanisms that have sabotaged workers' rewards in the past will continue to operate in the future. At this crucial point in our history, costs are increasing for our social insurance programs. Starting about now, we are relatively sure employer-sponsored pension costs will remain high for the next few years, and health benefit costs are an unknown over the next couple of decades. If history repeats itself, the fellow behind the tree is the American worker.

To show how that might come about, Steven Nyce and I used the results of the analysis presented in chapter 21 and some reasonable projections of program and benefit costs over the next couple of decades to analyze the implications of current policies for workers' incomes.[15] These projections are based on certain assumptions about the costs and how they would be distributed.

Richard Foster, the chief actuary at the Centers for Medicare & Medicaid Services, released an analysis of health reform shortly after the landmark legislation passed in 2010. His analysis projected health expenditures under the health reform law—the Patient Protection and Affordable Care Act—and under prior law. Expenditures under employer-sponsored health plans are estimated to climb from $847 billion in 2010 to $1,387.3 billion in 2019. Foster's projections of expenditures under employer-sponsored private health insurance suggests that in 2019, health benefits would cost 3.7 percent less under reform than under prior law.[16] Every little bit helps, but this is hard to get excited about, given the base projection of 64 percent growth in employer plan costs.[17]

Even Peter Orszag, who was the director of the Office of Management and Budget and a major architect of the health reform package, and Ezekiel J. Emanuel, a special advisor to the White House and the Office of Management and Budget as the reform was being developed, acknowledge that the hoped-for savings in the new regime "will be illusory if we do not reform health care delivery to bring down the long-term growth of costs."[18]

John Cogan, Glenn Hubbard, and Daniel Kessler evaluated insurance premium rates in Massachusetts around the implementation of their health reform law in 2007 because that law is generally considered to be similar to the national reforms. Cogan and his colleagues analyzed data over the

2004–2008 period and compared premium increases in Massachusetts to rising premiums elsewhere around the country. They used the 2004–2006 period as a control to determine whether Massachusetts' trends before health reform were different from those in other areas around the country. For individual coverage, the authors concluded the Massachusetts reform increased employer premiums by about 6 percent compared to elsewhere. For family coverage, the differential was only 1.5 percent across the state, but much higher in the Boston area compared to other metropolitan areas and for small employers.[19]

Increases to workers' health premiums have been averaging between 6 percent and 7 percent in recent years. Our baseline scenario assumes that employers' health benefit premiums grow by 6.72 percent per year, which includes compensation growth assumed to be 1.52 percent per year, plus inflation of 2.0 percent per year, plus an extra 3.2 percent per year to reflect the excessive inflation that has plagued health benefit plans. Because Richard Foster's projection of employer plan costs under health reform closely tracks his estimate of costs under the prior law, this seems to be a reasonable starting place for new-law projections. Even those who believe health reform will work admit that "bending the cost curve" is going to take time. Orszag and Emanuel suggest that under the new reform model, total U.S. health expenditures in 2030 will only be 0.50 percent less as a share of GDP than under prior law.

In addition to the assumptions about health benefit costs, we assumed that policymakers will raise the Social Security payroll tax rate as necessary to cover the benefit levels specified in current law over the next couple of decades. While policymakers may go a completely different route for Social Security financing reform, the approach we modeled would be fairly consistent with earlier patterns of financing adjustment, which allows us to demonstrate the implications of the traditional approach to program financing on workers' income prospects.

To link to other projections regarding economic growth and potential rewards for workers, the projections are calibrated to 1.1 percent wage growth over the 2015 to 2030 period, which is consistent with the actuaries' baseline projections of Social Security costs for the 2010 Trustees Report. The wage growth resulting from these projections up to 2015 is somewhat lower than the Social Security actuaries project because we do not believe they considered the extra pension contributions that will be required for the next few years. Employer contributions to pension and profit-sharing plans are assumed to grow by 9.7 percent per year from 2008 to 2014. This pattern of accelerated contribution growth is consistent with the 2000–2009 period and the extent of underfunding that existed at the beginning of 2010. As plans approach relatively full funding, contributions should level out. From 2017 onward, we assume that employer contributions to retirement programs increase at the rate of wage growth.

The results of our baseline projection appear in table 26.5, which also shows actual results from the 2000–2009 period taken from the underlying data presented in chapter 21. The projection results are shown separately for 2009 through 2015 and 2015 through 2030 and then combined. The results for both projection periods are worse than the results for 2000 through 2009—a time when many people and policymakers found wage growth disappointing to the point of being unacceptable. The projections suggest that wages would grow more slowly for the bottom half of the earnings distribution in the first projection period than in the second. The results are reversed for the workers in the top half of the earnings distribution.

Table 26.6 shows the shares of the growth in total compensation projected to be siphoned off by each component of the benefit package for both periods. In 2009 through 2015, the combination of higher contributions to

Table 26.5 Baseline Projections of Growth Rates of Annual Earnings across Income Deciles for Selected Periods

		Projection periods		
	Actual			
Income deciles	2000–2009	2009–2015	2015–2030	2009–2030
1	1.10%	0.60%	0.28%	0.37%
2	0.73%	0.52%	0.27%	0.34%
3	0.65%	0.44%	0.26%	0.31%
4	0.53%	0.38%	0.25%	0.29%
5	0.68%	0.38%	0.33%	0.34%
6	0.74%	0.36%	0.37%	0.37%
7	0.69%	0.41%	0.45%	0.44%
8	0.83%	0.42%	0.53%	0.50%
9	1.00%	0.47%	0.63%	0.58%
10	1.20%	0.61%	0.85%	0.78%

Source: Steven A. Nyce and Sylvester J. Schieber, "Treating Our Ills and Killing Our Prospects," Towers Watson and the Coalition for Affordable Health Care (June 2011).

employer retirement plans and higher health care insurance are the major culprits, although increases in Social Security contributions take a toll, too. From 2015 through 2030, employer contributions to retirement plans fall off dramatically, but Social Security costs accelerate and health benefit costs continue consuming a growing share of compensation rewards. Growing benefit costs absorb roughly two-thirds of compensation growth across most of the earnings spectrum during the first projection period and take out an even bigger bite during the second period, except for the upper 30 percent of the earnings distribution. The component elements of table 26.6 provide a framework for assessing the policy path we are now taking.

The short-term employer-sponsored retirement plan costs are partly the bill finally arriving for the baby boomers' retirement benefits—the cost of delaying funding until the latter part of their careers. The costs also reflect the residual effects of financial market turmoil during the first decade of the new millennium. There is no way out—the baby boomers are at or nearing retirement. An optimistic twist to this story is that retirement plan contributions will not curtail wage growth for long, provided we stay the course on improving funding in those defined benefit pensions still standing or systematically funding remaining obligations as they shut down. But we should learn from our mistakes. The late-career funding of the baby boomers' pensions—made much harder by an unscheduled recession—shows the merits of steady retirement saving throughout the career and should warn us off any policies that might delay retirement funding in the future.

During the 1980s, the payroll tax rate increased by a fraction more than 1.5 percentage points of covered payroll, which also increased significantly. In chapter 21, we saw that the payroll tax increase measurably dampened workers' pay rewards. According to the latest Social Security Trustees' Report, the cost rates for Social Security and the Hospital Insurance program, which are supported by payroll taxes, will increase by 4 percentage points between 2010 and 2030. If the Trustees' assumptions about wage growth pan out, average wages in 2030 will be 23 percent higher than they were in 2010 on an inflation-adjusted basis. If higher Social Security payroll taxes were the only other claim on a growing compensation base, it might be palatable. But given that we are potentially taking 80 percent of workers' rightful compensation gains for their added productivity when other claims are considered, it might be better to find a way to balance Social Security that is less punitive for workers. The discussion earlier in this chapter and elsewhere in this volume suggests that we need to consider the benefit side of the equation.

Table 26.6 Percentage of Total Compensation Growth Going to Finance Increased Costs of Specific Projected Benefits for Selected Periods

Decile	Employer retirement	Social Security and Medicare	Health benefits	Total
(2009 through 2015 period)				
1	8.5%	8.7%	39.1%	56.4%
2	14.4%	8.6%	38.4%	61.5%
3	19.4%	8.5%	38.5%	66.4%
4	22.8%	8.5%	38.3%	69.6%
5	26.3%	8.5%	35.1%	69.8%
6	29.4%	8.5%	33.1%	71.0%
7	30.2%	8.6%	29.9%	68.6%
8	32.9%	8.6%	26.2%	67.8%
9	34.4%	8.7%	21.8%	64.9%
10	34.7%	7.1%	13.9%	55.6%
(2015 through 2030 period)				
1	2.2%	17.7%	54.9%	74.9%
2	3.7%	17.5%	54.0%	75.3%
3	5.0%	17.3%	54.2%	76.5%
4	5.9%	17.1%	53.9%	76.9%
5	6.8%	17.2%	49.3%	73.3%
6	7.6%	17.2%	46.6%	71.4%
7	7.8%	17.3%	42.0%	67.2%
8	8.5%	17.4%	36.9%	62.8%
9	8.9%	17.7%	30.7%	57.3%
10	9.0%	14.3%	19.5%	42.8%

Source: Steven A. Nyce and Sylvester J. Schieber, "Treating Our Ills and Killing Our Prospects," Towers Watson and the Coalition for Affordable Health Care (June 2011).

The health care numbers in table 26.6 should be sobering to everyone. If we cannot constrain this system to some modicum of reasonable growth, it could literally suck the lifeblood out of the productivity of American workers and sap the prosperity gains we have secured for retirees over the last 80 years. During the recent health reform debate, there was a great deal of discussion about what we were willing to do for the dying—at some juncture, we also need to think about what we are doing to the living.

For the overwhelming majority of people, financing health care is much like an iceberg. They perceive they are paying for the part above water, while the massive bulk of the health bill remains out of view. In employer-sponsored plans, that hidden part is the premium covered by the employer's check. But in the context of the larger compensation picture, when an employer writes the check to cover workers' health benefits, it reduces the check written for wages. In that regard, employers aren't spending their own money for health benefits—they're paying with unseen withholding from workers' compensation. If we wish to engage workers in becoming more active in controlling health costs, the transaction has to become more transparent. Being unable to grasp the nature or magnitude of the costs that health benefits imply, we become convinced we are being cheated by the small rewards that show up in our paychecks for our improved productivity. We have to bring this transaction into the clear light of day, engaging everyone's interest in controlling costs and helping people understand the ramifications for failing to do so.

Reconciling Retirement Security and Worker Prosperity

This story is about retirement security, but generational equity must be considered as we move forward. Social Security is widely hailed as one of the greatest legislative accomplishments in our history and it has clearly contributed to the retirement security of our older citizens. But the munificence that it bought early participants has faded, and the deal held out to those now entering retirement and the workers who will follow has tarnished considerably. Making matters worse, the system lacks even the resources to deliver a not-very-good deal. The question we face is whether to invest more resources into an economically inefficient system or to modernize it so that it is viable in the future.

As I have noted at various points in the discussion, retirement benefits affect workers' behavior over time. In chapter 17, table 17.1 showed that by 2005, men were leaving the labor force 5.3 years earlier and living an average of 1.7 years longer than they were in 1950. A young man who joined the workforce at age 20 in 1900 stayed in the workforce 12.7 percent longer, measuring by chronological age, than the young man starting his career in 1950. The longer career meant more time to save for retirement—whereas the retirement the younger man was saving for was 58.3 percent longer than his grandfather's retirement. For women, the story is less clear cut because of their changing labor force patterns in the latter part of the 20th century. Still, the typical woman leaving the workforce between 2000 and 2005 enjoyed a retirement that was 69.9 percent longer than that for a woman a half century earlier.[20] The cost implications of longer retirements are profound—workers need more savings but have less time to accumulate them.

Defined benefit plan participants of the 1950s and 1960s were largely sheltered from the higher costs of changing retirement patterns and increasing life expectancies. Social Security was still being provided on a highly subsidized basis to anyone well into a working career. Employer contributions for supplemental pensions did not show up as deductions on workers' pay stubs and they often hardly noticed the plan until retirement approached. With benefits cheap and labor bountiful as the baby boom flooded the job market of the 1970s, early retirement seemed like such a good idea at the time. Ultimately, the stubborn rules of arithmetic caught up with the idyllic world we came to believe was our "entitlement."

One of the most politically sensitive subjects in the retirement policy arena is the age at which workers qualify for benefits. When increasing the retirement age is suggested, a barrage of criticism about cutting benefits follows. Nancy Altman's testimony discussed earlier in this chapter devoted several paragraphs to the subject. The websites of the National Committee to Preserve Social Security and Medicare, Save Our Security, and similar groups are full of the lamentations. When Congressman John Boehner, the House Republican Leader during the 2009–2010 legislative sessions, suggested raising Social Security's retirement age requirements during the 2010 campaign, he was lambasted by opponents.

It is interesting, though, to step back from the rhetoric and consider how our behaviors may be driven more by incentives than by necessity. How is it that men in the early 1950s could work five years longer, on average, than their counterparts at the beginning of the new millennium, or that women could work seven years longer a half century ago? People back then didn't live as long, on average, as they do today. No one could claim that work was easier in those days, because the economy was much more oriented toward manual labor than it is today. The reason we are retiring earlier than we used to is because our retirement system made it possible.

The retirement incentives in defined benefit plans are different from those in defined contribution plans. Workers with defined benefit plans, on average, retire earlier than those without them. As the prevalence of workers in defined benefit plans declines and dependence on defined contribution plans increases, there should be a natural response by workers to retire later. The higher workforce participation rates for retirement-age workers from 2000–2004 to 2005–2010 reflect the changing incentive structure of the retirement system. Table 26.7 shows average workforce participation rates for men and women by age group from 2000 to 2004 and 2005 to 2010. In every age class, average participation rates for both men and women increased in the second period, in several cases quite significantly. These shifts did not occur simply because people had a sudden urge to work longer. Lacking the luxury of a guaranteed annuity that will pay a living-standard sustaining income stream no matter what, people are working longer because they need to and because they can. As a way forward, that may be a far better solution to our retirement problems than simply putting our children behind the tree.

Table 26.7 Average Labor Force Participation Rates of Men and Women at Specified Ages during 2000 through 2004, and 2005 through 2010

Age	Men		Women	
	2000–2004	2005–2010	2000–2004	2005–2010
55–59	77.0%	77.9%	63.9%	67.7%
60–61	67.3%	68.3%	51.8%	57.0%
62	54.6%	58.8%	42.1%	48.2%
63–64	46.9%	51.4%	35.9%	41.1%
65	37.8%	42.4%	26.0%	31.8%
66–69	30.2%	31.8%	20.6%	24.2%

Source: Tabulations of the March *Current Population Survey,* various years.

27 SECURING THE SOCIAL SECURITY FOUNDATION

The world is awash with proposals to "fix" Social Security. The Social Security's Office of the Actuary has posted 45 to 50 detailed analyses of separate proposals to bring the program back into financial balance. The academic and think-tank worlds have released reams of recommendations for the health care system and its financing. Adding another tree in this dense forest would be of little notice or value. Instead, I present some of the thematic and component recommendations in existing proposals and specifically reference some that have been recently prominent in public conversation in order to present a frame of reference for the deliberations ahead. In approaching the policy discussion in this way, I present my conclusions for why certain proposals should be supported or not, and how I reached the positions I take. In some cases, I suggest that policy considerations should go much further than anything that has been put on the table thus far.

The Dilemma of Today versus Tomorrow

Each year when the Social Security actuaries project future operations for the annual Trustees' Report, they estimate the current funded status, taking into account the benefits expected to be paid out in future years, the trust fund assets and the interest they will accrue, plus the expected future tax revenues. As of January 1, 2011, the actuaries estimated that the system was underfunded to the tune of $6.5 trillion dollars over the next 75 years on a pay-as-you-go basis.[1] That means that if the trust funds held an additional $6.5 trillion dollars as of January 1, 2010, the assets plus expected tax revenues could pay expected benefits over the projection period. The Social Security actuaries estimate that if we had raised the payroll tax rate by 1.1 percent each on workers and their employers as of January 1, 2011, that would have filled the financing shortfall for the following 75 years.

Part two of this book, which focuses on the development and evolution of Social Security, discussed the controversies related to the trust funds, which were the specific focus of chapter 9. Because of the way the trust fund accumulates assets, there is a widespread belief that collecting additional payroll taxes would not ultimately increase savings; rather, it would increase spending elsewhere in the federal budget. As a result, there has been broad reluctance among policymakers to raise taxes now to narrow the projected shortfall. This might change as policymakers contend with the federal deficits. Social Security has been adding to the unified federal deficit since 2010 and is projected to continue to do so under current law until the trust funds are depleted somewhere around the mid-2030s.

When the final Advisory Council on Social Security was meeting during the mid-1990s, there was considerable discussion about the perception that an immediate increase in payroll taxes could not be saved under the current operations of the trust funds.[2] This was the Advisory Council that ultimately split into three groups, each making separate recommendations for addressing Social Security's long-term financing shortfalls. Two of the groups, including seven of the thirteen members, suggested increasing payroll taxes and establishing individual participant accounts, which would accumulate retirement savings over time.

I was a member of that council and have been publicly considered to have been a co-leader, with Carolyn Weaver, of the larger of the two groups—ours included five members. My motivation for advocating individual accounts— and I believe the reason for most if not all the other members—related to the long history of controversy about the system's funding. None of us believed that the trust mechanism in operation since 1937 would accumulate or save the added contributions, except as a bookkeeping entry in federal budgetary operations.[3]

Throughout this volume, the relative efficiencies of pay-as-you-go financing versus funding have been discussed, with the strong inference that funded retirement plans should be favored over the alternative. That is not to claim that funded retirement plans are risk-free. The economic collapse of many economies during the Great Depression led policymakers throughout the world to doubt the security of asset-backed retirement systems, and the turmoil in the financial markets since 2000 should be a reminder that asset returns can go both directions. Individual accounts confront the same risks as defined contribution plans, discussed at length in earlier chapters. Some workers will do a fine job of investing their accumulating savings, and others will not. For many workers, retirement will go as planned, but others will be struck by disability or foul labor market conditions that force them into retirement before they are financially prepared. Workers who must retire during the downside of a financial market cycle are likely to have less. It is important to consider the negatives of replacing some part of a universal annuity benefit—relatively impervious to the short-term ups and downs of economic gyrations—with an individually oriented capital accumulation program. There would be tremendous advantages to such a shift for some people, but we also have to think about those who might be disadvantaged.

For Social Security, the actuaries' estimates of the returns on lifetime contributions from workers turning age 65 in 2014 are sobering. A male earning about 60 percent of average pay—somewhere between $25,000 and $30,000 per year—will receive lifetime benefits worth only $0.91 for every dollar of payroll taxes put into the system on his behalf, accumulated with interest. Returns will be only $0.67 on each dollar of accumulated contributions for a medium earner, and only $0.48 on the dollar for a maximum earner.[4] These results will deteriorate even if policymakers reduce benefits or increase taxes. We should remember the conclusion that Edwin Witte and Arthur Altmeyer reached in the 1930s and 1940s—namely that this is not a desirable outcome under Social Security.

After considering the various plusses and minuses, I concluded that we would be better off with individual accounts in the policy proposal I helped to craft in the mid-1990s. But realistically, I have come to believe that we ought to drop the subject. The conversation about individual accounts has been so poisoned by the accompanying political discourse that all rationality has been lost. Further argument on the subject simply delays our progress in tackling an urgent problem. The ticking clock is taking us closer to Social Security insolvency every day, and the longer we go without a solution, the more drastic the adjustments that must be made. In this case, a second best solution is far superior to no solution at all.

Smoke-and-Mirrors Financing Is Not a Solution

Franklin Roosevelt opposed general revenue financing of Social Security because he did not want the program perceived as a welfare program—the "dole" in his terms. He knew that in a welfare program, retirees' benefits would get caught up in the annual budget appropriation debates in Congress. He was convinced that financing the benefits with payroll taxes would insure benefits against the varying political tides that sweep the body politic. His conviction that payroll tax financing would put Social Security in a unique class of federal activities has proven correct, but recently there have been chinks in his dike against the infusion of general revenues.

After the 2010 elections, President Obama reached an accord with senior Republican Congressional leaders to extend the Bush tax cuts, which were scheduled to expire January 1, 2011. Under that agreement, the Social Security payroll tax was reduced by 2 percentage points for 2011, but the trust funds were still credited with the full 12.4 percent contribution under current law. The credit will be made in the form of federal bonds like those the U.S. Treasury issues when there are surplus tax collections and for interest rate credits on the existing trust funds.

Recent years have witnessed a gradual loosening of the commitment to Franklin Roosevelt's principles in regard to contributory financing of Social Security, and the 2011 maneuver more directly assaults his abhorrence of general revenue infusions into Social Security. Since 1975, the Earned Income Tax Credit has provided refundable income tax credits to low- and middle-income individuals and couples, especially those with children. The credits can extend up to $6,000 on incomes up to $50,000 or so, and most of those qualifying have no income tax liability. In effect, this is a payroll tax rebate program operated through the income tax. Its operation obscures its effect.

Workers could also qualify for the Making Work Pay tax credit in 2009 and 2010. This was a credit of 6.2 percent of a worker's pay up to a limit of $400 for individuals and $800 for couples. The 6.2 percent exactly corresponds with the 6.2 percent payroll tax assessed against workers' taxable earnings for Social Security.

In the fall of 2011, President Obama rolled out a new set of proposals to stimulate the creation of additional jobs in the U.S. economy. His proposal called for extending the reduction of the payroll tax cuts for workers through 2012 and also providing them to employers. The resulting revenue reductions of $240 billion were the largest component of revenue reductions in his package of recommendations.[5] There is an interesting irony in this turn of events when juxtaposed against the discussions in 2004 and 2005 about President George W. Bush's recommendations to reform Social Security, including the creation of individual accounts. President Bush was criticized for putting forth a recommendation that would deprive the Social Security trust funds of the full revenue scheduled to be collected under the payroll tax. Senator John Kerry's and all of the Democratic presidential campaign ads of 2004 that touched on Social Security talked about the trillion-dollar hole that President Bush's proposals would create to finance his proposed individual accounts. Now President Obama has repeatedly advocated and presided over the implementation of policies that take away even more contributions than President Bush ever dreamed of and is not getting any saving toward individual retirement saving in return.

The latest payroll tax gambit is akin to the issuance of "pension obligation bonds" of the sort that Illinois has taken to issuing to finance its state pensions. In that case, the state actually has to sell the bonds to the public. In this case, policymakers have dispensed with the step of marketing the bonds—they simply printed them on a laser printer in Parkersburg, West Virginia, and "deposited" them in the Social Security trust fund binder as described in chapter 9. These bonds are a claim that our children will have to cover.

Franklin Roosevelt likely would not be amused with this "financing" scheme. Frances Perkins suggests that he was quite vehement in refusing to allow general revenue into the system.[6] As noted in chapter 10, one of Robert Ball's criticisms of me was that I strongly prefer "transparency" in Social Security's structure.[7] I plead guilty to the charge. The program extends the bulk of its benefits to people in the middle and upper end of the earnings distributions. I agree with President Roosevelt that we should not turn this program into the "dole." If payroll taxes must come down because they are too high, we should re-examine the benefits being provided. Backdoor general revenue funding without a broad and open discussion of the implications of changing policies is inappropriate.

Individual Accounts as an Element of Social Security Reform

Since the mid-1990s, many reform proposals have included an individual account element. It is impossible to discuss them all, but the one offered by Representative Paul Ryan, a Republican from Wisconsin who assumed chairmanship of the House Budget Committee in 2011, is worthy of mention. Representative Ryan has crafted what he calls a "Roadmap for America," which includes a legitimate proposal for Social Security reform that would allow workers to direct a portion of their payroll taxes into a personal account.[8] Representative Ryan and his fellow Republicans on the House Budget Committee have also crafted a package of fiscal reforms to rebalance the federal budget at sustainable levels.[9] It is notable that the latter does not include the Social Security reform elements from the "Roadmap." Representative Ryan's proposals have attracted ardent supporters and detractors.

After analyzing Representative Ryan's proposal, Stephen Goss, Social Security's chief actuary, has formally written that under the "Roadmap," Social Security "would be expected to be solvent and to meet its benefit obligations throughout the long-range period 2009 through 2083. The long-range OASDI actuarial deficit of 2.00 percent of payroll and the OASDI long-range unfunded obligation of $5.3 trillion [which grew to $6.5 trillion by January 1, 2011] in present value would be eliminated. In addition . . . the proposal meets the long-range criteria for sustainable solvency and would be expected to remain solvent for the foreseeable future."[10] The observation that this is a legitimate proposal is not an endorsement and does not suggest that it is achievable given the political realities that Social Security reform will face.

One criticism leveled at several legitimate proposals for Social Security reform that feature personal accounts, including Congressman Ryan's, is that they "carve out" the financing of the accounts from the existing 12.4 percent payroll tax. Critics point out that with the Social Security retirement and disability programs already operating in deficit and projected to deplete their trust funds within the next 30 years, diverting part of the payroll tax to individual accounts would further reduce program revenues. The benefits generated by the individual account accumulations would eventually reduce the benefits provided under Social Security, but this could take 10 to 15 years. To keep the "traditional" Social Security program solvent in the meantime, the system would either have to borrow money to pay benefits or scale back benefits substantially. Over the long term, moving from a fully pay-as-you-go system to one with a sizable funded individual account component should enable the system to pay off any short-term borrowing during the transition.

Because the existing system is underfunded, living within the current payroll tax rate means that some benefits would have to be cut. While individual accounts would pay higher returns to participants than the existing system, they would not fully make up for the current shortfall. Critics of Social Security reform proposals often attribute the estimated future benefit reductions under proposals like Representative Ryan's solely to the individual accounts, rather than identifying separately the benefit reductions made to balance the system and the costs attributable to the individual accounts.

Another criticism against individual account proposals is that they threaten retirement security by reducing Social Security's "guaranteed benefits." The argument that benefits defined in the current law are "guaranteed" is misleading. In the original legislation, Congress reserved the right to modify benefits at any time, and that provision remains in effect. Indeed, program changes adopted in 1977 and 1983 included benefit reductions relative to prior law. The fact that the program does not have borrowing rights means that full benefits cannot be paid once the trust funds are depleted, so the guarantee of benefits is good only to the extent that accumulating payroll taxes can pay them. Still, the concern that we not shrink the annuity benefits to an extent that threatens retirement income security is legitimate. In the context of the broader retirement system, we should also keep in mind that the private employer-based system has been largely converted to an individual account system, and some public plans are moving in that direction. With many economists and policymakers already worrying about retirees' longevity risks, we should be careful in considering the curtailment of the foundation annuity income Social Security provides retirees.

Republican policymakers have been the primary advocates of individual accounts as part of Social Security reform. Since the late 1990s, the Democrats have found campaigning against individual accounts to be extremely effective, and much of the public regards individual accounts with total disdain. The situation has not been helped by the performance of the economy and financial markets since the turn of the century. Remember, however, that President Bill Clinton was moving in exactly this direction on a Social Security reform proposal until his impeachment hearings got in the way. Ultimately, President Clinton put forward a proposal that would have established universal savings accounts—USA Accounts—independent of Social Security.

Many workers are not saving enough to meet their retirement needs, and added contributions accumulated in individual accounts could help. If we cannot fund Social Security through its current mechanisms and individual accounts as part of reform are off the table, we are trapped in a prisoner's dilemma—we have to either throw more money into a "broken" system or cut back existing benefits.

In the discussion in chapter 21 surrounding table 21.1, I demonstrated that an average worker retiring in 2011 paid more than twice the lifetime payroll taxes relative to earnings of one retiring in 1975 and more than six times the cost of retiring in 1955 to replace roughly the same share of earnings with Social Security benefits. A worker retiring in 2020 will pay about 20 percent more than a 2011 retiree under current law. Average-earning single workers and two-earner couples retiring today will get back only two-thirds to three-fourths of the economic value of their lifetime contributions, according to estimates by the Social Security actuaries.[11] Given that many low earners today are getting back less than the value of lifetime contributions on their earnings and higher earners are doing worse—and that every additional dollar we put into the system will make the outcome worse—how much more money do we want to pump into this system? With total obligations for benefits in excess of $20 trillion that have already been earned by people who are now alive we cannot walk away from the program but we can choose to constrain the future losses.

If we need to save more and already have an expensive system, shouldn't we try to develop an efficient way of accumulating additional saving? As an advocate of individual accounts in the past, I have always proposed that they be substantially financed by "add-on" contributions—new savings invested in real assets, thus making the most of the additional claims on workers' compensation. In the past, I have advocated that these individual accounts be an integrated part of Social Security but there is no reason the added savings and individual accounts couldn't be independent of Social Security. Other countries from Australia to Sweden have mandated savings programs to provide relief from the demands on their tax-financed, government-operated retirement programs, but that does not mean they have abandoned their social commitment to the retirement security of their elderly of today or the future.

Serious People Can Find Common Ground on Social Security Reform

Two recent commission reports shared a central theme: Our government should live within its means. The bipartisan National Commission on Fiscal Responsibility and Reform was created by President Obama to identify policies to improve the federal government's medium-term fiscal outlook and to achieve long-term fiscal sustainability. It was chaired by Erskine Bowles, former chief of staff in the Clinton Administration, and Alan Simpson, a former Republican senator from Wyoming. To simplify the discussion, I refer to this group as the Bowles-Simpson Commission. All but one of the other thirteen members, which included Representative Paul Ryan, were sitting members of the U.S. Congress, and the exception was Dr. Alice Rivlin, who was the first director of the Congressional Budget Office, the director of the Office of Management and Budget in the Clinton Administration, and a former vice chairman of the Federal Reserve.

The Bipartisan Policy Center is a non-profit organization established in 2007 by former Senate Majority Leaders Howard Baker (R), Tom Daschle (D), Bob Dole (R), and George Mitchell (D). The center is intended to be an "incubator for policy efforts that engage top political figures, advocates, academics, and business leaders in the art of principled compromise."[12] In January 2010, the Bipartisan Policy Center launched a Debt Reduction Task Force to develop a long-term plan to reduce the debt and place the nation on a sustainable fiscal path. The Task Force was chaired by Former Senator Pete Domenici, a Republican from New Mexico who served as chairman of the Senate Budget Committee for a period, and Dr. Alice Rivlin, who also served on the Bowles-Simpson Commission. The remaining 17 members were former White House and Cabinet officials, former Senate and House members, former governors and mayors, and business, labor and other leaders.[13] I refer to this group as the Domenici-Rivlin Task Force.

The Domenici-Rivlin Task Force released its final report, "Restoring America's Future," on November 17, 2010. An opening statement in the Executive Summary which was repeated in the full report indicated that "[t]o arrive at consensus on a plan of this size and complexity, each of the Task Force members made significant compromises. Not every member agrees with every element of this plan. But, each member agrees on the urgency of economic recovery and stabilizing the debt and believes that, as a whole, this plan offers a balanced, effective, and reasonable approach to the twin challenges at hand."[14] The Bowles-Simpson Commission released its final report, "Moment of Truth," on December 1, 2010.[15] The Commission's charter indicated that if 14 members voted to endorse the package, it would be submitted to the Congress as a comprehensive package for an up or down vote. In the end, it only received 11 favorable votes.

If individual accounts are off the table, the options narrow to adjusting the system's existing features. That is exactly the approach both the groups took in developing their Social Security reform packages. In many instances, their recommendations closely parallel each other and in some, they directly correspond. Their options provide a reasonable framework for discussing the policy issues involved in adjustments to the system.

Both groups suggested gradually expanding the share of earnings subject to the payroll tax. The 1977 Social Security Amendments scaled up the taxable earnings cap aiming to cover 90 percent of all earnings in the economy and roughly achieved that outcome by the early 1980s. Since then, earnings have grown at a higher rate at the upper end of the earnings distribution than across the whole and, as a result, only around 83 percent of total earnings are captured in Social Security financing. Both proposals call for gradually increasing the share of earnings subject to the tax, reaching the 90 percent target in 2050.

There has never been a rationale for the amount of total earnings covered under the payroll tax cap. The original tax base of $3,000 set in the 1935 Social Security Act came from the work done by the Committee on Economic Security. J. Douglas Brown, one of the architects of the original act, said that the staff that developed the package used "esthetic logic" in divining the original $3,000 level. He described "esthetic logic" in relating how the staff had hit upon age 65 as the appropriate retirement age in the original package: "It looked good. If you said 67 and a half, or 66, somebody would say, 'Why?' Sixty-five somehow fits. It's like saying 50-50. It settles the argument. It's emotional, I admit. I call it 'esthetic logic.' If you said 60-40, you'd still be arguing." In the case of the $3,000, Brown said, "Well, most of these things are compromises, and they come out with some element of esthetic logic. $3,000 looked very good. It was $250 a month."[16] Re-setting the cap has ramifications in an equity context. Given the already low value high earners receive relative to their contributions, raising the cap would make their bad deal even worse. Other elements of the proposals—specifically, proposals for cutting higher earners' benefits—exacerbate the inequity. In a broader context, however, taking into account participation and contributions in the private-sector side of the retirement system, the 90 percent becomes much less objectionable. But for it to remain less objectionable, we have to assume that the opportunity to save in the private element of the retirement system persists along the lines of current policy.

The Bowles-Simpson Commission, the Domenici-Rivlin Task Force, and Congressman Ryan independently in his "Roadmap" proposal call for increasing the minimum benefit for workers with long earnings histories. The Bowles-Simpson Commission calls for a benefit at 125 percent of the poverty line for workers with at least 30 years of covered earnings. It would be phased in by 2017 and indexed to wage growth beyond that so the benefit would gradually increase relative to the poverty line over time, since the latter is indexed to price inflation, which tends to lag behind wage growth over the long term. The Domenici-Rivlin Task Force would raise the minimum benefit for a 30-year worker to 1.33 times the poverty line in 2012 and index it by wage growth thereafter. Congressman Paul Ryan would increase the minimum benefit for a long-career worker to 120 percent of the poverty line with a longer phase-in period between 2018 and 2027.

Both of the commission reports and Representative Ryan's proposal would adjust the benefit formula over time to slow the growth of benefits for higher earners. Congressman Ryan embraced a proposal that has been around for some time called "progressive indexing." The idea is that benefits continue to grow at the rate of wage growth for workers with earnings in the bottom 30 percent of the earnings distribution. Above that, the growth rate for initial benefits would be slowed progressively at higher earnings levels, with benefits indexed entirely to price growth for the highest earners. This would gradually flatten the distribution of benefits over the existing benefit formula. Neither the Bowles-Simpson nor the Domenici-Rivlin proposal would reduce Social Security defined benefits as significantly as the Ryan proposal, but his complete package would include benefits paid out of the personal accounts that are not part of the other two approaches. The Bowles-Simpson Commission's proposals would have a larger effect on benefits at higher earnings levels in the future than the Domenici-Rivlin Task Force's recommendations.

Recognizing that life expectancies are still increasing, both the commission and task force propose to adjust benefits in the future, but their approaches are quite different. Under the Bowles-Simpson Commission's proposal, once the normal retirement age reaches age 67 in 2027, both the early retirement age of 62 and the normal retirement age would be indexed to further improvements in life expectancy. On the basis of the Social Security actuaries' estimates, the commission suggests increasing the normal retirement age to 68 by around 2050 and 69 by about 2075. The early retirement age would move up to 63 and 64 in lockstep. Rather than increasing eligibility ages, the Domenici-Rivlin Task Force suggested gradually slowing benefit growth by adjusting the benefit formula.

Both proposals addressed concerns about the effects of adjusting benefits based on life expectancy for workers at the bottom of the earnings distribution. The problem is that workers with few skills and low earnings histories may not have the ability or flexibility to extend their working lives to the extent those at higher earnings levels can. Many of them work in manual jobs where younger workers are far more competitive. Others are too broken down to work longer simply because life expectancies are rising in the general population.

In the Domenici-Rivlin Task Force package, the increments in the minimum benefit would override the effects of their longevity adjustments. The Bowles-Simpson Commission proposal would allow those who still needed to retire at age 62 to claim a half benefit, with the other half being paid later, and direct Social Security to establish a hardship exemption for those who cannot work beyond age 62. In the past, I have suggested exempting people in the bottom third of the lifetime earnings distribution from increases in the early retirement age because setting up a determination process is likely to become complicated and messy—as experience with the Disability Insurance program demonstrates—and letting those workers continue to retire early would not leak much productivity from the economy as many of them could find little or only marginal employment for the added few years.

Both groups called for shifting from the consumer price index (CPI) for all urban workers to the Chained CPI for all urban consumers, which more accurately reflects inflation. The latter is expected to grow 0.3 percentage points slower than the former, which would slow nominal benefit growth for retirees. The adjustment would address a long-standing concern that benefit indexing has been overly generous, and it is consistent with recommendations from former Senator Daniel Patrick Moynihan while he was on the Senate Finance Committee. Critics of this proposal are particularly concerned about its implications for individuals at lower benefit levels, especially those who live a fairly long retirement period. The difference in the two price indexes is based on assumptions about the extent to which consumers substitute goods for each other as prices change over time. At the lower end of the income distribution, consumption choices may be so limited that there is little flexibility in substituting goods to offset certain price variations. More importantly, reducing the indexation of benefits for someone who lives for 20 years beyond retirement will have a much greater effect on lifetime benefits than for someone who lives only 10 years beyond retirement. The Bowles-Simpson Commission also recommends bumping up benefits by 5 percent of the average benefit 20 years after early retirement age, with a 5-year phase-in period. The proposed benefit bump for long-living beneficiaries should ameliorate the high poverty rates that persist among the oldest retirees, especially widows. Still, critics point out that the 5 percent benefit bump in the Bowles-Simpson package would not make up for the 0.3 reduction in the indexation for someone affected for 20 years.

The Bowles-Simpson Commission and Domenici-Rivlin Task Force called for all state and local government workers hired after 2020 to be covered under Social Security. Today there are large concentrations of uncovered public workers in California, Colorado, Ohio, Texas, Louisiana, and Massachusetts. The politics of covering them are difficult. Costs for affected state and local governments may be an issue even in 2020 unless state plans are fully funded by then. Otherwise, while trying to catch up with their own plan funding, states would also have to pay Social Security payroll taxes on newly covered workers. To ameliorate the immediate costs, policymakers could gradually phase in payroll taxes on newly covered workers. This might not seem fair, but early participants in Social Security benefited from the slow phase-in of the payroll tax, and the transition relief would mitigate the financial hardship for states. Because of Social Security's pay-as-you-go operations, benefit claims for new hires would be minimal for some time. State and local governments could provide Social Security coverage on a highly efficient basis during the initial years, using it as an opportunity to coordinate their own plans with Social Security coverage. Without some enticement, experience suggests we will still have 6 or 7 percent of our workforce outside Social Security for the indefinite future. Social Security has a variety of benefit and cost features that include income redistribution, certain national retirement incentives, and other features that are mandated for more than 90 percent of all workers. Why should an elite group, with higher than average incomes, be exempted from participation? The only possible rationale is purely political.

Other Issues That Deserve Consideration

I believe there are two conspicuous voids in the Social Security reform packages put forward recently for public discussion, and both have major equity ramifications. One is the glaring need to modify the spousal benefits provided by Social Security. The Bowles-Simpson Commission, Domenici-Rivlin Task Force, and Ryan proposals would all prop up benefits for long-career low earners—a fundamental reaffirmation of the long-standing commitment to redistribution. In chapters 11 and 24, comparisons from the Social Security actuaries of hypothetical workers and the empirical results from various researchers showed that the spousal benefit is confounding the desired redistribution reaffirmed by policymakers time and again. A benefit that made sense when only 10 to 15 percent of those claiming benefits on their own earnings were women has become obsolete when 85 percent to 90 percent of women are claiming a benefit based on their own payroll tax contributions. No aspect of retirement income replacement theory or practice supports this benefit—it is one of the system's most inequitable features. One problem in eliminating this benefit is that some people would be left with little income support if the earning spouse dies before the one without an earnings history, which points to the second issue the proposals have failed to address.

The second lack is the failure to include the joint and survivor protection that a pension system like Social Security ought to provide. The lack of this benefit goes far beyond spouses with no retirement benefit earned in their own right or one that is less than half that of their partner's. The spousal benefit partially covers this void, but by perpetuating its inequitable existence and mitigating the need for a joint and survivor benefit, existing policy propagates another inequity. The longest living spouse in a two-earner couple receives absolutely no benefit relative to a single-earner couple where the high earners in each couple have equivalent lifetime earnings. The Retirement Equity Act of 1983 required that private employer-sponsored pensions offer a joint and survivor benefit, and the only way it can be waived is for both spouses to sign an affidavit saying they do not want it. These benefits can be self-financing at a moderate cost to the initial annuity and modest reduction in annuity payouts. Implementing a 100 percent joint and survivor benefit for couples where one spouse has limited or no covered earnings will provide as much protection as the current survivor system, and a minimum 50 percent joint and survivor benefit where both have substantial benefits of their own would likely have a positive marginal effect on survivors' income prospects. It is time to bring the same sorts of protections mandated on private pension plans to Social Security—there is no reason not to modernize the program where it makes sense to do so.

And Now a Word from the Boo Birds

Both the Bowles-Simpson Commission and the Domenici-Rivlin Task Force have received letters from Stephen Goss, the chief actuary at Social Security, indicating that their plans would restore long-term financing balance to the system. Despite the presentation of two major bipartisan models for resolving Social Security financing issues, opposition to the recommendations is strong. Stealing a catch-phrase from the health care reform debate, opponents to reform proposals dubbed the Bowles-Simpson Commission and the Domenici-Rivlin Task Force as "Social Security Death Panels."[17]

Opponents of the packages are framing the issue as policymakers trying to use Social Security to resolve the federal deficit. The *AARP Bulletin* puts it this way: "Many lawmakers, citing a need to control the ever-widening federal deficit, have floated proposals for lower-than-expected benefits for millions of workers retiring 20, 15, even 10 years from now."[18] In fact, it is not clear exactly what workers who will be retiring 10 to 20 years from now expect from Social Security. According to a July 2010 Gallup poll, 6 out of 10 workers have no hope of receiving benefits from the program, and two-thirds of workers between the ages of 36 and 64 do not expect to receive benefits.[19]

Some critics of the recent recommendations are at least willing to take them on in the context of Social Security financing, which merits consideration whenever the program is adjusted. Dean Baker is the co-director of the Center for Economic and Policy Research, a research arm of the AFL-CIO. Baker argues, "There is enormous public confusion (much of it deliberately cultivated) about the extent of the program's projected shortfall. This makes it far more likely that any changes to the program in the current environment will involve more cuts than would take place among a better-informed electorate."[20]

Baker cites the actuaries' projections that currently scheduled benefits can be paid for the next 27 years (reduced to 25 years under the 2011 Trustees Report) even if policymakers do nothing. But under that approach, Social Security monthly checks would be reduced by about 25 percent when the trust funds run dry. Of that possibility, Baker says, "After 2037, the projections show that Social Security would still be able to pay a benefit that is larger in real terms than what current retirees receive, even though it would be just 75 percent of the scheduled benefit. The payable benefit would continue to rise through time, so that even if nothing is ever done to change the program, a retiree in 2100 could anticipate a benefit that is more than twice as high as what current retirees receive today."[21]

Table 27.1 shows Social Security benefits payable at age 65 to medium, high, and maximum earners as estimated by the system actuaries in analyzing the Bowles-Simpson Commission and Domenici-Rivlin Task Force proposals. They show the initial benefits payable for the specified years under the proposals compared with benefits that could be paid if policymakers do nothing. For the medium-earning workers retiring in 2020 and 2030, there would be a slight dip in benefits relative to those payable under current law, but those retiring later would be better off. At the high and maximum earnings levels, beneficiaries would do somewhat worse under the Bowles-Simpson Commission proposal than under current law, but would fare better under the Domenici-Rivlin Task Force recommendation. The reason for the difference is that the former tilts benefits more heavily toward the low earners than the latter does. Some people would view the benefits for high- and maximum-earning workers retiring in the out years under the Bowles-Simpson Commission package as a reduction. But the purchasing power of the high earner's initial benefit in 2080 would be 63 percent higher than that for a comparable worker retiring today, and for a maximum-earner, it would be 56 percent higher.

Following the tendency to look at Social Security in isolation, the inclination likely would be to tilt more heavily toward the Domenici-Rivlin Task Force's Social Security recommendations over the Bowles-Simpson Commission package because the latter would slow the growth of high earners' benefits to a greater degree than the former. But if we also considered the potential future of private retirement saving becoming much more significant, as James Poterba, Steven Venti, and David Wise[22] have projected and as shown in chapter 19, it might be more reasonable to embrace the Bowles-Simpson Commission's proposal. Thinking more broadly is important.

Dean Baker advocates just letting things ride for 27 years because he believes Congress would then be forced to raise taxes. He says, "If a shortfall really was imminent, it is likely that Congress would make the necessary adjustments to keep the program paying full benefits. This is exactly what happened in 1982–83, when the program literally did run out of money. Congress took steps to ensure that benefits were paid each month. . . . Adjustments of

Table 27.1 Social Security Benefits Payable at Age 65 under the Proposals Postulated by the Commission on Fiscal Responsibility and Reform and the Deficit Reduction Task Force, as a Percentage of Benefits Payable under Current Law for Medium, High, and Maximum Earners in Specified Future Years

	Commission on Fiscal Responsibility			Deficit Reduction Task Force		
	Medium	High	Maximum	Medium	High	Maximum
2020	99	98	98	99	99	99
2030	96	91	88	97	97	96
2040	116	104	98	120	119	115
2050	108	91	83	114	112	107
2060	106	87	78	112	109	103
2070	106	86	77	111	108	102
2080	107	86	77	111	108	102

Sources: Letters from Stephen C. Goss to the respective groups, table B1 in each of the letters, which can be found at: http://www.socialsecurity.gov/OACT/solvency/index.html.

the size put in place in 1983 could keep Social Security fully solvent into the 22nd century even if we waited until 2030 to act."[23]

I put a slightly different twist on Baker's suggestion. In chapter 21, I analyzed the implications of the payroll tax increases on workers' disposable earnings during the 1980s. Looking at table 21.2 from that discussion, disposable earnings for the lowest-earning 25 percent of workers were stagnant because payroll tax increases and other benefit costs consumed their added compensation reward. The effects up the earning distribution were less severe but still significant. Much of the leakage between compensation payouts and cash in hand on payday was due to the payroll tax increases. The effects in the 2030s would almost certainly be exactly the same if we did what Baker proposes. Policymakers would rob my grandson and granddaughter of their chance to get ahead during their 30s in order to protect my generation's benefits from any adjustment at all. Baker is probably right that, if we do nothing, Congress would not dare allow benefits to fall and would adopt revenue-raising measures instead. Following the 1983 precedent would also mean jacking up the payroll tax rates. What Dean Baker has not told my granddaughter, Corinna, who will be 30 years old then, or my grandson, Miles, who will be 28, is that his solution will cost them at least 25 to 30 percent higher payroll tax rates over most of their working lives than we pay under current law—far more than we have been willing to assess on ourselves. Franklin Roosevelt called this sort of thing "immoral." I have difficulty believing this is the path we wish to take.

We Are All in the Boat—We Should Each Grab an Oar

I was born in 1946—the first birth cohort of the baby boom generation. My personal gripe about most of the Social Security reform packages of recent years is that they let the baby boom, especially the early cohorts, off too easily. When President George W. Bush was proposing to reform the system, he always started the discussion by saying no one currently retired or close to retirement would be affected. Representative Paul Ryan employs similar language in his "Roadmap" proposal. Dean Baker would let all the baby boomers off the hook until 2037 and then assumes that elected officials will simply reach deeper into our grandchildren's pocketbooks. The Bowles-Simpson Commission and the Domenici-Rivlin Task Force would make modest adjustments to the cost-of-living index, but the proposed index more closely reflects actual changes in the cost of living over time. An argument can be made that getting it right for the majority of Social Security beneficiaries as opposed to continuing to get it wrong should not be considered imposing a cost burden—it's more like eliminating a gratuity. If we are concerned about the benefits of those at the bottom of the earnings distribution, we should adjust them to fit our public sensibilities. That is what the redistributive benefit formula has been about for the 75-plus years that the program has been in operation.

I believe that current retirees and those about to retire should bear some of the cost of reform. While some complain that this is changing the rules of the game when current and near-term retirees have little or no time left to play, it appears that many of the rules must be changed regardless, and we should share in the burden of doing so. That is what the Bowles-Simpson Commission and the Domenici-Rivlin Task Force initiatives were all about. Social Security's financing problem is demographic—the baby boomers are a major element of the problem and they should also be an element of its solution.

28 SECURING TAX-FAVORED BENEFITS AND LIVING STANDARDS

One of the few things I remember from the keynote speaker at my college graduation was his quoting Mae West as saying, "I've been rich and I've been poor. Believe me, rich is better." In many ways, that seems to summarize our sentiments about employer retirement programs. The nostalgia for defined benefit plans of the late 1970s and 1980s is a recollection of earlier generations who walked out a plant door or office in their mid-50s with a lifetime benefit. For them, working hard and behaving themselves meant their jobs would last until they could grab that brass ring along with the gold watch, get in the Winnebago and be off on a blissful retirement odyssey. Today, most of us have to scramble on our own, socking away money out of our paychecks and family budgets while hoping for a few years' escape from the drudgery of work before our visit to the undertaker. In this modern world, a bunch of financial wizards can mess around packaging mortgage securities that blow up the financial markets, badly derailing our diligent efforts to finance our own retirement needs. In our world, Bernie Madoff can run a major investment house supposedly subject to government regulation and oversight yet embezzle billions of dollars, leaving investors out-of-pocket to try, again, to secure their future.

The private employer component of our retirement system has undergone a tremendous metamorphosis over the last 25 years, shifting from a predominantly defined benefit approach to an overwhelmingly defined contribution approach. While remnants of the defined benefit component are still operating among large employers, these plans are increasingly being closed to new hires. Most public-sector employees are still in the defined benefit golden age, but there are rumblings of a shift ahead for them, too. As the system that traditionally paid lifetime monthly pension checks to retirees closes down, there are moves afoot to try to make defined contribution plans behave more like those former plans.[1] As I noted in section III of this volume, increasing—and increasingly complex—regulations changed the incentives for employers, and the evolving regulatory framework played a major role in effecting many of the retirement plan changes over recent decades. The financial markets also exacerbated some of the problems employers have faced.

Maybe we can force defined contribution plans to look and operate more like defined benefit plans, but employers are unlikely to return to the traditional annuity pension offerings that were so prevalent in the early 1980s. The exploding pension liabilities in the new millennium and the financial market declines were the culmination of a slow-motion accident that crashed down on their financial operations, making many corporate boards and managers skittish over the volatility in financing these plans. At this juncture, there is widespread skepticism that the regulatory environment can be trusted to give defined benefit plan sponsors the options and stability they need to effectively manage retirement plan commitments that span many decades. There is solid grounding for the skepticism.

Déjà Vu on Tax Preferences All over Again

Confucius observed that there were three ways to learn wisdom: "First, by reflection, which is noblest; second, by imitation, which is easiest; and third, by experience, which is bitterest." For many private pension plan managers in the 1980s, knowing that surplus funds essentially could never be recovered meant they should make sure their plans were never overfunded. They did that by basing their contributions on minimum requirements rather than on accruing liabilities. As noted in chapter 16, Richard Ippolito, the chief economist at the Pension Benefit Guaranty Corporation, estimated that the excise taxes imposed on pension reversions in legislation adopted in 1986 and raised in 1990 resulted in well-funded plan sponsors reducing their contribution rates by 60 percent and the poorest-funded plan sponsors reducing theirs by 16 percent.[2] The contribution cutbacks ultimately led to funding shortfalls, which triggered plan closings and freezes. This was not learning wisdom by reflection; it was acquiring it by experience. But the question is open on what we have learned from this bitter experience.

The National Commission on Fiscal Responsibility and Reform (the Bowles-Simpson Commission) and the Debt Reduction Task Force (the Domenici-Rivlin Task Force) reviewed Social Security policy carefully. Their discussions about the remainder of the retirement system are scant, but their recommendations could have significant ramifications. In both cases, they framed the pension issue in the context of controlling tax expenditures—a major driver of regulatory policies for private employer-sponsored retirement plans over the past 30 years. The scope of the Bowles-Simpson Commission discussion on pension and retirement savings programs is their being the last in a five-bullet list of items to be addressed under the new tax code. In a figure that follows from the commentary is the substance of the commission's recommendation: "Consolidate retirement accounts; cap tax-preferred contributions to lower of $20,000 or 20% of income; expand saver's credit."[3]

The Domenici-Rivlin Task Force was a bit more expansive:

> The Task Force plan will let most individuals retain the ability to contribute enough to qualified retirement plans to accumulate enough tax-free assets to purchase an annuity that replaces a substantial share of their earnings in retirement. Individuals and employers combined will be able to contribute up to 20 percent of annual earnings to qualified plans, up to a maximum of $20,000 per year, indexed to inflation. However, qualified plans will no longer be a vehicle for wealthy individuals to convert a substantial share of their assets into tax-free retirement assets. In addition, to spur saving by rank-and-file workers, the plan will introduce an expanded and refundable savings credit for taxpayers in the 15 percent bracket.[4]

Not one member of either of these groups has any practical experience working with employer-sponsored retirement plans. None of them has contributed significantly to the economic or policy literature on the contribution these plans provide to retirement security. To those who are ignorant of how the retirement system works, employer-sponsored plans seem to be largely a tax-dodge for rich people, as the Domenici-Rivlin Task Force concluded.

In chapter 24 we saw that workers who are maxing out on the current qualified plan limits are incurring net economic losses when their aggregate lifetime tax benefits from their qualified plans are combined with their losses from Social Security. The estimated net economic losses for a maximum-earning worker were shown in chapter 24. The worker earned $106,800 in 2010, and the estimated net losses were the maximum for individuals in the cohort considered. Under both the Bowles-Simpson Commission's and the Domenici-Rivlin Task Force's proposals, at future incomes between $100,000 and $200,000 in today's dollars, the economic losses will be much greater than those under current law. Moreover, the proposal to reduce allowable contributions to retirement savings plans by as much as 60 percent is inconsistent with the Older Americans Act discussed in chapter 24.

There is an element of proportionality inherent in employer-sponsored retirement plans. It has evolved because of two constraints on the system. One is the complex array of discrimination requirements that the regulatory system imposes on employer-sponsored plans. The other is human nature. We can curse the latter all we want but we cannot regulate it out of existence. My own experience tells me that further cutbacks to middle-level managers' benefits will set off a chain reaction of curtailments that will eventually reach rank-and-file workers. Empirical analyses of the impact of similar changes have shown that the regulatory initiatives of the 1980s and 1990s resulted in lower coverage rates for lower-wage workers.[5]

If these recommendations were implemented, our children and grand-children would get less from employer plans than we did—and our benefits represent cutbacks from what our parents or grandparents enjoyed. From my perspective, this is the worst recommendation in the whole package of proposals coming out of either the Bowles-Simpson Commission or the Domenici-Rivlin Task Force.

The Domenici-Rivlin Task Force recommendation to simplify the prolifer-ation of different types of retirement accounts has much merit. Beyond that, it would be worthwhile to revisit the mass of regulations imposed on employer-sponsored pensions with a goal of simplifying the rules and reducing the costs of compliance. Simply slashing at the top earners and hoping that every-thing works out may be another endeavor that ends with nothing gained but wisdom through bitter experience.

Tax Preferences for Health Benefit Plans

In addition to imposing more restrictions on employer-sponsored retirement plans, both the Bowles-Simpson Commission and the Domenici-Rivlin Task Force recommend phasing out the favorable tax treatment of employer-sponsored health plans. The Bowles-Simpson Commission package would cap the exclusion at the "75th percentile of premium levels in 2014, with the cap frozen in nominal terms through 2018 and phased out by 2038."[6] The Domenici-Rivlin Task Force recommendation is: "Effective in 2018 . . . cap contributions by employers and employees who are eligible for tax-favored treatment, and then reduce the cap each year by equal dollar amounts, so that by 2028, all contributions to employer-based health insurance will be taxed."[7]

In the past, I have defended these tax incentives because the value of ben-efits delivered to low and moderate earners exceeds the value of the "tax expenditures" attributed to all employer-sponsored health benefits.[8] While that is still true, I have come to believe that this subsidy encourages plan structures and costs that are not in the economic or health interests of workers and their families. I recommend that we include 10 percent of the value of the health plan package offered in 2013 in taxable earnings, and then increase the amount included in taxable income by 10 percentage points per year until the full amount is taxable.

If we are going to tax workers on the cost of their health insurance benefits, then equity considerations suggest a wider application. Retirees pay a small share of the cost of their Medicare insurance, and the subsidies provide real economic value that should be subject to the same taxes imposed on workers. To value the benefits at the full premium rates might be unfair because of the added costs of health insurance for an elderly population, but taxing one-third of the premium value would put retirees on similar tax footing to the recommendation for the working-age population. Many retirees have sufficiently high incomes to participate in solutions to ensure the fiscal sustainability of our way of life.

Revisiting the Principles behind Pension Insurance

In recent years, federal regulation of private pensions has been largely shaped by concerns about Pension Benefit Guaranty Corporation obligations. The outcomes do not make sense in an economic or insurance framework—they appear to be the federal government's attempt to impose the cost of three decades of policy mistakes on the relatively small number of remaining pension sponsors, most of whom had no hand in creating the risk exposures the government now faces. The Obama Administration's intrusion into the bankruptcy settlements at General Motors and Chrysler shows how far the government will go to avoid claims on the pension insurance program.

I believe the pension insurance premium provisions introduced in the Pension Protection Act of 2006 should be revised. My reasoning and suggestion is based on a policy paper I developed with Julia Coronado on the financing provisions for the pension insurance program before the passage of the Pension Protection Act.[9]

There are two elements of the insurance financing problem discussed in chapter 18. The first is the legacy costs imposed by an inappropriately organized social insurance structure coupled with pension funding rules that encouraged moral hazard and adverse selection. These sunk costs are exacerbating pension terminations because they are being paid by plan sponsors who have followed the spirit of ERISA's funding rules—and are rewarded with outsized pension insurance premiums disproportionate to the minimal risks they pose. The other problem is the ongoing costs associated with continuing operations under the modified pension funding rules.

The existing sunk costs can be further split into two categories. The first includes the costs of plans already absorbed by the pension insurance agency. The second includes those that the program will potentially pick up in the future because of further bankruptcies by underfunded plan sponsors. The worst of both sets of obligations are concentrated in a few industries. To explore the policy alternatives for dealing with these unfunded obligations, consider those attributable to the airline industry. Through the end of fiscal 2009, Eastern, Pan American, TWA, US Airlines, United, and Delta had unloaded some $13.8 billion dollars of unfunded obligations to the insurance agency.[10] These obligations arose largely because of two situations. The first related to organizations offering workers pension benefits but not funding them as they were earned. The Pension Protection Act was supposed to eliminate this problem going forward but the financial market turmoil since 2006 set things back. The second situation relates to structural reorganization in the airline industry and the financial condition of the individual companies— especially those sponsoring defined benefit pensions—that led to a number of bankruptcies.

The market conditions that drove the listed airlines into bankruptcy were largely beyond their control. The unanticipated deregulation of the industry during the 1980s completely remade the business environment for these companies. Agreements between management and unionized workforces that made economic sense before deregulation put old-line companies at a competitive disadvantage compared with start-up entities born in the free-market world. Moreover, no one anticipated that foreign terrorists would use airliners as weapons against the United States, as they did in 2001, or the disruption to travel demand that would ensue.

The pension funding rules allowed the old-line airlines to accrue significant unfunded pension obligations, but it was the structural reorganization of this sector and, for several of them, the collapse of their market after the September 11 terrorist attacks that caused many of the bankruptcies that landed the Pension Benefit Guaranty Corporation with their unfunded liabilities. It is not clear why our public policies transfer the burden arising from the structural flaws in pension funding requirements and economic calamities affecting particular sectors to a relatively small number of companies that just happen to have sponsored defined benefit pensions in the past and have faithfully followed the rules on funding them. For example, why should a computer company that happens to sponsor a defined benefit plan be forced to pay for a problem which it did not create when direct competitors without such plans pay nothing? If the structural reorganization of the airline industry brought this problem to a head, shouldn't the industry bear the burden of paying it off?

An alternative to increasing the insurance premiums for compliant, well-funded defined benefit plan sponsors would be charging a head tax on all airline tickets for flights originating in the United States. In 2008, 726 million passengers embarked from U.S. commercial airports.[11] A $2 head tax per ticket over 10 years would raise the revenue needed to amortize the pension insurance agency's underfunding attributable to claims from the airline industry. Some might ask why airlines that do not sponsor a defined benefit plan should be required to help resolve this problem. The answer is that those airlines were part of the industry restructuring that was an element of the original problem. If all passengers were assessed the fee, no airline would be advantaged over another—the charge would simply be a user fee in the industry that caused the problem. Similarly, a levy could be put on every ton of steel produced in the United States or imported into the country in raw or finished form. Such a universal charge would spread the cost of paying off unfunded pension obligations in the industry among the remaining steel producers who helped to drive the old firms into bankruptcy. Imposing the surcharge on all steel produced in the country or entering it would grant no producer an unfair advantage. Nor would the levy put foreign producers at a disadvantage, thereby avoiding complaints of unfair trade practices from the World Trade Organization.

The Excise Tax on Surplus Funds Removed from a Pension

Allowing employers to run up pension liabilities that the assets in their plans cannot cover is clearly a recipe for trouble. But expecting plan sponsors to limit their funding to projected liabilities when financial markets are booming means that pensions will become underfunded whenever the market dips. And then the regulations require underfunded plan sponsors to quickly contribute their way out of the underfunding exactly when they can least afford it—during the low point of economic cycles. It should not be hard to understand that most rational business managers would not want to engage in this type of activity. The solution to pension underfunding is embodied in a biblical story that is thousands of years old. Joseph's interpretation of Pharaoh's dream tells us we should do extra saving in the good years so we can sustain ourselves in the lean ones. Many of us know this story but choose to ignore its relevance for our daily lives.

Because of the pension funding regulations, many pension plans were fully funded at the end of the 1990s—our dramatic years of plenty—but they were not allowed to do the extra saving that could have seen them through the subsequent decade of investment market drought and pestilence. To avoid this cycle, pension sponsors must be allowed to build up substantial funding buffers when financial markets are growing their assets for them. The Pension Protection Act offered some relief from the impossible environment of the 1980s and 1990s, but it came too late for many plans. Even for those it can help, however, there is still a catch which motivates me to make another policy suggestion.

If an employer attempts to tap into excess funds in an overfunded plan, current law taxes away virtually the entire amount, which discourages funding because plan sponsors do not want to tie up funds needlessly. I have seen plans so overfunded that it is hard to imagine liabilities ever catching up to assets. If we want to encourage employers to fund beyond projected liability levels in good times, we have to give them a safety valve when funding cushions get too plump. The excise tax came about partly because of the tax preferences accorded to pensions. Policymakers did not want plan sponsors parking tax-free income in these plans during high-income years and then tapping it when their tax rates were lower. The incentives discourage prudent funding practices, and the rules ought to be changed.

A modified policy could set a threshold, say 125 percent of projected obligations. If funding exceeded the threshold, the plan sponsor could take income on the trust fund assets that year for other corporate uses, as long as funding remained at least 125 percent of the plan's obligations. This situation would typically arise when financial markets are up and the excess income is unanticipated. If a sponsor wants to recoup unanticipated market rewards from its prudently overfunded plan, I propose taxing the reversion as regular income. After all, if the money remained in the trust, as it does now, the government gets no tax until benefits are distributed. If plan funding dropped below the 125 percent threshold after the sponsor had taken income from the plan, a requirement to amortize the losses over two or three years would restore the plan to a safe margin of funding.

Another reason for the special excise taxes on asset reversions was to prevent corporate raiders from swooping into companies with excess pension assets and walking off with the assets, which was occurring in the 1980s. A variety of provisions could prohibit such activities while still providing a more reasonable environment for stable companies with ongoing plans. In the 1980s, to protect themselves from pension raids, several companies adopted "poison pill" plan provisions that basically reverted any excess plan assets to participants in hostile takeovers. There could be anti-freeze or anti-termination provisions that limit acquirers in corporate takeovers from reducing benefits for some time—say up to 10 years—and requiring that accrued benefits continue to be paid on the basis of continuing increases in workers' earnings levels over the remainder of their careers.

Public Pension Plan Considerations

Every indication is that the retirement system that has served generations retiring in the past is no longer sustainable in many cases for the baby boom and future generations. Private defined benefit plans have already been restructured or curtailed. The proposals now emanating from publicly appointed commissions and pseudo public commissions to reform Social Security and Medicare reflect a growing seriousness about finally dealing with a problem that should have been dealt with 20 years ago, and will now be far more costly and disruptive to fix. Given the direction the private retirement system and Social Security policy are heading, public-sector workers will soon be the only retirees receiving publicly subsidized pensions in their 50s.

Late in 2010, the CBS program *60 Minutes* ran a segment on the fiscal challenges facing state and local governments. Among others, the segment included an interview with the comptroller of the State of Illinois, Dan Hynes, who said he had $5 billion in bills from contractors, suppliers, and other vendors and no money to pay them. He said that many gas stations in Illinois refuse to fuel the state highway patrol cars because it takes too long to receive payment on the state's credit cards. They now have "tens of thousands if not hundreds of thousands" of people waiting to be paid. Arizona has gotten so hard up that it has sold the state capitol, its Supreme Court building, and its legislature's chambers, and now lease them back. California was cited as now paying more in public pensions than it is contributing to the state university system. It cut back on contributions to the university system and hiked tuitions, but it is hogtied by its pension commitments to public workers, which are protected for another three decades. Governor Chris Christie in New Jersey told of canceling a much needed tunneling project to Manhattan that was being jointly funded by the federal government, New York, and New Jersey, which meant the loss of 6,000 construction jobs. When asked why, Governor Christie said, "The bottom line is I don't have the money. And you know what? I can't pay for those jobs if I don't have the money to pay them. Where am I getting the money? I don't have it. I literally don't have it." Governor Christie talked about cutting the primary and secondary school budget by $1 billion and laying off thousands of teachers. He described his initiative to roll back the public pensions and his fights with the public unions. He said he had told union leaders that if they didn't adjust their pensions now, they would have no pensions at all 10 years from now.[12] When we are cutting back on educating our children so we can pay retirees as young as 50 years old as much as 90 percent of their working salary, we have turned on its head the idea of leaving the next generation better off than our parents left us.

Much of the discussion throughout this volume has been about making commitments but deferring payment for them—passing the bill off to future generations. Looking at cases like Illinois, New Jersey, and California makes the ramifications of what we have been doing searingly clear. If I ran up a massive bill on someone else's credit card without their permission, it would be considered felony robbery. The idea that we can require that the next generation pay all these obligations we incurred, which will steal their own chance at getting ahead, is little different—we might call it generational robbery. We cannot undo all these obligations, but we can ameliorate the burden on the coming generations.

It does not take a Ph.D in finance to know that the path that Illinois, California, and New Jersey have been on is not sustainable. It does not require a Ph.D in economics to know that we cannot afford to have people retiring at age 50 or 55 whose retirements last longer than their careers. Trying to do this in a funded pension system would not work because few workers could afford to save enough during their working years. Doing it on a pay-as-you-go basis costs even more—but of course we leave that bill for later generations to pay.

The recent threat of bankruptcy in Harrisburg, Pennsylvania brought the state to the rescue, and some people have suggested that the federal government may have to help out states like Illinois. Leaving aside the fact that the federal government is busy trying to solve its own fiscal problems, rescuing states whose past pension policies have created their fiscal problems would be tremendously unfair to citizens in more prudent states. Rescuing the more profligate states will be a contentious issue.

A major problem with public retirement plans is the lack of transparency and enforcement. The Governmental Accounting Standards Board can stipulate disclosure rules but cannot force states to disclose or to follow its stipulated rules. After the elections in November 2010, three Republican representatives introduced the State and Local Pension Transparency and Accountability Act to push state and local governments to comply with accounting standards for their pension plans. If they fail to do so under this bill, their bonds would lose tax-exempt status under the federal income tax code. The three sponsors were Devin Nunes of California, who introduced the bill; Darrel Issa, also from California; and Paul Ryan from Wisconsin. Ryan is the chairman of the House Budget Committee and Issa is the chairman of the Committee on Oversight and Government Reform.[13] The record of private plans suggests that consistent and uniform disclosure encourages more rigorous oversight by stakeholders. It is time the federal government intervened to make sure that residents of state and local jurisdictions are fully aware of the pension obligations their local governments are creating for them. Beyond that, the states and local governments are going to have to adjust their commitments to levels that their taxpaying citizens can afford and will support.

The Defined Contribution Annuity Dilemma

In chapter 25, a number of issues associated with annuitizing accumulated defined contribution benefits at retirement were explored. Evidence suggests that people who have annuities in retirement are more sanguine about their retirement prospects than those who "go it on their own." Yet even after the adverse investment results many workers and retirees experienced over the past decade, the overwhelming majority of privately held retirement assets are still not being annuitized.

Constantijn Panis has analyzed the relationship between the Health and Retirement Study retirees' satisfaction in retirement and both the levels and forms of income. Panis found that in retirement plans other than Social Security, receiving annuities from at least a portion of that retirement wealth increased the percentage of retirees who reported being very satisfied in retirement. This shows the importance of having a pension annuity in giving retirees peace of mind. Panis looked separately at people across four income levels in 2000. At every income level, he found a substantially larger percentage of retirees with annuity supplements to Social Security reporting they were very satisfied with retirement.[14]

Panis based his analysis on survey responses gathered shortly after the beginning of the new millennium, and the past decade has probably caused more heartburn than peace of mind for those whose retirement assets are in capital. Businesses are not the only ones that have become increasingly concerned about financial market risk exposures. The challenge remains, however, in getting individuals to annuitize a larger share of their retirement assets.

In 2008 and again in 2009, the Life Insurance Marketing Research Association, the International Foundation for Retirement Education, and the Society of Actuaries sponsored a survey of a group of retirees ages 55 to 75 with $100,000 or more of investable assets. The first survey was done in February 2008 and the latter in April 2009, so the steep stock market drop was between the two. The results show that after the financial crisis, retirees felt less secure financially, less confident that they had saved enough for retirement, less willing to take risks in investing their savings, and more conservative in their spending patterns. Nevertheless, there was still little interest in purchasing annuities among retirees whose Social Security and defined benefit pension annuities were not adequate to cover basic living expenses.[15]

Policymakers are looking for ways to encourage people to convert some or all of their accumulated retirement savings into lifetime income streams at retirement. Given the success of default options in getting workers into 401(k) plans, which increases their contributions over time and moves them into reasonable investment allocations, some in the policy community are interested in a default mechanism to annuitize plan participants' retirement savings when they quit working.

I am skeptical that employers would be willing to choose specific "default" annuity companies or specific types of annuities. Despite regulations specifying "safe harbor" conditions under which employers can set up and administer such programs, if the chosen insurance company defaults a few years down the road, the legal system will almost certainly scrutinize every dotted i and crossed t to find culpability for making a wrong choice. The heirs of the individuals who die shortly after commencing annuity payments will seek restitution for a myriad of reasons we cannot begin to fathom now.

Furthermore, it is doubtful that workers will accept defaults that allocate all or a major portion of their retirement savings to an annuity given the widespread antipathy toward insurance companies and the purveyors of their products. It is clear that proper framing can encourage a retiring worker to take an annuity, but if employers are not willing to choose companies and annuity types as plan defaults, then participants will have to choose on their own. This will likely throw them into the individual annuity market, where take-up rates are extremely low. Alternatively, they would have to make a proactive choice in a group setting that puts them back into the investment versus income stream framing issues that were discussed in chapter 23.

It seems that most of these potential paths lead back very close to where workers are today, and we know that most people do not buy annuities when they cash out of their employer-sponsored retirement plans. We must resolve the problems with existing approaches to attain higher annuitization rates and address the role of employers. I have a proposal that could increase the annuitization of existing retirement savings and protect a significant share of workers' capital assets.

The proposal involves buying the annuity on an installment basis. Purchases should start at age 55 because that is when most workers start thinking about their retirement needs and there is more interest in assuring their future income than at younger ages. I suggest buying annuities in installments to ameliorate the timing risks workers face if they annuitize when they retire. Before describing the specific proposal, I evaluate its components in light of the research described in chapter 23.[16]

There are two aspects to the timing risks workers face by annuitizing on their retirement date: the first is the value of their accumulated assets and the second is the interest rate. To understand the implications of these, it is important to understand the effects of these timing risks separately and then in tandem. To do so, Brendan McFarland ran some additional simulations for me using the base model that was described in chapter 23. The simulations are based on hypothetical workers who start their careers at age 25 earning $10,000 per year. They receive pay increases of 2 percent per year and contribute 6 percent of pay to their retirement savings account each year. The workers earn an average salary of $20,815 over the last five years of their careers. The starting and ending salaries may seem low by today's standards, but the analysis period starts in 1915. To bring the numbers into the present, the pay levels and annuities in each example could be multiplied by two to four times as long as both the pay and annuities are multiplied by the same factor. Workers' accumulating savings are invested in a lifecycle fund, so they do not have to rebalance assets to stay aligned with retirement savings goals. Actual returns from the U.S. financial markets developed by Robert Shiller[17] are used to estimate the accumulating balances for a series of workers retiring on January 1 each year from 1915 through 2010. To see the asset values accumulated by all workers, look back to figure 23.1. The investment results of the lifecycle fund track closely with a portfolio that is invested 60 percent in equities and 40 percent in bonds and rebalanced each year over a worker's career.

In calculating annuities, we assumed a life expectancy consistent with workers reaching age 65 in 2010. We compared annuities that workers could purchase on their 65th birthdays, referred to as spot-market annuities, with annuities purchased in units beginning at age 55 and continuing to age 65, referred to as installment annuities. In the initial set of simulations, the unit purchases were equal to 12 percent of the accumulated balance in the retirement savings account, and, at age 65, any residual funds in the account are annuitized. For these results, we assumed that workers would pay a premium of 15 percent of the assets they spent as loading fees to cover marketing, profit, and annuity risk charges that insurance companies typically assess because purchasers of annuities tend to live longer than the rest of the population.

We first isolated the variations in how much annuity workers could afford based on how much their assets were worth on their retirement dates over financial market cycles. We held the interest rates used in calculating the annuities to a constant 5 percent. The results shown in figure 28.1 suggest very little downside risk from purchasing installment annuities versus spot-market annuities. Over the last 95 years, there were only three brief periods where spot-market annuities were superior to installment annuities. In all three periods, asset values were appreciating sharply, and in two of the three periods, the combined annuities workers could have purchased on an installment basis would have been rising year-over-year compared to what they could have bought the prior year. In all the market downturns, the installment annuities were clearly a better deal than the spot-market annuities.

The second component of the timing risk is the effect of varying interest rates over time. In this case, we assumed that all workers realized a 10 percent return on their equities and 5 percent return on the bonds throughout their careers. Thus, all workers ended up with the same asset balances to be annuitized. In calculating the annuities this time, we used the interest rates on the date the respective annuities were purchased. The results of this simulation are presented in figure 28.2. The spot annuities are slightly better than the installment annuities over most of the period from 1940 to 1980, and then spike up markedly in the early 1980s, which was quite an abnormal period for interest rates. The 10 individual years with the highest interest rates over the 95 years were from 1979 to 1989. Since interest rates fell in the mid-1980s, the installment annuities have been clearly superior to the spot-market annuities.

Ultimately, the interaction of these two risks would determine which option would be better for workers considering purchasing an annuity. The results of allowing both asset values and interest rates to vary are presented in figure 28.3. Once again, it is clear that the installment annuities are superior

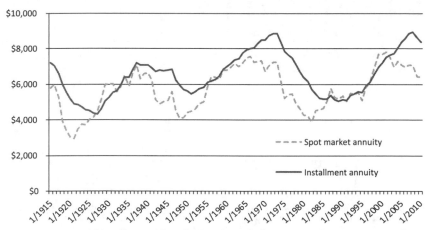

FIGURE 28.1 **Annuities from Lifecycle Funds with Constant Life Expectancies for a Hypothetical Worker Retiring Each Year from 1915 through 2010 Based on Spot-Market Purchase at Retirement Date and Installment Purchases from Ages 55 to 64 with Balance Annuitized at Age 65, Constant Interest Rates but Variable Asset Values**
Source: Calculated as described in the text.

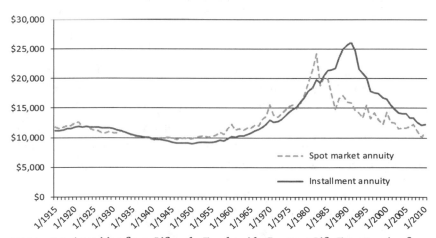

FIGURE 28.2 **Annuities from Lifecycle Funds with Constant Life Expectancies for a Hypothetical Worker Retiring Each Year from 1915 through 2010 Based on Spot-Market Purchase at Retirement Date and Installment Purchases from Ages 55 to 64 with Balance Annuitized at Age 65, Variable Interest Rates but Constant Asset Values**
Source: Calculated as described in the text.

to spot-market annuities during the down market cycles and may trail slightly during the up side. Over the last 45 years, the installment annuities beat the spot-market value in every instance. This suggests that getting workers to buy annuities in smaller bites potentially offers significant advantages for most workers with little downside costs for the rest.

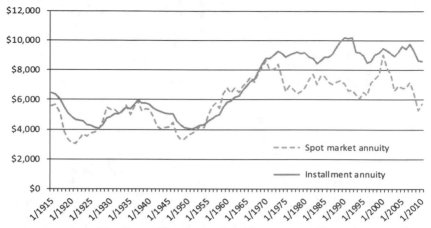

FIGURE 28.3 Annuities from Lifecycle Funds with Constant Life Expectancies for a Hypothetical Worker Retiring Each Year from 1915 through 2010 Based on Spot-Market Purchase at Retirement Date and Installment Purchases from Ages 55 to 64 with Balance Annuitized at Age 65

Source: Installment annuity calculations added to spot-market estimates from Brendan McFarland and Mark J. Warshawsky, "Balances and Retirement Income from Individual Accounts: U.S. Historical Simulations," *Benefits Quarterly* (Second Quarter 2010), p. 39.

The loading fees in the individual annuity markets significantly diminish the reach and efficiency of retirement savings. Purchasing annuities through a group market can likely reduce these costs by two-thirds. If a worker is spending $100,000 on a retirement annuity, reducing the loading costs by this amount would increase the lifetime stream of income by 11 percent to 12 percent—a boost clearly worth pursuing.

Creating an Environment to Encourage Annuitization

To understand the challenges we face in encouraging workers to annuitize more of their retirement savings, it is important to put several elements of this story together. First, most private retirement plan sponsors have moved away from providing retirement annuities, and most probably cannot be bid back into the process. They do not trust public policymakers to stay the course in regulating their plans over the decades of benefit obligations. Second, most employers will not want to wade through the fiduciary complexity and risks of picking annuity options for workers and then defaulting them into those choices. Third, if workers are left to buy annuities on their own at retirement, they face timing risks and inefficient annuity transaction pricing. Finally, workers seem to have an instinctive abhorrence to the idea of giving up hard-earned retirement savings and possibly not getting their money back. We have a seeming Gordian knot to unravel.

My suggestion is to create a central administrator to act as an intermediary between workers and retirees and the insurance industry. This could be a self-supporting quasi-public or private entity; call it the Retirement Insurance Clearing House or RICH for short. The administrators of all tax-qualified retirement plans that predominantly provide their benefit in lump sums could set up a default option system for plan participants. The default option could work differently for defined contribution plans than for cash balance and other hybrid defined benefit plans that provide benefits in the form of lump sums.

In defined contribution plans, the plan administrator would automatically enroll workers who turn age 55 in an annuity installment program and transfer 3 percent of their account balance to RICH in their own name. Participants who wanted to opt out could do so. For the others, RICH would pool their contributions and buy annuities from insurance companies that would bid on them in a competitive auction. The auctions would be similar to the auctions the U.S. Treasury now holds to sell government bonds to raise cash, except the cash would be flowing out to participating institutions rather than the other way around. No single individual's annuity would be placed with a single insurance firm—each annuity would be spread across the firms bidding to offer the annuities at the time, which would significantly reduce the default risks of purchasing from one vendor. If there were concerns about default risks, two additional measures could be taken. The federal government has left much of the regulation of annuities to the states but could stipulate certain conditions for companies providing annuities under this program. In addition, reinsurance could be provided by firms in the insurance industry that are not in the business of providing annuities.

For the sake of discussion, assume that this mechanism introduces efficiencies that reduce loading rates on annuities to 5 percent of retirees' accumulated assets. The 3 percent of the accumulated balance contributed to the program each year from ages 55 onward might not seem like much, but consider the annuities that it would throw off as a percentage of the spot-market annuity our hypothetical worker could buy with the total accumulation of retirement savings as reflected in figure 28.4. Over the whole period, the installment annuities purchased with the 3 percent contributions would average 33.7 percent of the full account being annuitized on a spot-market basis. Over the past 40 years, the installment annuity has been more than 30 percent of the full spot-market annuity in all but one year.

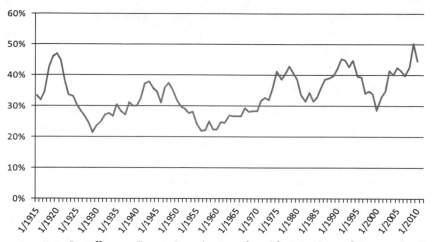

FIGURE 28.4 Installment Group Annuity Bought with 3 Percent of Accumulated Retirement Savings Contributed from Ages 55 Onward as a Percentage of an Individual Spot-Market Annuity Available to a Hypothetical Worker

Source: Calculated as described in the text.

I believe that a convincing case could be made to workers that this is an opportunity to secure a substantial and secure retirement income stream at a very reasonable cost. In a financial market that yields average returns, workers' accumulated retirement savings balances should continue rising even after the 3 percent annuity installment withdrawal. In a down market, the withdrawal would be small enough not to decimate their balance, and they could be increasing their retirement income guarantee even as their asset values were falling. In every case in the simulations, the worker would still end up with a cash balance at retirement equal to 75 percent of the balance without having bought the installment annuity. The system could guarantee that if a participant died before retiring or claiming benefits equal to his or her inflation-adjusted contributions, the net amount would be rebated to his or her estate. So participants would be buying income insurance with little risk to the net value of their assets. The transactions would not involve insurance salespeople or marketing costs but would employ the efficiency of buying group annuities.

Sponsors of defined benefit plans that provide benefits as lump sums could set up an internal annuity accounting system inside the plan and credit the 3 percent to their own annuity offering. Those that would prefer to get out of the annuity business could then transfer the amount to RICH, which would provide the annuities by efficiently tapping the insurance markets.

Workers could opt out of the automatic transfer program. They could also choose to contribute more than 3 percent of accumulated assets each year and would be given some flexibility in terms of making the annuity claim at the point of retirement. The actual annuity payout would depend on the retiree's age of claiming, whether a joint-and-survivor benefit was purchased in accordance with ERISA rules, and whether the benefit is indexed for inflation. After the retirement decisions were made, RICH would collect the payments from the insurance company and send a monthly check to the retiree.

The system would be fully funded at all times. It would provide an annuity supplement to Social Security benefits. The costs of running RICH would be covered by a slight fee applied against funds contributed. The annuities would be modest but the benefits would increase retirees' peace of mind and enhance their satisfaction with retirement.

It Is Better to Light a Candle than Curse the Darkness

It has been extremely encouraging in recent years to see the joint academic research and willingness of employers to experiment with ways to make retirement plans more effective which, in turn, has led to modifications of plan regulations to encourage widespread adaptation of new approaches to retirement savings. This is a fundamentally different approach to the development of new law and rules of the road than has gone on since the early 1970s. In some regards, this may be the optimal method of accumulating wisdom in the Confucian framework. The academics by nature are reflective in designing experiments to understand human reactions to a range of economic and other stimuli. By testing their experimental approaches and documenting their results, they develop wisdom that can be widely shared with policymakers, regulation writers, and the practitioners who run plans. When formulas that work are discovered, they can be passed on as wisdom acquired and adapted in the easiest fashion—by imitation of what works.

REMEMBERING THE FUTURE

Many people today credit Franklin Roosevelt for the magnificent success that Social Security has wrought in making today's retirees more economically secure than any other age group. FDR would be likely to smile broadly, acknowledge the importance of "[his] Social Security" but suggest the income security of today's retirees was based on more than this single program. When President Roosevelt talked about Social Security, he characterized it as the "foundation" of retirement security. It was meant to provide a "foothold" toward income security in old age.[1] Achieving the retirement security we have today has also required considerable initiative by many other players.

Other people blame Franklin Roosevelt for creating in Social Security a welfare program—the largest in the federal portfolio—that has made much of the middle and upper classes dependent on a government income-transfer program financed by the largest single tax burden on American workers. It is likely that FDR would suggest the blame is misplaced. In 1935, President Franklin Roosevelt called Frances Perkins, the secretary of labor, and Edwin Witte, the executive director of the Committee on Economic Security, to his office because he was upset about financing provisions in the package on its way to Congress. FDR feared that the pay-as-you-go financing would pass on costs and financing obligations to future Congresses and, by extension, taxpayers, which would not be "fair" or "moral." He insisted on a system based on insurance principles and opposed expanding the "dole."[2]

Broadening Our Perspective on Retirement Security

At the opening of chapter 22, I recounted one of Walter Cronkite's evening broadcasts on CBS News in the late 1960s, a story of older Americans being forced to eat dog food because they could not afford anything better. At the time, poverty rates were higher than 30 percent among retirees. As awareness of the elderly's predicament grew, our society recoiled and political leaders enhanced Social Security benefits. It is hard to fathom there coming a time when Americans would not be equally aghast to hear the same story. To give up on providing the mechanisms necessary for workers to achieve their own retirement security would be beyond the pale.

In the late 1960s, when we decided to do better by our elders, a full-career worker retiring at age 65 would have qualified for pension benefits financed by a cumulative 4 percent of lifetime earnings paid in Social Security payroll taxes. Assuming the worker also saved in a pension or capital accumulation plan, total retirement costs would have been around 10 percent of his lifetime pay. Employers would have diverted another 3 percent of compensation to health insurance. Medicare was just getting started, and while a late 1960s retiree would have qualified for full benefits, he or she would have paid virtually nothing out of lifetime earnings to do so. Around 1970, the cumulative costs of these benefits would have been around 13 percent of a worker's pay. Moving ahead to 2011, the lifetime payroll taxes on an average worker's earnings would have equaled 13 percent alone, supplemental retirement savings would have added another 7.5 percent of earnings, and health benefits were taking 10.6 percent of pay—adding up to roughly 31 percent of pay.

George Bernard Shaw said, "We are made wise not by the recollection of our past, but by the responsibility of our future." What my father had paid for his retirement package when he retired at age 65 in 1974 is really irrelevant. In fact, what I would have paid for mine had I retired in 2011 is equally irrelevant. What is important are the trends between those points and what they portend for my son, Sean, who will turn age 65 in 2041, or his son, Miles, who will reach that age in 2074. If we simply let current trends play out, our children and grandchildren will have to surrender most of the added rewards that earlier generations received for their part in improving productivity.

James Truslow Adams is often cited as having coined the phrase "The American Dream," which he described as the "dream of a land in which life should be better and richer and fuller for every man, with opportunity for each according to his ability or achievement."[3] *Forbes* quotes Adams as saying, "The whole of the American Dream has been based on the chance to get ahead, for one's self or one's children. Would this country have ever reached the point it has if the individual had always been refused the rewards of his labors and dangers?"[4] Are we going to risk abandoning the "dream" that our children and grandchildren will have a better life as the fruit of their toil because we refuse to get the financing of our retirement house in order?

When Franklin Roosevelt worried about the morality of leaving massive unfunded obligations for future Congresses to handle, he was expressing his responsibility for our future. Then there was J. Douglas Brown, one of the drafters of the Social Security legislation in 1935, who served with Edwin Witte on the 1939 Advisory Council on Social Security. When the council was deliberating the shift of Social Security financing to pay-as-you-go, Witte raised concerns about the inevitably higher future payroll tax rates under this approach. Brown dismissed those concerns by telling Witte that by then, "We will all be dead."[5] The costs that weren't J. Douglas Brown's concern are what our political leaders are now toiling to bring under control—exactly the prospect that FDR said was "immoral" and "unfair." The question we face is whether to emulate Franklin Roosevelt in addressing our retirement issues or J. Douglas Brown.

Not wanting to reduce our elderly to a diet for dogs should not mean abandoning the American Dream. We must figure out how to moderate both our retirement and our health costs or we risk doing so. Some people contend that excessive health inflation is the larger problem, stealing more of our rewards without providing any greater health dividends than much cheaper systems in other developed economies. They suggest leaving our retiree pension system alone to focus on the more serious problem of health care. This is akin to a man with cancer whose doctor ignores his broken leg. Of course, we need to address health cost inflation more aggressively, but we cannot ignore other maladies simply because that one is worse. Indeed, given the stubborn nature of health inflation, it reduces our flexibility to ignore other threats to our economic and fiscal health. Moreover, our retirement claims are worthy of concern on their own. If we dawdle away for the next 20 years and then raise taxes because we cannot reduce benefits on such short notice, we are effectively laying claim to an extra year and one-half of today's preschoolers' future earnings.

It Is Not 1939 Anymore for Social Security or Retirees

The late Robert Ball, the Social Security commissioner from the Kennedy Administration through the end of the first Nixon Administration and subsequently a prominent policy advocate for the program, summarized benefits as being essentially defined by the 1939 Amendments to the original 1935 Social Security Act. He said, "The pattern of the program was well set in the '39 amendments. One way to consider the whole history of the program from then on is as filling in the structure that had been created in '39."[6] Does this really make sense today?

By way of analogy, imagine the phone that sat on Arthur Altmeyer's desk as he carried out his duties as first commissioner of Social Security. That rotary dial phone could be connected to any other phone in America as long as the copper wires and operators' connections linked them together. Downstairs from Altmeyer's office in the Social Security Administration, there were no electronic computers, so administrative records were kept on Hollerith cards—paper keypunch cards—that were physically ordered and reordered by mechanical card sorters. Compare Arthur Altmeyer's world to what Commissioner Michael Astrue had available in the early 2010s for communicating with staff, participants, and the general public. Think of the way earnings records were processed before the computer and compare that to the massive electronic data storage, interchange, and processing facilities and capabilities available to Social Security today. The Social Security Administration no longer conducts its daily operations the way it did when Arthur Altmeyer was there because it would make no sense given developments since then. Nor does it make sense to remain strapped into the girdle of the 1939 benefits structure, ignoring all that has happened since in our economy and our society.

Social Security's benefit structure has not kept abreast of the times in many ways. For example, in 1950, less than 40 percent of women between the ages of 25 and 64 worked outside the home, and most of those who did were unmarried. Since then, the infrastructure to support working mothers—daycare facilities and preschool programs—has become widely available. If anything, women today may be preparing themselves for the modern economy better than their male counterparts as the latter are now the minority of enrollees in the higher education system. By the early 21st century, more than three of four prime-working-age women were employed outside the home, including the majority of those with children under school age. In light of these changes, shouldn't we revisit the spousal benefit and the equity issues it raises?

In the decade after World War II, a typical worker started a career after high school, around the age of 18. Most of their fathers had started working at an even younger age. In 1940, when Social Security benefits were first paid, remaining life expectancy at age 65 was just under 13 years. The typical retiree claiming his first benefit was older than age 65. Today, most young people pursue some college education, and many stay the full four years or even longer. The most frequent age for claiming Social Security benefits is 62, but life expectancy at age 65 is now up to 18 years. We have reduced the number of years we work by some two to four years, on average, yet we have increased the duration of our retirement by at least three years since 1940 simply by retiring earlier. Longevity improvements have added at least another five years to retirement. Some of the added cadre of retirees today results from people living longer in retirement with health conditions that cut short their working lives, but many are healthy and productive people who could make significant contributions.

While imposing higher taxes on rich people sounds like an easy fix, it would also violate the philosophical underpinning that Franklin Roosevelt believed was the foundation of the Social Security and its public support. Taxing people without giving them benefits in kind would turn the program into the "same old dole" that FDR clearly detested for his Social Security. We had a national policy debate about our federal "welfare" program in the 1990s when Congress replaced Aid for Families with Dependent Children with the Temporary Assistance for Needy Families. The changes were prompted by concerns that the old welfare system was generating a culture of long-term dependence that was at odds with the American Dream. If we worry about the economic dependence of mothers with young children in our welfare programs, how would we come to view much larger, more costly and far more expansive economic dependence on welfare for the middle and upper-class elderly if that is what we make of Social Security?

Social Security has always been a program for the masses of workers in our society—its very name suggests a collective sharing. If we need to change the program, shouldn't participants collectively share in the reforms to the extent they can? Because the baby boom is central to the current financing ills, it needs to be part of the cure. We all deserve a candid conversation about appropriate retirement ages in a modern society, the desirability of spousal retirement benefits for those who do not work outside the home, and affordable payroll taxes. Similarly, we should discuss appropriate growth levels in real purchasing power of initial benefits over time, especially for higher earners, and an appropriate benefit floor for those who toil for low pay over their careers.

The proposals developed by the Bowles-Simpson Commission, the Domenici-Rivlin Task Force, and the Debt Reduction Task Force addressed many of these issues. Yet Congress appears to have no appetite to move forward, nor has the Obama Administration been willing to embrace any of the suggested reforms for Social Security.

As an antidote to any serious discussion of the recommendations from the commission and the task force while the Obama Administration and Congressional leaders discussed federal deficits during the summer of 2011, AARP ran a series of television commercials in Washington, D.C.

and elsewhere around the country, urging its members to tell their Congressional representatives to oppose any adjustments to Social Security. AARP, the National Committee to Preserve Social Security and Medicare, the AFL-CIO, Social Security Works, and a host of other organizations will bring massive war chests to influence any political discussion about these programs. Schoolchildren—and those not yet born—will have no organized representation. As a society, we must decide whether to give those children their shot at the American Dream—as earlier generations gave us—and whether to stand behind Franklin Roosevelt's or J. Douglas Brown's principles in this case.

Private Role Is Vital in Securing Retirement Incomes

For much of the past 30 years, public policy has scaled back benefits in private employer-sponsored retirement plans. Social Security is backed by a large institutional staff that analyzes the implications of every elemental change to the program. As far as I know, no government agency has evaluated the effects on employer-sponsored pension plans of the comprehensive package of policy changes enacted over the past 30 years.

The Bowles-Simpson Commission and the Domenici-Rivlin Task Force have recommended limiting annual tax-deductible contributions to defined contribution plans to the lesser of 20 percent of earnings or $20,000. This would constrain the ability of workers earning more than $100,000 per year to accumulate sufficient resources to maintain their preretirement standard of living. If this policy were enacted, those most affected would be workers earning between $100,000 and $250,000.

Other recommendations in the two group's packages of proposals also single out higher earners, by raising the Social Security wage base—and thus this group's payroll taxes—and by reducing their benefits. When the National Commission on Fiscal Responsibility proposals are fully phased in, their effect would be to increase payroll taxes by 60 percent relative to current law for workers earning $200,000 in today's terms, cut their Social Security benefits by roughly a quarter, and reduce by half what they could get out of their private supplemental saving through an employer-sponsored retirement plan—a miserable trifecta for those affected. These workers are already getting a lousy deal from Social Security. Even under current law, their potential net benefits from the "tax preferences" in their employer-sponsored plans do not negate their Social Security losses, unless they have non-working spouses.

Both the Bowles-Simpson Commission and the Domenici-Rivlin Task Force are silent on the tax treatment of employer-sponsored defined benefit plans. This probably reflects a lack of understanding of how to go about adjusting defined benefit limits in line with their proposals for defined contribution plans. The groups were also silent about how the new limits would work for employers that sponsor both defined benefit and defined contribution plans. The proposals reveal a lack of experience with employer-sponsored plans and the tendency of policymakers to look at elements of the retirement system in isolation rather than as cogs in a functioning whole, thus missing the bigger retirement picture.

The financing of retiree health insurance offers a good case study of unintended consequences snaking their way through various components of the retirement system. When Congress limited the funding of retiree health benefits in the 1980s and the Financial Accounting Standards Board required companies to recognize retiree health costs and obligations on their financial statements, employers responded by shutting down the plans. After that, political pressure mounted to add a prescription drug benefit to Medicare in 2003 and then again under health reform. The latter has not yet been implemented, but the subsidization of drug benefits for older Americans well up into middle-income levels almost certainly will have many early retirees standing in line for their government-financed benefits after 2014. In fact, the subsidization of health insurance for older people who are younger than 65 under health reform will give them an incentive to retire earlier than planned—possibly negating any efforts to encourage workers to remain in the workforce longer.

Limiting the tax preferences for retirement savings plans might not prompt employers to shut down their plans, but some, possibly many, will scale back benefits—namely matching contributions for workers up and down the earnings spectrum, as plans are realigned to reflect the meager benefits that can be funded for mid-level managers and technical staff. These are complicated matters, and most policymakers cannot fully appreciate the nuances of these suggestions without acquiring an understanding of the issues. Tracking the changes that have occurred in employer-based segments of the retirement system over the past 30 years should serve as sufficient warning that regulatory changes affect plan structures and benefit levels. If the search for short-term federal revenue leads us to reduce tax expenditures for retirement savings at the expense of creating long-term demands for higher taxes and expenditures under Social Security, we will have played a game of double jeopardy with future generations of rank-and-file workers.

Of course, we must deal with our federal deficit, and all retirement benefits should be considered in the deliberations. While there is a tendency to commission things to death in Washington instead of acting, the regulatory environment affecting employer-sponsored retirement plans has gotten so complex and the implications of our actions so little appreciated that I believe we need a commission to study the issues and propose a rational way forward. It should include private-sector members who work with these plans on a regular basis, with representation from the plan sponsor community and the benefit consulting industry. Some of the academics who have been studying the operations of employer-sponsored plans should also be included.

The commission should not be populated with advocacy representatives from Washington or the think tanks, who might know plan statistics but have no grounded, practical knowledge of plan operations. Members should be broadly recognized as being knowledgeable about plan operations but should also understand policymakers' goals in regulating these plans over the last 35 years. The commission should also include members from legislative committees with jurisdiction over plan regulations or those closely affiliated with them—people like former Democratic Congressman Earl Pomeroy from North Dakota and Republican Senator Rob Portman from Ohio. They both know considerably more about the operation of private retirement plans than most of the members of Congress. This would provide a good blend of members who understand retirement plan operations—including the hurdles in structuring and delivering benefits to all workers—and others more sensitive to the fiscal and equity issues posed by a system that is given special considerations under the tax code.

Preserving Our Prosperity

My mother used to say that "God helps those who help themselves." I am not suggesting that we should turn to God to solve our retirement financing issues, but the suggestion that our fate depends on our own initiative could not be more apt. Various aspects of the discussion throughout this volume have pointed to increasing the age at which people retire. Generally, proposals to keep people working longer are made in the context of controlling retirement costs, but workers' extension of their careers would have even broader economic ramifications.

With the baby boom's retirement, the retiree population will grow much more rapidly than the working-age population—that is the nub of the worry that our retirement system could swamp the American Dream. Keeping people at work longer is an obvious and potent solution. Delaying retirement slows the growth of the retiree population and swells the ranks of the workforce, both of which are beneficial in producing more output and sharing it between workers and retirees. The question is whether we can convince people to do it.

"Keeping up with the Joneses" was a newspaper cartoon strip first run in the *New York Globe* in 1913. The Joneses weren't anyone in particular, but they were everyone's neighbors—the people next door.[7] The concept behind the strip was so relevant that the title made its way into our American lexicon, although the Joneses might have become more of a concept than people. When typical retirement ages dropped from the upper 60s to the early 60s and then even into the 50s, this was considered progress and we all wanted a piece of it. When "30 and out" pensions meant mill workers could escape the workaday world after 30 years of hard work, many of us who "worked in the office" wanted a piece of that, too. Giving it back is retrogression—acknowledging that the Joneses had it better than we will. In a society whose essence has been progress, this may be a bitter pill for some of us to swallow.

But as much as we aspire to progress, we are also a practical people. When political and economic demands have arisen, workers have responded. A classic example is reflected in "Rosie the Riveter," the icon representing the women of America who marched into factories during World War II to support the troops and provide for the nation. While that was a period of national peril, it is not the only or the most sustained example of changing labor force patterns to accommodate changing circumstances. Female workforce participation rates took a dramatic leap during the last half of the 20th century, especially among baby-boom women, who set off on very different paths than their mothers and older sisters had taken. Women working outside the home significantly grew the labor supply available to the U.S. economy and sent economic output soaring.

Diane Macunovich has studied the labor supply behaviors of baby boomers to explain why the baby-boomer women entered the workforce and stayed there at higher rates than women before them. She explains that the baby boom's numbers created an oversupply of workers, which drove down wages. The baby-boom women—seeing that their male counterparts were not earning enough to maintain the standards of living they had grown accustomed to in their childhood—entered and stayed in the workforce to boost family income and achieve their economic goals.[8]

If we applied the 1960 female labor force participation rates to the population and workforce patterns of women in 2009, as reported in the March 2010

Current Population Survey, the United States would have had roughly 45 billion fewer hours of labor input. This would have reduced our gross output by as much as $2 trillion—16 percent of our total production in 2009. Changing workforce patterns contributed to the goods and services available to American consumers, and the additional payroll and income taxes on women's earnings swelled government coffers.

Retirement trends may be in the process of reversing. There are signs that workers approaching retirement age are beginning to rethink their retirement decisions. The average labor force participation rates of men aged 62 to 65 increased by 4.5 percentage points from the first five years of the new millennium to the second. Among women aged 60 to 64, the rate increased by more than 5 percentage points.[9] The potential benefits for people who work a bit longer are tremendous. Barbara Butrica, Karen Smith, and Eugene Steuerle estimate that workers who work one additional year beyond age 50 can increase their retirement consumption by 9 percent per year if they annuitize the added net wealth accumulated in that year. Five more years of work can increase retirement consumption by 56 percent.[10] The estimates suggest that lower earners would actually gain more from extending their careers than higher earners. Encouraging workers to stay on the job a few years longer could enhance their own welfare while also lightening the burden on younger workers.

Inescapable Realities

On January 16, 2009, four days before his inauguration as president, Barack Obama met with the editorial board of the *Washington Post* to discuss a broad range of issues he would face in office. When the subject turned to the massive deficits the federal government was running, Mr. Obama outlined how he intended to bring spending under control. Among other things, he said:

> As soon as economic recovery takes place, then we've got to bend the curve and figure out how we get federal spending on a more sustainable path. . . . We are also going to have a discussion about entitlements and how we get a grasp on those. . . . As bad as these deficits that have already been run up have been, the real problem with our long-term deficits, actually, have to do with our entitlement obligations. . . . So we're going to have to shape a bargain. This, by the way, is where . . . some very difficult issues of sacrifice, responsibility and duty are going to come in because what we have done is kick this can down the road

and we are now at the end of the road. We are not in a position to kick it any further. . . . I have told my folks, to some consternation on their part, that we have to signal seriousness in this by making sure that some of the hard decisions are made under my watch and not under somebody else's because the usual game is to say, "well, here's what is going to happen but, by the way, it just happens to start in the ninth year from now." What we have to signal is that we are willing to make hard decisions now.[11]

Any serious discussion of entitlements must include Social Security, and when President Obama came into office, there were hopes he would lead a discussion aimed at finding an equitable way forward. By the time he gave his 2011 State of the Union address, however, he was sounding more tentative. In that speech, he said: "To put us on solid ground, we should also find a bipartisan solution to strengthen Social Security for future generations. And we must do it without putting at risk current retirees, the most vulnerable, or people with disabilities; without slashing benefits for future generations; and without subjecting Americans' guaranteed retirement income to the whims of the stock market."[12]

Representative Paul Ryan became chair of the House Budget Committee in January 2011 and led his fellow Republicans in developing a budget plan, "The Path to Prosperity,"[13] which the full House of Representatives adopted in April 2011 on a purely Republican vote. While this document discusses at length the modernization of Social Security to make it affordable and appropriate for the 21st century, instead of making specific recommendations, it calls on Congress to "[s]et in motion the process of reforming Social Security by establishing a requirement that in the event that the Social Security program is not sustainable, the President, in conjunction with the Board of Trustees, must submit a plan for restoring balance to the fund. The budget then requires congressional leaders in both the U.S. House of Representatives and U.S. Senate to put forward their best ideas as well."[14]

If any encouragement can be taken from the positions of President Obama and the Republican leadership in the House, it is that they acknowledge the need to get serious. But both are both employing a Tom Sawyer strategy for painting the fence—they are trying to get somebody else to do the work. When the new Social Security Trustees Report came out in May 2011, the results showed that the 75-year underfunding of the pay-as-you-go financing measure had grown by another $1.1 trillion over the prior year—to a total of $6.5 trillion—and the unfunded obligations had grown by $1.3 trillion—to a total of $21.6 trillion. The Social Security trust funds and incoming tax revenue were projected to be insufficient to pay promised benefits in 2036—one year sooner than the actuaries predicted a year earlier.[15] Undoubtedly Mark Twain could turn these circumstances into a tale at which we would have to laugh to keep from crying as he told it.

In its 2010 Annual Report, the Pension Benefit Guaranty Corporation reported an unfunded obligation of $20 billion in its single-employer plan insurance program—a $500 million increase over the prior year, despite increasing its assets by $10.2 billion since then. Its multiemployer insurance program was underfunded by $1.4 billion—an increase of $600 million over the prior year. With total assets of $79.4 billion, the underfunding is serious and unsustainable.[16] In February 2012, President Obama submitted his formal 2012 Budget proposals to Congress. Among other things, "The Budget proposes to give the PBGC Board the authority to adjust premiums and directs PBGC to take into account the risks that different sponsors pose to their retirees and to PBGC." The budget calls for the agency to raise an added $16 billion in premiums over the 10 years starting with the passage of the 2014 budget.[17] While this sounds like the agency will move to a more risk-based approach, the plans posing the greatest risks to the pension insurance program cannot possibly pay premiums that reflect the risks they impose as well as the amortized value of the insurance program's unfunded obligations. Once again, this portends large hikes in the flat premium. The diminishing number of employers that have stuck by their defined benefit commitments will continue paying the inequitable penalties to bail out the insurance agency from liabilities attributable to its own faulty structure.

During the first six months of 2011, seven private companies on the Fortune 100 list of public corporations closed their defined benefit plans to new hires, and another four froze their plans for future accruals. Only 13 companies on the list still sponsor traditional defined benefit pension plans and one of those, Walt Disney, has announced that it will freeze its plan in early 2012. Another 14 companies were still sponsoring a hybrid defined benefit plan at midyear 2011, but the recent trends in closing both traditional and hybrid plans seems firmly established. The Pension Benefit Guaranty Corporation will ultimately have to acknowledge being in a classic "insurance death spiral," where the only remaining program participants are those certain to make claims that far exceed their premiums. When that day arrives, the collapse of the private defined benefit system will be complete.

While there is much angst about the shift to defined contribution plans as the primary form of savings to supplement Social Security, it is the brightest ray of hope in the retirement story. Since the 1980s, workers have consistently saved more in these plans, on average, than the amount of contributions to the defined benefit system. Proposals to scale back 401(k)s have the potential to emasculate the only element of the retirement portfolio that is adding to workers' retirement wealth in this post-golden era.

Winston Churchill said, "You can always count on Americans to do the right thing—after they have tried everything else." When it comes to our retirement system, we might not have tried everything else yet, but it is time to get it right. At this juncture, our political leaders seem to have a studied understanding of the difficulties confronting Social Security and options for resolving them, although they have a blind spot about the program's function as one piece in the larger retirement system, and they have ignored options for modernizing the benefit structure. Moreover, policymakers seem paralyzed by our dysfunctional political dynamics. They are pretending to be Tom Sawyer but are really more like Billy the Kid, trying to get their opponents to draw first so they can slay them in the next political street fight.

As for the private supplementary components of the retirement system, there is a glaring lack of knowledge about plan operations, the incentives affecting them, and their outcomes. Until policymakers treat this component of the retirement system as something other than a revenue loss, we can expect our history of bad policy to continue.

Chapter 1 opened with lessons from *Alice in Wonderland*, and we might all be well served to reread the tale that Lewis Carroll told of Alice's wanderings. Much of the travail we have undergone with our retirement programs is because we forget to remember both ways. Despite all we had learned by the 1920s about the science of pension operations and the importance of pension funding, we have refused to remember those lessons time and again at our peril. Despite the fact that, in the 1930s, we knew that pay-as-you-go financing could get out of hand, we repeatedly refused to remember that what we were creating for our own comfort was an obligation for our grandchildren. If we continue to refuse to remember how these things work, future generations will also undoubtedly realize an even more dire predictable surprise than the one that now plagues us.

As James Truslow Adams wrote, "We have a long and arduous road to travel if we are to realize our American dream in the life of our nation, but if we fail . . . the alternative is the failure of self-government, the failure of the common man to rise to full stature, the failure of all that the American dream has held of hope and promise for mankind."[18]

GLOSSARY

Accumulated benefit obligation: The present value of benefits that have been earned by a worker under a defined benefit pension plan based on service and compensation up to the time for which the calculation is made.

Actuarial balance: A concept used by the Social Security actuaries to describe whether Social Security is sufficiently financed over the next 75 years. In developing the measure, they consider the available resources to pay benefits as the present value of the combination of the existing trust funds and anticipated revenues over the next 75 years. Against the estimated resources, they estimate the present value of anticipated benefits to be paid over the same time period. If the system's anticipated resources are estimated to be 0.5 percent less than anticipated costs, the system is considered to be out of actuarial balance.

Agency risk: In the context of retirement plans, it is the risk that plan managers improperly handle or dispose of plan assets for a purpose other than providing benefits to participants under the stated plan rules.

Average Indexed Monthly Earnings: The summarization of a worker's career earnings used in calculating the Primary Insurance Amount for determining Social Security benefit payments. A worker's history is converted into current earnings levels using the history of average wages over his or her working career up to age 61. Subsequent years are considered at their nominal or actual dollar value. The highest 35 years of earnings are used to calculate an average indexed earnings level. The sum of the selected 35 years of earnings are divided by 420—35 years x 12 months per year—to get the monthly indexed earnings average. If a worker does not have 35 years of covered earnings, all years with positive earnings are added together and the sum is still divided by 420. The result of this calculation is then subjected to the Social Security benefit formula to determine the Primary Insurance Amount.

Birth cohort: The group of people born in a single calendar year.

Default risk: In the context of retirement plans, it is the probability that a plan sponsor or its retirement plan will not be able to pay retirement benefits to workers who have earned them.

Defined benefit plan: A retirement plan in which the benefit is defined by specified provisions in the plan. Under a typical plan, a unit of benefit—which may be a flat monthly benefit or a specified percentage of covered earnings—accrues for each year of creditable service. Until recently, these plans typically paid out benefits in the form of a monthly annuity. Most private defined benefit plans today allow participants to take some or all of their accumulated benefits as a lump-sum cash distribution. Most public defined benefit plans still pay their benefits as annuities.

Defined contribution plan: A retirement plan in which workers accumulate funds under specified terms regarding contributions. It is common that both employers and employees contribute to these plans. In most cases, the accumulated account balance is paid to the plan participant as a lump sum upon termination of employment with the plan sponsor. The lump sum may be distributed as regular income or rolled into an Individual Retirement Account for gradual distribution during retirement.

Dependency ratio: The number of people receiving benefits from a retirement program divided by the number of active workers who are contributing to the plan or whose employers are contributing on their behalf.

Discount rate: The rate of interest used to calculate the present value of a future obligation. An obligation to pay someone $1,000 dollars a year from now is worth less now than the $1,000 because it can be secured by a bond or other asset that will pay interest over the intervening time.

Discrimination testing: The federal income tax code includes a variety of provisions to ensure that employers sponsoring retirement plans do not unfairly discriminate in favor of highly compensated participants in the plans relative to participants at lower earnings levels. In order to demonstrate compliance with these requirements, plans are subjected to a variety of tests comparing contribution rates, benefit accrual rates, and the like for the workers in the two earnings classes.

ERISA: The Employee Retirement Income Security Act, the major federal law regulating the operations of private pension plans. It was originally adopted in 1974 and has been amended many times since then. It includes elements of tax and labor law and is intended to secure workers' retirement benefits.

Fiduciary: A person or organization entrusted to manage another's money or property. ERISA specifies that anyone who exercises discretionary authority or control over the management or administration of a retirement plan or its assets or who renders investment advice for a fee or other form of compensation is a fiduciary.

Forfeiture risk: In the context of retirement plans, it is the likelihood of a worker's employment being terminated before he or she has earned a vested right to a benefit in an employer-sponsored retirement plan.

Fully funded pension: A retirement plan that hold assets in trust equivalent to existing benefit liabilities.

Funding ratio or funded ratio: The portion of a pension plan's liability that is covered by the plan assets.

Health and Retirement Study: A major longitudinal survey research project financed by the National Institute of Aging, which is part of the National Institute of Health. Samples of individuals ages 51 to 61 who were representative of people those ages in the general population were drawn in 1992, and they were interviewed regarding their health and economic status. They have been re-interviewed every other year since then, and younger birth cohorts were added in 1998 and 2004. This is an extremely valuable study for documenting the status of workers as they approach retirement age, transition into it, and then live out their remaining years.

Hidden pensioners: A term coined by Birchard Wyatt in his Ph.D. dissertation written in fulfillment of doctoral degree requirements at Columbia University in 1936. He was referring to aged workers whose productivity was declining below their level of pay due to age who continued working because they could not afford to retire. The implication was that such workers were effectively pensioned in jobs although their remuneration was not characterized as a pension.

Hybrid pension plan: A defined benefit retirement plan under ERISA's regulatory framework that is structured to operate like a defined contribution plan from the participant's perspective. Benefits are earned and communicated in the form of account balances which are typically paid in the form of a lump sum when a worker terminates employment with the plan sponsor.

Insurance principles: Insurance is related to the collection of large groups of individuals to "pool" the risks they face of incurring certain adverse events—such as car accident, fire loss, or death. The adverse events must be must be definite and determinable—the time, place, and cause of a loss should be objectively verifiable. The losses covered should be random or accidental, outside the insured individual's deliberate control. The loss must be meaningful—we don't insure against broken fingernails. The loss must be calculable—it is important to be able to determine the value of the loss in order to reimburse the person who has experienced it. The covered losses have to be limited so no single claim against the insurance pool bankrupts the pool. Finally, the premium for the insurance has to be affordable or no one will buy it.

Insurance principles and retirement plans: Retirement plans pose a particular problem in the context of insurance for a couple of reasons. Events like a house burning down or being involved in an auto accident are relatively rare, and so small premiums can cover significant claims. In the case of retirement, the vast majority of people who reach age 25 live to be old enough to retire. While life expectancies are longer today than they were decades ago, even in the 1940s, most people who reached their mid-20s could expect to reach age 65. The timing of retirement itself is clearly within the individual's own control in many cases. Because of these concerns, President Franklin Roosevelt and some of the architects of Social Security believed that workers' contributions should be "saved" or "reserved" in order to cover their ultimate highly likely claims.

Joint and survivor benefit: An annuity that pays a benefit to the individual who has earned or purchased it based on his or her life expectancy but also pays a survivor benefit to a surviving spouse. The benefit that is paid to the survivor can vary depending on the choice made when an annuitant starts receiving benefits. The added cost of providing the survivor benefit is covered by a marginal reduction in the annuity paid to the person who has purchased or earned it.

Money's worth: A comparison of the lifetime value of contributions on a worker's behalf to a retirement plan and the lifetime value of benefits that the worker will receive from the plan, assuming he or she lives a normal life expectancy.

Net intercohort transfers: The transfer of income or resources from one birth cohort to another. It has been used as a way to see how Social Security has treated various generations of participants in the program.

Normal cost: The share of a worker's lifetime pension benefit that is earned in a particular year.

OASDI: An abbreviation for Old Age, Survivors, and Disability Insurance, which covers the major provisions of Social Security's pension program.

Older Americans Act: An Act adopted by the U.S. Congress in 1965 that listed 10 objectives for older Americans. Among them was the goal that they enjoy an adequate income in accordance with the American standard of living.

Par value bond: A bond whose market value is always equivalent to its face value. These are the sorts of bonds in the Social Security trust funds.

Pay-as-you-go financing: Using current contributions to a retirement system to immediately pay benefits to people already retired.

Pension asset reversion: The process of a defined benefit sponsor taking assets out of a funded pension plan for purposes other than paying pensions to the participants.

Pension Benefit Guaranty Corporation: A government entity created under the Employee Retirement Income Security Act that provides insurance to participants in private defined benefit plans against default risks posed by plan sponsors. It is largely financed by a head tax levied against plan sponsors on the basis of participants in private defined benefit plans.

Pension expense: The calculated cost of sponsoring a pension plan in a given year. Pension accounting focuses on measuring the impact of a pension plan on the earnings and financial condition of the plan's sponsor. The sponsor's "pension cost" is calculated under rules promulgated by the Financial Accounting Standards Board. The expense is to recognize the cost of benefits earned in a given year based on the service of active plan participants, an interest cost that represents the growth in the plan's obligations from one year to the next, the expected return on assets, amortization of prior liabilities that have not been funded, and gains and losses in the plan's operation and valuations.

Pension funding: Putting aside money as workers earn future retirement benefits so the accumulating savings and the interest income they generate will be adequate to finance a worker's retirement benefits by the time he or she retires.

Pension wealth: An estimate of the present value of lifetime pension benefits an individual can expect to receive from a pension plan given a normal life expectancy. For a defined contribution plan, it would equal the amount of the plan balance at the point in time that it was measured.

Ponzi scheme: A 1920 investment scheme in Boston named after its founder, Charles Ponzi (1882–1949), who offered investors large returns on deposits but generated those returns for existing investors from new deposits rather than from returns on the investments themselves. The system collapsed in a few months because new investors could not be found fast enough to keep up with the returns paid to earlier investors.

Primary Insurance Amount: The basic benefit amount computed off of Average Indexed Monthly Earnings to determine a retiree's Social Security benefit. The actual benefit paid will vary based on the age at which the retiree claims it (see Social Security benefit actuarial adjustments).

Projected benefit obligation: The present value of benefits that have been earned by a worker under a defined benefit pension plan based on service up to the time on which the calculation is made and on compensation projected to the time that the benefit will be claimed. It is an estimate of the benefit that will ultimately be paid on the basis of service up to the calculation date.

Regressive tax: A tax that has a higher rate for low-income individuals than it does for those at higher income levels. Since earnings against which the Social Security payroll tax is levied are capped, workers above the earning cap pay a lower average tax rate on their total earnings than workers with earnings below the cap. Thus, the Social Security payroll tax is considered regressive.

Social insurance: A public insurance program that mandates participation for some or all members of a society that covers certain defined "risks" that participants face—such as disability and death when one still has economic dependents—and is financed by "contributions" or "taxes" on the participants.

Social Security Act: The enabling legislation adopted in 1935 that created the Social Security system. It included not only the retirement program that many of us now consider to be Social Security, but also other programs covering welfare benefits for low-income elderly, aid for low-income families with dependent children, and unemployment. The Act has been amended many times over the years—in some cases to expand the protections offered such as those to spouses and survivors in 1939, the disabled in 1957, and Medicare in 1965. Many other amendments over the years have changed contribution rates, covered earnings definitions, adjusted benefit levels, and set other important program parameters.

Social Security benefit actuarial adjustment: Social Security retirement benefits are based on a retiring worker's Primary Insurance Amount. This is the benefit that is payable to an individual retiring at age 66 in 2012. Benefits can be claimed as early as age 62 under the program but are subject to adjustment. Someone who retires at age 62 would have a normal life expectancy that is longer than one retiring at age 66. Because of this, the age 62 benefit is reduced, relative to the Primary Insurance Amount, to a level that, in theory, means the person retiring at age 62 would be paid the same cumulative lifetime benefit as he or she would if retirement was postponed to age 66. The reduction rates are at 6 2/3 percent for each of the 3 years prior to age 66 that someone retires and 5 percent for the fourth year of early retirement. This means a person retiring in 2012 at age 65 will receive a benefit that is 93.3 percent of the Primary Insurance Amount, dropping to 86.7 percent at age 64, 80.0 percent at age 63, and 75 percent at age 62. There is also an actuarial adjustment for people who work beyond age 66 up to age 70. These adjustments are 8 percent per year for each additional year a worker defers claiming Social Security benefits.

Social Security wealth: An estimate of the present value of lifetime Social Security benefits an individual can expect to receive from a pension plan given a normal life expectancy.

Spousal benefit: A benefit added to the program in the 1939 Amendments that provides benefits to spouses of retiring workers who do not work themselves in covered employment. For a worker and spouse claiming Social Security retirement benefits at the same age, the spousal benefit is 50 percent of the benefit paid to the retiring insured worker. If the spouse has earned some benefit on his or her own but that benefit is less than 50 percent of the retiree's benefit then the lower benefit is topped up to the 50 percent level. If a retired worker dies and leaves a spouse, the spouse's benefit is set equal to the retiree's benefit. The spousal and surviving spouse's benefit are subject to actuarial adjustment depending on the age at which they are claimed.

Tax expenditure: The measurement of the foregone tax revenues the government would collect but for special treatment of certain forms of income or deductions from income. For example, the deduction of interest paid on a home mortgage reduces a taxpayer's adjusted gross income and tax liability. This reduction in taxes is considered to be a form of government expenditures by many tax analysts.

Unified budget: The measurement and disclosure of all fiscal operations of the federal government, which consolidates the budgets of all federal governmental entities.

Windfall benefit: A gratuitous retirement benefit that exceeds the economic or actuarial value of workers' contributions or those of their employers on their behalf.

NOTES

PREFACE AND ACKNOWLEDGMENTS

1. Lewis Carroll, *Through the Looking Glass and What Alice Found There* (London: Macmillian, 1871), Chapter 6.

CHAPTER 1

1. *Summary of the 2011 Annual Report of the Board of Trustees of the Federal Old-Age and Survivors Insurance and Federal Disability Insurance Trust Funds*, http://www.ssa.gov/oact/trsum/index.html.
2. U.S. Department of Commerce, Bureau of Economic Analysis, *National Income and Product Accounts*, http://www.bea.gov/national/nipaweb/TableView.asp?SelectedTable=219&Freq=Year&FirstYear=2008&LastYear=2009.
3. Federal Reserve Board, *Flow of Funds*, http://www.federalreserve.gov/datadownload/Download.aspx?rel=Z1&series=51fafe7d7d6e4529e2873545a67534e5&lastObs=25&from=&to=&filetype=csv&label=include&layout=seriesrow&type=package.
4. *National Income and Product Accounts*, http://www.bea.gov/national/nipaweb/TableView.asp?SelectedTable=58&ViewSeries=NO&Java=no&Request3Place=N&3Place=N&FromView=YES&Freq=Year&FirstYear=2009&LastYear=2011&3Place=N&Update=Update&JavaBox=no.
5. U.S. Department of Commerce, Bureau of the Census, table 3, http://www.census.gov/hhes/www/poverty/data/historical/people.html.
6. U.S. Census Bureau, "Income, Poverty and Health Insurance Coverage in the United States: 2009," press release (September 16, 2010), http://www.census.gov/newsroom/releases/archives/income_wealth/cb10-144.html.
7. Murray Gendell, "Older Workers: Increasing Their Labor Force Participation and Hours of Work," *Monthly Labor Review* (January 2008), 42.
8. Paul Taylor and Rich Morin, "Different Age Groups, Different Recessions, Oldest Are Most Sheltered," Pew Research Center, http://pewsocialtrends.org/2009/05/14/different-age-groups-different-recessions.
9. Matthew Ricchiazzi, "To the Worst Generation: Stop Screwing Us Over," *The Cornell Daily Sun* (February 24, 2009), 1.

10. *Summary of the 2010 Annual Report of the Board of Trustees of the Federal Old-Age and Survivors Insurance and Federal Disability Insurance Trust Funds*, http://www.ssa.gov/oact/trsum/index.html.

11. *Summary of the 2011 Annual Report of the Board of Trustees of the Federal Old-Age and Survivors Insurance and Federal Disability Insurance Trust Funds*, http://www.ssa.gov/oact/trsum/index.html.

12. Jerry Geisel, "Caterpillar to Freeze Non-Union Pension Plan," *Chicago Business* (September 1, 2010), http://www.chicagobusiness.com/article/20100901/NEWS05/100909983/caterpillar-to-freeze-non-union-pension-plan#axzz18kIf92pP.

13. Pension Benefit Guaranty Corporation, *Pension Insurance Data Book 2009*, table S-36, http://www.pbgc.gov/docs/2009databook.pdf.

14. Brendan McFarland and Erika Kummernuss, "Pension Freezes Continue Among Fortune 1000 Companies in 2010," *Insider* 20, no. 9 (September 2010): 3, http://www.towerswatson.com/assets/pdf/mailings/September_Insider.pdf.

15. Towers Watson, "Towers Watson-Forbes Insights 2010 Pension Risk Survey," 4, http://www.towerswatson.com/assets/pdf/3220/TowersWatson-Pension-Risk-Survey-Rpt-NA-2010-17315.pdf.

16. U.S. Department of Labor, Employee Benefits Security Administration, "Historical Tables," *Annual Private Pension Plan Bulletin*, http://www.dol.gov/ebsa/publications/form5500dataresearch.html.

17. Ibid.

18. *CBS News*, "State Budgets: The Day of Reckoning," *60 Minutes* (December 19, 2010), http://www.cbsnews.com/stories/2010/12/19/60minutes/main7166220.shtml?tag=contentMain;cbsCarousel.

19. Robert Novy-Marx and Joshua D. Rauh, "The Liabilities and Risks of State Sponsored Pension Plans," *Journal of Economic Perspectives* 23, no. 4 (Fall 2009): 191–210.

20. Social Security Administration, Office of the Historian, Robert M. Ball, Oral History, http://www.socialsecurity.gov/history/orals/ball6.html.

21. Dean R. Leimer, "Cohort-Specific Measures of Lifetime Net Social Security Transfers," ORS Working Paper Series, no. 59 (Washington, D.C.: Social Security Administration, February 1994).

22. Paul A. Samuelson, "An Exact Consumption-Loan Model of Interest with or without the Social Contrivance of Money," *Journal of Political Economy* (December 1958): 467–82.

23. Paul A. Samuelson, "Social Security," *Newsweek* 69, no. 7 (February 12, 1967): 88.

24. Ibid.

25. See, for example, Sylvester J. Schieber and John B. Shoven, *The Real Deal: The History and Future of Social Security* (New Haven: Yale University Press, 1999), which explores at some length the debates and discussions about retirement plan financing that went on in both the political and academic arenas.

26. *1996 Annual Report of the Board of Trustees of the Federal Old-Age and Survivors Insurance and Federal Disability Insurance Trust Funds*, 6.

27. Pub. Law 89–73, July 14, 1965.

28. Franklin Delano Roosevelt, *Message to Congress of 16 January 1939*, http://www.ssa.gov/history/fdrstmts.html#message1.

29. Steven A. Sass, *The Promise of Private Pensions* (Cambridge: Harvard University Press, 1997).

30. *BBC News*, World Edition, "Last Yankee War Widow Dies," http://news.bbc.co.uk/2/hi/americas/2677095.stm.

31. D. C. Bronson, table 6 in "Social Security Act Amendments of 1939, Effects of the Amendments on Benefits and Costs of the Old-Age Insurance Program," attachment to memorandum to Oscar M. Powell, "Fourth Annual Report—Your Memorandum of August 23 to Mr. Williamson," August 31, 1939.

32. Social Security Administration, Office of the Actuary, "Unfunded Obligations and Selected Transition Costs for the Combined Old-Age and Survivors Insurance and Disability Insurance (OASDI) Programs" (unpublished data).

33. Sylvester J. Schieber, Statement before the U.S. House of Representatives' Select Committee on Aging, Subcommittee on Retirement Income and Employment, July 27, 1990.

34. See, for example, Ellen E. Schultz and Theo Francis, "How Lucent's Retiree Programs Cost It Zero, Even Yielded Profit: Trusts Paid the Tab—Till Now; Facing Need to Use Cash, Company Imposes Cuts," *Wall Street Journal*, March 29, 2004, 1; and "Companies Tap Pension Plans to Fund Executive Benefits," *Wall Street Journal*, August 4, 2008, 1.

35. *Summary of the 2011 Annual Report of the Board of Trustees of the Federal Old-Age and Survivors Insurance and Federal Disability Insurance Trust Funds*, http://www.socialsecurity.gov/OACT/TR/2011/lr4b1.html.

36. Dean Baker, "Action on Social Security: The Urgent Need for Delay," Center for Economic and Policy Research policy paper (Washington, D.C., 2010), 2, http://www.cepr.net/documents/publications/ss-2010-11-1.pdf.

37. President William J. Clinton, Speech at Gaston Hall, Georgetown University, Washington, D.C., February 9, 1998, http://www.ssa.gov/history/clntstmts.html.

38. Sylvester J. Schieber and John B. Shoven, *The Real Deal: The History and Future of Social Security* (New Haven: Yale University Press, 1999).

39. Michael Cooper and Mary Williams Walsh, "Alabama Town's Failed Pension Is a Warning," *New York Times*, December 23, 2010, 1, http://www.nytimes.com/2010/12/23/business/23prichard.html?_r=1&ref=us.

CHAPTER 2

1. W. Andrew Achenbaum, *Old Age in the New Land* (Baltimore: Johns Hopkins University Press, 1978).
2. Dora L. Costa, *The Evolution of Retirement* (Chicago: The University of Chicago Press, 1998).
3. Robert L. Clark, Lee A. Craig, and Jack W. Wilson, *A History of Public Sector Pensions in the United States* (Philadelphia: University of Pennsylvania Press, 2003).
4. Clark, Craig, and Wilson, *A History of Public Sector Pensions*, 167–70.
5. Birchard E. Wyatt, "Private Retirement Plans," Ph.D dissertation, Columbia University, New York, 1936), 38.
6. Edward Lazear, "Age, Experience, and Wage Growth," *American Economic Review* 66, no. 4 (September 1976): 548–58.
7. Dora L. Costa, *The Evolution of Retirement*, 90.
8. *Historical Statistics of the United States*, 15.
9. Committee on Economic Security, *Social Security in America* (Washington, D.C.: U.S. Government Printing Office, 1937), 14.
10. William C. Greenough, *It's My Retirement Money: Take Good Care of It* (Homewood, IL: Irwin, 1990).
11. Steven A. Sass, *The Promise of Private Pensions* (Cambridge, MA: Harvard University Press, 1997), 57.
12. Ibid., 58–60.
13. Clark, Craig, and Wilson, *A History of Public Sector Pensions*, 136.
14. Sass, *The Promise of Private Pensions*.
15. Ibid., 65–66.
16. Ibid., 62.
17. John B. Williamson and Fred C. Pampel, *Old-Age Security in Comparative Perspective* (New York: Oxford University Press, 1993), 26–27.
18. Issac M. Rubinow, *Social Insurance*, 15.
19. Sylvester J. Schieber and John B. Shoven, *The Real Deal: The History and Future of Social Security* (New Haven, CT: Yale University Press, 1999), 18.
20. Ibid., chapters 2 and 3.
21. Franklin D. Roosevelt, "Address to Advisory Council of the Committee on Economic Security," (November 14, 1934), http://www.presidency.ucsb.edu/ws/index.php?pid=14777.
22. Social Security Board for the Committee on Economic Security, *Social Security in America* (Washington, D.C.: U.S. Government Printing Office, 1937), 146.
23. W. Andrew Achenbaum, *Old Age in the New Land* (Baltimore: Johns Hopkins University Press: 1978), 129.
24. Arnold J. Toynbee in *Survey of International Affairs 1931* (London: Oxford University Press, 1932), 1.

CHAPTER 3

1. Frances Perkins, *The Roosevelt I Knew* (New York: The Viking Press, 1946), 167.
2. Edward D. Berkowitz, *America's Welfare State, from Roosevelt to Reagan* (Baltimore: Johns Hopkins University Press, 1991), 19.
3. William E. Leuchtenburg, *The FDR Years: On Roosevelt & His Legacy* (New York: Columbia University Press, 1995), 77–80.
4. Frances Perkins, *The Roosevelt I Knew*, 279.
5. Jerry R. Cates, *Insuring Inequality, Administrative Leadership in Social Security, 1934–54* (Ann Arbor: The University of Michigan Press, 1983), 22.
6. Frances Perkins, *The Roosevelt I Knew*, 294.
7. Berkowitz, *America's Welfare State*, 23.
8. Franklin D. Roosevelt, Message to Congress Reviewing the Broad Objectives and Accomplishments of the Administration, June 8, 1934.
9. Ibid.
10. Franklin D. Roosevelt, Executive Order no. 6757, June 29, 1934.
11. Frances Perkins, *The Roosevelt I Knew*, 285.
12. Edwin Witte, *The Development of the Social Security Act*, 12–13.
13. Interview with Arthur J. Altmeyer, Oral History Collection, Columbia University (1967), 192.
14. Theron F. Schlabach, *Edwin E. Witte: Cautious Reformer* (Madison: State Historical Society of Wisconsin, 1969), 220–31.
15. Interview with Barbara N. Armstrong, Oral History Collection, Columbia University (1967), 46, 48.
16. Franklin D. Roosevelt, Address to Advisory Council of the Committee on Economic Security on the Problems of Economic and Social Security, November 14, 1934.
17. Edwin Witte, *The Development of the Social Security Act*, 74.
18. Frances Perkins, *The Roosevelt I Knew* (New York: The Viking Press, 1946), 293.
19. Ibid.
20. Edwin Witte, *The Development of the Social Security Act*, 74–75.
21. Interview with J. Douglas Brown, Oral History Collection, Columbia University (1966), 18.
22. There is a full-blown discussion of the legislative development of the Social Security Act in Edwin Witte, *The Development of the Social Security Act*, 75–108.

CHAPTER 4

1. Senate Report no. 628, 74th Congress, May 13, 1935, 9.
2. Ibid.
3. John T. Flynn, "The Social Security 'Reserve' Swindle," *Harpers* (March 1939): 241.

4. Memorandum from Wilbur J. Cohen to A. J. Altmeyer, Social Security Board Interoffice Communication, "Reserves Vs. Pay-As-You-Go Plan," February 10, 1937.

5. Senator Robert J. Kerrey, CSPAN2 tape of Senate Finance Committee Hearing on Retirement Income Policy, August 1998.

6. Senators Arthur Vandenberg and Dr. Francis Townsend and Representatives Daniel Reed and Thomas Jenkins (quoted in Memorandum from Wilbur J. Cohen to A. J. Altmeyer, Social Security Board Interoffice Communication, "Reserves Vs. Pay-As-You-Go Plan," February 10, 1937).

7. Interview with J. Douglas Brown, Oral History Collection, Columbia University (1966), 19.

8. Interview with Barbara Nachtrieb Armstrong, Oral History Collection, Columbia University (1965), 234–35.

9. Arthur J. Altmeyer, *The Formative Years of Social Security* (Madison: University of Wisconsin Press, 1962), 88–89.

10. Ibid., 89–90.

11. Letter from Franklin D. Roosevelt to Arthur J. Altmeyer, April 28, 1938.

12. Theron F. Schlabach, *Edwin E. Witte, Cautious Reformer* (Madison: State Historical Society of Wisconsin, 1969), 163–64.

13. M. A. Linton, "Observations on the Old Age Security Program Embodied in the Social Security Act," box 199, Edwin E. Witte Papers, University of Wisconsin, Madison, WI.

14. Ibid.

15. Schlabach, *Edwin E. Witte: Cautious Reformer*, 168–71.

16. Edwin E. Witte, "The Concept of Social Insurance," handwritten note to W. Rulon Williamson, August 22, 1938, box 4, Edwin E. Witte Papers, University of Wisconsin, Madison, WI.

17. Martha Derthick, *Policymaking for Social Security* (Washington, D.C.: The Brookings Institution, 1979), 235 (quoting Brown as saying, *"Après nous le deluge"*)

18. Robert J. Myers, "History of Replacement Rates for Various Amendments to the Social Security Act," Memorandum no. 2 (Washington, D.C.: National Commission on Social Security Reform, 1982), 3.

19. Senate Report no. 628, 74th Congress, May 13, 1935, 9; and Senate Report No. 734, 76th Congress, 1st Session, 17.

20. Secretary of Treasury Henry Morgenthau, Jr., Statement before the Ways and Means Committee of the House of Representatives, March 24, 1939.

21. J. Douglas Brown, Statement before the Senate Finance Committee, June 13, 1939, 153–54.

22. Abraham Epstein, "1939 Marks Association's Greatest Victories," *Social Security* (September–October, 1939): 3.

23. Edwin E. Witte, "Social Security—1940 Model," *American Labor Legislation Review* 29, no. 3 (September 1939): 105.

CHAPTER 5

1. Edwin E. Witte, "The 'Bug-A-Boo' of 'The Welfare State,'" address at the Town Hall of Los Angeles, July 25, 1949, National Archives, RG47, MLR 6, Box 27, Records of the Office of the Commissioner.

2. If annual revenues (R) are equal to the number of workers (Nw) paying taxes times the average wages (W) covered under the system times the combined employer and employee tax rate (t) applied to these rates and annual expenditures (E) in these sorts of systems are equal to the number of beneficiaries (Nb) receiving benefits times the average benefits (B) paid to them and R = E, then the tax rate necessary to finance a system of this sort is the product of the ratio of average benefits to average wages times the ratio of beneficiaries to workers paying taxes. Specifically, if: (1) Nw x W x t = Nb x B, and then (2) t = (Nb/Nw) x (B/W).

3. The coverage data for 1940 to 1970 are from the U.S. Bureau of Census, *Historical Statistics of the United States* (Washington, D.C.: Government Printing Office, 1975), 348; and for 1971 to 1979, from the U.S. Bureau of Census, *Statistical Abstract of the United States* (Washington, D.C.: Government Printing Office), various years.

4. Beneficiary data for 1940 to 1969 are from the U.S. Bureau of Census, *Historical Statistics of the United States* (Washington, D.C.: Government Printing Office, 1975), 357; for 1970 from the *Social Security Bulletin* (March 1981), 73; for 1971 to 1974 from the *Social Security Bulletin* (December 1978), 75; and for 1975 to 1979, from the *Social Security Bulletin* (March 1982), 66.

5. The 2007 Annual Report of the Board of Trustees of the Federal Old-Age and Survivors Insurance and Federal Disability Insurance Trust Funds (table IV.B2 for the dependency ratios, Bureau of Labor Statistics for the employment levels, and U.S. Census Bureau for the population estimates of people age 65 and over).

6. Schlabach, *Edwin E. Witte: Cautious Reformer*, 179.

7. D. C. Bronson, table 6 in "Social Security Act Amendments of 1939, Effects of the Amendments on Benefits and Costs of the Old-Age Insurance Program," attachment to Memorandum to Oscar M. Powell, "Fourth Annual Report—Your Memorandum of August 23 to Mr. Williamson," August 31, 1939.

8. Author unknown, "Principles Concerning the Financing of the OAI Program" (paper found in the Social Security History section at the National Archives, Records of the Social Security Board, Chairman's File 1935–1942, Box 98, File 705).

9. D. C. Bronson, Memorandum to Mr. Oscar M. Powell.

10. Letter with attachment from Arthur J. Altmeyer to President Franklin D. Roosevelt, December 4, 1942.

11. Eighth Annual Report of the Social Security Board (October 31, 1943), 30–40.

12. Franklin D. Roosevelt, letter to Honorable Walter F. George, Chairman, Senate Finance Committee, and Honorable Robert L. Doughton, Chairman, House Ways and Means Committee, October 3, 1942.

13. Altmeyer, *The Formative Years of Social Security*, 137–61.

14. Franklin D. Roosevelt, statement accompanying the signing of H.R. 5564, "An Act to fix the tax under the Federal Insurance Contributions Act, on Employer and Employees for calendar year 1945," December 16, 1944.

15. Berkowitz, *America's Welfare State*, 57–61.

16. Edwin E. Witte, "Social Security—1948," in *Social Security Perspectives, Essays by Edwin E. Witte*, ed. Robert J. Lampman (Madison: The University of Wisconsin Press, 1962), 35.

17. J. Douglas Brown, quoted in Berkowitz, *America's Welfare State*, 64.

18. Memorandum from O. C. Pogge, Director of the Bureau of Old-Age and Survivors Insurance to all Bureau employees, July 27, 1950.

19. Social Security Administration, *Social Security Bulletin, Annual Statistical Supplement*, various years.

20. Social Security Administration, *Social Security Bulletin, Annual Statistical Supplement* (1976), 76, 96.

21. Wilbur J. Cohen and Robert J. Myers, "Social Security Act Amendments of 1950: A Summary and Legislative History," *Social Security Bulletin* (October 1950), 1.

22. Social Security Administration, *Social Security Bulletin, Annual Statistical Supplement* (1976), 76, 96; and Social Security Administration, *Social Security Bulletin, Annual Statistical Supplement* (1996), 184, 214.

CHAPTER 6

1. I. S. Falk, "Questions and Answers on Financing of Old-Age and Survivors Insurance," memorandum to Bureau of Old-Age and Survivors Insurance Director O. C. Pogge, February 9, 1945, 16.

2. Robert J. Myers, memorandum to Wilbur J. Cohen, "Relative 'Bargains' under the 1939 Act and under H.R. 2893," February 23, 1949 (Madison: State Historical Society of Wisconsin), Arthur J. Altmeyer papers, box 12, folder 4.

3. Arthur J. Altmeyer, memorandum to the president, July 5, 1939 (Madison: State Historical Society of Wisconsin), Arthur J. Altmeyer papers, box 2.

4. Senator Sheridan Downey, *Congressional Record*, 76th Congress, 3 sess., 1940, 86, pt.14: A1423.

5. The *actuarial value of benefits* is simply the amount of benefits that would be paid to a person based on the accumulated value of his or her contributions plus interest paid out over his or her life expectancy as estimated by actuaries. The estimate of benefits payable is based on the life expectancy for a person with a given set of personal characteristics.

6. While the $18 trillion to $20 trillion range was arrived at independently of the method used by the system's actuaries to estimate accrued liabilities, the estimate that the trust funds today would hold somewhere around $20 trillion if the early beneficiaries had not received the windfall benefits paid to them closely corresponds to the estimated unfunded accrued obligation in the program.

7. Sylvester J. Schieber and John B. Shoven, *The Real Deal: The History and Future of Social Security* (New Haven, CT: Yale University Press, 1999).

8. These prototypical workers are hypothetical individuals that Social Security has used historically to show how the system works and to compare the implications of alternative policies on various participants in the program.

9. In developing our calculations, we assumed that each worker would survive to age 65 and then have a normal life expectancy for his or her birth cohort for people in that cohort who lived to 65. We used government bond rates of return paid on the Social Security trust funds in calculating the accrued contributions for each worker for the years during which he or she was covered.

10. Monthly benefits for 1940 and every five years thereafter were calculated using the Social Security benefit calculator found at: http://www.ssa.gov/OACT; to calculate the present value of the lifetime stream of annual benefits, we used mortality tables provided by the Social Security Administration for cohorts born in 1875 and every fifth year from 1920 to 1995. Mortality tables for the cohorts born in 1880 to 1915 were constructed assuming a linear change in mortality from 1875 to 1920. The interest rate used to discount future benefits to the age of retirement for each cohort was the three-year average of the bond rates for the three years just before retirement.

11. U.S. Department of Labor, Bureau of Labor Statistics, *Handbook of Labor Statistics* (Washington, D.C.: Department of Labor, August 1989), Bulletin 2340, 13, 14, 19, and 20, and http://www.bls.gov/lau/table12full00.pdf.

12. Arthur M. Schlesinger Jr., *The Age of Roosevelt*, vol. 2, *The Coming of the New Deal* (Boston: Houghton Mifflin Co., 1959), 309–10.

13. These prototypical workers are hypothetical individuals that Social Security has used historically to show how the system works and to compare the implications of alternative policies on various participants in the program.

14. In developing our calculations, we assumed that each worker would survive to age 65 and then have a normal life expectancy for his or her birth cohort for people in that cohort who lived to 65. We used government bond rates of return paid on the Social Security trust funds in calculating the accrued contributions for each worker for the years during which they were covered.

15. Monthly benefits for 1940 and every five years thereafter were calculated using the Social Security benefit calculator found at: http://www.ssa.gov/OACT; to calculate the present value of the lifetime stream of annual benefits, we used mortality tables provided by the Social Security Administration for cohorts born in 1875 and every fifth year from 1920 to 1995. Mortality tables for the cohorts born in 1880 to 1915 were constructed assuming a linear change in mortality from 1875 to 1920. The interest rate used to discount future benefits to the age of retirement for each cohort was the three-year average of the bond rates for the three years just before retirement.

CHAPTER 7

1. Charles Schottland, Commissioner of Social Security from 1954 to 1958, makes it clear that he was preoccupied with matters other than Old Age and Survivors Insurance, and that Bob Ball was a strong and able administrator, philosopher, and exponent of the program. While Ball was the number two person in the operation, Schottland shows that he was a stronger, more dominating character than his immediate boss. Schottland also indicates that relations were smooth between him and the Bureau because he left it pretty much alone with Ball in charge. Schottland, Oral History Collection, Columbia University, 1967, 42, 78, 82, 125.

2. Arthur J. Altmeyer, *The Formative Years of Social Security* (Madison: University of Wisconsin Press, 1966), 142–43.

3. Frances Perkins, *The Roosevelt I Knew* (New York: Viking Press, 1946), 283–84.

4. Interview with Wilbur J. Cohen, by David G. McComb for the Lyndon Baines Johnson Library (1968) (quoted in Martha Derthick, *Policymaking for Social Security*, 26).

5. Robert M. Ball, "Policy Issues in Social Security," *Social Security Bulletin* 29 (June 1966): 3–9.

6. Ibid., 8.

7. President's Proposals for Revisions in the Social Security System, hearings before the House Committee on Ways and Means, 90th Congress, 1st session, part 1, 224 (presented in Martha Derthick, *Policymaking for Social Security*, 344).

8. Martha Derthick, *Policymaking for Social Security*, 345; and *Social Security Bulletin, Annual Statistical Supplement* (1996), 34.

9. See Sylvester J. Schieber and John B. Shoven, *The Real Deal: The History and Future of Social Security* (New Haven, CT: Yale University Press, 1999), chapter 10.

10. Derthick, *Policymaking for Social Security*, 346.

11. Paul A. Samuelson, "Social Security," *Newsweek* 69, no. 7 (February 12, 1967): 88.

12. Ibid.

13. 1975 Annual Report of the Board of Trustees of the Federal Old-Age and Survivors Insurance and Disability Insurance Trust Funds.

14. The average monthly wage indexing factors used to calculate this result were taken from the *Annual Statistical Supplement to the Social Security Bulletin* (2005), table 2.A16.

15. Assumptions were taken from the 1972 Annual Report of the Board of Trustees of the Federal Old-Age and Survivors Insurance and Disability Trust Funds; actual experience on prices was calculated from CPI data published by the U.S. Department of Labor, Bureau of Labor Statistics, and the actual growth of U.S. average real earnings was calculated from unpublished data provided by the Social Security Administration, Office of the Actuary.

16. Robert J. Myers, "Pending Legislation Puts Social Security Program on the Threshold of Long Range Expansionist Activities," *Weekly Bond Buyer* (December 27, 1971): 1, 36.

17. Memorandum from William Robinson, to James Schlesinger, Director Bureau of the Budget, Executive Office of the President, and accompanying "Staff Paper on the Implications of Future Changes in Benefit Levels of Social Security," April 29, 1970.

18. Ibid., 1.

19. Ibid., 10.

20. Robert M. Ball, *Managing the Social Security Program* (January 1973), 79–80, http://www.ssa.gov/history/pdf/ballpart4.pdf.

21. John Snee and Mary Ross, "Social Security Amendments of 1977: Legislative History and Summary of Provisions, *Social Security Bulletin*, U.S. Department of Health, Education, and Welfare, March 1978.

22. John Snee and Mary Ross, "Social Security Amendments of 1977: Legislative History and Summary of Provisions, *Social Security Bulletin*, U.S. Department of Health, Education, and Welfare, March 1978, 3–20.

23. Reported in "Social Security Commissioner Calls Improvements in Benefits Unlikely," *New York Times*, July 17, 1979, 10. This material also appears in W. Andrew Achenbaum, *Social Security: Visions and Revisions* (New York: Cambridge University Press, 1986), 69.

24. Assumptions are from the 1977 Annual Report of the Board of Trustees of the Federal Old-Age and Survivors Insurance and Disability Trust Funds; actual experience on prices was calculated from consumer price index data published by the U.S. Department of Labor, Bureau of Labor Statistics, and the actual growth of U.S. average real earnings was calculated from unpublished data provided by the Social Security Administration, Office of the Actuary.

CHAPTER 8

1. *HHS News*, U.S. Department of Health and Human Services, Statement of HHS Secretary Richard S. Schweiker, May 12, 1981.

2. Senator Moynihan (quoted in 1981 *Congressional Quarterly Almanac*, 284).

3. Senator Armstrong (quoted in 1981 *Congressional Quarterly Almanac*, 118).

4. Speaker O'Neill (quoted in "Senate Rejects Reagan Bid to Trim Social Security," *New York Times*, May 21, 1981, B14).

5. Speaker O'Neill (quoted in *Newsweek*, January 24, 1983, 20 [original quote by O'Neill was dated from May 1981]).

6. Charles M. Brain, *Social Security at the Crossroads: Public Opinion and Public Policy* (New York: Garland Publishing, 1991), 81.

7. Paul Light, *Artful Work: The Politics of Social Security Reform* (New York: McGraw-Hill, 1985), 120.

8. Ibid.

9. The Commission consisted of eight Republicans and seven Democrats; most were household names and included Senators Bob Dole (R-KS), Daniel Patrick

Moynihan (D-NY), John Heinz (R-PA), and William Armstrong (R-CO); and Representatives (or former Representatives) William Archer (R-TX), Barber Conable (R-NY), Claude Pepper (D-FL), Martha Keys (D-KS), and Joe Waggonner (D-LA). AFL-CIO chairman Lane Kirkland represented Labor, while business groups had Robert Beck of Prudential, Alexander Trowbridge of the National Association of Manufacturers and Mary Falvey Fuller, a management consultant from California who had been on the 1979 Advisory Council. Robert Ball was a member and served to represent the interests of Tip O'Neill and the Congressional Democrats.

10. W. Andrew Achenbaum, *Social Security: Visions and Revisions* (Cambridge, MA: Cambridge University Press, 1986), 81.

11. Robert Dole, "Reagan's Faithful Allies," *New York Times*, January 3, 1983, 14.

12. They were Republican Congressman Bill Archer from Texas, Republican Senator William Armstrong from Colorado, and former Representative Joe Waggonner, a Democrat from Louisiana who had been appointed to the commission by President Reagan.

13. Ibid., 89.

14. Ibid.

15. "Pension Changes Signed Into Law," *New York Times*, April 21, 1983, A1.

16. Harry C. Ballantyne, "Long-Range Projections of Social Security Trust Fund Operations in Dollars," Social Security Administration, *Actuarial Notes*, no. 117 (October 1983), 2.

17. The marginal effects of each factor can be found in appendix 1 of the *Report of the 1994–1996 Advisory Council on Social Security, Volume I: Findings and Recommendations* (Washington, D.C.: Social Security Administration, 1997), 163–64.

18. Arthur H. Vandenberg, "The $47,000,000,000 Blight," *The Saturday Evening Post* 209, no. 43 (April 24, 1937), 5–7.

19. Ernest F. Hollings, *Congressional Record* (October 13, 1989), S13411.

20. Daniel Patrick Moynihan, *Congressional Record* (October 9, 1990), S14754.

21. Ibid., S14753.

22. Transcript of the meeting of the 1994–1996 Advisory Council on Social Security, February 10–11, 1995, Washington, D.C., 190.

23. Ibid., 248.

24. James K. Glassman, "Moynihan's Social Security Plan," *Washington Post* (March 24, 1998), A19.

25. Social Security Administration, Office of the Historian, Robert M. Ball, Oral History Interview, May 22, 2001, http://www.ssa.gov/history/orals/ball5.html.

26. Ibid.

CHAPTER 9

1. The unified budget consolidates receipts and outlays from federal funds and the Social Security trust fund to create a single measure of the government's fiscal status.

2. President's Commission to Strengthen Social Security, *Strengthening Social Security and Creating Personal Wealth for All Americans: Final Report of the President's Commission to Strengthen Social Security* (Washington, D.C.: U.S. Government Printing Office, 2001), 38.

3. Peter A. Diamond and Peter R. Orszag, *Saving Social Security: A Balanced Approach* (Washington, D.C.: Brookings Institution, 2004), 200–04.

4. Sita Nataraj and John B. Shoven, "Has the Unified Budget Destroyed the Federal Government Trust Funds?" (paper presented at a conference sponsored by the Office of Policy, Social Security Administration, and Michigan Retirement Research Consortium, Washington, D.C., August 12–13, 2004).

5. Barry Bosworth and Gary Burtless, "Pension Reform and Saving" (paper presented at a conference of the International Forum of the Collaboration Projects, Tokyo, Japan, February 17–19, 2004).

6. Unpublished data provided by Social Security Administration, Office of the Chief Actuary, and *2011 Annual Report of the Board of Trustees of the Federal Old-Age and Survivors Insurance and Federal Disability Insurance Trust Funds*, http://www.ssa.gov/oact/trsum/index.html.

CHAPTER 10

1. For anyone interested in the deliberations of the Council, I have summarized my recollections of the proceedings in chapter 17 of Sylvester J. Schieber and John B. Shoven, *The Real Deal: The History and Future of Social Security* (New Haven: Yale University Press, 1999). An independent assessment of the Council's activities can be found in James Edward Gibson III, "The Last Council: Social Security Policymaking as Coalitional Consensus and the 1994–1996 Advisory Council's Institutional Turning Point," unpublished Ph.D dissertation, Virginia Polytechnic Institute and State University, 2007. Gibson conducted lengthy interviews with most of the major contributors to the deliberations within the Advisory Council.

2. *Report of the 1994–1996 Advisory Council on Social Security*, vol. 1, *Findings and Recommendations* (Washington, D.C.: The Social Security Administration, 1997), 2.

3. Dean Baker, "Privatizing Social Security: The Wall Street Fix," Economic Policy Institute Policy Brief 112 (April 29, 1996), http://www.epi.org/publications/entry/issuebriefs_ib112/.

4. Gerald Shea (quoted in Robert Pear, "Panel Advises U.S. to Invest Some Social Security Funds in Stock," *New York Times*, January 7, 1997, A1).

5. Social Security Administration, Office of the Historian, Robert M. Ball, Oral History Interview, http://www.socialsecurity.gov/history/orals/ball6.html.

6. Steven M. Gillon, *The Pact: Bill Clinton, Newt Gingrich, and the Rivalry that Defined a Generation* (Oxford: Oxford University Press, 2008), 194–200.

7. Ibid., 210.

8. Will Marshall (quoted on the back dust jacket of Sylvester J. Schieber and John B. Shoven, *The Real Deal: The History and Future of Social Security* (New Haven, CT: Yale University Press, 1999)).

9. Steven M. Gillon, *The Pact: Bill Clinton, Newt Gingrich, and the Rivalry that Defined a Generation* (Oxford: Oxford University Press, 2008).

10. Ibid., 211–13.

11. Ibid., 215.

12. Douglas W. Elmendorf, Jeffrey B. Liebman, and David W. Wilcox, "Fiscal Policy and Social Security Policy during the 1990s" (Cambridge, MA: National Bureau of Economic Research, September 2001), NBER Working Paper no. w8488, 39.

13. *The Progressive*, "Social Security Hysterics—President Clinton's proposal to privatize Social Security," June 1998, http://findarticles.com/p/articles/mi_m1295/is_n6_v62/ai_20645726/?tag=content;col1.

14. http://www.progressive.org/mission.

15. *The Progressive*, "Social Security Hysterics."

16. Elmendorf et al., "Fiscal Policy during the 1990s," 30.

17. Ibid., 45–46.

18. Steven M. Gillon, *The Pact: Bill Clinton, Newt Gingrich, and the Rivalry that Defined a Generation*, (Oxford: Oxford University Press, 2008), 224.

19. Ibid., 268.

20. Elmendorf et al., "Fiscal Policy during the 1990s," 42–43.

21. Ibid., 43.

22. Ibid.

23. Social Security Administration, Office of the Historian, Robert M. Ball, Oral History Interview, http://www.socialsecurity.gov/history/orals/ball6.html.

24. Transcript of part of the presidential election debate held between George W. Bush and Al Gore, October 4, 2000, http://www.socialsecurity.org/daily/10-04-00.htm.

25. These commercials can be found at http://pcl.stanford.edu/campaigns/2000/gore/index.html.

26. The appointments and charter can be found at http://govinfo.library.unt.edu/csss/index.htm.

27. Joe Conason, Al Franken, and James Roosevelt Jr., *The Raw Deal: How the Bush Republicans Plan to Destroy Social Security and the Legacy of the New Deal* (Sausalito, CA: PoliPointPress, 2005), 52–56.

28. Commission to Strengthen Social Security, *Strengthening Social Security and Creating Personal Wealth for All Americans*, Final Report (December 2001), http://govinfo.library.unt.edu/csss/reports/Final_report.pdf.

29. Peter A. Diamond, "Reducing Benefits and Subsidizing Individual Accounts: An Analysis of the Plans Proposed by the President's Commission to Strengthen Social Security" (Washington, D.C.: Center on Budget and Policy Priorities and New York: The Century Foundation, 2002), table 8.

30. Peter A. Diamond and Peter R. Orszag, "Saving Social Security: The Diamond-Orszag Plan," *The Economists' Voice* 2, no. 1 (2005), http://www.brookings.edu/views/papers/orszag/200504security.pdf.

31. Ibid.

32. Diamond, "Reducing Benefits and Subsidizing Individual Accounts," table 9.

33. *2010 Annual Report of the Board of Trustees of the Federal Old-Age and Survivors Insurance and Disability Insurance Trust Funds,* supplemental table, http://www.socialsecurity.gov/OACT/TR/2010/lr4b10.html.

34. Charles Blahous, *Social Security: The Unfinished Work* (Palo Alto, CA: The Hoover Institute Press, 2010).

35. Elmendorf et al., "Fiscal Policy during the 1990s," 39.

36. Andrew G. Biggs, "Personal Accounts Are No Cure-All," *National Review* (August 30, 2010), http://www.nationalreview.com/articles/print/245052.

37. Found at: http://georgewbush-whitehouse.archives.gov/news/releases/2005/02/20050204-7.html.

CHAPTER 11

1. See, for example, Alan L. Gustman and Thomas L. Steinmeier, "How Effective is Redistribution under the Social Security Benefit Formula?," NBER Working Paper 7597 (Cambridge: National Bureau of Economic Research, 2000); and Jeffrey R. Brown, Julia Lynn Coronado, and Don Fullerton, "Is Social Security Part of the Social Safety Net?," NBER Working Paper 15070 (Cambridge: National Bureau of Economic Research, 2009).

2. Social Security Administration, Office of Retirement and Disability Policy, *Income of the Population 55 or Older* (Washington, D.C.: 2009), table 11.1.

3. Franklin Delano Roosevelt, Message to Congress, 17 March 1935, http://www.ssa.gov/history/fdrstmts.html#message1.

4. Franklin Delano Roosevelt, Radio address on the third anniversary of the adoption of the Social Security Act, August 14, 1938, http://www.ssa.gov/history/fdrstmts.html#message1.

5. Franklin Delano Roosevelt, Message to Congress, January 16, 1939, http://www.ssa.gov/history/fdrstmts.html#message1.

6. Social Security Administration, http://www.ssa.gov/history/oldmans.html, http://www.ssa.gov/history/motherchild.html, and http://www.ssa.gov/history/oldlady.html.

7. W. A. "George" Hale, "The Real Truth about Social Security," http://www.lewrockwell.com/orig5/hale1.html.

8. See, for example, James F. Moore and Olivia S. Mitchell, "Projected Retirement Wealth and Savings Adequacy in the Health and Retirement Study," in *Forecasting Retirement Needs and Retirement Wealth,* ed. Olivia S. Mitchell, P. Brett Hammond, and Anna Rappaport (Philadelphia: University of Pennsylvania

Press, 2000); and James Poterba, Steven Venti, and David A. Wise, "New Estimates of the Future Path of 401(k) Assets," NBER Working Paper 13083 (Cambridge, MA: National Bureau of Economic Research, 2007).

9. Poterba, Venti, and Wise, "New Estimates of the Future Path of 401(k) Assets," 6.

CHAPTER 12

1. William C. Greenough, *It's My Retirement Money* (Homewood, Ill.: Irwin, 1990), 5–16.

2. Murray Webb Latimer, *Industrial Pension Systems in the United States and Canada* (New York: Industrial Relations Counselors, Incorporated, 1932), 35–36.

3. Leslie Hannah, *Inventing Retirement: The Development of Occupational Pensions in Britain* (London: Cambridge University Press, 1986), 24.

4. Steven A. Sass, *The Promise of Private Pensions* (Cambridge, MA: Harvard University Press, 1997), 51.

5. Ibid., 635–36.

6. Ibid., 846–47.

7. Dan M. McGill, *Fundamentals of Private Pensions*, 4th ed. (Homewood, IL: Richard D. Irwin, Inc., 1979), 23–28.

8. Committee on Economic Security, *Social Security in America* (Washington, D.C.: United States Government Printing Office, 1937), 202.

9. Dan M. McGill, *Fundamentals of Private Pensions*, 1st ed. (Homewood, IL: Richard D. Irwin, Inc., 1955), 35.

10. Sylvester J. Schieber and John B. Shoven, *The Real Deal: The History and Future of Social Security* (New Haven, CT: Yale University Press, 1999), 132.

11. J. K. Lasser and Walter Roos, "You Are Richer Than You Think," *Nations Business* (October 1951): 25.

12. Ibid., 84.

13. Marion B. Folsom, Oral History Collection, Columbia University, 1970, 50–51.

14. Sass, *The Promise of Private Pensions*, 118.

15. James A. Wooten, "'The Most Glorious Story of Failure in the Business': The Studebaker-Packard Corporation and the Origins of ERISA," *Buffalo Law Review* 49 (2001): 686–739.

16. U.S. Department of Commerce, Bureau of the Census, *Historical Statistics of the United States* (Washington, D.C.: Government Printing Office, 1975), 132.

17. M. F. Lipton, "Trends in Company Pension Plans," *Studies in Personnel Policy* (National Industrial Conference Board (1944)), no. 67, 8 (quoted in Wooten, "The Most Glorious Story of Failure in the Business," 687).

18. *Inland Steel Company v. United Steel Workers of America* (CIO), 77 NLRB 4 (1948).

19. Wooten, "The Most Glorious Story of Failure in the Business," 687–90.

20. James A. Wooten, *The Employee Retirement Income Security Act of 1974* (Berkeley: University of California Press, 2004), 36–37.

21. The pension participation data are taken from Alfred M. Skolnick, "Private Pension Plans, 1950–1974," *Social Security Bulletin* (June 1976); the employment data for calculating the participation rate was taken from the U.S. Department of Labor, Bureau of Labor Statistics, *1981 Economic Report of the President*, table B-35, 273.

22. Skolnick, Alfred M., "Private Pension Plans, 1950–1974," *Social Security Bulletin* (June 1976), 4.

CHAPTER 13

1. Wooten, *The Employee Retirement Income Security Act of 1974*, 4.

2. Ralph C. James and Estelle D. James, *Hoffa and the Teamsters: A Study of Union Power* (Princeton, N.J.: D. Van Nostrand Company, Inc., 1965), chapters 14, 21.

3. *Encyclopedia Britannica*, http://www.answers.com/topic/jimmy-hoffa.

4. Merton C. Bernstein, *The Future of Private Pensions* (New York: The Free Press of Glenco, 1964), part 2, 51–140.

5. Ibid.

6. Wooten, "The Most Glorious Story of Failure in the Business," 70.

7. Ibid., chapter 2.

8. Ibid., 700–16.

9. Sass, *The Promise of Private Pensions*, 183–184.

10. President's Committee on Corporate Pension Funds and Other Private Retirement and Welfare Programs, "Public Policy and Private Pension Programs: A Report to the President on Private Employee Retirement Plans," January 15, 1965.

11. Wooten, "The Most Glorious Story of Failure in the Business," 80–81.

12. Ibid., 77–78.

13. Ibid., 78–79.

14. Walter J. Blum, "The Effects of Special Provisions in the Income Tax on Taxpayer Morale," in Joint Economic Committee's *Federal Tax Policy for Economic Growth and Stability*, 84th Congress, 1st Session (1955), 250–51.

15. Stanley S. Surrey, speech to Money Marketeers, New York, November 15, 1967.

16. Ibid.

17. Wooten, "The Most Glorious Story of Failure in the Business," 116–65.

18. Ibid., 166.

19. Ibid., 164.

20. Karen W. Ferguson, "Mert Bernstein: Pension Pioneer," *A Tribute to Professor Merton C. Bernstein, Washington University Law School Quarterly* (1993), vol. 71, p. 999.

21. *Time*, "The Press: Who Decides Fairness?" (February 4, 1974), found at: www.time.com/time/magazine/article/0,9171,908437,00.html.

22. Thomas G. Krattenmaker and Lucas A. Powe, Jr., *Regulating Broadcast Programming* (Cambridge, MA: MIT Press, 1994), pp. 264–266.

CHAPTER 14

1. The following brief description of the legislative content of ERISA draws on Dan M. McGill et al., *Fundamentals of Private Pensions* (Philadelphia: University of Pennsylvania Press, 1996), 35–37.

2. U.S. Department of Labor, Pension and Welfare Benefits Administration, *Private Pension Plan Bulletin Historical Tables and Graphs: 1975–2007*, table E-19, http://www.dol.gov/ebsa/pdf/19752007historicaltables.pdf.

3. U.S. Department of Labor, Pension and Welfare Benefits Administration, *Private Pension Plan Bulletin*, http://www.dol.gov/ebsa/pdf/1975-2007historicaltables. pdf.

4. U.S. Department of Labor, Pension and Welfare Benefits Administration, *Private Pension Plan Bulletin*, no. 8 (Spring 1999): 67.

5. U.S. Department of Labor, Pension and Welfare Benefits Administration, *Private Pension Plan Bulletin*, http://www.dol.gov/ebsa/pdf/1975-2007historicaltables. pdf.

6. U.S. Department of Labor, Pension and Welfare Benefits Administration, *Private Pension Plan Bulletin Historical Tables and Graphs: 1975–2007*, table E-19, http://www.dol.gov/ebsa/pdf/1975-2007historicaltables.pdf.

7. Ibid.

8. Watson Wyatt Worldwide, *1983 Survey of Actuarial Assumptions and Funding*, 15, *1986 Survey of Actuarial Assumptions and Funding*, 4, and *1991 Survey of Actuarial Assumptions and Funding*, 4 (Bethesda, MD: Watson Wyatt Worldwide).

9. U.S. Department of Labor, *Private Pension Plan Bulletins Abstract of Form 5500 Annual Reports*, http://www.dol.gov/ebsa/publications/bulletin/tbl_f20.htm.

10. U.S. Department of Labor, *Private Pension Plan Bulletins*, 1975 data is from (1995), no. 4, 63, and 1984 data is from (2001–2002), vol. 11, 83.

11. President's Commission on Pension Policy, *Coming of Age: Toward a National Retirement Income Policy* (Washington, D.C.: Government Printing Office, 1981), 26.

12. Unpublished data from the Department of Treasury, Office of Tax Analysis as published in Alicia H. Munnell, *The Economics of Private Pensions* (Washington, D.C.: Brookings Institution, 1982), 44.

13. U.S. Department of Labor, *Private Pension Plan Bulletins Abstract of Form 5500 Annual Reports*, http://www.dol.gov/ebsa/publications/bulletin/tbl_f20.htm.

14. Munnell, *The Economics of Private Pensions*, 45.

15. Ibid., 60–61.

16. U.S. Office of Management and Budget, *Special Analyses, Budget of the United States Government (various years)* (Washington, D.C.: U.S. Government Printing Office, 1989), 183.

17. For example, see Dan M. McGill et al., *Fundamentals of Private Pensions*, 9th ed. (Oxford: Oxford University Press, 2010), 90–91.

18. This is $5,000 * (1.08)^{15}$ in mathematical terms.

19. This is $5,392.69 \div (1.08)^{15}$ in mathematical terms.
20. Roth 401(k)s are more advantageous because contribution limits for both types of plans are based on contributions to the plans rather than the income used to generate the contributions. It takes more pretax income to generate a $30,000 contribution to a Roth 401(k) than to generate a similar amount to a traditional plan. Because of that mathematical fact, workers contributing to Roth 401(k)s or IRAs are subjecting more of their pretax earnings to the tax-favored treatment offered to tax-qualified plans than those using traditional forms of these plans.
21. Robert L. Clark and Elisa Wolper, "Pension Tax Expenditures: Magnitude, Distribution and Economic Effects" in *Public Policy Toward Pensions*, ed. Sylvester J. Schieber and John B. Shoven, (Cambridge, MA: MIT Press, 1997), 41–84.

CHAPTER 15

1. Office of the Management and Budget, *The President's Budget, Historical Tables* (Washington, D.C.: 2010), table 1.2, http://www.whitehouse.gov/omb/budget/Historicals/.
2. U.S. Office of Management and Budget, *Special Analyses, Budget of the United States Government* (Washington, D.C.: U.S. Government Printing Office, various years from 1980 to 1989).
3. When ERISA was originally passed, section 415 limits allowed the funding of a maximum defined benefit of $75,000 per year or the maximum contribution of $25,000 per year to a defined contribution plan. With the consumer price indexing of these limits, they had grown in lockstep at the three-to-one ratio. Under the Tax Relief Act of 1986, the limit on defined contribution plans was to be frozen until the ratio between the two reached a four-to-one level, at which point the indexing was to again move in lockstep.
4. See Sylvester J. Schieber, "The Evolution and Implications of Federal Pension Regulation," in *The Evolving Pension System*, ed. William G. Gale, John B. Shoven, and Mark J Warshawsky (Washington, D.C.: The Brookings Institution, 2005), 11–50.
5. The Wyatt Company, *The Compensation and Benefits File*, vol. 3, no. 11 (November 1987).
6. Sylvester J. Schieber, "The Employee Retirement Income Security Act: Motivations, Provisions, and Implications for Retirement Security" (paper presented at ERISA After 25 Years: A Framework for Evaluating Pension Reform, conference sponsored by The Brookings Institution, TIAA/CREF and the Stanford Institute for Economic Policy Research, Washington, D.C., August 1999).
7. Ibid.
8. Schieber and Shoven, "The Consequences of Population Aging on Private Pension Fund Saving and Asset Markets," 219–46.
9. Watson Wyatt Worldwide, *Survey of Actuarial Assumptions and Funding* (Arlington, VA: Watson Wyatt Worldwide, 1980).

10. Ibid.
11. Pension Benefit Guarantee Corporation data as published in Mitchell A. Petersen, "Pension Reversions and Worker-Stockholder Wealth Transfers," *The Quarterly Journal of Economics* 107, no. 3 (August 1992): 1036.
12. U.S. Department of Labor, *Private Pension Plan Bulletins*, Historical Tables, http://www.dol.gov/ebsa/pdf/historicaltables.pdf.
13. David A. Cather, Elizabeth S. Cooperman, and Glenn A. Wolfe, "Excess Pension Asset Reversions and Corporate Acquisition Activity," *Journal of Business Research* 23 (1991): 337–48.
14. Mitchell A. Petersen, "Pension Reversions and Worker-Stockholder Wealth Transfers," *The Quarterly Journal of Economics* 107, no. 3 (August 1992): 1033–56.
15. Ibid., 1052.
16. Ibid., 2.

CHAPTER 16

1. U.S. Department of Labor, Pension and Welfare Benefits Administration, *Private Pension Plan Bulletin*, no. 8 (Spring 1999): 78. These pension participation rates are slightly different from those discussed later because of the method under which the two series were developed. The DOL series used here is based on numbers of active participants in private pension plans from Form 5500 filings and estimates of the U.S. workforce, including the unemployed, for the respective years. The later calculations are based on full-time, private-sector workers reporting pension coverage on the Current Population Survey for various years.
2. Edwin C. Hustead, "Trends in Retirement Income Plan Administrative Expenses," in *Living with Defined Contribution Plans: Remaking Responsibility for Retirement*, ed. Olivia S. Mitchell and Sylvester J. Schieber (Philadelphia: The University of Pennsylvania Press, 1998), 171.
3. Robert L. Clark, Janemarie Mulvey, and Sylvester J. Schieber, "Effects of Nondiscrimination Rules on Private Sector Pension Participation," in *Private Pensions and Public Policies*, ed. William G. Gale, John B. Shoven, and Mark Warshawsky (Washington, D.C.: Brookings Institution, 2004), 259–79.
4. U.S. Department of Labor, Pension and Welfare Benefits Administration, *Private Pension Plan Bulletin Historical Tables and Graphs: 1975–2007*, tables E-2 and E-3, http://www.dol.gov/ebsa/pdf/1975-2007historicaltables.pdf.
5. Clark, Mulvey, and Schieber, "Effects of Nondiscrimination Rules on Private Sector Pension Participation," 272.
6. Peter R. Orszag, Comment, in *Private Pensions and Public Policies*, ed. William G. Gale, John B. Shoven, and Mark Warshawsky, (Washington, D.C.: Brookings Institution, 2004), 280–87.

7. Conversion to 2010 dollars used Urban Consumer CPI series from the U.S. Department of Labor, Bureau of Labor Statistics, and pension data from U.S. Department of Labor, Pension and Welfare Benefits Administration, *Private Pension Plan Bulletin Historical Tables and Graphs: 1975–2007*, tables E-8 and E14, http://www.dol.gov/ebsa/pdf/1975-2007historicaltables.pdf.

8. Internal Revenue Code, section 415.

9. For a discussion of this phenomenon, see Steven G. Allen, Robert L. Clark, and Sylvester J. Schieber, "Have Jobs Become Less Stable in the 1990s? Evidence from Employer Data," in *On the Job: Is Long-Term Employment a Thing of the Past*, ed. David Neumark (New York: Russell Sage Foundation, 2000), 196–226.

10. Alan Greenspan, "The Challenge of Central Banking in a Democratic Society," remarks at the Annual Dinner and Francis Boyer Lecture of the American Enterprise Institute, December 5, 1996.

11. Robert J. Shiller, *Irrational Exuberance* (Princeton, NJ: Princeton University Press, 2000).

12. Watson Wyatt Worldwide annual surveys of a sample of plans with more than 1,000 active participants.

13. Richard A. Ippolito, "The Reversion Tax's Perverse Result," *Regulation* 25, no. 1 (Spring 2002): 46–53.

14. Ibid., 51.

15. Ibid., 53.

CHAPTER 17

1. U.S. Department of Commerce, Bureau of Economic Analysis, *National Income and Product Accounts*.

2. Susan Grad, *Income of the Population 55 and Older, 1990*, U.S. Department of Health and Human Services, Social Security Administration (Washington, D.C.: U.S. Government Printing Office, 1992) (reported in Virginia P. Reno, "The Role of Pensions in Retirement Income," *Pensions in a Changing Economy*, ed. Richard V. Burkhauser and Dallas L. Salisbury (Washington, D.C.: The Employee Benefit Research Institute, 1993), 21.

3. Bureau of Economic Analysis, U.S. Department of Commerce, *Survey of Current Business* 74, no. 7 (July 1994): 77, 92.

4. Sylvester J. Schieber, "Why Do Pension Benefits Seem So Small?" *Benefits Quarterly* 11, no. 4 (Fourth Quarter 1995): 57–70.

5. Ibid., 61.

6. Note this is a slightly different definition of filing unit than Susan Grad used in developing her analysis. In her work, Grad also included people over 65 who were living in extended family arrangements where the elderly person was not the head of the family unit or married to the head of the family unit. She also

considered the income available to other members of the family unit in these cases as providing support to the elderly person in the extended family.

7. Sylvester J. Schieber, "Why Do Pension Benefits Seem So Small?" 62.
8. Pension Benefit Guaranty Corporation, *Pension Insurance Data Book*, various years, http://www.pbgc.gov/publications/default.htm.
9. Federal Reserve Board, *Flow of Funds*, http://www.federalreserve.gov/apps/fof/DisplayTable.aspx?t=l.225.i.
10. James M. Poterba, Steven F. Venti, and David A. Wise, "Personal Retirement Saving Programs and Asset Accumulation: Reconciling the Evidence," Working Paper no. 5599 (National Bureau of Economic Research, 1996).
11. Steven F. Venti and David A. Wise, "Have IRAs Increased U.S. Saving: Evidence from Consumer Expenditure Surveys," *Quarterly Journal of Economics* 105 (August 1990): 661–98.
12. Ibid., 692.
13. Ibid., 691–92.
14. William G. Gale and John Karl Scholz, "IRAs and Household Saving," *American Economic Review* 84, no. 5 (December 1994): 1233–60.
15. Eric M. Engen, William G. Gale, and John Karl Scholz, "The Illusory Effects of Saving Incentives on Saving," *Journal of Economic Perspectives* 10, no. 4 (Fall 1996): 113–38.
16. James M. Poterba, Steven F. Venti, and David A. Wise, "How Retirement Saving Programs Increase Saving," *Journal of Economic Perspectives* 10, no. 4 (Fall 1996): 91–112.
17. Mathew Sobek, "New Statistics on the U.S. Labor Force, 1950–1990," *Historical Methods* 34 (2001): 71–87, table 9.
18. McGill et al., *Fundamentals of Private Pensions*, 9th ed., 38–39.
19. *2010 Annual Report of the Board of Trustees of the Federal Old-Age and Survivors Insurance and Disability Insurance Trust Funds*, supplemental table, www.socialsecurity.gov/OACT/TR/2010/lr4b2.html.
20. Diane J. Macunovich, *Birth Quake* (Chicago: University of Chicago Press, 2000).
21. Ibid.
22. Ibid.
23. For example, see Gary Burtless and Robert A. Moffitt, "The Effect of Social Security Benefits on the Labor Supply of the Aged," in *Retirement and Economic Behavior*, ed. Henry J. Aaron and Gary Burtless (Washington, D.C.: The Brookings Institution, 1984); Peter A. Diamond and Jerry A. Hausman, "The Retirement and Unemployment Behavior of Older Men," in *Retirement and Economic Behavior*; Gary S. Fields and Olivia S. Mitchell, *Retirement, Pensions, and Social Security* (Cambridge, MA: MIT Press, 1984); Jerry A. Hausman and David A. Wise, "Social Security, Health Status and Retirement," in *Pensions, Labor, and Individual Choice*, ed. David A. Wise (Chicago: University of Chicago Press, 1985); Gary Burtless, "Social Security, Unanticipated Benefit Increases and the Timing of Retirement," *Review of Economic Studies* 53 (1986): 781–805; Alan L. Gustman and

Thomas L. Steinmeier, "A Structural Retirement Model," *Econometrica* 54 (1986): 555–84; and Glenn T. Sueyoshi, "Social Security and the Determinants of Full and Partial Retirement: A Competing Risks Analysis," Working Paper no. 3113 (Cambridge, MA: National Bureau of Economic Research, 1989).

24. See, for example, D. Bell and W. Barclay, "Trends in Retirement Eligibility and Pension Benefits, 1974–1983," *Monthly Labor Review* 110 (April 1987): 18–25; Edward Lazear, "Pensions as Severance Pay," in *Financial Aspects of the United States Pension System,* ed. Zvi Bodie and John B. Shoven (Chicago: University of Chicago Press, 1983), 57–89; and Olivia S. Mitchell and Rebecca A. Luzadis, "Changes in Pension Incentives Through Time," *Industrial and Labor Relations Review* 42, no. 1 (1988): 100–08.

25. Richard A. Ippolito, "Toward Explaining Earlier Retirement after 1970," *Industrial and Labor Relations Review* 43, no. 5 (July 1990): 556–69; see esp. table 2.

26. In addition to some of the research cited earlier throughout this chapter, see Richard V. Burkhauser, "The Pension Acceptance Decision of Older Workers," *Journal of Human Resources* 14, no. 1 (1979): 63–75; Roger H. Gordon and Alan S. Blinder, "Market Wages, Reservation Wages, and Retirement Decisions," *Journal of Public Economics* 14 (October 1980): 277–308; Joseph F. Quinn, "Microeconomic Determinants of Early Retirement: A Cross-Sectional View of White Married Men," *Journal of Human Resources* 12 (Summer 1977): 329–46; and Rebecca A. Luzadis and Olivia S. Mitchell, "Explaining Pension Dynamics," *Journal of Human Resources* 26, no. 4 (1991): 679–703.

27. Tabulations of the U.S. Census Bureau's *Current Population Survey,* various years.

28. Ibid.

29. Ibid.

30. Paul A. Samuelson, "Social Security," *Newsweek* 69, no. 7 (February 12, 1967): 88.

CHAPTER 18

1. Federal Reserve Board, *Flow of Funds,* https://www.federalreserve.gov.

2. Based on tabulations of Compustat U.S. disclosure database compiled from annual financial reports filed with the U.S. Securities and Exchange Commission.

3. Ibid.

4. Pension Benefit Guaranty Corporation, http://www.pbgc.gov/res/factsheets/page/pbgc-facts.html.

5. Pension Benefit Guaranty Corporation, *Pension Insurance Data Book,* various years, http://www.pbgc.gov/practitioners/plan-trends-and-statistics/content/page13270.html.

6. Ibid.

7. Pension Benefit Guaranty Corporation, *Pension Insurance Data Book,* 2009, http://www.pbgc.gov/practitioners, 43 and 79.

8. Ibid.

9. Ibid.

10. Ibid.

11. Ibid., 105.

12. Ibid., 108.

13. U.S. Department of Labor, Employee Benefits Security, *Private Pension Plan Bulletin Historical Tables and Graphs*, 13, http://www.dol.gov/ebsa/pdf/historicaltables.pdf.

14. Pension Benefit Guaranty Corporation, *Pension Insurance Data Book*, 97.

15. Pension Benefit Guaranty Corporation, *PBGC's Guarantee Limits: An Update* (2008), http://www.pbgc.gov/documents/guaranteelimits.pdf.

16. Dan M. McGill et al., *The Fundamentals of Private Pensions*, 8th ed. (Oxford: Oxford University Press, 2005), chapter 16.

17. For an extended discussion on this point, see Robert L. Clark and Sylvester J. Schieber, "Taking the Subsidy Out of Early Retirement: Converting to Hybrid Pensions," in *Innovations in Retirement Financing*, ed. Olivia S. Mitchell, Zvi Bodie, and P. Brett Hammond (Philadelphia: University of Pennsylvania Press and the Pension Research Council, 2002), 149–174; and Robert L. Clark and Sylvester J. Schieber, "An Empirical Analysis of the Transition to Hybrid Pension Plans in the United States," in *Public Policies and Private Pensions*, ed. William Gale, John Shoven, and Mark Warshawsky (Washington, D.C.: The Brookings Institution, 2004), 11–42.

18. See *Cooper v. IBM*, 274 F. Supp. 2d 1010 (S.D. I11 2003).

19. Pension Benefit Guaranty Corporation, *Pension Insurance Data Book 2004*, 60.

20. *Cooper v. IBM Personal Pension Plan*, 457 F.3rd 636 (7th Cir. 2006).

21. Pension Benefit Guaranty Corporation, *Pension Insurance Data Book 2009*, 73–74.

22. Ibid., 75–76.

23. Brendan McFarland and Erika Kummernuss, "Pension Freezes Continue among Fortune 1000 Companies in 2010," *Insider* (September 2010), http://www.towerswatson.com/united-states/newsletters/insider/2761.

24. Brendan McFarland, Towers Watson, previously unpublished tabulations from the authors on the firms in lists for all seven *Fortune 1000* lists from 2004 through 2010.

25. General Accountability Office (GAO), *Defined Benefit Pensions: Plan Freezes Affect Millions of Participants and May Pose Retirement Income Challenges*, Report GAO-08-817 (Washington, D.C.: GAO, 2008).

26. Form 5500 is the federal pension disclosure form that pension plan sponsors must submit to the IRS and Department of Labor each year to report their tax-qualified plan details.

27. GAO, *Defined Benefit Pensions: Survey Results of the Nation's Largest Private Defined Benefit Plan Sponsors*, Report GAO-09-291 (Washington, D.C.: GAO, 2009).

28. McGill et al., *Fundamentals of Private Pensions*, 9th ed., 625.

29. Ibid., 635.

30. Sylvester J. Schieber, "Prepared Statement before the Subcommittee on Retirement Income and Employment," Select Committee on Aging, U.S. House of Representatives, July 27, 1990.

CHAPTER 19

1. U.S. Department of Labor, Pension and Welfare Benefits Administration, *Private Pension Plan Bulletin Historical Tables and Graphs: 1975–2007*, tables E-8 and E14, http://www.dol.gov/ebsa/pdf/1975-2007historicaltables.pdf.

2. Conference Report 93–1280, 305.

3. See http://en.wikipedia.org/wiki/Black_Monday_(1987).

4. U.S. Department of Labor, Pension and Welfare Benefits Administration, *Private Pension Plan Bulletin Historical Tables and Graphs: 1975–2007*, various tables, http://www.dol.gov/ebsa/pdf/1975-2007historicaltables.pdf.

5. Ibid.

6. Ibid.

7. Richard R. Hinz and John A. Turner, "Pension Coverage Initiatives: Why Don't Workers Participate?" in *Living With Defined Contribution Pensions: Remaking Responsibility for Retirement*, ed. Olivia S. Mitchell and Sylvester J. Schieber (Philadelphia: University of Pennsylvania Press, 1997), 17–37.

8. For example, see Robert L. Clark and Sylvester J. Schieber, "Factors Affecting Participation Rates and Contribution Levels in 401(k) Plans," in *Living With Defined Contribution Pensions: Remaking Responsibility for Retirement*, 169–97.

9. Bridgette C. Madrian and Dennis F. Shea, "The Power of Suggestion: Inertia in 401(k) Participation and Savings Behavior," *Quarterly Journal of Economics* 116, no. 4 (November 2001): 1149–87.

10. Ibid.

11. Ibid.

12. Ibid.

13. See, for example, James Choi et al., "Defined Contribution Pensions: Plan Rules, Participant Decisions and the Path of Least Resistance," in *Tax Policy and the Economy*, ed. James M. Poterba, vol. 16 (Cambridge: MIT Press, 2002), 67–113; and John Beshears et al., "For Better or Worse: Default Effects and 401(k) Savings Behavior," in *Perspectives on the Economics of Aging*, ed. David A. Wise (Chicago: University of Chicago Press, 2004), 81–121; "The Importance of Default Options for Retirement Savings Outcomes: Evidence from the United States," NBER Working Paper 12009 (Cambridge, MA: National Bureau of Economic Research, 2006), http://www.nber.org/papers/w12009; "Simplification and Saving," NBER Working Paper 12659 (Cambridge, MA: National Bureau of Economic Research, 2006), http://www.nber.org/papers/w12659; and "The Impact of Employer Matching on Savings Plan Participation under Automatic Enrollment," NBER Working Paper 13352 (Cambridge, MA: National Bureau of Economic Research, 2007), http://www.nber.org/papers/w13352.

14. Richard Thaler and Shlomo Benartzi, "Save More Tomorrow: Using Behavioral Economics to Increase Employee Saving," *Journal of Political Economy* 112, no. 1 (2004): pt. 2, S164–87.

15. B. Douglas Bernheim, "Financial Illiteracy, Education, and Retirement Saving," in *Living With Defined Contribution Pensions: Remaking Responsibility for Retirement*, ed. Olivia S. Mitchell and Sylvester J. Schieber (Philadelphia: University of Pennsylvania Press, 1997), 38–68.

16. Aaron Smith, "More Employers Make 401(k) Enrollment Automatic," *CNN Money* (August 24, 2010), http://money.cnn.com/2010/08/24/news/economy/schwab_401k_retirement/index.htm.

17. Fidelity Investments, "Evaluating Auto Solutions," *Fidelity Perspectives* (Summer 2009), 5.

18. Vanguard, *How America Saves 2009*, https://institutional.vanguard.com/iam/pdf/HAS09.pdf, 18,.

19. Fidelity Investments, "Evaluating Auto Solutions," 5.

20. Ibid., 5–11.

21. Madrian and Shea, "The Power of Suggestion," table 2.

22. Ibid; and James Choi et al., "Optimal Defaults and Active Decisions," NBER Working Paper 11074 (2005).

23. Alicia H. Munnell et al., "Investment Returns: Defined Benefit vs. 401(k) Plans," Issue Brief no. 52 (Boston: Boston College Center for Retirement Research, 2006).

24. Fidelity Investments, "Evaluating Auto Solutions," 13.

25. Federal Reserve Board, *Flow of Funds*, https://www.federalreserve.gov.

26. James H. Moore Jr. and Leslie A. Muller, "An Analysis of Lump-Sum Pension Distribution Recipients," *Monthly Labor Review* (May 2002), 31.

27. Alicia H. Munnell et al., "An Update on 401(k) Plans: Insights from the 2007 Survey of Consumer Finance," CRR Working Paper 2009–26 (Boston: Center for Retirement Research at Boston College, 2009), 32.

28. Andrew A. Samwick and Jonathan Skinner, "How Will 401(k) Pension Plans Affect Retirement Income?," *American Economic Review* 94 (March 2004): 329–43.

29. Ibid.

30. James M. Poterba, Steven F. Venti, and David A. Wise, "Rise of 401(k) Plans, Lifetime Earnings, and Wealth at Retirement," NBER Working Paper 13091 (Cambridge: National Bureau of Economic Research, 2007), http://www.nber.org/papers/w13091.

CHAPTER 20

1. Pew Center on States, *The Trillion Dollar Gap: Underfunded State Retirement Systems and the Roads to Reform* (Philadelphia: The Pew Center on States, 2010).

2. For example, see Jeffrey R. Brown and David W. Wilcox, "Discounting State and Local Pension Liabilities," *American Economic Review* 99, no. 2 (2009): 538–42; Robert Novy-Marx and Joshua D. Rauh, "The Liabilities and Risks of State Sponsored Pension Plans," *Journal of Economic Perspectives* 23, no. 4 (Fall 2009): 191–210; and Andrew G. Biggs, "Public Pensions Cook the Books," *Wall Street Journal*, July 6, 2010, A13.

3. U.S. Census Bureau, *2008 Survey of State and Local Public Employee Retirement Systems*, http://www.census.gov/govs/retire/.

4. Ibid.

5. Government Accountability Office, *State and Local Governments' Fiscal Outlook*, GAO-10-358 (Washington, D.C.: GAO, 2010), 11.

6. National Association of State Retirement Administrators, "Myths and Misperceptions of Defined Benefit and Defined Contribution Plans" (NASRA White Paper, February 2005), http://www.nasra.org/resources/myths%20and%20misperceptions.pdf, 3.

7. Robert L. Clark, Lee A. Craig, and John Sabelhaus, *State and Local Retirement Plans in the Twentieth Century* (Northampton, MA: Elgar Publishing, 2010), chapter 10.

8. For example, see Cynthia Moore, *Is Your Pension Protected? A Compilation of Constitutional Pension Protections for Public Educators* (Washington, D.C.: American Association of Retired Persons, 2000).

9. Sharon P. Smith, "Government Wage Differentials by Sex," *Journal of Human Resources* 11, no. 2 (1976): 185–99.

10. James M. Poterba and Kim S. Rueben, "The Distribution of Public Sector Wage Premia: New Evidence Using Quantile Regression Methods," Working Paper 4734 (Cambridge, MA: National Bureau of Economic Research, 1994).

11. Keith A. Bender and John S. Heywood, "Out of Balance: Comparing Public and Private Compensation over 20 Years," (National Institute on Retirement Security and Center for State & Local Government Excellence, 2010).

12. Ibid.

13. Bureau of Labor Statistics, "Employer Costs for Employee Compensation," news release, June 9, 2010, http://www.bls.gov/news.release/ecec.nr0.htm.

14. Andrew G. Biggs, "Are Government Workers Underpaid? No," *The American* (June 9, 2010), http://www.american.com/archive/2010/june-2010/are-government-workers-underpaid-no.

15. Sylvester J. Schieber, "Political Economy of Public Sector Retirement Plans," *Journal of Pension Economics and Finance* 10, no. 2 (April 2011): 269–89.

16. Mary Williams Walsh and Amy Schoenfeld, "Padded Pensions Add to New York Fiscal Woes," *New York Times*, May 20, 2010, A1.

17. Michael W. Grynbaum, "$239,000 Conductor among M.T.A.'s 8,000 Six-Figure Workers," *New York Times*, June 2, 2010, A1.

18. Fred Grimm, "Compensation Issues Demand Miami's Attention," *Miami Herald*, September 1, 2010, http://www.miamiherald.com/2010/09/01/1803902/grimm-compensation-issues-demand.html.

19. Craig Karmin, "Pension Calculus Draws New Scrutiny," *Wall Street Journal*, July 20, 2009, http://online.wsj.com/article_email/SB124804047828063059-lMyQjAxMDI5NDI4MDAyNDAwWj.html.

20. *Chicago Sun Times*, "A Year after Retiring, Jones to Get 51% Boost," September 11, 2009, http://www.suntimes.com/news/politics/1764559,CST-NWS-pension-jones11.article.

21. http://www.honda-tech.com/showthread.php?t=2611207.

22. Pew Center on States, *The Trillion Dollar Gap: Underfunded State Retirement Systems and the Roads to Reform* (Philadelphia: The Pew Center on States, 2010).

23. Governmental Accounting Standards Board, Statement No. 25, *Financial Reporting for Defined Benefit Pension Plans and Note Disclosures for Defined Contribution Plans.*

24. Robert Novy-Marx and Joshua D. Rauh, "Public Pension Promises: How Big Are They and What Are They Worth?" *Journal of Finance,* (forthcoming), http://www.kellogg.northwestern.edu/faculty/rauh/.

25. F. Modigliani and M. H. Miller, "The Cost of Capital, Corporate Finance and the Theory of Investment," *American Economic Review* 48 (1958): 261–97; M. H. Miller and F. Modigliani, "Dividend Policy, Growth and the Valuation of Shares," *Journal of Business* 34 (1961): 411–13; and F. Modigliani and M. H. Miller, "Corporate Income Taxes and the Cost of Capital: A Correction," *American Economic Review* 53 (1963): 433–43.

26. Cynthia Moore, Nancy H. Aronson, and Annette S. Norman, *Is Your Pension Protected? A Compilation of Constitutional Pension Protections for Public Educators* (Washington, D.C.: American Association of Retired Persons, 2000).

27. Morrison & Foerster, LLP, and Greenebaum Doll & McDonald, PLLC, "Index by States" (2007), http://finance.ky.gov.NR/rdonlyres/275A2978-5DDE-4138-A7F5-AF02D17D7F97/0/State-bystatememo10.pdf.

28. Jeffrey R. Brown and David W. Wilcox, "Discounting State and Local Pension Liabilities," *American Economic Review* 99, no. 2 (2009): 538–42.

29. Novy-Marx and Rauh, "Public Pension Promises."

30. Robert Novy-Marx and Joshua D. Rauh, "The Crisis in Local Government Pensions in the United States," http://www.kellogg.northwestern.edu/faculty/rauh/.

31. For example, see Norman L. Jones, Brian M. Murphy and Paul Zorn, "Actuarial Methods and Public Pension Funding Objectives: An Empirical Examination" (paper presented at the Society of Actuaries Public Pension Finance Symposium, May 2009), http://www.soa.org/files/pdf/2009-chicago-ppf-paper-jones-zorn-murphy.pdf.

32. Governmental Accounting Standards Board, *Preliminary Views of the Governmental Accounting Standards Board on Major Issues Related to Pension Accounting and Financial Reporting by Employers* (June 2010), 16–17.

33. Joshua D. Rauh, "Are State Public Pensions Sustainable?" (2010), 26–27, http://ssrn.com/abstract=1596679.

34. Joseph Heller, *Catch-22* (New York: Simon and Schuster, 1961).

35. Daniel W. Hynes, "Pension Obligation Bonds, A Four-Year Review" (2007), http://www.comptroller.state.il.us/FiscalFocus/article.cfm?ID=286.

36. Barry B. Burr, "Another Round of Pension Bonds for Illinois Possible," *Pensions and Investments* (July 1, 2010), http://www.pionline.com/apps/pbcs.dll/article?AID=/20100701/DAILYREG/100709979/1034/PIDailyUpdate&issued ate=20100701.

37. Ibid.
38. CBS News, "State Budgets: The Day of Reckoning," *60 Minutes* (December 19, 2010), http://www.cbsnews.com/stories/2010/12/19/60minutes/main7166220. shtml?tag=contentMain;cbsCarousel.
39. Alicia H. Munnell et al., "Pension Obligation Bonds: Financial Crisis Exposes Risks," CRR Brief no. 19, 2 (Boston: Center for Retirement Research, 2009).
40. Amy B. Monahan, "Public Pension Plan Reform: The Legal Framework," *Education Finance and Policy* (2010), 622.
41. Ibid..
42. Ibid., 629.
43. Stephen C. Fehr, "States Tackling Public Employee Retirement Benefits in 2010," *Stateline.org* (February 19, 2010), http://www.stateline.org/live/details/ story?contentId=461796.
44. Ibid.
45. Joseph Lawler, "Another Look at Reform in New Jersey," *The American Spectator* (September 20, 2010), http://spectator.org/blog/2010/09/20/another-look-at-reform-in-new.
46. For the fact sheet prepared by the Governor's Office, see http://www.state.nj.us/ governor/news/news/552010/pdf/20100914_Fact_Sheet_Pension.pdf.
47. Administrator, "Details of N.J. Public Worker Pension and Health Benefits Reform Bill," www.pension.net (June 19, 2011), http://pensioned.net/2011/ details-of-n-j-public-worker-pension-and-health-benefits-reform-bill/.
48. Lisa Fleisher, "Governor Christie Outlines Cuts to N.J. Workers' Pension Benefits" (September 15, 2010), http://www.nj.com/news/index.ssf/2010/09/gov_ christie_outlines_cuts_to.html.
49. Michael Symons, "NJ Pension Reform Act Target of Lawsuit by 26 Unions," *Asbury Park Press* (September 1, 2011), http://www.app.com/article/20110901/ NJNEWS11/309010016/NJ-pension-reform-act-target-lawsuit-by-26-unions.
50. Office of Management and Budget, *Budget of the United States Government, Fiscal Year 2010: Analytical Perspectives* (2009), 345.
51. U.S. Department of Defense, *Valuation of the Military Retirement System* (December 2010), table 9, 19.

CHAPTER 21

1. Benjamin D. Sommers, "Who Really Pays for Health Insurance? The Incidence of Employer-Provided Health Insurance with Sticky Nominal Wages," *International Journal of Health Care Finance and Economics* 5 (2005): 89–118; and Katherine Baicker and Amitabh Chandra, "The Labor Market Effects of Rising Health Insurance Premiums," NBER Working Paper No. 11160 (Cambridge, MA: National Bureau of Economic Research, 2005).

2. Steven A. Nyce and Sylvester J. Schieber, "Treating Our Ills and Killing Our Prospects" (paper presented at Controlling Costs: The Price of Good Health, conference sponsored by the Coalition for Affordable Health Care and the U.S. Chamber of Commerce, Washington, D.C., July 12, 2011), www.ThePredictableSurprise.com.

3. Steven A. Nyce and Sylvester J. Schieber, "Health Care Inflation, Must Workers Bear the Brunt," *Milken Institute Review* (Second Quarter 2010): 46–57.

4. Nyce and Schieber, "Treating Our Ills and Killing Our Prospects."

5. T. Lynn Fisher, "Estimates of Unreported Asset Income in the Survey of Consumer Finances and the Relative Importance of Social Security Benefits to the Elderly," *Social Security Bulletin* 67, no. 2 (February 2007): 47–53.

6. Towers Watson, *Accounting for Pensions and Other Postretirement Benefits, 2010 Reporting Under U.S. GAAP Among the Fortune 1000* (Towers Watson, 2010), http://www.towerswatson.com/assets/pdf/3178/TW-AcctngForPension-NA-2010-17799_perspective-EF.pdf, 12.

7. U.S. Department of Labor, Pension and Welfare Benefits Administration, *Private Pension Plan Bulletin Historical Tables and Graphs: 1975–2007*, table E-19, http://www.dol.gov/ebsa/pdf/1975-2007historicaltables.pdf.

CHAPTER 22

1. See table 3 at: http://www.census.gov/hhes/www/poverty/data/historical/people.html.

2. Bob Adelmann, "Social Security: No COLA for You," *New American* (October 18, 2010), http://www.thenewamerican.com/index.php/usnews/politics/49Figure 24-social-security-no-cola-for-you.

3. U. S. Census Bureau, press release, "Income, Poverty and Health Insurance Coverage in the United States: 2009" (September 16, 2010), http://www.census.gov/newsroom/releases/archives/income_wealth/cb10-144.html.

4. Alan Gustman, Thomas Steinmeier, and Nahid Tabatabai, *Pensions in the Health and Retirement Study* (Cambridge, MA: Harvard University Press, 2010).

5. Ibid., 170.

6. John R. Woods, "Pension Benefits among the Aged: Conflicting Measures, Unequal Distributions," *Social Security Bulletin* 59, no. 3 (Fall 1996): 3–30.

7. Ibid., 25–26.

8. Barry Bosworth and Gary Burtless, "Capital Income Flows and the Relative Well-Being of the Elderly" (paper presented at Challenges and Solutions for Retirement Security, 9th Annual Joint Conference of the Retirement Research Consortium, Washington, D.C., August 9–10, 2007), 1.

9. Gustman, Steinmeier, and Tabatabai, *Pensions in the Health and Retirement Study*, 178–279.

CHAPTER 23

1. Annamaria Lusardi, Olivia S. Mitchell, and Vilsa Curto, "Financial Literacy and Financial Sophistication in the Older Population: Evidence from the 2008 HRS," Working Paper WP 2009–216 (Ann Arbor: University of Michigan Retirement Research Center, 2009).

2. Ibid.

3. Tara L. Queen and Thomas M. Hess, "Age Differences in the Effects of Conscious and Unconscious Thought in Decision Making, Psychology and Aging" *Psychology and Aging* 25, no. 2 (June 2010): 251–61.

4. *Science Daily*, "Age Doesn't Necessarily Affect Decision Making, Study Shows," June 29, 2010, http://www.sciencedaily.com/releases/2010/06/100629094147. htm.

5. Ibid.

6. See a summary of the literature by Jeffrey R. Brown, "Rational and Behavioral Perspectives on the Role of Annuities in Retirement Planning," NBER Working Paper 13537 (Cambridge, MA: National Bureau of Economic Research, 2007).

7. Jeffrey R. Brown et al., *The Role of Annuity Markets in Financing Retirement* (Cambridge, MA: The MIT Press, 2001), 18–19.

8. Ibid., 72.

9. Ibid., 96.

10. Jeffrey R. Brown et al., "Why Don't People Insure Late Life Consumption? A Framing Explanation of the Under-Annuitization Puzzle," NBER Working Paper 13748 (Cambridge, MA: National Bureau of Economic Research, 2008).

11. Ibid.

12. Ibid.

13. William G. Gale et al., "Increasing Annuitization in 401(k) Plans with Automatic Trial Income," paper no. 2008–2 (Washington, D.C.: The Retirement Security Project, 2008).

14. White House Task Force on Middle-Class Working Families, "Fact Sheet: Supporting Middle Class Families" (January 2010), http://www.whitehouse.gov/ sites/default/files/Fact_Sheet-Middle_Class_Task_Force.pdf.

15. Jeffrey R. Brown, "Automatic Lifetime Income as the Path to Retirement Income Security," Colloquium on Tax Policy and Public Finance, Spring 2010, New York, NYU Law School, February 2010.

16. *Federal Register* 75, no. 21 (February 2, 2010): 5253–58, http://webapps.dol.gov/ FederalRegister/HtmlDisplay.aspx?DocId=23512&AgencyId=8&DocumentT ype=1.

17. See http://www.dol.gov/ebsa/pdf/1210-AB33-356.pdf.

18. Craig Copeland, "IRA Balances and Contributions: An Overview of the EBRI IRA Database" Issue Brief no. 346 (September 2010): 9.

19. Brendan McFarland and Mark J. Warshawsky, "Balances and Retirement Income from Individual Accounts: U.S. Historical Simulations," *Benefits Quarterly* (Second Quarter 2010): 36–40.

20. Robert J. Shiller, *Irrational Exuberance* (Princeton: Princeton University Press, 2000). His data can be found at: http://www.irrationalexuberance.com/index.htm.

21. See McFarland and Warshawsky, "Balances and Retirement Income from Individual Accounts," 37.

22. Mark J. Warshawsky, statement before the Joint Hearing of the Departments of Treasury and Labor on Certain Issues Relating to Lifetime Income Options for Participants and Beneficiaries in Retirement Plans, September 15, 2010, http://www.dol.gov/ebsa/pdf/TowersWatson091510.pdf.

23. Walter Welsh, James Szostek and Shannon Salinas, comment on the Departments of Treasury and Labor Request for Information on Certain Issues Relating to Lifetime Income Options for Participants and Beneficiaries in Retirement Plans, May 3, 2010, http://www.dol.gov/ebsa/pdf/1210-AB33-637.pdf, 3–4.

24. Greg Burrows, letter commenting on the Departments of Treasury and Labor Request for Information on Certain Issues Relating to Lifetime Income Options for Participants and Beneficiaries in Retirement Plans, October 13, 2010, http://www.dol.gov/ebsa/pdf/Principal101410.pdf, 2.

25. Allison R. Klausner, Assistant General Counsel for Honeywell International, Inc., on behalf of the ERISA Industry Committee, testimony before the Joint Hearing of the Departments of Labor and the Treasury on Lifetime Income Products, September 14, 2010, 3–4.

26. Janet Boyd, Director of Government Relations for The Dow Chemical Company, on behalf of the American Benefits Council, testimony before the Joint Hearing of the Departments of Labor and the Treasury on Lifetime Income Products, September 14, 2010, 3.

27. David L. Wray, President of the Profit Sharing/401(k) Council of America, testimony before the Joint Hearing of the Departments of Labor and the Treasury on Lifetime Income Products, September 14, 2010, 3.

CHAPTER 24

1. Michael Clingman et al., "Money's Worth Ratios under the OASDI Program for Hypothetical Workers," Social Security Administration, Office of the Actuary, *Actuarial Note* no. 7 (July 2010), http://www.socialsecurity.gov/OACT/NOTES/ran7/index.html.

2. The derivation of the scaled earnings levels is discussed in detail by Michael Clingman and Kyle Burkhalter, "Scaled Factors for Hypothetical Earnings Examples under the 1009 Trustees Report Assumptions," Social Security Administration, Office of the Actuary, *Actuarial Note* no. 2009.3 (July 2010), http://www.socialsecurity.gov/OACT/NOTES/ran3/index.html.

3. The Social Security actuaries have compiled a distribution of actual career earnings levels for workers who retired at age 62 in 2008 to compare to those of their hypothetical workers retiring that year. The results of that compilation can be found in Clingman and Burkhalter, "Scaled Factors for Hypothetical Earnings Examples under the 1009 Trustees Report Assumptions," 3, http://www.socialsecurity.gov/OACT/NOTES/ran3/index.html.

4. Social Security Administration, *Social Security Bulletin, Annual Statistical Supplement* (2008), table 5.b5.

5. Alan L. Gustman and Thomas L. Steinmeier, "How Effective Is Redistribution under the Social Security Benefit Formula?" Working Paper No. 7597 (Cambridge, MA: National Bureau of Economic Research, 2000).

6. Jeffrey R. Brown, Julia Lynn Coronado, and Don Fullerton, "Is Social Security Part of the Social Safety Net?" Working Paper No. 15070 (Cambridge, MA: National Bureau of Economic Research, 2009), 4.

7. Public Law 89–73, July 14, 1965.

8. President Franklin D. Roosevelt, "A Social Security Program Must Include All Those Who Need Its Protection," Radio address on the third anniversary of the Social Security Act, August 15, 1938, http://www.socialsecurity.gov/history/fdrstmts.html#radio.

CHAPTER 25

1. Jay V. Strong, *Employee Benefit Plans in Operation* (Washington, D.C.: Bureau of National Affairs, Inc, 1951), 175.

2. *The World Almanac for 1948* (New York: New York World Telegram, 1948), 448.

3. Strong, *Employee Benefit Plans in Operation*, 182.

4. Social Security Administration, "Chronology of Health Insurance Proposals, 1915–76," *Social Security Bulletin* 39, no. 7 (1976): 37.

5. Ibid.

6. Dorothy P. Rice, "Health Insurance Coverage of the Aged and Their Hospital Utilization in 1962: Findings of the 1963 Survey of the Aged," *Social Security Bulletin* 27, no. 7 (1964): 9.

7. G. Lawrence Atkins, "The Employer Role in Financing Health Care for Retirees," in *Providing Health Care Benefits in Retirement*, ed. Judith F. Mazo, Anna M. Rappaport, and Sylvester J. Schieber (Philadelphia: University of Pennsylvania Press and the Pension Research Council, 1994), 108.

8. Steven A. Sass, *The Promise of Private Pensions* (Cambridge, MA: Harvard University Press, 1997) 65–66.

9. Ibid., 62.

10. Lawrence H. Thompson, Assistant Controller General, Human Resources Division, testimony before the Subcommittee on Oversight, Committee on Ways and Means, House of Representatives (September 15, 1988), http://archive.gao.gov/d39t12/136835.pdf.

11. Sass, *The Promise of Private Pensions*, 62.

12. Financial Accounting Standards Board, *Summary of Statement No. 106*.

13. Towers Watson, *Accounting for Pensions and Other Postretirement Benefits, 2010 Reporting Under U.S. GAAP Among the Fortune 1000* (2010), http://www.towerswatson.com/assets/pdf/3178/TW-AcctngForPension-NA-2010-17799_perspective-EF.pdf, 12.

14. Ibid., 20.

15. Governmental Accounting Standards Board, Statement No. 45, *Accounting and Financial Reporting by Employers for Post-employment Benefits Other Than Pensions (OPEB)* (2004), http://www.gasb.org/st/index.html.

16. Pew Center on States, *The Trillion Dollar Gap: Underfunded State Retirement Systems and the Roads to Reform* (Philadelphia: The Pew Center on States, February 2010).

17. Alfred M. Skolnik, "Private Pension Plans, 1950–1974," *Social Security Bulletin* 39, no. 6 (June 1976).

18. U. S. Department of Labor, *Private Pension Plan Bulletin, Abstract of 2007 Form 5500 Annual Reports* (June 2010), http://www.dol.gov/ebsa/PDF/2007pensionplanbulletin.pdf.

19. Derived from the U.S. Department of Labor, Bureau of Labor Statistics' Urban Consumer Price Index data and Social Security Administration, Office of the Actuary's average wage index series.

20. Watson Wyatt Worldwide, *Group Benefits Survey* (1980–1988).

21. Kaiser Family Foundation and the Health Research and Education Trust, *KFF/HRET, Employer Health Benefits* (2008), http://ehbs.kff.org/images/abstract/7791.pdf, 6.

22. Sylvester J. Schieber and Roland D. McDevitt, "From Baby Boom to Elder Boom: Providing Health Care for an Aging Population" (Watson Wyatt Worldwide, 1996), www.ThePredictableSurprise.com; and Roland D. McDevitt, Janemarie Mulvey, and Sylvester J. Schieber, "Retiree Health Benefits: Time to Resuscitate?" (Watson Wyatt Worldwide, 2002), www.ThePredictableSurprise.com.

23. Robert Clark and Melinda S. Morrill, "The Funding Status of Retiree Health Plans in the Public Sector," NBER Working Paper 16450 (Cambridge, MA: National Bureau of Economic Research, 2010).

24. Philip Bredesen, "ObamaCare's Incentives to Drop Insurance," *Wall Street Journal*, October 21, 2010, Op-Ed page.

CHAPTER 26

1. Congressional Budget Office, *The Long-Term Budget Outlook* (Washington, D.C.: CBO, August Revision, 2010), 1, http://www.cbo.gov/doc.cfm?index=11579.

2. Ibid.

3. Richard S. Foster, "Statement of Actuarial Opinion," *2010 Annual Report of the Board of Trustees of the Federal Hospital Insurance and Federal Supplementary Medical Insurance Trust Funds*, 282.

4. Virginia P. Reno, testimony at Hearings on Social Security at 75 Years: More Necessary than Ever, Statement for the National Academy of Social Insurance at the Subcommittee on Social Security, U.S. House of Representatives, Committee on Ways and Means, July 15, 2010, 5, http://waysandmeans.house.gov/media/pdf/111/2010Jul15_Reno_Testimony.pdf.

5. Nancy J. Altman, quoting Robert Ball in testimony at Hearings on Social Security at 75 Years: More Necessary than Ever, Statement for the National Academy of Social Insurance at the Subcommittee on Social Security, U.S. House of Representatives, Committee on Ways and Means, July 15, 2010, 5, http://waysandmeans.house.gov/media/pdf/111/2010Jul15_Altman_Testimony.pdf.

6. Gustman, Steinmeier, and Tabatabai, *Pensions in the Health and Retirement Study*.

7. Ibid., 305.

8. Ibid., 306.

9. Steven A. Nyce and Sylvester J. Schieber, *The Economic Implications of Population Aging: The Costs of Living Happily Ever After* (Cambridge, UK: Cambridge University Press, 2005).

10. Reno testimony, 7.

11. Altman testimony, 9–11.

12. Robert Mann, *Legacy to Power, Senator Russell Long of Louisiana* (Lincoln, NB: iUniverse, Inc., 2003), 329.

13. Ibid., 333.

14. *The Bryan Times*, November 21, 1975, 1, http://news.google.com/newspapers?id=hRwLAAAAIBAJ&sjid=VVIDAAAAIBAJ&pg=2898,4424130&dq=you+me+behind-that-tree&hl=en.

15. Steven A. Nyce and Sylvester J. Schieber, "Treating Our Ills and Killing Our Prospects," Towers Watson and the Coalition for Affordable Health Care (June 2011),

16. Richard S. Foster, "Estimated Financial Effects of the 'Patient Protection and Affordable Care Act,'" https://www.cms.gov/ActuarialStudies/Downloads/S_PPACA_2010-01-08.pdf, 5.

17. Richard S. Foster, "Estimated Financial Effects of the 'Patient Protection and Affordable Care Act,'" as Amended (April 22, 2010), table 5, http://burgess.house.gov/UploadedFiles/4-22-2010_-_OACT_Memorandum_on_Financial_Impact_of_PPACA_as_Enacted.pdf (the data cited in the derivations are from table 5 of the analysis).

18. Peter R. Orszag and Ezekiel J. Emanuel, "Health Care Reform and Cost Control," *New England Journal of Medicine* (June 16, 2010), http://healthpolicyandreform.nejm.org/?p=3564.

19. John F. Cogan, R. Glenn Hubbard, and Daniel Kessler, "The Effect of Massachusetts Health Reform on Employer-Sponsored Insurance Premiums," *Forum for Health Economics and Policy* 13, no. 2 (April 2010), http://www.bepress.com/cgi/viewcontent.cgi?context=fhep&article=1204&date=&mt=MTI5MTIzNzQ2MA==&access_ok_form=Continue.

20. Murray Gendell, "Older Workers: Increasing Their Labor Force Participation and Hours of Work," *Monthly Labor Review* (January 2008): 42.

CHAPTER 27

1. Unpublished data from the Office of the Actuary, Social Security Administration.
2. *Report of the 1994–1996 Advisory Council on Social Security*, vol. 1, *Findings and Recommendations*, (Washington, D.C.: The Social Security Administration, 1997).
3. For anyone interested in the deliberations of the Council, I have summarized my recollections of proceedings in chapter 17 of Sylvester J. Schieber and John B. Shoven, *The Real Deal: The History and Future of Social Security* (New Haven: Yale University Press, 1999). An independent assessment of the Council's activities can be found in James Edward Gibson, III, *The Last Council: Social Security Policymaking as Coalitional Consensus and the 1994–1996 Advisory Council's Institutional Turning Point*, unpublished Ph.D. dissertation, Virginia Polytechnic Institute and State University, 2007.
4. Michael Clingman et al., "Money's Worth Ratios under the OASDI Program for Hypothetical Workers," Office of the Actuary, Social Security Administration, *Actuarial Note* no. 7 (July 2010): 9–10, http://www.socialsecurity.gov/OACT/NOTES/ran7/index.html.
5. Benyamin Appelbaum, "Plan's Focus on Social Security Taxes Reflects Its Modest Ambitions," *New York Times* (September 8, 2011), p. A1, found at: http://www.nytimes.com/2011/09/09/us/politics/09tax.html?pagewanted=all.
6. Frances Perkins, *The Roosevelt I Knew* (New York: The Viking Press, 1946), 293.
7. Robert M. Ball, Oral History Interview, http://www.socialsecurity.gov/history/orals/ball6.html.
8. http://www.roadmap.republicans.budget.house.gov/Plan/#retirementsecurity.
9. See http://paulryan.house.gov/Issues/Issue/?IssueID=12227.
10. Stephen C. Goss, letter to the Honorable Paul D. Ryan presenting estimates of the financial effects of his Social Security proposals, April 27, 2010, http://www.socialsecurity.gov/OACT/solvency/index.html.
11. Michael Clingman et al., "Money's Worth Ratios under the OASDI Program for Hypothetical Workers," 9–10, http://www.socialsecurity.gov/OACT/NOTES/ran7/index.html.
12. See http://www.bipartisanpolicy.org/about.
13. See http://www.bipartisanpolicy.org/projects/debt-initiative/about.
14. Bipartisan Policy Center, Debt Reduction Task Force, "Restoring America's Future" (Washington, DC, 2010), http://www.bipartisanpolicy.org/.
15. The National Commission on Fiscal Responsibility and Reform, "Moment of Truth" (Washington, DC, 2010), http://www.fiscalcommission.gov/.
16. J. Douglas Brown, Oral History Collection, Columbia University (1966), 4.

17. Stephanie Condon, "Pelosi Opposed to Raising the Retirement Age," *CBS News*, July 24, 2010, http://www.cbsnews.com/8301-503544_162-20011573-503544.html.

18. Thomas N. Bethell, "Social Security: Where Do We Go from Here?" *AARP Bulletin* (July 1, 2010), http://www.aarp.org/work/social-security/info-07-2010/social_securitywhere_do_we_go_from_here.html.

19. Frank Newport, "Six in 10 Workers Hold No Hope of Receiving Social Security," *Gallup* (July 20, 2010), http://www.gallup.com/poll/141449/six-workers-hold-no-hope-receiving-social-security.aspx.

20. Dean Baker, "Action on Social Security: The Urgent Need for Delay," Center for Economic and Policy Research policy paper (Washington, DC, 2010), http://www.cepr.net/documents/publications/ss-2010-11-1.pdf, 1.

21. Ibid., 1–2.

22. Poterba, Venti, and Wise, "Rise of 401(k) Plans, Lifetime Earnings, and Wealth at Retirement."

23. Dean Baker, "Action on Social Security," 2.

CHAPTER 28

1. Jeffrey R. Brown, "Automatic Lifetime Income as the Path to Retirement Income Security," *Colloquium on Tax Policy and Public Finance, Spring 2010* (New York: NYU Law School, February 2010).

2. Richard A. Ippolito, "The Reversion Tax's Perverse Result," *Regulation* 25, no. 1 (Spring 2002): 46–53.

3. The National Commission on Fiscal Responsibility and Reform, "Moment of Truth," 26–27.

4. Bipartisan Policy Center, Debt Reduction Task Force, "Restoring America's Future," 39.

5. Robert L. Clark, Janemarie Mulvey, and Sylvester J. Schieber, "The Effects of Nondiscrimination Rules on Private Sector Pension Participation," paper presented at the Conference on Public Policies and Private Pensions, sponsored by the Brookings Institution, Stanford Institute for Economic Policy Research, and TIAA-CREF, Washington, D.C., September 21, 2000).

6. The National Commission on Fiscal Responsibility and Reform, "Moment of Truth," 27.

7. Bipartisan Policy Center, Debt Reduction Task Force, Restoring America's Future, 49.

8. Sylvester J. Schieber, Prepared Statement before the Subcommittee on Retirement Income and Employment, Select Committee on Aging, U.S. House of Representatives, July 27, 1990.

9. Julia N. Coronado and Sylvester J. Schieber, "Saving Private Pension Insurance: An Evaluation of Current Proposals to Shore up the PBGC," *Journal of Compensation and Benefits* 21, no. 2 (March/April 2005): 13–20.

10. Pension Benefit Guaranty Corporation, *Pension Insurance Data Book*, various years, http://www.pbgc.gov/practitioners/plan-trends-and-statistics/content/page13270.html.

11. U.S. Department of Transportation, Bureau of Transportation Statistics, "Airport Enplanements by State and Air Carrier Category: 2008," http://www.bts.gov/publications/state_transportation_statistics/state_transportation_statistics_2009/html/table_01_12.html.

12. CBS News, "State Budgets: The Day of Reckoning," *60 Minutes* (December 19, 2010), found at: http://www.cbsnews.com/stories/2010/12/19/60minutes/main7166220.shtml?tag=contentMain;cbsCarousel.

13. Michael Corkery, "Pension Woes Prompt GOP Move," *Wall Street Journal*, December 10, 2010), http://online.wsj.com/article/SB10001424052748703350104575653290661576692.html.

14. Constantijn W. A. Panis, "Annuities and Retirement Satisfaction," *Rand Labor and Population Program* Working Paper Series 03–17 (April 2003), http://www.rand.org/pubs/drafts/2008/DRU3021.pdf.

15. Sally A. Bryck et al., "What a Difference a Year Makes," http://www.soa.org/files/pdf/news-pub-2009-difference.pdf.

16. Brendan McFarland and Mark J. Warshawsky, "Balances and Retirement Income from Individual Accounts: U.S. Historical Simulations," *Benefits Quarterly* (Second Quarter 2010).

17. Robert J. Shiller, updated data used in developing *Irrational Exuberance* (Princeton, NJ: Princeton University Press, 2000), http://www.irrationalexuberance.com/index.htm.

CHAPTER 29

1. Roosevelt, radio address, http://www.ssa.gov/history/fdrstmts.html#message1.

2. Perkins, *The Roosevelt I Knew*, 294; and Berkowitz, *America's Welfare State*, 23.

3. James Trunslow Adams, *The American Epic* (New York: Blue Ribbon Books, Inc., 1931), 404.

4. Adams as quoted by *Forbes*, http://thoughts.forbes.com/thoughts/james-truslow-adams.

5. Derthick, *Policymaking for Social Security*, 235 (quoting Brown).

6. Robert M. Ball, Oral History Collection, Interview #6, http://www.socialsecurity.gov/history/orals/ball6.html.

7. *The Phrase Finder*, http://www.phrases.org.uk/meanings/216400.html.

8. Macunovich, *Birth Quake*.

9. See table 26.7 in chapter 26.

10. Barbara A. Butrica, Karen E Smith, and C. Eugene Steurele, "Working for a Good Retirement," Discussion Paper 06-03 (Washington, D.C.: Urban Institute Retirement Project, 2006), 24, table 1.

11. Barack Obama, comments at a roundtable discussion with editorial board of the *Washington Post* (January 2009), www.washingtonpost.com/wp-dyn/content/audio/2009/01/16/AU2009011601671.html?sid=ST2009011504146.

12. President Barack Obama, State of the Union Address (2011), www.whitehouse.gov/the-press-office/2011/01/25/remarks-president-state-union-address.

13. House of Representatives, House Committee on the Budget, "Path to Prosperity" (2011), http://budget.house.gov/UploadedFiles/PathToProsperityFY2012.pdf.

14. Ibid., 47.

15. Unpublished data from the Social Security Administration, Office of the Actuary, and *Summary of the 2011 Annual Report of the Board of Trustees of the Federal Old-Age and Survivors Insurance and Federal Disability Insurance Trust Funds*, http://www.socialsecurity.gov/OACT/TR/2011/lr4b1.html.

16. Pension Benefit Guaranty Corporation, *2010 PBGC Annual Report* (Washington, DC: 2011), http://www.pbgc.gov/documents/ar2010.htm.

17. Budget of the United States Government, Fiscal Year 2012, http://www.whitehouse.gov/omb/.

18. Adams, *The American Epic*, 416.

INDEX

Aaron, Henry, 89
AARP, 341, 368–69
abuses, with public pensions, 220–22
accounting rules, 158–59, 163–64
accrued liabilities, 390n6
accumulated benefit obligation, 377
accumulation, 135, 283t, 285t
  economic savings and retirement
    plan, 174–75
  large pension wealth, 259–62
  for low earners, 213–14
  trust funds, 86–91
Accuracy in the Media, 143–44
Achenbaum, Andrew, 29
ACLI. See American Council of Life
  Insurance
actuarial balance, 377
actuarial cost methods, 158f
actuarial value of benefits, 390n5
actuaries, 390n6, 415n3
Adams, James Truslow, 365, 376
Advisory Council on Economic Security,
  34–35, 54
  1947, 57
Advisory Council on Social Security,
  xvii, xx, 102–3, 106, 108, 329
AFL. See American Federation of
  Labor
age. See also claiming age; early
  retirement; OASDI; old-age
  dependency; Old-Age Pension bill
  average for retirement and claiming
  benefits, 180t, 240

45 and accrued benefits with cash
  balance plan and traditional
  pension, 193f
men and women as labor force
  participants at specified, 327t
retirement, 84
30 and accrued benefits with cash
  balance plan and traditional
  pension, 192f
women age 62 or older receiving
  benefits, 291t
age discrimination laws, 177
agency risk, 136–37, 218, 377
Air Force, U.S., 234. See also Military
  Retirement System
Alaska (AK), 216–17, 225, 299
Alice's Adventures in Wonderland
  (Carroll), 307, 376
Altman, Nancy, 313–14, 318
Altmeyer, Arthur, 12, 54, 56–57, 367
  on economic fairness, 60–61
  with financing, 46–47
  with insurance principles, 63
  with national retirement program,
    35, 36, 38
  on pay-as-you-go flaws, 66–67, 72–73,
    90
Amendments
  Clark, 40
  Morgenthau, 39
  1939, 50–52, 56, 71, 79, 122, 124, 382
  1950, 57–58
  1965, 70

Amendments (*continued*)
 1972, 73, 76, 80
 1977, 78–80, 336
 1983, 84–86, 91
American Council of Life Insurance
 (ACLI), 272, 275
American Dream, 365–66, 369
American Express, 24
American Federation of Labor (AFL),
 134
American Motors, 138
amortization, 138, 147, 222
Andrews, John, 28, 35
angst, 8–9, 11–12
annuities, 121–22. *See also* retirement
 annuities
 with defined contribution plan,
  355–60
 installment group, 362*f*
 interest rates and asset required to
  fund, 183*t*
 joint and survivor benefits with,
  340–41, 380
 from lifecycle funds for hypothetical
  worker for 1915 to 2010, 359*f*, 360*f*
 loading fees for, 360
 resistance to, 267–68
 retirement plan calculations for, xx
 retirement risks with, 270–72
 tax-favored benefits to encourage,
  360–63
anti-cutback provisions, 230
Apfel, Kenneth, 45, 91
Archer, Bill, 105, 394n12
Archer, William, 393n9
Arizona (AZ), 299, 353
Armstrong, Barbara, 36, 38, 39, 46
Armstrong, William, 81, 393n9,
 394n12
Army, U.S., 234. *See also* Military
 Retirement System
Aronson, Nancy, 223

assets
 annuity funding with interest rates
  and required, 183*t*
 depletion of, 225
 401(k) plans and private tax-flavored,
  204*f*
 managed by workers and
  participants, 200–203
 mean household dedicated
  retirement, 281*t*
 pension, 152, 159–60, 380
 trust funds from 1975 to 1982, 151
Astrue, Michael, 367
Atkins, Lawrence, 296
Australia, 335
automatic enrollment, 206, 208–9
Automatic Minimum Tax, 310
average earners, 64, 67, 284
 benefits payable at age 65 for, 343*t*
 benefits reduced for, 78, 114
 401(k) projected wealth for, 214
 2011 benefits for, 114
average indexed monthly earnings, 377,
 381, 392n14
AZ. *See* Arizona

babies, notch, 79
baby boomers, 155
 as biggest claim on system, 16,
  176–77, 251, 371
 Clinton on, 20
 funding delay with, 159
 labor force participation rates
  of, 179
 prefunding with, 45
 retirement of, 7, 11
 shortfall in benefits for, 86–87,
  99–100, 157
 Social Security financing influenced
  by, 12, 14
 women, 69, 372–73
baby bust generation, 11

Baker, Dean
  on funding crisis, 19–20, 341–42
  on individual accounts, 102
Baker, Howard, 82, 84, 335
Baker, James, 83
balanced funds, 210
Ball, Bob, 9–10, 71–73, 366, 393n9
  on financing crisis, 82–83
  with flawed pay-as-you-go funding,
    76–78, 90, 392n1
  on individual accounts, 102–3, 108
  with transparency, 332
  with trust funds, 88–89
Ballantyne, Harry, 85
banking principles, 48
bankruptcies, 13, 23, 137, 139, 349
Bardenwerper, Walter, xx, 9
Beck, Robert, 393n9
Bender, Kcith, 220
benefit calculator, 391n10, 391n15
benefit equity, 50
  concerns, 61–64
  uneven, 64–66, 150–52, 261
benefit formula, redistributive, 120
benefits. *See also specific benefits*
  accumulated benefit obligation, 377
  for age 30 with traditional pension
    and cash balance plan, 192*f*
  for age 45 with traditional pension
    and cash balance plan, 193*f*
  average age for retirement and
    claiming, 180*t*, 240
  default risks with, 191–95
  early changes in, 49–51
  early retirement with lower, 81
  final earnings replaced by, 79*f*
  in Germany, 27–28
  for government workers, 8
  initial equity concerns and start-up,
    60–61
  living standards secured with tax-
    favored, 345–63

with multi-employer pension plan
    insurance flaws, 189–90
with new pension funding rules,
    198–99
paid out in 1990, 173
paid out in 2009 and 2010, 5
payable at age 65 for medium, high
    and maximum earners, 343*t*
pension conversions to closures with,
    195–98
pension funding collapse amid
    financial market chaos, 182–84
pension insurance flaws with
    exploding claims and, 184–86
with private pension insurance
    defects, 186–89
private retirement and controversy
    with measurement of, 172–74
program maturity with expansion of,
    71–74
reduced, 78
regulations influencing, 166, 167*f*
Santa Claus increases with, 57
shortfalls, 29, 86–87, 99–100, 157
spousal, 120–21, 289–92, 340, 382
supplemental, 176
survivor retirement, 120
for UAW, 176
windfall, 64–66, 67–68
Bernanke, Ben, 100–101
Bernatzi, Schlomo, 207
Bernheim, Douglas, 207
Bernstein, Merton, 137, 141, 143
betrayal, 8–9, 11–12
Beveridge, William, 71
Biden, Joe, 268
Biggs, Andrew, 115, 220
bipartisan accord, 105–7
birth cohorts, 377
  benefit equity between, 61–64
  intercohort transfers paid to specific,
    62*f*, 66

birth cohorts (*continued*)
  money's worth for, 281–82
  with net intercohort transfers, 61–62,
    66, 380
  1937 members, 63
  1938 through 1950 members, 64
  1949 members, 284
  1957 through 2010 members, 64
  windfall benefits estimated with,
    67–68
Bismarck, Otto von, 27
Black Monday, 201. *See also* stock
  market
blacks, with automatic enrollment, 206
Blahous, Charles, 114
Blue Cross-Blue Shield, 294, 303
Blum, Walter, 141
BNP Paribus, xx
Boehner, John, 326
bonds, 228*t*. *See also* trust funds
  par value, 380
  pension obligation, 225
  U.S., 42–43, 67, 94*f*
Bosworth, Barry, 88–89, 97, 261–62
Bowman, Michele, xxi
Bowles, Erskine, 103, 105, 108, 335
Bowles-Simpson Commission, 335–39,
    342, 347–48, 368–70
Boyd, Janet, 276
Breaux, John, 106
Bredesen, Philip, 304
Breheny, Ann Marie, xx
bridge jobs, with five-legged stool
    metaphor, 4
Bronson, Dorrance, 17, 54–55
Brown, J. Douglas, 36, 38, 39, 46–47,
    366, 369
  with 1935 Social Security Act, 336–37
  old-age dependency, 50
  on pay-as-you-go financing, 48, 57
Brown, Jeffrey, 223, 268, 290–91
Brown, Kyle, xix, xx

Buck, George B., 26, 138
Bureau of Old-Age Survivors Insurance,
    9–10
Burr, Barry, 227
Burrows, Greg, 275
Burtless, Gary, 97, 261–62
Bush, George W., 95–96
  on beneficiaries to workers ratio,
    115–16
  with financing crisis, 101
  no-new-taxes rule of, 115
  with reform, 110–16, 344
  with reform roadblocks, 116–17
  tax cuts, 310, 331
Bush commission. *See* Commission to
  Strengthen Social Security
Butrica, Barbara, 373

California (CA), 339, 354
Campbell, Nancy, xix
Canada, 97, 315
capital accumulation plans, 135
car accident, 379
Career Status Bonus/redux, 234
Carnegie, Andrew, 25, 129
Carroll, Lewis, xviii, 3, 307, 376
Carter, Jimmy, 78, 80, 150
cash balance plan
  benefits accrued for age 30 with
    traditional pension and, 192*f*
  benefits accrued for age 45 with
    traditional pension and, 193*f*
cashing out, 211
cash surpluses, 94–96, 96*f*
Catch 22 (Heller), 227
Caterpillar, 7
Cather, David, 160
Cato Institute, 112, 115
CBO. *See* Congressional Budget
  Office
Census, U.S.
  1967, 5

1970, 75
1993, 205
Census Bureau, U.S., xx, 172, 216, 243
  on poverty rate, 5, 253
Charles Schwab, 208
chicken in every pot campaign, 34
children, 47
  orphans, 58
  poverty rate, 253
Children's Health Insurance Program,
  311
Christie, Chris, 230–32, 353–54
Chrysler, 138, 349
Churchill, Winston, 376
CIO. See Congress of Industrial
  Organizations
Civil Service Retirement System (CSRS)
  populations, liability and funding
    status for October 2008, 234, 235t
  workers covered under, 233
Civil War, 16, 24, 25
Clague, Ewan, 142
claimants, against PBGC single-
  employer pension plan insurance,
  187t–188t
claiming age
  average, 180t, 240
  in 1950s, 5
  in 1935, 176
  present day, 5
claims
  baby boomers with system's biggest,
    16, 176–77, 251, 371
  pension insurance flaws with
    exploding, 184–86
Clark, Bennett, 40
Clark, Robert, xix, xxi, 303
Clark amendment, 40. See also Clark,
  Bennett
Clinton, Bill, xvii, 22, 95, 292, 334
  with bipartisan accord on reform,
    105–7

with financing crisis, 101
  on funding crisis, 20, 90–91, 102
  health care reform and, 249
  with reform, 103–5, 108–11, 115
  with reform proposal, 107–8
  with reform roadblocks, 116–17
close actuarial balance, 85
CO. See Colorado
Coast Guard, U.S., 232
Cogan, John, 320–21
Cohen, Wilbur, 35, 71–72
collapse
  financial market, 15
  pension, 13–14, 25–26, 182–84
  Studebaker, 13–14, 16, 137–39
Colorado (CO), 217, 339
commissioners, Social Security, 392n1,
  393n9
Commission to Strengthen Social
  Security, 112–16. See also Bush,
  George W.
Committee on Corporate Pensions
  Funds, 140–41, 142. See also
  Kennedy, John F.
Committee on Economic Security, 1, 44
  with funding question, 39
  national retirement program
    formulated by, 34–38
Commons, John, 28, 35
companies. See also specific companies
  Fortune 500, 205–6
  Fortune 1000, 197t, 298
  participant-directed investing at, 202f
  pension collapse in, 25–26
  private insurance, 119
  vulnerable to hidden pensioners, 25
compensation
  benefits story with, 247–50
  compound annual growth rates with
    hourly, 246f
  gains provided with more expensive
    benefits, 250t

compensation (*continued*)
  growth financing increased benefit
    costs, 324t
  increases absorbed by payroll taxes,
    248t
  with pay levels for workers in 2009,
    244t
  public pensions in context with,
    219–20
compound interest, 74
  power of, 121
  with unfunded obligations, 98–101
Conable, Barber, 393n9
  on financing crisis, 82–83
concerns
  with defined contribution plans,
    210–12
  with do-it-yourself pensions, 205–7
  with financing, 46–49
  funding controversy and, 43–46
  nagging and persistent early,
    42–51
  pay-as-you-go financing, 52–56
  program financing and benefit
    structure, 49–51
  start-up benefits and initial equity,
    60–61
  with trust fund operations, 42–43
Confucius, 346, 363
confusion, 8–9, 11–12
Congress, U.S.
  commission recommendations for,
    83–85
  with Greenspan Commission, 83–85
Congressional Budget and
    Impoundment Control Act of 1974,
    144–45, 151
Congressional Budget Office (CBO)
  federal spending and revenues under,
    312t
  with too hot perspective, 309–12
Congressional Research Institute, xx

Congress of Industrial Organizations
    (CIO), 134
Connecticut (CT), 225
consequences, for elderly without
    retirement, 1
consumer price index (CPI), 112, 234,
    300, 338
contributions, 16. *See also* defined
    contribution plan; savings
  automatic enrollment influencing, 206
  banking, 48
  benefits value with accumulated
    lifetime, 283t, 285t
  of birth cohorts, 63–64
  concerns plaguing, 210–12
  defined plans and automatic features
    with, 208–10
  with do-it-yourself pensions,
    205–7
  earnings replacement rates from
    lifecycle funds, 271f
  employer, 18–19
  with ERISA, 148
  Fortune 500 and average defined
    expenses of benefits and, 197t
  401(k), 174–75, 203–5, 212–14
  health benefits and employer, 248t
  of higher and lower earners, 174
  holidays, 168
  IRA, 174–75
  from 1975 to 1982, 151
  profit-sharing and money-purchase,
    135
  with retirement plan participants as
    investment managers, 200–203
  Roosevelt on, 37, 44
  state-level public pension plans with
    funding and, 223t
  tax-deferred status of, 130–31
  from tax-qualified savings accounts
    versus net benefit gains, 289t
  for teachers in IL and LA, 226t

controversy
  funding, 43–46
  legal protections and public pension,
    229–32
  over public plan generosity, 218–19
  private retirement plans and benefits
    measurement, 172–74
  public plan generosity over, 218–19
  with trust funds and savings, 94–96
Cooperman, Elizabeth, 160
Copeland, Craig, 270
Coronado, Julia, xx, 290–91, 349
corporate boards, 19
Corzine, John, 231
Costa, Dora, 25
cost methods
  entry age normal, 158–59
  projected-unit-credit, 158–59
cost-of-living adjustments, 75, 81, 231
costs
  of benefits with measurement of
    rewards, 242–47
  compensation growth financing
    increased benefit, 324t
  health benefits, 242
  health care, 252
  1980 Social Security program, 17
  of paying for retirement systems,
    318–19
  of pension with 40-year career, 158f
  program maturity and rising, 69–70
  public pensions, 222–24
  retirement health, 241t
  retirement income security and
    implications of, 240–42
  Social Security participation with
    payroll tax, 281–83
  transition, 113, 115
  2010 Social Security system, 22
countries, quasi-retirement income
    replacement rates for, 316t
couples, one-earner, 284

CPI. See consumer price index
CPS. See Current Population Survey
cradle to grave program, 71
crisis
  financing, 82–83, 100–101, 393n9
  funding, 12, 17–20, 60, 81–91, 102,
    110–12, 341–42
  Greenspan Commission with
    funding, 83–85
  new surprised in aftermath of, 85–86
  political dialogue to address
    financing, 82–83
  trust fund accumulation and déjà vu
    with, 86–91
Croft, Dan, 229
Cronkite, Walter, 253, 364
CSRS. See Civil Service Retirement
    System
CT. See Connecticut
Current Population Survey (CPS), xx,
    172–74, 219, 243, 260, 373
Curto, Vilsa, 264–65

Darman, Richard, 83
Daschle, Tom, 335
death, before full life expectancy, 59,
    379. See also mortality tables
Debt Reduction Task Force, 346, 368.
    See also Domenici-Rivlin Task Force
debts, 87
  federal, 43, 44–45
  state, 229
decoupling, 76, 78
defaults
  employer pensions with forfeitures
    and, 137–40
  enrollment, 206–7
  investments, 210
  risk, 136, 191–95, 377
Defense Department, U.S., 235. See also
    Military Retirement System
Deficit Reduction Act, 19, 154, 297

deficits
  legislation, 19, 154, 297
  with Old-Age Pension bill, 39
  with Social Security benefits, 6–8,
    17–18
defined benefit plan, 166–67, 377–78
  lumpsum payouts with, 211
defined contribution plan, 135, 147, 149,
  271f, 378
  with annuities, 355–60
  automatic features of, 208–10
  concerns, 210–12
  ERISA with, 200–201
  roll overs with, 212
Delta Airlines, 14, 187t, 350
Democratic Leadership Council (DLC),
  104
demographics, xviii
  costs influenced by, 69
  policy stalemate with, 102–17
  retirement programs influenced
    by, 4
denial
  funding crisis and policymakers in,
    12, 18–20, 110–12
  negative human consequences from,
    21, 23
  with saving for retirement, 121,
    242–43
Denmark, 97
Department of Health, Education and
  Welfare (DHEW), U.S., 71
Department of Labor, Pension and
  Welfare Benefits Administration,
  U.S., 7, 402n1
dependency ratio, 378
  with pay-as-you-go financing, 52–55,
    57, 69, 70f, 71
  from 2000 to 2030, 84
depletion
  of assets, 225
  of trust funds, 19, 75, 225

Great Depression, 13, 28–29, 33, 69, 329
DeWitt, Larry, xxi
DHEW. See Department of Health,
  Education and Welfare, U.S.
Diamond, Peter, 96, 113, 114
Dickens, Charles, 237
disability insurance, 50, 119–20
discount rate, 378
discrimination testing, 378
DLC. See Democratic Leadership
  Council
do-it-yourself pensions, 7. See also 401(k)
  plans
  retirement security concerns with,
    205–7
Dole, Bob, 84, 335
  on financing crisis, 82–83,
    393n9
Domenici, Pete, 335
Domenici-Rivlin Task Force, 336–39,
  342, 347–48, 368–70
double indexing, 76, 79
Dow Chemical Company, 276
Downey, Sheridan, 61
Duberstein, Kenneth, 83

early-out provisions, 176–77
early retirement, 3
  at age 55, 177
  at age 62, 176
  benefits level tied to, 177
  lower benefits in, 81
Earned Income Tax Credit, 331
earnings
  average indexed monthly, 377, 381,
    392n14
  benefits replacing percentage of final,
    79f
  cap, 156–57
  growth rates of annual, 322t
  household social security wealth by
    lifetime, 258t

hypothetical workers and defined contribution, 271*f*

payroll taxes and ratio of benefits paid to covered, 16, 17, 19, 52, 69, 70*f*

rate of workers, 64–65

ratio of price-to-, 169*f*, 183*f*

workers retiring in 2030 with 401(k) and lifetime, 213*t*

of younger workers in relation to older workers, 176

earnings replacement rate, 53, 271*f*

Eastern Airlines, 16, 187*t*, 350

Eastman, George, 133

economic fairness, 60–61

Economic Growth and Tax Relief Reconciliation Act of 2001, 310

Economic Recovery Tax Act of 1981, 153

economics

boom and irrational exuberance, 168–70

employers retrenching on benefits and irrationality of, 300–303

knowledge, 21

retirement programs influenced by, 4

savings and retirement plan accumulations, 174–75

The Economic Implications of Aging Societies. The Costs of Living Happily Ever After (Nyce and Schieber), xix

education funding

for college professors, 129

pension costs edging out, 6, 8

elderly

income relief for, 33–34, 37

poverty rate, 253

without retirement and consequences, 1

elections, 4

Emanuel, Ezekiel J., 320–21

Employee Retirement Income Security Act. *See* ERISA

employer pensions, 129

benefits paid in 2009, 5

benefits paid out 1990, 173

with contributions to health benefits, 248*t*

early federal regulations for, 130–31

employment termination and disposition of benefits with, 264*t*

encouragement of, 131–33

ERISA with, 146–52

with five-legged stool metaphor, 4

flaws with multi-, 189–90

with forfeitures and defaults, 137–40

insurance and claimants against PBGC single-, 187*t*–188*t*

origins, 13

with other factors stimulating plan creation, 133–35

problems with, 12–15

employers

compensation gains and more expensive benefits paid by, 250*t*

contributions, 18–19, 248*t*

cumulative lifetime payroll taxes for workers and, 241*t*

economic irrationality and retrenching of benefits by, 300–303

practices with accounting rules, 158–59, 163–64

with retiree health insurance and regulatory conflicts, 296–97

Engen, Eric, 175

enrollment

automatic, 206, 208–9

default, 206–7

entitlement, 9, 37, 326, 373

claims, 116

programs, 100

entry age normal cost method, 158–59

Epstein, Abraham, 28, 35, 36, 38

on 1939 Amendments, 51

equity. *See* benefit equity
ERISA (Employee Retirement Income
 Security Act), 13–14, 21–22, 130,
 144, 145, 276
 with accounting rule changes, 159,
 163–64
 components, 146
 with defined contribution plans,
 200–201
 definition, 378
 early operations under, 147–50
 funding, 401n3
 with funding limits, 166–67
 with hybrid pension plan, 379
 private sector under, 230
 public pensions exempt from most,
 216
 with retiree health benefits,
 298–300
 with tax treatment of pensions,
 150–52
estimates
 trust funds and insurance principles,
 63
 windfall benefits, 67–68
Every Man a King (Long), 34
excise tax, 201, 211, 351–53

farmers, 53
Farris, Susan, xxi
Federal Communications Commission
 (FCC), 143–44
federal debt, 43, 44–45
Federal Deposit Insurance Corporation,
 139
Federal Employee Retirement Systems
 (FERS)
 CPI, 234
 populations, liability and funding
 status for October 2008, 234, 235t,
 236
 workers covered under, 233

federal pension disclosure form. *See*
 Form 5500
federal pensions, 232–36
Federal Reserve System, U.S., 232
*Federal Tax Policy for Economic Growth
 and Stability*, 141
Federal Thrift Savings Plan, 233, 236
Feinlieb, Joel, xxi
Ferguson, Karen, 143
FERS. *See* Federal Employee
 Retirement Systems
fertility rates, 69
Fidelity Investments, 208–9, 210
fiduciary, 378
Fields, W. C., 94
Financial Accounting Standards Board,
 158, 296–97, 370, 380
financial market
 collapse of, 15
 pension collapse amid chaos of,
 182–84
financing, 324t. *See also* pay-as-you-go
 financing
 baby boomers' influence on Social
 Security, 12, 14
 benefit structure and program, 49–51
 crisis, 82–83, 100–101, 393n9
 for Medicare, 240
 revisited, 46–49
 smoke-and-mirrors, 330–32
financing structure. *See also* pay-as-you-
 go financing
 early changes in, 49–51
 faux pas, 74–78
 funded, 11, 12, 26–27, 47, 52
Finland, 97
firefighters, 24, 220–21, 231
fire insurance example, 118–19
fire loss, 379
fireside chats, 292
five-legged stool metaphor, 4
Florida (FL), 217, 225

Folsom, Marion, 132–33
Ford, Gerald, 78, 82, 145
Ford Motor Company, 134, 138, 142
forfeiture risk, 136, 378
forfeitures, employer pensions with
    defaults and, 137–40
Form 5500, 406n26
Fortune 500, 205–6
Fortune 1000, 298
    average defined benefit and
        contribution plan expense, 197t
Foster, Richard, 310–11, 320
401(k) plans, 6, 7, 15, 18, 22, 147. See also
    Profit Sharing/401(k) Council of
    America
    annuity values in traditional balanced
        fund versus guaranteed minimum
        withdrawal fund, 274t
    birth of, 160–62
    do-it-yourself pensions and, 205–7
    growing role of, 203–5
    high- and average earners with
        projected wealth of, 214
    household social security wealth
        with, 258t
    lifetime earnings for workers retiring
        in 2030, 213t
    in 1984, 161, 205
    participant-directed investing of, 202f
    private retirement plans
        outperforming, 209
    reality of, 212–14
    rules and influence on low earners,
        165
    safe harbors with, 208
    savings, 174–75
    share of private tax-flavored plan
        assets in, 204f
    with traditional balanced fund versus
        guaranteed minimum withdrawal
        fund, 273t
freezes, plan, 7, 375

Fromm, Al, 104
Fuller, Ida Mae, 9, 10, 60
Fuller, Mary Falvey, 393n9
Fullerton, Don, 290–91
fully funded pension, 378
The Fundamentals of Private Pensions
    (McGill), xix, 132
funded financing structure, 11, 12,
    26–27, 47, 52
funded ratio. See funding ratio
funding
    accounting rule changes and delay in,
        158–59, 163–64
    controversy and concerns, 43–46
    crisis, 12, 17–20, 81–91, 90, 102,
        110–12, 341–42
    ERISA, 401n3
    limits, 18–19, 156, 157t, 166–67
    of Medicare in part by payroll taxes,
        240
    over, 159, 168, 170–71
    prefunding as, 45–46
    questions arise at outset, 39
    regulations, 198–99
    regulations curtailing, 166, 167f
    shortfall, 29, 86–87, 99–100
    state-level public pension plans with
        contributions and, 223t
    Wizard of Oz, 227–28
funding ratio, 378
funds, balanced, 210
The Future of Private Pensions
    (Bernstein), 137, 141

Gale, William, 175, 268
GDP. See gross domestic product
Geithner, Timothy, 268
General Motors, 134, 138, 349
generational considerations, 20–21, 23
    benefit equity with, 61–64
Gephardt, Dick, 103, 105, 108
Germany, retirement program in, 27–28

Gillon, Steven, 105–6
Gingrich, Newt, 103, 105–6, 108
golden age of retirement, xvii, 117, 170,
    242, 345, 376
Goodfellow, Gordon, xx
Gore, Al, 105, 110–12
Goss, Stephen, 332, 341
Goss, Steven, xxi
government, U.S.
    benefits for workers in, 8
    benefits paid out in 2009, 5
    federal debt of, 43, 44–45
    taxpayers taking on Medicare burden
        with, 303–5
Governmental Accounting Standards
    Board, 222, 224, 298
Grad, Susan, 403n6
Gramlich, Ned, 88
Greenebaum Doll & McDonald, 223
Greenspan, Alan, 88
    on economic boom and irrational
        exuberance, 169
    on financing crisis, 82–83, 100–101
Greenspan Commission
    creation of, 82–83
    recommendations to Congress,
        83–85
Gregg, Judd, 106
gross domestic product (GDP), 154
    federal spending and revenues under
        CBO as percentage of, 312t
    health care out-of-pocket
        expenditures with, 301f
growth rates
    of annual earnings across income
        deciles, 322t
    of compensation financing increased
        benefit costs, 324t
    hourly compensation and compound
        annual, 246f
    hourly wages and compound annual,
        245f

wage and, 76–77
Gustman, Alan, 254–58, 259–62, 290,
    314

Hannah, Leslie, 130
Hansen, Alvin, 47–48
Hawaii (HI), 225
hazards, 119
Health and Retirement Study, 379
    costs, 241t
    employer-sponsored benefits with
        employment termination, 264t
    findings, 254–59
    household social security wealth by
        lifetime earnings for, 258t
    with mean household dedicated
        retirement assets, 281t
    original cohort with pension receipt
        and monthly benefits in, 260t
    respondents in plan types among
        alternative cohorts, 256t
    on tax benefits and benefit taxes,
        279–93
    wealth among ages 51 to 56, 257t
health benefits, 294
    burden shifting to government or
        taxpayers, 303–5
    costs, 242
    employer contributions to, 248t
    employers retrenching on,
        300–303
    Medicare, 3, 295
    pay-as-you-go funding prevails with,
        298–300
    regulatory conflicts with employers'
        retiree health insurance and,
        296–97
    tax-favored benefits and tax
        preferences for, 348–49
    union plans with, 302
health care, 4, 22
    costs, 252

out-of-pocket expenses and GDP
  spent on, 301*f*
reform, 249
Heinz, John, 88, 393n9
Heller, Joseph, 227
Hess, Thomas, 265
Heywood, John, 220
HI. *See* Hawaii
hidden pensioners, 25, 379
high earners, 64–65, 67. *See also*
  maximum earners; windfall
  benefits
  benefits payable at age 65 for, 343*t*
  benefits reduced for, 78, 114
  contributions of, 174
  401(k) projected wealth for, 214
  2011 benefits for, 114
  uneven benefit equity for, 151, 261
Hinz, Richard, xx, 205
Hispanics, with automatic enrollment,
  206
Hoffa, Jimmy, 136–37
Hollings, Ernest, 87, 88, 95
Homestead Act, 28
hourly compensation, compound
  annual growth rates with, 246*f*
hourly wages
  compound annual growth rates with,
  245*f*
  private-sector, 38, 40–41
Hubbard, Glenn, 320
hybrid pension plan, 379
Hynes, Daniel W., 225–27, 229, 353

Illinois (IL), 225, 332, 353
  annual required pension
  contributions in, 226*t*
  as deadbeat, 229
  distribution of 2003 pension bond
  revenues in 2009 for, 228*t*
  pension-plan deficits in, 8
  public pension laws in, 229, 232

IN. *See* Indiana
incentives, retirement, 21, 177
income, personal. *See* personal income
income adequacy, 120
income relief, for elderly, 33–34, 37
income replacement rates, for selected
  countries, 316*t*
income-spiking, 221–22
income tax, 162, 378
Indiana (IN), 225
individual accounts
  as reform element, 332–35
  shift to, 113
  support for, 102–3, 108
individual retirement accounts (IRAs),
  147, 151–52, 378
  household social security wealth
  with, 258*t*
  savings, 174–75
  share of private tax-flavored plan
  assets in, 204*f*
industrialization
  in Germany, 27
  in U.S., 24
inflation, 75, 122–23
installment group annuities, 362*f*
insurance
  against bad labor market outcomes,
  120–21
  default risks with requirements for
  funding and, 191–95
  disability, 50, 119–20
  against inflation, 122–23
  against longevity risks, 121–22
  against myopia with saving for
  retirement, 48, 121
  preretirement survivor, 119
  protections of Social Security, 119
  role of, 118–19
  spousal survivor, 122
insurance principles, 59, 63, 379. *See
  also* pension insurance principles

insurance principles and retirement
plans, 379
intercohort transfers, 64
negative, 11
net, 61–62, 66, 380
paid to specific birth cohorts of
retirees, 62f, 66
positive, 62–63
interest
compound, 74, 98–101, 121
with discount rate, 378
for hypothetical worker with expected
value of benefits, 283t
rates, 93
rates and assets for funding
annuities, 183t
on trust funds, 44
Internal Revenue Code, 130–31, 140, 148
Internal Revenue Service (IRS), U.S.,
140, 160, 201
401(k) regulations and, 161
Tax Files with, 173–74
International Foundation for
Retirement Education, 356
investment managers, 200–203
investments, default, 210
Ippolito, Richard, 171, 177, 346
IRAs. *See* individual retirement
accounts
Irrational Exuberance (Shiller), 169–70,
270
IRS. *See* Internal Revenue Service, U.S.
Issa, Darrel, 355
Iwry, Mark, 268

Janeway, Gertrude Grubb, 16
Janeway, John, 16
Japan, 97
Javits, Jacob, 142–44
jobs
bridge, 4
elimination of, 239

employer-sponsored benefits with
termination of, 264t
Jobs and Growth Tax Relief
Reconciliation Act of 2003, 310
Johnson, Lyndon B., 71–72, 140, 141, 142,
253
joint and survivor benefit, 340–41, 380
Joss, Dick, xx

Kennedy, John F., 9, 71, 139–40, 295, 366
Kennedy, Robert, 136–37
Kennedy, Ted, 319
Kennelly, Barbara, 116–17
Keogh plans
household social security wealth
with, 258t
share of private tax-flavored plan
assets in, 204f
Kerrey, Robert, 45, 89, 90–91
Kerrey-Moynihan bill, 89
Kerry, John, 331
Kessler, Daniel, 320
Keys, Martha, 393n9
Kirkland, Lane, 393n9
Klausner, Allison, 276
Klein, Joe, 108
knowledge economy, 21
Kolbe, Jim, 106
Kulash, Marjorie, xx

LA. *See* Louisiana
labor force participation rates. *See also*
workers
of baby boomers, 179
for men, 65, 178, 179f, 325, 327t
for women, 65, 178, 179f, 250, 325–26,
327t
Labor-Management Relations Act, 134
labor market, insurance against bad
outcomes in, 120–21
labor unions. *See* unions
Latimer, Murray Webb, 36, 130–31

laws, xix
  age discrimination, 177
  public pensions, 229–32
Lazear, Edward, 25
legal protections, with public pensions,
  229–32
legislation, 144–45. *See also*
  Amendments; laws; *specific*
  legislation
  on age discrimination, 177
  for public pensions, 229–32
  Social Security Act, 40–41
  tax, 153–63
  Title I, 37, 46
  Title II, 37–38, 46
Leimer, Dean, 10, 11, 61–63, 66, 72
lessons, retirement, 15–21
Lewinsky, Monica, 108
liabilities
  accrued, 390n6
  CSRS and MRS, 234, 235t
  FERS, 234, 235t, 236
  funding ratio with, 378
  teachers with contributions and
    unfunded accrued, 226t
life expectancy, 5, 84, 121, 210, 338,
  390n5
  of birth cohort at retirement, 64, 67
  death before full, 59, 379
  with hypothetical workers and
    annuities from lifecycle funds,
    359f, 360f
  longer, 249, 271, 283
  normal, 284
Life Insurance Marketing Research
  Association, 356
limits, funding, 18–19, 156, 157t, 166–67
Linton, M. Albert, 47–48
living standards, with tax-favored
  benefits, 345–63
loading fees, 360
lock box, 90, 93, 111

Long, Huey, 33–34, 318–19
Long, Russell, 319
longevity risk, 121–22
losses, 379. *See also* insurance principles
Louisiana (LA), 225, 339
  annual required pension
    contributions in, 226t
  debt in, 229
low earners, 64, 67
  accumulations for, 213–14
  with automatic enrollment, 206
  benefits reduced for, 78, 114
  contributions of, 174
  401(k) plans and influence on, 165
  IRS Tax Files with, 173
  2011 benefits for, 114
  uneven benefit equity for, 151, 261
lumpsum payouts, 211
Lusardi, Annamaria, 264–65

MA. *See* Massachusetts
Macunovich, Diane, 176, 372
Madoff, Bernie, 345
Madrian, Brigitte, xxi, 205–7, 209
Making Work Pay tax credit, 331
management, pension, 136–37
managers, investment, 200–203
Mandatory Universal Pension system,
  150
Marine Corps, U.S., 234. *See also*
  Military Retirement System
Marshall, Will, 104
Massachusetts (MA), 339
maturity. *See* program maturity
maximum earners
  benefits payable at age 65 for, 343t
  top coding with, 243–44
McFarland, Brendan, xx, 270, 357
McGill, Dan, xix, 132
Medicare, 3, 4, 70, 71–72, 89, 117, 326
  burden shifted to taxpayers or
    government, 303–5

Medicare (*continued*)
  expenditures for 2009, 5
  movement to establish, 295
  payroll taxes partially financing, 240
medium earners. *See* average earners
men. *See also* spousal benefits; workers
  average age for retirement and
    claiming benefits, 180*t*, 240
  early retirement for, 176
  labor force participation rates for, 65,
    178, 179*f*, 325, 327*t*
  in plan types among alternative
    cohort populations, 256*t*
  poverty rate among, 123
  private and public pensions for, 315*t*
  with spousal survivor insurance,
    122
  with stock market, 265
  windfall benefits in 2009 for single,
    68*t*
  women as participants compared to,
    205
  in workforce in 1943 and 1944, 133
Michigan (MI), 216–17
military pensions, U.S., 24
  Navy, 26
military retirees, 2009 pension benefits
    paid out to, 5
Military Retirement System (MRS), 232
  Career Status Bonus/redux in, 234
  populations, liability and funding
    status for October 2008, 234, 235*t*
  underfunding of, 235–36
  workers covered under, 234
Miller, Lex, xx
Mitchell, George, 335
Mitchell, Olivia, xx, 264–65
momentum, for pay-as-you-go
    financing, 56–58
Monahan, Amy, 229–30
money market funds, 209
money purchase plans, 135

money's worth, 281–82, 380
Montana (MT), 217
Moore, Cynthia, 223
Moore, James, 211
Morgenthau, Henry, 39, 49
Morgenthau amendment, 39
Morrill, Melinda, 303
Morrison and Foerster, 223
Morris Packing Company, 25–26
mortality tables, 391, 391n10, 391n15
mothers, widowed, 28. *See also* women
Moynihan, Daniel Patrick, 81, 84, 95,
    339, 393n9
  with Bush commission, 112
  on financing crisis, 83
  pay-as-you-go financing supported
    by, 88
  with trust fund accumulation, 89–91
MRS. *See* Military Retirement System
MT. *See* Montana
Muller, Leslie, 211
multi-employer pension plan
    insurance, 189–90
Mulvey, Janemarie, xx
Munnell, Alicia, 104, 209, 211
Myers, Bob, 76–77, 82
Myers, Robert J., 36, 39, 60–61
My Lai approach, reform with, 89

Nader, Ralph, 143
Nataraj, Sita, 97
National Association of State
    Retirement Administrators, 216
National Commission on Fiscal
    Responsibility and Reform, 335,
    346, 369. *See also* Bowles-Simpson
    Commission
National Committee to Preserve Social
    Security and Medicare, 326
national elections, 4
National Income and Product Accounts,
    173, 243, 246

National Institute of Health (NIH), 379
National Institute on Aging, 254, 379
National Labor Relations Act, 294
National Labor Relations Board (NLRB), 134
National Oceanic and Atmospheric Administration, U.S., 232
Navy, U.S., 26, 234. *See also* Military Retirement System
NC. *See* North Carolina
ND. *See* North Dakota
Nebraska (NE), 216
negative intercohort transfers, 11
Netherlands, 315
net intercohort transfers, 61–62, 66, 380
Nevada (NV), 225
New Deal, 33
New Jersey (NJ), 225, 227, 353–54
  pension-plan deficits in, 8
  public pension laws in, 230–32
  public pension plans in, 218
Newman, Edwin, 143
Newsweek, 73–74
New York (NY), 225, 229, 353
NIH. *See* National Institute of Health
9/11. *See* September 11
Nixon, Richard, 73, 137, 144–45, 366
NJ. *See* New Jersey
NLRB. *See* National Labor Relations Board
no-new-taxes rule, 115
normal cost, 158–59, 380
Norsman, Annette, 223
North American Benefits Consulting, xvii
North Carolina (NC), 225
North Dakota (ND), 217
notch babies, 79
Novy-Marx, Robert, 224
Nunes, Devin, 355
NV. *See* Nevada

NY. *See* New York
Nyce, Steven, xix, 243, 320

OASDI (Old Age, Survivors, and Disability Insurance), 132, 333, 380, 392n1
  benefits paid in 1990, 173
Obama, Barack, 95, 368, 421n11
  with annuitizing retirement savings, 268
  with bankruptcy settlements, 349
  budget proposals of, 375
  with reform, 116
  on spending, 373–74
  with taxes, 310, 331
obligations
  accumulated benefit, 377
  compound interest with unfunded, 98–101
  fiscal threat of unfunded public pension, 224–29
  projected benefit, 381
OECD. *See* Organization for Economic and Cooperative Development
Ohio (OH), 217, 339
Oklahoma (OK), 225
Old Age, Survivors, and Disability Insurance. *See* OASDI
old-age dependency, 50
Old-Age Pension bill, 28, 39, 49, 56, 71, 92, 123–24
Older Americans Act, 12, 292, 347, 380
older worker problem, 27. *See also* workers
Omnibus Budget Reconciliation Act, 160, 166
  of 1987, 19, 155–56
  of 1989, 297
  of 1990, 168, 297
one-earner couples, 283t, 284, 285t, 288, 289t

O'Neill, Tip, 81, 82–83, 84, 393n9
OPEB. *See* Other Post Employment
    Benefits
operations
    ERISA's early, 147–50
    pay-as-you-go financing, 69–80
    trust funds, 42–43, 92–94
Organization for Economic and
    Cooperative Development (OECD),
    97, 313
orphans, 58
Orszag, Michael, xxi
Orszag, Peter, 320–21
    on political policy, 113, 114
    with regulations, 165
    on trust funds, 96
Other Post Employment Benefits
    (OPEB), 303
overfunding, 159, 168, 170–71

Packard, 138–39
Pan American Airlines, 187t, 350
Panel Study of Income Dynamics,
    290–91
Panis, Constantijin, 355
Parkersburg, WV, 93, 332
Parsons, Richard, 112
participants. *See also* workers
    assets managed by workers and,
        200–203
    money's worth for, 281–82
    private firms with investments
        directed by, 202f
    women compared to men, 205
par value bond, 380
Patient Protection and Accountable
    Care Act, 304, 311, 320
pay-as-you-go financing, 10, 46,
    48, 88
    backside of shift to, 66–67
    benefits expanded before reaching
        program maturity, 71–74

concerns with shifting to, 52–56
definition, 378
dependency ratio with, 52–55, 57, 69,
    70f, 71, 378
difficulty with making social security
    policy with, 78–80
faux pas, 74–78
as flawed, 12, 14, 53–55, 57, 66–67,
    72–73, 76–78, 90, 380, 392n1
Ford Motor Company and, 138
with health benefits, 298–300
operations, 69–80
resistance to and momentum for,
    56–58
with rising costs as program
    matures, 69–70
Roosevelt's opposition to, 12, 54, 58
underfunding with, 74–78, 113
Witte's opposition to, 53–55
payroll taxes, 10, 29. *See also* trust funds
    banking *versus* social insurance with,
        48
    compensation increases absorbed by
        increases in, 248t
    with costs and benefits of
        participation in Social Security,
        281–83
    cumulative lifetime employee plus
        employer, 241t
    increase delayed on, 56–57
    increases, 57, 72–73
    increase to prevent funding crisis,
        19–20, 60
    Medicare partially funded by, 240
    in 1975, 6
    ratio of benefits paid to covered
        earnings with, 16, 17, 19, 52, 69, 70f
    ratio of number of beneficiaries to
        workers with, 16–17, 52, 115–16
    reduction, 89
    Roosevelt on, 56–57, 66
    with Social Security Act, 40–41

surplus revenue from, 45–46
today, 6
with U.S. Treasury, 42–43
PBCG. *See* Pension Benefit Guaranty
    Corporation
Pelosi, Nancy, 253
penalty taxes, 292
Penn, Mark, 103, 104
Pennsylvania Railroad, 26
pension asset reversion, 159–60, 380
pension assets, other uses for, 152,
    159–60
Pension Benefit Guaranty Corporation
    (PBGC), 13, 146–47, 170–71, 375,
    380. *See also* ERISA
    claimants against single-employer
        pension plan insurance, 187*t*–188*t*
pension collapse
    companies experiencing, 25–26
    financial market chaos with, 182–84
    with union plans, 13–14
pension envy, 222
Pension Equity Act of 1981, 254
pension expense, 26–27, 380
pension funding, 380
    curtailment of private, 167–68
    education edged out by, 6, 8
pension insurance principles, 349–51
pension management, 136–37
pension movement, 24–30. *See also*
    public pensions
pension obligation bonds, 225
pension plans
    claims and flaws in, 184–86
    conversions to closures with,
        195–98
    federal, 232–36
    households and respondents with
        existing, 255*t*
    military, 24
    with summary characteristic for state
        and local workers, 217, 218*t*

tax treatment with, 150–52
    termination of, 159–60
Pension Protection Act of 2006, 208–10,
    350
Pension Research Council, xix, xx
Pension Rights Center, 143
pension wealth, 381
Pepper, Claude, 84, 393n9
Perkins, Frances, 35, 39, 332, 364
personal income, U.S. total in 2009 and
    2010, 5
personal savings plans, with five-legged
    stool metaphor, 4
Petersen, Mitchell, 160
Pew Research Center, 6, 222, 298
Pickle, J. J., 83–84
plan freezes, 7, 375
plans, top-heavy, 156
Podoff, David, 89
police officers, 24, 220–21, 231
policymakers. *See also* Greenspan
    Commission
    denial of, 12, 18–20
    with faux pas of pay-as-you-go
        financing, 74–78
    with income relief for elderly, 33–34
    with lower taxes, 153–55
    reform roadblocks for, 116–17
political dialogue
    financing crisis creating, 82–83
    with public pension legal protections,
        229–32
political policy
    Clinton's bipartisan accord with
        Social Security reform, 105–7
    with development to rhetoric,
        110–12
    with pay-as-you-go financing, 78–80
    with private pension curtailment,
        167–68
    on Social Security reform, 102–17
    with tax benefits, 292–93

Pomeroy, Earl, 371
Ponzi, Charles, 381
Ponzi scheme, social insurance as, 11, 74, 181, 381
population
    confusion, betrayal and angst of, 8–9, 11–12
    poverty rate in 1967 for total, 5
    recession's influence on, 6
population, 65 and over
    poverty rate in 1967, 5
    recession's influence on, 6
Portman, Rob, 371
positive intercohort transfers, 62–63
Poterba, James, 125, 174–75, 212–13, 258
poverty rate
    in 1967, 5
    for children, 253
    among elderly, 253
    among men, 123
    among older women, 123
    among widows, 122–23
prefunding, 45–46
preretirement survivor insurance, 119
President's Commission on Pension Policy, 150. See also Carter, Jimmy
prices
    benefits with inflation of, 122–23
    wage increase ratio to increase in, 76–77, 113–14
price-to-earnings ratio, 169f, 183f
Prichard, Alabama, 23
Primary Insurance Amount, 377, 381–82
private insurance companies, 119
private pension insurance system. See also ERISA
    for men at early and normal retirement, 315t
    structural defects in, 186–89

private retirement plans
    accumulations and economic savings with, 174–75
    with benefits measurement controversy, 172–74
    benefits paid in 2009, 5
    from committee to family rooms, 142–44
    curtailment of, 167–68
    failing, 7–8
    forfeitures and defaults in employer pensions and, 137–40
    401(k) plans outperformed by, 209
    growing pains, 136–45
    legislative twins with, 144–45
    principal agent problems in pension management with, 136–37
    with reform, 140–42
    regulations influencing, 164–65
    with tax benefits, 279–81
private sector
    hourly wages, 38, 40–41
    workforce, 135
problems. See also crisis
    with employer-sponsored plans, 12–15
    with pay-as-you-go financing, 12, 14, 380
    pension management and principal agent, 136–37
professors, college, 129
Profit Sharing/401(k) Council of America, xxi, 201–2, 275, 277, 414n27
profit-sharing plans, 5, 135
program maturity
    benefit expansion prior to, 71–74
    cost drivers trending upward with, 69–70
The Progressive, 106–7
projected benefit obligation, 381
projected-unit-credit cost method, 158–59

proposals
  Bush commission's, 112–13
  Obama's budget, 375
  reform, 18, 107–8
prototypical workers, 391n8,
  391n13
Public Health Service, U.S., 232
public pensions
  abuses and agency risk issues with,
    220–22
  challenges with costs and paying for,
    222–24
  in compensation context,
    219–20
  with controversy over public plan
    generosity, 218–19
  early motivations behind, 24–30
  as exempt from most ERISA
    requirements, 216
  federal pensions and, 232–36
  fiscal threat of unfunded obligations
    with, 224–29
  funded status and contribution
    measures for state-level, 223t
  income-spiking in, 221–22
  legal protections and controversy
    with, 229–32
  for men at early and normal
    retirement, 315t
  for state and local employees,
    215–18
  tax-favored benefits and
    considerations with, 353–55
Public Policy Toward Pensions (Shoven
  and Schieber), xix
public utilities, 24

Queen, Tara, 265
Quinn, Pat, 229

railroads, 13, 40–41, 129
Rangel, Charles, 153–54

ratios
  of benefits paid to covered earnings
    with payroll taxes, 16, 17, 19, 52,
    69, 70f
  dependency, 52–55, 57, 69, 70f, 71, 378
  funding, 378
  number of beneficiaries to workers
    with payroll taxes, 16–17, 52, 115–16
  price increase to wage increase,
    76–77, 113–14
  stocks with price-to-earnings, 169f,
    183f
  workers to retirees, 5, 11
Rauh, Joshua, 224–25
Reagan, Ronald, 81, 150, 394n12
  with financing crisis, 82–83
  on 1983 Amendments, 84–85
  tax proposals of, 153–55
  tax reform package of, 162
realities
  of 401(k) plans, 212–14
  of Social Security future, 373–76
The Real Deal. The History and Future
  of Social Security (Schieber and
  Shoven), xix, xxi, 104–5
redistributive benefit formula, 120
Reed, Bruce, 105–6
reform, health care, 249
reform, Social Security
  Clinton's bipartisan accord on, 105–7
  commission on, 112–16
  derailed by unrelated events, 108–10
  forward movement in, 140–42
  My Lai approach to, 89
  with policy development to political
    rhetoric, 110–12
  policy stalemate with, 102–17
  political stirrings, 103–5
  proposal for, 18, 107–8
  Reagan with, 82
  roadblock to, 116–17
regressive tax, 381

regulations, xix. *See also* ERISA
  with accounting rules and employer
    practices, 158–59, 163–64
  benefits and funding influenced by,
    166, 167*f*
  with birth of 401(k), 160–62
  employer pensions and early, 130–31
  employers' retiree health insurance
    and conflicts with, 296–97
  401(k), 161
  funding, 198–99
  with pension assets tapped for other
    uses, 159–60
  with pension change, 164–65
  reversal of, 15
  tax collections maintained with lower
    tax rates, 153–58
regulatory structure, 4
Reno, Virginia, 312–14, 316, 318
resistance, to pay-as-you-go financing,
  56–58
retirees
  health insurance, 4, 22
  intercohort transfers paid to specific
    birth cohorts of, 62*f*, 66
  with Medicare, 294
  military, 5
  ratio of workers to, 5, 11
  windfall benefits paid in 2009 to
    single, 66, 68*t*
retirement, 22–23. *See also* private
    retirement plans; retirement plans
  age, 84
  with applied lessons, 15–21
  average age for claiming benefits
    and, 180*t*, 240
  of baby boomers, 7, 11
  background, 4–6
  consequences for elderly without, 1
  early, 3, 81, 176–77
  fault lines in foundation of, 6–8
  in Germany, 27–28

  golden age of, 117, 170, 242, 345, 376
  implications of retirement patterns
    on, 180–81
  insurance against myopia with saving
    for, 48, 121
  national program formulated for,
    34–38
  plan accumulations and economic
    savings, 174–75
  plans and workers' retirement,
    176–80
  with public confusion, betrayal and
    angst, 8–9
  Roosevelt on individual's
    responsibility for, 13, 121, 123–25
  Social Security as foundation of, 9–12
  workers encouraged into, 131–33
retirement annuities
  concerns over move away from,
    263–66
  retirees with choice and avoidance of,
    266–68
  with retirement savings automatically
    annuitized, 268–70
  with risks and annuitization as
    automatic, 270–72
  without solution to retirement
    security dilemmas, 272–78
Retirement Equity Act of 1983, 122, 340
retirement incentives, 21, 177
retirement income security
  benefit costs factored into reward
    measurement with, 242–47
  with benefits story in compensation,
    247–50
  cost implications of, 240–42
  documentation of, 254–59
  with workers' residuals, 239–52
Retirement Insurance Clearing House
    (RICH), 361–63
retirement plans. *See also* defined
    contribution plan; private

retirement plans; *specific retirement plans*

accumulations and economic savings, 174–75

annuity calculations, xx

default risk with, 136, 191–95, 377

defined benefit plan with, 166–67, 211, 377–78

insurance principles and, 379

participants as investment managers with, 200–203

retirement of workers with, 176–80

for state and local workers, 215–18

retirement savings. *See* savings

retirement systems. *See also* civil service retirement system; federal employee retirement systems; military retirement system

findings, 320–25

just right perspective of, 314–17

major forces in development of, 4

paying for, 318–19

too cold perspective of, 312–14

too hot perspective of, 309–12

worker prosperity and security of, 325–27

World Bank's tiered characterization of, 4

Reuther, Walter, 134, 139, 141

Revenue Act

1938, 131

1942, 56, 131

1945, 56

1978, 160

reversion taxes, 160, 171. *See also* termination/reversions

Revolutionary War, 24

RICH. *See* Retirement Insurance Clearing House

risks

agency, 136–37, 218, 377

with annuitization at retirement, 270–72

default, 136, 191–95, 377

forfeiture, 136, 378

insurance against longevity, 121–22

public pensions and abuses

demonstrating agency, 220–22

spending, 121–22, 373–74

Rivlin, Alice, 335. *See also* Domenici-Rivlin Task Force

robber baron environment, 160

roll over, 212

Roosevelt, Franklin D., 10, 11, 56, 82, 379. *See also* New Deal

on contributions, 37, 44

cradle to grave program and, 71

delayed payroll tax increase and objections from, 56–57

on economic fairness, 60

with elderly and income relief, 33–34, 37

fireside chats with, 292

on individual's responsibility for retirement, 13, 121, 123–25

with insurance principles, 63

on Old-Age Pension bill, 28, 39

with pay-as-you-go flaws, 66–67

pay-as-you-go opposed by, 12, 54, 58

on payroll tax, 66

with Social Security Act, 40–41

Social Security as visualized by, 59, 364

Rosie the Riveter, 372

Ross, Stanford G., 80

Rostenkowski, Dan, 161

Roth, William, 152

Roth 401(k)s, 401n20

Roth IRAs, 151–52

Rubinow, Isaac, 28, 35, 36, 38

rules. *See also* regulations

no-new-taxes, 115

Russia, 29

Ryan, Paul
  with public pension plan
    considerations, 355, 374
  with Social Security foundation,
    332–33, 335, 337

safe harbor, 208, 276–77, 356
salaried workers, 38
Samuelson, Paul, 10–11, 73–74, 181
Samwick, Andrew, 211–12
Santa Claus
  benefit increases, 57
  welfare state, 54
Sarbanes-Oxley Act, 19
Sass, Steven, 26, 130, 296
Save Our Security, 326
savings, 268–70, 281–83. *See also*
    personal savings plans
  in context with Social Security, 87, 98
  401(k), 174–75
  insurance against myopia with
    retirement, 48, 121
  IRA, 174–75
  retirement plan accumulations and
    economic, 174–75
  risks, 121–22
  surplus unsaved as, 97
  tax benefits and private retirement,
    284–89
  trust funds as, 94–96
  younger workers' attitudes about, 177
SC. *See* South Carolina
Schieber, Sylvester J., xix, xxi, 104–5,
    116, 259–61
Scholz, John Karl, 175
Schottland, Charles, 392n1
Schweiker, Richard, 81
self-employed workers, 53
self-reliance, 13, 50
September 11, 81, 350
share the wealth campaign, 34
Shaw, George Bernard, 365

Shaw, Miles, 365
Shaw, Sean, 365
Shea, Dennis, 205–6, 209
Shea, Gerald, 102
Shiller, Robert, 169–70, 270, 357
shortfalls, in funding, 29, 86–87, 99–100
Shoven, John, xix, xxi, 64, 97, 104–5, 157
Simpson, Alan, 335. *See also* Bowles-
    Simpson Commission
single-employer pension plan
    insurance, claimants against
    PBGC, 187t–188t
single retirees, 66, 68t
60 Minutes, 143, 229, 353
Skinner, Jonathan, 211–12
Slover, Michael, xx
Smith, Karen, 373
social insurance, 27–28, 381
  banking principles *versus*, 48
  as Ponzi scheme, 11, 74, 181, 381
Social Security
  advisory council for 1994–1996,
    102–3, 106, 108, 329
  baby boomers influencing financing
    of, 12, 14
  benefits and deficits, 6–8, 17–18
  commissioners, 392n1, 393n9
  with dilemma of today *versus*
    tomorrow, 328–30
  financing concerns, 46–49
  five-legged stool metaphor for, 4
  foundation secured, 328–44
  funds invested in stock market, 111,
    159, 169–70
  insurance against bad labor market
    outcomes and, 120–21
  insurance against inflation and,
    122–23
  insurance against lack of retirement
    savings and, 121
  insurance against longevity risk and,
    121–22

insurance protections, 119
in modern times, 118–25
as one part of retirement security,
123–25
other issues with, 340–41
participation costs with payroll tax,
281–83
program costs, 17, 22
as retirement foundation, 9–12
role of, 118–19
Roosevelt's vision for, 59, 364
savings in context with, 87, 98
with smoke-and-mirrors financing,
330–32
Social Security, foundation of
with common ground on reform,
335–40
individual accounts as reform
element with, 332–35
other issues, 340–41
securing, 328–44
smoke-and-mirrors financing as
problematic, 330–32
today *versus* tomorrow, 328–30
Social Security, future of
1939 and, 366–69
perspectives broadened with, 363–66
private role with, 369–71
prosperity preservation with, 371–73
realities with, 373–76
Social Security Act, 10, 52, 69, 381
critics of, 46
demand for income relief for elderly
with, 33–34
from design to legislative action,
40–41
development and passage of, 33–41
funding question at outset with, 39
national retirement program
formulated with, 34–38
1935, 47–48, 336–37
pension goals of, 131–32

Social Security Advisory Board, xvii,
xxi, 116
Social Security benefit actuarial
adjustment, 381–82
Social Security Bulletin, 260
Social Security wealth, 258*t*, 317*t*, 382
Society of Actuaries, 356
soldiers. *See* Military Retirement
System
Sophocles, 127
South Carolina (SC), 217
S&P 500, 273
spending risks, 121–22, 373–74
Sperling, Frank, 221
Sperling, Gene, 107, 110
spousal benefits, 120–21, 289–92, 340,
382
spousal survivor insurance, 122
Stanford Institute of Economic and
Policy Research, xix
State and Local Pension Transparency
Act, 355
states. *See also specific states*
debts, 229
public pension laws in, 229–32
with unfunded public pension
obligations, 224–29
Steinmeier, Thomas, 254, 259, 262, 290,
314
Stenholm, Charlie, 106
Steuerle, Eugene, 373
Stockman, David, 83
stock market, 21
crash of 1929, 29
crash of 1987, 201, 203
price-to-earnings ratios in, 169*f*, 183*f*
Social Security funds invested in, 111,
159, 169–70
women and men's knowledge of, 265
stool metaphor, five-legged, 4
Studebaker Company, collapse of,
13–14, 16, 137–39

Summers, Larry, 107, 110
supplemental benefits, 176
Supreme Court, U.S., 230
surpluses
    cash, 94–96
    evidence of unsaved, 97
    payroll tax revenue, 45–46
    trust fund, 45–46, 85
Surrey, Stanley, 141–42
surveys, recession's influence on
        population, 6
survivor retirement benefits, 9–10, 120.
        See also joint and survivor benefit;
        OASDI; preretirement survivor
        insurance
Sweden, 97, 335

Tabatabai, Nahid, 254, 259, 262, 314
A Tale of Two Cities (Dickens), 237
tax benefits
    payroll tax costs and benefits of Social
        Security with, 281–83
    private retirement plans with, 279–81
    private retirement savings with,
        284–89
    with results into stated retirement
        policy, 292–93
    spousal benefits and implications
        with, 289–92
tax credits, 331
tax-deferred status, 130–31
Tax Equity and Fiscal Responsibility Act
        for 1983, 162, 166
Tax Equity and Fiscal Responsibility Act
        of 1982, 154–56
taxes. See also payroll taxes
    automatic minimum, 310
    Bush with, 115, 310, 331
    excise, 201, 211, 351–53
    income, 162, 378
    increase to prevent funding crisis,
        19–20

legislation, 153–63
    no-new, 115
    Obama on, 310, 331
    penalty, 292
    pensions with treatment of, 150–52
    Reagan's proposals, 153–55, 162
    regressive, 381
    reversion, 160, 171
tax expenditure, 141–42, 151–52, 382
    1980s and rise in, 154
tax-favored benefits
    annuitization encouraged with,
        360–63
    with defined contribution annuity
        dilemma, 355–60
    with excise tax on surplus funds,
        351–53
    living standards secured with,
        345–63
    pension insurance principles with,
        349–51
    public pension plan considerations
        with, 353–55
    with tax preferences for health
        benefit plans, 348–49
    tax preferences with, 348–49
Tax Files, 173–74
taxpayers, Medicare burden shifted to,
        303–5
tax rates, 389n2
    of average-wage workers, 44
    tax revenue increase without hike in,
        14, 153–58
Tax Reform Act
    1984, 161
    1986, 155–56, 160, 211
Tax Relief Act, 1986, 401n3
tax revenue, increase without tax-rate
        hike, 14, 153–58
teachers, 24, 129, 354
    unfunded accrued liabilities and
        contributions for, 226t

Teachers Insurance and Annuity Association, 129
Teamsters Unions' Central States Pension Fund, 136–37
Tennessee (TN), 304
termination/reversions, of pension plans, 159–60, 378, 380
terrorists, 81, 350
testimony, on funding crisis, 18–19
Texas (TX), 339
Thaler, Richard, 207
30-and-out union contracts, 176–77
Thornton, Kate, xxi
Through the Looking Glass and What Alice Found There (Carroll), xviii, 3
Title I, legislation, 37, 46
Title II, legislation, 37–38, 46
TN. *See* Tennessee
top coding, 243–44
top-heavy plans, 156
Towers Watson, xvii, xix, xx, 7, 9, 298
Townsend, Francis E., 33–34
Toynbee, Arnold, 29
transfers. *See* intercohort transfers
transition costs, 113, 115
transparency, 332, 335
Treasury, U.S., 161. *See also* trust funds
    bonds, 42–43, 67, 94f
    with tax treatment of pensions, 150–52
    with trust fund operations, 92–94
Troncoso, Fernando, xxi
Troncoso Consulting Group, xxi
Trowbridge, Alexander, 393n9
Truman, Harry, 134, 295
Trustees Report
    1975, 75
    1982, 82, 84
    1985, 86
    2010, 251
    2011, 7, 86, 374

trust funds, 390n6, 391n9, 391n14, 394n1
    accumulating, 86–91
    assets from 1975 to 1982, 151
    cash surplus and unified budget with, 96f
    depletion of, 19, 75, 225
    estimates with insurance principles, 63
    evidence of unsaved social security surpluses, 97
    federal pension, 232–36
    funding concerns and controversy, 43–46
    interest on, 44
    operations, 42–43, 92–94
    with power of compound interest and unfunded obligations, 98–101
    as savings and controversy, 94–96
    with savings in context, 87, 98
    surplus, 45–46, 85
Turner, John, 157, 205
TWA, 350
Twain, Mark, 375
2030, funds exhausted in, 111
TX. *See* Texas

UAW. *See* United Auto Workers
UK. *See* United Kingdom
underfunding, 17–18
    of MRS, 235–36
    with pay-as-you-go financing, 74–78, 113
unemployment, 29
unfunding
    of accrued liabilities in IL and LA, 226t
    fiscal threat of public pension obligations and, 224–29
    of obligations with compound interest, 98–101
unified budget, 96f, 382

union plans
  with health benefits, 302
  pension collapse with, 13–14
  30-and-out, 176–77
  UAW, 176
unions, 13, 133–34. *See also specific
  unions*
  Hoffa and, 136–37
United Airlines, 187*t*, 350
United Auto Workers (UAW), 134, 137,
  139, 141, 176
United Kingdom (UK), 315
United Steel Workers (USW), 134
Universal Savings Account, 110
Urban Wage and Clerical Workers, 234
U.S. Steel, 26
USA Accounts, 110, 111
US Airlines, 350
USW. *See* United Steel Workers
Utah (UT), 217

VA. *See* Veterans Administration
Vandenberg, Arthur, 45, 46, 47, 52, 87,
  91
  on cash surpluses, 95
Vanguard Investments, 208, 210
Vaughn, Genevieve
Vaughn, Terry, xxi
Venti, Steven, 125, 174–75, 212–13, 258
Veterans Administration (VA), 232
Vietnam War, 70

Wade, Alice, xxi
wages
  funding limits with, 157*t*
  price increase ratio to increase in,
    76–77, 113–14
  private-sector hourly wages, 38, 40–41
  tax rates for workers with average, 44
  workers' earnings rates with, 64–65
Waggonner, Joe, 393n9, 394n12
Walker, David, 100

Walt Disney, 375
Warner, David, xxi
Warshawsky, Mark, 270
Watergate, 144–45
Watson Wyatt, xvii, xviii, xix, xx, xxi. *See
  also* Towers Watson
wealth. *See also* share the wealth
  campaign
  accumulation of large pension,
    259–62
  among ages 51 to 56 in health and
    retirement study, 257*t*
  average earners with 401(k) and
    projected, 214
  401(k) plans and household Social
    Security, 258*t*
  pension, 381
  Social Security, 382
  Social Security and 401(k) lifetime
    projected, 317*t*
Weaver, Carolyn, xx, 104, 329
West, Mae, 345
Wharton School, xx
White House Task Force on Middle-
  Class Working Families, 268. *See
  also* Obama, Barack
"Why Do Pension Benefits Seem So
  Small?" (Schieber), 259–60
WI. *See* Wisconsin
Wickes, Gene, xx
widows, 28, 47, 58, 122–23. *See also*
  women
Wilcox, David, 223
Williams, Debi, xxi
Williams, Harrison, 142–44
Williams, R. Scott, 23
windfall benefits, 60, 132, 382
  estimating, 67–68
  given away, 63
  paid to single retirees in 2009, 66, 68*t*
  for workers, 64–66
Wirtz, Willard, 139

Wisconsin (WI), 218
Wise, David, 125, 174–75, 212–13, 258
Witte, Edwin, 12, 35–36, 38–39, 47, 71
　on banking payroll taxes, 48
　on economic fairness, 60
　on funded financing structure's
　　importance, 52
　with insurance principles, 63
　on 1939 Amendments, 51
　on pay-as-you-go flaws, 53–55, 57, 66,
　　72–73, 90
Wizard of Oz funding, 227–28
Wolfe, Glen, 160
women. *See also* spousal benefits;
　　workers
　average age for retirement and
　　claiming benefits, 180*t*, 240
　baby boom, 69, 372–73
　benefits received for age 62 or older,
　　291*t*
　early retirement for, 176
　labor force participation rates for, 65,
　　178, 179*f*, 250, 325–26, 327*t*
　as participants compared to men,
　　205
　in plan types among alternative
　　cohort populations, 256*t*
　poverty rate among, 122, 123
　with spousal survivor insurance, 122
　with stock market, 265
　widows, 28, 47, 58, 122–23
　windfall benefits in 2009 for single,
　　68
Woods, John, 259–61
Wooten, James, 136, 142, 144
workers. *See also* average earners;
　　baby boomers; high earners; low
　　earners; maximum earners
　benefits for government, 8
　cashing out early, 211
　compensation and pay levels in 2009
　　for, 244*t*

compound annual growth rates
　with hourly compensation for,
　　246*f*
compound annual growth rates with
　hourly pay for, 245*f*
CSRS, 233
cumulative lifetime payroll taxes for
　employers and, 241*t*
entitlement of, 37
FERS with, 233
401(k) by lifetime earnings in 2030
　for retiring, 213*t*
funding limits and influence
　on, 157*t*
German, 27–28
in households with existing pensions,
　255*t*
as investment managers with
　retirement plans, 200–203
MRS, 234
older, 27, 176
private-sector, 135
prototypical, 391n8, 391n13
ratio of retirees to, 5, 11
retirement encouraged for, 131–33
retirement plans and retirement of,
　176–80
retirement plans for state and local,
　215–18
retirement programs influenced by
　desires of, 4
retirement security and prosperity of,
　325–27
salaried, 38
self-employed, 53
Social Security and projected 401(k)
　wealth for, 317*t*
summary characteristics of pension
　plans for state and local, 217, 218*t*
tax rates of average-wage, 44
2009–2010 benefits paid to, 5
urban wage and clerical, 234

workers (*continued*)
 without value as economic burdens,
  239
 windfalls for, 64–66
workers, hypothetical, 61, 64, 219, 282,
  284
 annuities from lifecycle funds with
  life expectancies for, 359*f*, 360*f*
 benefits from accumulated lifetime
  contributions with interest for, 283*t*
 combined value net benefit gains
  versus contributions for, 289*t*
 defined contribution earnings
  replacement rates from lifecycle
  funds for, 271*f*
 installment group annuity for, 362*f*
 value of lifetime contributions and
  expected benefits for, 285*t*

value of lifetime net benefits from
  tax-qualified retirement savings
  for, 287*t*
workers, younger
 older workers' earnings in relation
  to, 176
 retirement savings and attitudes of,
  177
workers' residuals. *See* retirement
  income security
World Bank, xx, 4
World Economic Forum, xix
World Trade Organization
  (WTO), 351
World War II, 13, 19, 30, 75, 133, 372
Wray, David, xxi, 276–77
WTO. *See* World Trade Organization
Wyatt, Birchard, 24–25, 379